D1088816

International City/County **ICMA** Management Association

The International City/County Management Association (ICMA) is the professional and educational organization for appointed administrators and assistant administrators in local government. The mission of ICMA is to create excellence in local governance by developing and fostering professional local government management worldwide. To further this mission, ICMA develops and disseminates new approaches to management through training programs, information services, and publications.

Local government managers—carrying a wide range of titles—serve cities, towns, counties, councils of governments, and state/provincial associations of local governments. They serve at the direction of elected councils and governing boards. ICMA serves these managers and local governments through many programs that aim at improving the manager's professional competence and strengthening the quality of all local governments.

ICMA was founded in 1914, adopted its Code of Ethics in 1924, and established its Institute for Training in Municipal Administration in 1934. The institute provided the basis for the Municipal Management Series, popularly known as the "ICMA Green Books." By 1994, the institute had evolved into the ICMA University, which provides professional development resources for members and other local government employees.

ICMA's interests and activities include public management education; voluntary credentialing and standards of ethics for members; an information clearinghouse; local government research and development; data collection and dissemination; technical assistance; and a wide array of publications, including *Public Management* magazine, newsletters, management reports, and texts. ICMA's efforts toward the improvement of local government—as represented by this book—are offered for all local governments and educational institutions.

Advisory Board

Douglas P. Forsman
P. Michael Freeman
Bob Hart
Gerard J. Hoetmer

Barrie J. Lough
Warren E. McDaniels
Anthony R. O'Neill
Denis Onieal

Contributors

Maureen Brodoff
Timothy R. S. Campbell
Steven C. Carter
William H. Clark
Dennis Compton
Jim Crawford
David T. Endicott
Stephen N. Foley
Douglas P. Forsman
P. Michael Freeman
Robert P. Gannon
John Granito

Bob Hart
William M. Kramer
Murrey E. Loflin
Wm. D. Morrison
James O. Page
Robin Paulsgrove
Kevin M. Roche
Russell E. Sanders
James L. Schamadan, M.D.
Gail Stephens
Lyle J. Sumek

Municipal Management Series

Managing Fire and Rescue Services

A completely revised and updated version of *Managing Fire Services*

Editors

Published
for the
ICMA University

Dennis Compton
Fire Chief
Mesa, Arizona

By the
International
City/County
Management
Association

John Granito
Fire and Public Safety Consultant
Professor Emeritus and
Retired Vice President
State University of New York

International
City/County
ICMA
Management
Association

ICMA UNIVERSITY

Municipal Management Series

Managing Fire and Rescue Services

Advanced Supervisory Practices

Effective Communication

The Effective Local Government Manager

Effective Supervisory Practices

Emergency Management

Local Government Police Management

Management of Local Public Works

Management Policies in Local Government Finance

Managing Human Resources: Local Government Cases

Managing Local Government: Cases in Decision Making

Managing Local Government Finance: Cases in Decision Making

Managing Small Cities and Counties

The Practice of Local Government Planning

The Practice of State and Regional Planning

Service Contracting: A Local Government Guide

Library of Congress Cataloging-in-Publication Data

Managing fire and rescue services / editors, Dennis Compton, John Granito.
    p.   cm. — (Municipal management series)
    Includes bibliographical references and index.
    ISBN 0-87326-128-3 (hardcover : alk. paper)
    1. Fire departments — Management.   2. Emergency medical
services — Management.   I. Compton, Dennis.   II. Granito, John
III. Series.
    TH9145 .M253 2002
363.37'0068 — dc21   2002009018

Printed in the United States of America

2009 2008

10 9 8 7 6 5 4

04-306   12/08
42810

Foreword

As this book goes to press, the events of September 11, 2001, are fresh in the minds of U.S. citizens and their public servants. The attacks on the World Trade Center and the Pentagon had a profound impact on the fire service, whose members responded with round-the-clock rescue efforts, in the course of which 343 fire service personnel lost their lives. Many citizens who had taken their local fire departments for granted developed a new appreciation for the role the fire service play in their communities and their nation.

With the publication of this volume, the International City/County Management Association (ICMA) continues its long-standing presence in the field of fire service management. ICMA's first book on the subject appeared in 1935, and the most recent in 1988. The volume has become one of the most popular of ICMA's Municipal Management Series (popularly called "Green Books"), providing state-of-the-art management information and insights for fire service administrators, city and county managers, elected officials, training officials and students, and candidates for promotion through the ranks.

For fire department administrators, the book offers guidance on policy issues and decision making in areas ranging from risk management and mutual aid agreements to performance measurement, leadership training, and leadership strategies for the political process. For local government managers and elected officials, it presents a detailed discussion of the management issues that affect the fire service—a vital, costly, and highly visible part of local government. For fire service training officers, *Managing Fire and Rescue Services* is the complete textbook. And for students in fire science, fire technology, or public administration (and candidates for promotion), this is an authoritative, readable text that draws on decades of experience—a text without equal in the field.

The changing titles reflect the changing fire service. In 1967, it was *Municipal Fire Administration*; in 1988, *Managing Fire Services*; and now, *Managing Fire and Rescue Services*. During the past several decades, change has been a constant theme in the fire service—not only in technological advances but also in the services provided. These changes are examined throughout the book.

While fire protection is a highly technical field, this book is written from a managerial rather than a technical perspective. It identifies and discusses the key managerial issues that face the fire chief and other departmental managers, the chief administrative officer, and local elected officials. While the book encompasses relevant theory and research, it does so primarily as background for practical management decision making.

This book, like others in the Municipal Management Series, has been published for the ICMA University, which offers in-service professional development and training specifically designed for local government officials whose jobs are to plan, direct, and coordinate the work of others. To assist those who wish to learn from this book on their own, ICMA has developed a self-study guide to accompany *Managing Fire and Rescue Services*.

Many individuals contributed their efforts to the preparation of this book. First and foremost are the editors, Dennis Compton, fire chief, Mesa, Arizona, and John Granito, fire and public safety consultant and professor emeritus and retired vice president, State University of New York. They worked tirelessly with the authors and the ICMA staff to ensure that the present volume represents the state of the art in professional fire service management and that it transcends differences that occasionally arise between and among our constituencies.

The editors were assisted by members of an editorial advisory board who provided valuable guidance as this project took shape. Members (with affiliations at the time of publication) were Douglas P. Forsman, fire chief, Union Colony Fire/Rescue Authority, Greeley, Colorado; P. Michael Freeman, chief, Los Angeles County Fire Department; Bob Hart, city manager, Huntsville, Texas; Gerard J. Hoetmer, executive director, Public Entity Risk Institute, Fairfax, Virginia; Barrie J. Lough, chief (retired), Winnipeg City Fire Department, Winnipeg, Manitoba, Canada; Warren E. McDaniels, superintendent, New Orleans Fire Department; Anthony R. O'Neill, vice president (retired), Government Affairs, National Fire Protection Association (NFPA), Arlington, Virginia; and Denis Onieal, superintendent, National Fire Academy, Emmitsburg, Maryland.

ICMA is also grateful to the chapter authors, many of whom provided continuing assistance throughout the editorial and revision process; to the many individuals (acknowledged throughout the text) who contributed sidebars; and to fire departments throughout the country who provided program descriptions and illustrations. Special thanks go to Thomas Healy, chief, Daisy Mountain Fire Department, Phoenix, Arizona, who made helpful contributions to the coverage of health and wellness issues; and to Doug Forsman, who contributed supplementary text and sidebars for several chapters.

Finally, a number of ICMA staff members contributed to the volume: Barbara H. Moore, Director of Publishing and Information Resources, provided general oversight; Verity Weston-Truby laid the editorial groundwork; Jane C. Cotnoir coordinated editorial and production activities; Dawn M. Leland supervised production; and Nedra James provided administrative support and ensured that editorial changes were accurately incorporated into the chapters. Working with ICMA as a consultant, Jane E. Lewin edited the book and worked with the authors to resolve queries.

The publication of this text at this particular time means a great deal to me personally. I will retire as ICMA's executive director on October 2, 2002, at the conclusion of the association's annual conference in Philadelphia. My father, William H. Hansell Sr., was a career firefighter in the city of Philadelphia from 1944 to 1964, so I became familiar with the fire service at an early age. I began my career in city management in 1961 as a management trainee in the Philadelphia fire department, where I served for three years while earning a master's degree in public administration at the Fels Institute of Government at the University of Pennsylvania. During that time I was privileged to work for former chiefs George Hink and James McCarey—two of the giants of the fire service in the mid-twentieth century. I hope my dad and chiefs Hink and McCarey would be as proud as I am as this book joins the roster of ICMA's major texts.

William H. Hansell
Executive Director
International City/County
   Management Association
Washington, D.C.

Contents

Preface

Managing Fire and Rescue Services is the successor to ICMA's well-received and widely used *Managing Fire Services,* the second edition of which was published in 1988. This successor volume is designed to be an equally useful text and reference book for the many practitioners, students, and others who are concerned with providing effective and efficient fire and rescue protection in their communities, or with having such protection provided. The book will serve as a resource for both new and experienced officials of the fire service and local government, and for concerned citizens; it will also serve as a college-level textbook and as a commonly used study document for promotional examinations. The intended audience, in short, embraces subject-matter beginners and experts alike.

Producing a volume for this broad an audience required that great attention be paid to the choice of authors and topics. For that reason, an advisory group of experts from the fields of fire administration, local government, and education carefully chose both the authors and the subjects of the chapters. The authors are all experienced and expert practitioners. The topics reflect the vast amount of change that has occurred in both the local government environment and the fire service since publication of the predecessor volume. Just as the challenges and problems facing fire service and local government leaders today are significantly different from those that faced them fourteen years ago, so, too, the topics covered in

this book differ significantly from those covered in the earlier book.

This volume consists of sixteen chapters divided into five sections:

I   *The Context of Fire and Rescue Services*   an overview of contemporary service delivery, the process of evaluating local risk and planning to meet local needs, and leadership strategies for interacting with the political process

II   *Resource Management*   an overview of fire department organization and concepts of resource deployment, and an in-depth look at the management of human, financial, and capital resources

III   *Improving Resources*   a focus on leadership, training, performance measurement, and the health and well-being of firefighters

IV   *Prevention*   a description of comprehensive fire and life safety prevention programs and of regulations, standards, and issues of liability

V   *Managing Support Services*   a review of information management, communication systems and emergency response centers, and intergovernmental cooperation.

To guide the managers of fire and rescue services, each author not only gives an overview of his or her subject but also elaborates on the subject's main aspects (topics and subtopics), illustrating them with real-world examples and exploring possible future developments. The state-of-the-art content of each chapter, which experienced professionals will appreciate, is paired with a "reader-friendly" writing style that makes all chapters (no matter how technical) accessible even to readers who are building up their knowledge of the fire and rescue service.

The degree of expertise and professionalism required of fire department administrators has increased significantly over the years and will continue to increase. A fire chief is the chief executive officer (CEO) of a large, medium, or small service delivery organization staffed with career employees, volunteers, or a combination of the two. He or she must work effectively within the community and with other officials. To be effective in meeting customer needs and in leading the organization internally and externally, the CEO must have technical knowledge and a keen business sense, as well as management and leadership skills. Furthermore, at the same time that the CEO is attending to sound management and business practices and to the resources and internal programs that are critical to the organization's success, he or she must also provide critical lifesaving programs. And all of this plays out within the context of a unique relationship among service providers, support personnel, local government officials, and customers. Thus, a systems approach to managing the fire and life safety infrastructure component of our communities is important to the sustained success of fire departments.

No book about the fire and rescue service can ignore the events of September 11, 2001. The four terrorist attacks that day not only had incalculable significance for the United States as a whole but also will mark the fire and life safety community, in

particular, for a very long time to come.

Among the thousands of people who lost their lives because of the attacks were 343 fire service personnel (340 firefighters, 2 paramedics, and a chaplain). They died trying to save the lives of others. Consciously and unhesitatingly, each of these fire department members took the ultimate risk. They ran out of time, but they never ran out of courage and dedication.

For years, many fire service leaders had expressed their concern to Congress and federal agencies about the possible impact of a terrorist attack. In disaster exercises, cities simulated events that killed and injured thousands, and these scenarios led fire service leaders to warn that among the casualties in an actual incident would be large numbers of first responders—especially firefighters. Fire service leaders lobbied, debated, and argued to get more federal funding to address training, equipment, and personnel needs, typically without the desired effect. The events that unfolded on September 11 may well draw increased attention to some of these issues.

Already in the fifteen years before September 11, a very high number of significant changes had occurred in fire and rescue organizations, motivated by the desire to improve service delivery and internal processes as well as by profound transformations in the surrounding culture and environment. Among the most important and lasting of these changes was the increase in service delivery specialties, which now include emergency medical, technical rescue, hazardous materials, public safety education, and special disaster operations as part of integrated emergency management. In addition, departments responded to new industry standards and regulations involving response and operational protocols, required training, and the availability of department accreditation and individual certification. Strong professional group affiliations, the U.S. Congressional Fire Services Institute, and the Congressional Fire Caucus, and the focus on fire safety and necessary resources by a variety of groups and agencies, all made a difference.

Technical advances in protective clothing and equipment and in operational equipment have been made and continue to be developed. Training and educational programs have proliferated, and the body of technical and managerial literature has vastly increased. Professional organizations offer more and more in support of their members, and diversity of membership continues to be emphasized.

These and many other changes have improved the fire and rescue service, yet the effort to match what is needed with what is provided is never-ending. We conclude with the words of Garry Briese, executive director of the International Association of Fire Chiefs, who has offered us his observations about the future:

"Like most of the business world today, the fire service must examine every facet of the services and products it provides, the quality and nature of the delivery of these services and products, and the involvement of its stakeholders.

"Change occurs in every organization and business sector, and the fire service is no exception. What is different is the effect of tradition on all fire service organizations. Traditional attitudes in the fire service are perhaps the greatest impediment to change—yet *not* changing can itself do severe damage.

"For change to be effective it must be efficient, timely, and meaningful. For change in the fire service to be meaningful, the service must embrace its stakeholders and involve them in the implementation of change. Specifically, for the fire service to maximize its resources, it must ensure that the recipients of fire service products and services, the legislative and executive decision makers, and the delivery agents of products and services all provide high-quality input into the process of making changes.

"One change on which the future of the fire service largely depends is that of fostering good relationships between labor and management. Traditional labor-management relationships must undergo a metamorphosis so that the participants cease to be adversaries and become partners. Confrontational-style labor-management relationships are no longer effective in the fire service. In fact, there are no examples of successful, thriving fire departments that rely on confrontational relationships. An increasing number of departments throughout the United States now include labor in the leadership of the fire department. When labor and management leaders are united, they can improve their departments by combining resources, empowering each other to accomplish common goals, and establishing the fire department as a professional, focused organization.

"Making the transition to true partnerships will take a sustained commitment from both labor and management. Hence, the principal international organizations representing fire service labor and management must model a positive attitude toward cooperation. To date, the International Association of Fire Chiefs and the International Association of Fire Fighters have done this by becoming partners in high-quality programs to enhance the fire service— programs such as the Fire Fighter Health and Wellness Initiative, the Candidate Physical Ability Test, and the Fire Service Leadership Partnerships. These are examples of labor and management's commitment to working together.

"But even with the need to change in an increasingly complex society, the fire service must not lose its traditional focus. People in need call the fire department, and firefighters arrive to save lives and protect property—a very simple premise, and one that should not be lost sight of. To be sure, the fire service will seek to diversify the products and services that it provides, becoming increasingly involved in community outreach while learning to respond to new challenges. Nevertheless, all of the fire service must remain vigilant about fulfilling its primary mission."

As coeditors of *Managing Fire and Rescue Services,* we express our thanks to the chapter authors, to the advisory committee, and to the staff of ICMA. We are proud to present this new book to those who are interested in learning about, improving, working with, and progressing within the fire and rescue service, and we appreciated the opportunity to be this book's coeditors.

Dennis Compton

John Granito

Part one:
The context
of fire and
rescue services

Modern fire protection, emergency medical, and rescue services

The common denominator for fire protection, emergency medical, and rescue services is people. People require the basics of life (food, water, shelter, employment) as well as discretionary goods, services, and luxuries. These demands entail the use of raw materials to produce goods, transportation of all kinds, and disposal of what is left over or wasted. Inherent in the pursuit of all these activities are risks to the public's health and safety.

As the number of people increases, hazards tend to increase proportionately. For example, the greater the number and density of housing units, the more likely it is that fire, medical, and rescue emergencies will increase. In addition, the greater the population, the more need there is for transportation of both people and commodities; therefore, aircraft and auto crashes, railroad derailments, spills of hazardous materials from overturned trucks, and so forth will occur more frequently.

Increased population also translates into increased consumption of manufactured goods. Manufacturing operations often involve the storage, heating, and mechanical processing of raw materials, some of which are inherently hazardous, either alone or in combination with other materials.

Finally, increased population means increased numbers of places of employment and increased demand for entertainment in places of public assembly. Some of the most disastrous emergencies in U.S. history have occurred in places of employment and entertainment (see sidebar on page 4).

U.S. population growth—not only the numbers but also the pattern of the growth—raises new issues for the fire service. The context within which these issues will have to be resolved is dominated by the fire department's relationship with the public and by the policy environment for local government management. In addition, it must be recognized that in the early twenty-first century, fire departments generally do more than suppress (and try to prevent) fires. A high percentage of fire departments in the United States also provide emergency medical services and rescue services.

U.S. population growth and emerging fire service issues

In the twenty years after publication (in 1979) of the first edition of ICMA's book *Managing Fire Services,* the U.S. population increased by about 40 million people. During the last thirty years of the twentieth century, it increased by about 65 million people. These increases were accompanied by a rise in the number of risks to public health and safety. During this period of growth the fire service used engineering, education, and code enforcement to moderate the frequency and severity of fires and fire losses, but at the same time the frequency and complexity of other risks, including medical emergencies and dangers from hazardous materials, grew in proportion to the growth in population.

As the population increased, it also shifted. While the older cities and suburbs continued to gain population, mostly from births and immigration, smaller towns and communities as well as rural areas also grew, but from migration rather than births. Both developments have presented problems for fire departments.

Disasters at three places of congregation   The Triangle Shirtwaist Company in New York City, the Cocoanut Grove nightclub in Boston, and the MGM Grand Hotel in Las Vegas, Nevada, were the scenes of especially disastrous fires during the twentieth century.

On March 25, 1911, the deadliest manufacturing facility fire (excluding explosions) in U.S. history occurred at the Triangle Shirtwaist Company in New York. Five hundred women were employed at the company, and to keep them at their sewing machines, the proprietors had locked the doors leading to the exits. Workers were on the eighth, ninth, and tenth floors, but the fire department's ladders extended only to the sixth floor; and life nets broke when workers jumped in groups of three and four. In less than fifteen minutes, 146 women died. One result of the ensuing investigations was the establishment of New York City's Bureau of Fire Investigation, which increased the city fire department's powers to improve safety in factories.[1]

On November 28, 1942, a fire at the Cocoanut Grove nightclub in Boston took the lives of 492 people and seriously injured many others. The decorations in the nightclub were flammable; the main exit consisted of two revolving doors, not doors that swung outward; and the occupant capacity of the structure had been exceeded. The Cocoanut Grove fire had a major effect on fire prevention and control for nightclubs and related places of assembly.

On November 21, 1980, eighty-five people died in a fire at the MGM Grand Hotel in Las Vegas. The industry responded with an unprecedented degree of code compliance and with the adoption of proven fire protection systems even before such adoption was required.

[1] See Leon Stein, *The Triangle Fire* (Philadelphia: J. B. Lippincott, 1962).

Metropolitan and suburban areas

The population of metropolitan areas grew by 6.9 percent in the 1990–1996 period. This growth compounded the familiar problems associated with big cities: demands for fire protection and emergency medical and rescue services generally have increased in urban areas, whereas housing and business buildings have grown older and produced decreased levels of property tax revenue. The challenge of providing more services with less revenue is worsened when job-producing employers move their businesses to nonmetropolitan areas.

Meanwhile, there are signs that older suburbs—those areas from which people and their employers are migrating—are becoming much like the older cities from which they sprang. "If they are not careful, they could end up with slums," commented one land use consultant.[1]

Outlying areas

Growth in the more outlying areas presents a different picture and a different set of problems. The 2,304 U.S. counties classified as nonmetropolitan in 1993 gained nearly 3 million residents between 1990 and 1996, compared with a gain of 1.3 million between 1980 and 1989.[2] This growth, attributed to migration rather than births, characterizes all but a few nonmetropolitan counties, although the rates of growth vary. The trend seems to be influenced by growth in rural manufacturing and by the location of universities, military installations, recreational facilities, and prisons (all of which are industries that create jobs), not to mention families' attempts to improve their quality of life.

Also growing from migration are the new "micropolitan" areas, a term devised in 1998 in recognition of the demographic trend of suburbanites migrating to smaller towns and communities.[3] Although the suburbs surrounding the big cities were a popular alternative to the cities during the last half of the twentieth century, eventually they drew criticism for the proliferation of fast-food restaurants, strip malls, town house tracts, high prices, and traffic jams. Micropolitan areas, populated by those fleeing the suburbs, are the result.

Although there is no official government definition, a micropolitan area has been described as containing at least one central city and one surrounding county. It is not part of an officially designated metropolitan statistical area (MSA). The central city contains at least 15,000 residents, and the surrounding county has at least 40,000 (including the central city). There are more than 190 micropolitan areas in the United States.

A drive across the United States on interstate highways makes these trends visible. The so-called micropolitan areas are growing and many will ultimately become MSAs. Undeveloped land for miles surrounding both metropolitan and micropolitan areas is being developed as businesses, industries, and their employees migrate to new environments.

With that migration will come increases in the frequency, severity, and complexity of public health and safety emergencies. For example, a community of 5,000 might expect 180 requests for emergency ambulance service per year (an average of one request every other day). That level of demand can usually be met with an all-volunteer ambulance service. But if the population doubles to 10,000, the demand is likely to double as well, averaging one call per day (360 per year).[4] In many communities that may be too great a burden for an all-

---

Issues for small communities   The small community of Stroud, Oklahoma, is located about midway between Oklahoma City and Tulsa along Interstate Highway 44. Although a few travel-related businesses were located directly adjacent to the highway, Stroud was primarily a farming community with a very slow growth trend.

Then a national chain of outlet malls decided to build a 40- to 50-store complex in the community, and the complex was successful. Other businesses, such as restaurants, convenience stores, and motels, followed. Established businesses in the community flourished as well.

Stroud quickly found itself playing catch-up with its services and started making major commitments for street, utility, and other service improvements to meet the demands of this new economic growth. Fire services were no exception. New facilities and equipment were desperately needed to

protect against significant new hazards.

Approximately five years after the mall began operating, a major tornado devastated the facility, rendering it completely useless. To the shock of the community, the national chain opted not to rebuild the facility but merely cleaned up and then abandoned the site. The huge income from sales taxes that had allowed the city to upgrade its services was gone. Orders for new fire apparatus had to be reconsidered. Although the demand for services had decreased dramatically, the long-term costs of the upgrades were still a reality.

In the budgets of small communities, development peaks and valleys are seriously magnified. Whether the valleys result from a tornado or just the economics of a given industry, big projects can wreak havoc when small communities must scramble to increase services and then risk losing the funding base of the single entity that makes a difference.

volunteer service, but at the same time it may not be adequate to support a private, for-profit ambulance service. As this inexorable evolution occurs, small communities throughout the United States will continue to face new and unfamiliar issues, including the need for improved fire prevention, fire protection, and emergency medical and rescue services.

For example, when the XYZ Pharmaceuticals Corporation decides to build its new half-million-square-foot manufacturing facility on the outskirts of Smalltown, who will ensure that modern requirements for fire protection are included in the building's design? Smalltown may have only a volunteer fire department, organized as a nonprofit association with officers elected by the membership. Does the fire department have the expertise to interpret fire code requirements during construction of a building that will greatly influence the future of Smalltown? Does it have code enforcement authority? Will the local water system be able to meet the fire flow requirements of a half-million-square-foot building? Does the fire department have the equipment and staffing to deliver that water in emergency conditions? What would the cost be to the community if fire were to damage or destroy the facility? Will the pharmaceutical corporation's manufacturing operations create the potential for leaks or spills of hazardous materials? If so, can such accidents be handled by local resources? Once the plant is in operation and employs hundreds of workers, what agency will be able to respond promptly to industrial accidents and medical emergencies?

These are but a few of the difficult questions facing public officials in smaller jurisdictions. In many areas the existing public health and safety infrastructure is essentially a remnant of simpler times. Urban-to-suburban and suburban-to-rural shifts of population, and the activities entailed by such shifts, will require an investment in and upgrading of that infrastructure.

The fire service's relationship with the public

All these issues will have to be addressed within the context of the fire department's relationship with the public. This relationship has two components: the public's view of the fire department, and the status accorded the department in most communities.

The public's view of the fire department

In 1997, a national poll studied the relative levels of trust the public accorded various community services and institutions, ranging from the police to public schools and from the media to the local, state, and federal governments (see sidebar on facing page). The institution that the highest percentage of adults trusted "a lot" was their own fire department. With a rating of 78 percent, fire departments ranked 32 points ahead of the next highest (their own police department) and 64 points ahead of city or local government (even though most fire departments are part of city or local government).

This public vote of confidence may be due to a number of things, including the fire department's reliability. As the conflict between demand and resources has escalated in many areas of public service, promptness and level of service have often been compromised. Calls for police assistance are often queued, with only the most urgent calls getting an immediate response. Reports of potholes, downed tree limbs, missing street signs, or broken sidewalks may not be acted on for days or weeks. But a telephoned report of a fire or medical emergency almost always produces an immediate lights-and-siren response from the local fire department.

Not only that, but firefighters tend not to worry about getting dirty. And they carry an impressive array of tools and equipment with them. Then, too, in most

"Whom do you trust?"   According to a 1997 *USA Today* survey, these are the percentages of adults who said they trusted the following institutions "a lot":

Their fire department	78%
Their police department	46%
Their public schools	32%
Local TV news	24%
Local daily newspapers	22%
City or local government	14%
Their state government	9%
Federal government	6%

Source: *USA Today*, 12 September 1997, p. 1. Copyright 1997, *USA Today*. Reprinted with permission.

cases they dig into a problem or task without issuing exculpatory warnings (i.e., without waiting until the customer signs a statement acknowledging and accepting the risks) or without asking for liability waivers. What all this adds up to is that aside from the obvious—containing and extinguishing fires—firefighters are increasingly called to assist in other emergencies. Whether the problem is a flooded basement or a natural gas leak, an overturned automobile or an elderly person who cannot get out of a bathtub, the local fire department has become a prompt and reliable source of assistance in most communities.

Fire service agencies themselves have done much to cement a positive relationship with the public. Increasingly they have been complementing technical expertise and an effective arsenal of tools with a customer service attitude. Nearly every fire chief receives letters of thanks from people who have received emergency services—and while most of those letter writers comment briefly on how quickly the response occurred and how technically skilled the fire personnel were, they comment at length on how much the firefighters seemed to care about the victims of the emergency and the victims' property. This common response brings to mind the slogan "Nobody cares how much you know till they know how much you care."[5]

Status of the department: Responder of first and last resort

Promptness and reliability; a customer service attitude; crews that are physically capable, trained, disciplined, and well equipped—in the public mind these characterize the fire and rescue department and underlie its status in most communities as the response resource of first and last resort.

For a wide range of emergency situations—a person suffering chest pains, a train that has been derailed, or the unmistakable shuddering and sounds of an earthquake—the first resource to be dispatched is usually the local fire and rescue department. Similarly, in situations when a service agency, public or private, is on the scene of a nonemergency problem or mishap and determines that it lacks the tools, equipment, or personnel to resolve the situation, the local fire and rescue department is likely to be called as a last resort. And first or last, in cases of building collapse, hazardous material (HAZMAT) spills, or brushfires, the fire department will remain on the scene long after the media, spectators, and other organizations have lost interest and gone home.

Of all public health and safety services, the local fire and rescue department is usually the only one that cannot pass a difficult emergency to another agency. A local health department can call on state or federal health agencies to assume responsibility for major public health emergencies. A local police department

Figure 1–1   Emergency service personnel in various nonemergency situations: (Top) Firefighters at a rail car derailment on Grand Avenue in Glendale, Arizona. (Center) A HAZMAT team plugging a leaking drum in Houston, Texas. (Bottom) Firefighters at a small plane crash site in Stillwater, Oklahoma.

facing civil disobedience or a major crime can seek assistance from the county sheriff or from a host of law enforcement agencies at the state and federal levels. But except for possible assistance on large wildland fires, the local fire department and neighboring mutual aid organizations essentially own their emergencies until those emergencies are resolved.

The public largely takes for granted the fire and rescue department's status as the trusted response resource of first and last resort: public reliance on the local fire department is usually subconscious. Yet these public expectations and this trust may have serious policy and financial implications for local government managers as they attempt to deal with issues of fire protection and emergency medical and rescue services.

The policy environment

The local government policy environment for fire protection and emergency medical and rescue services is complex and presents local government managers and fire department leaders with several types of pitfalls to avoid and challenges to meet. These range from the risk of complacency, at one extreme, to the danger of legal liability, at the other extreme.

Complacency

Human beings tend to become complacent when all seems well and when years pass without challenge. As long as the fire and rescue service enjoys a virtual love affair with the U.S. public, the risk of complacency will be present, affecting both fire service leaders and the public officials who bear responsibility for all local government services.

Fire service leaders   Although some fire service leaders will work to ward off complacency within their organizations, others will be less perceptive and less energetic. The greatest danger is when fire service leaders take the public's trust and confidence for granted. In these circumstances, complacency is usually manifested by inattentiveness to changes in the local environment and, on a larger scale, to changes in the industry's state of the art. When this inattentiveness develops, within a few years an organization that once excelled can lose touch with industry standards, innovations, and behavioral norms and with the people it is supposed to serve. Effective leadership is needed to prevent this from happening.

Public officials   Complacency toward fire, emergency medical, and rescue services may also characterize the public officials who are responsible for local government services. Usually the reason is that "squeaky wheels get greased first." If the public trusts and has confidence in the services provided by its fire and rescue department, public officials are not likely to hear complaints and demands for improvement or expansion.

Nevertheless, such complacency can erode the vitality and strength of the agencies for which the officials are responsible. When officials fail to provide both good leadership and the recognition and resources that a community's fire protection and life safety service needs, the result is usually deterioration that may take decades to reverse.

It is not only equipment and physical facilities that are subject to deterioration. The organizational culture of the public safety agency may also be transformed over time from positive to negative. This culture is the behavioral engine of most fire protection and emergency service organizations. Like a large ship at sea, the culture develops momentum, whether heading in a positive or a negative direction. Likewise, the culture is very difficult to turn around once

Third-party assessment   Third-party assessment of fire department services has been in place for many years. In setting fire insurance rates for a community, the insurance industry's Insurance Services Office (ISO) has periodically assessed a fire department's fire defense capability by applying ISO's self-generated standards and a graduated numerical schedule. The ISO Grading Schedule deliberately focuses mainly on the protection of property assets, however, and does not evaluate a number of programs and services that the modern fire service regards as important.

In the mid-1980s a group of concerned fire chiefs and local government managers developed an accreditation program designed specifically for local fire departments. Through a memorandum of understanding between the International Association of Fire Chiefs and the International City Management Association, a separate organization was created to operate the accreditation program. Responsibility for administering and maintaining this popular program now rests with the Commission on Fire Accreditation International (CFAI).

Regardless of size, fire departments that wish to be accredited are required to complete a detailed self-assessment that causes managers to examine more than 240 separate performance indicators, 98 of which are considered "core" or required competencies. The remaining competencies relate to activities and services that are considered local options and may or may not be offered by any given fire department. (The performance indicators fall into ten categories: governance, risk assessment, goals and objectives, finance elements, program elements, human resource practices, physical assets and facilities, training and competency assurance, internal support structure, and external relationships.)

Once the self-assessment is complete and has been reviewed by the CFAI, a team of site evaluators is assigned to visit the fire department to verify and clarify the material in the self-assessment document. At the end of the visit (whose duration will vary with the size of the department), the site team will recommend either final accreditation or more work. A reasonable fee and the cost of the site visit are the responsibility of the fire department.

Departments can use the self-assessment process without ever applying for accreditation, but no agency can be accredited without completing the documentation and undergoing the review and examination process.

The CFAI sponsors regional meetings to help prepare fire department and local government officials for this rigorous process. In addition, many fire departments that have been accredited will provide helpful advice to those considering this very significant undertaking. Although accreditation may not be the only way to measure the effectiveness of fire and rescue services in a community, it is a comprehensive tool and will provide benchmarks for many of the services offered by a modern fire department.

Departments interested in registering for the accreditation process should contact the Commission on Fire Accreditation International, 4500 Southgate Place, Suite 100, Chantilly, VA 20151, (703) 691-4620.

Source: Some of this information was provided by Chief Robert L. Ridgeway of the Gastonia, North Carolina, Fire Department. Additional information was provided by Ronny J. Coleman, FiFireE, CFC, chairman, CFAI Board of Trustees.

the momentum has developed. Official complacency is the environment in which the cultural transformation from positive to negative commonly occurs.

Competition with other local government agencies

Another challenge to public administration acquired new force in June 1978, when California voters overwhelmingly approved a tax limitation measure known as "Proposition 13" and thereby sparked a nationwide rebellion against local government taxation. The effect has been a reduction in the resources for building and maintaining local government infrastructure and for providing necessary services.[6] This happened while the U.S. population was growing by 40 million people.

In this atmosphere, intense competition developed among the public needs of local government, including fire and emergency response services. Internally, the competition pits streets, sewers, parks, libraries, schools, crime prevention, and fire protection and emergency medical and rescue services against one another. Externally, local governments are competing for funds that are apportioned at the state and county levels and redistributed to local jurisdictions.

In this competitive atmosphere, being trusted by the public has actually become a disadvantage. Citizens who are impressed by and satisfied with their community's fire protection and emergency medical and rescue services are not inclined to clamor for a bigger investment in those services.

In jurisdictions with career (full-paid) fire and rescue departments, more than 85 percent of the department's total budget often goes to salaries and fringe benefits. From the perspective of the local government administrator, investing in more fire department personnel offers little payoff because there will be no clear performance indicators that can be used to justify the investment (except for potential increases in revenue directly linked to new firefighter positions, such as staffing an additional ambulance that will generate net revenues). For example, a 10 percent increase in the fire department budget is not likely to produce a measurable reduction in fire losses in that budget year or the next.

The inability to measure outcome compared with investment may be the greatest management challenge facing fire service administrators in a competitive environment. An expansion of the local library is likely to produce a measurable increase in patronage. Construction of a park or public golf course is likely to produce measurable increases in public use as well as in user fees and concessionaire payments. The employment of additional parking enforcement officers is likely to generate larger fines and forfeitures. But the employment of additional firefighters is not likely to produce measurable outcomes that can be used for competing with the budget requests of other local government agencies.

Increasing the number of firefighters may ultimately trigger a reduction in the local jurisdiction's fire insurance rating, but the reduction is not likely to occur for a year or more. Since local government administrators seldom hear from citizens about their fire insurance premiums, an incremental rating change in an urban community is not likely to be persuasive in the internal competition for local government budgets. In rural or developing communities, in contrast, there is the potential for significant improvements in ratings, and the local jurisdiction's investment in fire department personnel may be more justifiable in a competitive atmosphere.

Competition with the private sector

A second form of competition is with the private sector, involving mainly the right to provide emergency ambulance services. With respect to fire protection, although for many years a small number of jurisdictions have contracted with private companies, in the United States and Canada this alternative to public fire protection has never achieved widespread acceptance. In contrast, in many areas of the country public fire departments have long struggled with private ambulance companies.

This conflict is largely about money, in that medical transportation services can generate revenue from a number of payment sources, yet it is often clothed as a conflict between government and free enterprise. Many fire service leaders view emergency ambulance service as a natural extension of their public health and safety responsibilities. Private ambulance companies have opposed this expansion of fire service roles, claiming it constitutes government incursion into the sphere of private enterprise.

This claim is questionable. The characteristics of free enterprise are unregulated retail competition; the opportunity to control pricing and payment terms; freedom to develop and sell new, innovative products and services; and management of cash flow. The field of medical transportation lacks these characteristics. It is highly regulated, and competition is precluded through exclusive contracts. Services and prices are prescribed by contract or regulation. In some of the privatized systems, contractors are prohibited from billing customers; instead, they receive predetermined payments from a governmental or quasi-governmental management entity that actually owns the ambulances. In essence, instead of being exemplars of free enterprise, the private companies have become little more than labor contractors.

The widespread impression that ambulance service throughout the United States and Canada is undergoing privatization is mostly incorrect. Although many small ambulance companies were acquired by or merged into the larger companies, very few communities with public ambulance service abandoned it or turned it over to private companies. In contrast, during the 1990s a number of jurisdictions stopped using private services and transferred responsibility for emergency ambulance transportation to their fire and rescue departments.[7]

In all locales where public fire departments have replaced private companies as primary providers of emergency ambulance service, improvements in response times and customer service have been reported. In addition, by increasing the productivity of their existing workforce and using marginal cost allocations, most fire chiefs are able to provide this additional service at a net cost that is less than a private company's. Once a fire and rescue department is a producer of net revenues, it is better able to compete with other public needs for funding and expansion.

As economic realities shape public-private competition, it is likely that a cooperative model will evolve. With public fire departments responsible for emergency ambulance service, private companies will be able to concentrate on the more profitable, less time-sensitive forms of nonemergency medical transportation.

Volatility in local government

Since the 1970s, a variety of factors have combined to make the policy environment of local government less stable and predictable. The noble pursuit of open government has created a public forum for every citizen, including those who look askance at all government activities.

The resulting volatility imposes a serious burden on public agency administrators. In addition to focusing on the legitimate goals of local government, managers must maintain respect for the principles of openness, honesty, and courtesy without overreacting to ignorant or grossly unfair criticism. The requisite composure and maturity may not be part of one's position description but are nonetheless necessary.

Risk aversion

Volatility in the local government policy environment as well as a growing volume of litigation against public agencies has caused many local governments to become very averse to taking risks. Unfortunately this aversion can discourage innovation and encourage a siege mentality.

For the fire service administrator who seeks excellence from his or her workforce, the local government's preoccupation with the need to avoid risk may pose a dilemma. Preoccupation with risk avoidance tends to deter progress and can paralyze an organization, whereas industry standards and public expectations change almost continuously. At the same time, though, most fire and rescue organizations contain persuasive people who wish their organization to excel. The resulting frustration among these people will have negative effects on the organizational culture.

Turnover of elected officials

Although it is the essence of representative government that elected officials have ultimate control of local government, the reality of this control can be troubling to the fire service administrator. Many elected officials come to their positions with noble intentions and ambitious plans but little technical background in the operations of local government. Fire chiefs and other agency heads may need to spend a great deal of time and energy orienting their elected leaders in the months or years following each election. Although the need to do this may seem an imposition, a drain on one's time and energy, it has become a reality of public administration.

Effect of special interests

Dealing with special interests is another challenge to the fire service administrator. Part of this challenge is a side effect of the increased cost of campaigning for public office. Even in relatively small jurisdictions, it is not uncommon for candidates for elective positions to spend several thousands of dollars on their campaigns—for positions that may be unpaid or may provide only token compensation. Thus, unless the official has abundant personal financial resources, he or she may be quite dependent on campaign contributors and unduly influenced by the opinions of people representing special interests.

This dependence may mean, for example, that a conflict between the fire service and a property owner over fire or building code violations will generate an inquiry or intervention from a local elected official. A second example concerns fireworks: in jurisdictions where the fire department has sought to ban fireworks, fire chiefs may experience political end runs from representatives of special interests. But the most prevalent source of political pressure on fire service issues since before 1990 has been the private ambulance industry. (Issues connected with ambulance service are discussed later in this chapter.)

Presumably every plan, proposal, or program put forth by a fire service administrator will balance divergent interests while making public health and safety dominant. The intervention of special interests to weaken, alter, defuse, or kill a proposal or program can be maddening. Nonetheless, it is the obligation of a professional administrator to respond with proper decorum, to calmly offer additional information or supportive evidence, and to accept the outcome as a product of the democratic process.

Another part of the challenge of dealing with special interests centers on purchasing and contracting for services. The marketing budget of manufacturers of fire apparatus and equipment includes money for entertaining potential purchasers. Although a free dinner or a round of golf is not likely to clinch a decision to purchase one brand rather than another, if the dinner or golf outing is reported in the local newspaper it is certain to raise questions. Even a trip to the factory to inspect apparatus under construction may be described by critics as a "junket" if it is linked to a family vacation.

To maintain public confidence, managers need to avoid situations that appear to compromise their integrity. If the chief administrator of the jurisdiction is a member of ICMA, he or she is subject to the ICMA Code of Ethics and is likely to be particularly sensitive to appearances of influence. In fact, the city manager may advise that if an inspection trip to the factory is desirable, it should be paid for by the local government rather than by the equipment manufacturer.

More than a few situations can become ethical traps and career disasters for local government administrators. Obviously the only way to avoid all risk is to do nothing. However, the true professional will plan and pursue ongoing improvements while keeping an eye open for situations that could appear inappropriate.

Legal issues: Civil and criminal liability

Fire, emergency medical, and rescue service agencies are the target of relatively few allegations of civil or criminal liability, compared with law enforcement and public transportation. Furthermore, the laws of most states provide certain forms of immunity for various levels and categories of emergency medical service (EMS) workers and providers. Still, the topic warrants serious and continuing attention.

Of the many areas of civil law (ranging from corporate to probate), the one that most directly affects fire, emergency medical, and rescue services is the law of negligence (sometimes referred to as "torts"). A basic principle of the law of negligence is that a person who is careless (negligent) and whose carelessness causes injury or damage to another person should be required to make that other person whole.

Under the law of negligence, when a lawsuit is filed by a person or entity against another person or entity, the person suing (plaintiff) is seeking monetary compensation from the defendant and has the burden of proving duty, breach, causation, and damages—the burden of proving that

1. The defendant had a legally recognized *duty* to perform in a particular way. Under the law of negligence, it is one's duty to always perform or behave as a reasonable, prudent, properly trained person in that position would perform or behave under the same or similar circumstances.
2. The defendant *breached* that duty with regard to the plaintiff. This is a question of fact: on the basis of all the available evidence, did the defendant violate or breach the duty he or she owed to the plaintiff?
3. The defendant's breach of duty was the proximate *cause* of the damage, injury, or loss suffered by the plaintiff. To prove causation, the plaintiff must show not only that the defendant breached his or her duty to the plaintiff but also that the breach of duty was the actual cause of the injuries or damage suffered. In other words, the plaintiff must prove that the injury or damage would not have occurred *but for* the negligence of the defendant.
4. The *damages*, injuries, or losses suffered by the plaintiff can be compensated with an award of money. Various types of compensable damages (as defined by state law) include damage to reputation, damage to property, lost earnings, emotional distress, physical disability, pain and suffering, medical expenses, wrongful death, and funeral expenses.

There are two degrees of negligence: ordinary and gross. Violation of the "reasonable, prudent, properly trained person" standard of duty is generally considered to be *ordinary negligence*. Behavior that is so extreme that even an unreasonable person would have done better is generally considered to be *gross negligence*.

As mentioned above, immunity laws (sometimes referred to as "Good Samaritan laws") in most states provide some level of protection. That is, even if ordinary negligence occurred, the plaintiff may not be able to recover damages from the negligent emergency medical technicians, paramedics, or their employers. However, if the deviation from the standard was so extreme as to be considered gross negligence, the immunity may not apply.

Understanding these basics of the law of negligence is imperative for every manager of fire and rescue services because, to a great extent, the risk of causing injury to others through negligence—thus suffering the process of litigation and the price of compensation—can be avoided. Identifying risks in advance and mitigating them proactively should be a high priority for every local government manager.

Although there is no national database, anecdotal and media reports suggest that the most frequent causes of suits and claims against U.S. fire departments are collisions involving emergency vehicles. Those reports also suggest that very large settlements and awards against fire departments often occur when a collision causes death or disability to one or more citizens. In contrast, published studies involving urban fire department paramedic ambulance services in Florida and Illinois reveal one claim or suit alleging defective medical care, on average, for every 18,000 patient transports (with an average settlement cost of less than $10,000).[8] It is reasonable to assume that those findings are typical of communities nationwide.

With regard to criminal law, the most frequently reported incidents involving the fire service arise from suspected arson. Other criminal charges that have been filed against public employees include theft of public property, assault and battery, sexual molestation, and illegal possession or use of controlled substances.

Just as the law of negligence is governed by basic principles, criminal law is governed by the principle that a person accused of a criminal act is innocent until proven guilty. Accordingly, every public agency should be guided by well-considered policies and procedures that will protect the rights of the accused while also protecting the public health and safety.

Legal issues: Interpretation of laws and codes

Another type of legal issue that fire and rescue departments must deal with is the interpretation of laws, codes, and standards.

Despite the best intentions of legislators, laws passed to create new rights and protections are usually followed by numerous legal conflicts. The reason is that legislative (including congressional) language is most often a product of compromise; thus, it leaves open various questions as to intent and application.

Legal questions and challenges ultimately produce written opinions by appellate courts (the only courts that set precedents and are required to produce written opinions). Usually these opinions introduce still more questions for those who must apply the law. For example, laws forbidding discrimination on the basis of sex, age, and race must be assessed in the context of infinitely variable situations of fact. Since these laws apply across the full range of public agencies, most local governments employ human resource and legal specialists who monitor the legal status of such issues on an ongoing basis. The fire service manager should recognize the pitfalls of "freelancing" in this area of public policy and should seek expert assistance when necessary. More detailed information on personnel issues is available in Chapter 5.

In addition, the codes and standards that govern or influence fire, emergency medical, and rescue services have a legal dimension. For example, safety standards applied to the fire service by state and federal occupational safety and health agencies have the authority of law. And local government managers are confronted with the potential legal effect of consensus standards adopted by such organizations as the National Fire Protection Association (NFPA), the American Waterworks Association, and ASTM (known as the American Society for Testing and Materials until the 1980s; some people continue to use the former name). These standards and related legal responsibilities are addressed in Chapter 13.

The remainder of this chapter will survey the three areas of responsibility of most fire departments: fire protection, emergency medical service, and rescue service.

Fire protection

The fire service exists to protect people and their property from fires, and that remains the service's core mission even as firefighters have learned new skills and taken on new responsibilities. Protecting against fires has three components: defining and addressing the problem, improving fire prevention, and suppressing fires when they do break out.

The fire problem: Past, present, and future

In 1973 the National Commission on Fire Prevention and Control issued a report, *America Burning,* to President Nixon. At that time the annual fire toll in the United States was estimated at 12,000 deaths, 300,000 injuries, and $11 billion in property losses, not counting indirect losses such as business interruption, loss of sales and property tax revenues, and the cost of unemployment when jobs were lost because of fires.[9]

The commission's report recommended six changes:

More emphasis on fire prevention

Better fire service training and education

Public fire safety education

More attention to flammability and toxicity of materials

Improved fire protection features in buildings

Research into firefighting, treatment of burn and smoke victims, and protection of the built environment from combustion hazards.[10]

To some degree all these recommendations have been addressed, apparently with good effect. For example, updated fire and building codes are being applied to virtually all new construction and to major modifications of older structures (the effect of the updated codes is improved fire protection features in buildings); the nation's older building stock, including many combustible wood structures, is being replaced with more fire-safe construction, including built-in fire protection where required by code. The availability and quality of firefighter and fire officer training have vastly improved; in this effort, the National Fire Academy (established in 1975) has been a major influence. Millions of elementary school children have received education in fire safety, including how to conduct fire safety inspections in their homes; they have been exposed to the "Stop, Drop and Roll" escape procedure, the *Learn Not to*

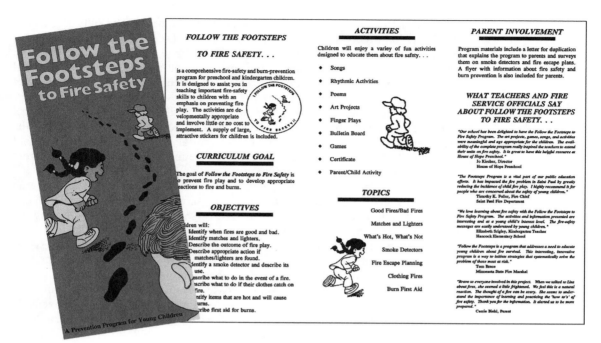

Figure 1–2   Brochure for a comprehensive fire safety and burn prevention program in Saint Paul, Minnesota, for preschool and kindergarten children.

Burn® campaign, and the EDITH (Exit Drills in the Home) program. Flammable and toxic materials, in products ranging from children's toys and sleepwear to home furnishings and airplane seats, have been the subject of numerous statutes and government programs. Finally, the products of continuing medical research have reduced morbidity and improved the survival rate for victims of burn injuries.

Although no research has been conducted to measure cause and effect, between 1977 and 2000 the annual U.S. fire toll (as reported by NFPA) dropped from the estimated 7,400 civilian fire deaths to 4,045 and from 31,190 civilian injuries to 22,350 (but rose from $4.7 billion in property damage to $11.2 billion [in 2000 dollars]). Between 1977 and 2000 the number of fires reported in the United States fell by nearly one-half, from more than 3.2 million to 1.7 million per year.[11] These improvements occurred during a period of substantial population growth.

The solid progress made by the U.S. fire service in dealing with the national fire problem has largely erased the sense of urgency. At the national, state, and local levels, public policy makers have tended to put the fire problem on the back burner. As fire officials seek funds to continue the task of reducing the fire problem, they find themselves competing with other priorities, such as crime, sewers, roads, and public transportation.

In addition, as fire departments have become more involved in related emergency activities (such as medical first response, ambulance service, technical rescue, and HAZMAT management), public policy makers have tended to trivialize the fire problem. But in fact, as mentioned above, the nation still suffers about 4,000 fire-related deaths annually. Thus, increased emphasis on comprehensive fire prevention systems and public education is essential.

Learn Not to Burn® is a registered trademark of the National Fire Protection Association (NFPA), Quincy, MA 02269.

Furthermore, adequate numbers of personnel must be on duty or readily available for timely response to and control of fires and other emergencies. Because fire suppression and rescue work, by their nature, are time sensitive and labor-intensive, analogies to the use of labor in manufacturing or retail sales are illogical. When automobile sales are depressed, car manufacturers can reduce capacity by laying off workers. Fire and rescue emergencies are unpredictable as to time and place, and properly trained and equipped personnel must be available around-the-clock to respond to those emergencies. If the frequency of fires declines 30 percent, the on-duty roster of firefighters cannot be reduced proportionately because the next fire may require a full complement of people to contain and extinguish it.

To ensure adequate resources, local government managers should make an unrelenting effort to keep the issue of fire safety on the front burner. They should not allow the issue to be trivialized or shelved simply because progress has been made and further progress may be expensive.

At the same time, though, the reduction in the frequency of fires raises issues of efficiency and productivity in career fire departments. These issues are addressed by the conversion of fire departments into multirisk agencies, a conversion that was coincidental in some cases, responsive in others. This conversion is often misunderstood, for many local elected officials and citizens do not grasp the logic or the economics of expanding the roles of firefighting personnel to include other functions.

Typically, a "standing army" of fire suppression personnel is available for prompt mobilization in the event of fires, floods, building collapses, and so forth. When additional emergency functions (such as EMS, technical rescue service, and HAZMAT management) are taken on and firefighters cross-train for these additional roles, the cost of fire protection is spread over a wider array of emergency services.

Thus, an additional goal in addressing the fire problem is to continue the conversion from single-function fire departments to multirisk fire, EMS, and rescue organizations. When the organization becomes multirisk and spreads its cost over a larger number of emergency service needs, the expense of maintaining adequate human resources for fire protection becomes more defensible. In fact, some of those emergency service needs, such as emergency ambulance service, may actually produce nontax revenue that can help offset the cost of staffing for fire suppression.

Of course, a strong case can be made for fire protection as one of the central reasons for local government. The human and monetary cost of fire deaths, injuries, and property loss should be sufficient in itself to justify the cost of adequate staffing for fire protection. However, most fire losses are insured, the cost of full-paid firefighters is relatively high, and the competition for local government resources is intense; thus, single-function fire departments have generally suffered gradual reductions in staffing. Multirisk fire, EMS, and rescue organizations for the most part have held their own or increased their staffing. They are therefore better able to pursue the primary goal of further reducing fire deaths, injuries, and associated costs.

A three-pronged approach to prevention

When possible, the most logical solution to the fire problem is prevention. But fire prevention lacks the physical challenge and excitement of fighting a fire, so it is generally perceived as less glamorous. Still, it is a universally accepted principle that fire prevention is the responsibility of every member of a fire service organization. Fire prevention is achieved with engineering, education, and enforcement; these topics are covered in detail in Chapter 12.

Fire suppression: Evolution of apparatus, tools, and equipment

As late as 1960, U.S. fire apparatus tended to be overweight, cumbersome, and dependent on frequent maintenance and repairs. Pumpers (engines) were designed around their primary function: moving large volumes of water. Ladder trucks tended to be ungainly and expensive to maintain. Most aerial ladders were limited to eighty-five feet in length.

The 1970s were marked by major improvements, including diesel power, rugged and dependable automatic transmissions, faster acceleration, better braking, and more reliable pumps and hydraulics. Reflecting both inflation and the cost of improvements, the price of fire apparatus more than doubled in a single decade.

Also in the 1970s, the primary service role of fire apparatus began to change. Neighborhood fire companies became the first line of defense in medical as well as fire emergencies. Thus, as the frequency of fire calls began to decline, the typical fire pumper essentially became a sixteen-ton personnel carrier on EMS calls in the intervals between its firefighting assignments.

Some argued that this was inefficient and that smaller, more mobile vehicles would be better for responding to EMS calls. But the use of firefighters in multiple roles—for fire suppression and EMS, for example—requires that all their tools and equipment (and pumping capacity) be with firefighters at all times. It is better to respond to a medical emergency with a pumper than to respond to a fire in a small vehicle that cannot pump water.

By the 1990s, when the nature of the fire service mission had substantially changed, the demands on its rolling stock had changed accordingly. In the 1970s many fire departments retired low-mileage 1950s-era fire apparatus because of age, but by the 1990s some fire apparatus purchased in the 1970s and 1980s was being retired because of excessive mileage. The price of fire apparatus had also changed: a typical pumper in the 1990s was at least three times as expensive as its predecessor in the early 1970s.

Tools and equipment also changed during the last third of the century. Although water remained the basic element of fire suppression, foam additives were increasingly used to create a more efficient and effective extinguishing agent. Many new pumpers were being ordered with built-in compressed-air foam systems for extinguishing fires in a wide variety of fuels, from residential structures to combustible vegetation (in fire protection/suppression, anything that will burn is a fuel).

The almost universal adoption of large-diameter hose and quick-connect couplings—a break with many decades of tradition—allowed for the delivery of more water faster. Power equipment used to breach walls, floors, and roofs was greatly improved and more reliable than the tools of earlier generations. Even some of the firefighter's most basic hand tools, such as the pike pole, axe, and spanner wrench, were improved with such features as fiberglass handles and harder, lighter, metal surfaces.

Heavy canvas salvage covers gave way to lighter but more durable plastic materials. Manila rope was replaced by kernmantle (a type of braided rope). Finicky gas-powered smoke ejectors, saws, hydraulic pumps, and generators became obsolete as more reliable equipment was invented and marketed. Burlap sacks filled with sawdust, long used by firefighters to control water damage, were replaced by materials that can absorb many times their weight and volume.

During the last thirty years of the twentieth century, the U.S. fire service changed more than at any other time in its history. To be sure, the invention of steam pumpers in the nineteenth century and the conversion from horse-drawn to self-propelled fire apparatus early in the twentieth were important developments. But the continuous stream of innovation and development since about 1970, along with the expansion of the fire service's role, makes the most recent period momentous in terms of change.

Fire suppression: Innovations in organization and management

In an earlier time, when the U.S. fire service was highly autocratic, virtually all organization and management of emergency fire and rescue situations centered on one person—the fire chief. But if the emergency worsened or grew after the arrival of the fire department, the numbers of on-scene people and apparatus increased, sometimes exponentially, beyond the numbers that one person could manage effectively.

When emergencies are mismanaged, the possibility of injury and death for firefighters and civilians, not to mention unnecessary property losses, grows. When the resources of multiple agencies are deployed (through automatic or mutual aid, both of which are prearranged deployments of resources), these risks—and the complexities of managing the emergency—are compounded.

Since 1970, at least two incident management system (IMS) designs have been developed to better organize and manage fire suppression operations and responses to other emergencies.[12] Structurally, the IMS design merely subdivides responsibility and accountability into functional subgroups. Ultimately a national IMS standard was developed.[13] In addition, standard nomenclature is used throughout the system so that resources from multiple agencies can function together effectively. Variations of the fire department IMS have been developed and used for multiple-casualty incidents.

Whether used for fire incidents or for other protracted emergency situations,

---

Usefulness of incident management systems Incident management systems provide a framework for effective delivery of emergency services and make the incident scene significantly safer. Several tragic incidents during the 1990s cost firefighter lives and pointed to the need for strong and effective incident management.

At fires in several states, firefighters died when they were trapped or lost in perilous positions. The lack of a structured accountability system for personnel on the scene might have been a significant factor in these deaths. A standardized incident management system (IMS) provides for the accountability of personnel and integrates this important information into a process that keeps people aware of one another's activities and locations and provides for the welfare of personnel working on the scene.

A second factor in these incidents was the difficulty of maintaining communication between the personnel in danger and those who might have been able to provide assistance. In two cases in particular, radio transmissions seeking help were not heard because of high levels of ambient noise in the command officers' area of operations. Again, a strong IMS takes advantage of the best available command environments and a defined communications process, both of which are significant assets when one is dealing with the unforeseen.

Nearly identical situations involving firefighter deaths have occurred at single-family residence fires. Although these would appear to be much less complicated incident management situations, the factors were much the same. These incidents and many others like them lend credibility to the concept of putting an IMS in place and using it with literally every incident.

IMS can facilitate the smooth expansion or contraction of the emergency response organization as needed. When other, nonfire agencies are involved, such as police agencies and disaster relief organizations, the system can embrace them without disruption or loss of control.

Coincidental with the development of IMS, electronic data and the tools to store and access the data have been made available to many fire, EMS, and rescue organizations. Thus, an incident commander and his or her staff, using a common laptop computer and portable printer, can produce maps, building plans, pre-fire inspection reports, resource inventories, emergency procedure checklists, HAZMAT information, and on-scene equipment and personnel rosters.

Emergency medical services

At the beginning of the twenty-first century, a high percentage of the work of many fire departments consists of responding to medical emergencies. No other chapter in this book focuses on such emergencies, so the discussion here includes a fair amount of detail.

Historical perspective

As early as the 1920s, a few U.S. fire departments expanded their traditional roles to include first aid for victims of illness and accidents. Those departments were in the minority, however. Most U.S. and Canadian fire departments ignored or resisted the opportunity to provide any service beyond fire protection.

Meanwhile, a revolution was occurring in the field of prehospital emergency medical care and transportation. New techniques and treatments were approved, improved training programs and textbooks were adopted, and in the early 1970s the title "emergency medical technician" (EMT) was devised for those who successfully completed the 80- to 120-hour EMT training course and certification exams. *EMS (emergency medical service)* became the umbrella term to describe all the services and processes involved in caring for sick or injured people before they reach the hospital.

At the same time, the term *basic life support (BLS)* was put forth to distinguish the new level of training and skill from first aid, which had been the standard of care for firefighters and ambulance personnel for decades. BLS includes such skills and functions as CPR, administration of oxygen, maintenance of airway without invasive equipment, spinal immobilization, splinting of fractures, control of external hemorrhage, emergency childbirth, and ambulance transportation of patients.

A quantum leap occurred in about 1970, when experimental paramedic programs in Columbus (Ohio), Miami (Florida), Seattle, and Los Angeles trained firefighters to deliver what came to be known as advanced life support (ALS). Within months the level of EMS delivered in those four locales jumped from first aid to sophisticated coronary care—care more advanced than was available in some hospitals at the time.

ALS includes all of the BLS skills and functions as well as electrocardiogram analysis, use of adjunctive airway devices, establishment and maintenance of intravenous lines, administration of approved solutions and medications, and other advanced procedures as approved by a local medical director (an M.D., who is a liaison between local medical authorities and the fire and rescue department). Although the official titles for ALS personnel vary from state to state, in day-to-day parlance such personnel are almost universally referred to as paramedics.

The four experimental programs might have been temporary but for the effect of entertainment television. A veteran producer became aware of the Los An-

Meeting community expectations: Emergency medical service   With public expectations for emergency medical service (EMS) driven by very visible and successful systems throughout the world, small communities often face the dilemma of how to meet those expectations when resources are very limited. A number of small suburban and rural communities in and around Milwaukee County, Wisconsin, devised a way to cope with the problem of high expectations and low resources. Local government and fire service officials developed a plan to pool their resources by developing EMS zones. Within each zone, a single fire service agency was designated to train for and provide advanced life support services. The remaining agencies were responsible for training for and providing first-responder/basic life support services, a much less expensive process.

The resulting system provides a highly qualified and effective tiered response to emergency medical incidents throughout the protected area. It does so at a cost that is manageable for all communities inasmuch as the sharing of resources spreads the effect over the entire area. The citizens are winners, as the service is excellent. The fire services are also winners in that they are providing a valuable and very popular service to their communities by sharing resources and avoiding costly duplication.

With the wise use of fire service resources, each community's high expectations were met.

geles paramedic program and used it as the basis for a weekly action-adventure series, *Emergency!* Seven years later, more than half of all U.S. residents were within ten minutes of a paramedic unit, and a majority of those units were operated by fire departments.

Probably no other organizational concept in health care has swept the nation so rapidly and changed public expectations so dramatically. In many cases, it was public expectations that drove reluctant fire departments to expand their services and become multirisk organizations. By the end of the twentieth century, some of the most respected fire service leaders acknowledged that their agencies had become EMS providers that also occasionally fought fires.

EMS and the fire service

By the mid-1990s, most fire and rescue department first responders were equipped to provide the full range of BLS functions, and many were also equipped with automatic or semiautomatic portable electric defibrillators (see sidebar on page 24). During the decade the trend among fire departments nationwide was to upgrade their first responders to the ALS level; the use of defibrillation equipment was a major factor in the upgraded service.

Many fire departments strive to maintain all members at the basic life support (EMT) level as a minimum. Others have found that their budgets cannot cover the costs of continuing education and periodic recertification exams (especially if all or a portion of the training/testing time must be compensated at overtime rates mandated by the Fair Labor Standards Act). If at all possible, however, BLS is the ideal baseline level of training and certification for firefighters. (As each state created laws and regulations for EMS, EMTs were labeled with additional identifiers indicating various levels of proficiency. During the 1990s, when the national standard training curriculum for BLS was revised, the title of the training program was changed to EMT-Basic, or EMT-B.)

Figure 1–3   An automatic external defibrillator being used to resuscitate a victim.

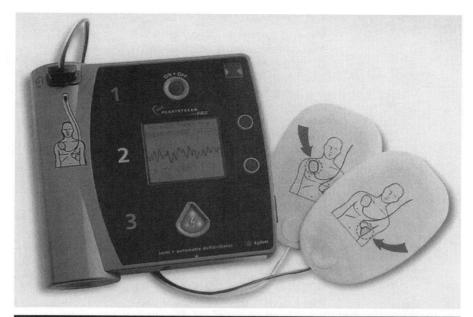

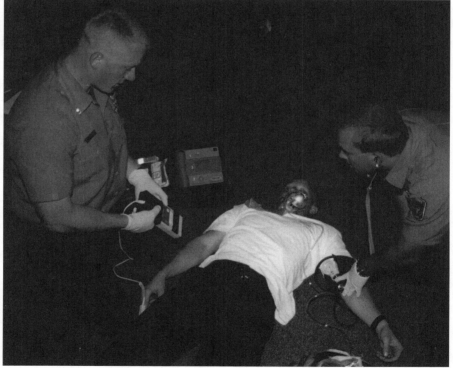

Fire department first-response service   As the fire service role in the United States and Canada expanded to include first aid and medical rescue services, some coincidental relationships and effects became apparent. For example, the placement of fire stations in a typical community had always been related to time (getting to the scene and applying water to a fire before it reached the point of "flashover" [the point when fuel and superheated air, in an enclosed space, finally ignite])—and increasingly since the 1960s, medical research has

Meeting community expectations: Automated external defibrillation   An accepted adjunct to BLS is automated external defibrillation. The most sudden and lethal cardiac malfunction is known as ventricular fibrillation, or V-fib. It is a condition in which the electrical impulses that control the rhythmic pulsation of the heart become uncoordinated. A human heart in V-fib quivers in a manner that resembles a jelly-like mass. In this state, it cannot pump blood. Very quickly after the onset of V-fib, the victim loses consciousness (as the flow of oxygenated blood to the brain ceases). About six minutes after onset, brain damage begins to occur in most victims. At about ten minutes, unless effective CPR has been performed, there is very little chance that the victim can be resuscitated.

The only effective remedy for V-fib is electrical defibrillation. This is accomplished by a machine (the automatic external defibrillator, or AED) that delivers a powerful shock of direct current in a controlled waveform to repolarize the heart. If defibrillation is successful, the heart will immediately convert to an effective rhythm, and pulse and blood flow will be restored. The prognosis for recovery without neurological damage depends greatly on the time elapsed between the onset of V-fib and the administration of the electrical shock by an AED.

Technology has resulted in smaller, lighter, more durable defibrillators that now include computerized logic systems to automate the analysis of cardiac rhythm and activation of shock.

AEDs have found their way into the expectations of citizens when it comes to their fire and emergency medical services. Many fire departments have an AED unit on every fire engine and ladder truck. Several communities have equipped police patrol cars with AED devices. The visibility of these devices, not only on television but also in the workplace and even on airliners, has greatly increased the public's awareness of their potential lifesaving value.

Fire departments, small and large alike, are faced with the problem of meeting the expectation that high-tech AEDs will be available with the very first arriving units at a cardiac emergency. The standard AED unit sells for several thousand dollars and requires some ongoing battery and electronic maintenance. In addition, anyone who will be operating the unit requires training, which varies from just a few hours to the acquisition of full EMT credentials, depending on the state or province having jurisdiction.

Many fire departments have used their strong community base to get started on an AED project for their community. Thousands of AEDs have been purchased with funds provided by various service clubs in local communities, particularly in small communities where public resources are very limited. Because nearly every family can relate to the need for emergency cardiac care at some time, the AED is a particularly attractive project for civic organizations.

Although most of the expense of training and maintenance must naturally be borne by the fire service, the initial purchase and even the replacement of an AED is often a win/win proposition for the community and for one or more of its civic organizations.

revealed the significance of time in saving lives from cardiac arrest ("sudden death") and in extricating and transporting trauma victims.

From an EMS standpoint, it is known that cardiac arrest is universally lethal unless timely and appropriate interventions occur within five to ten minutes of the arrest. In communities with on-duty career or volunteer firefighters, an engine company can usually be at the scene of a medical emergency within approximately five to ten minutes of being called. The timely availability of trained firefighters was the greatest influence in expanding their role to include medical first-response services. In addition to BLS skills such as CPR, these personnel bring with them oxygen, devices for maintaining a patient's airway, splinting and immobilization equipment, and, increasingly, defibrillators. In providing these services, first-response fire companies "stop the clock" for ambulances that are traveling from more distant locales.

The use of local fire companies as medical first responders entails other advantages in addition to promptness in administering emergency procedures. First and foremost, in-depth knowledge of their districts helps them to locate the site of the patient promptly. Second, in cases in which elderly fall victims are locked inside their dwellings and unable to admit rescuers, the special skills of forcible entry are important. Third, if the individual who requires assistance is heavy, moving him or her rapidly to an uncluttered area where there is a flat, hard surface may require several personnel working together.

Once an ambulance crew arrives at the scene, primary responsibility for medical care, along with all available information, may be transferred. If more than one patient is to be transported or if conditions require both ambulance personnel in the patient compartment, a firefighter may drive the ambulance to the hospital.

These value-added services are delivered millions of times each year throughout the United States and Canada and have become an integral part of the standard of emergency care that is expected in most communities in these two countries. Removal of the first-response service from the mix of resources that is EMS would greatly reduce the effectiveness of the system, increase the cost, or do both.

Paramedic fire companies   Many of the early fire service EMS systems have evolved into different operational profiles. One of the most important evolutionary changes has been the concept of paramedic fire companies. Originated in Santa Monica, California, in 1972, the ALS engine company is seen as an economical way to deliver paramedic-level emergency care rapidly. Although some fire service EMS systems have restricted paramedic (ALS) status to a few firefighter positions, others have trained all or most firefighters to the ALS level. The ideal is probably somewhere between those extremes.

Again, the placement of fire stations (for fire protection purposes) has the coincidental effect of quick responses by fire units to medical emergencies. A neighborhood fire company, with a staff that includes one or more firefighter paramedics, equipped with all the ALS equipment except a gurney, can receive a call for assistance, respond to it, and initiate ALS more quickly than any other operational profile. In many cases, by the time an ambulance arrives at the scene the ALS fire company personnel will have the patient resuscitated or stabilized and packaged for transport.

Another advantage of ALS fire companies is that even when paramedic firefighters receive promotions, they can continue to use their ALS training and skills. For example, a fire apparatus operator or engineer, or a lieutenant or captain, may perform in that role while also serving as a paramedic on incidents involving ill or injured people. This "career ladder" option reaps greater public benefit from costly training programs, and it optimizes the patient care and emergency command experience gained by paramedics while serving as firefighters.

In some locales, fire departments have, in effect, "marketed" ALS first-response services to private ambulance companies. When private companies are bound by contract to meet certain response-time standards and when the cost of meeting those standards is prohibitively expensive, contracts have been devised whereby the fire department's paramedic-staffed fire engines and ladder trucks "stop the clock," so to speak, upon arriving at the scene. This gives the private ambulance company a longer response time (which translates into lower operating costs). A portion of the private company's savings is paid to the local government to cover the marginal cost of the ALS first-response services.

The managed care environment

Fire department EMS at the beginning of the twenty-first century operates in a managed care environment. *Managed care* is an umbrella term referring to a variety of methods, processes, concepts, and organizations whose purpose is to ensure the provision of adequate levels of health care at acceptable costs. Off-shoots of the umbrella term are managed care organization (MCO) or plan and other labels and acronyms, such as health maintenance organization (HMO), preferred provider organization (PPO), and primary care physician (PCP).

In the managed care environment, the most elementary issues for fire and rescue agencies are competition and customer orientation. From the beginning, fire service customers were victims of fires or other emergencies who had immediate needs and no real choices: when one's house is burning, one is oriented toward receiving an immediate response and does not engage in comparison shopping to select a fire department to fight the fire. The local fire department was, in essence, a monopoly. In contrast, managed care arose from financial desperation, and the need to contain the costs of health care led to the use of competition to reduce costs and increase customer (member) satisfaction. Typical fire and rescue departments, having no real experience with market competition and no historic need to be concerned with customer satisfaction, have been ill equipped to compete with, for example, private ambulance companies in the evolving managed care environment.

A central problem is that of geographic boundaries. MCOs and their affiliated insurers recruit members (customers) and sell memberships throughout large geographic areas—areas that may include dozens or even hundreds of cities, towns, and counties and may even cover parts of two or more states. Fire and rescue departments, by contrast, are usually monojurisdictional. That is, they serve only areas within their own jurisdictional boundaries. And even if those boundaries include multiple communities, they never cover as large an area as the total area in which a major MCO operates.

Accordingly, the jurisdictional priorities of a typical fire and rescue department may often be at odds with the needs and expectations of a managed care plan. If the fire and rescue department is unable to get the plan's members to (what the plan considers) the right bed at the right clinic or hospital the first time, the MCO may seek medical transportation providers who can meet its needs.

A solution, it appears, is for fire departments to develop regional networks or consortia that allow for regionwide allocation of resources. For example, if a fire department ambulance service transports an MCO member out of the department's own jurisdiction to a hospital or clinic affiliated with the plan, it might rely on neighboring fire departments to provide coverage for its territory while it is engaged in that transport.

Managing such a network or consortium generally requires greater flexibility and more prompt decision making than are possible in many local governments. Therefore, it may be necessary to organize and create such a network or consortium in the form of a separate corporation (either for profit or nonprofit). Regardless of the form it takes and the various forms of alliances and agreements it enters into, the separate organization would fit the category of a management service organization (MSO)—that is, an organization that, for a managed care network, coordinates services provided by a multiplicity of agencies.

To forge an appropriate role in a managed care environment, a fire and rescue agency needs to develop internal expertise and then educate or inform local policy makers, from city or county managers to elected council members or commissioners. Given the complexity of health care services generally and of managed care specifically, this informational and educational task may become the fire service manager's greatest challenge.

Pathway management

The strategies used by managed care to save costs include achieving economies of scale, shifting risks, limiting members' (patients') freedom of choice, and —especially significant for fire and rescue agencies—controlling members' "pathway" through the health care system. It is generally recognized that the goal of pathway management is to direct people to the appropriate care in the most efficient manner at the appropriate time. Pathway management is intended not to restrict access to care but to direct traffic.

In the days before pathway management, people who believed they had medical problems could select any doctor they wanted and doctors could order any tests, prescribe any medications, and refer patients to any specialists. Neither access nor cost was controlled, as both are with managed care. Under managed care's system of pathway management, people who believe they have medical problems are required to go first to a primary care physician who is employed by or allied with their plans. The primary care physician's compensation arrangement is likely to include a strong incentive to limit the patient's care and treatment to only what is necessary. Before referring a patient to a specialist, the primary care physician will make certain that the specialist referral is absolutely necessary.

Pathway management is not so straightforward, however, with respect to prehospital care and transportation. Prehospital care has two components: dispatching and first response. Transportation is an especially complex issue with a strong economic component.

Dispatching   For many decades, public safety dispatching—now an integral part of the emergency services system—was generally thought to involve little more than receiving information and notifying emergency units. In many locales, dispatcher positions were filled with injured or disabled firefighters or police officers.

Two types of change have affected the dispatching function: the dispatcher may now give prearrival instructions to callers, and the dispatcher may go through what is called "structured interrogation" to determine actual medical need.

As early as 1974, a few fire departments assigned one or more EMTs or paramedics to their dispatch centers for the purpose of helping callers while rescue units were en route—helping them, for example, by giving instructions on how to clear a choking victim's airway or how to perform CPR. This process came to be known as prearrival instructions, and it has been credited with saving the lives of thousands.

Originally it was thought that those providing prearrival instructions needed EMT or paramedic training and experience. Subsequently, however, the EMT or paramedic background was found to be unnecessary; the specialized position of emergency medical dispatcher (EMD) was created; and EMD training programs have come to be recognized as providing more than adequate preparation for this function.

The other aspect of dispatching (structured interrogation) also changed significantly. Before 1980, the accepted procedure for dispatching emergency units to reported medical emergencies was predetermined and invariable. The traditional assumption was that any request for EMS involved a sudden, unexpected onset of potentially life-threatening circumstances. For example, a report of a male adult with abdominal pain would trigger a worst-case presumption —even though the relative medical risk does not justify extraordinary efforts to save time. In most locales, the nearest fire company would be dispatched as first responders, an ambulance would be dispatched simultaneously, and in most cases a police patrol unit would be assigned to assist and maintain order at the scene. The fire company and the ambulance would respond "hot" (with red lights and sirens).

Largely from concern about the frequency of emergency vehicle collisions, the long-standing worst-case dispatch procedures were challenged.[14] It was determined that the use of red lights and siren on a typical emergency medical response saved little time. In addition, in 1998, of 100.4 million emergency department visits in the United States (more than half of which did not involve a fire and rescue response), only 31.3 million were classified as "urgent."[15] Some amount of careful discrimination therefore seemed advisable. It was determined that a structured interrogation process would allow dispatchers to elicit enough information from callers to ascertain more accurately the gravity of the event. Dispatch protocols were then devised to base responses on actual medical need and on a recognition of local traffic flow problems, construction areas, and other area-specific variables. In the year 2000 some fire departments were staffed to "triage" calls for EMS assistance and to route calls for non-emergency assistance to more appropriate agencies.

Some public safety dispatch agencies resisted adopting priority medical dispatching, often justifying the resistance by invoking the potential risk of liability. However, in the first two decades in which the concept was applied in ever-increasing numbers of systems, no losses due to legal liability were reported.

Pathway management in prehospital EMS can therefore be applied at the dispatch stage by the use of medically approved protocols, carefully designed interrogation processes, and continuous quality improvement. Once an EMD determines that the call does not involve an acute emergency, he or she has several options.

If the EMD determines that the sick or injured person is a member of an MCO and identifies the plan, a call center service may be available through the plan. If so, the EMD may be able to transfer the call to that call center— which is operated by or contracts with the caller's MCO. At the call center, a nurse or other qualified person will be able to quickly access the member's computerized records, including physician recommendations for responding to that member's emergencies.

Whether or not a call center is accessed, the EMD may have other alternatives. For example, the EMS protocols may allow the EMD to select a private ambulance responding "cold" (without warning lights and siren). Or the protocols may allow an appointment to be made for a home health care nurse to visit the caller's home. Or, if the patient has a means of transportation and the condition is determined not to be acute, the patient may be directed to his or her MCO's ambulatory clinic. Thus, the member's pathway through the system may be managed.

In many cases, even with medical priority dispatch protocols and structured interrogation, the possibility of a life-threatening condition cannot be safely ruled out. In those situations the EMD will dispatch a normal response, including a first-response unit and an ambulance. When the first-response unit arrives at the scene, however, a second opportunity for pathway management occurs.

First response When first-response personnel assigned to fire companies have additional training, they can conduct an in-depth physical assessment of the patient at the scene and obtain information about recent medical history. They can make telephone contact with a pathway manager at the patient's MCO. Preestablished protocols for this patient probably would be accessible on the call center's computer. On the basis of those protocols, one of several courses of action may be chosen. The first-response fire company may be instructed to arrange for transportation of the patient to the closest appropriate hospital or to a hospital that is affiliated with the plan. It may be instructed to issue an appointment slip and arrange for alternative transportation to the plan's ambulatory care clinic. Or it may be instructed to make the patient comfortable and arrange for a home health care nurse to visit. At the very least, the first-response fire company has an opportunity to provide the plan with an updated assessment and patient history information regarding its member.

Providing these services enables first responders to play an important role in pathway management. To the extent that such a service requires additional training and equipment as well as on-scene time and risk, it should be treated as a potential source of revenue. In other words, if the fire and rescue organization uses its personnel and resources to help reduce the costs of health care plans, at least by providing information that has value, the plans should be willing to pay for those services.

Traditionally, only medical transportation services have been reimbursable under Medicare and Medicaid regulations and the policies adopted by most private insurers. In the late 1990s the major fire service organizations were participating in a national fee-setting process, including discussions over first-responder reimbursement. Although first-responder reimbursement was not adopted in the national fee schedule, it could be reconsidered in the future.

Of course, in all cases when a true emergency is indicated, EMS personnel should respond immediately; and at the scene, if the initial assessment shows that the patient has suffered a life-threatening illness or injury, emergency care and transportation should begin at once, without concern for the economics of managed care.

Medical transportation

In 1982, 19 percent of the 100 most populous cities in the United States provided emergency ambulance service through municipal or county EMS agencies.[16] These are often referred to as "third-service" agencies, meaning that fire, police, and EMS departments are all separate entities of local government. By 1998, that proportion had been reduced to 8 percent.[17] Weighing the economics of operating a separate, single-function public agency against the potential benefit from merging the single-function agency with a multirole agency that has cross-trained personnel, several major jurisdictions turned their third-service EMS agencies over to their local fire departments. Among them were Hillsborough County (Florida), Louisville (Kentucky), New York City, Norfolk (Virginia), St. Louis, and San Francisco.

During the 1990s, entrepreneurs purchased hundreds of small private ambulance companies and combined them into large, investor-owned companies that controlled about 25 percent of all medical transportation in the United States and Canada. By 1998, however, changes in the U.S. government's reimbursement practices were reflected in the profit performance and stock prices of those companies.

The pressure to meet Wall Street's expectations exacted a toll on local operations and employee morale. In many (possibly most) communities served by the two largest companies, service deficiencies were numerous. It became increasingly clear that the public sector would have to provide a medical transportation safety net. That safety net was lodged in the fire department.

The most prevalent form of medical transportation by fire departments is emergency-only service using multirole personnel (sworn, uniformed firefighters with EMS training and certification). Less prevalent are, first, emergency-only service using single-role personnel and, second, the provision of non-emergency as well as emergency medical transportation. Emergency-only service using multirole personnel seems most compatible with the culture and strengths of most fire and rescue services.

Emergency transportation with multirole personnel   Given not only the fire department's preparedness in areas ranging from dispatching to vehicle maintenance but also the advantages conferred by station locations and organizational discipline, most fire and rescue organizations using multirole personnel are able to provide emergency medical transportation services that meet or exceed medical and community expectations.

From an economic point of view, emergency ambulance service (compared with nonemergency service) requires a high state of readiness, subjects vehicles to greater wear and tear, carries greater potential for civil liability, and involves a higher percentage of uncollectible fees for service. Very few private ambulance companies could survive if they limited their services to emergency transportation. If they provide any emergency services at all, they must balance the proportionally higher cost with a higher percentage of revenues from nonemergency medical transportation. Ideally the ratio of billable to nonbillable transportation events will be two to one: two-thirds nonemergency and one-third emergency.

These economic facts raise the question of whether a fire department—with higher salaries and more generous fringe benefits than most private ambulance companies offer—can provide emergency ambulance service on a competitive, cost-recovery basis. Much depends on the demographics of the community, the payer mix, the prevailing reimbursement rates, and the effectiveness of the billing and collection processes. In most cases, however, if the transportation system is staffed with people who are paid for by the fire protection function, the marginal costs will be sufficiently low to allow for full cost recovery. In

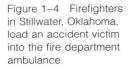

Figure 1–4   Firefighters in Stillwater, Oklahoma, load an accident victim into the fire department ambulance.

addition, prices charged for service can be lower than those charged by private companies in the same geographic area.

Before a fire and rescue agency, whether career or volunteer, decides to offer transportation services, it should contract with experienced consultants for a feasibility study. Medical transportation is very complex, and although many fire and rescue agencies provide excellent service on a full cost-recovery basis, designing a system requires anticipating and avoiding numerous pitfalls.

Emergency transportation with single-role personnel   For a variety of reasons, some fire and rescue agencies have elected to staff emergency ambulance operations with single-role personnel. That is, the EMTs or paramedics employed to operate the transportation system have no status or role as firefighters.

Since 1970, however, efforts in a number of cities to operate single-role emergency ambulance systems as a separate service of the fire department have been troublesome, to say the least. In most places where the effort has been made, it was motivated by the desire to hire EMS personnel for less money than what firefighters were paid. However, once the firefighters and EMS personnel began to work together, the disparity became apparent and seemed unfair. The EMS personnel responded to many more emergencies, operated with less supervision, encountered more stress than their firefighter counterparts, but were paid less. The resulting conflict was very destructive to morale and labor-management relations.

Furthermore, any savings achieved through salary disparity were eliminated by the high percentage of disability pension claims from single-role EMS employees of public fire and rescue agencies. Even though single-role EMS personnel employed by a fire and rescue agency of local government have a reasonable expectation of career-length employment and retirement with a pension, the demands of the position make it difficult for most people to remain in good health until retirement age.

An alternative developed by three fire departments in California—in Huntington Beach, Newport Beach, and Oceanside—may be applicable elsewhere. In those departments, emergency ambulance EMTs and paramedics are hired as temporary employees at minimum wage rates. Their temporary employment is limited to three years, a period during which they work under the supervision of fire company officers and are expected to prepare for and compete in the department's firefighter recruiting process. In essence, this body of personnel becomes a pool of potential career employees for the agency. Because the temporary employees are paid at the minimum wage and have few fringe benefits, the cost of providing emergency ambulance service with them is competitive with the cost of providing single-role, private sector ambulance services.

This concept works well in regions where competition for employment in the career fire service is intense. For the participants, it is an opportunity to get a foot in the door of a career fire department, prove themselves to the organization, and add fire service experience to their résumés. For the employer (the fire and rescue department), it is an opportunity to attract a diverse work group (including minority candidates) into the program and then spend as long as three years training the members of the group in preparation for a successful career with the organization. A primary disadvantage of this concept, however, is that it does not contribute substantially to the productivity of the residual firefighter workforce.

Emergency as well as nonemergency (scheduled) medical transportation   A few U.S. and Canadian fire departments, both career and volunteer, provide nonemergency (scheduled) medical transportation services in addition to emergency ambulance service. In most cases a fire department's assumption of this service is related to local history, such as the abrupt business failure of a private ambulance company.

Generally speaking, nonemergency medical transportation is more profitable than emergency service. The level of service (typically BLS) requires less training and less-expensive equipment. There is no legal obligation to transport people requiring nonemergency transportation unless they have a source of payment. There is less wear and tear on vehicles and less exposure to potential liability from collisions with other vehicles. The net revenues from this level of service may seem attractive to local government administrators.

Among the major issues surrounding this profile of service is staffing (sworn or nonsworn, temporary or permanent, single-role or multirole). There is also the question of whether to use emergency units for nonemergency transports when the former are available or whether to have dedicated fleets of emergency and nonemergency units. All these questions have serious financial and human resource implications.

Before a department makes a commitment to nonemergency medical transportation, it should carefully evaluate the adaptability of a fire and rescue organization's culture. The nature of the work is far afield from the expectations of most people who are motivated by the excitement of emergency action. And the work can be monotonous or even unpleasant.

Other value-added services

"Value added" refers to additions to or enhancements of existing services that add value for the benefit of the community, the customer (patient), and/or the customer's insurers (including MCOs). Some fire and rescue organizations already provide value-added services without recognizing them as such. Most organizations could fortify their importance to the community by making minor alterations or additions to their existing services.

Two examples of value-added services are community health education and health screening.

Community health education   Just as prevention is considered the first responsibility of fire protection, prevention is also the foundation of public health, and the larger health care community has looked with envy at the success of fire-prevention initiatives. Thus, as the fire service has expanded its role to encompass EMS, many public health authorities have invited the fire service to expand its fire prevention efforts to the analogous task of preventing accidental falls and bicycle injuries, heart disease, child drowning, poisoning, and medication overdoses.

Indeed, the residual public trust enjoyed by the fire service creates unrivaled opportunities for success in community health education. There is a fire station within about five minutes of most urban and suburban U.S. residents, and at least since the late 1970s most of those stations have been opened to citizens needing blood pressure checks. Many stations have also offered the public free training in CPR and first aid. In some locales, fire departments offer free home-safety inspections, combining fire safety with the mitigation of health and accident hazards (such as loose throw rugs, uncapped prescription bottles, and unsecured swimming pools).

Successful fire safety education programs can be expanded to include information on bicycle and skateboard safety and on nutrition and exercise. Firefighters in many communities already provide junior high and high school students with training in CPR and the Heimlich maneuver.

As time passes and the fire service becomes more comfortable with its expanding role, some fire stations may become public health resource centers. Conveniently located, they may be ideal sites for periodic "well-baby" clinics and inoculation programs. Indeed, such programs may be revenue opportunities for fire departments. Public health grants may be available for providing health screening services (discussed below) and immunization programs. MCOs may be willing to pay fire departments to help with preventive health services and the updating of patient histories for their members.

Health screening   A second possible value-added service, health screening, usually consists of a few straightforward tests—blood pressure, pulse, and respiration rate—as well as some standardized questions. These tests and questions can provide early warning for such conditions as heart disease, lung disease, and stroke. Periodic tests can also show trends in an individual's overall health. Given the convenient locations of fire stations and the availability of personnel who have been trained to perform physical assessments, fire stations might be designated health screening sites during specified hours.

The information obtained from testing individuals could be forwarded to their MCOs for inclusion in health profile records. A growing number of health care plans are emphasizing preventive care, and to them, this service and the resulting information has value. Accordingly, these health care plans may be willing to compensate the fire and rescue organizations that acquire and forward the information.

Technical rescue services

Rescue generally refers to assisting, retrieving, or extricating people who are entrapped or otherwise in perilous situations from which they cannot escape. EMS is often spoken of in the context of rescue, but here *rescue* refers to physical situations, even when the entrapment or peril may be related to illness or injury.

Typical rescue situations include entrapment in an automobile after a collision, or having a finger, arm, or leg caught in farm or industrial equipment. Construction sites often present rescue situations: workers may be trapped in collapsed trenches or overcome by fumes in confined spaces. Recreational activities present an almost endless variety of rescue situations, triggered by anything from avalanches to swift water and involving altitudes that range from mountains to caves.

Until about 1930, rescue situations in the United States and Canada usually produced a response by untrained and ill-equipped volunteers, both organized and unorganized. Farmers, mechanics, and manual laborers were numerous and

Essential rescue situations and functions   Seven essential rescue situations and functions are referenced in the National Fire Protection Association (NFPA) Standard on Operations and Training for Technical Rescue Incidents. All fire and rescue organizations, whether career or volunteer, should be trained and equipped in accord with NFPA Standard 1670 or should have agreements or affiliations with other organizations that can provide these services reliably and competently. The seven situations and functions are as follows:

1. Structural collapse
2. Rope rescue
3. Confined space rescue
4. Vehicle and machinery rescue
5. Water rescue
6. Wilderness search and rescue
7. Trench and excavation rescue.

Source: NFPA 1670, Standard on Operations and Training for Technical Rescue Incidents (1999 edition).

often willing to assist someone in peril. Still, the outcome of these events was often fatal for the victim.

The Roanoke Lifesaving Crew in Virginia is credited with being the first organized volunteer rescue organization in the United States. Founded in 1928, the Roanoke group received much favorable publicity in its early years. The publicity prompted the creation of thousands of similar groups, mostly in the eastern and southern states.

During the post–World War II period, thousands of volunteer rescue organizations formed, many of them specializing in mountain and wilderness search and rescue, high-angle and technical rescue, water rescue, and cave rescue.

Until the 1970s, many rescue organizations seldom had opportunities to practice their skills and use their equipment in real emergencies. However, increases in and the migration of population, the invention of riskier recreational equipment (from all-terrain vehicles and snowboards to hang gliders and modern rock-climbing and white-water equipment), and the growing popularity of adventurous outdoor sports and recreation placed more and more people in perilous situations in nearly inaccessible areas. Additionally, transportation accidents and industrial-construction accidents became more frequent.

The role of the fire department as a provider of technical rescue services was significantly affected following World War II, when important changes were made in the engineering and manufacture of passenger vehicles. The newer vehicles were faster, heavier, and bulkier; when they collided, passengers were more likely to be trapped inside the twisted metal. When this happened, police officers at the scene increasingly called for assistance from the fire department.

In 1949, an event in the Southern California community of San Marino raised the public's and the fire service's awareness of the need for properly trained and equipped rescuers at the local community level.[18] A child named Kathy Fiscus fell into an abandoned water well shaft and was trapped there.

The incident occurred shortly after commercial television had begun broadcasting. Television stations KTLA and KTTV, upon hearing of the girl trapped in the well, sent remote broadcast units and reporters to the scene. The event became the television medium's first live, on-scene report of a breaking news event to reach an audience of significant size. The broadcast was continuous for 27½ hours.

Local emergency services were not adequately equipped or trained to effect a rescue effort. Among the heroes of that event was a construction worker named Bill Yancey, who first learned of the trapped child from television coverage. The on-scene reporters described the suspense and frustration as efforts to dig a parallel access hole were frustrated by repeated cave-ins. Yancey had no car; he took public transportation to the scene. Once there, he and other civilians ("sandhogs") stepped into the leadership void, organizing the volunteers and equipment that had congregated around the abandoned well.

Finally, as was considered fitting in those days, the television crews discreetly shut down and left the scene as Kathy Fiscus was removed from the well and pronounced dead. Previously accidents, disasters, and other calamities had been presented to the public in newspapers, magazines, and brief newsreel clips, but only television made it possible for ordinary citizens to watch for hours on end, becoming emotionally involved in a frantic life-or-death struggle.

Many viewers questioned whether their own communities were adequately prepared to face similar emergencies. Probably more than any other event, the televised attempt to rescue Kathy Fiscus inspired the fire service to try to broaden its role and to organize and equip itself for potential emergency situations other than fires.

In the 1970s, the evolution of traditional fire service roles was fueled by the invention of a cleverly named tool that captured the public's imagination, the Jaws of Life. Introduced in 1971, it gave firefighters an alternative to the

Figure 1–5 Television crews cover the frantic but ultimately futile attempt of civilian volunteers to rescue Kathy Fiscus from the well.

manual Porto-Power hydraulic spreader, the mechanical "come-along," and oxyacetylene cutting torches for auto extrication.

In the public's eye, the fire service role in rescue was confirmed by the popular television series *Emergency!* which played weekly from 1972 to 1978 (and remained in syndication for twenty-five years thereafter). For an entire generation of television viewers, the image of firefighters John Gage and Roy DeSoto responding on Rescue Squad 51 to skillfully and dramatically deploy the Jaws of Life and other rescue tools and techniques created an indelible impression and expectation.

In virtually all of the world's industrialized nations, when transportation and workplace hazards cause entrapment of people, there is an organized emergency response by trained and equipped rescuers. In the United States and Canada, it is the fire service that responds most frequently. Alone among public or private agencies, the fire service has reliable, trained, and physically fit people who are promptly available around-the-clock, organized into functional units, and equipped for almost any contingency.

Summary

Since 1988, when the previous edition of this book was published, the fire and rescue service has undergone transformations on several fronts. One of the most important of these transformations has resulted from increases in population and migratory shifts of people and industry away from traditional urban centers: these developments have increased the public safety burden on the limited resources of small communities.

Another significant transformation has been the expansion of the fire service's roles to include providing emergency medical services and technical rescue services. In its handling of these additional roles, the fire service has more than met the public's expectations for promptness, skill, and caring attitudes. Nevertheless, the cost of operating a capable, multirisk fire and rescue agency remains a thorny issue for many local government administrators. And in locales where the ability to charge for medical transportation and to finance it on a marginal cost basis has led fire departments to expand into this area of service, their doing so has sometimes given rise to territorial and policy confrontations between fire departments and private ambulance companies.

Despite the difficulties involved, these transformations have emphasized the fact that from medical emergencies to the most calamitous events confronting a community, the local fire department is the emergency resource of first (and, often, last) resort. Usually no other resource has the tools, the training, and the organization to cope with the situation. Late-twentieth-century improvements in incident management, communications, training, and equipment have reinforced this reliability. But along with the responsibility and community's trust have come greater complexity, cost, and conflict.

Thus, the administrator of a modern fire and rescue organization faces challenges unimaginable to his or her predecessors. The context from which those challenges emerge has been delineated in this chapter.

1 Douglas Porter, quoted by Eric Lipton, "Fairfax Considers Plan to Freshen Up the Place," *Washington Post*, 13 May 1997, Metro section, B1.

2 Kenneth M. Johnson, Loyola University of Chicago, http://www.luc.edu/depts/sociology/research.html, referenced by Brad Edmondson and Matthew Klein, "A New Era for Rural America," *American Demographics Magazine*, September 1997. See http://www.marketingtools.com.

3 Kevin Heubusch, "Small Is Beautiful," *American Demographics Magazine*, January 1998. See http://www.marketingtools.com.

4 These estimates are provided by JEMS Communications, Carlsbad, Calif.

5 Attributed to motivational speaker Zig Ziglar.

6 In 1998, the California Business Roundtable released the findings of a year-long study showing that (1) $90 billion would be needed in the following ten

years to maintain and improve that state's infrastructure and (2) state government would be able to cover only two-thirds of that amount.

7 Among these jurisdictions were Sacramento, Huntington Beach, Ventura, San Diego, and Newport Beach, all in California; Birmingham, Alabama; and several cities in Florida.

8 J. M. Soler et al., "The Ten-Year Malpractice Experience of a Large Urban EMS System," *Annals of Emergency Medicine* 14 (October 1985): 982–985; and R. J. Goldberg et al., "A Review of Prehospital Litigation in a Large Metropolitan EMS System," *Annals of Emergency Medicine* 19 (May 1990): 557–561.

9 The National Commission on Fire Prevention and Control, *America Burning* (Washington, D.C., 1973), x.

10 Ibid., xi.

11 *The U.S. Fire Problem*, annual report of the Fire Analysis and Research Division, National Fire Protection Association (NFPA) (Quincy, Mass.: NFPA, November 2001).

12 Alan V. Brunacini, *Fire Command* (Quincy, Mass.:

NFPA, 1985); and FIRESCOPE of California (*FI*refighting *RES*ources of *C*alifornia *O*rganized for *Po*tential *E*mergencies), http://firescope.oes.ca.gov.

13 NFPA 1561, Standard on Fire Department Incident Management System (updated in 2002 as Standard on Emergency Services Incident Management System).

14 Jeff J. Clawson, MD, and Kate Boyd Dernocoeur, EMT-P, *Principles of Emergency Medical Dispatch,* 2nd ed. (Salt Lake City, Utah: National/International Academy of EMD, 1998).

15 National Center for Health Statistics, Centers for Disease Control and Prevention, U.S. Department of Health and Human Services, *Advance Data Report* #313, May 10, 2000 (Hyattsville, Md.).

16 "The Profile of EMS in America's 100 Most Populous Cities," *JEMS (Journal of Emergency Medical Services)* 7 (January 1982): 71.

17 "EMS in the Nation's Most Populous Cities," *JEMS* 23 (February 1998): 50.

18 "Real Life Became Drama: A Rescue That Changed the World," *Rescue Magazine* (November/December 1994): 4.

Evaluating local risks and planning for the necessary resources

As fire and rescue departments continue to take on additional responsibilities, chief officers often find that their budgets, staffing, and general resources are diminishing while workloads are growing. Under such constraints, if a fire department is to serve the community efficiently and provide competent and effective services, the fire chief has to initiate a strategic planning process. The goal of the process is to ensure that adequate levels of resources, including staffing, are allocated to meet the community's needs for the services delivered by the fire department.

Because the primary goal of the fire department is to prevent fires and—when they do occur—eliminate loss of life and reduce property loss, the strategic planning process must include (1) a fire risk assessment of the community; (2) an internal audit (quality assurance) of current services provided by the department (which may include fire suppression, fire prevention, related code enforcement, public fire and all-risk life safety education, fire investigation, and other assigned emergency responses—e.g., emergency medical service [EMS], hazardous-materials mitigation, technical rescue operations, and emergency management); and (3) the culmination of the whole process—a written strategic plan that projects fire department goals over a minimum of five years.

Determining the current level of risk and then the level that a community is willing to accept makes it possible for the fire and rescue department to set objectives for minimizing or reducing risk—not only the risk of fire but also that of other hazards (see the next section). Setting these risk-management objectives is necessary in terms of evaluating current services and planning for both future services and the resources that will make possible the provision of future services at the agreed-upon level.

The strategic planning process for the fire department brings together the department, elected officials, civic organizations, planning officials, local business owners, and involved citizens. Although the department initiates the process, the community's involvement is essential. The community is a vital partner in identifying particular needs, evaluating the quality of current services (emergency and nonemergency), determining the level of future services that will be necessary, and, most importantly, providing fiscal support.

Definition and types of community risk

For the purposes of this chapter, risk is defined by National Fire Protection Association (NFPA) Standard 1250, Recommended Practice in Emergency Service Organization Risk Management (2000 edition), as "the measure of probability and severity of adverse effects that result from exposure to a hazard." Each jurisdiction decides what degree of risk is acceptable in that jurisdiction; the determination is based on criteria that have been developed to define the levels of risk (e.g., of fire) within all sections of the community. The decision about what levels of risk are acceptable will determine the extent of fire department capabilities that must be available.

The risks faced by the community begin with fire. Every community faces the risk of fire, although in some communities the risk threat is greater because of population, type and age of building construction, lack of fire protection features such as sprinklers, or other contributing factors. Another risk is that of mass-casualty incidents. This risk may be greater in communities where large groups of people are gathered or transported. Terrorism is yet a third very real risk. Although terrorism is relatively new to the United States and Canada, no community is immune to it. A fourth risk is posed by hazardous materials, if hazardous or toxic materials are transported through a community or are manufactured, stored, or used within it. A fifth risk is that of natural disasters (e.g., tornadoes, hurricanes, earthquakes, floods, or meteorological extremes), which may affect any community. Because none of these risks can be entirely prevented from materializing, communities must use effective evaluation and planning to minimize loss of life and property. Control measures may include building, fire, and life safety codes (see Chapter 12); pre-incident planning (see a later section of this chapter); adequate fire department deployment and staffing (see Chapter 4); and effective emergency management techniques.

Community fire risk assessment

To identify the magnitude and scope of the probable fire risk, the fire department should conduct and periodically update a community fire risk analysis, or assessment. A universally available tool that allows the entire community to be evaluated in relation to the risk of fire is the Risk, Hazard, and Value Evaluation (RHAVE) model, which the Commission on Fire Accreditation International developed as a way to classify individual properties in relation to protecting lives and property. The RHAVE software and documentation are available at no cost from the U.S. Fire Administration. Using the RHAVE

Fire department operational risk Just as the community faces risks, so does the fire department, which is at risk both operationally and organizationally.

Fire department operational risk results from the department's primary mission: fire suppression and rescue to limit the negative consequences of fires involve significant risks to the service providers. Some of these risks are unpredictable and unavoidable, but others are well-known and can be effectively controlled or avoided with the application of operational risk management protocols and techniques. Control measures include training and adequate standard operating procedures. For example, having a backup hose line at every fire is an operational risk-management measure.

National Fire Protection Association (NFPA) 1500, Standard on Fire Department Occupational Safety and Health

Program (2002 edition), calls for a fire department to develop an official written internal risk management plan based on the activities that are conducted. The purpose of preparing such a plan is to develop a process that effectively manages the risks encountered daily by a fire department in both an emergency and a nonemergency context. Under the direction of the fire chief and staff, the department must develop and administer appropriate policies, procedures, and programs that will reduce or control identified risks and thereby help protect members, equipment, facilities, and so forth. The internal risk management plan should address risks encountered in connection with the following: administration, facilities, training, vehicle operations, protective clothing and equipment, emergency incident operations, and operations at nonemergency incidents.

model, a department can collect and organize a standard set of risk evaluation information about individual properties and, on the basis of the rated factors, can derive a "fire risk score" for each property. The score is then used to categorize the property as one of low, moderate, or high/maximum risk. The program also creates a database of information that can be used to manage the fire department interaction with each property (e.g., the scheduling of fire prevention inspections and pre-incident planning surveys) and to identify locations in the community where particular hazards are present. After completing the initial survey, a department should maintain the database by adding information on new and changing properties and by periodically verifying the information for all properties in the community.

The risk ratings of individual properties can be aggregated to establish a risk level of low, moderate, or high/maximum for each geographic area of the community. (Occupancies rated as "excessive" risks should be identified separately for individual consideration.) These area ratings can then be used to establish the fire suppression capabilities (personnel, equipment, and vehicles) to be deployed for the initial arriving company, the full alarm assignment, and the additional alarm assignments for each level of risk. These data will be compatible with a community's geographic information system so that additional data, including population and economic factors for each geographic area of the community, can be considered.

The RHAVE model requires a department to gather information using an extensive questionnaire: the more information the department has, the easier the RHAVE process will be. Thus, a department should lay the groundwork by identifying the community's fire risks, analyzing them, and then classifying them.

Risk identification

The identification of risk considers both actual (historical) and potential losses. Actual losses are those that have occurred, have been documented, and may be expected to occur again. Potential losses are those that have not yet occurred but probably or possibly will.

Risk identification needs to be as complete as possible. The following information, which will be necessary later in the risk assessment process, should be collected during this stage:

The nature, extent, and magnitude of the risk (e.g., of fire) within the community

The community's actual experience with the particular risk, including trends distilled from the analysis of data (for a discussion of data analysis, see Chapter 14)

Changes or anticipated changes in population relative to the built environment

Current capabilities of the fire department

Analysis of selected fire protection methods

Effect of the building and fire codes, code enforcement, and public education programs in relation to fatalities, injuries, and property losses from fire

Existence or availability of mutual aid, automatic aid, and other agreements with local communities (for a discussion of interagency cooperation, see Chapter 16)

Defined level of the EMS expected, and the ability to provide this level

Ability to provide reliable communications—a prerequisite for the ability to deliver prompt fire, EMS, and technical rescue responses (for a discussion of communications, see Chapter 15)

Identification of hazards that would precipitate a need for technical rescue activities.

Risk analysis: Frequency and severity

After risks are identified, they must be analyzed; that is, their effect on the community must be specified. The two measures used to specify this effect are *frequency* and *severity*. Frequency is defined as *how often* a particular incident may occur or is likely to occur (i.e., how many incidents may or are likely to occur as a result of a particular risk?). Severity is defined as *the consequences* of an incident once it has occurred (i.e., how serious might the incident be?). However, although the two measures are addressed individually, they are typically analyzed as a unit, or simultaneously. Simultaneous analysis makes it possible to assess the significance of each identified risk more accurately (see the sidebar below). Figure 2–1 represents graphically how frequency and severity together produce an overall risk rating.

Risk as a measure The fire service uses the word *risk* to define or measure both the possibility that an emergency incident (e.g., a fire) will occur and the potential outcome of this event (e.g., lives lost, property damaged, or economic harm to the community). If a type of incident occurs frequently and with significant severity, the risk is severe. At the other end of the spectrum, if an emergency incident occurs infrequently and with little or no severity, the risk of the incident is low. Hospitals and nursing homes, for example, are high-risk facilities—even though the frequency of incidents there may be low—because the potential severity (or the consequence) is extremely high.

Each building and occupancy is different, but risk profiles for similar properties within the community (e.g., single-family dwellings of identical construction) may be identical. The equivalences of risk profiles allow the fire department to use a small number of categories for risk assessment.

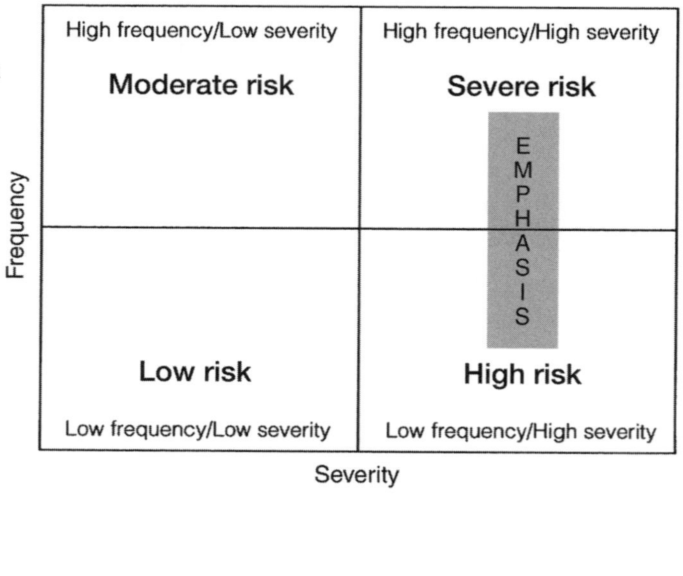

Figure 2–1 Frequency and severity produce an overall risk rating.

Although on the surface the two measures seem easy to establish, there is no numerical scale that one can use to calibrate either frequency or severity. Certainly numerical factors (such as cost, effect on the organization, time, and resources used) can serve as benchmarks, but if the analysis is to be productive, much hard nonquantitative work is required (especially to measure potential, rather than actual, frequency).

In measuring frequency, one has the information that was collected during risk identification. The frequency of actual fire incidents can be determined on the basis of fire department statistical data, such as incident reports. But determining the frequency of potential incidents requires something more. One may reasonably ask, "How can frequency be determined for things that have not yet happened?" The fact that a major fire in the downtown area of a community has not occurred in several decades does not mean that it will never occur. Such an incident is therefore a risk that must be identified, even if the frequency of the occurrence will, it is hoped, be extremely low; and in assigning a frequency to this risk, those who make the determination rely on their judgment and experience. The frequency assigned can be modified as additional information is gathered. This information as to frequency will be a factor later, when priorities among risks are established.

Determining severity—the second half of risk evaluation—requires deciding what constitutes a severe loss. Cost (i.e., the dollar amount of the damage done by the fire) is often used as a proxy for severity, but is the cost of a fire that destroys the entire downtown of the community the most important aspect of the loss? The incident described in the sidebar below illustrates the problem.

The complexity of measuring the severity of a fire A community of 18,000 experiences a major fire in the central business district, where the vacancy rate is already high. The fire has destroyed four businesses and offices. Furthermore, because the fire occurred during a weekday morning, it created staffing problems for the volunteer fire department, a majority of whose members were at work in their primary occupations. The department subsequently submits a request for additional staffing. Economic issues in the community ensure that this request will be closely scrutinized.

At the same time, a new office park and mall are being developed in a recently annexed area in the western part of the city. Before the fire, many of the city's businesses were considering moving to this new area.

Thus, city officials and community leaders are struggling with the dilemma of whether to support the central business district—the city's hub—or to support the development of the new office park and mall. The mall will generate considerable revenue for the city, and this revenue will be able to provide funding for additional fire department staffing.

Among the questions the decision makers have to consider are the following:

What economic impact will each course have on the community, which currently has few retail and business facilities?

What will the economic impact of each be in terms of lost jobs and wages?

Will the businesses destroyed by the fire rebuild within the community or will they move away?

What effect will each course have on the community's economic growth?

Risk prioritization, or classification by level

After risks have been identified and analyzed, they are prioritized, or classified by level. This is necessary before risk management can be undertaken because many factors contribute to community risks and, in many communities, the range of potential risks is wide.

As previously noted, risks can be classified under three headings, or at three levels: high/maximum, moderate, and low. High/maximum risks are normally concentrated in larger communities, for the area classified as high risk typically (but not always) is of substantial size and contains a concentration of properties (or occupancies) representing, in the event of a fire, a high risk of loss of life, loss of economic worth to the community, or loss of property. These occupancies require high water-flow capabilities; they may or may not have built-in fire protection capabilities; and occupants may not be capable of self-rescue. High-risk occupancies might include shopping and business centers, malls, multistory offices, and hotels; entertainment centers; concentrations of high-risk industrial or commercial properties; hospitals, nursing homes, and other occupancies that house people who may require assistance; and high-rise buildings with or without built-in fire protection capabilities. An incident in any of these occupancies requires a multiple-alarm response and a concentration of resources. A fire department must identify these occupancies in order to ensure its ability to control and minimize the loss once a fire or other type of emergency has occurred in this classification.

The moderate-risk classification, also typically found in large cities and towns, designates an area with concentrations of properties representing, in the event of a fire, a moderate risk of loss of life or financial effect on the community, and an unusual likelihood of damage to property. Examples of moderate-risk areas are strip shops (which every community has) and business areas; single- and/or multistory properties with high fire load (i.e., significant concentrations of combustible material or storage of hazardous material); multistory properties with significant potential loss of life (e.g., office buildings, apartment buildings); schools and government facilities; and some industrial occupancies.

Low-risk areas can be found in suburban areas, large and medium-sized cities, and concentrated areas of small towns; they are districts of average size with a minimal risk of loss of life or property damage in the event of fire in a single structure. The concentration of properties may vary. Low-risk areas also consist of small, single-story commercial occupancies; detached residential structures; and low concentrations of any type of structure.

Determining the seriousness of a risk to the community can be a challenge, and a risk that is serious in one community may have little effect in another (see the accompanying sidebar).

Community risk management

After risks have been assessed (identified, analyzed as to frequency and severity, and classified [prioritized] on a scale of high to low), risk management begins, with risk control as the key. Determining the appropriate control measures entails choosing from among three techniques (which are not unique to emergency services, for these techniques are generally accepted and universally applied by all forms of business). The three risk control techniques are (1) risk avoidance (making sure that the conditions giving rise to the risk are eliminated or not allowed to arise), (2) risk transfer (e.g., to another agency or to an insurance company), and (3) risk control (making sure that conditions for mitigating the risk are in place). A combination of the three techniques may be

Determining the seriousness of a risk A potential for risk, requiring thorough evaluation, exists in a community of approximately nine thousand residents. The center of town is divided by a major rail line, with rail traffic consisting of more than twenty freight trains a day plus six passenger trains a week. Cargo carried by rail includes coal, household products, and hazardous materials. Public fire protection, emergency medical service, and hazardous-materials response are provided by a combination department that has paid drivers for fire apparatus on duty Monday through Friday from 7 A.M. to 5 P.M., supplemented by volunteer firefighters. Train traffic is the community's only target hazard because no industry exists in the community. (A target hazard is a property where the potential for loss of life or property is large.)

Risk analysis shows that the overall risk is medium to high: the frequency of an incident (given the number of trains per day) is low to medium, but the severity of an incident is judged to be medium to high because even though no derailments or accidents have occurred in recent times, the potential still exists—and if a derailment did occur, there would be risk of loss of life, damage to commodities, an adverse impact on the environment, and an adverse impact on the well-being of the community.

This community must develop a strategy to effectively manage a derailment if one were to occur. The strategy requires developing a plan (one that includes detailing the resources that would be needed if the incident were to involve hazardous materials or a passenger train); determining the resources that would have to come from outside the fire department; developing a response matrix or plan (which would include automatic or mutual aid [see Chapter 16], training for personnel, and a practical drill); and reevaluating and completing the plan.

For another community, one that is basically similar to the first but has no major transportation routes other than primary and secondary roadways, the result of a risk analysis is drastically different. Overall risk is low, as are frequency and severity. The fire and rescue department must develop a response document that outlines the necessary response and needed resources in the event of an incident involving hazardous materials—but the only hazardous materials expected to be encountered are the "common" ones (e.g., gasoline, motor oil, and pesticides).

necessary, and the degree to which one technique is applied will affect the use of the others.

Risk avoidance means not allowing conditions of risk to exist. For example, if a community establishes a sprinkler ordinance requiring the installation of sprinklers in all one- and two-family residences, the community will be avoiding the risk of fire in the type of structure in which, in the United States, fire is most prevalent (see the sidebar on pages 46–47).

Risk transfer means that instead of being avoided, the risk is transferred to another department or agency by some form of contract. Commercial insurance programs would be used to fund loss from a fire if the level of public fire protection were not met by the contract. Funds should be available to pay for loss from a fire if the fire department lacked the resources to provide adequate public fire protection or the fire completely overwhelmed the resources that the department did have (e.g., if there were a conflagration). (Fire department internal risk transfer is discussed in the sidebar on pages 48–49.)

Risk control—the third technique for controlling risk—is the one most commonly used by fire departments, and it has the greatest effect on operations and services. It consists of implementing measures that will help control the frequency and severity of losses and reduce the overall impact of community risk. Examples of such measures are requirements for a higher level of fire protection in the form of smoke detectors, fire alarm and detection systems, automatic sprinklers, and the use of noncombustible construction materials. Moreover, a fire/all-risk life safety education program, which develops a level of all-risk awareness within the community, greatly enhances a fire department's ability to manage and reduce the fire risk and fire loss within the community (see the sidebar on pages 50–51).

Risk control measures in general

Effective measures to control risk take different forms (there is no magic list of them) and are limited only by the imagination and ingenuity of those responsible for designing and implementing them. Some of the most effective risk control measures may be designed by creative personnel and may have specific applicability in particular situations. One example is requiring the dem-

---

Fire sprinkler systems: Saving lives in the home Fire sprinkler systems have effectively protected lives and property in public buildings for more than one hundred years, yet less than 1 percent of the structures where most fire deaths occur have fire sprinkler systems. These structures are people's homes.

According to National Fire Protection Association (NFPA) statistics, 85 percent of fire deaths and nearly 78 percent of fire injuries occur in residential structures.[1] Automatic home fire-sprinkler systems can reduce those statistics and play a vital role in the fire and life safety infrastructure of communities.

The greatest potential for increasing the installation of home fire-sprinkler systems lies with the new-construction market. Every year, more than one million single-family homes are built in the United States, yet lack of awareness prevents consumers from having fire sprinklers installed in their new homes.

To inform and educate consumers about the life- and property-saving benefits of residential fire-sprinkler systems, the Home Fire Sprinkler Coalition (HFSC) was founded in 1996 by NFPA, the American Fire Sprinkler Association, and the National Fire Sprinkler Association. In its efforts to increase awareness, the HFSC has encountered many challenges. The first is the need

to dispel common myths associated with fire sprinklers.[2] A major concern of consumers centers on the possibility of accidental discharges and the belief that the entire system activates when a fire starts. The odds of an accidental discharge due to manufacturing defects, however, are 1 in 16 million. And despite what is often depicted in television situation comedies, each sprinkler is individually activated by heat, not by smoke, and only the sprinkler closest to the fire will activate, spraying water directly on the fire. In fact, 90 percent of fires are contained by the operation of just one sprinkler.

A second myth has to do with appearance and cost. The latest residential sprinkler systems, however, are designed to be inconspicuous and can be flush-mounted in walls or ceilings. Some can even be concealed behind decorative coves and molding. New technology has also made sprinkler systems much more affordable and easier to install. On a national average, sprinkler systems in new construction add only 1–1.5 percent to total building costs. A growing number of insurance carriers help make sprinkler systems affordable by offering 5–15 percent discounts on coverage for homes with fire sprinkler systems.

The HFSC also realized that members of the fire service, too, need to become more aware of residential fire-sprinkler

olition of abandoned structures; another is marking the exterior of abandoned buildings to indicate exterior firefighting only. Other types of risk control measures take the form of community planning, preparedness (one very important form of preparedness—pre-incident planning—is discussed below), training and education (see Chapter 9), public service programs, fire prevention operations (see Chapter 12), and disaster management. (See the sidebar "Control Measures against the Risk of Hazardous Materials" on page 52.)

The participants in the risk management process weigh the probability of different outcomes, the losses expected to result from a fire or other emergency incident, and possible control measures (i.e., possible changes in level of service or in response, or in the installation of automatic detection, alarm, and sprinkler systems); prioritize the identified possible control measures; and ultimately arrive at acceptable levels of risk and service. The acceptable levels of risk and service are the focus of the planning process described below.

The prioritized list of control measures is based on the following factors:

---

facts, resources, and availability. Fire service awareness is vital because consumers often look to their local fire service as an information resource.

Another challenge the HFSC faces is the resistance of home builders. Often builders reinforce the myths, do not believe fires occur in new construction, or do not have a relationship with contractors who install residential fire-sprinkler systems. Part of the HFSC effort is to help builders understand the value and marketability of installing fire sprinkler systems in new homes.

One of the HFSC resources that is most popular, especially with the fire service industry, is *The Scottsdale Report,* prepared by the Scottsdale (Arizona) Rural/Metro Fire Department. This report summarizes fire records spanning the ten years after the Scottsdale local government passed a new construction ordinance requiring sprinklers. During those ten years, there were 598 home fires, 44 in homes with sprinklers.[3] In the homes with sprinklers, there were no deaths, whereas in the unsprinklered homes, there were ten deaths. The report also demonstrates that sprinkler systems reduce the amount of damage from a fire: the average fire loss in a house without sprinklers was $17,067, but in a house with sprinklers the average amount of loss was only $1,945—a reduction of nearly 90 percent.[4]

Much of the savings was due to reduced water damage. Not only do sprinklers extinguish fire before it spreads, often before the fire department arrives, but they also use far less water to do so. According to *The Scottsdale Report*, sprinkler systems release an average of 209 gallons per fire incident, compared with 3,290 gallons used by firefighter hoses.[5]

Primarily through its grassroots efforts, the HFSC believes that more people are beginning to realize that fire sprinklers are an accessible, cost-effective option for their own and their families' safety. Specifically, as more members of the fire service recognize that residential sprinkler systems are an important piece of the fire and life safety profile, residential fire-sprinkler systems will become more common in homes and, over time, will save lives.

[1]Michael J. Karter Jr., *Fire Loss in the United States during 2000* (Quincy, Mass.: NFPA, September 2001), ii. Copyright © 2001. NFPA, Quincy, MA 02269.
[2]All information in this and the subsequent three paragraphs has come from Home Fire Sprinkler Coalition, "Fire Sprinkler Facts." Available at www.homefiresprinkler.org/hfsc.html.
[3]Scottsdale (Arizona) Rural/Metro Fire Department, *Saving Lives, Saving Money: Automatic Sprinklers, a 10 Year Study (The Scottsdale Report)* (Scottsdale, Ariz., 1997), 33.
[4]Ibid., 32.
[5]Ibid.

Source: Gary Keith, vice president for code development, NFPA.

Fire department internal risk management and risk transfer   Fire department risk management is a rather new concept for fire departments and associated emergency response organizations, but it is an excellent tool for strengthening existing health and safety guidelines and should therefore be supported by all levels of the organization, by labor unions, by community leaders, and by local government elected bodies.

Fire department risk management requires the department to examine all aspects of protecting assets, including personnel, resources, and property. The department must identify the exposures associated with each examined component and then apply an industry-standard model of the risk management process to help control risks. A standard risk management model consists of the following steps:

Identify and analyze loss exposures

Examine potential risk management techniques

Select the best techniques available for the exposure

Implement the techniques

Monitor the program.

Once adopted and applied, this model will enable fire departments to bring ongoing safety control measures to bear systematically on identified hazards in their environments.

When an exposure is too large to be managed using only proper training, guidelines, and planned expenditures of money, fire departments must transfer the risk—or a portion of it—to a reputable insurance company. For example, even the best driver training programs cannot guarantee that accidents involving emergency vehicles will not happen. Furthermore, because today's emergency apparatus is extremely expensive and technologically advanced, maintenance and repair are complex. Fire and local government administrators must therefore provide insurance to cover the portions of losses that cannot be either self-repaired to current standards or budgeted for. Some fire and rescue departments are part of self-insurance pools that are coordinated by the local governments whose citizens they protect. Self-insurance is most common in large jurisdictions.

Cost-benefit analysis (relationship between the cost of the losses and the reduction in cost if the losses were to be controlled)

Cost of the control measure

Ease of implementation of the control measure

Time required to implement the control measure

Effectiveness of the control measure.

Placing specific values on the costs and benefits of different plans for providing different levels of service for different risks is not easy, yet cost-benefit analysis, with its relationship to the cost of the control measure, is probably the most critical of the five factors. The projected loss estimates should include factors for injuries and loss of life as well as for insured and uninsured properties. The total cost of all control measures should be compared with the anticipated resulting reduction in all types of losses. The cost-benefit analysis should be supported by good research, logic, and judgment. Once the costs of the losses that would be incurred have been identified, the anticipated reduction in those costs, if whatever identified potential control measures were implemented, can be considered.

From a financial and refinancing standpoint, a manager can examine fire department exposures by dividing the organization into four categories: properties, personnel, vehicles, and portable equipment. Properties include real and personal properties, such as land, buildings, facilities, electronic data equipment, communications equipment stored in the buildings, maintenance supplies, and furniture (tables, chairs, etc.). Personnel are uniformed members and civilian staff. Vehicles are fire apparatus, ambulances, support vehicles, and vehicles with special applications (e.g., all-terrain vehicles and boats). Portable equipment is any piece of equipment that is not permanently attached to a vehicle and is placed into service at an emergency (e.g., hose lines and nozzles, turn-out gear, and exhaust fans).

Fire chiefs and local government leaders must recognize that the fire department is a specialized organization with unique exposures, requiring additional energies to ensure proper risk management and refinancing strategies. With respect to risk management cost transfer, every fire chief or local government leader should consider the following:

Does the insurance company offer measurable programs that support the fire department's internal risk management program?

Does the insurance company have extensive knowledge of fire department exposures and loss ratios? Does it offer professional assistance to help formulate a complex and ongoing risk management plan?

Are claims paid rapidly so that the fire department can rapidly reestablish the existing level of service?

In sum, fire department risk management is a highly technical operation requiring the fire department to search for assistance and demand performance from the insurer or the local government risk manager. If the insurance company being used does not provide proper assistance and coverage, the leaders of the fire department or the local government should explore the coverage provided by a specialized company.

Source: William L. VanGorder, loss control consultant, Emergency Services Insurance Program, Cortland, N.Y.

The cost factor—direct and indirect costs of control measures—is linked to the cost-benefit analysis. Thus, the administrator who conducts this prioritization process must have accurate and specific information about the direct and indirect costs of the control measures. The cost of providing a control measure —whether the right or the wrong measure—often determines whether the action is taken. (On costing, see Chapter 6.)

A prime example of the way in which cost-benefit analysis and cost are linked is the case of a community that is considering purchasing a new piece of fire apparatus but has not yet appropriated the money for it (approximately $375,000). The community has recently suffered several large fires, and this piece of equipment would greatly enhance the department's fire suppression capabilities. Citizens and merchants have been very vocal about the need for the purchase and are pressing the local government to appropriate the funds. Because of the recent unexpected fire losses and the community's pressure, the local government decides to appropriate the funds in order to improve the department's ability to suppress fires in the future.

The third factor—ease of implementation of a control measure—affects or may affect the priority assigned to that measure: some measures are easier and quicker to implement than others and will therefore receive higher priority, all

Recognizing the importance of public fire and life safety education In *America Burning*, its landmark 1973 report on the status of the nation's fire safety problem, the National Commission on Fire Prevention and Control called for (among other things) the emphasis at the local, state, and national levels to be shifted from fire suppression to fire prevention. But despite great strides in both the development and the use of safety technology in the decades since 1973, public fire and life safety education in most fire service systems remains chronically understaffed and underfunded.

There are signs, however, that emerging leaders in the fire service are beginning to recognize that their departments' skilled public educators are experts in community risk reduction, cost containment, and public outreach and are therefore vitally important to achieving the department's public safety mission. Progressive fire service managers recognize the benefit of supporting a strong public education program as an essential element of their departments' overall service delivery plans. The departments led by these managers include a public education function that is fully staffed with well-trained, highly motivated people, who are respected as valued members of a well-balanced team. These managers hire or groom fire and life safety educators to acquire twenty-first-century skills in advocacy, business management and finance, communication, community health planning and development, coalition building, leadership, computing and technology, cultural competency, evaluation, and strategic planning.

Many of tomorrow's leaders will probably have had direct public education experience at some point in their careers, and the system will be the better for it. But at a minimum, every effective manager will demonstrate his or her own commitment to prevention and education through personal example—for instance, by installing residential fire sprinklers in his or her own home, requiring the use of seat belts by all department personnel, and displaying as much facility in communicating accurately and effectively about injury prevention as in describing an engine company's response to a structure fire.

Future fire service and local government managers will also understand the fire problem as part of the larger picture of injury prevention—not as a safety issue only, but as one facet of a public health epidemic that exacts an enormous toll in disability and premature death, consuming dollars for health care and undermining the nation's productive capacity. This conceptual shift requires us to move from the traditional paradigm of preventing accidents to a paradigm of embracing the full range of proven public health tools and perspectives. Modern approaches

other things being equal. The fourth factor, time needed to implement, may also affect the priority assigned: a solution that takes too long to implement or to show results may, for that very reason, be ineffective. The final prioritization factor is the effectiveness of the control measure. The challenge here is to predict the effect or success of a particular program or decision. For example, fire departments use some form of ongoing fire prevention program or effort, yet the commitment of personnel and other resources to the fire prevention effort does not guarantee success: fires still occur. In this context, therefore, the key issue is not the fact that fires still occur but their frequency (actual number) and severity (damage and monetary loss).

On the basis of these five factors, possible control measures are prioritized to address the risks that have already been identified, analyzed, and classified. Establishing the priorities is extremely important because in all probability actions cannot be taken to control all the risks at once.

to injury prevention are grounded in a public health framework, drawing on the interdisciplinary strategies of

Education and behavioral change to increase awareness of the risk of injury and to encourage the adoption of more-positive behaviors

Engineering and technological interventions to alter the physical environment or modify the design of products

Legislation and enforcement to pass and enforce new laws and increase the enforcement of existing laws.

From the standpoint of community education, the days of simply putting on a puppet show and passing out a few brochures are over. Research clearly indicates that successful community-based programs require the use of multiple strategies that are integrated into the community and adapted to unique community characteristics. The most successful programs actively involve community stakeholders in the development and delivery process, and use techniques of ongoing evaluation to document measurable outcomes and improve the effectiveness of programs.

And because no fire department—for that matter, no single agency of any kind—can possibly amass the breadth of talent needed to tackle such a complex set of tasks, the future of public

safety lies in successful coalition building and management. Through its work with the *Risk Watch*® school-based injury program, the National Fire Protection Association (NFPA) has experienced firsthand the advantages of multiagency collaboration. These include gaining access to a wider audience, to the strengths of a broader and more diverse talent pool, to better data, and to more resources.

With a demonstrated track record in reducing fire deaths and injuries in the last two decades of the twentieth century and with a high degree of public trust and approval, the fire service has a legitimate leadership role to play in the arena of injury control. The challenge is to articulate a clear and compelling vision of a safer society and to attract others in the community to work in cohesive, collective action toward that vision. Without compromising high standards of fire and emergency response, fire and local government managers must advocate for increased investment in injury prevention and fire and life safety education. And finally, through personal conviction and persistent repetition, community leaders must model safe behaviors themselves so that others can learn from their unwavering example.

Risk Watch® is a registered trademark of the National Fire Protection Association (NFPA), Quincy, MA 02269.

Source: Meri-K Appy, vice president for public education, NFPA.

Pre-incident planning

One particularly effective risk management technique is pre-incident planning —a way of preparing for emergency incidents by assessing the risks associated with particular occupancies, thereby gathering vital information for use during emergency response incidents at those occupancies. Pre-incident planning takes into account such factors as a building's size, height, and configuration, special life risks, exposures, construction types, occupancy classifications, and other hazards. The pre-incident planning process has great bearing on the successful outcome of an incident (and on the safety of personnel operating at that incident), allowing the fire and rescue department to perform efficiently and effectively (and ensuring the safety and welfare of responding members). Basically, a department must identify the types of potential risks to which members may

Control measures against the risk of hazardous materials   Legislation enacted during the 1980s addressed the control and mitigation of hazardous materials with respect to community risk assessment. Title III of the Superfund Amendment and Reauthorization Act of 1986 (SARA), known as the Emergency Planning and Right-to-Know Act, established requirements for federal, state, and local governments; industrial facilities; and other businesses to develop planning for reporting hazardous and toxic materials through the community's "right-to-know" program. The purpose of the law is to help local communities by ensuring that chemical hazards specific to a community and its environs are identified.

The law also requires communities to develop and implement a planning process that complies with various mandates. The level of commitment expected of local officials should be commensurate with the risk of hazardous materials manufactured, stored, and/or transported through a community. A small community whose sole exposure is hazardous chemicals that are transported through it by rail will have a different risk assessment and strategic plan from a community that contains industrial plants that manufacture, store, and transport hazardous chemicals.

For more about the regulation of hazardous and toxic materials, see Chapter 13.

The staffing and deployment of fire companies   A community's fire risk analysis and the department's pre-incident planning process should determine the number and type of engine companies, truck companies, heavy-rescue companies, EMS units, and command officers assigned to respond to a reported fire. A staffing and deployment plan is based on the premise that the demand for public fire protection resources is directly linked to the fire risk characteristics of each geographic area and that these characteristics can be quantified through the ap-

plication of a systematic survey system (e.g., the Risk, Hazard, and Value Evaluation [RHAVE] model). The staffing and deployment plan also assumes that reasonable objectives can be established for the timely delivery of adequate fire department resources (i.e., staffing and equipment) to each category of risk. The plan concludes that the fire department's levels of resources overall and the geographic deployment of those resources can be tailored to have the appropriate level of service delivered to each geographic area.

respond and must plan accordingly. Members must understand the importance of the pre-incident planning process and must use it to their benefit.

Above all, fire departments must conduct pre-incident planning at major target hazards to familiarize department members with the significant hazards or risks present at the facility. Target hazards are defined as large structures with multiple floors (or large floor areas) or properties that pose significant hazards and represent a potentially large loss of life or property. Examples of major target hazards are hospitals, nursing homes, bulk-storage facilities, chemical plants, refineries, and any other occupancy or property with a potentially high risk of fire or loss of life.

Pre-incident plans must be maintained and stored so as to be readily accessible during an incident. Many fire departments store pre-incident plans and

Defining the level and placement of resources in the United Kingdom   In the United Kingdom, where the fire service is considerably more centralized than in the United States and Canada, the standards used to define the level and placement of resources to be provided throughout the country are constantly being revised in response to a process of risk assessment.

In the late 1990s an audit commission concluded that the existing standards (called "standards of cover") placed too much emphasis on property and that the method of assessing fire risk should be updated. In response, the British Fire Service and a consultant determined that five types of risk would have to be considered: individual, societal, property, heritage, and environmental.

Individual risk is the risk of death for individual members of the public; it can be measured in terms of frequency of fatality for individuals in a given area or situation. *Societal risk* is the risk of the deaths of a large number of people in one incident; it can be estimated in terms of the probability of incidents involving more than a specified number of fatalities. *Property risk* is the risk of loss of property, estimated in terms of the probability of losses having a specified cash value. *Heritage risk* is property risk where the possible loss to the nation's heritage goes beyond the replacement value of a given property. *Environmental risk* is the risk of environmental damage.

The risk factors that were developed correlate with fire service response times, which are the basis of decisions about the allocation of resources.

According to the new standards, a certain level of risk to life is considered intolerable and another level is considered negligible. Between these two levels is an area where the risk to life may be described as tolerable but should be kept "as low as reasonably practical." Most individual and societal risks in a response area fall within this intermediate category.

Tool kits were developed to help each fire service assess the risk of its coverage area and were tailored for common risk sources. The "dwelling tool kits" help the fire service assess the individual risk due to fire in large areas of similar housing: each fire service uses its own incident data to quantify the risk to life in such areas. The "other buildings tool kit" offers a structured way of assessing societal, property, heritage, and environmental risks, as well as risks of firefighter deaths, due to fire in specific buildings.

The scientific basis of the system and the process for conducting the risk assessment[1] are available from the Department of Transport, Local Government and the Regions in the United Kingdom (DTLR) through its Fire Experimental Unit, c/o The Fire Service College, Moreton-in-Marsh, Gloucestershire GL56 0HR, England.

[1] As of spring 2002, this system had not yet been adapted nationally.

Source: Adapted by permission of the British Home Office from "Fire Service Emergency Cover Risk Assessment," *Fire Research News* 22 (winter 2000): 6–7.

other pertinent information on mobile data terminals that will access and display the information quickly and easily. Other departments use laptop computers with software that is able to diagram the site plan of the structure, facility, or complex. These software programs offer a two-dimensional look at the site plan, providing information that can be invaluable during emergency operations. Regardless of the particular technology, it is important to make the pre-incident plan convenient to use so that it will in fact be used.

For more details about how pre-incident planning is conducted, see the sidebar on pages 54–55.

The pre-incident planning process

Today's fire service professionals and community leaders realize that pre-incident planning gives tremendous advantages to incident commanders and companies operating at emergencies. Pre-incident planning allows emergency response departments to capture critical information—before an incident occurs—about buildings, contents, infrastructure, technological processes, and the like within the department's initial response or contracted areas (i.e., areas that are outside the department's normal jurisdiction but to which the department delivers services in accordance with the terms of a written contract [see Chapter 16]). During an incident, these data allow incident commanders to make timely decisions that support successful outcomes.

To obtain qualitative and quantitative data for pre-fire planning and community risk assessments, fire officers must work with other community decision makers and organizational boards. For example, the superintendent of the community's water authority will be able not only to provide civil engineering layouts of the existing water distribution system but also to elaborate on the system's pressures and volume in relation to specific target hazards. Another excellent source of pre-incident planning data is the code enforcement department: the local code enforcement officer frequently tours buildings, facilities, and complexes during all phases of construction and operations and typically archives documentation about construction alterations and additions; creates floor plans, plot plans, and photographs; witnesses acceptance testing of fire protection and detection systems; obtains knowledge of condemned structures; issues or revokes certificates of occupancy; and so forth. The fire chief must require that all relevant intelligence created in the code enforcement office or building department be accessible to the incident command structure, either by electronic means or in hard copy stored in a command vehicle.

Other emergency organizations (e.g., the police department and—if not directly associated with the fire department—the emergency medical service) must also be consulted for expertise, guidance, and affirmation of strategies and tactics. In addition, legal counsel must be kept cognizant of pre-incident planning operations and must become involved when needed. Legal expertise may be required during inter- and intra-state contract developments involving the provision of mutual aid by emergency organizations. During pre-incident planning, for example, fire department officers may (1) determine that some specific needs must be handled by contract, (2) do planning for a piece of property whose owner has had several fires at other facilities, and (3) discover serious fire code violations that must be corrected immediately. Thus, pre-incident planning may require legal assistance that local government leaders had not taken into account. Other departments or community groups with which fire departments may interact during pre-incident planning include the highway department, which provides information about highways and other roads and about specialized equipment that may be made available

Monitoring risk management

After possible control measures are weighed and prioritized and acceptable levels of risk and service are decided on, the final step in risk management is to circle back and conduct a periodic evaluation, or monitoring, of the risk management process itself. The purpose of this monitoring is to identify any weakness in the process so that steps can be taken to modify and improve it. The intention is to determine what is working, what is not working, and what may have to be done to make risk management more efficient and effective.

on request; the parks department, which also provides information about specialized equipment that may be made available on request; all other local government departments and offices; and the Boy Scouts, Girl Scouts, and business, religious, and other civic organizations, which provide information about emergency shelters, food, supplies, and pastoral services. A matrix may be used to display the personnel needed to accomplish pre-incident planning and community risk management.

After pertinent pre-incident data have been gathered, additional steps are necessary. First, fire department administration must evaluate the data collected, including their accuracy, and must classify them according to adopted risk assessment parameters. Second, fire officers must ensure that the department's procedures do not conflict with the emergency procedures of the facility for which the planning is being conducted. For example, many health care facilities have evacuation plans that require patients or residents to be evacuated first into another horizontal compartment instead of to the exterior, as is traditionally done. It is critical that rescue companies be familiar with a health care facility's specific evacuation plan and support the efforts of the facility's staff with a progressive horizontal migration. A vertical migration will be necessary only if the structure is higher than one story and either the fire is not controlled quickly or structural collapse is imminent.

Third, pre-incident information must be disseminated appropriately. It must be directed to the department's training officer to help that person evaluate existing—and create new—training programs, objectives, and job performance standards. The information must be introduced into the department's incident command operating structure for multicompany training exercises and emergency applications. Information gathered during pre-incident planning events must be funneled to the department's safety officer for review. This person is responsible for ensuring that safety levels are adequate both tactically and strategically with respect to the overall theater of operations. In addition, the dissemination of pre-incident planning data should not be limited to the administrative level of the fire department. The information must be forwarded to the local government elected body to communicate about the fire department's activities and to initiate community-wide risk management evaluations and measurements.

Community risk management is synonymous with community disaster planning, and obviously the fire department's pre-incident plans provide essential information for the officials who are engaged in identifying and classifying potential exposures in case of major disasters. The effective application of fire department pre-incident plans by any community and its leaders depends greatly on the amount of cooperation and support extended to the fire department during all aspects of the planning process.

Source: William L. VanGorder, loss control consultant, Emergency Services Insurance Program, Cortland, N.Y.

There are no hard and fast rules or numerical scales that will do this. Participants should review operations, activities, data, and the components of the risk management plan to determine if community change has occurred for the better or for the worse or if the risk management process itself is still producing satisfactory results. In other words, risk management is a process that must be continually evaluated and updated. As new problems occur—as the risks and hazards in the community change—the fire department must continually evaluate and reevaluate them to determine their effect on the community's risk management plan and, if necessary, take new corrective actions. The challenge is to stay ahead—to be able to forecast potential problems and develop solutions.

Fire department organizational statement

To formalize its responsibilities and capabilities to meet the community's needs for service, a fire and rescue department may create an organizational statement. This statement defines the legal justification for operating the department, specifies the services the department is authorized to perform, and outlines

The position of the department in the governmental structure

The types and levels of services provided

The number of employees and the personnel structure needed to provide these services

The training required to enable these employees to provide these services

The authority and accountability of selected members or key positions.

The community, through its elected officials, civic organizations, and citizens, is responsible for determining the types and levels of services provided by the fire department (i.e., the resources to be deployed and the level of staffing). The fire department is responsible for providing the community with a description of services (e.g., fire protection, fire suppression, and other assigned emergency response capabilities) based on the organizational statement; this description must include the necessary costs and resources associated with each service, and the parameters for delivering the service. The fire department must identify in writing the requirements that will enable it to (1) prepare for anticipated incidents and (2) provide effective, competent, and safe services aimed at preventing fires, reducing the risk to lives and property if fires do occur, and responding to nonfire emergency incidents.

NFPA 1710, Standard for the Organization and Deployment of Fire Suppression Operations, Emergency Medical Operations, and Special Operations to the Public by Career Fire Departments (2001 edition) addresses the organization and deployment of fire suppression operations, EMS, and special operations by substantially all career fire departments. This standard also addresses the functions and objectives of fire department emergency service delivery, response capabilities, and pre-incident planning. NFPA 1720, Standard for the Organization and Deployment of Fire Suppression Operations, Emergency Medical Operations, and Special Operations to the Public by Volunteer Fire Departments (2001 edition), addresses the same matters for volunteer fire departments.

Within the governmental entity, the fire and rescue department is no different from any other department whose authority is constrained, and whose services are delineated, by the governing authority. (Legal counsel within the jurisdiction will ensure that the types and levels of services are being met.) The majority of fire and rescue departments are established under the stipulations of their governing bodies or by the adoption of charters. These ordinances—stipulations or charters—define the legal parameters for operating a fire department, the mission of the fire department, the duties and responsibilities of all members, and the authority and accountability of key members to direct the operations and services of the fire department. The department must be responsible for establishing documentation that pinpoints the legal basis of its own existence and for demonstrating that the services it provides are the ones it is legally responsible for providing. Moreover, especially for a volunteer fire department or a department that is, or is part of, a fire protection district (see Chapter 4), this documentation might already be part of a state, county, or municipal charter or of an annual allocation of funding. In any case, this information should become part of the organizational statement.

A credible personnel structure is what enables the department to provide the services it is required (and has agreed) to provide, and the foundation of a credible personnel structure is job classification—a defining of roles and responsibilities for all positions within the organization. Job classification is based on job analysis (see Chapter 5), which is a means of identifying the skills, behavior, knowledge, and abilities that an employee needs to perform a job

Figure 2–2 Sample training matrix.

Certification level	Certification hours	Recertification hours	Expiration
Driver's license			5 years
Defensive driving	8 hours	4 hours	3 years
Cardiopulmonary resuscitation	8 hours	4 hours	1 year
Infection control	4 hours	1 hour	Annually
HAZMAT team		16 hours	Quarterly
HAZMAT awareness	16 hours	8 hours/OSHA[1]	Annually
HAZMAT operations	48 hours	8 hours/OSHA	Annually
HAZMAT technician	80 hours		
HAZMAT specialist	136 hours		Annually
HAZMAT incident command	48 hours	8 hours/OSHA	Annually
Radiological response training	24 hours		Annually
Emergency medical technician	110 hours	30 hours/test	4 years
Emergency Vehicle Operator's Course (EVOC)	16 hours	Test	5 years
Firefighter II	45 hours	Test	5 years
Firefighter III	42 hours	Test	5 years
Driver/pump operator	64 hours	Test	5 years
Aerial operator's course	32 hours	Test	5 years
Fire officer I	116 hours	Test	5 years
Fire officer II	48 hours	Test	5 years
Fire officer III	Pilot		
Instructor I	24 hours	Test	5 years
Instructor II	24 hours	Test	5 years
Instructor III	24 hours	Test	5 years
Inspector II	120 hours	16 hours/test	2–5 years
Inspector III	120 hours	Test	2–5 years
Investigator II	240 hours	40 hours/test	2–5 years
Investigator III		Test	2–5 years
Rope Level I	16 hours	Not required	
Rope Level II	32 hours	Not required	
Rope Level III	24 hours	Not required	
Confined space rescue	16 hours	Not required	
Trench rescue	16 hours	Not required	
Vehicle extrication	16 hours	Not required	
Helicopter operations	8 hours	8 hours	Biannual
Automatic weapons training	24 hours	8 hours	1 year
Technical team		16 hours	Quarterly
Rescue specialist	20 hours		
Helicopter rig master	24 hours		
Structure collapse awareness	20 hours		

[1]OSHA = Occupational Safety and Health Administration.

task successfully. Job analysis consists of gathering and evaluating facts about each position: the tasks involved, the methods or tools used, the qualifications needed to perform the job, and the level of performance required. Job analyses, and the job descriptions that are based on them, need to be periodically reviewed to ensure that they reflect the changing type and level of work; the need for new knowledge, skills, and abilities; and changes in organizational structure.

Job descriptions define the initial training and education needed for each position as well as the continuous and ongoing training and education needed to maintain certification (see Figure 2–2). They therefore allow a fire department to develop a training matrix for each certification and position. A training matrix must use as its conceptual base the various competencies for which training is to be provided.

Training, in fact, is basic to any organization, regardless of the type of service or business provided. The fire department's training program should support the mission and scope of the department as a whole and must be directly correlated with the department's organizational statement, thus ensuring that the department is meeting the community's needs. Training and education provide a solid foundation for the delivery of competent and effective services. An improperly or ineffectively trained fire department greatly increases the risk to the community inasmuch as the department is less able to control and extinguish fires of any magnitude. In addition, training has a direct relationship to the safety and health of fire department personnel. A training program should ensure that the necessary knowledge, skills, and abilities are established, maintained, and enhanced, and in that sense the training and education of department members should remain consistent even as the needs of the community change and the services delivered by the organization continue to increase.

The fire chief has to accept responsibility for the overall direction of the fire department, and staff members within the department must be aware of their roles in the system and must accept responsibility for completing assigned tasks. The chief is responsible for establishing the rules and regulations of the department, and management within the department must enforce them. Enforcement implies taking proper action to ensure compliance.

Evaluation of current services and resources

To ensure that the department's performance is in accord with the organizational statement and that the department is meeting community needs as defined by the risk assessment and risk management processes discussed above, the department must evaluate the types and levels of services it provides. The evaluation should thoroughly examine and assess the needs of both the department and the community with respect to each of these services and will show whether changes are needed. Evaluation at some level should occur continuously, after each response, but a more formal evaluation may take place as part of the local government's annual goal-setting and budgeting cycle, as part of a community-wide strategic planning process, or at specified intervals when a more comprehensive review of organizational goals and performance is conducted. NFPA 1201, Standard for Developing Fire Protection Services for the Public (2000 edition), serves as an excellent toolbox to help a department ensure that the basic services of public fire protection are provided.

Evaluations of fire department services must consider the questions listed below. (Having a clear idea of the questions that should be asked will help fire service managers explain the evaluation process and results to the media, political leaders, citizens' groups, fire department members, labor, and other local government departments.)

Description of primary services provided by fire and rescue departments

Fire suppression The activities involved in controlling and extinguishing fires by using the necessary equipment, apparatus, and staffing that will provide rescue, forcible entry, ventilation, and application of water within a manageable system. These services are provided by a company fully staffed with firefighters and an officer.

Fire prevention Universally accepted as the most effective means of accomplishing the mission of the fire service. Prevention covers the next three items in this list: public fire safety education, inspections and code enforcement, and fire and arson investigations. It also covers arson prevention programs. One of the major prevention strategies is passage of laws and ordinances requiring built-in fire protection systems, such as sprinklers.

Public education Activities that address fire safety issues, such as residential fire prevention and personal fire safety. These activities include educational programs for young people, families, and people who are elderly, deaf, or blind or whose mobility is reduced.

Code adoption and enforcement The adoption of minimum codes and standards to prevent fires from starting and to limit the spread of fires that do start. Inspections of occupancies are conducted to identify risks and hazards, to ensure compliance with code requirements, and to record any existing violations.

Fire investigations Investigations to identify the causes of fires in order to determine their origin and prevent future fires. Early fire investigations identified nonregulated construction standards and occupancy hazards, thereby strengthening the need for codes to be adopted and enforced. This process as a whole is intended to systematically identify the factors involved in the start and spread of fires.

Emergency medical services Delivery of prehospital medical care in the form of basic and advanced life support services at the scene of a medical emergency and while the patient is being transported to a medical facility.

Hazardous materials mitigation Operations that involve the regulation, planning for, management, mitigation, and cleanup of hazardous and toxic substances, as prescribed by regulation. Specialized training and equipment are required.

Technical rescue operations Operations that involve incidents requiring specific and advanced training and specialized tools and equipment. These incidents may involve water rescue, extrication, confined-space entry, high-angle rescue, trench rescue, and any other operations involving specialized training.

Emergency management Activities that involve preparedness for, response to, mitigation of, and recovery from incidents such as earthquakes, hurricanes, tornadoes, floods, acts of terrorism, and disasters (whether caused by an act of nature or by human action).

If the fire department is charged with providing some of the various emergency response services identified in the second paragraph of this chapter and described in the sidebar above, how well is it providing them?

If the fire department does not directly deliver a service that it provides, which agency does deliver it, and with what degree of success?

Has an effective community risk assessment been conducted and is it currently operational?

Are the goals and objectives of the department clearly stated, widely accepted, and appropriate to the community's risk assessment and future needs?

Is the department structured and managed in the most practical, efficient, and effective manner?

Is a more comprehensive and extensive prevention and code administration program needed?

Do trained members, properly equipped, arrive at fire and other emergency incident locations within the recommended time frame and with sufficient staffing?

Are suppression and emergency management strategies and tactics appropriate, safe, and effective?

Are major functions of emergency management written down, understood, and operational?

Is a standard risk-benefit assessment part of firefighting and incident management training?

As the evaluation proceeds, the fire department has to address—in addition to the questions already listed—unique and specific circumstances particular to the organization. These should include the following:

Perceived effectiveness of, and improvements needed by, the fire department as reflected by citizen surveys or other measures

Depth and magnitude of service needed by the community

Level of risk acceptable to the community

Condition of the local economy

Competence and concerns of the department's members

Frequency of emergency responses

Availability of automatic or mutual aid

Type and condition of equipment, apparatus, and facilities (see Chapter 7)

Composition of the emergency communications system

Status of support services

Magnitude of approval from public officials and citizens

Status of and competition for funding

The community's interest in effecting change

Competence and effectiveness of departmental leadership (see Chapter 8).

To promote citizens' support of the fire department, the department must explain to its citizens the types and levels of services available. If the department cannot adequately provide a particular service, the public needs to understand why. For example, if a volunteer fire department has trouble providing adequate staffing during weekdays, the citizens need to understand what level of service is possible during those hours and how they may be affected. If some of the shortcomings are critical, the fire department must address them by developing strategies to provide alternative solutions.

An assessment of the department's resources will greatly help not only in conducting the evaluation but also in improving the quality of service provided. The assessment of resources involves asking and answering the questions that follow. The assessment will affect the department's operations, planning, and future provision of services.

Personnel (see also Chapter 5)

What are the recruitment and retention requirements?

Does the department use competent members to operate the personnel management process?

Are members given a relevant and competent performance-based assessment annually?

Does the organization have short-, medium-, and long-range internal personnel goals and objectives, including that of responding to customer service needs?

Equipment (see also Chapter 7)

Does purchased equipment meet applicable NFPA standards?

Does the department have warehouse or storage capabilities for the equipment it purchases?

Does the department have procedures for selecting, caring for, using, and maintaining equipment?

Is equipment maintained so that it is safe, reliable, and in good working order?

Does the department have an equipment replacement program that is recognized by the governing authority?

Apparatus (see also Chapter 7)

Is the type of apparatus (including its staffing, resources, and equipment) appropriate to the kind of fire encountered, whether it be a brushfire, vehicle fire, residential-structure fire, commercial fire, etc.? The fire department has to equip the fire apparatus for the types of incidents to which it will respond and for the type of community served (urban, suburban, or rural).

Is there adequate pumping capacity and are there proper ladder requirements so that—with the inclusion of automatic or mutual aid response—initial operations can be sustained?

Does apparatus purchased meet applicable NFPA standards?

Are all fire department vehicles properly maintained and do they meet applicable motor vehicle inspection requirements?

Are reserve apparatus available and in proper working order?

Does the department have an apparatus replacement program that is recognized by the governing authority?

Facilities (see also Chapter 7)

Are fire stations located so that incidents in extreme- or high-hazard occupancies can be responded to by the first-due company within the number of minutes established as the department's standard?

Are unstaffed fire stations located in areas accessible to responding members? A fire department may operate a fire station that houses fire apparatus and provides minimal space for offices, one or more meeting rooms, and other functions, but that lacks space for facilities where firefighters can sleep, eat, or maintain the necessary hygiene. The primary function of these fire stations is to be located in an area that is accessible for personnel who must get to the fire station from work or home, assemble, and then respond to an incident with fire department vehicles.

Do all fire stations have enough room for housing the required personnel? NFPA 1500, Standard on Fire Department Occupational Safety and Health Program (2002 edition) recommends—and the federal Occupational Safety and Health Administration (OSHA; see Chapter 13) requires—that the number of members assigned to a fire station be governed by the facilities available for sleeping, eating, maintaining personal hygiene, etc. The fire department is responsible for ensuring that a fire station meets the fire and life safety requirements and the health mandates established by OSHA.

Are all areas in fire stations properly maintained in terms of housekeeping, maintenance, and health and safety?

Can individual study, classes, and practical drills be adequately conducted?

Alarm, dispatch, and communications (see also Chapter 15)

Are current provisions adequate for handling daily operations, including during peak periods?

What are the projected service needs and requirements in the short, medium, and long terms?

Are there any mandates or requirements, service needs, or other issues that will have to be considered?

Health and safety provisions (see also Chapter 11)

Does the department use current and recognized medical and physical fitness requirements for candidates and incumbent members?

Is the health and wellness program an ongoing process that helps maintain the well-being of department members?

Does the department have a functional occupational safety and health committee?

Is a competent incident-safety officer present at designated incidents?

Does the department use sound firefighter safety and health standards as a basis for its occupational safety and health program?

Is safety a departmental value?

Pre-incident planning (see above)

What are the community's past, current, and future fire risk issues?

Does the department encounter any special risks, such as airports, waterfronts, hazardous materials, and so forth?

What are the nonfire risks?

Is pre-incident planning used as part of the department's incident command system?

Funding sources (see also Chapter 6)

What are the funding sources for the department?

Does the department generate income from the services it provides? If so, does that income affect the annual budget?

Does the governing authority have a public safety or fire department tax that contributes to the departmental budget?

The strategic plan: Road map for the future

To ensure that the operation of the fire department meets all the internally and externally established requirements, a process to produce a written strategic plan is important. The strategic plan is the organization's road map for the future. As such, the plan must be reflected in the department's budget. Few goals are achieved without money, so the plan should serve as a blueprint for constructing the department's budget. Thus, it is critically important that the department's strategic planning and budget development cycles be synchronized with each other. (For more detail on planning, see Chapter 6.)

Developing the strategic plan

Initiating and facilitating the planning process is ultimately the responsibility of the fire chief. In smaller organizations, the chief is often the person responsible for managing the planning process, whereas in larger organizations, facilitating the process is often delegated to a staff member. Regardless of the size of the organization, soliciting participation from stakeholders, both internal and external, is important. (The foundation of the plan is the organization's mission statement, as explained in the accompanying sidebar.)

The participation of stakeholders is achieved with an analysis of *s*trengths, *w*eaknesses, *o*pportunities, and *t*hreats (a SWOT analysis). Often, but not always, strengths and weaknesses are defined as *internal* to the department, and opportunities and threats as *external*. (SWOT analyses are also discussed in Chapter 6; see especially Figure 6–6.)

The analysis of the internal environment (the department's strengths and weaknesses) examines the existing bureau and department plans, special programs, and budgets, and it evaluates each bureau's performance and available resources. The analysis of the external environment (opportunities and threats) is a review of other public and private sector agencies (e.g., the police department, EMS if a separate department, the water company, the health department, disaster and emergency services, and neighboring fire departments). These agencies' missions, goals, objectives, and available resources should be considered. After this information is collected and analyzed, a narrative should be developed to delineate all the external factors that may either affect fire department operations adversely or present the department with opportunities.

After the SWOT analysis is concluded, a final review of the mission state-

The plan and the mission statement

The foundation of the organization's plan is its mission statement. (For a detailed discussion of drawing up a fire and rescue service mission statement, see Chapter 8.) Thus, the first step in developing a plan for the future should be to review the mission statement. Further, the mission statement should be reviewed several times during the planning process because it is the key to maintaining proper focus during that process. A copy of the department's mission statement should be displayed in every fire company and bureau. All members should be familiar with it and should continually question it, asking, "Do the services we currently provide fit the broad language of the mission statement? Does the mission statement imply services that we are not providing? Are we capable of providing services needed by our customers that do not fit the current language?" These and similar questions will ensure that the mission statement accurately reflects the services provided by the department.

ment is in order. The statement may now need to be revised to incorporate any pertinent information from the internal and external analyses.

The SWOT analysis is an effective way to get every member of the organization involved in the planning process. Members work in small groups with team leaders, who facilitate brainstorming to encourage a free flow of ideas about what the organization does well and where it is lacking, and to identify potential opportunities and threats.

At the conclusion of the brainstorming sessions, the same small groups should complete two additional steps. First, they should seek common themes among the many responses. This step often requires extensive dialogue and debate, and it is important to remember that the purpose of the SWOT analysis is not to address individual grievances but to find consensus on the organization's strengths, weaknesses, opportunities, and threats.

Second, the small groups should clearly define the identified strengths, weaknesses, opportunities, and threats in operational terms. For example, an operational definition of a weakness could be this: "The department does not have an effective training program to prepare midlevel officers for commanding hazardous material (HAZMAT) incidents." These definitions must be very specific so as not to become confused with the later process (discussed below) of developing goals and objectives.

In a large organization, the SWOT analysis is the most time-consuming but also the most important part of the planning process. There are two reasons for its importance. First, involving all members ensures that planning is not conducted in a vacuum. Those on the front lines who deliver the organization's services are closest to the customers and have an excellent understanding of their needs and wants. Second, involving all members creates a feeling of ownership for those who will ultimately be called on to meet the goals and objectives identified in the organization's plan.

Another layer of the external environmental analysis is an exploration of *p*olitical, *e*conomic, *s*ocial, and *t*echnological issues (a PEST analysis). Determining how political, economic, social, and technological factors may either affect the department adversely or present it with opportunities is typically the responsibility of senior staff members, working with experts from both inside and outside the department. Often the necessary expertise can be found at local universities or colleges, at the chamber of commerce, at professional associations, in other government agencies, or in private sector organizations. The PEST analysis, like the SWOT analysis, is conducted from the viewpoint of the community. In other words, what is best for the long-term interest of the community is best for the department.

Like the SWOT analysis, the PEST analysis helps the department's planners avoid planning in a vacuum. Often the success of established goals depends on political, economic, and/or social support, and a recent technological advance may prove to be the catalyst enabling a particular project or program to gain political support and/or financial resources. This analysis, too, serves as a reality check. An in-depth understanding of the relevant factors will enable planners to avoid building up unrealistic expectations.

Setting goals, objectives, and timetables

Armed with information obtained from both of the environmental analyses, the planners must then develop and prioritize goals and objectives, and establish timetables.

Goals Goals are broad statements directed at accomplishing the department's mission, and they identify what needs to be done to carry out specific projects or programs that were identified in the SWOT analysis. Goals are written in clear, precise, measurable terms. The weakness mentioned above that might have been identified in the SWOT process, for example, may give rise to this goal: "Implement a department-wide HAZMAT command training course for midlevel officers." Not only was such a goal identified in the SWOT process, but it is also consistent with the department's mission statement.

Objectives   Objectives are narrowly focused, defined steps directed at accomplishing a goal. Typically several objectives are required to accomplish a single goal. To accomplish the goal stated above, for example, the objectives may be the following: (1) Form a task force of community partners with expertise and interest in the subject. (2) Survey all fire departments serving populations of 100,000–150,000 to identify existing programs. (3) Evaluate the strengths and weaknesses of existing programs. (4) Prepare the first draft of a proposed program, review it, and evaluate it. (5) Submit the final program to the appropriate manager for approval.

Timetables   Just as an overall time frame must be established for accomplishing the department's plan, each goal and objective must be tied to a specific timetable. Timetables for accomplishing all goals should be submitted to the program manager for approval. The timetables should be reasonable and flexible, but the people responsible for accomplishing specific goals should be held accountable.

Monitoring the plan

Once a program to determine the department's needs and resources has been developed and implemented, a process of continual monitoring must be established. Managers of fire and rescue organizations must periodically step back and survey the successes and deficiencies of this program (as they must with the risk management program). Each time an individual goal is met, the program should be reevaluated and perhaps strengthened by the addition of new goals. In addition, these periodic evaluations, or mini-evaluations, serve to ensure that the goals and objectives are being met.

Conclusion

What is the future of fire and rescue department operations and programs? As local governments continue to face challenges in funding the services they offer, it is up to fire and rescue departments to develop strategies enabling them to fully meet the requirements set by the governing authorities. Fire departments must also establish benchmarks (see Chapter 10) to indicate that the services they are providing are improving the quality of life in the community.

At present, the traditional service of firefighting is complemented by other vital fire department operations. As the need for each new essential service arises, the fire department must be willing to step in and provide it. In the future, the services that might be offered are limited only by the focus and vision of the fire department itself.

An excellent process for forecasting potential problems and controlling them as they arise, using resources that have already been developed, is risk management. Risk management, however, has only scratched the surface of what can be done to align the fire service's capabilities with the needs of the community.

Leadership strategies for the political process

As the twenty-first century begins, the major policy issues facing fire and emergency services are more numerous and more complex than ever before—and very critical. In fact, the decisions reached on some of these policy issues will define the future of the fire service. These crucial policy decisions are being made in the public arena by elected officials, with input from the community. Fire chiefs and managers therefore need to be involved in the public arena, framing policy issues and options as well as mobilizing support for the department and its needs. The key for fire managers is to understand the political dynamics of their communities so that they can participate effectively in the policy formulation process.

Focusing on the fire service's relationship to the public arena, this chapter discusses (1) major policy issues to be resolved in that arena, (2) the community context, (3) the local political arena, (4) ethical behavior as the foundation for public trust and confidence, and (5) the role of the fire chief within the public arena.

Major fire issues for the public arena

The policy issues that make collaboration with citizens and elected officials necessary generally vary from community to community, but ten such issues are common to many fire departments across the United States and Canada. All ten of them will need to be addressed in the foreseeable future, and they are all likely to have a substantial effect on fire agencies. These policy issues are as follows:

1. *Mission and range of services*   Services provided by fire agencies have expanded considerably since the 1970s. Fire responses now account for a very small percentage of activity in most agencies and have been exceeded especially by emergency medical calls. What should the fire service's mission be? What services should it provide? How will the answers to these questions affect the local community?
2. *Funding*   Few agencies would admit to having adequate funding. When economic conditions are weak or funding is limited, agencies sometimes experience serious budget reductions. Or they are required to provide services over a rapidly expanding population while resources remain static. What alternative funding options are there? Are fees consistent with the mission? Where will funds be spent most effectively? If funding is not adequate, what is the most reasonable place to reduce expenditures? Would privatizing or alternative organizational arrangements be more cost-effective? In the cities of Champaign and Urbana, Illinois, the answer to the last question was yes: the cities contracted with the University of Illinois to provide it with fire services, at considerable savings to the cities and the university.
3. *Regional cooperation*   Potentially greater effectiveness and efficiency are two strong inducements for increasing regional cooperation. Would greater cooperation benefit more agencies? What type of cooperation

would be most effective—consolidation, functional consolidation, mutual aid, automatic aid, or some other type? (Consolidation is the merging of two or more agencies; functional consolidation is the merging of a function, such as training, of two or more agencies; mutual aid is an agreement between departments to respond when specific assistance is requested; and automatic aid is having the closest unit automatically respond to a call regardless of political boundaries.) Sarasota, Florida, consolidated its fire services with those of a countywide department. Beaverton, Oregon, consolidated operations with the Tualatin Valley Fire and Rescue Fire Protection District. El Cerrito, California, assumed fire service responsibilities beyond its boundaries through functional consolidation. In an example of mutual aid, the Chicago metropolitan area developed the Mutual Aid Box Alarm System, an extensive program that encompasses approximately 250 fire departments from Kenosha, Wisconsin, to Kankakee, Illinois. An example of a "seamless" automatic aid response system (a system without consideration of jurisdictional boundaries) is the one operated by the Phoenix metropolitan area.

4. *Privatization and contracting* A growing number of communities have considered privatization or contracting. Are there services or activities that others can provide more cost-effectively—for example, emergency medical response, fire code inspection, training of fire personnel, public education? Some communities contract with private organizations for all of their fire services. Examples are Scottsdale, Arizona (Rural Metro Corporation); Overland Park, Kansas (Overland Park Fire Department, Inc.); and Elk Grove, Illinois (American Emergency Services Corporation). Other communities have chosen to retain certain fire functions internally, such as fire prevention and code enforcement, while contracting for the remainder; one such community is Knox County, Kentucky (Rural Metro Corporation). More commonly, communities contract for specific functions, such as emergency medical service (EMS) or airport fire service. Among the communities that contract for EMS are several in the Chicago suburbs (PSI Paramedic Services of Illinois); among those that contract for airport fire service are the Northwest Arkansas Regional Airport (the Wackenhut Corporation), and Eau Claire, Wisconsin (American Emergency Services Corporation).

Interlocal agreements, from sharing resources to providing contract service Since 1980, cities in California have been responding to decreases in resources and revenues. They have had to explore ways of getting the resources necessary to maintain quality basic service, including fire service. The El Cerrito Fire Department has developed an aggressive strategy of resource sharing. The role of the fire chief is to be the chief negotiator in developing interlocal agreements.

With the city of Richmond, the El Cerrito department has joint dispatch and training programs and a joint response agreement, all of which are used daily. These arrangements have saved dollars and enhanced the quality of services in both communities.

With the Kensington Fire District, the El Cerrito department has a contract for service; it hired the district's staff and is now the service provider. Services and programs of the El Cerrito Fire Department have been expanded to the Kensington area, and the city of El Cerrito has enhanced services to both communities and has spread its overhead over a larger service area.

5. *Entrepreneurship*   Some agencies have developed more of a private enterprise approach themselves, offering their services to other jurisdictions for a fee, selling public information programs they have developed, and so forth. Is this sort of thing appropriate for public agencies? Champaign, Illinois, markets a locally produced fire prevention video through Fire Service Publications, Oklahoma State University. Rock Island, Illinois, provides dispatch services to several communities in the region.

6. *Diversity*   Census numbers show that communities and their workforces are becoming increasingly diverse, yet the workforces of many agencies still do not reflect the diversity of the communities they serve. In many instances this has resulted in litigation; it has also, and perhaps more importantly, negatively affected the relationship between the agency and segments of the community. (The International Association of Black Professional Fire Fighters, the National Association of Hispanic Firefighters, and Women in the Fire Service, Inc., have an increasing presence in departments nationwide.) How do community groups feel about such underrepresentation? Is there an ongoing, constructive dialogue on this issue in the department? In the community?

7. *Facilities*   The growth of communities has strained the fire service's capacity, as the cost of new stations and staffing is high. In older sections of the community, stations built twenty or more years ago may no longer be adequate for new service, equipment, staffing, and health and safety needs. Are stations located where they need to be? How can these needs be addressed? As an example, some municipalities construct stations jointly, to be staffed by departments in both municipalities.

8. *Equipment and technology*   Purchase of a new or replacement ladder truck at approximately a half-million dollars is a major expenditure in many communities. Specialized functions (e.g., water rescue, high-angle rescue) create additional funding needs. New technology, from computers to infrared sensors, seems to become available more frequently than ever before. How does the agency decide when to purchase new equipment or technology, and how is the purchase funded?

9. *Staffing, compensation, and work hours*   Increases in costs of fire service are due mainly to labor costs—higher salaries and shorter hours of work. Some departments have begun to consider alternative staffing arrangements, including a combination of paid and volunteer staff, use of paid on-call employees (paid by the hour or incident for responding to alarms or participating in drills), or staffing shared with other jurisdictions.

10. *Working conditions and safety*   Outside agencies, such as the National Fire Protection Association and the federal Occupational Safety and Health Administration, have set standards and requirements that will significantly affect local operations. (One such requirement is the "two-in/two-out" rule as described in the sidebar on page 70.) How will local agencies address these requirements, which have emerged from heated debate inside the fire service?

Fire and rescue services in the context of communities

How those policy issues are addressed will depend to some extent on the relationship between the fire and rescue service and its community. In the 1990s in local governments there was an increased awareness of and emphasis on communities (citizens and community groups). Local governments were challenged by citizens to provide more citizen-friendly services, to find different ways of involving the community in the affairs of local government, and to initiate community-oriented programs—for example, community-oriented po-

---

"Two-in/two-out" rule The "two-in/two-out" fire ground-procedures regulation published by the Occupational Safety and Health Administration (OSHA) on September 25, 1998 *(Inspection Procedures for the Respiratory Protection Standard)*, states that once firefighters begin the interior attack on a structural fire, the atmosphere is assumed to be immediately dangerous to life and health and the buddy system must be used inside the structure. Two more firefighters must be outside the structure ready to render immediate assistance to those inside if needed. The two or more firefighters inside the structure must have direct visual or voice contact with each other and must have direct voice or radio contact with firefighters outside the structure.

OSHA regulations recognize deviations from regulations in an emergency operation when immediate action is neces-sary to save a life. For fire department employers, this means that initial attack operations must be organized to ensure that adequate personnel are at the emergency scene before any interior attack on a structural fire but that if initial attack personnel find a *known* life hazard situation in which immediate action could prevent the loss of life, deviation from the two-in/two-out standard may be permitted as an exception to the fire department's organizational plan. However, such deviations from the regulations must be *exceptions* and not de facto standard practices. The exception is for a known life rescue only, not for standard search and rescue activities. When the exception becomes practice, OSHA *de minimis* citations are authorized (these citations are warnings for minor violations).

Source: Adapted with permission of the International Association of Fire Chiefs from a press release issued by IAFC on October 13, 1998.

---

licing. As governments tried to respond, they found themselves questioning and modifying the processes of governance, management, and service delivery. The accepted model of local government shifted: professionalism was displaced by the bond to the community. Local governments balanced a professional approach with responsiveness to community needs as identified by community members.

Fire service managers need to understand both the nature and the implications of the shift in model. They need to understand (1) how the professional model itself generated the community-based model, (2) what community-based government is like in action, (3) how they can draw up profiles of their own communities, (4) what their communities expect of them, and (5) how they can build strong relationships with their communities.

Background: Professional local government

Starting in about 1960, most local governments tried to attain and sustain a professional approach. Professional local government assumed the desirability of

1. Separation between politics (elected officials) and administration (managers), with policy set by the elected officials and implemented by staff
2. Centralization of organizational processes (including employee recruitment and selection, salary policy and administration, and purchasing and financial management)
3. Development of professionally based standards (such as zoning, development standards, life safety codes, sprinkler ordinances)
4. Increased emphasis on and resources for employee development (e.g., fire academies for new firefighters, in-service training programs to expand skills)

5. Support for technology (e.g., new safety equipment, more highly engineered fire apparatus, and computers in vehicles) as a tool for management and fire suppression
6. Greater emphasis on planning for the future (pre-fire [pre-incident] planning, participation of fire managers in reviewing development plans and land use proposals, studies of the locations of fire stations, and so forth)
7. Experimentation with innovative programs (such as water rescue units, high-angle rescue, hazardous material [HAZMAT] programs)
8. Expansion of services and service areas (by incorporating full emergency medical services in the fire department, contracting for service outside the jurisdictional boundaries, and so forth)
9. Limitation of citizen involvement to large formal committees or the public hearing process.

The fire service was changed for the better by these efforts and now has a strong professional foundation.

In the late 1980s, however, individual citizens and community groups increasingly challenged professional government, arguing that local governments had become insensitive to the needs of the community and to the effect their services and actions had on citizens. Basically, in many communities citizens felt that local government officials had gone too far in professionalizing. Citizens cited the following perceptions:

Arrogance of local government officials (from elected officials to managers to employees) in minimizing citizen concerns or issues

Bureaucratic approach to rules and procedures, reflecting a rigidity that sometimes led to decisions or actions that made no sense to the community

Seemingly predetermined outcomes in decision making, with the "participative" process simply an attempt by the professionals to manipulate and placate citizens

Punitive actions toward the average citizen, especially in code enforcement and inspections

Patronizing attitude—belief that the professionals know what is best for the community

Inbreeding of membership on boards and commissions, giving the impression that citizen involvement was for the select few.

Decision making based on thorough research and analysis but paying no attention and giving no weight to citizen concerns.

Certainly, some staffs and elected officials had assumed less visible roles than their more political predecessors had, and participated less in community events. As for fire chiefs and managers, they spent more of their spare time on professional activities and matters related to professional associations. This emphasis was encouraged by local government managers and elected bodies, who put a high value on recognition by peers and professional organizations. In addition, few fire suppression personnel were involved or known in the community: public education programs became concentrated in a small staff, whose members may or may not have been firefighters or had credibility with firefighters, and often noncommissioned inspectors were hired to enforce the codes. As fire departments got caught up in the drive for an internally prized professionalism, the image of the firefighter as the trusted friend in the community sometimes faded.

Emergence of community-based local government

During the 1990s, local elected officials and managers began to reemphasize the importance of community. In the new model of local government, the professional approach is balanced with what is best for the community as determined by the elected officials. This balancing sometimes means that the line between policy and administration is blurred.

The new model is based on the following assumptions:

1. Localities in fact actually consist of a number of communities, defined by geography, race or ethnicity, age, income, and so forth.
2. Local governments need to reach out to citizens, inviting them to participate as partners.
3. Local government employees should be empowered to use their discretion to proactively solve problems in the community.
4. Elected officials, managers, and employees must listen to citizens' expressions of their needs and desires, help them define problems that require attention, and help them clarify their expectations of local government and the outcomes they want.
5. Citizens need to be included in a decision-making process early, not just when it is time to react to the final report.
6. Goals should focus on outcomes for the communities and should be checked out with citizens.
7. Staff should focus its energy on meeting the community's needs first and other needs later.
8. Guidance from values and goals should take priority over rules and regulations.
9. Local officials and managers need to increase their visibility in the community by participating in community events or celebrations, becoming active in service or civic organizations, attending meetings, and listening.
10. Evaluating and adjusting services and programs is essential to success.

Police departments were quick to pick up on this trend. They began programs like DARE (Drug Awareness and Resistance Education), COPS (community-oriented policing), and problem-solving policing. Other departments were slower.

Community-based government in action

How does community-based local government really work? The foundation is the community, beginning with citizens who form neighborhood associations or cultural/religious organizations. There are special-interest groups that are advocates for a specific cause. There are numerous civic and community groups that have access to and participate in local government decision making. In addition, elected officials appoint committees and task forces as well as boards and commissions to help them (the officials) in the governing process. The ultimate representatives of the community are the individuals who are elected to the governing body, and it is they who decide on what is going to get accomplished (see lower half of Figure 3–1).

The local government organization (top half of Figure 3–1) is represented first by the employees who are in the field, providing services and delivering products. Supervisors and division directors translate the goals, mission, and organizational values to employees. Department directors have the dual concern of supporting policy development and leading the departmental organization. The city manager or administrator is the organization's key link to the governing body—to the political process. The organization's purpose is to determine

Figure 3–1 Community-
based local government.

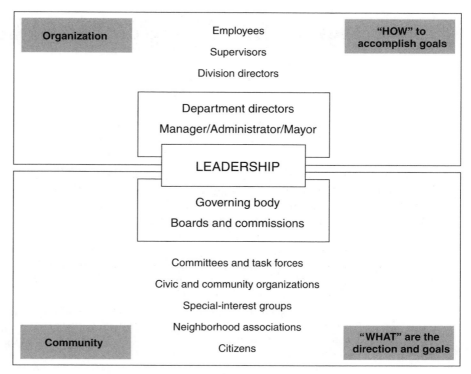

how to accomplish goals set by, and implement decisions made by, the governing body.

Under the model of community-based local government, fire service managers should be guided by the following "commandments":

1. Know your communities: who they are, what is unique to each one, who their leaders are, what they perceive to be their problems and needs.
2. Define desired outcomes for community goals and fire service goals, with measurable benchmarks.
3. Involve citizens in fire service decisions and programs as appropriate.
4. Make decisions about what is best that balance professional standards and the community.
5. Empower employees and managers to solve problems and make decisions.
6. Negotiate on policy decisions to achieve a viable, realistic compromise whenever possible.
7. Develop approaches to educating citizens about the fire department and department-related services.
8. Anticipate community issues and opportunities that lie over the horizon.
9. Evaluate the effect that programs have on the community.
10. Have a personal presence in the community.

The profile of the community

Communities are the building blocks of local governments. They constitute the framework within which people live, work, play, and raise a family—the framework within which people come together in pursuit of common interests. Every locality consists of multiple communities, and they all need services and amenities from local government in order to survive and prosper. Thus, it is important for a fire department and the entire local government organization to look beneath the surface; understand the communities being served, their needs, and their expectations of the department and the local government; and recognize that communities—along with their needs and expectations—change over time.

Four important characteristics of communities to look for are age, nationality or ethnicity, geographic location, and religion.

Age   Senior communities may expect a more formal local government, may pay bills in cash, may prefer city hall to open at 7:00 A.M., and may expect a timely response from the fire department in any emergency, including falls and other physical difficulties. In contrast, communities made up of young families are tied together by school activities, by youth development groups (such as the Boy Scouts and Girl Scouts), or by sports groups.

Nationality or ethnicity   Some communities are linked to the countries of their ancestors by a common language, cultural traditions, or experiences and expectations. Examples are African Americans, Asian Americans, Irish Americans, and Hispanic Americans. And even within an ethnic community there can be significant differences.

Geographic location or neighborhood   Communities are sometimes defined by physical place, by where people live: historic district, agricultural or rural area, gated community, new subdivision, or planned development.

Religion   Some areas of the United States are home to various religious communities whose members are tied together by common beliefs and values; desire local government to adopt specific rules and regulations; and meet regularly on a predetermined schedule.

For all communities whatever their age, ethnicity, location, or religion, it is important that fire service managers recognize their unique values, what they need from local government, what they expect of local government (from services to the behavior of its employees), their level of trust in government, their experiences in dealing with local government, and their perspectives and views on issues.

Fire service managers need to reach out to each community, not only to understand it but also to appreciate each community's relationship and contribution to the local government. In other words, fire service managers need to truly value the diversity of the communities they serve.

Citizens' expectations of the fire service

Within each local jurisdiction, the various communities will have differing expectations of the fire service. Some expectations, however, are widely held:

Responds quickly to emergency situations, including fires and medical crises, and handles the emergency with minimal inconvenience

Is sensitive to citizens' problems and concerns, recognizing that a problem really does exist and should not be minimized or made light of

Focuses services on the basic mission, attributing limited value to "innovative" programs that detract from basic services

Maintains professional appearance and demeanor (employees' uniforms are professional and consistent with the locale; stations are attractive but functional)

Is located nearby but not next door (i.e., close enough for a quick response but far enough away that residents are not inconvenienced by sirens or noise)

Helps solve problems rather than simply enforcing the rules strictly (e.g., explains how a code violation can be fixed as inexpensively as possible)

Works with other jurisdictions, especially in sharing resources, just as long as its own community benefits and cost-effectiveness increases

Adopts technical innovations in medical services and fire suppression (e.g., uses advanced computers and other new equipment).

To translate these general expectations to one's own community, one might ask at an upcoming staff meeting, "What do our citizens expect of the fire service, in terms of what services should be provided and how the services should be delivered?" One might also ask, "What do the city manager and elected officials expect of the fire service, in terms of services provided and the manner of their delivery?"

In general, citizens rate fire services high in surveys. Citizens expect a lot, but they appreciate the superior quality of service received. This satisfaction provides a very positive base on which the fire service can build a strong relationship with the community.

Tools for working with communities

Fire service managers have used many tools to understand and respond to their different communities. It is recognized that no set of tools will work in all locales or among differing communities, but tools that have worked for some fire managers are presented below. Beyond the specifics of these six tools lies the fact that each locale, and the public arena along with it, is changing. The fire service needs to be sensitive to its communities now and in the future.

Tool 1: Develop a community profile   Fire managers, working with the city manager and other departments or with their own staffs, can develop a profile of who really makes up their communities and how their communities are changing. In many cases, perceptions do not match the reality. Fire managers should begin with basic demographic data, such as age, educational level, and income level; establish a baseline; and examine trends over time. They should then expand the profile to identify expectations of local government, including programs and service delivery mechanisms. This information can guide fire managers as they define their mission (tool 2) or develop a new program (tool 4).

Tool 2: Reevaluate the departmental mission and core values   Managers should look up on the wall and dust off the old mission statement. Most fire departments have developed mission statements and statements of core operating values, but many of the statements are generic and look alike. Fire managers need to begin by looking at the needs and expectations of their own communities and citizens. An aging housing supply or a population of elderly people calls for a different mission from that of a department in a community with a younger citizenry and newer homes built under modern codes. Core values, too, should be reviewed: how should the fire department provide services and work with citizens? How the department does its work will determine its image in the community. Fire managers need to align the department's values with the community's values.

Tool 3: Create a citizen task force   Fire managers have continuing opportunities to involve citizens through task forces. (Some task forces may be created by the elected officials, others by the fire service manager.) A task force has (1) a defined assignment (usually to define the problems or issues, to bring into focus desired outcomes for the community, to identify and evaluate options, and to make recommendations); (2) small membership (seven to nine is optimal, there should be no more than eleven, and members should be identified not by special interest but by communities to be represented; elected officials can be asked to identify potential members); (3) a defined time frame (three to six months is best, and twelve months is the absolute limit); (4) regular agendas (prepared in advance of all meetings) and minutes (recording the decisions made); and (5) for complex issues, special reports to serve as discussion guides. The key for citizens is that their participation on a task force makes a difference and produces tangible results.

Tool 4: Develop a community-based program Identifying a community issue that relates to fire services and developing a neighborhood-based program in response is a way for fire managers to engage the community proactively. For example, Lake Oswego, Oregon, implemented a Community Emergency Response Team (CERT) program in which firefighters teach neighborhood teams to handle minor fire and medical emergencies, perform light rescue, and avoid hazards for seventy-two hours after a disaster has occurred. The concept originated with the Los Angeles City Fire Department for earthquakes and has been expanded by the Federal Emergency Management Agency to cover all emergencies.[1] In another example, the city of Cincinnati created neighborhood action teams; with members from several city departments, they work closely with neighborhood groups in solving neighborhood problems.

The keys to community-based programs are

1. Developing and maintaining a philosophy within the department that supports community-based programs, as demonstrated by an enthusiastic commitment of resources and staff time
2. Addressing "real" community issues and concerns
3. Involving citizens as partners so that they have a responsible role
4. Producing results that are visible in the community, generating a sense of making progress
5. Making the experience positive and fun for both citizens and firefighters.

Remember also that such a program cannot satisfy everyone.

Neighborhood emergency action team The El Cerrito (California) Fire Department participated in the 1991 Oakland Hills firestorm firefight. From that experience, the department learned that individual neighborhoods can be cut off from city services during a disaster and therefore need to develop their own capacity for self-governance and action. El Cerrito has exposure to wildfires coming over the crest of the Berkeley Hills from Wildcat Canyon, as well as significant earthquake exposure. Therefore, the fire department took the initiative and developed the NEAT program—Neighborhood Emergency Assistance Teams.

The purposes of NEAT (which is an ongoing effort) are to increase citizens' awareness of earthquakes, fires, and other possible disasters and of the potential impact of these disasters on the city and their own neighborhoods; and to develop each neighborhood's capacity for local action. The fire department worked with individual neighborhoods through education and organization to develop their capacity to act. This is a real effort of community-oriented fire management that strengthens citizens' capacity to be responsible for their neighborhoods in a time of crisis and ultimately to make their communities safer.

Tool 5: Maintain a greater community presence   Fire managers should get out into the community, setting the example by increasing their personal presence and staff's presence in the community. They should begin by drawing up a list of key community events or festivals, key civic and community organizations, and key businesses and institutions. Next they should evaluate the involvement of the fire department and staff with an eye to who should be involved and to what extent.

Community presence may include

Visiting community organizations

Meeting one-on-one with citizens, ranging from key community leaders to "average" citizens

Participating in community events (e.g., celebrations)

Opening fire stations to the community (the chief alone cannot be everywhere, but the department's presence can be enhanced)

Developing a department Web site.

Community involvement: "Baby Shots"   The Phoenix (Arizona) Fire Department is widely known for its innovative approaches to many issues. Community involvement is not an exception. In the late 1990s, fire department management and local health officials collaborated to address a serious community health problem and to use a valuable community resource.

A program called "Baby Shots" was put in place to address the problem of immunization of children. Under the supervision of both health and fire service professionals, the program uses Phoenix Fire Department paramedics to administer early childhood immunizations free of charge at strategic times and places around the city. The vaccines and other medical supplies are provided by the local public health agency, and the paramedics volunteer for the activity, typically held on weekends. Other fire department personnel provide record keeping and "TLC" for the little recipients of the shots.

Public health records are used to identify target areas in the community, and the fire department uses its public education and information network to notify area residents of the time and place of the sessions.

Feedback to the fire department and to its individual members has been highly favorable. This program is an excellent example of the use of fire department resources in meeting a community need.

Figure 3–2   A paramedic administering immunizations as part of the Phoenix (Arizona) Fire Department's community service work.

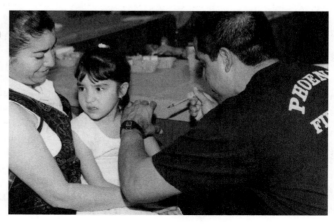

Tool 6: Check out citizens' needs and satisfaction   Fire managers should survey their citizens. Many local jurisdictions conduct regular surveys of the community, and fire managers can participate in these efforts by incorporating questions related to fire services—or they can develop their own surveys. These surveys are a reality check and can provide valuable feedback to enhance management and the delivery of service. The survey results can be discussed in staff meetings and used in developing programs and budgets. One alternative to general surveys is periodic phone surveys on specific issues (the scope needs to be narrowly defined). Another alternative—to get more in-depth feedback

---

A volunteer department's community involvement   Many volunteer fire departments are heavily involved in their communities as a function of essential fund raising. Others take the approach that their contribution to the community is fulfilled in the many person-hours devoted just to training, responding to emergencies, and maintaining the department. However, some volunteer departments recognize the need for and importance of additional community involvement.

A suburban volunteer fire department in the Midwest noted that many of the required child-restraint seats in automobile accidents did not function properly because they had not been properly installed. This same department had long sponsored fund-raising car washes using department members, helped by family members and citizen volunteers.

In the mid-1990s the fire department decided to add an important new community service to its car-wash program. At each session, full members of the volunteer fire department were on hand for the sole purpose of checking the installation of child restraints and, if necessary, instructing parents in the proper mode of installation.

The fire department obtained detailed instructions on installation from a wide variety of manufacturers of child restraints and automobiles. Training sessions were held for the volunteers to make sure that proper methods were used and taught. The tools and some nuts and bolts were provided by the fire department at each session.

Local media gladly advertised and covered the event whenever possible. The net result was that a large number of young parents learned how to install child restraints, and an unknown number of youngsters were saved from serious injury or death. In addition, the number of people attending the car washes, and thus making a goodwill donation, increased dramatically. This organization's community involvement paid several kinds of dividends.

Community involvement: Fire station community room   During the 1990s the city of Kent, Washington, constructed four new fire stations and renovated two others. In each case, management made a conscious decision to include opportunities for public participation. Each station contains a "community room," which is available free of charge for community meetings of all types. Not only do community groups (and fire prevention education classes) use the rooms, but the city council has held neighborhood outreach meetings there as well. In addition, each of the stations features a front counter just inside the entry, where on-duty personnel can greet the public. Finally, management included "Hoops for Youth" basketball goals in the parking lots so that neighborhood kids can congregate at the station and interact with the firefighters in a positive way.

—is to use focus groups. In all these cases, the key is listening to communities and using the messages in managing the fire service.

Fire and rescue services in the local political arena

To be effective, fire service managers also need to understand and operate successfully in the local political arena. This means that they need to understand the governing process—the role of elected officials—and the significant ways in which the political world for local government managers changed during the 1990s. During that decade new political challenges arose, and a new breed of elected official began emerging from the electoral process. This section describes the governing process, the new political challenges, and the new breed of elected official, and then, within that framework, it outlines a set of guidelines for working with elected officials.

Understanding the governing process: The responsibility of elected officials

Governance is the responsibility of the elected officials—the mayor and city council, board of aldermen, county commission, county board of supervisors, board of fire trustees, and so forth. Governance focuses on defining what the local government is going to be: its vision for the future, goals for the community, allocation of resources, and decisions on key policy issues. The governing process has nine basic elements; and each elected body has its own style of governing. In addition, elected boards all have in common a standard life cycle that reflects the phases of the political season.

Governance: Basic elements and styles   The nine basic elements by which elected bodies govern are (1) listening to the community (making themselves available to hear the ideas and concerns of a wide variety of citizens); (2) informing citizens about the local government, its vision and goals, policies and plans, programs and services; (3) defining the future direction of the community by articulating a focused vision that is simple, understandable, and usable and has outcome-based goals for which there are benchmarks of future success; (4) making decisions on policy direction, resource allocation, solutions to problems, issues to be addressed during the next year, and level of services; (5) setting the tone for the way business is conducted in the local government and for the image of government that is transmitted in the community and to the outside world; (6) representing the local government—serving as its spokesperson—to federal and state officials, to other local governments at the elected-official level, and to the outside world (including businesses that desire to relocate to the local community); (7) monitoring the performance of the local government (the results of local government services and actions and the effects on, and reactions of, citizens); (8) seeking feedback from citizens and adjusting policies and resources accordingly; and (9) mobilizing support from community partners—community groups, public institutions, schools, key businesses and business leaders, neighborhood associations—who can help achieve a goal.

Each elected body develops its own style of carrying out these basic elements of governing. Even in situations in which only one or two positions change, style and process of governing will change. By observing the governing process, a fire service manager can define his or her elected body's own style of governing:

Are the elected officials problem solvers, focusing on specific problems and expecting quick and timely action by staff?

Are they crisis managers, responding to the phone calls and complaints of citizens by directing staff to take short-term actions?

Are they visionaries, developing long-term goals and bringing into focus a vision for the community's future?

Are they legislative leaders, balancing long-term goals with short-term results, individual citizens' desires with what the legislators see as best for the overall community?

Every elected body has a dominant style, and it is important that fire service managers understand the style of the elected body and, in working with the elected officials, adapt their approach to that style. For example, if the members of the elected body do not read the agenda and supporting materials, the manager should think about alternative ways to get information on a policy issue to them—perhaps by taking them on a field trip, meeting with them one-on-one to discuss the issue, and so forth. However, fire service managers' actions should be guided by this principle: think political (put yourself in their shoes) but act apolitical (focus on the policy background rather than on lobbying).

The political season—The life cycle of an elected board   The political season is the period from election to election. It can be broken down into four phases (assuming for purposes of discussion that the season is two years long). The phases may vary in length, depending on who is running and what the issues are.

Phase 1: Preseason (months 1–3)   The preseason is when the elected officials get to know each other and staff, define how they want to operate, establish goals and direction, and learn about the local government. It is a time for translating political promises and commitments made during a campaign into goals and issues for the local government. It is not a time for major policy decisions.

Phase 2: Time for action (months 3–18)   The time-for-action phase is the time to study issues in depth; seek input and involvement from stakeholders in the community; address major policy issues and make decisions; and evaluate and adjust program direction, service levels, or resource allocations. This is the least "political" phase. In this phase elected officials concentrate more on governance (doing what is best for the local government) than on their political futures.

Phase 3: The stretch drive (months 18–23)   The stretch-drive phase has many names, from "the silly season" to "the time for weirdness." Elected officials often see the next election on the horizon, and citizens sense potential political vulnerability. The stretch drive is the time when elected officials avoid making controversial or major policy decisions (a manager who pursues the issues involved may get decisions that do not address the issues); it is a time when managers should produce results by taking visible actions in the community, respond to situations involving "political" favors by handling a citizen complaint (even one that would not be handled during other phases), and recognize the political side to governing.

Phase 4: The legacy (months 20–24)   This phase is applicable to elected officials who have decided not to run for reelection or have been defeated in the election. The legacy is their time to think about what they really want to leave behind. Perhaps they answer by making the final effort to secure approval of a program or project, by being a true statesman on an issue, or by championing a cause, and by leaving with grace and dignity. Or they may choose to drop out and not attend (or not prepare for) the meeting. Some may speak out and perhaps be "politically incorrect" now that the next election is not a restraining influence.

Fire service managers need to be aware of the political season and its phases and act accordingly. For example, the stretch drive (phase 3) is not the time to introduce a new sprinkler ordinance, propose to build or design a new fire facility, or negotiate a mutual aid agreement with another agency. A practical suggestion for managers is to develop with the city manager a policy calendar in which the months of the season are laid out with specific issues for deliberation or tasks to be done in preparation for issue discussions. Doing so can increase the effectiveness of fire service managers as they participate in the governing process.

Political challenges for local government

Against the basic backdrop of the governing process, a number of challenges for local government have arisen—challenges for political leaders and fire service managers alike. These challenges add new complications to the governing process and must be dealt with by fire service managers.

Challenge 1: The growing influence of the negative 20 percent
Populations in local communities often fall into a 20–20–10–10–40 political distribution: 20 percent have positive opinions of local government, 20 percent have negative opinions, 10 percent lean toward the positive, 10 percent lean toward the negative, and 40 percent are (in effect) bystanders (see Figure 3–3).

The positive 20 percent are generally satisfied with services and trust government and local officials. They may or may not vote, depending on their interests or available time. Increasingly they are not running for elected office and, in fact, may be discouraged from running by the negative 20 percent.

The negative 20 percent—a growing force in the local political arena—are never satisfied with any response; basically distrust local government, political leaders, and managers; and make personal attacks on staff. They misrepresent facts and information when speaking to the news media and community; their behavior is less than civil; they increasingly show up at meetings; they manipulate the Freedom of Information Act and the public hearing process; they increasingly network with other "negative" forces; and they intimidate average citizens to the extent that the latter withdraw from the political arena. The negative 20 percent do vote. They argue for greater citizen involvement, but if that approach is in fact taken and results in views contrary to their own, they criticize the approach and the process.

In the middle are the 10 percent who lean to the positive and the 10 percent who lean to the negative. Most elected officials come from this segment of the population. People in this segment are concerned about issues, worry about the future, and are willing to compromise (seek the middle ground and avoid extremes). This segment may or may not vote, depending on the tone of the campaign, the quality of the candidates, and the importance of the election.

Finally there are the 40 percent who are bystanders, politically speaking.

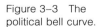

Figure 3–3   The political bell curve.

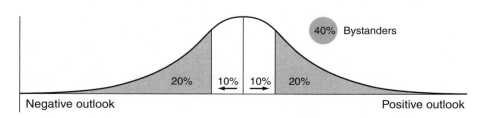

Negative outlook   Positive outlook

They may not know what city, county, or fire district they live in. They usually do not vote in local elections, and their views are not represented on boards and commissions. Although most of the time they have little or no patience with the negative 20 percent, their nonparticipation has the effect of strengthening that 20 percent, particularly in states where financial issues require a "super-majority" vote by the governing board.

In the 1990s the negative 20 percent became a significant force in the political arena for several reasons. First, local governing bodies did not say a loud "no" to the personal attacks and did not make sure to explain their decisions. Second, local governing bodies appointed the negative 20 percent to citizen committees and boards/commissions and then allowed them to dominate and, in many cases, take over the political process. Third, public officials, by not identifying or correcting errors, allowed inaccurate public statements to appear credible. Fourth, the negative 20 percent themselves—by disrupting public meetings—made local government seem no different from *Monday Night Football* or a comedy show on television. And finally, the negative 20 percent swayed elections by turning out in large numbers.

At times and in some communities, the negative 20 percent are getting elected to political office. When that happens, there is a resistance to setting goals and a desire to investigate past actions; civility decreases; and meetings of governing boards last longer.

For fire service managers, the challenges are to help political leaders deal with the growing influence of the negative 20 percent and to reach out in a positive manner to the other 80 percent. To do both of these things, fire service managers can take the following actions:

1. Present timely and accurate information and reports that are easily understood by citizens, and do so more proactively.
2. Invite the 80 percent to be on a departmental citizens' advisory team or to attend a citizens' fire academy.
3. Share background information with the media before the issue becomes political (i.e., before it enters the political arena).
4. Listen to, but avoid reacting to, the charges and attacks by the negative 20 percent. Although factual inaccuracies should be corrected, negativity and name-calling should not be engaged in.
5. Support and use the local government's goals and department mission as the framework for action, not just giving them lip service but really using them.

Challenge 2: The "McGovernment" attitude of citizens   The United States has increasingly become a "fast-food" society, and citizens bring to local government the same attitudes they bring to the purveyors of fast food. In other words, citizens have a "McGovernment" attitude and expect local government to provide

Services now

Services cheap

Services my way

Services without hassle or personal inconvenience

Services that are readily accessible

Services that are consistent.

This attitude is intensified by the rapid growth of electronic communication. The advent of Web pages and e-mail has given rise to an expectation that answers should be available instantaneously. A further complication is that many citizens have little understanding of local government—what it does, how it works, and how they fit into it. They may not understand their responsibilities as citizens in a democratic society, and they may not appreciate the importance of their vote. They may think that the politician runs the organization and have no conception of the role of the administrator or manager.

For fire service managers, the challenge is to help citizens understand both local government (from governance to service delivery) and their own responsibilities as citizens. In most communities the traditional methods of getting information out to citizens are not effective: citizens are not reading newspaper articles on local government issues and policies unless there is a scandal or controversy, nor are they reading the newsletters they are inundated with. So managers need to go to the citizens. Fire service managers can bring government and the political arena to citizens by taking the following actions:

1. Incorporate public spaces and meeting rooms in fire stations, to be available for public forums and neighborhood meetings.
2. Include "Local Government 101" in a public education program covering, among other things, the responsibilities of citizenship, and address the program to employees first.
3. Develop public education programs for cable television (five- to seven-minute shorts) that can be shown repeatedly.
4. With other departments, set up an information booth at a shopping mall.
5. Provide access to services through a Web site.

Challenge 3: Agenda of the unimportant   Local elected officials may not always know how to put meetings to good use. Their agendas may not differentiate between relatively unimportant issues and major issues that establish a policy framework. As a result, policy decisions may get short shrift. Part of the reason for this is a desire to be responsive to citizens and to demonstrate concern about the community. This desire often leads local elected officials to increase the number of items on their meeting agendas, loading the agendas with minor policy issues or managerial issues raised by citizens. And if "unimportant items" are placed at the beginning of an agenda, major items are not considered until the hour is late and the meeting is winding down. For example, elected officials may spend a lot of time on the color or specifications of fire vehicles, the specific design features of fire facilities, or recreational/fitness facilities in stations, all of which are relatively unimportant issues that managers could resolve with minimal policy direction or outside the political process. As a result of the time spent on those issues early in the meeting, major policy issues concerning fire and emergency medical services may never get an adequate discussion or policy direction. These issues may concern local government's role in emergency medical services, new building codes (including sprinkler requirements), or the sharing of facilities and equipment with neighboring jurisdictions.

Many fire service managers have thus been forced to fill the political void and make policy decisions. They have encountered local elected officials who do not want to make a policy decision but instead want the flexibility of being able to disavow any responsibility if a problem arises. Or the local elected officials may enjoy the operational side of fire services and truly dislike and avoid policy decisions in which they feel technically deficient.

For fire service managers, the challenge is to help local elected officials focus on the "important, non-urgent" issues that will provide the policy framework and shape the future of the fire service. (See Figure 3–4, which shows categorization of topics by importance and by time frame, or urgency.) When one is uncertain about the community politics or desired outcome, it is very easy to avoid the major issues. Focusing on them requires trust in the governing

Figure 3–4 Effective use of time by leaders.

		Low	High
Urgency	High	Response driven • Reaction to individual request or complaint • "Crisis" for one person only • New "fad" • Reaction to news media story	Problem solving • Emergency situation • Ethical problem • Public safety issue • Employee safety issue
	Low	Time wasting • Daily frustrations • Minutiae • Rumors • Minor technical or operational details	Leadership focused • Long-range plans • Policy direction • Training • Relationship building
		Low	High
		Importance	

process and in elected officials and respect for the differing roles and responsibilities.

The fire service manager can help frame policy issues and support the policy deliberations of elected officials by taking the following actions:

1. Use work or study sessions to ask the elected officials about their desired outcomes or guidelines before completing policy research.
2. Make brief (five- to ten-minute) visual presentations that begin with the policy questions that need to be addressed and include key background information (no overloading or lobbying).
3. Use on-site visits or tours of the community to bring issues and problems into focus.
4. Provide a brief (one- to two-page) summary of a policy report, highlighting issues, options, and recommendations.
5. Ask the question: Is this issue a policy issue or a management issue?

Challenge 4: Use of "power politics" Traditionally, local election campaigns in many communities were relatively short and low-key. In the 1990s, however, candidates (including incumbents) made the tone of campaigns and the whole campaign process more "political." They solicited larger amounts of money, especially from special-interest groups that wished a favorable reception for their concerns, and attributed less importance to small, individual contributions. With larger budgets, candidates (including incumbents) hired professional campaign managers to do polling and give political advice, no longer relying on friends as their campaign chairs. In many communities the personal approach began giving way to a media-based approach. In addition, campaigns started earlier and therefore lasted longer.

Local government employee unions have long understood the importance of the political process. Firefighter unions have traditionally been involved in local elections by holding candidate forums and providing volunteers to distribute campaign literature and the like. Some firefighter unions have begun playing a more active role in the electoral process. If from their point of view management has not appropriately addressed an issue, they are more likely to take the issue to candidates running for office. The issues raised may involve bargaining, the performance of the fire chief and managers, and operational and service-related matters, and at times they may cause embarrassment to the chief and others. This more active role is a high-risk one, however. If the union's candidate loses, whoever won may not look sympathetically on union issues or even, by extension, on fire department issues. If the union's candidate wins, that person may support the union on some of its issues, but even so, with many competing interests and only limited resources, the final decisions may still not reflect the union's position.

For fire service managers, the challenge is to avoid becoming involved in local elections, either personally or through others. When the fire chief is appointed by and serves at the pleasure of the mayor, there may be an expectation that the chief will be involved in the mayor's campaign. Such involvement may take many forms, from providing information to doing actual campaigning. With neutrality as the desired outcome, the chief needs to negotiate his or her role with the mayor. The decision, whatever it is, will have consequences for both the chief and the department.

Fire service managers can minimize their political involvement in elections by taking the following actions:

1. Avoid endorsing candidates or serving on a campaign committee—and avoid making negative comments about candidates.
2. Develop a policy of not permitting candidates to use fire facilities and personnel in political advertisements.
3. Be sensitive to the political nature of your comments: others may see these comments as a political agenda.
4. Treat candidates the same by providing the same information to all.
5. Frame policy issues in discussions with the candidates without taking a political stance or mentioning a solution. If you mention a solution, candidates will quickly pick up on it and will either promote or attack the idea.

Challenge 5: Lack of civility at the governing table   The lack of civility at governing board meetings became a concern of the National Association of Counties and the National League of Cities in the late 1990s. More particularly, the arena for conducting the public's business has seen actual and threatened violence between elected officials and between elected officials and citizens, personal (verbal) attacks and abusive language, lack of agreement on ground rules for appropriate behavior (i.e., absence of an agreed-upon code of conduct), and disrespect for the governing process, all of which have detracted from public debate.

Some elected officials have lost sight of the process—the manner in which the public's business is conducted. Before laws were passed mandating open meetings, disagreements that got out of hand were dealt with in private. Now they are often on television. (Lack of civility does not always take the form of extreme behavior. Lack of civility may find expression in a nice comment with an edge, a personal putdown, or a comment that demonstrates the speaker's competence in contrast to the alleged incompetence of staff or a fellow elected official.)

For fire service managers, the challenge is to help elected officials act with civility—while remembering that the only behavior one can control is one's own. The fire service manager can support civility on the part of elected officials by taking the following actions:

1. Know the code of conduct of elected officials (if there is one) and act accordingly; in the absence of one, develop staff ground rules for meetings with elected officials.
2. Avoid escalating a conflict, even with subtle comments: remember that once a conflict is escalated, control is lost.

3. Act in a professional manner, making sure that remarks deal with content and not people.
4. Do not take things personally, although this is easier said than done.
5. When discussion has wandered, refocus it on the issues (on definitions, outcomes, options, and recommendations).

Challenge 6: Elected officials' feeling that their power of choice has been preempted   Local government and its missions, services, programs, and resources sometimes seem to elected officials to be under attack. One source of attack is mandates from state and federal governments that dictate policy direction even though this policy direction may have costs or may threaten sanctions. Another source is the news media, whose coverage of local government policy issues is superficial and whose editorials often concentrate on the negative aspects of government and reflect personal bias rather than concern for the community. A third source of attacks is litigation on frivolous issues—and sometimes, even though the local government and elected officials believe they are in the right, the attorney advises them to settle the case because settling is cheaper than pursuing the matter in court. To elected officials, these "attacks" may seem to define the issues and leave them little discretion in making a decision.

The challenge for the fire service manager is to help officials overcome their feeling of helplessness, and the way to do that is to focus on policy decisions in which the officials have a choice. Fire service managers can take the following actions:

1. Know the legal and policy constraints affecting fire service in the jurisdiction, including federal and state laws, administrative codes, or legislative mandates.
2. Support the lobbying efforts that the jurisdiction's elected officials make at federal and state levels: identify potential legislative changes, monitor (through fire service professional organizations) legislative bills and political actions, and participate in the lobbying efforts as needed (on the basis of an understanding with elected officials).
3. Develop and maintain an ongoing relationship with the news media: respond to their calls and inquiries in a timely manner, have prepared news items for television or newspaper reporters, treat each reporter with respect, and provide honest responses.
4. Identify issues that could result in legal action if policy direction were not provided by elected officials.
5. Know when it is best to "fold": neither the local government nor the fire department benefits if a losing position is adhered to once a decision has been made.

The changing types of local elected officials

The governing process is being modified not only by the new political challenges but also by the new political types responding to these challenges. There is a shift from the traditional type of elected official to a new breed.

Traditional elected officials   Certain types of elected officials were prevalent in the past and may still be evident in some communities. To generalize, one can call them community leaders, community stewards, "moms," and "new-new rookies."

Community leaders—recognized by the community as leaders—gained experience in local government by serving on boards and commissions; wish to do what is best for the community; trust staff and value staff's information and recommendations; conduct efficient meetings; are effective spokespersons for the local government; and, if needed, are facilitators or consensus builders.

Community stewards are involved in civic groups or local government; concentrate on making the best decision for the overall community; value staff (their ideas and recommendations); come to meetings prepared, with homework done and questions answered; are respectful to those in leadership positions in the community; and make decisions.

"Moms" know the community, its people, and its issues; are loyal to the community and the local government; take a personal approach, wanting staff to fix the problem or handle the complaint; require significant staff time; want staff to handle sensitive items; defend staff actions; and want things to be "nice," with personal conflicts avoided. They do not forget, so a fire manager should never make them angry.

"New-new rookies" have little or no experience in civic affairs or local government; are on a very steep learning curve, covering everything from terminology to processes; are excited about being elected, open to learning, and eager; can be swayed by a reasonable-sounding negative 20 percent person; and have unrealistic expectations about what it means to be an "elected official." This group is generally easier to work with than the other types, believes in local government, and respects its role in local government and the roles of other participants.

New breed   The general types of elected officials that have appeared more frequently since the late 1990s can be called zealots for a cause, amateur politicians, pseudomanagers, and antagonists.

Zealots for a cause reflect a special-interest group and view all issues from the perspective of their primary issue. Desiring to win and to defeat the other position, they are unwilling to compromise and may attack individuals who disagree.

Amateur politicians believe they are the political experts, and their agenda is to run for higher political office. Thus they view issues from a political perspective (will their actions gain voter support?) and are easily influenced by political pressure from special interests. They do not know how to really negotiate in a political arena and may not be trusted by others.

Pseudomanagers may be retired executives or managers; they love details, trust their own facts over the information and data supplied by staff, are likely to micromanage issues, and even if they know the answer will always ask questions (just to test staff). They will prolong the debate with more questions or will extend the process with their detailed involvement.

Antagonists basically distrust staff and local government and serve as self-appointed government watchdogs. Elected by the negative 20 percent, they are never satisfied with the report, recommendation, or results; question staff, particularly in an accusatory manner; attack people and the process; and strive to mobilize political support in the community.

More and more of the new breed are getting elected, driving the traditional types away from the political arena. The presence of the new breed has modified the governing process in a number of ways: more time is spent in meetings; policy is less emphasized and personalities more so; debate is longer and less substantive; citizens' distrust of government and officials is pandered to; and citizens are driven from the political process.

Fire service managers must be able to work with all types of elected officials. Guidelines for doing so are presented on the next page.

Guidelines for working with elected officials

This section contains two sets of guidelines. The first set outlines what local elected officials at the start of the twenty-first century expect of fire service managers. The second set suggests approaches that managers can take to prepare for their work in the political arena.

In general, elected officials expect managers to use their professional expertise within the context of the community they are serving. Specifically, their expectations are that fire service managers will

Know the community as a whole and specific communities in the jurisdiction

Anticipate community needs, problems, and concerns

Look over the horizon for innovative opportunities for service

Manage public dollars and resources prudently

Prepare staff work in which the issues are well defined, the options thoroughly evaluated, and the recommendations clear

Keep elected officials and city managers informed about major incidents in the community.

Managers should bear in mind, however, that each political unit has its own personality and therefore will have its specific expectations, and these should be discussed.

General guidelines on preparing to work in the political arena are as follows:

1. Define the fire service's mission and core operating values and get the approval of the elected body
    What is the department's purpose?
    What services are critical?
    What values should guide management and operations?
2. Develop and use a strategic (five-year) plan for fire and emergency services, including
    Measurable goals, with benchmarks of success
    Plans that outline actions
    Mechanisms for reporting on progress.
3. Train staff in writing policy reports
    Incorporate goals from both the strategic plan and the elected body
    Clearly define the problem and the desired outcome
    Discuss the history, including previous action by the legislative body

---

Guidelines for working with all types of elected officials

1. Begin discussion of issues by defining (a) the problem, (b) the desired outcomes, and (c) the parameters for staff research.
2. Share information with all elected officials equally.
3. Get to know each elected official as a person by going to lunch, inviting him or her to the office for a discussion of a current topic, and so forth.
4. Do not stereotype an elected official; recognize that a person may be a combination of types.
5. Help elected officials see the successes, not just the problems.

      Present and analyze options
      Acknowledge any public input
      Make a recommendation
      Check for proper spelling and grammar and for factual accuracy.
4. Develop an annual legislative agenda
      Incorporate policy issues as set forth by the elected officials
      Anticipate fire-related policy issues and gather relevant information
      Make sure legislative suggestions are consistent with all the policies of the elected officials
      Work with others in your jurisdiction or professional organization to advise legislative representatives.
5. Report on progress
      Keep goals in the forefront so that elected officials are less likely to forget them
      Provide updated policy reports using reader-friendly formats
      Seek advice and redirection on policy issues as they are developed or as programs are implemented.
6. Celebrate successes with elected officials and citizens
      Say "thank you" for participation and partnership
      Demonstrate results and link others' decisions and actions to these results
      Include elected officials and citizens in celebrations.

Ethics: Maintaining public confidence

A cornerstone of public service is having the public's trust and confidence. At best, public confidence is the foundation for the community's engagement and financial support, which are crucial for effective local government. At worst, lack of public confidence can mean that people refuse to participate, refuse to support funding needs, or even initiate a "throw the rascals out" movement. That reaction can seem even worse when the person considered "the rascal" is oneself.

People expect their government officials to do the right thing, the ethical thing. When a fire manager acts other than in the public's best interest, public confidence in government is undermined. All the community support painstakingly developed by use of some of the tools and strategies discussed above can evaporate instantly with one serious lapse in ethical decision making, or even the appearance of one.

This section discusses (1) ethical decision making as good management, (2) the types of ethical problems that are likely to arise, (3) remedies when an error in judgment has been made, and (4) steps that can be taken to achieve consistency in ethical behavior.

Ethical decision making as good management

If earning and maintaining public confidence were not reason enough for fire managers to be concerned about ethics, there is also a practical benefit: ethical decision making is good management and good politics. Ethics covers such basic matters as how services are allocated, how resources are managed, and how people are treated.

Decisions about services carry a major ethical component, often associated with equity. Are services provided that favor a particular income level or part of town? Are services excluded that those with little political influence need?

Decisions about how resources are managed involve things on which public funds are spent. Are the funds spent on a legitimate public purpose? Did those funds really have to be spent? And what about the way the funds were spent: Was a fair bid process used? Were any personal benefits received from vendors?

Decisions about how people are treated strike at the very heart of the employee-employer relationship. Are employees put in a situation in which they are expected to take an ethically questionable action? In addition, for employees as well as employers, effectiveness, motivation, and job satisfaction depend on how well they identify with the organization's values, whether the organization's values are consistent with their own, and whether the values the organization professes are consistent with what the organization actually does.

Types of ethical problems likely to arise

Perhaps the biggest challenge of all is to recognize that the problems, concerns, and issues fire managers face daily do have ethical ramifications—and to recognize what these ramifications are. Recognizing potential problems allows time to keep them from materializing. Recognizing them after the fact is usually too late. A few types of potential ethical (possibly even legal) problems are discussed here.

Criminal activity   The most damaging ethics problem for the fire and rescue service is arson by fire personnel or theft from fire or medical victims. Criminal activity may also include theft from the department—for example, taking equipment, overcharging for travel expenses, seeking compensation for a non-duty-related injury that is presented as duty related, and requesting pay for time not worked. Crimes committed by fire employees off duty can have the same negative effect on the department's reputation in the community as on-duty crimes.

Racial and sexual discrimination   Historically, fire and rescue agencies have not reflected adequate racial and sexual diversity in their workforces. Actions ranging from blatant discrimination to a seemingly unjustified decision, and including insensitivity to those who are different, have prompted discrimination complaints and lawsuits pertaining to appointment, promotion, discipline, and discharge.

Sexual and other forms of harassment   Treatment of employees, particularly female employees, by supervisors, peers, and the public is regulated by law and agency policy. A 1998 court decision, *Oncale v. Sundowner Offshore Oil Services* (523 U.S. 75, 118 S.Ct. 998), also recognized "same-sex" sexual harassment as actionable. Yet incidents that can create a hostile work environment or deny equal opportunity continue to occur.

Drug or alcohol abuse   A small but significant portion of any workforce is likely to have a problem with drug or alcohol abuse. The problem is often reflected in high absenteeism, a high accident rate, or strained relationships with other employees.

Acceptance of gifts   By the nature of the fire service's work, people like to give fire employees gifts. An inexpensive gift (e.g., a plate of cookies) as an expression of appreciation for helping a family member with a medical emergency may be harmless, but an expensive gift in return for favored treatment is entirely different. (Employees charged with enforcing the fire code may be more likely to attract expensive gifts.) Discounts on food and other merchandise for fire employees are not uncommon but are probably inappropriate. Was the gift meant to influence a decision? What value would be acceptable? Would a gift be perceived by others as improper influence? There should be a clear organizational standard as to what is acceptable.

Irregularities in purchasing   Buying goods and services from employees and diverging from the regular process to buy from a "friendly" business are both improper. Also improper is accepting travel, entertainment, or other things of personal value from equipment manufacturers, yet in some areas this practice is still engaged in.

Incompatible employment   With so many employees holding second jobs, potential conflicts between the two jobs need to be carefully monitored. Examples of possible incompatibility are when a fire inspector works for an establishment that he or she is responsible for inspecting and when an employee provides a service that may be needed after an inspection (e.g., recharges fire extinguishers).

Endorsements of private products   With an ever-increasing variety of public-private partnerships, endorsements may or may not be proper. Personal benefit from an endorsement is clearly unacceptable. The main consideration is the message conveyed by the endorsement (e.g., by a photograph in a professional magazine of fire chiefs and chief officers in front of a particular brand of fire apparatus). The general rule of caution in such matters, regardless of any personal benefit received, definitely makes this sort of thing questionable.

Political activity   Some political activity by employees is permitted under state laws. But the law usually frowns on using one's official position in support of political candidates. And even though some political activity may be allowed by law, that does not make it wise. Political candidates seem to be attracted to fire equipment or personnel for campaign ads, but this pairing should not be allowed.

Disclosure of confidential information   What is legally considered "confidential" varies by state. "Confidential" may apply to personnel information, medical information, collective bargaining information, identity of complainants, and so forth. Care should be taken to identify what is confidential and to maintain that confidentiality. By the same token, it is important not to restrict disclosure of public information and to encourage the sharing of information that is helpful to other agencies; for example, the fire department would identify a home with unhealthy living conditions to the local agency responsible for child welfare.

Illegal meetings   State statutes define requirements for public meetings (i.e., the conditions under which a gathering is a meeting that is required to be open to the public). If fire managers are not sensitive to those requirements, they may put elected officials in a difficult situation. A politically active union may also put elected officials in the position of violating an open-meeting law if the union is not careful when hosting incumbent elected officials.

Use of public equipment or facilities for private benefit   The nature of this unethical act can vary, from taking an office pen or pad of paper for use at home to taking or "borrowing" expensive tools or other equipment.

Remedies for errors in judgment

After making an error in judgment, many people rationalize their error and hope the matter goes away quickly. The sidebar "Mind over Manner" lists

Mind over manner: Excuses for wrongdoing

Denying or trivializing its significance	"Show me a victim." "It's not illegal." "You can't legislate morality." "It's just a technicality."
Invoking the double standard	"Morality is a personal matter." "I don't mix business with my personal feelings."
Arguing necessity	"It's cutthroat out there." "If I don't do it, someone else will." "It's my job." "It will save some jobs."
Arguing relativity	"It's not illegal elsewhere." "In the United States, ideals are turned into laws." "No act is inherently illegal." "We are no worse or better than society at large."
Professing ignorance	"I wasn't told." "Ethics is a gray area." "The rules are inscrutable."

Source: Gary B. Brumback, "Institutionalizing Ethics in Government," *Public Personnel Management* 20, no. 3 (1991): table 1. Reprinted with permission of *Public Personnel Management*, published by the International Personnel Management Association (IPMA), 1617 Duke Street, Alexandria, VA 22314; 703/549-7100, http://www.ipma-hr.org.

many of the common forms that such rationalization may take. Unfortunately, in the public's mind this kind of excuse only compounds the error.

When managers and employees find themselves considering the use of one of these excuses, they would do better to redirect their responses as described below. They should

Tell their boss(es) everything　　Before the bosses learn of an error from someone else, the erring person should meet with them at the absolutely earliest time and ask for no interruptions; should explain what happened as fully as memory allows (making some notes in advance is a good way to make sure that nothing is forgotten); should be most explicit about the part that is most difficult to explain (otherwise, when that part comes out in the open later, the person will seem to have been trying to hide something); and should not only have a plan in mind for dealing with the problem but also ask for suggestions.

Make a complete public disclosure　　The erring person should not succumb to the tempting thought that no one else will ever discover the problem. A "voluntary" statement at a public meeting or news conference allows one to take the initiative in addressing the problem, as well as ensure that the media get all the relevant facts. If the issue is strictly internal to the organization, a meeting with staff can be substituted for the public meeting—but one should not be surprised if someone in attendance makes the "internal" issue public.

Apologize to all interested parties　　There is no substitute for a timely, sincere, personal apology.

Providing ethical leadership   Ethical behavior is essential for all of us involved with public administration. If we as chief fire officers violate the ethical expectations of our communities and departments, our personnel will most probably refuse to follow us and the public will likely attempt to have us removed from our positions.

It is essential that we provide ethical leadership for our organization. We need to attempt to avoid any situation that could be interpreted as a conflict of interest, we need to refrain from making decisions based on our personal preferences, and we must diligently ensure that we do not abuse the power of our position.

If we are in doubt about a proposed action, we should ask what we would like to see reported on the front page of the local newspaper. If we wish to keep our actions from public view, it is a strong indicator that we may not think our actions are ethical.

The following is the current adopted Code of Ethics of the International Association of Fire Chiefs (IAFC), which represents the leadership of America's fire and rescue departments and those of forty other nations.

Every member of the IAFC shall with due deliberation live according to ethical principles consistent with professional conduct and shall

Recognize that we serve in a position of public trust that imposes responsibility to use publicly owned resources effectively and judiciously.

Keep in mind our obligation not to seek advantages or favors for ourselves, friends, or family.

Use information gained by virtue of our positions only for the benefit of those we are entrusted to serve.

Conduct our personal affairs in such a manner that we cannot be improperly influenced in the performance of our duties.

Recognize and avoid situations wherein our decisions or recommendations may have an impact on our personal financial interests.

Seek no favor and accept no form of personal reward for influence or official action.

Engage in no outside employment or professional activities that may impair or appear to be in conflict with our primary responsibilities as fire officials.

Handle all personnel matters on the basis of merit.

Carry out policies established by elected officials and policy makers to the best of our ability, even when they are contrary to our recommendations.

Refrain from financial investments or business that conflict with, or are enhanced by, our official position.

Source: Adapted with permission from the International Association of Fire Chiefs, "Fire Chief's Code of Ethics," IAFC Board of Directors, 2002.

Take corrective action   The erring person should do whatever he or she can to minimize the effect of the immediate problem and should then act to prevent its recurrence. The preventive action, too, should be explained publicly.

Have a résumé ready in case it is needed   Sometimes the only way to restore the public's trust is for the erring person or the person in charge to resign.

Steps toward greater consistency in ethical behavior

Obviously there is no foolproof formula for ensuring ethical perfection, and in fact perfection does not exist. However, there are certain simple steps that fire service managers can take to help achieve greater consistency over time and throughout the organization. Taking these steps should make decision making in the department still more ethical and should increase the public's confidence in the department and the department's effectiveness in the public arena.

Clearly define organizational values and expectations Management consultant and author Ken Blanchard wrote: "An organization needs to know what it stands for and on what principles it will operate. Once it has a clear picture of its purpose and values, it has a strong basis for evaluating its management practices and bringing them into alignment."[2] An ethical framework for an organization can be provided by one of the following: (1) a set of legal requirements, (2) a statement of values, (3) an ethics policy or ordinance, or (4) performance standards or expectations.

Set of legal requirements Some organizations use the collection of federal, state, and local laws that cover ethical violations. Obviously the coverage varies considerably by state, and it changes regularly. In addition, being legal does not make something the right thing to do in all cases.

Statement of values Some organizations have identified several values that they expect employees to be guided by in their behavior (see Figure 3–5).

Ethics policy or ordinance Some local government bodies have enacted comprehensive ethics policies or ordinances detailing requirements in areas such as conflict of interest, financial disclosure, and representation of outside interests.

Performance standards or expectations Some local government bodies have defined what they expect of their employees in their daily performance (see the sidebar on "Integrity: Expectations of City Employees" on pages 96–97).

Hire employees who are sensitive to ethical issues In its recruitment material the organization should cover values, and in interviews it should include questions involving ethical situations. However, the best way to determine whether prospective employees are sensitive to ethical issues is with reference checks.

Offer regular ethics training and education for employees Regular formal training is important for all employees, especially managers and supervisors. And it is particularly important that this training be interactive. Most effective, however, may be discussions between supervisors and employees as issues come up: evaluating the issues from different perspectives, weighing alternative courses of action, and clarifying the organization's position or decision.

Provide consultation on ethical issues for employees Employees need to be able to get advice they can rely on to keep them out of trouble with their employer. Ultimately this advice may have to come from the city manager or attorney for the organization. However, employees may be more inclined initially to seek counsel from their supervisor. Although supervisors are not qualified to provide legal advice to their employees, they can help employees analyze the situation. A sample decision-making guide is presented in the sidebar on "Guidelines for Ethical Decision Making."

Figure 3–5   City of El Cerrito organizational philosophy.

CITY OF EL CERRITO
Organizational Philosophy

We respect: Ourselves,

Our work,

Our people,

Our community.

Respect means:

R esponsibility—We produce results.

E thics—We have integrity.

S ervice—We serve our community.

P ride—We care.

E nthusiasm—We are positive.

C ommunications—We listen, we share.

T eamwork—We work together.

Respect builds trust

Maintain reasonable means for monitoring and control   Monitoring key processes and decisions to make sure there are no problems in the department is very important. The way to do this is to check periodically. For example, it is management's responsibility to check payroll, long-distance telephone service logs, or Internet usage records; review travel reimbursements; verify purchases or any handling of cash; or ask employees in protected classes if they are being treated in a manner that is consistent with relevant laws, policies, or organizational values.

Respond to ethical problems by correcting systems and holding employees accountable   When an ethical problem occurs, one of the first questions to ask is, "How could this have happened?" In some cases the cause may simply be an employee error, and disciplinary action (up to and including discharge) may be appropriate. In other cases the cause may be a faulty procedure or system, such as an ambiguous purchasing policy, requiring a change in the procedure or more training for employees.

Guidelines for ethical decision making

1. What are the facts?
2. What are the options?
3. What ethical values and principles are at stake?
4. Who will be affected by your decision?
5. Who needs to help determine the course of action?
6. Which options benefit which groups? Are any fundamental rights involved?
7. Are your personal values in conflict with the organization's values? Are they in conflict with the values of others who must participate in the decision? With those of affected groups?
8. What are the short- and long-term costs of your decision?
9. What adjustments do you need to make on the basis of unexpected consequences or new information?

Source: Adapted from Jane G. Kazman and Stephen J. Bonczek, *Ethics in Action: Leader's Guide* (Washington, D.C.: International City/County Management Association, 1999), 33–34, 40–42.

Set a good personal example In *Leading without Power*, Max DePree, a prominent business executive, observed, "Trust in organizations depends on the reasonable assumption by followers that leaders can be depended upon to do the right thing."[3] When a leader models the kind of behavior expected of employees, the employees will display that behavior more consistently themselves.

Fire chiefs and managers: Roles in the public arena

What roles should fire chiefs and managers play in the public arena in the twenty-first century? Historically two roles for fire chiefs have predominated; one served as the model until about 1970, when the other replaced it. In the 1990s, however, as the accepted model of local government shifted (see "Fire and Rescue Services in the Context of Communities" above), fire chiefs learned to blend the two roles. Since then, the most effective fire chiefs have in common a number of ways of blending the two historical roles.

Traditional roles: Political chief to professional chief

In most communities the fire service began as a volunteer service. The fire chief was elected by the volunteers and was retained by their votes. If chiefs wanted to continue holding the position, they had to develop allies within the

---

Integrity: Expectations of city employees

1. Integrity in communications
   a. Be truthful in communications with other employees, council, and customers.
   b. Be a good listener. Seek to understand and then to be understood.
   c. Share all information that relates to a decision or incident or event, except when the sharing would be prohibited by policy or law.
   d. If a matter is confidential, maintain the confidence and let the person seeking the information know that it is confidential and why it is.
   e. Be forthcoming with information. If the information would help provide better service, do not wait to be asked.
   f. When presented with unverified information (e.g., rumors, gossip), seek the facts. When the information is of a strictly personal nature, forget it, as it does not belong in the workplace.
2. Integrity in relationships with others
   a. Put organizational and community needs above personal preferences in the workplace.
   b. Strive to resolve conflicts promptly.
   c. Speak directly and personally to others involved in situations in which conflict exists.
   d. If you have an agenda or concern, reveal it early.
   e. Try to appreciate all sides of an issue.
   f. Support others in efforts to implement city policies.
   g. Treat people seeking city services and resources in a fair and unbiased manner.
3. Integrity in the use of resources and times
   a. Use work time for work, always giving your best effort in the job you were hired to perform.
   b. Use city resources and equipment for work-related responsibilities only.
   c. Strive to improve your work efforts and add "value" to the services that you help provide.

Leadership Strategies for the Political Process   97

department who would support them in the next election, and they had to know their potential opponents—candidates at the next election. Thus was born the "political chief."

In about 1970, the fire service began providing new services and expanding its use of technology. Educational and training opportunities also expanded. Accordingly, potential candidates for fire chief were evaluated more on their technical competence and professional/managerial competence than on their personal relationships and political acumen. Thus was born the "professional chief."

The pure model of the political chief   In this model's purest form, political chiefs are a major political force in their communities. Many would minimize their political roles and their ability to influence politics, but they understand their community and know those who are or could be political allies. Their power is based on personal relationships and the power of their associates. They have attained their position through an election or a political appointment, not necessarily through their managerial or technical skills. Their approach to the public arena is characterized by the following:

Visible presence in the community: They are members of organizations, and —generally in "dress" uniform—they attend fire and nonfire events, community events or socials.

---

    d. Use professional and personal development resources to improve your work.
4. Integrity in the use of position
    a. Reveal financial and personal interests in work-related matters as soon as possible, and seek direction when appropriate.
    b. Avoid even the appearance of a conflict of interest or other impropriety.
    c. Use all elements of your position, including information that you obtained as a function of your position, for official duties only and not for personal gain or political or commercial endorsements.
5. Integrity in daily work activities
    a. Follow the letter and spirit of the law, professional codes of ethics, city policies, and the organizational philosophy, and support others who do the same.
    b. Accept personal responsibility for your decisions.
    c. Share credit where credit is due.
    d. Admit, accept responsibility for, correct, and learn from your mistakes.
    e. Do what you promise to do.
    f. Support the city, its departments, and its employees in the face of unfounded criticisms, and support council and managerial decisions and employees who act in support of these decisions.
    g. Make recommendations and take actions that are based on commonly held principles and values of the organization.
    h. Be sensitive to potential ethical issues, and when a question arises that may involve integrity, ask your supervisor for advice.
    i. Report unethical conduct or dishonesty.
    j. Treat others as you want to be treated.
    k. Accept differences (of opinion, of racial or ethnic background—all differences) and build from them.

Source: Adapted from "Integrity Expectations," a document of the city of Champaign, Illinois, 1995.

"Street smarts": They do not have a lot of formal education and training, although they may be highly skilled in firefighting.

Strong personal relationships with their command staff: Staff serve at the pleasure of the chief and are expected to help enlist support for the chief and the department.

Expectation of loyalty: Accountability is based more on loyalty to the chief than on performance of job duties.

Friendly, outgoing manner: They know the firefighters, hold regular coffee get-togethers and informal discussions, and show concern about the firefighters' families and personal lives; yet they may also isolate themselves as much as possible from internal problems.

Maintenance of a loose set of rules and operating procedures: Individuals are allowed to use their discretion more.

Aura of power and influence: Local elected officials who may want support in a future election perceive them as powerful and influential.

Knowledge of the community, its history, families, and politicians.

Political chiefs who were good politicians served for long periods of time and were able to obtain valuable resources for the fire department.

The pure model of the professional chief   In this model's purest form, professional chiefs emphasize the development of a professional fire department, with defined goals and performance measures and with professional firefighters who are well trained and technically competent and have the best equipment and resources, enabling them to perform their jobs effectively and efficiently. Professional chiefs' duties include insulating the fire department—its command staff and managers, supervisors, and firefighters—from politics and political influence. The basis of their power in the community and in the political arena with elected officials is technical expertise. They are skilled managers and administrators who can maximize service levels from available resources and can solve problems. They become chief through a competitive process, often involving written testing, and are typically appointed by a jurisdiction's chief administrative officer. They let the administrator handle the elected officials, while they themselves serve as technical expert and supporter. Their approach to the public arena is characterized by

Active involvement in professional organizations like the International Association of Fire Chiefs, the National Fire Protection Association (NFPA), and other professional organizations, which meet periodically to discuss professional issues

Lobbying through their associations for fire codes, federal dollars for training, and standards for ISO (Insurance Services Office) ratings

Sensitivity to community needs and interest in expanding the responsibility of the fire department, as a professional department, to new service areas such as emergency medical and HAZMAT

Well-prepared and well-supported budget requests based on data analysis, and thorough staff work in the form of well-written policy reports that present options and recommendations

Internal (departmental) focus on developing the organization (departmental rules, standardized procedures, pre-fire plans, process for critiquing responses to fires, etc.) and on building the skills of employees

Openness to new ideas about equipment for, and methods of, fire suppression

Commitment to staffing the public education and public information positions—positions that may have more contact with the public arena than the fire chief does.

Professional chiefs are proud of the department's professionalism and nonpolitical nature. They are effective in a setting characterized by strong professional management.

Choosing roles in the twenty-first century

To be effective leaders in the twenty-first century, fire chiefs will need to demonstrate skills associated with both of these two models, as will their command staff and managers. But there is no one best way or set of tools for all circumstances, and no simple recipe for success. Fire chiefs and managers may approach the public arena in many different ways, any of which can be right for their own community and their local political arena.

Each fire chief and manager makes choices on what roles to play in the public arena. A fire chief can share these roles with the immediate command staff. The choices made should reflect both one's personal skills and the expectations of the community at large and of the local government (elected officials and city managers). The choices made may have little to do with what one personally enjoys doing.

Chiefs and managers should begin this decision process with a self-examination, using personality profiles like the Myer–Briggs Inventory, performance evaluations, and feedback from professional colleagues, peers, and friends. People can test themselves on such personal traits and skills as

Flexibility

Openness in the face of controversy (positive outlook and optimism)

Tolerance of ambiguity

Ability to think "outside the box"

Ability to translate abstract ideas into concrete messages

Willingness to learn from others

Willingness to work on teams

Ability to put personal ego aside

Enjoyment of politics—the exercise of power and influence

Skill in conflict resolution and negotiation

Skill in marketing

Ability to communicate consistent messages to different groups and individuals

Skill in putting technical knowledge and information to appropriate use

Ability to make decisions with little or no guidelines

Ability to establish policy on the basis of goals and plans

Ability to develop processes for accomplishing a political agenda.

This list is a beginning. To develop the political sensitivity necessary for effectiveness in the public arena, one might need other qualities and strengths, depending on the community.

After evaluating oneself, a chief or manager should also evaluate the community. This means talking with people, observing the community, and learning about its history, especially if one is new to the community. The evaluation should cover

History and traditions

Local political customs

Expectations held by elected officials, both collectively and individually

Expectations held by supervisors of the fire chief and managers

Types of political and community issues affecting the fire service

Time demands on the chief and managers

The public's attitude toward government's role in society (this attitude varies by region).

After evaluating oneself and the community, it is time to choose an appropriate role (or several of them—see below). There are no criteria to meet in making the choice. The decision is purely individual and is made with the recognition that roles change over time. All a person can do is use discretion and make the best effort—while remembering that one does not have to make a perfect choice and that trying to do so will create paralysis. One needs to make a decision, seek feedback, evaluate, and adjust. It might be useful to identify a fire chief or manager who has been effective in the public arena and talk to that person, using him or her as a coach or mentor, an advisor.

Seven major roles of effective chiefs and managers

In evaluating fire chiefs and managers who are effective in the public arena, a manager will realize that certain roles are fairly common, although style and approach may differ. These roles are not mutually exclusive: a chief may combine aspects of several of them. In addition, a chief may delegate roles to subordinates.

Community ambassador Community ambassadors work with their communities. They begin by getting to know the community: identifying it; listening to it; helping it focus on issues and problems related to the fire service; and knowing influential individuals, groups, and organizations. They also represent the fire department and its services to the community, serving as spokespersons, sharing information about the department and its services, and functioning as symbolic leaders who are present in the community. They assume responsibility for educating citizens about the fire department and fire-related issues. They make sure that key citizens and stakeholders are brought to the table with fire department staff to define issues and explore opportunities. They are recognized by people in the community and are invited to participate in community activities. The role of community ambassador, therefore, requires a presence in the community, a willingness to listen, the ability to relate to an individual as a person, and the ability to communicate ideas through brief messages.

Futurist Futurists have their eyes on the horizon. With regard to the community, they anticipate potential policy or political issues that may affect and should involve the fire department. With regard to the profession, through professional organizations and journals they keep abreast of innovations in the fire service and of services that might be useful to the community. They anticipate change and plan for it. They work with the community and fire staff to test new ideas—to see whether the ideas add value to fire programs and services and whether they are likely to work in the particular community. After determining that a concept is worth pursuing, they frame the issue and present it to the elected officials and to the community. Being a futurist requires reading, attending professional meetings, searching for real opportunities, avoiding the latest fad, and being willing to take risks and experiment.

Political strategist   Political strategists work with elected officials and community leaders, with whom they have developed credible relationships based on mutual trust and respect. They respect role boundaries. They help the elected officials define the problem and bring possible outcomes into focus, and once goals are decided on, they make suggestions and advise these leaders on everything from strategies for involving the community to strategies for building support for action. Political strategists must be able to relate to various kinds of people, find a personal link with each politician, think strategy and not just project or program, develop an action plan, and advise without directing.

Negotiator   Negotiators represent the fire department to other agencies and departments and represent the local government to other government entities. They help negotiate local agreements on fire services, contracts with other entities (such as hospitals), arrangements for emergency medical and labor contracts, and so forth. This kind of negotiating involves the ability to seek options and arrive at a compromise—a compromise that must be represented to and owned in the fire department and must be acceptable to elected officials and community. Negotiators must be willing and able to be a member of a negotiating team, articulate and argue a point of view, seek a middle ground, and sell the agreement to others.

Lobbyist   Lobbyists work with the state and federal governments to protect the rights of local government to make decisions about fire services. These lobbying efforts are generally made through professional organizations—for example, the Congressional Fire Caucus—and take place both at the legislative level and with agencies. Legislative lobbying involves representing defined positions on legislative proposals, monitoring potential and proposed legislation, drafting legislative bills and potential amendments, and taking time to develop personal relationships. Agency lobbying focuses on administrative regulations and requirements and is directed at attempts to reduce or remove the local government's authority in setting policy or to extend mandated costs. Agency lobbying also supports programs to improve safety, and it supports funding for desirable programs. Lobbying requires an outgoing personality, the ability to develop personal relations and credibility with a variety of politicians of different personality types, the ability to translate technical issues into easily understandable messages, a tolerance for ambiguity, and a willingness to act without needing to see results.

Navigator   Navigators first help others focus on the end results and desired outcomes and then help them maneuver through an obstacle field in the community and in the political arena. They develop the "process"—how to get to the defined destination—recognizing that the political environment is fluid and can change at a moment's notice. Navigators monitor the community and the political arena for these changes and, when they happen, suggest alternative routes for consideration by elected officials and managers. Navigators need an astute political sense, a concern for the process, flexibility in proposing alternatives, the ability to suggest a route without asserting control, and a willingness to remain in the background so that the elected officials and managers take credit for the progress and for the final results.

Champion   Champions are boosters of the fire service, the fire department, and local government without being self-promoting. They look at ways of getting others to believe in the fire department and of inspiring others to act in support of the fire service. They look for and create opportunities to celebrate successes in the community, in the local government, and in the fire department —successes such as the completion of projects and the accomplishment of established goals. Champions say "thank you" to partners and supporters and share successes with others, rather than claiming personal credit. They also market the department to others. Champions need an optimistic outlook, skills in marketing, and the willingness to take time for the little niceties of thanking others and having a party to celebrate success.

Concluding thought

Perhaps more than any other local government service, the fire service has enjoyed a long and close relationship with the community served. From the volunteer fire brigades that were formed in towns in colonial America through the continued use of volunteer departments, the fire service has been an integral part of its community. It has embodied the identity of the community and provided valued services to citizens. Thus, as society changes—as new patterns develop in how people look at things, how they behave, what they expect— and as the fire service itself takes on many new duties, the ways in which fire chiefs and managers relate to their communities must change as well.

As of the early twenty-first century, communities have grown larger, more complex, and more interdependent, but with a diminished sense of community. At the same time, fire departments face fewer fires but more demands from citizens for services. In response, fire departments have taken on the added responsibilities of code enforcement, education, disaster management, emergency medical services, HAZMAT responses, and an assortment of specialized rescue services, requiring more and more specialized skills. The result of these and other changes both in the community and in the fire service has sometimes been a shift in the relationship between departments and the communities they serve.

From this perspective, fire chiefs and managers can be successful leaders only if they are effective in the public arena. To be effective in the public arena, they should be guided by the principle that underlies all the guidelines and tools presented in this chapter: *Think political, act apolitical.*

1   Phil Sample, "Making Certain with CERT: Firefight- ers Teach Neighbors to Help Neighbors," *American Fire Journal* (January 1997): 15.

2   Ken Blanchard and Michael O'Connor, *Managing by*

VALUES (Escondido, Calif.: Blanchard Training and Development, 1995), vi.

3   Max DePree, *Leading without Power* (San Francisco: Jossey-Bass, 1997), 129.

Part two:
Resource management

4 Organizing and deploying resources

Unwanted and uncontrolled fire is a force that human beings have contended with for millennia. Out-of-control fire can injure and kill living things, destroy property, and disrupt important natural ecosystems. The United States, like many other countries, has periodically suffered from large fires. In 1871 a tinder-dry Chicago, with its wooden buildings, burned for nearly twenty-four hours; more than three hundred people were killed and ninety thousand were left homeless. Thirteen months later, the great Boston fire wiped out nearly sixty acres of downtown Boston. In the last decade there were three large-loss fires: the 1991 firestorm of Oakland, California, in which twenty-five people died, more than twenty-five hundred homes were destroyed, and the property loss amounted to more than $1.5 billion; the 1993 bombing and fire at the World Trade Center in New York City, which killed six people, injured a thousand, and resulted in a loss of more than $500 million; and the 2001 disasters at the World Trade Center and the Pentagon, which killed more than three thousand people and have resulted in as yet incalculable property loss.

Organized fire protection may date from as early as 24 B.C., when Augustus was ruler of Rome. Night watches, called *vigiles,* were used to enforce regulations and prevent fires. They also carried buckets and axes to combat the many fires that did break out. In 872 A.D., fire protection regulations were enacted to ensure that hearth fires would be extinguished at specified times each day.

As cities and population centers grew, with their burgeoning mercantile and closely built residential areas, the risk of large fires dramatically increased. And as property values increased along with risks, the fire insurance industry was born. So was the concept of organized fire departments. In the American colonies, firefighting organizations—whether created by insurance companies to protect their insured properties or formed by local communities to protect themselves using volunteers—became the forerunners of the fire department of today. In 1648 Peter Stuyvesant of the colony that would become New York initiated an early effort at fire prevention by appointing fire wardens. In 1679 Boston created the first paid fire department in the American colonies, and in 1736 in Philadelphia Benjamin Franklin founded the first volunteer fire department in the colonies.

At the beginning of the twenty-first century, fire service organizations are of several kinds (e.g., state, local) and several types (e.g., volunteer, career). Whether small or large, they tend to have in common a basic organizational structure. And to fulfill their mission of protecting the community from uncontrolled fire, they deploy the resources of fire stations, vehicles and other equipment, and staff. This chapter discusses all those topics. In addition, it surveys the expanded array of services that contemporary fire departments provide. Some of these services come under the heading of emergency responses, whereas others are proactive ways of making the community a better place to live. The chapter then touches on some revenue-enhancing aspects of the fire service and on two arrangements for controlling fire department costs. A brief conclusion mentions essential challenges at the beginning of the twenty-first century.

Kinds of fire departments

Although the basic reason for having a fire department (the need to protect people from unwanted, uncontrolled fire) is universal, local circumstances quite often influence the details of how a fire department is structured and how it fulfills the common mission of protecting life and property from fire. Thus, the kind of fire department varies around the world. "Kind of department" refers to the source of the department's authority, the entity that provides overall funding and policy direction. In the United States, there are seven kinds of fire departments: military, federal, state, local, county, intergovernmental, and private.

Military fire departments

At those U.S. military installations where the firefighting is highly specialized or where there are overriding defense concerns, uniformed members of the armed services function as the fire department. This is the case, for instance, at some air force bases, where aircraft rescue and firefighting duties are performed by U.S. Air Force enlisted personnel and officers.

Federal fire departments

At other military posts, bases, and installations, fire protection is routinely handled by federal firefighters. These are nonmilitary personnel who are employed by the federal civil service system and are trained to provide every type of fire department service. They serve in all areas of the continental United States as well as in Alaska, Hawaii, and Puerto Rico, staffing conventional fire stations and fire apparatus as well as using specialized equipment. Federal firefighters protect huge naval shipyards, restricted military installations, training centers, and military housing complexes. In many areas federal firefighters interact and respond with their military counterparts as well as with nonmilitary local government firefighters from communities that adjoin the federal facility.

The number of federal civil service firefighters needed fluctuates with changes in U.S. defense budget appropriations: as dollars are diverted from military and defense programs, military facilities are closed, and a closure often diminishes the number of federal firefighters needed. In some cases federal firefighters who would have been laid off or transferred across the country have been hired instead by a local fire department. When a military base or installation is closed, fire protection services often become the responsibility of the local civilian fire agency or department.

Also on the federal level, the U.S. Department of the Interior and U.S. Department of Agriculture maintain firefighting forces. Under the latter, the Forest Service has firefighters who are trained to fight forest and wildland fires in the national forests. The agencies of the Department of the Interior that have firefighters are the National Park Service, the Bureau of Land Management, and the Bureau of Indian Affairs.

State fire departments

Some countries and certain regions of the United States have provincial or state-level fire departments. Such departments are usually a natural outgrowth of widespread fire risks that clearly extend beyond the jurisdiction of local governmental entities. These fire risks are generally related to forests, logging concerns, or highly flammable natural fuels that would pose serious threats to life, property, and the economy of the particular region if fires occurred and were not controlled.

In Canada, the Ministry of Public Security of the province of Quebec co-operates with local fire departments and operates an extensive firefighting air force, using Canadian-built SuperScooper aircraft, to combat the annually occurring forest fires. In the United States, the California Department of Forestry and Fire Protection (CDF) employs full-time career and seasonal firefighters to conserve and protect state-owned lands. Much of the area protected by CDF is sparsely populated, but the abundant volatile vegetation makes it susceptible to large-scale wildland fires. CDF's operation is state of the art, with a statewide network of fire stations, bases for heavy equipment, and airfields from which rotary and fixed-wing air tankers are dispatched (see Figure 4–1).

CDF also protects wildland areas where residential and some commercial development has extended into lands with highly flammable vegetation that poses serious threats to the structures. (This presence of structures adjacent to or within wildland areas is referred to as urban interface or intermix.) In addition, CDF provides routine municipal-like fire protection services through contract in a number of incorporated cities in California.

Other states, including North Carolina, Texas, and Washington, also have state-managed fire departments. For the most part, these departments deal primarily with fire protection related to less-populated rural areas where protection and conservation are equally important objectives. The suppression of fires by state-level fire departments often serves the important purpose of conserving state resources, such as wildlife and forests, while also protecting water resources and ecosystems that would be disrupted by major unabated fires.

Local government fire departments

In the United States and Canada, probably the greatest number of personnel and the largest amount of firefighting equipment are amassed in local fire departments. As contrasted with federal, military, or state-level departments, local

Figure 4–1   A California Department of Forestry and Fire Protection S-2 air tanker, which carries eight hundred gallons of fire retardant.

fire departments are operated by such governmental entities as cities, towns, or, in some cases, counties (see below). Local fire departments provide fire protection services, usually some level of emergency medical service (EMS), and technical rescue capabilities.

Funding for local fire departments usually comes from the local government's general fund and is allocated to the fire department in an annual budgeting process. Annual budgets are prepared by the fire chief within guidelines established by the local government manager. (Preparation of annual budgets is discussed in detail in Chapter 6.) Once the annual budget is prepared, it is submitted to the elected officials, who exercise final approval authority. Generally speaking, more than 85 percent of a local fire department's annual budget covers the cost of salaries and employee benefits, with less than 15 percent covering all other aspects of the department's operation.

Some local fire departments, particularly in small communities, are staffed by volunteer firefighters, who receive either no pay or a nominal stipend for their services. In these situations, all that the municipality or town budgets for is equipment, supplies, and structural facilities. Local fundraising events conducted by the volunteers often help defray the costs of new or specialized equipment.

County fire departments

Within the United States, local fire protection services are provided by some county governmental agencies rather than by municipalities; overall funding and policy direction are provided by county elected or appointed officials. Usually the formation of a county fire department originates in a local need that could not be met by a single local fire department. An example is the Los Angeles County Fire Department, which was established because many of the forty-four hundred square miles within the county were unincorporated areas covered with highly flammable brush. Fires that occurred were driven by steep natural gradients and seasonal Santa Ana winds. Frequently thousands of acres burned, threatening populated areas within the county. After such fires, the denuded hills and mountains threatened homes with potential mudslides and created imbalances in the water percolation cycles so important to this region in southern California.

Accordingly, in 1923 the Los Angeles County Board of Supervisors formed the Department of Forester and Fire Warden to conserve the wildland areas by carrying out fire prevention and fire suppression activities. Over the years the department's responsibilities broadened, and as of October 31, 2000, they included providing consolidated contractual fire services to fifty-seven incorporated cities within Los Angeles County.

Many other counties in the United States have fire departments, including De Kalb (Georgia), Fairfax (Virginia), and Miami-Dade (Florida). In most in-

---

U.S. fire department profile, 2000

286,800 career firefighters

777,350 volunteer firefighters

$21.3 billion in total expenditures (1999)

26,354 fire departments

49,200 fire stations

68,200 pumper vehicles (at least 500 gallon-per-minute pumps)

6,400 aerial ladder apparatus

Source: Michael J. Karter Jr., *U.S. Fire Department Profile through 2000* (Quincy, Mass.: National Fire Protection Association [NFPA], December 2001), 3, 15, 18, and 25. Copyright © 2001. NFPA, Quincy, MA 02269.

stances, the emergency response services provided by county fire departments are similar to those provided by many local fire departments (emergency medical, technical rescue, and hazardous material [HAZMAT] response services).

Intergovernmental fire protection

In some localities and counties, the desire to contain costs, improve the level of service, solve problems innovatively, or do all of these has led to the development of intergovernmental agreements for providing fire protection. Such agreements abide by local laws authorizing governmental entities to join together for purposes of providing fire protection and related emergency services.

Basically, in such an arrangement two or more jurisdictional bodies form a separate governmental unit to carry out the functions of fire protection. In some states, these units may be created through a joint powers agreement; in others, a fire protection district may be created. When such approaches are used, provision must be made for funding, decision making, and overall control, but the collective power created can benefit a large area and its citizens by pooling firefighting resources and personnel while eliminating some duplication and spreading the costs over a wider area.

In a joint powers agreement, local jurisdictions form a special authority to deliver fire services. The Orange County Fire Authority of Southern California (OCFA) is an example of this kind of arrangement. Through the OCFA, a board of elected officials (one from each city served and two from Orange County) sets policy, establishes the budget, and governs the fire authority. Where permitted by state law, a fire authority enables local cities to pool their tax dollars so that the participating localities may benefit from a wider range of services with greater efficiencies.

A fire protection district is governed by a board of directors elected from the area to be protected. Funding for the district may come from a portion of local taxes, from special fees, or from some type of assessment. Usually the particular laws of each state establish the limits within which special fire districts can function.

Also in the realm of intergovernmental arrangements, a local governing body may contract for fire protection with another agency. This has occurred when a town or community contracts with a state-run fire department for local services or when one locality contracts with another for fire protection. Usually such contracts for service reflect a desire to contain costs while maintaining service levels.

Private sector fire protection organizations

There are also private fire departments. Some large, complex industrial plants have organized their own fire brigades to provide fire services (and possibly a wide range of other services) to the plant and its employees. In some cases, private fire brigades are helped in emergencies by the local fire department. Conversely, there are cases in which a private fire brigade routinely responds with the local fire department in areas adjacent to the particular industrial complex, especially when the private brigade has specialized equipment or supplies for HAZMAT incidents.

There are also companies that market fire and emergency medical services to communities, industrial sites, and governmental facilities. Such services are similar to those provided by local fire departments but are delivered by employees of the company rather than by the local government. The company (or corporation) is accountable to the locally elected policy-making body for the quality and efficiency of service delivery. For example, the city of Scottsdale, Arizona, has been served for many years by Rural Metro, a privately owned and publicly traded corporation that provides fire protection and EMS. Wackenhut Services, Inc., provides fire, EMS, and rescue protection to industrial corporations and governmental sites.

In some cases, localities have contracted with private firms for fire services as an alternative to providing the services as a direct local governmental function. In other cases, the local government fire departments themselves have entered into limited partnerships with private firms to deliver emergency ambulance service; contractual terms address all aspects of the operation, including how revenue and costs are shared. At some airports in the United States and in other countries, private sector companies provide specialized fire protection (such as aircraft rescue and firefighting). Private fire protection service organizations may also protect many governmental sites, such as those maintained by federal agencies.

Types of fire departments

As just discussed, the *kind* of fire department is a function of the entity that controls the department's overall funding and policy direction. The *type* of department is a function of the employment relationship between the firefighters and the parent organization. This relationship produces four types of fire departments: volunteer, career, combination, and public safety.

Volunteer departments

A volunteer fire department is one in which the firefighters are not employed by the department and do not work full time in their capacity as firefighters. In the United States, volunteer fire departments are the most numerous type: according to the National Fire Protection Association (NFPA), 777,350 of the nation's 1,064,150 firefighters in the year 2000 were volunteers.[1] A volunteer department depends on the personal commitment of its civic-minded members to deliver fire protection services. Even in some private fire brigades, the firefighting duties of the employees of the firm may be carried out on a voluntary basis and would classify the brigade as being private in kind but volunteer in type.

Figure 4–2 A small, rural, volunteer fire station in Andeas, New York.

Volunteers protect approximately 80 percent of the area of the United States, whereas career firefighters protect approximately 60 percent of the nation's population; the majority of volunteer fire departments serve rural areas with populations of less than 2,500. Yet some larger and more complex urban communities are also protected by volunteer (or combination career and volunteer) fire departments. One such community is Pasadena, Texas, with a volunteer fire department that operates eight fire stations and protects a population of 120,000 within the fifty-two square miles that constitute the city.

At the beginning of the twenty-first century, some volunteer fire departments are having difficulty recruiting enough people willing to volunteer their services. Many factors enter into this difficulty, but often communities in need of volunteers are predominantly residential, with most residents commuting long distances to their places of employment. During the day few residents are at home or near enough to respond to fire calls, and at night most are tired and unable to devote time to training and the other duties required of volunteer firefighters.

Some volunteer fire, emergency medical, and rescue departments are operated by colleges and universities. St. Michael's College Fire and Rescue, located in Colchester, Vermont, is an example. It is a student-run organization and was the first of five or six college-affiliated fire and rescue squads in New England. Twenty-five active student members and a number of local alumni members receive training in advanced first aid and CPR as they progress to the level of emergency medical technician. The basic firefighting apprenticeships meet state training requirements before interior firefighting certification is awarded. St. Michael's College Fire and Rescue serves the college and neighboring towns and highways. College-based volunteer fire and rescue programs like the one at St. Michael's can offer dependable fire services to college communities.

Whether affiliated with a college or not, many volunteer fire departments do require members to bunk in (sleep) at the fire station periodically so that the fire units they staff can respond more quickly when a fire or other emergency occurs.

Inasmuch as the majority of fire protection organizations in the United States are volunteer, volunteer firefighters will continue to play a significant role in providing fire protection services to their communities. The depth of community spirit that motivates people to prepare themselves as volunteer firefighters in order to respond with help to those in need is a lasting tribute to them and the fire service at large.

Career (fully paid) departments

The career type of fire department is one in which all firefighters are fully paid for their firefighting services and all have made a full-time commitment to the duties of firefighting. Career firefighters may be found within federal, state, county, and local government departments. Usually their employment is governed by a civil service system, whether federal or local; by the work schedule of the given fire department; and by a labor contract, if one is in force for a given department.

Civil service   Federal career firefighters are employed through the federal civil service system. Personnel issues, such as hiring, promotions, and salary step advancements, are administered according to the civil service rules. The different ranks are based on government pay ratings and categories, which are applicable throughout the federal fire service regardless of the assignment location. The civil service structure is intended to provide order and fairness in these matters that are so important to the individual firefighter.

Local career fire departments also commonly take a civil service system approach to firefighter personnel issues. Unlike the federal model, however, local government civil service rules are applicable to only one locality, not to multiple jurisdictions. Each locality has its own personnel department, which handles hiring, promotional examinations, and other administrative matters (see the sidebar below).

Work schedules Once career firefighters complete the basic training provided in a fire academy setting, they are assigned to fire station duty. Such duty involves working a given shift, or tour of duty, that in most localities lasts for 24 hours. On duty and subject to emergency response for this period, career firefighters are given time for meals and sleep, although interruptions can occur at any time during the work shift. Firefighters working 24-hour shifts will work one shift of 24 hours and then be off for 48 hours, after which they will work another 24-hour shift. Although a 24-hour shift can be mentally and physically demanding, most firefighters prefer it, and localities find it to be cost-effective and very workable.

Schedules of 24 hours on and 48 hours off constitute a 56-hour workweek average and require three platoons of firefighters, one on duty and the other two off duty. This weekly hour level is lowered if several extra 24-hour shifts are allowed off during the year. These days off, which are in addition to vacation time and holidays, are deducted from the yearly total a firefighter works, to reduce the weekly average hours worked. Or some fire departments schedule firefighters' duty so that strings of days off can be arranged. Such alterations benefit the firefighters (by permitting four days off in a row) without measurably increasing the costs borne by the local government.

Other work-shift schedules for firefighters include a 10-hour and 14-hour arrangement that uses two shifts of personnel to cover a given 24-hour period. This schedule has firefighters on one shift working 10-hour day tours with nights off, while their counterparts on the other shift come in to work the nighttime 14-hour shift. Such schedules produce a 42-hour workweek average

---

Civil service The term *civil service* refers to a set of rules and procedures for hiring, promoting, and terminating government employees. The underlying rationale of a civil service system is the merit principle, which holds that the most qualified individuals shall be hired or promoted and that employees shall be removed from public service only when there is a clear showing of just cause.

The embodiment of a civil service system is the civil service examinations. These examinations are given to candidates who meet the minimum qualifications as to knowledge, skills, and abilities. Such tests must necessarily be free of any cultural, racial, or ethnic bias. They must also be administered fairly and impartially so that all candidates have an equal opportunity to

demonstrate their qualifications and abilities to gain the desired position.

Most public agencies have established an independent body to oversee the administration of its hiring, promotion, and termination procedures. That body is usually referred to as a civil service commission. The jurisdiction of a civil service commission commonly extends to all facets of personnel administration for the purpose of ensuring that the merit principle is observed. Civil service commissions are a way of assuring citizens that a public agency does not operate on the basis of patronage, spoils, or nepotism. Between 1975 and 2000 there were several important procedural reforms in civil service procedures, but the underlying purpose of preserving the merit principle remained constant.

Fire academies   Before someone can fully function as a career firefighter engaged in interior, structural fire suppression requiring the use of a self-contained breathing apparatus, that person must successfully complete training. Many states have adopted firefighter training curricula that specify exactly what courses and class length are required for certification as a firefighter.

Many fire departments also require additional training for specific firefighter duties beyond basic fire protection. This additional training may cover advanced first aid, CPR, and the skills required of an emergency medical technician. These additional classes are often taken during basic fire training programs delivered through training academies.

Some fire training academies operate within particular local government fire departments so that students (or "recruit firefighters," as they are often called) are hired first and then become qualified firefighters for that department. In other arrangements, usually with community colleges, fire academies provide basic firefighter training for men and women seeking certification as firefighters to improve their chances of being hired as entry-level firefighters by fire departments that may not have their own fire training academies.

Whether a fire academy is completely supported by a fire department or is associated with a college, what constitutes it as a fire academy is its dedicated training staff, its established firefighter curriculum, and its primary objective of delivering basic firefighter training.

but generally require a fourth platoon of firefighters. The additional platoon makes such shift arrangements more expensive for the locality, since 25 percent more personnel are required.

Labor relations   Most career firefighters have formed associations or labor unions to represent their interests. Even when there are associations rather than formally established labor unions, many of these associations are affiliated with national labor groups. Some localities have ordinances that prohibit labor unions from engaging in formal collective bargaining for government jobs such as firefighting. In other localities, there may be formally adopted labor contracts between the firefighters' union and the locality, establishing pay, benefits, and agreed-upon working conditions for the firefighters during the term of the contract. In the interest of public safety, such contracts usually contain provisions that prevent a strike by the firefighters.

Combination departments

In some communities, fire protection and EMS are provided by a fire department that relies on both volunteer firefighters and paid, career firefighters. Both groups respond to emergencies, where they function together. The paid firefighters provide full-time staffing and routinely drive emergency vehicles to the reported incident. They are joined at the emergency by volunteers, who come in their own vehicles and augment on-scene firefighter staffing levels. In some combination departments, volunteers may stay over at the fire station for their tours of duty and respond on the fire apparatus with paid personnel. Volunteer firefighters in combination departments perform many different duties.

Combination departments have evolved in communities where adequate daytime coverage is not possible because many volunteers are employed long distances from the communities they serve or because quicker response times are desired. Although less common than fully volunteer departments, combination departments offer communities an economical way to have full-time coverage, rapid emergency response, and the benefit provided by a group of volunteer firefighters. Of particular importance in combination departments is the need for regular, joint training and drilling, with career and volunteer firefighters participating together so that their skill levels are well coordinated for emergency services when the need arises.

Public safety consolidations

In some parts of the United States and Canada a consolidated approach to providing fire department services is taken: local law enforcement personnel as well as firefighters are used. Public safety consolidations are most common either in smaller communities or in newer ones where most structures have built-in fire protection features. Quite often law enforcement demands are minimal; accordingly, police officers can engage in firefighting and the other emergency responses typically handled by the fire department.

In concept, public safety consolidations depend on having on-duty law enforcement officers respond to fires in their police vehicles, whereupon they assist in actual fire suppression activities. Police officers are cross-trained in basic firefighting techniques and carry personal protective gear in their vehicles. Law enforcement officers basically augment the firefighter personnel, who come to the scene on firefighting apparatus. Day-to-day fire department responsibilities for fire prevention, public education, equipment and station maintenance, and administrative functions are normally carried out by the fire chief and fire department staff.

Local government officials under pressure to increase service while holding the line on taxes have viewed consolidation as a solution.[2] Consolidated public safety operations seek to reduce operating costs by having a smaller cadre of firefighters on duty, augmented by the on-duty staff of police officers. Although this type of operation seems to work in some localities, the reality of simultaneous service demands for police and fire personnel prevents the consolidated public safety approach from being seriously considered in most communities. And although the public safety concept of consolidating fire and police services is attractive from the point of view of efficiency, it is usually controversial because law enforcement and fire protection are often viewed as two distinct disciplines.

There are five forms of consolidation:

Administrative Both departments maintain separate operations, but administrative functions, such as clerical and personnel, are combined.

Functional The departments may or may not be administratively consolidated, but some operational functions, such as dispatch, are combined.

Area Joint operations are performed in certain areas, such as residential neighborhoods where demand is relatively low, and separate operations are performed in areas with higher service demand (e.g., in downtown business sections of a city).

Partial The fire and police departments are administratively consolidated and most of the operations are integrated. This type of consolidation model uses a combination of public safety officers, firefighters, and police officers.

Full   All administrative and operational functions are integrated into a single department of public safety. Cross-trained public safety officers perform fire and police services, primarily suppression and patrol, while other public safety officers perform specialized services, such as fire and crime prevention and fire and crime investigations.

The most common form of consolidation is the functional type, followed in descending order by full, administrative, partial, and area.[3]

The consolidations that have worked better are those in places where previously separate fire and EMS departments have been merged. The concurrent emergency response of fire units staffed by firefighters and emergency medical personnel staffing an ambulance makes such consolidations sensible and workable.

Organizational structures in fire departments

Like any organization, a fire department must have some type of organizational structure that effectively divides responsibility for critical functions and distributes authority so that service is delivered in a timely, orderly, and safe manner. But given the emergency nature of most services provided, many fire departments operate in a paramilitary fashion regardless of the organizational structure used.

Traditional approaches

Traditionally fire department organizational structures begin with the fire chief. The chief—or the highest-ranking fire officer, whatever the title—is simultaneously the chief administrator of the fire department and the chief firefighter.

When a fire department is small (having only one or two fire stations), the fire chief maintains responsibility for most functions, including incident command at large incidents, budgeting, policy development, and personnel actions such as hiring. If there is an assistant-level chief officer, responsibilities for that position typically relate to fire prevention and operational matters.

Basic approaches that work in medium-sized departments seek to divide authority and responsibility in accordance with operational service delivery efforts (line functions) and administrative support (staff) functions (see Figure 4–3).

Although in larger fire departments the fire chief responds to only the largest of fires, he or she is just as responsible for firefighting as for fire prevention, budgeting, and personnel issues. The extent of such responsibilities leads to the traditional division of responsibility among bureau chiefs, who command bureaus charged with assigned areas. In fact, given the wide range of services delivered and the need for expertise in the critical support functions, even fire departments of modest size often go beyond the most basic line and staff assignments and use a slightly more extensive organizational design to accomplish their mission.

Figure 4–3 Basic organizational approach that works in medium-sized departments.

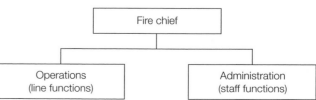

With the fire chief serving as the chief executive officer, major areas are placed beneath the command of bureau chiefs, who report directly to the fire chief. Commonly the major bureaus consist of operations (fire suppression or emergency services), administrative, services, and prevention. Within each bureau, divisions carry out various related functions under the managerial oversight of division chiefs (see Figure 4–4).

When workload or complexity requires a broader organizational structure, divisions may be further divided into sections. Sections are managed by section managers, or chiefs, who are generally on the same organizational level as the platoon battalion chiefs, although nonuniformed personnel may have a slightly lower pay status.

Operations bureaus   Operations bureaus, under the command of senior fire officers, are responsible for the actual delivery of emergency fire department service. This includes responses to fires of all types, responses to specialized-rescue and HAZMAT incidents, and possible provision of EMS. Such services must be delivered around the clock, whenever an emergency or fire occurs, so the majority of personnel assigned to operations bureaus work schedules that ensure staffing twenty-four hours a day, seven days a week.

Firefighters, company-level fire officers, and other emergency response service personnel staff response vehicles housed in fire stations. Usually each fire unit is under the command of a company officer. When there are several fire stations in a geographical area, these stations collectively constitute a battalion, with their personnel and officers functioning under the command of a battalion or district chief officer, who works a similar schedule.

Such organizational arrangements provide consistent managerial presence and oversight for both routine matters and emergencies, regardless of the time of day. When the majority of firefighting personnel are assigned to shift work, it follows that management and command staff (at least up to the division level) should work the same hours. In addition to addressing the routine administrative matters, the division chief can respond to larger-scale fires and emergencies when incident command-and-control requirements are complex.

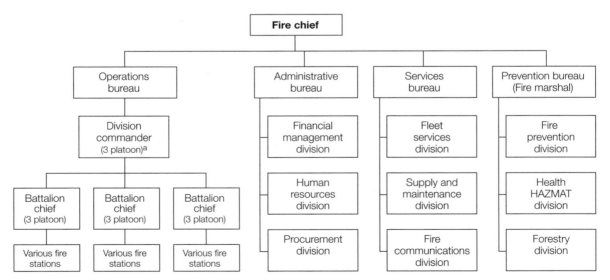

a Normally the operations personnel who work platoons cover the position twenty-four hours a day, seven days a week, working whatever shift is common in the jurisdiction.

Figure 4–4   Traditional division of responsibility among bureaus and the divisions under them.

Commonly used terms

Company: A group of firefighters who staff a given firefighting unit, supervised by a company officer; there are engine companies, truck companies, and other types of fire companies, depending on the structures in any given locality.

Company officer: A fire officer, usually a captain or lieutenant, who is in charge of a fire company.

Station: The building that houses one or more fire companies with support equipment and facilities.

Battalion: Usually a group of fire stations (and companies assigned to them), commanded by a battalion chief.

Battalion chief: A senior fire officer who oversees the operations of the several fire stations and personnel within a battalion.

Division: Two or more battalions administratively commanded by a division-level chief, who, in turn, reports to a bureau-level chief officer.

Platoon: Firefighting personnel assigned the same work schedule to provide round-the-clock staffing for fire companies; commonly referred to as A, B, and C platoons.

Shift: The duration of a given work period for firefighters, such as a twenty-four-hour shift.

There are wide variations from community to community in how upper-level operations bureaus are organized. Usually when the platoon presence of chief officers extends up just to the battalion level, the frequency of larger-scale fire emergencies is low. Conversely, when larger fires occur more often, the shift work schedule extends up to a division-level chief officer. This is generally the rule in large cities with high population densities, aged and complex building stock, and frequent larger fires. Of course, whenever platoons are used, whether the personnel are rank-and-file firefighters or chief officers, the salary and employee benefit costs will be greater because three or more people are needed to staff each position.

In most fire departments it is common for each fire station to be under the supervision or command of a station officer. Here, too, if there is paid twenty-four-hour staffing rather than volunteer-type service, the station officers will work platoon duty, being responsible for their shift only. Other platoons will have a station officer assigned as well.

Station officers report directly to the battalion chief and are responsible for the personnel assigned to their respective stations and shifts—including paramedic personnel when such services are provided from that station. When more than one fire company operates from a given fire station, the additional companies are commanded by an officer who is usually subordinate to the station commander. The most common practice is for a fire captain to be in charge of the fire station and a single company; additional fire companies within a given station are commanded by a fire lieutenant or a junior-level captain. (Fire officer ranks in many departments consist of battalion chief, captain, lieutenant, and engineer/driver.)

When a fire department provides prehospital EMS, a division or section (usually within the operations bureau) has responsibility for it. This division provides for the coordination of medical training and the administrative oversight specifically associated with firefighter paramedics and the services they provide. (Fire department EMS is discussed in a little more detail later in this chapter, and in much more detail in Chapter 1.)

Administrative bureaus   Functioning under the command and management of the bureau chief, administrative bureaus in fire departments are responsible for overall budgeting, financial management, human resources, and procurement. Authority and responsibility for these functions are further delegated to division managers. Administrative division managers may be people who are not uniformed fire officers but are civilian managers with expertise in the relevant administrative fields.

Most local fire departments function as part of a larger local governmental entity, which may have a well-established civil service system and local government departments of purchasing, human resources, and financial management. Even so, there is often sufficient need for an administrative bureau within the fire department, providing expertise for the fire department alone.

Of course, when the scope of fire department operations is smaller, administrative duties can be carried out by a division, a subordinate unit of the fire chief's office. In such cases the fire department is more likely to depend on other local government departments because it lacks sufficient personnel and expertise to provide full administrative services itself.

Services bureaus   Fire departments require a wide range of special services, including fleet purchasing and maintenance; facility design, construction, and maintenance; upkeep of tools and equipment; stocking of supplies of all types; and stocking of specialized protective clothing and appliances used by firefighting personnel. These critical and highly technical responsibilities are handled by a services bureau, which may function under a bureau chief or be provided by the fleet maintenance and facilities management departments of the general government.

Routine duties require services bureau personnel to prepare numerous contracts with external vendors and to maintain significant quantities of parts and supplies for immediate distribution and use in support of the department's main mission. Divisions within the bureau are assigned specially trained personnel who repair and maintain the departmental vehicles and fire apparatus; other crafts personnel provide repair and maintenance services to fire stations and facilities.

Usually a special division of the services bureau is responsible for fire department communications, both wireless and telephone. The communications division handles incoming emergency calls, assigns appropriate fire and/or EMS units, and dispatches these units (see the subsequent section on handling emergency calls). Associated responsibilities include maintaining computer-aided dispatch components, global positioning systems for individual emergency units, and telecommunication systems of various types. Given the predominance of computer technology in both emergency and routine electronic communications, many fire department services bureaus have a computer specialty staff assigned to a computer section or, in some cases, constituting a separate division, with a manager who reports to the services bureau chief. (For more detail on electronic and other communications, see Chapter 15.)

Prevention bureaus   When the scope of fire prevention activities exceeds the capability of the fire marshal and a modest-sized staff, fire departments customarily create a prevention bureau. Functioning under a bureau chief (who may carry the title and responsibility of fire marshal), the prevention bureau is responsible for fire code enforcement, interaction with other local code enforcement agencies, and fire-cause investigation and reporting activities for statistical purposes. A number of fire departments have specially trained firefighters who conduct arson fire investigations, including arresting suspected arsonists and following up in court.

Depending on the complexity of the community, the prevention bureau can be assigned some collateral responsibilities in addition to code enforcement and fire investigation. A number of city fire departments have made prevention bureaus responsible for public fire safety education and other special functions (such as nightclub inspections and special-event fire safety support). Another important aspect of the prevention bureau's responsibility is close coordination with community needs. As growth, urban renewal, and occupancy changes occur in commercial properties, fire safety needs must be addressed in a proactive, cooperative way through coordination with other city departments, developers, and prospective tenants. (Fire code enforcement is discussed at greater length later in this chapter in the section called "Fire Prevention.")

Other functions   Other functions within fire departments may be designated divisions or sections within the organizational structure and may be placed under different bureaus, depending on local needs and good management practices in the given setting. These functions include, among others, training, research and planning, community services, disaster services, emergency preparedness (some fire departments have this function), information management, public information, employee relations, and internal affairs.

Beyond traditional approaches

In some communities, special circumstances (or a different approach to fire protection) have resulted in organizational structures that depart from or go beyond the more traditional approaches to organizing a fire department.

In Los Angeles County, for example, specialized services of considerable magnitude present a need for a different approach to fire department organization. The county fire department protects fifty-seven incorporated cities, many of which are contiguous to one another, as well as all the unincorporated areas of the county, including urban and wildland areas. Covering forty-four hundred square miles with traditional fire and paramedic services as well as helicopter-supported fire attack and air squad, dozer operations, ocean lifeguard services, and brushfire-fighting hand crews requires a departure from the norm.

A unique organizational structure has been implemented in the Los Angeles County Fire Department to address the diverse needs of the large geographic area it serves (see Figure 4–5). Emergency and nonemergency services have been divided among three regional operations bureaus. Each region is commanded by a deputy chief, who is accountable for all service delivery within that geographic region. (One region includes all ocean lifeguard services in addition to the other services.) The regional operations bureau chiefs and their support staff are housed within their respective regions, bringing executive management closer to the actual point of service delivery. Inherent in the structure are challenges related to communication, coordination, and continuity across regional lines as the operations bureaus fulfill the department's mission.

Deployment concepts

The fire department's organizational mission is to protect life and property from fire. Accordingly, the characteristics of fire influence virtually all aspects of the department: the location of fire stations, the vehicles and equipment used, and staffing practices.

When a fire has adequate fuel and oxygen, it grows larger and more intense very rapidly. In a private residence, for example, a curtain blown into the open flame of a candle can burn intensely enough for heat and smoke to spread incredibly quickly throughout the room and into the rest of the house. Within six minutes that room of origin and all its contents may be engulfed by flames. The point at which this occurs is known as "flashover," and once this point is reached, life inside the structure is in great peril because the fire's further spread is inevitable.

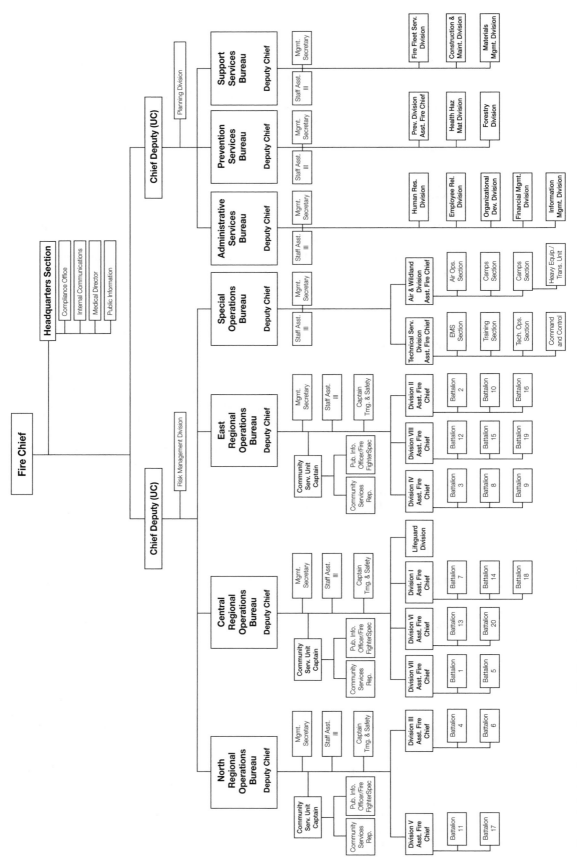

Figure 4–5   Los Angeles County Fire Department organizational chart.

This rapid growth and spread of fires involving ordinary combustibles has been well documented in laboratory tests, and it challenges firefighters over and over as they respond to the call. The critical difference between a small, easily controlled fire and a large fire that threatens to destroy an entire building is time. (Time is also a big factor in saving lives because once respiratory and cardiac functions cease, four to six minutes is as long as a human being can survive without intervention and resuscitation.)

Thus, response time for fire departments is a very important component for success in the main mission. As usually measured, response time counts the minutes and seconds from the moment an emergency call is received in the dispatch center until the emergency unit arrives at the location of the emergency. Given that it may take three-quarters of a minute or longer to process a call and dispatch responders, the reaction time of the firefighters and the driving or travel time become tremendously important. (Of course, the one thing that neither firefighters nor dispatch staff can control is the time elapsed between ignition of the fire, a citizen's discovery of the fire, and the subsequent call to 911. This is why response time is only one of several components critical to minimizing losses from fire. Prevention efforts, code enforcement, and public fire education are among the other critically important components.)

Locating fire stations

In a fire or medical emergency, excessive travel times may mean an increased risk to the public experiencing the emergency. Therefore, the basic deployment concept, or model, for a fire department calls for fire stations to be located to form an orderly pattern or network of stations from which emergency service is delivered in a timely manner. Each fire station is an integral part of the fire station network and serves as a base from which emergency fire units respond. The network as a whole seeks to optimize coverage with short travel distances, while giving special attention to natural and man-made barriers that can create response-time problems. Where such barriers to optimum response times exist, some areas may require more fire stations.

Fire station planning is therefore a critical component of managing local fire protection services. And because stations should last fifty years or more, location has a long-term effect on the community to be served. Accordingly, fire chiefs and local government managers perform an important community service if they thoroughly lay out the rationale for optimal fire station locations. Sometimes neighbors of a proposed fire station may object because of concerns about noise, fire vehicular traffic, and devaluation of property. Such concerns are generally not warranted, and once the station is operational, neighbors often learn that firefighters are good neighbors and valuable additions to the neighborhood.

Sound planning of fire station locations can be done in various ways. With the help of accurate historical response data and realistic computer modeling, factually based decisions can be made. Computerized programs are available, as are private consultants who specialize in such efforts. A computerized database of local streets, roads, and thoroughfares can help the fire department planning staff by simulating responses from a proposed fire station site along all streets at various average miles per hour. When completed, the "web of coverage" (as shown in Figure 4–6) provides an accurate visual projection of a station's coverage area, using computer-generated response times defined by actual street configurations. Obviously, the more realistic the average response speeds, the better the projected coverage area can be defined.

The decentralized network of fire stations constitutes the basic level of first-responder coverage for a community or a fire department jurisdiction. In large

Figure 4–6 "Web of coverage" for a Los Angeles County Fire Department station.

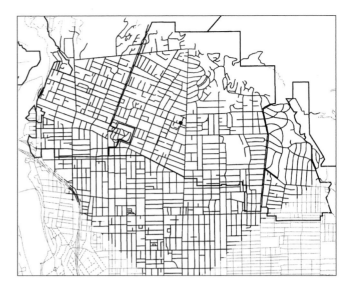

communities or jurisdictions where the risks are accentuated by high population densities and heavy traffic, departments usually have more fire stations, fire-fighters, and fire companies per thousand population than do departments in communities without such features.[4] Excessively high demands for service, geographical barriers such as rivers and railroad rights-of-way, or major shifts in community infrastructure may require the reevaluation of station locations

---

Using computer software to analyze problems and identify solutions   To see how a computer software program can make both problem analysis and solution-path identification easier, consider the following example of a project that involved more than forty fire departments that protect a very large county:

While parts of the county are urban, most of it is suburban and rural, and a good portion of it has no municipal water supply. Working with a consultant, county officials and fire department officers designed a plan to improve the ISO/CRS [Insurance Services Office/Community Rating System] public protection classification for structures that are located within five miles of a fire station but have no water main service.

The fire suppression rating schedule now credits the delivery of water to an incident, not just through a pressurized hydrant system, but also by tanker shuttle or relay and by drafting from certified sites. A department's ability to

deliver a sustained, specified fire flow for at least two hours may with certain detailed stipulations result in significant insurance savings.

"Using our computer program," says Mark Morse, vice president for Public Safety Programs at MMA Consulting Group, Inc., in Boston, "officials easily identified all structures within five road miles of an existing station, plus areas where a new or relocated station might be possible. Still using the computer, we then hypothetically redeployed existing tankers and portable tanks to key stations, taking into account the certified year-round drafting sites and hydrants already in place and the ISO-required fire flows."

In such situations, the computer reveals that a redeployment of existing resources among departments willing to engage in a detailed "functional consolidation" program may give property owners impressive savings. As Morse notes, "the beauty of the computer is that it enables us to play

---

and fire units. Sometimes budgetary constraints, downsizing, and the reengineering of city services may also affect station location.

Structure fires and labor-intensive emergencies will draw fire companies from more than one station because a single station rarely houses all the fire companies and personnel needed for such emergencies. Since most departments respond to structure fires with two or three engine companies and a ladder company (see the discussion of vehicles that follows), some fire stations in the network will house both an engine and a ladder company.

Vehicles and equipment

Regardless of its range of services, every fire department, large or small, relies on a fire engine, or pumper, to transport firefighters, hoses for firefighting, and tools that are essential at the scene of a reported fire. Fire engines have a fire pump that is used to increase pressure on water taken from fire hydrants or other sources so that powerful firefighting streams can be developed in fire hoses. Many engines also carry three hundred to five hundred gallons of water for use on small fires where a hydrant hookup is unnecessary. Most fire departments rely on the engine because of its versatility. With a trained crew, the engine company is versatile enough to handle—or at least begin to make a difference at—almost every fire emergency. In most communities, the engine company is supported by a truck company (a ladder truck with its crew). A quint vehicle, which is discussed below, can perform as an engine or as a ladder truck.

The ladder truck, specially designed for the purpose, carries more than 300

---

out this scenario long before a department has to agree to move a tanker, or buy large-diameter hose, or identify rural drafting sites that meet the specs."

GIS- [geographic information systems-] based computer analysis is the type of analysis most frequently discussed by departments undertaking a master plan, analyzing staffing, or locating or relocating a station. However, other tools are just as valuable.

Spreadsheet and data-based computer applications allow for a more thorough analysis than would have been thought possible twenty years ago. And as a result of this analysis, fire departments are often able to accurately measure their activities and service delivery or capacity, to reconsider the conventional wisdom, and to develop more appropriate strategies.

It is important in this era of cost-consciousness to be able to determine the true costs of services. How much

does the department's public education program cost: What is the price of enforcement? How much do volunteers cost? Valid cost data often provide the documentation fire service administrators need to make informed decisions or persuasive arguments to local legislators.

It is clear that fire departments expect sophisticated reasoning and justifications for major recommendations, especially when those recommendations have substantial cost implications. The use of advanced computer software programming greatly enhances a department's ability to analyze and understand program inputs and outgoing services.

Source: John A. Granito, "From Hoselines to Online," in *Fire Services Today: Managing a Changing Role and Mission,* ed. Gerard J. Hoetmer (Washington, D.C.: International City/County Management Association, 1996), 226–227. Reprinted with minor adaptations by permission from *NFPA Journal* 89 (January/February 1995) Copyright © 1995. National Fire Protection Association (NFPA), Quincy, MA 02269.

feet of different ladders of various lengths; some are extension ladders. Most often, the ladder truck also has a hydraulically operated aerial ladder that may be from 75 to 135 feet long. Aerial ladder vehicles are commonly found in urban areas and cities where building heights exceed three stories.[5]

When responding to structure fires, the engine company's personnel lay and advance hose lines for the purpose of confining and extinguishing the fire. Firefighters arriving on ladder trucks search for lost or trapped occupants, use specialized hand tools to gain entry into locked buildings, and place ladders to gain access to rooftops, where they cut holes to allow superheated fire gases and smoke to escape from the structure that is on fire. They may effect cross ventilation by opening windows and doors, taking advantage of prevailing breezes or of forced air introduced by mechanical blowers brought by the fire department.

All firefighters, whether they staff engine companies or truck companies, are trained in various aspects of firefighting to accomplish specific objectives at fires. These fire ground objectives are necessary for saving lives and protecting property (see sidebar on fire ground objectives). Therefore, in communities that may not have a ladder truck company, engine company members perform the tasks necessary for the particular incident.

To emphasize versatility, some departments use quints. A quint is a firefighting vehicle that can perform five important firefighting functions: it carries water, has a pump, is loaded with hose, carries many ladders, and has a hydraulically operated aerial ladder. With assistance from another unit at the scene, the quint can sometimes handle both engine and truck functions. The St. Louis Fire Department placed a quint in every fire station to reduce costs (by not having to have engines and trucks) and increase versatility (by having a quint respond from every station).

In addition to the basic firefighting engines and trucks, ancillary fire vehicles also respond to fires and other emergencies and are housed in fire stations, but

---

Fire ground objectives   The specific goals to be accomplished at the scene of a fire (i.e., on the fire ground) are as follows:

1. *Rescue* is the highest-priority objective and encompasses all necessary fire ground commitments of firefighters to search for and remove victims endangered by fire.

2. *Exposure protection* is the objective with the second-highest priority and encompasses all efforts to confine the fire to the building of origin if at all possible.

3. *Confinement* is the fire ground objective of holding the fire to the smallest area, with emphasis on preventing the fire from traversing any other avenues.

4. *Extinguishment* is the process of extinguishing the flames and cooling the fuels involved to below ignition temperature.

5. *Ventilation* can be performed at any point in the firefighting effort and involves the planned, systematic removal of smoke, fire gases, and heat from the involved structure.

6. *Salvage* (conservation of property) is defined as any actions taken to conserve property, including contents, from heat, smoke, and water.

7. *Overhaul* ensures the complete extinguishment of the fire and the safety of the structure, and establishes at least a probable cause of the ignition of the fire.

Figure 4–7   Fire department vehicles and equipment: (Top left) Oklahoma City fire engine at hydrant. (Center) Oklahoma City firefighters operating the deck gun of a fire engine at a warehouse fire. (Bottom) Blackwell and Ponca City (Oklahoma) aerials operate streams at a major downtown fire.

in lesser numbers than pumpers or trucks. These specialized vehicles include HAZMAT units, rescue trucks, ambulances, battalion chief vehicles, and mobile command posts (see Figure 4–8 and the sidebar on specialized equipment).

Staffing fire units

Once a suitable network of fire stations is in place, fire departments use different levels of staffing on fire companies to balance cost with the need for an adequate number of fire units and firefighters for structure fires and other emergencies. Different staffing schemes prevail depending on budgetary considerations, actual fire frequency, and demand for such fire department corollary services as EMS. In fact, fire company staffing levels vary from department to department. They may be influenced not only by the factors just mentioned but also by population protected (which may be different from the census population, as explained in the next paragraph), population density, types of structures, and response distances; by response and workload data; or by local labor agreements. But although fire unit staffing levels vary from department to de-

Figure 4–8   (Top) Hazardous materials (HAZMAT) vehicle, Santa Fe Springs (California) Fire Department. A HAZMAT unit responds to HAZMAT incidents, which can vary from industrial spills to air contamination releases and transportation accidents. The unit carries a variety of tools and equipment (including decontamination equipment) to accomplish its tasks. It also has a database of chemical listings. (Bottom) Urban search and rescue (USAR) vehicle, Los Angeles County Fire Department. Firefighters assigned to USAR units are prepared to rescue people who become trapped during earthquakes, floods, or terrorism incidents; on cliffs; after construction accidents or mountain accidents; in confined spaces; and in other situations that require advanced rescue techniques. These units are equipped with state-of-the-art technology to find trapped people and remove them from harm. USAR units also respond to large fires in order to rescue victims or trapped firefighters.

Specialized equipment To handle a wide range of emergencies effectively, many fire departments have developed specialized vehicular equipment. This equipment includes heavy rescues (called "urban search and rescue" in some departments), water tenders and fuel tenders (which carry water or fuel to incidents), food dispensers, de-icing units, mobile air compressors, hazardous materials (HAZMAT) response units, command posts, and watercraft.

HAZMAT units are designed to carry hundreds of tools for specially trained firefighters to use in controlling leaks and spills at HAZMAT emergencies. Such units are often staffed twenty-four hours a day, seven days a week, and are dispatched to incidents other than those involving hazardous materials so that the capabilities of the personnel assigned to them are put to additional use. Alternatively, some fire departments staff these special units only when a HAZMAT emergency is reported; at all other times, the HAZMAT firefighters staff an engine or truck company.

Mobile command posts are designed to accommodate radios, communications equipment, maps, and support supplies for incident command staff. Whenever a fire or other large-scale emergency warrants its use, the mobile command post is set up to facilitate on-scene command and control of the emergency. When an emergency involves other responding agencies in addition to the fire department, their mobile command posts can be positioned near the fire department's to ensure on-scene coordination.

partment, most departments establish minimum staffing levels (i.e., the minimum number of personnel necessary to operate each unit of firefighting equipment) on the basis of the aforementioned factors.

Fire departments in core communities will protect more people than the community's census population because of commuters who work in such areas during work hours. For a city of 900,000 that is a business hub, with employees at work and visitors in town for conventions and trade shows, the protected population may exceed one million people. According to the NFPA *Fire Protection Handbook*®, fire staffing levels for cities with a population of 250,000 or more range from 0.5 to 2.7 firefighters per thousand population, with a median of 1.0 to 1.5 per thousand.[6] Nevertheless, communities must assess their local needs, analyze fire frequency and loss data, and determine the staffing level that meets their own requirements. NFPA Standards 1710 and 1720 provide information concerning staffing.

Another influence on staffing decisions is regulations issued by the federal Occupational Safety and Health Administration in 1998 and applicable to paid firefighters. These regulations do not specify fire company staffing levels, but they do require that when firefighters enter an atmosphere immediately dangerous to life and health, at least two of them must enter together and two more must be available outside to assist if the first two require it. This "two-in/two-out" rule affects fire ground operational policies and procedures in that initial fire attack decisions must consider the number of firefighters on scene as interior operations begin.[7] (For more detail on the "two-in/two-out rule," see Chapter 3.)

There are many computer models that can help fire departments and local government managers make sound, demand-based decisions about deployment of staff. Good management requires the effective use of expensive, life-saving

Fire Protection Handbook® is a registered trademark of the National Fire Protection Association (NFPA), Quincy, MA 02269.

resources—stations, vehicles and equipment, and personnel. Effective use, in turn, requires that deployment strategies be periodically revisited and reevaluated in the context of ever-changing local circumstances and in conjunction with local fire education and fire prevention efforts.

Expanding the services delivered

The role of fire departments varies from community to community. In some places, the department is strictly a line of defense when a fire breaks out. In those places, even when the fire department's response to a fire is swift and of the highest quality, the department is primarily reactive. When and if the need arises and someone calls, the fire department reacts.

For many years, reactive fire protection was all that most communities expected or desired. But when a fire department is able to extend its resources and empower its personnel to do more than just fight fires, the number of ways the department can contribute to the safety and overall good of the public is almost unlimited.

Proactive fire departments identify needs within the community that they can meet. In the 1990s fire departments made significant strides in applying their capabilities to local problems. Such outreaches moved fire departments into the forefront of responding to other emergencies besides fire: prehospital emergency medical care and transportation of the sick and injured, HAZMAT response, disaster preplanning, and technical rescue services. Fire departments also increased their delivery of nonemergency services: fire prevention programs (including code enforcement), public education programs, and various community-oriented services.

When a local government funds the fire department and its career fire protection personnel, one can expect the range of departmental services to blend the reactive with the more proactive. Proactive fire department services, besides increasing the value of budgetary expenditures for the department, benefit the community by improving public safety. And as the fire department assumes a role in improving the quality of life in the community, the department gains public support.

Handling emergency calls

Because emergency response to fires and medical situations must be rapid once a call for service is received, most fire departments share some basic similarities in how they handle these calls. They have a central dispatch center that receives and processes telephone requests for service so that the closest appropriate fire and/or EMS units are dispatched. The actual dispatching of the units is often done with radio signals that activate radio receivers inside fire stations. (Emergency response units also have radios installed so that continuous radio contact between them and the dispatch center is maintained.) The speed with which the dispatch center handles emergency calls is vitally important because time lost there cannot be made up on the road by responding units; excessive road speeds are impractical and unsafe. Thus, as mentioned above, a properly laid out network of decentralized fire stations is critical—and is found in most communities.

In the United States the most common arrangement for handling emergency calls for fire or EMS is to have the local police agency answer the initial call, especially if a 911 system is in use. If the need is for fire services, the call is immediately transferred to the fire communications center for processing and dispatch. In some instances the police dispatcher processes and dispatches fire and EMS calls in addition to police calls. In some localities the fire dispatchers are in the same facility as their police counterparts but handle fire department dispatching separately. (For detailed information about the 911, 311, and seven-digit telephone numbers for emergencies, as well as about the technological advances mentioned in the next paragraph, see Chapter 15.)

Many fire departments and localities have put technological advances to good use in their operations: computer-assisted dispatch, global positioning systems, mobile data computers, and hand-held instruments of all kinds have improved the delivery of emergency services, the gathering and retrieval of data, and overall operations. There is little doubt that technological advances in the first decade of the twenty-first century will bring even more improvements in emergency response operations.

Emergency medical service

Although firefighters have rendered first aid to injured people for decades, many fire departments have expanded the duties of firefighting personnel to include, as well, basic and advanced life support medical services. At the beginning of the twenty-first century, EMS accounts for 70 to 80 percent of annual emergency responses made by fire departments.

Usually fire departments that provide EMS also rely on the expertise of a medical doctor, who functions as medical director and is responsible for overall medical control issues and liaison with local medical authorities within the community being served.

Some fire departments (although comparatively few) provide EMS using personnel other than cross-trained firefighter paramedics, but most use firefighting personnel who have received special medical training for basic and advanced life support service. (For an extensive discussion of fire department EMS, see Chapter 1.)

Hazardous materials response

As fire departments have entered the realm of HAZMAT response, they have become the primary line of defense and control against chemical emergencies caused by illegal drug laboratories, industrial accidents, and the clandestine dumping of hazardous waste. Some fire departments also work extensively with industry to prepare for potential HAZMAT accidents, playing a partnership role with local firms in developing mitigation plans as well as response plans. In many communities the fire department is the lead agency in planning, writing, and updating local emergency disaster plans. This proactive role benefits the community and the fire department by preparing the community, other governmental agencies, and local hospitals for a better-coordinated response in the event of some type of HAZMAT disaster.

Technical rescue services

Recognizing special needs within their area, a number of fire departments have established technical (specialized) rescue units or teams. These include swift-water rescue teams for rescues in rapidly moving waters, and urban search and rescue (USAR) teams trained and equipped for search and highly technical rescues in collapsed structures or in other complex rescue situations. Where there are large bodies of water, a number of fire departments operate special marine rescue units.

Following the 1993 World Trade Center bombing in New York City, a national effort to prepare for acts of terrorism began in America, with Congress allocating federal funds for fire department training and equipment. When the

Alfred P. Murrah Federal Building in Oklahoma was bombed in April 1995, taking 168 lives, the Federal Emergency Management Agency flew in USAR task forces to conduct extensive search efforts in the rubble.

Then, on September 11, 2001, terrorists struck again, using hijacked airliners as huge bombs deliberately flown into both World Trade Center towers in New York City and the Pentagon in Washington, D.C. Responding in great numbers, firefighters, EMS personnel, and police officers rushed to the scenes and saved thousands. Still, the unthinkable happened: both World Trade Center towers collapsed, killing more than 2,800 human beings—among them an unprecedented 343 New York City fire service personnel, who died in the rescue effort.

As first responders on that Tuesday morning, fire departments and firefighters stood prominently on the front lines of the response to terrorism. But given the catastrophic damage and extensive loss of life, the critical need for advanced equipment, more training, and the use of fire department USAR teams in domestic terrorism preparedness has become that much more evident—and another example of the expanding range of services that fire departments are expected to provide.

Fire prevention

In addition to timely and effective response to emergencies in general and to fire emergencies in particular, many fire departments also provide a wide range of preventive services (see Chapter 12). Proactive fire prevention programs, which seek to prevent fires before they start, involve both suppression personnel and prevention services personnel. Believing that fires can be prevented by the development, adoption, and enforcement of fire codes and that this is a proactive, constructive way to protect lives and property, fire departments commit significant energies and resources to this endeavor.

In many local areas, firefighting personnel carry out routine fire prevention inspections within their jurisdictions, with the more specialized occupancies (e.g., institutions, schools, and hospitals) given annual or even quarterly inspections by specially trained prevention staff. In the case of structures proposed for construction, fire prevention personnel (operating under authority of the fire marshal) ensure code compliance by reviewing plans and checking the fire alarm and fire sprinkler plan. During the actual building process, personnel conduct on-site inspections.

When communities consider modifications to their fire and building codes, the fire chief, the fire marshal, or specialized staff usually furnishes input aimed at ensuring the inclusion of fire safety provisions that are based on the latest experience and technology. Codes, with their emphasis on built-in elements for fire detection and suppression, have decreased the risks of commercial fires in many communities; but alert fire officials must ensure that as commercial occupants change, subsequent occupants do not significantly alter the processes and contents of commercial properties in a way that could overwhelm built-in fire protection features in the event of a fire.

In its routine fire code enforcement efforts, a proactive fire department will also consider the needs of the business proprietor: the department will approach fire safety requirements as a friend of the business, always explaining the code requirements and working to assist with compliance. Recognizing the costs associated with code compliance should not deter a department from enforcing the code but should lead fire department personnel to promote the business value of code compliance.

In the larger localities that have older buildings, dense populations, and dramatic demographic changes, fire prevention efforts require an extensive commitment of staff time. On occasion, local desires to revitalize urban centers by attracting businesses back can place fire prevention personnel on the cutting

Figure 4–9 Urban search and rescue teams work with their dogs to find, uncover, and rescue victims following the September 11, 2001, attack on the World Trade Center.

edge of change. However, if fire code requirements appear to be standing in the way of progress and revitalization, they will undergo intense scrutiny.

New development and growth may also create challenges to fire prevention: with extensive construction projects and subdivisions, water and access requirements come into play. In addition, fire staff workloads increase during periods of rapid growth, and there is a rising demand for plans to be checked more rapidly.

An element that is important to quality of life in urban areas and to a financially sound future for many metropolitan communities is effective planning for growth, but new development is often controversial. Local government, led by elected officials, must balance the demand for new commercial, multifamily, and residential properties with the existing communities' opposition to more congestion, unsightly structures, and loss of natural local features. Sometimes both the proponents and the opponents of growth use the fire department and its fire code in an effort to further their own particular interests.

Here again, many fire departments are proactive—first, by anticipating the probability of growth and the differing local views that accompany it and, second, by developing a reasonable code-supported department position that is well communicated to all interested parties. In the best cases, with the fire department and planning officials working together, local government managers and elected officials will have gotten a community master plan—or at least some basic guidelines—adopted in advance of major growth initiatives.

When fire departments plan proactively for growth, they often become influential in areas of special risk. For example, when excessively large warehouse facilities or high-risk structures are planned, special advance preparation and even fire code changes may be in order. In regions where growth and development are planned in areas susceptible to brush, wildland, or vegetative fires, special features such as buffer zones may be advisable and arranged for in advance of any large-scale development.

Fire departments that are proactive in fire code applications, day-to-day operations, and such special circumstances as urban growth and development can serve the community well as a stabilizing, rational force that can be counted on to put public safety first without being unreasonable or arbitrary.

Public education

Beyond routine fire prevention activities, many fire departments, both career and volunteer, are extensively involved in public fire and life safety education programs. Some of these programs are designed by fire department personnel and delivered at local schools and community events and in the news media. Public service–type announcements are used on radio and television stations to announce fire safety tips. Cable television stations are excellent vehicles for fire departments to use in conducting public education throughout the community.

Some fire departments fashion seasonal messages around their fire safety education outreach as a way of keeping fire safety a year-round topic. There are prepackaged fire safety education programs available as well. For example, in 1999 NFPA's *Learn Not to Burn*® program was available as a grant to qualifying fire departments and partner school districts, where teachers deliver the classroom portion of the program.

Available in 1998 was the NFPA program called *Risk Watch.*® *Risk Watch*

Learn Not to Burn® and *Risk Watch*® are registered trademarks of the National Fire Protection Association (NFPA), Quincy, MA 02269.

goes beyond fire safety lessons and focuses on preventing the eight leading causes of unintentional injury and death to children: motor vehicle crashes; fires and burns; choking, suffocation, and strangulation; poisoning; falls; unintentional firearm incidents; bike and pedestrian hazards; and water hazards.

Fully engaged fire departments use all types of ways to conduct public education. (Public education programs are discussed in detail in Chapter 12.) With the technological advances that seem imminent and the many more that seem likely in the decades to come, it seems fair to say that Internet Web sites, compact discs, and interactive television are only the beginning of new ways to conduct fire safety education.

Community partner and customer-oriented services

Consistent with fire departments' proactive multiservice approach, firefighting forces and their facilities have become more involved in the communities they protect and are seen as community partners. Plans for new fire stations sometimes include meeting rooms suitable for use by local government officials and citizens, and fire stations and emergency response personnel have been used in numerous ways to further assist and support important community efforts. For example, stations and personnel offer medical screenings (such as blood pressure checks), safety inspections for infant car seats, distribution of residential smoke detectors, and voter registration; and stations serve as polling places for elections. Some communities have identified fire stations as "safe places," with standardized signage that lets parents and youngsters know that the fire station is a safe place for a child who needs help (see accompanying sidebar and figure on page 134).

Learn Not to Burn® and Risk Watch® programs The National Fire Protection Association (NFPA) is a nonprofit organization dedicated to reducing the number of fires, fire deaths, fire-related injuries, and unintentional injuries (as opposed to injuries from child abuse, assault, etc.) that occur in the United States and Canada each year.

Since 1979, *Learn Not to Burn® (LNTB)* has been the theme and focus of NFPA's comprehensive public fire safety education initiative. Based on NFPA's belief that fire safety information should be presented in a positive, nonthreatening manner, LNTB teaches preschoolers, grade-school children, and their families how to make responsible choices about health and safety. LNTB and NFPA's other fire and life safety campaigns (e.g., National Fire Prevention Week) have been credited with saving more than five hundred lives in twenty-one years.

Risk Watch® is NFPA's comprehensive injury prevention curriculum. Launched in 1998, *Risk Watch®* was developed by NFPA with cofunding from the Lowe's Home Safety Council and in collaboration with a panel of respected safety and injury prevention experts. Designed for children from preschool through grade eight, *Risk Watch®* can be taught as a stand-alone unit or can easily be integrated into such core curriculum subjects as health, language arts, and physical education. *Risk Watch®* links teachers with community safety experts from local fire, law enforcement, and health agencies. It also includes special parent and caregiver activities to help prepare youngsters for the bright, challenging, and safe future they deserve.

Further information can be obtained from these National Fire Protection Association Web sites: http://www.nfpa.org, http://www.firepreventionweek.org, and http://www.riskwatch.org.

The use of fire stations and personnel for community services and the forging of partnerships are becoming more common as local government managers and fire chiefs realize the convenience associated with an existing network of fire stations located throughout a community, especially when a jurisdiction is geographically large. With a community-focused approach and the desire to function as a strong partner in a locality, fire departments more often see the public being served as "the customer" and less often as just a "victim" who requires help. Customer-centered service has had a pervasive effect on the fire service.

For example, in some fire department ambulance operations, patients who are medically stable enough are being transported to the hospital of their health care provider, even if it is not the nearest hospital. Such customer-oriented service results in greater user satisfaction, the user in this case being both the

---

Safe Place program   Some local fire departments have joined with youth shelters to collaborate with school districts, police departments, businesses, parents, and community members in establishing the Safe Place program. Participants in the program accept a shared responsibility for the well-being of young people living in their communities.

A "safe place" is a fire station or any other place (e.g., a business, public building, or police station) where a young person can receive help when encountering a dangerous or threatening situation. Safe Place locations are marked with a distinctive diamond-shaped yellow sign or decal for easy identification.

Fire departments that participate and display the Safe Place sign make each fire station a "safe place" for children or youth who may need assistance. Because of the fire station's visibility in the community, it can be the first stop

for the child who needs to escape from a potentially violent situation or who experiences some problem. In case firefighters are out, these young people can easily access emergency telephones installed on the outside of fire stations to call the Safe Place number indicated there.

Fire station personnel provide assistance to children by doing the following:

Temporarily placing a fire department unit out of service while providing assistance

Telephoning the Safe Place number to connect with professional help and transportation for the youth

Reassuring frightened, lost, or endangered children

Initiating the response of emergency medical personnel for children who have medical emergencies or calling appropriate law enforcement authorities if necessary for immediate safety concerns

Assisting children who fear becoming imminent victims of crime, intimidation, or abuse

Reporting crimes to law enforcement officials and providing descriptions of vehicles and suspects when possible.

Source: Adapted from information provided by the National Safe Place Office, YMCA National Safe Place, Louisville, Kentucky; http://www.safeplaceservices.org.

patient and the health care organization; such service may also save time and money by eliminating the need for subsequent, costly hospital transfers.

Other customer-related programs cover virtually all aspects of what fire departments do. Pamphlets aimed at preventing fires and injuries outline home and business fire safety tips. Many fire departments provide detailed guidance to owner-occupants who experience a fire, so that they can take immediate steps to limit further damage, preserve unaffected contents, establish fire scene security, and initiate recovery efforts.[8] Fire departments also notify social service organizations, such as the American Red Cross and the Salvation Army, and solicit help for fire incident victims.

Probably gone forever are the days when a fire department, whether fully paid or volunteer, simply suppressed fires that started. Fire department personnel, fire chiefs, local government managers, elected officials, and the citizens they serve have all seen how much a proactive, community-based, customer-oriented department can accomplish when it looks beyond being there *just* in case of fire.

Raising revenue and controlling costs

Money is always a concern, and the presence of a fire department within a community can be financially beneficial, as can multijurisdictional arrangements.

Raising revenue

Good, dependable fire protection services with adequate water supplies, sound communication systems, effective training programs, and a strong network of properly placed, sufficiently staffed fire stations can save a community dollars through good insurance ratings and lower premiums (see the sidebar on the Insurance Services Office). But besides saving dollars, such fire services can also help raise dollars.

The civic pride that a community feels when it has a good fire department and fire personnel who take an interest in the wider spectrum of local issues is intangible, but civic pride may also have a tangible financial offshoot. In some communities where service is provided by volunteer firefighters, many citizens not only admire those who answer the call but also make significant financial contributions toward purchasing equipment and apparatus for the fire department.

Some fire department services have been used more directly as a source of additional (albeit limited) revenue to the community. Although basic emergency response service for fires is free, a number of localities have levied fees for extraordinary services provided by their fire departments: fees have been assessed for welding permits, firework stands, oil well permits, and many other kinds of permits. Some fire departments charge a reinspection fee if fire code violations are not corrected after the first reinspection. The revenue from such fees usually flows into the general operating funds of the local government.

In jurisdictions where the fire department provides ambulance service, a fee is usually charged for ambulance transportation to a hospital and for medical supplies used for the patient's care. Many of these charges are paid by third-party providers of medical and health care insurance, health maintenance organizations, or government subsidies such as Medicaid. But in communities where a majority of those who require fire department ambulance service are not insured or financially able to pay ambulance fees, ambulance revenue may be exceeded by the cost of the EMS program. Often this excess of costs over income creates budgetary challenges for a locality. To generate a more predictable revenue stream and evaluate the actual cost effect of an ambulance

Insurance Services Office   The Insurance Services Office (ISO) is an independent statistical, rating, and advisory organization that provides the property and casualty insurance industry with up-to-date information about localities' fire protection services to help insurance companies determine appropriate fire insurance premiums for residential and commercial properties.

ISO collects information on a community's fire protection and analyzes the data, using its Fire Suppression Rating Schedule (FSRS). ISO then assigns the community a public protection classification from 1 to 10. Class 1 represents the best public protection and Class 10 indicates that the community does not meet the minimum criteria found in the FSRS. Ten percent of the overall rating is based on the fire department's capability to dispatch emergency calls; 50 percent on the number of engine companies, staffing, equipment, training, and related matters; and 40 percent on the community's water supply.

To evaluate the dispatching services provided by a fire department, the FSRS takes into account the number of dispatchers, the communication

infrastructure, the number of telephone lines coming into the center, and various other components of the communication system.

In addition to the number of engines and ladder trucks/service trucks needed, the FSRS also evaluates the equipment and the type of training provided to fire company personnel, the number of firefighting personnel who participate in the training, and the number of firefighters responding to emergencies.

The water supply rating is based on the sufficiency of the local water supply for fire suppression beyond what may be used for daily maximum consumption. ISO surveys all components of the water supply system, including pumps, storage, and filtration. ISO also conducts fire flow tests from fire hydrants at representative locations in the community to determine the actual rate of flow through water mains.

Communities are evaluated whenever there are changes to their fire protection services that are significant enough to warrant a change in protection class.

Source: Adapted with permission from Insurance Services Office, *Product Spotlight* (New York: ISO, 1998).

---

transportation fee, some communities have instituted fire department ambulance "subscription-fee" programs. Such programs enlarge the number of payers by encouraging all citizens to pay a small subscription fee that will ensure them a "free" ambulance ride to the hospital if they should need one during the subscription year. Visitors to the community and residents who do not subscribe pay a higher ambulance transport fee if they require the service.

From the basic fire suppression and preventive services to specialized fire department programs, communities benefit from what fire departments do. Quality of life and community safety are closely related, so the more ways a fire department serves its residents, especially when user fees generate revenue, the greater the returns.

Controlling costs

Seeking to control costs, particularly on high-value items such as firefighting vehicles and fire hose, some fire departments have formed consortia with other fire departments so that joint purchasing becomes possible. Similar consortia have achieved cost controls in joint services such as entry-level testing, basic firefighter training programs, and dispatching services. Some fire departments have also entered into arrangements to share facilities such as vehicle maintenance, training centers, and in some cases fire stations (where the response areas of different communities can be served from a common fire station).

Another practice, one that benefits both the customer and the taxpayer, is the formation of automatic aid agreements between fire departments. Unlike mutual aid agreements, whereby departments agree to send help to one another in the event of a major fire or emergency, automatic aid agreements address routine, small emergencies. The parties to automatic aid agreements agree to dispatch the fire department unit nearest to the emergency, regardless of the jurisdiction in which the emergency occurs. In other words, automatic aid agreements ignore jurisdictional boundaries in favor of sending the closest appropriate fire unit. Such arrangements have to be equally advantageous for both parties and usually require prior, formal approval by the governing body of each locality. When automatic aid is in effect, a fire department may be able to avoid the cost of an additional fire station or fire unit and the associated personnel.

A new millennium—New challenges

Whatever the approach to providing fire protection and first-responder services in medical emergencies, the local government manager, the chief fire administrator, and elected officials face an array of challenges. On the one hand, the need for adequately trained personnel, dependable tools and equipment, and necessary infrastructure (stations, radios, dispatching capability) will continue to place economic demands on the community. Yet, on the other hand, a deficiency in any of these critical elements will place human life and valuable property at greater risk in case of fire, illness, accident, or other emergency.

The fire service has entered a new millennium in which greater accomplishments lie ahead, thanks to technology. In the twenty-first century, high priorities for fire and local governmental managers will be adaptation to the changing health care system, preparedness for acts of domestic terrorism, and use of new technology to improve fire and rescue services while controlling costs. As the new millennium unfolds, other issues will emerge. Nevertheless, judging by its long history of contributions already made, the fire service will undoubtedly remain a key force in making tomorrow even safer for the communities and places where people live and work.

1   Michael J. Karter Jr., *U.S. Fire Department Profile through 2000* (Quincy, Mass.: National Fire Protection Association [NFPA], December 2001), 2. Copyright © 2001. NFPA, Quincy, MA 02269.

2   Leonard A. Matarese and Kenneth R. Chelst, "Forecasting the Outcome of Police/Fire Consolidation," *Management Information Service Report* 23 (April 1991): 25.

3   John E. Steen, "What about Consolidation?" *The International Fire Chief* 48 (November 1982): 17–19.

4   For additional information, see Arthur E. Cote, ed., *Fire Protection Handbook®: NFPA Codes, Standards and Recommended Practices,* 18th ed. (Quincy, Mass.: NFPA, 1997). *Fire Protection Handbook®* is a registered trademark of the NFPA, Quincy, MA 02269.

5   NFPA 1901, Standard for Automotive Fire Apparatus (1999 edition). The NFPA catalog contains a complete listing of current editions of NFPA documents that address fire apparatus

6   NFPA, *Fire Protection Handbook.*

7   U.S. Department of Labor, Occupational Safety and Health Administration, Occupational Safety and Health Administration Regulations (Standards 29 CFR), Respiratory Protection 1910.134, Procedures for IDLH Atmospheres (section g3), and Procedures of Interior Structural Firefighting (section g4).

8   Alan V. Brunacini, *Essentials of Customer Service* (Stillwater, Okla.: Fire Protection Publications, Oklahoma State University, 1996).

5 Human resource management

Communities large and small appreciate the wide array of emergency response services provided by their fire and rescue departments. Besides taking on pre-hospital emergency medical care, the fire service has branched into such new fields as hazardous materials (HAZMAT) mitigation and high-angle and confined-space rescue. Citizens' appreciation for these services is almost universal, and the services delivered by the fire department earn high marks. To a large extent, the reason is the quality of personnel who have chosen to enter the fire service despite the long hours and dangerous working conditions.

Fire and rescue departments are labor-intensive. In career departments (those whose personnel are full time and fully paid), the vast majority of expenses are for salaries and fringe benefits, which in medium and large cities normally constitute about 90 percent of the total fire budget. In communities served by volunteer departments, human resources are without doubt the most vital ingredient in the delivery of fire and emergency medical protection.

The public often judges the worth of a fire department by its bright and shiny apparatus and equipment, but the best fire departments do not necessarily have the best apparatus, the best stations, or the best equipment. What they have is quality personnel. Spending hundreds and thousands of dollars on the latest electronics and designing all systems to perform flawlessly cannot overcome the disadvantage of having improperly trained or insufficiently motivated personnel.

The author of a 1988 production-oriented book for businesses showed that effectiveness requires many things: plant and equipment, financial resources, a way of marketing whatever product or service is created, and human resources. Although all of these are important to organizational effectiveness, the technology, financing, and customer connections (marketing) can be easily copied. The only factor that represents a potential competitive advantage is human resources. Like businesses in the private sector, public service agencies such as fire and rescue departments excel on the strength of their personnel.[1]

In any organization, the management of human resources faces numerous internal and external challenges. The challenges are much the same whether the organization is private or public; however, public organizations are certainly open to a greater level of scrutiny and are often held to much higher standards of conduct, even if those standards are perceived rather than mandated. Close scrutiny is not in itself a challenge, but it does mean that public sector managers must pay careful attention to the rules, the rights of individuals, and the productivity of an organization.

Human resource management involves all management decisions and practices that directly affect or influence the people—or human resources—who work for the organization.[2] And progressive fire chiefs are seeing the results of an interest in human resource management: the results of involving their employees in organizational decision making, of having the right people to do the job, and of genuinely caring about their people.

This chapter first touches briefly and broadly on two issues that overarch human resource management in the fire service: the differences (and similarities) between career and volunteer departments, and the role of external mandates. It then comments on human resource management functions and specialists, and on human resource planning and job analysis. The next subjects discussed are recruitment and selection (incentives, diversity, and the selection process); the work environment (details about the relevant legislative mandates); proficiency, career development, and employee evaluation; promotion; labor relations; and future challenges. The chapter concludes by focusing squarely on the term *human resources.*

Overarching issues: Career/volunteer departments and external mandates

As indicated below in the section on promotion, the majority of U.S. fire service agencies are volunteer or combination career/volunteer departments. Given the vital role played by volunteer departments, therefore, questions of human resource management in the fire service cannot be addressed only from the perspective of career departments. Rather, the differences (and sometimes the similarities) between human resource management in career departments and in volunteer departments must be kept in mind. A second and equally profound consideration is the legislative and regulatory constraints that affect all aspects of human resource management.

Human resource management in career and volunteer departments

The level of sophistication needed to perform human resource management tasks does not depend on whether the agency is volunteer or career. Instead, it depends on the size of the organization, local political priorities, and quality of leadership. Many volunteer fire departments use the same intensity of recruitment strategies, grievance management, and other human resource management activities that career organizations use. Usually a volunteer fire department has less personnel stress, but it also has less control over its members. Although volunteer firefighters are dedicated employees, in personnel hearings they are less affected by legal mandates than are career firefighters because their legal stake or "property interest" in the job is obviously much less. Instead of legal mandates, the common sense and good judgment of the volunteer fire chief are often counted on to deliver fair and proper personnel management.

In terms of providing the leadership necessary to build team strength and keep the department accountable to the community, career and volunteer fire officers have the same basic responsibilities. They need to train and equip fire personnel to deal with the challenges associated with the mission and goals of the fire service. Training systems, promotion processes, evaluation techniques, and employee support programs are equally important for all firefighters.

Both volunteer and career personnel

must be selected, utilized, and rewarded properly in order to make an organization effective.

Most volunteers begin their fire service involvement with a high degree of commitment. Significant effort must be put forth to retain and nurture this commitment, or serious organizational and economic problems are likely to occur. . . .

There is often much pressure to make the selection and performance standards for volunteer firefighters lower than those for career fire service personnel. The volunteer fire service organizations that have recognized the necessity of maintaining equal standards have found not only a cadre of volunteer personnel willing to conform, but also a degree of resentment when the volunteer is asked to play a technically inferior role.

The National Fire Protection Association [NFPA] 1000 series standards, which address fire service personnel standards, do not differentiate between volunteer and career personnel.[3]

The future of the volunteer fire service

The future of the U.S. volunteer fire service, like its past, is filled with challenges. Although a list of them could probably be as long and as wide as one's imagination, such a list can undoubtedly be boiled down to two elements—time and money.

We live in an age of heightened customer expectations. The public we serve demands more, better, and cheaper services. Teams specializing in urban search and rescue, swift-water rescue, still-water rescue, high-angle rescue, low-angle rescue, trench rescue, and just about every other kind of rescue abound. There is every indication that this expansion of services will continue into the foreseeable future. Furthermore, the public expects us to increase public education and inspection as well as improve suppression—all at less cost, if possible. This means more training, which translates into more time.

Unfortunately, the volunteer fire service is already confronting a time dilemma. U.S. workers spend more time at their jobs than ever before. Two-earner couples have become the norm, and many people are forced to take second jobs. Consequently, the time available for training is being reduced just when the time demand is increasing dramatically. This places the fire service in the unenviable position of competing for members' time. When the fire department competes against churches, school groups, community obligations, and the members' own families, some group is going to lose. This is not an encouraging scenario.

The money challenge merely compounds the time challenge. Many, if not most, volunteer fire departments spend a substantial amount of time on fund raising. As a result, local governments have enjoyed the benefit not only of donated services but also of reduced operating costs. As volunteers' discretionary time shrinks, however, something obviously has to give. If that "something" is the time spent on fund raising, governmental units will have to assume responsibility for providing adequate funding for those who protect them. This will reduce or eliminate the money problem, and it will ease the time problem.

But it will not eliminate the time problem. Volunteer fire departments in the first decade of the twenty-first century will address this problem in a number of ways. Some will realize that the demand for services has outrun their resources. Many of these departments will add some paid personnel to fill the gaps. In particular, departments in areas experiencing rapid population growth will move toward combination departments. Consolidations, too, will increase as more departments seek the resulting economies of scale in terms of both time and money. Changing the organizational structure of a department is stressful, however, and will be done well only when the factors involved are properly appreciated. This is especially true for consolidations, which typically involve a loss of identity for the merged departments.

Time constraints will also be addressed in other ways. Most notably, recruitment practices will change. Rather than concentrating exclusively on people interested in suppression, departments will recruit specialists. They will attract persons interested in contributing computer skills, accounting and administrative know-how, maintenance skills, aptitude in fire and life safety education, and the like. Releasing people charged with suppression duties from also performing these tasks will ease the time crunch and will, in addition, open the volunteer service to those who are not interested in suppression activities because of physical disabilities, lack of time, or personal preferences.

What the first decade of the twenty-first century will hold for the volunteer fire service obviously remains to be seen. What the first decade will *not* hold is the demise of the volunteer fire service. Prophets of doom to the contrary, adequate numbers of persons dedicated to donating their time and talents to their communities will step forward. The challenges of the future will be met as they have been for the past 350 years —with ingenuity, enthusiasm, and dedication.

Source: Philip C. Stittleburg, chief, La Farge (Wisconsin) Fire Department, and president, National Volunteer Fire Council.

One issue—recruiting and retaining volunteer personnel—is especially critical to the large number of local governments that rely on volunteers to deliver service in a manner that is affordable and effective. Clearly, social changes have affected the time most people have available for volunteer service, and the increasing mobility among the general population has seriously diminished the number of people who have a strong sense of community and are willing and able to make long-term commitments to their communities' volunteer fire departments. Any recruiting/retention program must be cognizant of these factors. Each year a number of publications and magazine articles explore the issue.

External mandates: Legislative and regulatory constraints

Laws have a major effect on the operations of both career and volunteer fire service organizations, and legal requirements often change. Moreover, state governments are affected by the actions of the federal government, and local governments are influenced by federal, state, and county policies. Thus, fire service leaders must exercise constant vigilance.

There is no reason to believe that the mandates placed on local government will diminish over time. Rather, the forces of social change are more likely to lead the federal and state governments to continue addressing employment issues for both career and volunteer entities. In addition, labor unions will continue pushing their issues in relation to both legislation and consensus standards, generating additional pressures on human resource managers to be aware of mandates in place and mandates in process.

Much of the system of governmental pressures focuses on ensuring fairness to all in the delivery of services. Because of widespread concern over civil rights for all people, the federal government has created directives, regulations, and laws that directly affect personnel issues for fire and rescue departments. Laws are also aimed at protecting workers' safety. As a National Fire Academy publication points out:

> While some managers tend to view the rules and regulations from outside authorities as burdensome, these rules typically are designed to protect personnel and to promote better service. The function of the U.S. Fire Administration (USFA), an arm of the Federal Emergency Management Agency (FEMA), is to assist in human resource development functions, such as training and education. The U.S. Department of Labor and the Occupational Safety and Health Administration (OSHA) are examples of regulatory agencies that exercise authority related to safety in the workplace.[4]

External mandates are discussed in far more detail below under "The Work Environment: Relevant Legislation."

Human resource management functions and specialists

In both career and volunteer fire service organizations, even the most basic personnel management program must have certain responsibilities, as listed in Figure 5–1. These functions need to be properly assigned and carried out. In larger organizations, one or more individuals may be spending all or much of their time on these functions, but even in the smallest fire department someone needs to be given the authority and responsibility to manage human resources. Figure 5–2 suggests some levels of responsibility for certain functions, but these are only suggestions; the assignments by position may vary widely from department to department. Those performing the assignments could be considered "organizational specialists."

Personnel assigned to human resource management tasks need to be trained for those tasks. Money is well spent when it provides local, distant, or online training for fire officers who are charged with managing the most important asset of the fire department—its personnel.

The very first rung on the personnel management ladder within the fire department itself is the line officer (or first-line supervisor). The actions and attitudes of line officers directly affect the personnel serving under them. Whether the organization is career or volunteer, line officers are responsible for the command and control of personnel in both emergency and routine conditions and are therefore in a position to strengthen or weaken their unit mem-

Figure 5–1 Human resource functions in career and volunteer fire departments.

Recruitment (career)	Recruitment (volunteer)
Pretesting; orientation/training	Promotional appointments
Entry-level testing	Transfers
Candidate selection	Grievances
Orientation and training of new personnel	Commendations and disciplinary actions
Project and work duty assignments	Personnel status records (time in service, leave records, etc.)
Salary and/or benefit classifications	
Probationary clearances	Salary and benefits package adjustments (primarily for career personnel)
Establishment of leave entitlement	
Performance evaluations	Injury, disability, and medical records
Maintenance of personnel folders	Separation or retirement and pension data
Training and educational accomplishments	

Figure 5–2 Organizational specialists responsible for human resource functions in career and volunteer fire departments.

Personnel	Function
Fire chief	Supervises personnel functions overall.
Training officer	Develops team and individual strengths by targeting weak areas for future training. Develops training programs and agendas.
Operations officer	Implements departmental personnel procedures through the organizational hierarchy and makes sure the plan of action is being closely followed.
Personnel officer	Is responsible for making sure that personnel procedures (e.g., hiring, promotion, transfer, evaluations, pay increases) are being properly implemented; makes sure that employee rights (e.g., grievance procedures, employee right to bargain for changed working conditions, contract rights) are properly protected according to personnel law; is a direct contact to a union, if one exists; may assign teams of specialists to specific duties, such as recruitment and testing, affirmative action plan implementation, and employee-employer negotiations; may be appointed departmentally or may serve the entire local government.
Finance officer	Is responsible for payroll, insurance (health insurance, worker's compensation, unemployment insurance, etc.), retirement, and related compensation benefits; may assign teams to specific areas, such as payroll and employee benefits.
Program coordinator	Works on employee assistance programs to support and develop employee effectiveness: employee health, career, personal and family counseling, career development, and other related human resource development activities.
Legal assistance	Personnel law is a special legal entity, and legal advice is often required when the organization is dealing with sensitive personnel matters such as potential loss of employee property rights (e.g., salary reduction, demotion, layoff, termination). The organization may have a legal advisor who understands personnel law, or it may retain legal advisors who specialize in personnel law.

Note: In many fire departments, some or all of these functional areas will probably be combined into one or more positions.

bers' positive attitudes and skill levels. To have a positive effect, line officers need both developmental skills and supervisory skills.

Developmental skills come into play inasmuch as company-level line officers are directly involved in shaping the career firefighter's workday or the volunteer firefighter's time spent serving with other members. The line officer can make this time productive by assigning and performing training, and by guiding individual and team performance in completing company work assignments.

Supervisory skills come into play during both emergency and routine activities, as the line officer directs individuals at structure fires and serious auto accidents as well as during training drills designed to enhance skill levels for these operations.

Human resource planning and job analysis

As the fire service mission expands in most communities, local governments are taking steps to determine the number of people required to accomplish standard tasks and the skills that are necessary to those people. Projects such as the FireDAP program (Fire Department Analysis Project, initiated by NFPA's Urban Fire Forum and the Phoenix Fire Department) seek to establish direct relationships between resources and standard outcomes at various types of emergency incidents. (For more details on the FireDAP program, see Chapter 10.) It is hoped that the complicated process of establishing such relationships will yield useful information—information that will enable communities to deploy their resources innovatively while achieving results that can still be measured in a standard manner.

For example, having dual-trained firefighters/paramedics who can handle whichever kind of emergency first occurs may prove better than having crews who can handle only one kind or the other. An analogy from private industry is General Motors' decision to institute "round-the-clock production and flexible, lean manufacturing" at its plant in Lordstown, Ohio: to support its decision, GM retrained its workers to handle a variety of jobs rather than endlessly repeating a few rote tasks.[5]

Central to any scheme for deploying human resources more effectively is the need for thorough job analyses. Job analyses provide a deeper understanding of the behavioral requirements of jobs and therefore create a solid basis for making job-related employment decisions—and for defending such decisions in court, if necessary. When employment practices (e.g., interviews, tests, performance appraisal systems) are challenged, job analyses are a major part of the defense because they demonstrate that the practices in question are "job related." Requiring a potential fire recruit to lift a ladder, for example, is more likely to be ruled valid than requiring the potential recruit to lift an identical amount of dead weight. (For more on legal requirements and challenges, see the sidebar on the next page.)

The following list presents ten key steps in properly placing and retaining fire service personnel, and the foundation of all the steps is job analysis.[6]

1. *Job evaluation and compensation*   Before jobs can be either ranked in terms of their overall worth to an organization or compared (for purposes of pay surveys) with jobs in other fire departments, their requirements must be understood. To those responsible for making decisions about job evaluation and compensation, job descriptions and specifications provide such understanding.
2. *Recruitment*   The information most important to a recruiter is full knowledge of the job(s) in question, a knowledge gained from job analysis. In cities and other large governmental entities, the fire and rescue department should remain involved even when the primary task of recruiting is done by a human relations or personnel department.

Court ruling on job-related tests

A case involving hiring practices is *Zamlen v. City of Cleveland*, 906 F. 2d 209 (6th Cir. 1990).

Only twenty-one females out of nearly three hundred female applicants [for firefighter positions in the city of Cleveland] scored high enough on the written and physical portions of the exam to be placed on the eligibility list. Even then they were ranked far too low to have any reasonable prospects of being hired. Ultimately, a group of female applicants brought suit against the city challenging the rank ordering and the written and physical selection examinations. The trial court concluded that the possibility of hiring unqualified firefighters posed such a significant risk to the public that it was appropriate to hold the city to a lighter burden of proving that the employment criteria were job related. The court concluded that the examinations had been appropriately validated and were job related. Finally, the trial court ruled that there was sufficient correlation between higher test scores and job performance to warrant a rank order hiring procedure. Unsuccessful female applicants appealed.

[The court's holding read (in part) as follows:] HELD: The purpose of fair employment laws is to achieve equality of employment opportunities through eradication of employment barriers which discriminate on the basis of race, gender, religion, and other protected classifications. Employment practices, which on the face are neutral, but are discriminatory in practice, have given rise to the theory of liability commonly known as the disparate impact theory. Under this bias for liability, a specific employment practice may be deemed unlawful without proving the employer's subjective intent to discriminate. But even a procedure that has disparate impact may still be permissible if it is shown to be validated as a job-related test. Here the trial court concluded that the examination was properly validated according to federal guidelines. Each event in the physical examination was designed to test a representative firefighting task. The barbell lift was designed to simulate the use of a pike pole to tear out ceilings. The fire scene mock-up and tower climb event was intended to duplicate firefighting tasks performed where speed is the most critical factor, such as setting up ladders and climbing stairs. The dummy drag simulated the rescue of a disabled person under circumstances where heat and smoke make it difficult to stand upright. The would-be female firefighters challenged the procedure because it did not measure aerobic qualities, but rather placed emphasis on anaerobic performance. Although a simulated firefighter examination that does not test for stamina (aerobic capacity), in addition to short-term speed and energy, may be a less effective barometer of firefighting abilities than one that does include an aerobic component, the deficiency does not rule the test unlawful. Because the examination did parallel the actual tasks which firefighters perform on the job and the city did demonstrate a direct correlation between higher test scores and better job performance, the examination withstands the challenge of the unsuccessful female applicants. Affirmed for the City.

Source: Reprinted with permission of the National Fire Academy, *Personnel Management for the Fire Service*, Course Guide (Emmitsburg, Md.: National Fire Academy, 2000), 4-13 to 4-14.

3. *Selection*   Any method used to select or promote applicants must be based on a keen, meaningful forecast of job performance. To make such a forecast, one first needs to understand just what a worker is expected to do on the job; one then uses job-related interviews or test questions to predict how a particular worker will perform in the particular job. The selection process continues, almost seamlessly, to the next phase: placement.

4. *Placement* In many cases, applicants are first selected and then placed in one of many possible jobs. When the needs of a job and the abilities of workers to meet those needs are clearly understood, placement decisions will be accurate. Since full-time fire service careers are coveted and competition is keen, a fire department usually has a large pool of applicants; the important thing is to select and place the applicant who best matches the job, not necessarily the applicant who is most intelligent or most physically fit.

5. *Orientation, training, and development* First, efforts should be made specifically to show new employees and their families what to expect and what is expected of them. This orientation helps set the stage for a career that rewards the employee and the organization. Second, training a firefighter begins early and is costly. Training programs that do not reflect actual job requirements are not effective uses of funds. Up-to-date job descriptions and specifications help ensure a good match between training and the actual job. A worthwhile motto, one that should in fact reflect reality, is "What you learn in training today, you'll use in the field tomorrow." Third, as employees avail themselves of specialized training, they experience personal development.

6. *Performance appraisal* If firefighters are to be judged in terms of how well they do the parts of their jobs that really matter—the parts that distinguish effective from ineffective performers—it is important to specify critical and noncritical job requirements. (Positive corrective follow-up is important, too.)

7. *Career-path planning* Firefighters advance through the ranks and become officers and chiefs. If the organization (as well as the individual) does not have a thorough understanding of how ranks at succeeding levels relate to one another, effective career-path planning is difficult. The organization should use good job analyses to define performance expectations at each rank level and should provide opportunities for employees at one level to prepare for the next level.

8. *Labor relations* The information provided by job analyses is helpful to both management and unions for contract negotiations as well as for grievance resolution. (Labor relations are discussed below.)

9. *Safety* NFPA Standard 1500 on firefighters' safety is well known and has been responsible for many improvements. During job analysis, unsafe conditions (environmental conditions or personal habits) are often discovered, and the discovery leads to safety improvements both in the station and on the fire ground.

10. *Vocational guidance and rehabilitation counseling* Comprehensive job descriptions and specifications enable personnel to make informed decisions about career choices. For example, a firefighter may choose fire prevention, fire suppression, emergency medical service (EMS), or a combination of the three.

Recruitment and selection: Incentives and diversity

The fire and rescue profession has become one of the most desirable in the United States, and career fire service jobs typically draw large numbers of applicants. Volunteer positions, however, are often hard to fill. And even in career departments where there is little difficulty attracting numerous candidates, attracting the proper mix of candidates to comply with federal civil rights guidelines is far more difficult. This section discusses recruitment incentives in both career and volunteer departments and then turns to the law on diversity and various approaches to achieving a diversified workforce.

Incentives in career and volunteer departments

To career-oriented people, standard employee benefit packages are attractive. The fire service typically offers some work schedules that are attractive as well, even though the number of hours worked exceeds the typical forty-per-week average.

Some forms of benefits may also be attractive to volunteer or paid on-call candidates (i.e., paid by the hour or incident for responding to alarms or participating in drills). For example, some communities have used retirement programs to attract volunteer personnel and retain them for long periods. However, trends at the turn of the millennium indicate that to most volunteers, benefit programs with very distant payouts are not persuasive reasons for staying in the service. To recruit and retain volunteer firefighters, fire departments continue to look for other forms of incentive, often tied to level of participation.

Recruiting may also be affected—positively or negatively—by the expanded role of the fire department in the community. In past years, the role of the fire service was rather traditionally defined as that of firefighting and rescue, but now there are other assigned duties that may draw some potential candidates and deter others. Functions such as EMS, responses to HAZMAT incidents, technical rescue, and public education have provided the fire service with new challenges and opportunities.

Diversity in recruitment: Nondiscrimination in law and in practice

Ensuring nondiscrimination in recruitment (as in other personnel practices) is a goal of numerous pieces of federal legislation. On the basis of the Civil Rights Act of 1964 (Title VII), fire departments are legally mandated to ensure that every person regardless of race, color, religion, sex, or national origin is given fair, just, and equitable treatment in both employment and promotion processes.

To meet legal requirements and achieve diversity, various approaches to recruitment are possible. One authority on human resource management mentions four approaches, all of which are applicable to both career and volunteer fire departments.

Passive nondiscrimination is a commitment to treat all races and both sexes equally in all decisions about hiring, promotion, and pay. No attempt is made to recruit actively among prospective minority applicants. . . .

Pure diversity-based recruitment is a concerted effort by the organization to actively expand the pool of applicants so that no one is excluded because of past or present discrimination. . . .

Diversity-based recruitment with preferential hiring goes further than pure diversity-based recruitment: it systematically favors women and minorities in hiring and promotion decisions. This approach is known as a "soft quota" system.

Hard quotas represent a mandate to hire or promote specific numbers or proportions of women or minority-group members.[7]

Both private and public employers find hard quotas an unpalatable strategy for rectifying the effects of past or present discrimination. Nevertheless, the courts have ordered "temporary" quotas in instances when discrimination has obviously taken place and no other remedy is feasible. In 1973, for example, the fire department in the city of Cincinnati signed a federal court decree to actively recruit black men until that group's percentage within the department equaled its percentage within the city's population.[8] In that year the percentage of African Americans in the Cincinnati Fire Department began growing, and by 1990 the terms of the court decree had been met.

Diversity in recruitment: Expanding the pool

Effort is required to ensure that the large number of applicants to career fire and rescue departments includes enough women and members of minority groups to make it likely that some of the applicants from those groups will be successful. If the number of female and minority candidates is insufficient, intervention in the selection process becomes necessary. According to the National Fire Academy, this intervention is usually done by creating separate eligibility lists or certifying applicants individually, with attention directed at selecting women and minorities to the greatest degree possible without compromising overall fairness. These methods have often generated substantial controversy and litigation.[9]

During the recruitment process, chiefs must use their influence to ensure that a solid and assertive effort is made to overcome the bureaucratic obstacles to achieving diversity. All governmental agencies should cooperate because the problem belongs to the entire governmental entity, not just to the fire department or the personnel department.

Some elements of successful selective recruitment are as follows:[10]

Involvement of the chief in public appearances and announcements

Use of minority media

Use of minority and women's activist groups

Use of minority and female firefighters as recruiters

Outreach to minority churches and other focused organizations

Outreach to spas and fitness centers with female clientele

Chief's close cooperation with African-American, Hispanic, and women's firefighter organizations

Role model–based recruiting.

Polygraph testing and psychological evaluation

During the selection process, the chief and other fire officials should set a positive tone. Transferring responsibility for the outcome of the recruitment process to the personnel or human resources department is an easy way out but should be avoided.

Two techniques that are often used as component parts of the selection process are polygraph testing and psychological evaluations. Both, however, should be used—if at all—with great care.

Although polygraph testing has become popular in some organizations, its validity and usefulness have been called into question. The information that it is obviously illegal for an employer to seek on a job application is information that it is also illegal to seek in a polygraph test. An employer may not ask questions about, for example, an employee's color, race, creed, religion, sex, national origin, and disability. Nor may an employer under any circumstances require a new hire (or, for that matter, any employee) to submit to a polygraph test, a voice stress test, or any other test that purports to measure "truth" as opposed to measuring "employment suitability."

Psychological evaluation, long used in law enforcement selection, is now gaining acceptance in the fire service. It responds to the need to select individuals who fit the behavioral requirements for the job. Such considerations as temperament, character, reaction to stress, flexibility, and traits of personality are profiled in psychological evaluations. But although these evaluations may help predict future behavior under varied conditions, they should be used cautiously. If taken at face value, they can have an adverse effect and can unfairly exclude suitable candidates.

The following is a list of possible weaknesses of psychological evaluations:[11]

Cultural characteristics may not be differentiated from character flaws.

Assertive women tend to be classified as aggressive, defensive, or defiant.

Applicants who give short, abrupt responses tend to be called uncommunicative.

Strong personalities are often deemed unsuitable for the fire station environment.

Soft-spoken, humble applicants are profiled as lacking initiative or not having "take-charge" ability.

Given the emphasis on equal-opportunity recruitment and selection, the first two of these possible weaknesses may be particularly invidious. As one observer has noted,

There is evidence of cultural bias in some of the standard tests. There are observations of prejudices reflected by the psychologists themselves in some of the respondents' written comments. There were a number of concerns expressed regarding apparent bias when female applicants were evaluated by male psychologists.

The impact of cultural bias was most evident in its effect on female, black, Hispanic and Asian subjects.[12]

The National Fire Academy course on personnel management offers five suggestions for making psychological evaluations beneficial and for minimizing any adverse effect they may have on affirmative hiring:[13]

1. Consider them to be advisory only.
2. Do not use them as a basis on which to eliminate candidates.
3. Review the track record and techniques of the psychologist.
4. Attempt to corroborate the psychologist's observations with oral interviews.
5. Discuss your concerns with the psychologist before the testing begins.

The work environment: Relevant legislation

As employees are hired and promoted and as they advance through their careers, fire and rescue departments have no choice about whether to observe equal employment opportunity (EEO) requirements. The only choice they have is how best to create a work environment that lives up to both the letter and the spirit of the civil rights laws. It is important to note that besides meeting federal and state civil rights requirements, an employer must also check local regulations. Many localities have requirements for employers that federal or state laws may not have. (Another aspect of the work environment—drug testing—is discussed in the accompanying sidebar.)

People who are covered under EEO laws are referred to as "members of a protected class." To implement laws barring discrimination against members of protected classes, several regulatory agencies have developed guidelines and regulations. The following discussion of the relevant laws has been adapted slightly from the National Fire Academy's *Personnel Management for the Fire Service*.[14]

The work environment: Drug testing
In career departments, both labor unions and administrators openly seek drug-free environments, although often unions also want to ensure the privacy rights of their members. Volunteer fire departments support drug-free initiatives as well, but they often lack the finances and logistical support necessary for programs that test for drug use.

Personnel procedures for prohibiting the distribution, dispensing, or use of a controlled substance or alcohol in the workplace should be developed and properly implemented. The courts have held that drug testing (a part of personnel procedures) is permissible within the "unreasonable searches and seizures" provision of the Fourth Amendment to the Constitution and can be carried out under the categories of preemployment, periodic, and postaccident drug testing as well as testing for cause.

Equal Pay Act of 1963   The equal pay provisions of the Fair Labor Standards Act [FLSA], as amended in 1963, 1968, and 1972, prohibit wage differentials based on sex. . . . [The Equal Pay Act was an amendment to the FLSA of 1938.]

1964 Civil Rights Act, Title VII   This federal law is the keystone of federal EEO legislation. Two of its important provisions, Sections 703(a) and 704(b), are as follows:

Section 703(a)
It shall be an unlawful employment practice for an employer (1) to fail or refuse to hire or to discharge any individual, or otherwise to discriminate against any individual with respect to his compensation, terms, conditions, or privileges of employment, because of such individual's race, color, religion, sex, or national origin, or (2) to limit, segregate, or classify employees in any way which would deprive or tend to deprive any individual of employment opportunities or otherwise adversely affect employee status, because of such individual's race, color, religion, sex, or national origin.

Section 704(b)
It shall be an unlawful employment practice for an employer, labor organization, or employment agency to print or publish or cause to be printed or published any notice or advertisement relating to employment by such an employment agency indicating any preference, limitations, specification, or discrimination based on race, color, religion, sex, or national origin.

Age Discrimination in Employment Act (ADEA)   The ADEA of 1967, as amended in 1978 and 1986, makes it illegal for an employer to discriminate in compensation, terms, conditions, or privileges because of an individual's age.

Older Workers Benefit Protection Act of 1974 (OWBPA)   The OWBPA restricts an employer's ability to obtain waivers of age discrimination claims when terminating or laying off older employees.

Pregnancy Discrimination Act of 1978 (PDA)   The PDA, passed as an amendment to the Civil Rights Act of 1964, requires that women employees "affected by pregnancy, child birth, or related medical conditions will be treated the same" as any other employees or candidates for employment.

Americans with Disabilities Act (ADA)   The ADA was passed in 1990, and its requirements for employers were phased in from 1992 to 1994 (employers with twenty-five or more workers were required to comply with them by July 26,

Job analysis and the Americans with Disabilities Act of 1990 The Americans with Disabilities Act of 1990 (ADA) "makes it clear that job applicants must be able to understand what the essential functions of a job are before they can respond to the question, 'Can you perform the essential functions of the job for which you are applying?'"

Essential job functions are functions that require relatively more time and in which error or nonperformance has serious consequences. A function may be essential because it is the reason that the position exists at all (e.g., a firefighter must necessarily be able to carry or drag a 200-pound person or mannequin).

Essential job functions can be systematically identified by the use of job analysis. If the physical, environmental, or mental demands of a job change or expand, the job analysis must be updated. Job analysis results are normally summarized in writing in the form of a job description. For the fire service, this summary might be better presented through a video job description that provides an applicant with visual evidence of the job's physical and environmental demands. (Environmental demands might include belligerent or combative EMS patients.) Candidates whose physical or mental disabilities render them unable to perform a job may then self-select out, making it less likely that the department's hiring decisions will be challenged in court.

To ensure that the required knowledge, skills, abilities, and other characteristics on which candidates are assessed are job related, the department must be able to link this knowledge (etc.) to essential job functions.

Under the ADA, "essential" job requirements must be distinguished from "nonessential" job requirements *before* a job opening is announced. "If a candidate with a disability can perform the essential functions of the job and is hired, the employer must be willing to make 'reasonable accommodations' to enable the person to work." Examples of such accommodations are

Restructuring a job so that someone else does the nonessential tasks a person with a disability cannot do

Modifying work hours or work schedules so that a person with a disability can commute during off-peak periods

Reassigning a worker who becomes disabled to a vacant position

Acquiring or modifying equipment or devices (e.g., a telecommunications device for the hearing-impaired).

Source: Adapted with permission of The McGraw-Hill Companies from Wayne F. Cascio, *Managing Human Resources*, 5th ed. (Boston: Irwin McGraw-Hill, 1998), 138.

1992; employers with fifteen or more workers, by July 26, 1994). The equal access measures took effect in 1992: employers with twenty-five or more employees are prohibited from discriminating against qualified disabled employees. The law defines a "qualified disabled person" as a person who, with reasonable accommodation, can perform the essential functions of the position. "Reasonable accommodation" is defined as steps an employer can take to help a disabled person perform the job; an example of such a step is providing a reader for a blind employee. If the accommodations would cause the employer "undue hardship," however, the employer is not obligated to accommodate a disabled employee. The ADA also forbids preemployment physicals unless the physical examination tests for job-related functions, is a business necessity, and is required only after the employer has made an offer of employment to the applicant.

National Labor Relations Act of 1935 (NLRA)   The NLRA prohibits employers from interfering with the rights of employees to form unions or engage in union activity.

Immigration Reform and Control Act of 1986   The Immigration Reform and Control Act prohibits employers from knowingly employing illegal aliens.

Veterans' Readjustment Assistance Act of 1974   The Veterans' Readjustment Assistance Act of 1974 provides that employees who leave their jobs to serve in the armed forces are entitled to reinstatement when their tours of duty are completed. To be covered by the statute, the veteran must have completed a tour of duty and must apply for a job within ninety days of release from active duty or within one year of service-related hospitalization. If the veteran meets these requirements, he or she must be either returned to his or her former position or placed in an equal position unless circumstances have changed so drastically that this would be impossible. After reemployment, the veteran may not be discharged except for just cause.

Fair Labor Standards Act (FLSA)   The FLSA has applied to public sector workers, including firefighters and medics, since 1985. For personnel whose main job is EMS or firefighting, the FLSA requires that overtime be paid for hours in excess of an *average* of 53 hours per week.[15]

Proficiency, career development, and employee evaluation

Once personnel are recruited and selected and are on the job, it becomes important to maintain their proficiency, help them develop their careers, and evaluate their performance.

Proficiency

Despite a department's best efforts to recruit quality personnel, maintaining high standards among employees requires effort in both career and volunteer departments. Continuous quality training is often what differentiates professional fire departments (whether career or volunteer) from the less capable ones.[16] And to ensure that the efforts made to recruit quality personnel are not negated by substandard performance on the job, meaningful training should be accompanied by assertive supervision. Occasionally discipline is needed, but discipline does not have to be negative. The term *disciplined soldiers* is actually positive. Most supervisors find that preventive disciplinary procedures are superior to corrective procedures. Dennis Compton, chief of the Mesa, Arizona, Fire Department, uses safety procedures as an example: "Rather than spend a lot of time simply discussing what to do with people who don't follow safety procedures, I find it beneficial and productive to discuss ways to prevent people from operating outside of our expectations in the first place."[17]

Career development

In career development, training must be augmented by education. As personnel develop throughout their careers, a mix of education and training, in varying proportions, helps them become increasingly proficient. But experience, too, plays an important role:

Education and training in the fire service are complemented by an equally important third factor: experience. The three component parts—education, training and experience—make up what has been described as a "learning triad." A healthy mix of all three is required

Figure 5–3 The learning triad.

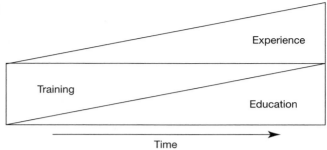

for an effective fire officer, but as he or she moves through a career, the mix and the proportion of each tend to vary, with education becoming more and more important over time. [Figure 5–3] gives a capsulized description of each of these three and shows their changing proportional relationship through a career.[18]

Employee evaluation and performance management

In any organization, one of management's major responsibilities is evaluating employees in an effort to guide overall performance. Fire service organizations do not materially differ either in the need for this activity or in the process. A wide variety of evaluation and performance management systems are used throughout the service, ranging from the extremely informal to some that provide for extensive feedback. One of the most detailed and extensive systems of performance management has been developed by the Plano, Texas, Fire Department. Unique to this system is its process of ensuring that performance goals for individuals are properly tracked for the benefit of both the organization and the employee.

Volunteer and paid on-call departments also require a level of performance management. To be sure, the relationship between management and unpaid (or marginally compensated) workers may introduce into the review process some elements that are different from those in a traditional employee-employer relationship. Nevertheless, it is still incumbent on managers to provide meaningful feedback to all personnel.

An excellent discussion of employee evaluation and performance management, applicable to all organizations, is available in the ICMA publication *Employee Performance: Appraisal and Management.*[19]

Promotion

Most firefighters are quite interested in promotion because it provides them with an opportunity to exercise more authority, rise within the organization, and (in career departments) receive greater remuneration. A successful organization requires a process of building future leaders and promoting capable people. Career management on the part of fire department supervisors blends concern for personal ambition and choice with concern for departmental strength.

This section discusses promotion with respect to (1) type of department, (2) certification standards, and (3) helpful tools.

Promotion by type of department

The three types of fire department discussed here are (1) fully volunteer; (2) combination volunteer and career (with two subtypes: the mostly volunteer departments, where more than half the personnel are volunteer, and the mostly career departments, where more than half the personnel are career); and (3) fully career (i.e., full time and fully paid). Because new fire departments are constantly being formed and consolidations of smaller departments into larger ones are regular occurrences, the number of fire departments in the United States varies over time.

NFPA estimates that as of 2000, there were more than 26,000 fire/rescue departments in the United States, distributed by type and subtype as follows:

73.0 percent—fully volunteer

14.6 percent—mostly volunteer

5.3 percent—mostly career

7.1 percent—career[20]

In Canada there are approximately 7,000 fire/rescue departments of similar types and distribution.

Interestingly, although most fire and rescue departments remain volunteer, most of the U.S. population is protected by fully career departments. The 12 percent of all departments that are either fully or mostly career protect 62 percent of the population, whereas the 89 percent of all departments that are fully or mostly volunteer protect 38 percent of the population.[21]

According to the National Fire Academy, by the year 2000 it had become harder to distinguish between career and volunteer "because many volunteers now receive some form of remuneration, direct, indirect, or deferred, for their part-time service. Also, there are personnel who function only as 'call firefighters,' paid by the hour or per response for their part-time work."[22]

Promotion in volunteer departments   Volunteer departments may use one of several methods for promoting members to higher rank. Many volunteer departments have business or civil officers (president, vice president, secretary, treasurer, etc.) as well as firefighting officers (chief, assistant chiefs, captains, lieutenants, engineers, etc.). In most volunteer departments the civil officers are elected, although positions such as secretary may be appointive. Firefighting (or online) officers may also be elected (by fellow members at an annual election), but in some volunteer departments the volunteer chief has the power to appoint subordinate officers.

In some cases there are citizen-elected [or appointed] commissioners who may select the chief, or may reserve the right to approve whoever is elected chief by the volunteer members. Some volunteer departments set a limit on the number of consecutive years an individual may hold the chief's position. This is done to ensure that junior officers will remain motivated toward promotion and will be able to move up through the ranks within their own lifetime.[23]

Although in completely volunteer departments the promotion process typically involves election by members, the governing documents of a high percentage of these departments contain bylaw provisions that stipulate, for various ranks, such prerequisites as years of prior service, levels and types of training, certification in types and levels of specialties, depth of involvement in department functions, and so forth. In addition, some communities and some states push volunteer departments toward meritorious promotions rather than what used to be called popularity contests. With federal laws and some states imposing clear requirements for training in safety procedures, HAZMAT response, incident command, and other areas, the days of popularity votes for volunteer officers are in fact fast disappearing.

Volunteer firefighters suitable for promotion are often active in the community in many ways. Some, for example, have had to resign from the fire department to serve as local elected officials.[24]

Volunteer firefighters promoted to officer positions face a special challenge. The volunteer leader has been described as a "part-time officer with full-time responsibility."[25] Volunteer officers function most effectively when the reason for their appointment is their knowledge and merit, when they maintain a high level of dedication, and when they have written job descriptions.

Promotion in career departments   The promotion practices used in most career departments are outlined in the following passage from NFPA's *Fire Protection Handbook*®:

In the vast majority of fire departments, various officer ranks are filled by personnel serving in the next lower rank or ranks, although more fire departments are recognizing the potential benefits of allowing lateral entry, transfers, and promotions of well-qualified personnel from other areas and departments. Promotion procedures are designed to take into account technical qualifications for the particular rank and fire department experience. It is essential that examination procedures in the civil service be fully competitive and nondiscriminatory.[26]

In general, promotion procedures in career departments are administered by personnel departments or by state or local civil service authorities, who usually take the advice of people who have experience with and knowledge about the particular job classification. Such advisors include fire chiefs and technical consultants. Normally their advice includes guidance as to the relative weight that should be given to experience and to written examinations covering the technical qualifications of the position.

In some systems, experience and written examinations are supplemented by performance ratings, but these tend to introduce bias, even if such bias is quite unintentional. Some supervisors, for example, tend to be much more demanding than others when rating performance, and their subordinates often have lower performance grades than other employees who may actually be less qualified for promotion. For this reason, subjective performance ratings should be used sparingly in the promotion process. If performance has not been satisfactory, the matter should be dealt with before the promotion process gets under way.

Promotion in combination departments   In combination departments, the percentage of career personnel can vary considerably, and the several officer ranks, including that of chief, may be either career or volunteer. Thus, the procedures for promotion in combination departments vary widely. Generally, in departments with career officer ranks in both career and volunteer categories, promotions in each category follow the procedures as outlined in the two sections just above. However, in combination departments with paid skeleton crews (e.g., paid drivers only), there usually are no career officers. In combination departments that are predominantly career, there may be only one or two volunteers in the officer ranks, and they may be either elected by fellow volunteers or appointed by the paid chief.

Certification standards

Many U.S. states and Canadian provinces as well as many local governments use the NFPA professional qualification standards as the basis for certification of individuals. The standards are used to develop written and skill tests that,

---

Fire Protection Handbook® is a registered trademark of the National Fire Protection Association (NFPA), Quincy, MA 02269.

when used in a credible testing process, are highly effective in ensuring that individuals meet the job performance requirements for a given position and level.

All NFPA standards are consensus documents and are updated at least every five years to reflect changes in technology and in the fire service itself, particularly in the United States and Canada.

Many agencies affiliate with a national certification testing group, one of which is the International Fire Service Accreditation Congress. Another is the National Board on Fire Service Professional Qualifications.

This section discusses (1) NFPA Standard 1201 and its relationship to promotion, (2) NFPA Standard 1021 (fire officer professional qualifications), and (3) chief officer certification.

NFPA Standard 1201 and its relationship to promotion   NFPA 1201, Standard for Developing Fire Protection Services for the Public (2000 edition), addresses a number of personnel-related issues. Section 7-4.1, quoted below, is pertinent to the promotion process and stands as recognized good practice in the industry:

> **7-4.1** The fire department shall establish a documented job-related personnel evaluation program for internal and lateral entry promotion to the various ranks. The program shall be coordinated with the procedures of municipal or other personnel or civil service agencies having jurisdiction.

This standard refers its users to a number of other standards that have been developed specifically to assist in the training and promotion of fire service personnel. Known as the Professional Qualifications Standards (see Figure 5–4), the standards describe in detail the job performance requirements and requisite knowledge and skills to do specific fire service jobs at specific levels. (Fire departments should not overlook well-organized education programs available locally, regionally, and nationally. Some of these may include community colleges, universities, state fire academies, and the National Fire Academy.) The standards do not discriminate between career and volunteer personnel or jobs.

Figure 5–4 NFPA Professional Qualifications Standards.	NFPA 1001 Standard for Fire Fighter Professional Qualifications (1997 edition)
	NFPA 1002 Standard for Fire Apparatus Driver/Operator Professional Qualifications (1998 edition)
	NFPA 1003 Standard for Airport Fire Fighter Professional Qualifications (2000 edition)
	NFPA 1006 Standard for Rescue Technician Professional Qualifications (2000 edition)
	NFPA 1021 Standard for Fire Officer Professional Qualifications[a] (1997 edition)
	NFPA 1031 Standard for Professional Qualifications for Fire Inspector and Plan Examiner (1998 edition)
	NFPA 1033 Standard for Professional Qualifications for Fire Investigator (1998 edition)
	NFPA 1035 Standard for Professional Qualifications for Public Fire and Life Safety Educator[b] (2000 edition)
	NFPA 1041 Standard for Fire Service Instructor Professional Qualifications (2002 edition)
	NFPA 1051 Standard for Wildland Fire Fighter Professional Qualifications[c] (2002 edition)
	NFPA 1061 Standard for Professional Qualifications for Public Safety Telecommunicator[d] (2002 edition)
	NFPA 1071 Standard for Emergency Vehicle Technician Professional Qualifications (2000 edition)
	NFPA 1081 Standard for Industrial Fire Brigade Member Professional Qualifications (2001 edition)

[a]Contains the requirements for incident safety officer.
[b]Contains the requirements for public information officer and for juvenile fire setter interventionist.
[c]Contains the requirements for wildland/urban interface officer.
[d]Requirements apply to dispatch personnel who service fire service, law enforcement, and/or emergency medical service.

NFPA Standard 1021: Fire officer professional qualifications   NFPA 1021, Standard for Fire Officer Professional Qualifications, was first published in the mid-1970s and describes, in the terminology of job performance requirements, four different levels of fire officer qualification: first-line supervisor, midlevel supervisor, manager, and executive officer (Levels I through IV). These qualifications, or performance requirements, are common to most career and volunteer organizations. The standard acknowledges that not all departments require personnel certified at each level, but many of the performance items it discusses are required for an effective organization. The standard addresses both emergency response and routine performance requirements.

NFPA 1021 also addresses certain fire officer positions related to the four listed above, most notably that of incident safety officer. The job performance requirements for this and other specialized positions are designed to be used in a separate certification process.

Chief officer certification   In late 1998, the International Association of Fire Chiefs (IAFC) initiated a program to certify chief fire officers. This program is designed to provide a set of criteria that a candidate must meet in order to be certified. The criteria were initially developed in Canada and were then modified by an IAFC task force. The certification process is extensive and thoroughly professional. Some chief-officer recruiting efforts list this certification as a preferred or required qualification.

Promotion: Helpful tools

Figure 5–5 provides a partial list of the advantages and disadvantages of several common promotion tools. Three of these tools—assessment centers, written tests, and interviews—are discussed in the rest of this section.

Assessment centers   Some fire and rescue departments rely on assessment centers as a way to select candidates for promotion. Assessment centers, which are expensive, have been used for quite some time by industry. They use problem-solving, role-playing, and other exercises that require candidates to demonstrate certain abilities. Each candidate's performance is observed and scored by a trained assessment team. Some people believe the assessment center is the most realistic way to determine a candidate's suitability for a particular position. Assessment centers are most reliable when outside consultants work with inside officials to evaluate candidates objectively.

Written tests   Written tests that are used for promotion contain bona fide job-related questions that, ideally, can be validated by a test review board. Personnel specialists administer the testing process: they make sure that all candidates are treated equally; oversee the test's timing and environment; oversee the

Figure 5–5 Promotional tools compared.

Tool	Advantage	Disadvantage
Seniority	Easy to calculate	Disregards merit
Performance success	Based on work	Dependent on supervisor
Extra merit	Encourages brave acts	Unrelated to needs of the job
Credit for military service	Compensates	Discriminates
Written tests	Job-related questions	Unrealistic, discriminates
Interviews	Flexible approach	Can be discriminatory and unreliable
Evaluation process	Job related	May be biased
Assessment centers	Job related	Complex and costly
Recommendations	Past performance evaluated	Negative statements perhaps withheld because of fear

security of the test documents; correct the test; and place the scores in rank order, which becomes the promotional list. All candidates are notified of their test scores and their rankings on the list. The fire chief (or appointing authority) reviews the candidates who are highest on the list. Local personnel policy may allow the holders of a certain number of top-ranking positions (e.g., the top three to ten test scores) to be reviewed for appointment. Other jurisdictions give the appointing authority the "rule of the list"—that is, the opportunity to pick anyone on the list. In all cases a promotional list has a defined life span (e.g., one year), although the operating authority may have the option (depending on written personnel policy) of extending the life of the list by six to twelve months.

Local personnel policies can allow individual scores to be increased in recognition of military service, seniority, or meritorious action. The overriding purpose of the civil service system, however, is to encourage promotions based on merit. The old days of political appointment to administrative positions based on political favors or family relationships are essentially over.

Interviews   Often at some point in the promotion process an interview takes place. The interview may be brief and simple, with the applicant meeting only one interviewer, or it may be longer and more formal, with a selection team. All interviews should be carefully planned and conducted. They must be standardized and equitable.

The interview provides an opportunity for the organization to judge candidates' potential worth or value to the organization. A value-based hiring process requires that interviews be conducted under the close scrutiny of a personnel specialist so that any questions about hiring or promotional procedures can be answered. There should be more than one interviewer, and each should ask the same question or questions of each candidate to help ensure fairness and uniformity. Personal questions or inquiries about race, religious beliefs, or other topics irrelevant to the position should be avoided, but a few personal questions may be necessary. An interviewer could ask, for example, "Is your family prepared to relocate?"

Labor relations

Human resource management is often defined in terms of formal organizational processes, and the organization's employee policy manual often provides guidelines and standards for desired employee behavior. But management's desires must be constantly balanced with the rights of employees.

When career firefighters are unionized, their rights (which include wages, fringe benefits, living conditions, and a grievance procedure) can be formalized through collective bargaining between management and local union leaders and are usually spelled out in a written contract.

The union movement, with durable roots in U.S. history, received important protections under two New Deal laws: the Norris-LaGuardia Act of 1932 and the National Labor Relations Act of 1935. Then in 1947 the Taft-Hartley Act placed controls on unions, and in 1959 the Landrum-Griffin Act exacted accountability from union leadership. Those laws were enacted, and were interpreted in the courts, with a view toward economic stability and industrial harmony. By and large, these goals were met.

All the significant labor relations legislation that was enacted, modified, and updated from 1935 to 1959 had to do with the private sector. Public employees were excluded from consideration because they were thought to work in an environment insulated from the entrepreneurial attitudes and competition that had produced labor inequalities and unionism.

But whereas labor relations in private industry have become much more stable and less acrimonious, in the public sector employees have become more vocal and the labor relations climate more volatile. The official beginnings of the public sector labor movement have been traced to Executive Order 10988, issued in January 1962. With that order, "President John Kennedy extended the rights of union organization and a truncated system of collective bargaining to federal employees. This action exerted pressure at the state level and laws giving public employees the right of union organization and collective bargaining soon were enacted in major states."[27]

Even without the federal impetus, however, public employee unions and the corresponding organizational attitudes might very possibly have come to be as much in evidence as they are now. After all, the separation between private and public modes of employment that has persisted since the Industrial Revolution is disappearing, mainly for two reasons. First, fiscal pressures are forcing public organizations to operate more like competitive businesses. Second, the common denominator in employment, whether public or private, is the employee—a human being who has needs, desires, and aspirations that transcend the traditional barrier between private and public.

This section discusses labor relations in fire departments generally, collective bargaining, mutual gains bargaining, relations by objective, and committees and teams.

Labor relations in fire departments

The fire department is a special type of public service agency, and whether or not its employees are union members, good labor relations are possible for the fire administrator who is willing to research labor relations issues adequately and exercise professional understanding in dealing with employees.

In both unionized and nonunionized fire departments there is a contractual relationship between employer and employee; usually both employees and administrators find it beneficial to have some form of labor agreement committed to writing. Nonunion fire departments should have at least a basic set of written guidelines. The result of professionally conducted labor relations is a cooperative atmosphere and a working relationship that is productive for both management and employees.

When employees attempt to organize, it is unwise for fire department management to react defensively. It is far better for all concerned (especially the public) if management recognizes employee organizing as a social trend that must be dealt with in a professional manner. Studies of private employers' early aggressive actions against employees' attempts to organize show that these employer actions were negative, expensive, and futile. It is much better for management—in private industry and the fire service alike—to treat employees in such a way that the reason unions arise is to organize employees and not to oppose management.

The role of the IAFF As public employee unionism became more widespread, the firefighters' union—the International Association of Fire Fighters (IAFF)—grew in equal measure. As of 2001, it represented more than 80 percent of the career firefighters in the United States and Canada.

The IAFF offers assistance and guidance to its many local organizations, small and large, scattered throughout the United States, and it is often influential in resolving labor disputes at the local level.

Collective bargaining

The set of rules, procedures, and laws under which today's leaders must perform is subject to judicial scrutiny. Thus, management is necessarily becoming more legally astute in labor relations and collective bargaining. Managers who understand the collective bargaining process and who exercise good judgment as leaders are successful in developing effective labor agreements and productive workforces.

Although the term *collective bargaining* has become a household word, it also has a precise legal definition. Section 7(d) of the 1947 Taft-Hartley Act describes collective bargaining as follows:

For the purposes of this section, to bargain collectively is the performance of the mutual obligation of the employer and the representative of the employees to meet at reasonable times and confer in good faith with respect to wages, hours, and other terms and conditions of employment, or the negotiation of an agreement, or any question arising thereunder, and the execution of a written contract incorporating any agreement reached if requested by either party, but such obligation does not compel either party to agree to a proposal or require the making of a concession.[28]

A community that has established a working collective bargaining procedure with its firefighters can expect (and will need) numerous and sometimes lengthy negotiating sessions. Only the insignificant, inexpensive items can be handled in single sessions. Sufficient time must be allowed not only for the negotiating sessions themselves but also for each side to consider proposals and counterproposals and to conduct necessary research. And the union team may require time to confer with its general membership, while the management team will need to conduct its own consultations, including some with the elected and appointed officials who are involved in the labor negotiations. If, in addition, the negotiating teams are dealing with potential major changes that are already in the hands of long-standing committees, time for liaison will usually be necessary.

In the end, a written labor contract provides a blueprint for personnel operations—a blueprint that is as helpful to management as it is to labor.

When labor-management negotiations result in an impasse, four standard options have been used to overcome the impasse. They have been identified as mediation, arbitration, fact finding, and strike.[29]

Mediation   When the two parties to a labor negotiation are diametrically opposed on one or more issues or are unsuccessful in reaching agreement, a neutral third party can often play a vital role. This third party is the mediator, who is usually a member of the Federal Mediation and Conciliation Service or some similar state agency. The role of the mediator is to help the opposing parties find common ground and reach agreement on various issues. At this stage, however, nothing is binding on either party.

Arbitration   When management and union leaders remain unsuccessful in reaching agreement on some contract issue, grievance case, or disciplinary action, even after mediation attempts, they are said to be at an impasse. At this point the climate is ripe for arbitration, a process in which a neutral third party reaches a decision that is *final and binding;* the arbitrator actually dictates what the agreement will be. Arbitrators can be obtained through the American Arbitration Association.

Since arbitration is binding, compulsory arbitration is often considered an alternative to a strike. Since strikes in fire departments have particularly undesirable consequences, arbitration is common and is often mandated by state law.

Fact finding Fact finding is one method for resolving an impasse that has proved extremely helpful in the public sector. Fact finding uses arbitrators but lacks the binding quality of arbitration. It points the parties in a common direction and returns them to the bargaining table for further negotiations.

Strike Strikes are by no means an inevitable conclusion to a collective bargaining process, particularly if both sides adopt the professional approach advocated above. Yet strikes do occur, and it is well known that when they do, both management and the union suffer. When a fire department goes on strike, the public also suffers. Nobody can win. In most states, strikes by firefighters are prohibited by law. Fire departments are legally required, instead, to submit to binding arbitration.

Collective bargaining, along with labor-management relations and contract administration (administration of the contract between the union and the local government), has historically had a major effect on the human resource function in fire service organizations. In dealing with firefighter unions—in particular, the International Association Fire Fighters—management has been forced to be methodical, fair, and progressive in handling personnel issues. This effect will grow as departments become larger and as more departments unionize.

The collective bargaining process, however, is changing as new attitudes emerge and new management approaches to organized labor are devised. Some new approaches that are already being used are described below: mutual gains bargaining, relations by objective, and committees and teams.

Mutual gains bargaining

Although collective bargaining is often seen as a "zero-sum" process—that is, a process in which a gain for one side causes a loss for the other—a more recent approach aims at making it possible for both sides to achieve desired results. This "win-win" approach in collective bargaining is referred to as mutual gains bargaining. When both parties emerge from the collective bargaining negotiations with something gained, the community is the ultimate winner. The welfare of the community takes prominence in its own right as a focal point of the negotiations instead of being a proxy for each side's interests in an "us versus them" struggle.

Relations by objective: Action plans and teams

At the beginning of the twenty-first century, it is common for management and labor unions to be more collaborative than confrontational. They have adapted what for many years was one of the key techniques of sound management: management by objectives (MBO), a system in which supervisors and subordinates establish objectives jointly. In 1984, the Phoenix Fire Department (PFD) and Phoenix Firefighters Union Local #493 used the MBO concept in creating their labor-management cooperative program called Relations by Objective (RBO).

The goal of RBO is to establish a positive relationship between labor and management, one built on trust and mutual respect. The process brings labor and management together to work on shared objectives and to discuss areas of disagreement or conflict. The relationship is then used to create action plans designed to meet the needs of both internal customers (PFD members) and external customers (the public being served).

The major RBO goals and objectives for the coming year are developed at a labor-management meeting attended by participants from each side. The participants express the goals and objectives in the form of action plans. Each action plan includes, first, a statement identifying an achievable goal and, second, quarterly objectives that can be measured and reviewed throughout the year. The action plans are then assigned to one or more of the RBO teams.

The RBO process works because the leadership on both sides wants it to work.

The RBO process can be useful in the paid on-call or volunteer environment. Although the personnel who work in paid on-call or volunteer departments are not typically thought of as labor, they do indeed provide labor to perform the department's work and they generally have interests that need to be communicated. An RBO process provides the forum and methodology for high-quality, constructive input from all levels. Further, it offers a volunteer organization the same sense of "buy in" to management decisions that it offers a career department. As the pressures of a changing society affect the availability of volunteer firefighters, finding avenues for individual input in volunteer organizations becomes particularly important.

Committees and teams

Another example of a management-employee partnership—one that could be used by any size or type of fire department—is provided by the Mesa (Arizona) Fire Department (MFD). This kind of partnership makes enhanced use of teams to research issues and make decisions on external and internal delivery of services.

According to MFD chief Dennis Compton, using teams does not and should not eliminate conflict, nor is it an easier way of doing business and making decisions. To the contrary: using the group often takes longer, but almost always the process yields better decisions.

Mesa's enhanced team approach follows year 2001 management models that private sector organizations are using. But, according to Chief Compton, "It really doesn't matter what the groups are called; what matters is that they have the leadership and guidance necessary to be effective."[30]

A tool that the MFD finds useful for its purpose is the team profile (Figure 5–6). Each MFD standing team and project team must complete this one-page document, circulate it internally, and keep it current. As the end of the profile admonishes, in order to make the process as open and effective as possible, all the teams should use agendas and action plans and should post or distribute minutes of their meetings.

Chief Compton provides the following suggestions for any supervisor-employee participation program:

Management should never constitute a team to review and rubber-stamp an issue that they have already made the final decision on. . . . This is patronizing to the team members.

The team's recommendation may not be exactly what Management would have done, but it may be just as good (or better). There is more than one "right" way to go about something. Don't discard the work of the team over a few details that would probably work just as well anyway.

Be certain that the scope and parameters are defined as clearly as possible. If the team's work is going to be used in an "advisory" capacity that will be significantly refined by Management later, tell them so up-front.

Being members of teams encourages people to "participate" in decisions that relate to their work and/or issues on which the organization is seeking their input. It doesn't set anyone up as being in a position to dictate policy or work outside the scope of the team. If a team is getting away from their scope, or operating outside of the parameters that were established, the Sponsor and/or Chair(s) should redirect their efforts.[31]

In labor-management relations, the conversion from an authoritative or dictatorial management structure to a team effort is becoming easier because of changes in social attitudes. Most fire service leaders have been exposed to

The following profile must be completed, communicated, and kept current for all standing and project teams that are constituted in the Mesa Fire Department.

Name of team: _____

Scope of team's work: _____
_____
_____
_____
_____

Team sponsor: _____
                              Name   Division

Team facilitator or chair: _____
                              Name   Work assignment

Team recorder: _____
                              Name   Work assignment

Check one:
☐ Standing team
☐ Project team _____
                                       Duration of assignment

Frequency and location of team meetings: _____
_____

Team members:

_____   _____
_____   _____
_____   _____
_____   _____
_____   _____
_____   _____
_____   _____

Special instructions or predictable parameters for this team (if any): _____
_____
_____

All teams should utilize agendas and action plans and publish minutes in an effort to make these procedures as open and effective as possible.

Figure 5–6   Mesa (Arizona) Fire Department team profile.

participatory management concepts, and employees readily adapt to them. It is helpful if management ensures that employees understand and respect the culture of the industry they have chosen to enter and the culture of their specific organization within that industry. The fire service is rich in tradition, and most employees quickly come to feel an affinity with it. "Mature organizations have their own unique and distinctive culture. The key to effecting change is to recognize and understand that culture."[32]

Future challenges and conclusion

As the twenty-first century progresses, the fire service will be facing a number of challenges affecting its workforce, whether career or volunteer. These challenges will require innovation and adjustment in the human relations approaches of many fire and rescue departments.

For example, the growing diversity of the workforce will require policies that recognize and respect the diversity of employees' needs. The demographics of the fire service will mirror the demographics of society, and the changed demographics will be accompanied by changes in priorities and attitudes, mobility, and other elements that affect the workforce and performance.

In addition, the complexity of tasks assigned to the fire service will continue to increase. Technological change will affect what the built environment is constituted of, thereby increasing the intensity and complexity of the fire problem. Technological change will also require that personnel have the knowledge and skills necessary to operate complex machines and complicated systems.

Customers' expectations will continue to rise, and fire service personnel will have to be prepared to maintain attitudes and levels of productivity commensurate with the changing expectations of their customers.

The volunteer fire service will continue to be under incredible pressure to recruit and retain viable personnel (i.e., personnel who are healthy, energetic, available, compassionate, and committed). Changing social values, increased demands for productivity in regular employment, dual-income households, and increased mobility are just a few of the issues that will have an effect on established volunteer systems.

The fire service is not alone in recognizing the vital role played by people, for the term *human resources* is now widely accepted as a primary focus of attention in both public sector and private sector organizations. This term was introduced during the working careers of many people who were still on the job as the millennium began in 2001. Until the 1970s, the term generally used to describe the courses and literature purporting to guide management was *personnel management*. But because people are the most vital of the resources used by any organization, including the fire service, the broader term *human resources* gives this topic its proper billing.

Regardless of whether a fire and rescue department is career, combination, or volunteer, it relies heavily on personnel and the ability of human beings to deliver its range of vital services. This reliance has remained constant.

The management of human resources can be complex. Local elected officials and fire service leaders must manage personnel within limits defined by law, by national labor initiatives, by the civil service system, and by a complicated web of human motivations. Nevertheless, the concepts and guidelines presented above will help fire service leaders properly harness the boundless energy of their most complex but most valuable "human resources."

1   Robert Levering, *A Great Place to Work: What Makes Some Employers So Good (And Most So Bad)* (New York: Avon, 1988), 69.

2   Cynthia D. Fisher, Lyle F. Shoenfeldt, and James B. Shaw, *Human Resource Management* (Boston: Houghton Mifflin, 1996), 5.

3   Douglas P. Forsman, "Resource Management," in *Managing Fire Services,* ed. John A. Granito and Ronny J. Coleman, 2nd ed. (Washington, D.C.: International City Management Association, 1988), 177.

4   National Fire Academy, *Personnel Management for the Fire Service*, Course Guide (Emmitsburg, Md.: National Fire Academy, 2000), 1–7.

5   Wayne F. Cascio, *Managing Human Resources,* 5th ed. (Boston: Irwin McGraw-Hill, 1998), 134, citing "General Motors: Open All Night," *Business Week,* 1 June 1992, pp. 82, 83.

6   The steps presented here are based on and adapted from the National Fire Academy, *Personnel Management,* 4-4 to 4-5.

7   D. Seligman, "How 'Equal Opportunity' Turned into Employment Quotas," *Fortune* (March 1973): 160–168, as cited in Cascio, *Managing Human Resources,* 172–173.

8   Cincinnati Fire Division, internal document, synopsis of federal consent decree, 1973.

9   National Fire Academy, *Personnel Management,* 4-6.

10 Adapted from National Fire Academy, *Personnel Management,* 4-7.

11 Adapted from National Fire Academy, *Personnel Management,* 4-8.

12 Robert E. Osby, "Guidelines for Effective Fire Service Affirmative Action," *Fire Chief* 35 (September 1991): 54.

13 Adapted from the National Fire Academy, *Personnel Management,* 4-9.

14 Ibid., 4-10 to 4-13.

15 John Rukavina, "Recent Decision Leaves FLSA Situation Still at Sea," *Fire Chief* 43 (March 1999): 22–24.

16 Fisher et al., *Human Resource Management,* 534.

17 Dennis Compton, "Safety Leadership by the Company Officer," *Firehouse* (July 1998): 99.

18 William M. Kramer, "Training and Education," in *Fire Chief's Handbook,* ed. Joseph R. Bachtler and Thomas F. Brennan, 5th ed. (Saddle Brook, N.J.: Fire Engineering Books and Videos, 1995), 328.

19 Lydia Bjornlund, *Employee Performance: Appraisal and Management,* Training Package (Washington, D.C.: International City/County Management Association, 1997).

20 Michael J. Karter Jr., *U.S. Fire Department Profile through 2000* (Quincy, Mass.: National Fire Protection Association [NFPA], December 2001), 15. Copyright © 2001. NFPA, Quincy, MA 02269.

21 Ibid., 23.

22 National Fire Academy, *Personnel Management,* 4-3.

23 Ibid., 5-3 to 5-4.

24 Philip C. Stittleburg, "Double Duty Can Be Double Trouble for Volunteers," *Fire Chief* 43 (May 1999): 33–36.

25 This paragraph is based on William Beetschen, "Part-Time Officer, Full-Time Responsibility," *Fire Engineering* 152 (May 1999): 10–12.

26 William Peterson, "Fire Department Administration and Management," in *Fire Protection Handbook: NFPA Codes, Standards and Recommended Practices®,* ed. Arthur E. Cote and J. L. Linville, 17th ed. (Quincy, Mass.: NFPA, 1991), 9–44.

27 Ralph J. Flynn, *Public Work, Public Workers* (Washington, D.C.: The New Republic Book Company, 1975), xi, as cited by William M. Kramer and William V. Donaldson, "Labor Relations: No Arena for Amateurs," in *Managing Fire Services,* ed. John L. Bryan and Raymond C. Picard (New York: International City Management Association, 1979), 336.

28 Quoted in Kramer and Donaldson, "Labor Relations: No Arena for Amateurs," 342.

29 Ibid., 347–351.

30 Dennis Compton, "Labor Management Teams," Mesa (Arizona) Fire Department, 1995.

31 Ibid.

32 John Lee Cook Jr., "Change and the Lost Art of Followership," in *Fire Engineering* (September 1998).

6 Fiscal management

As other chapters in this book point out, the world of the fire service is changing. Building and fire codes, technology, and education have caused a massive decline in the number of working fires that require the mobilization of many human and physical resources. (Working fires are fires with the potential to progress rapidly and involve other components of a building or property.) Numerous incidents are now confronted in their early stages, when the level of resources that must be brought to bear is quite low. With the reduction in the number and size of incidents, even the busiest fire trucks are used on average only about 5 percent of the time. The fundamental question, therefore, is what is happening during the remaining 95 percent. It is the use of this time that provides the fire and rescue organization with an opportunity to engage the citizen in terms of enhanced and valued customer service and to carry out effective fiscal management.

What is fiscal management? Fiscal management is calibrating the use of resources with citizens' perceptions of need; it is managing the financial resources that have been attributed or allocated to the fire and rescue organization in such a way as to ensure that the organization can remain true to its vision, carry out its mission, and achieve its objectives in the context of organizational values. In other words, fiscal management is an approach to governance that insists on a positive link between the public service department and citizens —and between the department's planning and the planning done by the local government as a whole.

Most managers of fire departments are familiar with such accounting practices as financial record keeping and auditing. These processes, aimed at keeping records of revenues and expenditures, are in place as a matter of law in all city and county government systems. Fiscal management encompasses and extends well beyond these important processes of tracking an organization's financial resources. Fiscal management views financial resources as a critical input that is required if specific outcomes are to be achieved, but what fiscal management focuses on is the outcomes. It is certainly important to know how much of the taxpayer's dollar is spent on a given service, but from the perspective of fiscal management, it is even more important to determine what the citizen sees as important before then directing financial, human, and material resources at some given objective. In other words, an organization that is involved in fiscal management must shift its focus from inputs to the customers and to the services that will make customers' lives better.

To prevent fiscal management from becoming an unrewarding exercise that consists only of reporting after-the-fact financial realities and implications, the organization must ask such fundamental questions as these:

In what context—as customers or as citizens (the former have choices; the latter do not)—is the public receiving service?

Has a risk assessment been completed, and has the public been consulted about what level of service it requires in the context of community risk?

What does the citizen/customer want?

By what methods can the organization deliver service?

By what measures will the organization determine success in achieving objectives?

Can the organization afford the service?

What methods will the organization use to communicate with key stakeholders (the public, politicians, and city/county administrators)?

Sound fiscal management is therefore an integral part of a much larger planning, management, and performance framework; it participates in the higher strategic plan that is established jointly by public and political will and is implemented by the local government administration. Sound fiscal management cannot be separated from management of the whole local government. In other words, fiscal management is a means to effective governance rather than an end in itself. It must occur before, during, and after the organization's planning phases and must be integrated with all operational choices and decisions. Achieving effective fiscal management requires not only focusing on the methods and ideologies of effective governance as they apply to the local administrative and political context but also selecting and implementing the proven best practices of accountable government.

However, public fiscal management systems, including those for emergency response services, must cope with certain difficulties, some of which are the following:

Given the nature of the service, determining the level required is very hard to do.

That which constitutes value is infused with a high degree of public perception.

Performance measures with which to determine whether the type or method of service and its delivery are right for the community are rarely in place.

The political and cultural focus has been fixed on financial inputs (resources allocated in the budget process) rather than on outputs (services).

Traditionally, fire and rescue organizations were managed within a framework grounded mainly in operational goals and objectives and very little in goals having to do with fiscal management. Either voluntarily or through coercion, fire departments generally passed financial or fiscal matters off to higher civic management authorities and systems. But by the year 2000, citizens were expecting to receive value for their tax dollars; at the same time that they care about efficient services, they are also concerned with property tax levels. Thus, fiscal management and stewardship must be integral to all operations of the emergency response organization.

The fiscal management agenda must include

Developing strategies to strengthen the financial position of the organization

Developing and delivering financial information that is appropriate for decision making

Making visible the costs of delivering individual services and outcomes, thus illuminating the path toward cultural and structural change and enhancing accountability within the organization (for details on organizational cultures, see Chapter 8)

Integrating financial effects with operational decision making, organizational planning, and strategic direction

Managing financial risks and exposures.

This chapter discusses fiscal management first by describing its context—the management system of local government—and then by zeroing in on one part of that system: the business planning conducted by each local government department. Business planning directly connects the mission and goals of the department with those of the local government as a whole. Then the chapter focuses on the financial techniques and areas that support effective fiscal management: budgeting, full costing, monitoring and reporting, managing financial information, managing financial risks and exposures, managing assets, and identifying funding mechanisms and potential sources of revenue.

The management system of local government

Inasmuch as fiscal management must be viewed as a component of the broader framework of local government, one should understand what this broader framework may entail. Local governments spend a considerable amount of time, effort, and resources developing processes that operate as a management system linking three groups: elected officials, administrative staff, and the larger community. This management system of local government can be expressed diagrammatically, as shown in Figure 6–1.

The relationships among the three groups produce three primary products: political leadership (or vision), organization-wide strategy, and value for service. When the exchanges among the groups are working well, the quality of these products is high: the local legislative body exhibits strong leadership, senior administration provides sound strategic direction in the form of planning, and the services offered to the public provide good value. When the exchanges are not working well, these three products suffer.

Managing the system effectively is a matter of managing the processes that produce the three products. See, for example, Figure 6–2, which represents how one Canadian city—Winnipeg—manages its processes. In Winnipeg, those processes collectively constitute what is called the city's planning framework. The purpose of the framework is to ensure consistency in thought and action, extending from the broad community vision to the services delivered by staff on a daily basis.

For its management system to work, the city of Winnipeg has identified six processes that must be aligned (see sidebar on page 171). All the processes occur simultaneously rather than in lock-step order, and each process goes through many iterations before the elected body's approval is sought. The first of the processes, led by elected officials, is one of defining a community vision

Figure 6–1 Local government management system.

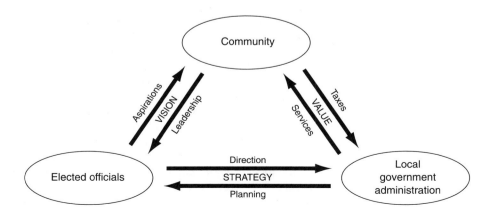

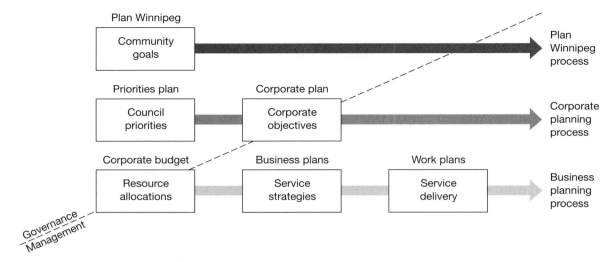

Note: The diagonal dotted line ascending from left to right indicates the separation of policy from management. In practice, however, the boundary between the two may sometimes be blurred.

Figure 6–2　Winnipeg's planning framework for processes and products.

and setting policy. (Many jurisdictions have their own local terms to designate where they are going, but *vision* and sometimes *policy* are usually synonymous with *goals*.) This process results in the local government's long-range strategic plan—a document called *Plan Winnipeg*.[1] An excellent example of a five-year strategic plan is the one for the Mesa (Arizona) Fire Department. Figure 6–3 presents those sections of the Mesa plan that are most relevant in the present context: the sections on the plan's purpose, development, and assumptions.

The second of the six processes in Winnipeg's management system involves setting political priorities that reflect the community vision and outlining goals that are intended to span the length of the legislative term. This second process results in the elected officials' priorities plan, which sets out specific financial and/or service goals and targets to be achieved by the administrative staff. Together the first two processes, which have produced the strategic plan and the priorities plan, provide direction to administrative staff and set in motion the third process, that of overall operational planning, whereby senior administrative staff determine organization-wide objectives. These objectives must be consistent with *Plan Winnipeg* (the strategic plan) and with the priorities plan. In the fourth process, the city's finance department allocates resources, supporting the organization-wide objectives of the third process. In this fourth process, individual departmental budgets are approved for expenditure. (Of course, final approval can come only from the elected officials.)

In conjunction with the resource allocation process, the departments undergo the fifth process in the city of Winnipeg's management system, a departmental business planning process, in which each department develops a plan for delivering its own services. (The business planning process is looked at in greater detail in the next section.) The departmental plans are guided by a financial strategy, which is developed through the political administrative process and which the local government administrative staff has provided to the department. Each department presents its own fiscal realities, which it then negotiates with financial administration. (Ultimately, the local legislative body and the financial administration must view the fiscal ramifications of each department's plan within the broader context of all departments in order to approve the overall city budget, which in Canada must then be approved by the provincial legislature.)

The sixth and final process—like the fifth, undergone by each department

---

City of Winnipeg's planning framework Winnipeg's planning framework, or management system, consists of six processes that produce the following documents:

1. Strategic plan (elected officials: community vision, broad policy)

2. Priorities plan (elected officials: specific financial and/or service goals and targets for administrative staff)

3. Financial strategy (senior administrative staff: overall operational planning and overall organization-wide objectives; all proposed departmental budgets are rolled up into one financial document that allows senior administrators to juggle demand, resources, and priorities)

4. Budget, or allocation of resources (city or county finance officials: examination of the expenditure and revenue categories of the single budget into which all individual departmental budgets have been rolled)

5. Departmental business plans (management of each department: planning for delivery of the department's services)

6. Departmental operational plans (managers of each department: responsibilities of individual staff members).

Figure 6–3 Sections from the Mesa (Arizona) Fire Department's five-year plan, 1998–2003.

Purpose of the plan

The plan is designed to be "reader friendly" and to guide the department through major issues.

The plan is not intended to address all departmental issues but to provide general guidance and direction to the organization.

The plan will serve as a communication tool to policy makers within the local government and to department members, in an effort to define the organizational vision and to chart progress.

Budget elements and proposals will be driven to a large extent by the plan and will be addressed during regular budget cycles. The plan will be updated regularly at approximately eighteen-month intervals.

Development of the plan

The plan is a result of input from all divisions and sections of the department derived from regular meetings with the fire chief. Input is provided by senior staff direction, local government administration, other departments, the business community, and the citizens of Mesa. Anonymous information is also accepted.

Captains, battalion chiefs, division chiefs, the fire chief, labor representatives, and support staff conduct the strategic planning process.

Updates also incorporate input from industry leaders and citizen groups.

The plan is presented, on a periodic basis, to the city council's fire committee.

Assumptions

The primary mission is protecting the lives and property of the citizens and customers of Mesa.

The major focus of effort is to provide quality customer service, externally within the community and internally within the organization.

The organization is committed to maintaining current staffing levels.

The city will continue to grow in terms of population, industry, and geographic area.

Financial resources will remain limited.

The population center will shift, and commercial development will continue to grow in order to support the growing population.

individually—results in completed operational plans for the delivery of services. These plans reflect the resources that the department has allocated to each service and the financial strategy the department has developed in connection with it. A department can have multiple operational plans, especially when it is multifaceted and engages in a wide variety of public services. Operational plans detail the responsibilities of individual staff members, thereby closing the circle that connects vision with action.

The rigor and tools that promote disciplined adherence to this planning framework are inherent in the term *fiscal management.*

Business planning

The fifth process described above is the departmental business planning process. The business plan is essentially an accountability agreement that sets current-year budget amounts and multiyear projections of financial and operational performance targets for the emergency services organization. The budgets and financial projections reflect the intended results and outcomes for the operation, in alignment with the overall direction of the local government. Business planning does not require a consultant, but a consultant may be hired to educate the department on how to complete proper business planning.

This section looks at business planning as a whole before discussing the business planning template and the procedure for doing a business plan.

Departmental business plans are based on the directions issued from the administrative staff under the overall strategic plan (which emerged from the first process); these directions are basically the jurisdiction's political and administrative priorities and, in most cases, must reflect the financial parameters established administratively (in the fourth process). Each department must develop its own business plan for service delivery based on a template provided by the chief administrative and financial officers; the template is called a business planning framework. The template includes financial guidelines, which help the department create a business plan that will be close to previously agreed-on priorities established in the political administrative arena. (The template is discussed below.)

Put another way, business planning is the action taken jointly by departments and the administrative body of the local government to balance inputs (taxes and revenues) with outputs (services and expenditures). After being given the template and financial guidelines, the department sets about writing its own plan while keeping the financial reality in mind; the department will then defend its plan to the financial officers of the local government administration, who, once sold on it, will have to sell it politically. Business planning is the direct link between the operational planning of departments (the sixth process) and the overall political agenda (the second process). In this context, therefore, the challenge of effective public fiscal management for emergency response organizations is to

Operate within an acceptable level of taxation by managing expenditures effectively and maximizing opportunities for nontax revenue

Effectively partner with operations branches of all local government departments to reduce duplication of effort, thereby reducing overall costs; such reductions ensure that both the financial effects of operational decisions and sound fiscal management become integral to all management decision making

Provide good value to taxpayers

Create capacity (i.e., generate a surplus of financial resources) in the fire and rescue organization to make possible strategic investment in people and technology; the investment would be geared to achieving the goals laid out in the business plan.

A working definition of business planning in fire and rescue organizations (in fact, in any public sector organization or agency) could be the following:

Business planning is the process of arriving at a document that outlines how the organization will achieve its objectives in conjunction with the fiscal constraints set by the budget process. The document outlines both the major tasks to be performed to a specified level of service (e.g., responding in a certain number of minutes in at least a certain percentage of calls, or having a certain number of firefighters on the scene within a certain number of minutes for at least a certain percentage of all reported working fires) and the associated costs.

In short, the value of business planning lies in both the process and the product. The process (1) engages managers and staff in a healthy dialogue, (2) stimulates creative and critical thinking, (3) focuses employees on the strategies and actions critical to success, and (4) ensures a link to political priorities and the goals of all the other departments within the local government structure.

The product (1) encourages communication between a public organization and its stakeholders (its customers and staff as well as the local government, elected officials, and citizens who receive services directly or indirectly); (2) enhances accountability; and (3) documents where the fire and rescue services organization is, where it is going, and how it will get there.

As mentioned above, a successful business plan ties the department's action plan at the operational level (the sixth process) with the local government above the department. A successful business plan ensures that programs and services will support the local government's strategies and goals.

Although the quality of the critical thinking behind the business plan is important to the plan's success, numbers and the financial implications of the decisions that go into the plan are paramount. Part of the process of completing a business plan is identifying and allocating the resources required for achieving stated objectives—the human and financial resources, the equipment, the information systems, the materials, and the technology.

Business plans also provide an outline of how a program's performance can be measured against stated objectives so that variances from targets can be identified and explained. Essentially, therefore, departmental business planning allows the political and administrative arms of local government to review actual results and compare them with intended results, rather than simply engage in after-the-fact monitoring of inputs. It is this outline of performance measures that makes a business plan an accountability document. (Performance measurement is the subject of Chapter 10.) The business plan also helps the decision makers focus on results and on what has been planned but not yet accomplished, rather than on what is being done now.

At least in concept, a business plan (or accountability document) allows a fire and rescue organization to achieve increased operational and financial autonomy: once a business plan is in place, the department should be allowed to pursue it without interference from either the administrative or the political body. Thus, the organization could shift to a more entrepreneurial culture by decentralizing decision making and giving managers greater control over the operations of a program or service through increased accountability for results. (On leadership and management, see Chapter 8.)

When the legislative body approves each department's business plan, it also approves the department's budget. Each department's budget is a component of the department's business plan. In other words, the legislative body will approve the goals and actions that are named in the business plan and that have a cost or revenue associated with them, and it will be prevented from arbitrarily reducing or increasing a department's budget without knowing the consequences of its decision in terms of impact on particular goals or policies. The business planning/budget process is an attempt to educate the main financial decision makers (local elected officials) about the tight bond between all departmental actions and costs, making it impossible for them to say, "We've reduced your budget by $1 million, but keep up the good work."

Consistency of format: Business planning template

Once each department has created its own business plan, city or county financial planners will roll up all the individual department plans into a single jurisdiction-wide financial plan that reflects the elected body's political priorities and will require political approval.

To create the broader fiscal and operational understanding required at the political and administrative levels, consistency of style across all the departmental plans is very important. A business planning template in which the requirements of the citywide strategic plan and priorities plan are met must be established. (Figure 6–4 presents a comprehensive table of contents for a typical business plan of a fire and rescue organization.) The template is basically a guide for all departments to use in creating their own business plans. Without consistency across all the plans, the elected decision makers would find it difficult to grasp the larger financial picture without having to rummage through several documents seeking the pertinent points of each. But if all plans are created in a consistent format, decision makers know that financial information is in section 5, for example, or that departmental goals are in section 2, and so forth. Consistency of format not only considerably speeds up the budget approval process but also, and most importantly, provides a readily accessible foundation for performance measurement.

Environmental scan, analysis of services, and customer profile

The department's business plan must make clear how departmental goals and objectives will intersect with the needs of the citizen/customer. In other words, the focus is on outputs of goods and services (meeting the needs of the citizen/customer) and not on inputs of resources; focusing on inputs tends to reinforce the status quo.

To begin, the organization conducts an environmental scan, which determines the context of the business plan—the internal and external context that is the department's working environment. The department has to understand as much as possible about this context. In the scan a department may find that it has customers it did not know about. The scan helps the department know its customers and determine its service in terms of those customers.

In addition, to ensure that operational output is not misdirected and that all facets of the organization are providing a service or product that meets the criteria set out in the local government's strategic and priorities plans, the organization must conduct an inventory (or audit) of itself and the services it provides. And it must draw up a profile of its customers.

The environmental scan Implementation of the strategies formulated within the business plan begins with the environmental scan, which as already mentioned is a method of determining the internal and external realities of the organization. The scan is grounded on one simple but fundamental question: what factors (i.e., what dependent and independent variables) shape the organization's present working environment? "Seat-of-the-pants" management may work for some fire officers, but generally too many factors are in play, creating a chaotic environment, for that kind of management to work. Goals can prob-

Figure 6–4 Table of contents, typical fire service business plan.

1.0 Executive summary

2.0 History, mission, and goals
Historical overview
Vision, mission, values
Goals (long term)
Objectives (short term)

3.0 Analysis of services
Service profile: Who are the customers, what are their needs, what is the value of the service to the customer, how satisfied are the customers with the service, what are the service objectives (stated in measurable terms)?
Environmental scan: Industry trends, similar organizations, comparable organizations in other regions/countries
Challenges and opportunities: Strengths, weaknesses, opportunities, and threats (SWOT) analysis
Strategies/action plans

4.0 Information technology

5.0 Human resource planning

6.0 Asset management

7.0 Finance

8.0 Performance measurement

9.0 Marketing and public information

10.0 Supporting appendixes
Organization chart
Performance framework
Detailed financial data
Other

ably not be achieved without knowledge of what makes the particular organization tick. Because the working environment of any organization is shaped by both internal and external forces, real and perceived, the department must understand these forces to the greatest extent possible if it is to provide an effective and fiscally prudent public service.

Analyzing the working environment requires one to look within and examine the organization's vision, mission, values, and competencies, seeking to identify *strengths* and *weaknesses.* One must also look to the external environment to identify *opportunities* and *threats.* Thus the name: SWOT analysis. (See the discussion of SWOT analyses in Chapter 2.) Fiscal management can then be seen as the ability to link the organization's internal strengths with its external opportunities so that the organization is positioned effectively in the context of its environment and in alignment with both the strategic plan and the priorities plan of the local government.

Calculating strengths and weaknesses is fairly straightforward. It requires a focus on the present to determine what the organization does well and what it does less well; making this determination requires consultation with employees, stakeholders, and citizens/customers. In contrast, calculating opportunities and threats is much more difficult because they are external to the organization, and much can be hidden. Opportunities can take several forms, some of which are mentioned below in the section on potential sources of revenue. Some threats may be very real and very powerful (e.g., downturns in the economy or labor unrest), but others may be more subtle (e.g., another large department may have better financial leverage, as when a police department bases its budget on perceived levels of crime). Surveys and polls can be effective but, to ensure some degree of accuracy, they have to be methodologically consistent with the requirements of good social research. For instance, the size of the sample must be appropriate.

In any case, an examination of external opportunities and threats will require significant innovative and critical thinking, which can be quite successful if it is done in a sequestered, off-location environment.

Strategy is created at the point where the results of the two appraisals, internal and external, intersect. Internal strengths can exploit external opportunities, while threats and risks are managed and weaknesses circumvented. Henry Mintzberg, a noted Canadian political scientist and theorist of organizational behavior, developed a model (illustrated in Figure 6–5) that depicts the point of strategy creation at the intersection of the external and internal appraisals.

When a department evaluates the choices available to it and makes decisions that ultimately lead to implementation, other elements must also be taken into account. For the fire and rescue organization, these will be politics and policy, administrative values, social responsibility, fiscal and budgetary constraints, organizational culture, quality of leadership, and timing/tempo.

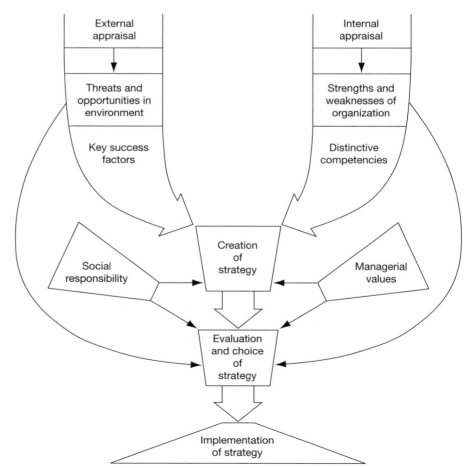

Figure 6–5   Model of a SWOT analysis.

That is essentially all there is to an environmental scan (or SWOT analysis), but the process of doing one does not come easily because it requires a department to examine its own fundamental tenets and assumptions. The process must be learned (essentially by case study) and practiced. Figure 6–6 provides a brief example of the internal and external parts of a SWOT analysis.

Analysis of services Inasmuch as services rendered by fire and rescue organizations are generally very direct and visible, they attract extensive public and media attention. Therefore, managers must be clear and explicit about the services they provide, the objectives undergirding services, and the standards or benchmarks by which performance will be measured. An analysis of services serves as the foundation of comprehensive performance measurement.

Typical emergency response service deliverables include fire suppression, emergency medical responses, and technical rescue. Other direct deliverables include fire prevention/inspection, code enforcement, and public education activities. All these deliverables fall generally into the category of public services —services a government provides that have a direct and tangible effect on, or benefit to, its citizens. Organizational units also provide internal or support services for the benefit of other organizational units.

Like private corporations, emergency response services become more diversified the larger they get. Mintzberg argues that as an organization becomes large, it saturates its traditional core competency and looks elsewhere for avenues of expansion: "It diversifies its product-market and then splits itself into units, each dedicated to a particular strategy."[2] The year 1997–1998 saw many Fortune 500 corporations fail because, in expanding into new markets, they found themselves out of their competency base; their strategies had been poor.

Internal		External	
Strengths	Weaknesses	Opportunities	Threats
Staff	Staff	State or provincial	State or provincial agencies
Dedicated, well-trained	Staffing shortages	agencies	Stagnant community growth
Paramedic III capability	Training resources	Alternative training ideas	Aging population
Volunteers	underutilized	Private partnerships/grants	(demographics)
	Staffing flexibility restricted	Collective agreement	Urban sprawl
Equipment/resources	Resistance to change	negotiations	Potential for further industrial
High-quality equipment	(preventing the	Supplier relations (access	development
EMS utility budget	achievement of critical	to purchasing power of	Loss of key personnel
(revenue account for	mass)	hospitals for medical	Assumptions held by any
receipt of fees from		products)	person, agency, or
patients transported to	Equipment/resources	Training partnerships/pre-	organization outside the
hospitals by	Aging equipment	entry	department
ambulance)	Constrained budgets	Alternative service	IAFF/NFPA/government-
Similarity of roles or	Aging technology	delivery models	mandated codes
outputs in some areas	Separate dispatch/	Public perceptions	
(medical director,	communication systems	NFPA	
protocols, stations)	Organizational	Legislation, codes, and	
Merging of responsibilities	communications	standards	
and infrastructure	Station locations		
Other	Other		
Business planning	EMS response times		
Response times	Highly political		
	environment		

Notes: EMS = emergency medical service; NFPA = National Fire Protection Association; IAFF = International Association of Fire Fighters.

Figure 6–6   Brief example of a SWOT analysis.

Core competencies are the meat and potatoes of any organization, public or private; they represent the value that an organization offers to the customer, and they provide strength and position in the marketplace. In the context of fire and rescue services, the core competencies are the skills and attributes that meet a real public need. They are the things the organization does best.

Emergency response providers must continually review the fundamental question of why they are providing x or y service. Can the service be provided better and more efficiently by a different supplier or through alternative processes (contracting out, partnering, charging user fees, establishing special operating agencies, etc.)? An organizational model premised on services may be a helpful tool for analyzing services under the local government umbrella, including fire and rescue services. For some ideas about such models (the word is used here to indicate a potential reality), see the section below on potential sources of revenue. The concept of alternative service delivery is key here: any model of service delivery in which the value of outcomes to the community (as opposed to the value of inputs to the department) is held dear should prove beneficial.

An emergency response organization that is focused on services (outcomes) as opposed to inputs (budgets based on requests for service) is better prepared to be proactive and is likely to have an increasingly positive effect on the community it serves. The organization can have this effect by (1) establishing a business planning process that takes into account all of the organization's internal and external stakeholders (see the discussion above of SWOT analyses); (2) integrating the financial imperatives into the political context; and (3) completing the process by establishing service-based budgets, which value the cost outcomes of a service, as opposed to line-item accounting, which considers only inputs. The business planning process used by the city of Winnipeg and discussed above accomplishes all of that. However, moving from inputs to outputs is not easy and requires the extensive education of, and commitment from, all employees.

Two cities that practice alternative service delivery are Indianapolis (Indiana) and Portland (Oregon). Others practice it as well, although they may not call it by that name.

Customer profile   To identify service deliverables properly, an organization must understand who its customers are. Services cannot be delivered effectively unless the types of customers that receive them are understood. Services and customers must be linked in some meaningful fashion. Too often, public organizations offer services that in fact can be delivered more effectively through other means. The service delivered must match exactly what the customer wants or demands. Understanding the customer profile is essential when a department is analyzing its services.

There are three types of customer sets: external, internal, and stakeholders. External customers include people from outside the organization who are customers for the services—generally, the entire population. The entire population can be divided into direct users of emergency response services and indirect users. Direct users are people who use and receive emergency response services (e.g., an emergency medical response). Indirect users are people who receive or benefit indirectly from the collective good and from the preventive nature of the service or who may be direct users in the future, for example, by receiving conflagration protection or being targeted by a public education effort.

For the fire service generally, internal customers are personnel of the department itself. This group of internal customers, however, also represents the larger local governmental structure in that it is composed of people who depend on others within other departments (such as administration and finance) to complete or add value to a product or service.

Stakeholders are those who have a role in developing or delivering services. For an emergency response service, stakeholders include state or provincial authorities having jurisdiction, such as the fire marshal's office, the office of the medical director, or various health authorities.

Budgeting

As mentioned, a budget is drawn up in conjunction with the business plan. Historically, emergency response services have generally not been subject to the same monetary constraints in the budget process as have other local government departments. However, in periods when debt loads increase, infrastructure decays, transfer payments from higher levels of government decrease, and the desire to lower property taxes makes itself heard, local governments become less willing to sacrifice other services to maintain emergency response services at existing levels. Fire and rescue departments then face the same scrutiny as other local government departments.

Developing a department budget in conjunction with the local government budget is perhaps the single most important and time-consuming administrative activity of a fire and rescue service. The budgetary amounts for the current year, and the financial projections for the next several years, are set within the business plan discussed above. The financial projections should accurately reflect the financial resources needed to accommodate the service strategies (including the strategies for managing human resources, information technology, and physical assets) proposed to achieve organizational goals. A sample form for displaying three-year financial projections is presented in Figure 6–7.

Figure 6–7　Sample form for three-year financial projections.

Department Name

THREE-YEAR FINANCIAL PROJECTIONS
for the years ending 2002 to 2006 (000's)

CURRENT OPERATING PROJECTIONS BY PROGRAM

	2002 Unaudited Actual	2003 Esti-mate	2004 Esti-mate	2005 Esti-mate	2006 Projec-tion
Revenues					
Program A	——	——	——	——	——
Program B	——	——	——	——	——
Program C	——	——	——	——	——
Expenditures					
Program A	——	——	——	——	——
Program B	——	——	——	——	——
Program C	——	——	——	——	——

Note: A listing of services may be more appropriate for those departments whose services relate to only one program.

Surplus/(Deficit)	——	——	——	——	——
Full-time equivalents	——	——	——	——	——

The objectives of public budgeting are

To formalize policy by allocating dollars among the priorities within the local government mandate

To present decision makers and the public with information that allows decision makers to decide how to allocate public dollars among competing priorities and that educates the public about public assets, programs, and services

To supply operational managers with specific information that enables them to monitor, assess, and respond to financial surprises or to the effects of inaccurate internal/external environmental predictions

To provide a mechanism for controlling expenditures and balancing them against the revenues collected by the local government.

A draft budget can be prepared from one of two possible starting points, and it can use one of two possible formats.

Starting points for preparing a draft budget

Whether for a small volunteer department or for a career department in a large city, preparing a departmental budget is often a difficult task requiring considerable amounts of time, effort, and human resources. The process generally begins in one of two ways. Either the local government administration establishes a fixed financial target or (as when a new department is established) the chief of the department determines the financial resources required to provide a level of service established through a political or administrative process.

Fixed financial target   At the turn of the millennium, with pressures on local governments to provide better services while lowering taxes, use of the fixed financial target is becoming widespread. Preparing a budget under this style of financial leadership can be very trying, but it can also be rewarding and informative: Often the constraint of a fixed target serves as a catalyst for new and innovative service delivery methods that enhance the quality and effectiveness of the service. The fixed financial target requires the chief to determine what can be provided within the limit set, and the department may be forced to do any or all of the following: reduce staffing levels, decrease levels and types of services, decrease response capability, and seek alternative methods of funding or of delivering services. As with every budget, the draft is submitted to local elected officials for approval.

Target set by the department   Increasingly less common is the department-initiated budget. Generally such a budget is prepared after a risk assessment has been performed to determine the level of risk to life and property in the community. Often the assessment is performed by consultants who specialize in the subject (even though smaller departments often cannot afford the expensive process of conducting a consultant-based risk assessment), for if a department conducted its own risk assessment and ended up advocating a higher level of funding for itself, the chief could be viewed as empire building. Moreover, only large departments may have risk reduction units (which focus on things like demographics, population and structural densities, trends, etc.—things that have a huge effect on how service is actually delivered). In a risk assessment and risk management process (see Chapter 2), the levels of human resources, physical assets, and so forth that respond to the identified risks are determined and costed, usually in a line-item budget format (see below). This budget, too, must be presented to local elected officials for approval.

Two budgetary formats for public sector organizations

The most common budgetary format for public sector organizations is the traditional line-item budget, which focuses on inputs (the objects of expenditure).[3] An alternative format is the service-based budget, which focuses on outputs (results, or services).

The line-item budget   The line-item budget lists items purchased, and the list is organized by department, division, or some smaller organizational unit. Dollars are appropriated for specific items, and failure to expend can be perceived as a lack of need for such monies. In addition, any unexpended amount for the current fiscal year is lost to the department, as is an equal amount in succeeding years. Thus, absolute expenditure of all appropriations is almost inevitable.

A line-item budget format has several advantages: adding up lists of items purchased is relatively simple, so the total budget is easy to derive; the level of operational detail enables departmental supervisors to monitor, revise, and control day-to-day operations and prepare and justify the next year's budget; and because the purchasing and payroll systems are linked directly to actual financial amounts within specific budgetary line items, budgetary control can be effected through the accounting control system.

A line-item budget format also has several disadvantages. First, although easy to balance, it does not lend itself to cutting expenditures because a cut in one line item may have ramifications throughout the budget. To understand why this is so, one has to realize that desired outcomes, which are reflected in the budget, are interrelated in terms of both human and physical resources, all of which are linked not to single actions but to a variety of outcomes. Thus, when budget reductions are arbitrary (i.e., when the financial authorities reduce the whole budget, leaving managers to fend for themselves), the consequences of the cut may be unforeseen; the budget itself will give no information on the operational implications of reductions. For if the financial authorities do not understand the complex nature of the fire and rescue service, they do not understand how cuts will affect the overall picture. But as discussed below, when the financial authorities make a cut in a service-based budget (as opposed to a line-item budget), they have an idea of what is being affected—that is, of which specific service levels will be reduced.

A second disadvantage of the line-item format is that the emphasis is on the objects of expenditure (inputs) rather than on the results (outputs, or services). A third disadvantage is that the level of detail tends to reduce operational flexibility: monies are appropriated for specific items, but if circumstances change significantly between the time the budget is prepared and the time it is implemented, moving monies between and among line items may require getting various approvals. Fourth, precisely because the budget is easy to control, there is a risk of overcontrolling and of stifling innovation.

Figure 6–8 is an example of a line-item budget.

The service-based budget   In contrast to the line-item budget with its focus on inputs, a service-based budget focuses on outputs—on the services provided by the local government. Service-based budgeting can be defined as the allocation of activity costs on the basis of service cost centers, which represent the smallest segments or areas of responsibility for which costs are accumulated. A service cost center should be defined in a manner that (1) facilitates decision making, (2) is consistent with legislation, and (3) aligns the cost center with a specific set of goals or objectives for serving a specified target group or customer population. Service cost centers must also be aligned with the overall organizational mandate and should not be limited by functional groupings within the organizational structure. Examples of service cost centers are listed

Figure 6–8 Example of a line-item budget.

THE CITY OF WINNIPEG
DETAIL ESTIMATES

15-Apr-1999

Page 3

Company: 01   Centre: 210301   Operations
Department: Fire Department
Division:
Group:

	1998		1999	Variance	2000	Custom Account Description
Adopted	Actual	Estimate	Amount	Projection	/ Explanation

552xxx   SERVICES

552101	Profes & Consult Services					
18,200	15,036	15,000	(3,200)	15,500	Normal requirement	
552201	Allocated Dept Costs					
	239	250	250	270	Nominal amount based on experience	
552302	Auto Allowance					
4,000	5,335	5,500	1,500	5,700	Normal requirement	
552401	Heat-Gas,Oil,Steam & Elec					
113,000	120,566	111,000	(2,000)	113,000	Normal requirement.	
552402	Light And Power					
145,000	158,841	154,000	9,000	155,000	Normal requirement.	
552403	Water					
30,000	35,990	33,000	3,000	33,000	Normal requirement.	
552404	Real Prop Con-Const& Mtce					
275,000	27,601	324,000	49,000	278,000	Normal requirement - $189,000 Fire station #26 exterior concrete repair - $40,000 Roof repairs at several halls - $20,000 Concrete repairs at several halls - $75,000	
552503	Cleaning And Laundry					
9,000	5,902	8,300	(700)	8,500	Normal requirement	
552505	Other Equipment Servicing					
15,000	15,025	22,000	7,000	23,000	Normal requirement	
552606	Drivers' Licenses					
10,647	13	0	(10,647)	0	No longer required per new collective agreement	

in Table 6–1, which shows how budgeting under a service-focused regime (rather than under a department/division categorization) might look.

For a description of each of the service lines in Table 6–1, see Figure 6–9. For an illustration of the difference between a traditional (line-item) budget profile and a service-based budget profile, see Figure 6–10.

The advantages of service-based budget systems are that they allow managers to

Concentrate on services and service levels instead of on dollar inputs and line-item objects

See their budgets not as a pure control function but as decision-making tools for policy makers and managers

Link results, and measure and assess performance, by service

Cumulate the costs of related services to the higher level of local govern-

Table 6–1 Service-based budget allocation, fire protection and public education division.

Allocation by service	Salaries and benefits ($)	Services ($)	Materials and supplies ($)	Asset purchases ($)	Total ($)
Public event support	15,803	1,574	0	0	17,377
Fire safety promotion	209,153	11,579	9,319	9,825	239,876
Injury awareness and prevention	43,462	805	0	0	44,267
Fire safety consultation	78,473	1,150	0	0	79,623
Fire prevention code enforcement	799,567	68,887	3,106	32,475	904,035
Fire code compliance—buildings	106,732	4,700	0	0	111,432
Fire code compliance—licensing	159,690	14,275	0	0	173,965
Fire code compliance—confirmation	17,315	75	0	0	17,390
Fire cause investigation	38,362	2,700	0	0	41,062
Fire permits	20,061	925	0	0	20,986
Total	1,488,618	106,670	12,425	42,300	1,650,013

Service	Offered to	Provides
Public event support	Special-event organizers	On-site risk assessment of fire and rescue requirements
Fire safety promotion	Fire safety students	Educational encounter to increase knowledge of fire safety
Injury awareness and prevention	Schoolchildren and adults	Presentations on injuries sustained as a result of accidents and on injury prevention
Fire safety consultation	Fire safety information seekers	Information relative to the seekers' fire safety concerns and questions
Fire prevention code enforcement	Building owners, building managers, and occupants	Assurance of compliance with the fire prevention bylaw (fire code) to prevent or reduce the impact of fire
Fire code compliance—buildings	Building occupants	Approval to occupy a building with the assurance that the building complies with the fire code
Fire code compliance—licensing	Business	Regulation and control, for the purpose of fire safety, of various trades operating from commercial or residential property
Fire code compliance—confirmation	Property buyers	Information (for a fee) on the fire code compliance of the properties
Fire cause investigation	Fire victims	Determination of cause of fire, and help to the state fire marshal when appropriate (for fires of suspicious origin, supports other agencies; for fires of known origin, makes the determination itself)
Fire permits	Fire safety applicants	Permit entitling the applicant to conduct a high-risk fire-related activity in a safe manner

Figure 6–9 Description of service lines listed in Table 6–1.

Figure 6–10 Allocation categories, traditional vs. service-based budget.

Traditional organizational-unit budget	Service-based budget
Firefighting operations	Emergency response—fire and rescue
Ambulance operations	Emergency response—medical
	Nonemergency response—fire and rescue
	Nonemergency response—patient transport
	Neonatal medical team transport
	Public event support—fire
	Public event support—ambulance

ment programs (i.e., view expenditures or services in relation to the whole organization).

The disadvantages of service-based budgets are, first, that *service* and *program* are often hard to define and, second, that in the application of a service-based budget, line-object detail—which is useful for day-to-day management decision making—is lacking.

Full costing

Budgets are ways of organizing costs, but costs can be defined in different ways. These ways are often referred to as *cost accounting techniques,* which accountants use to link various expenditures from various budgets (or types of budgets) to specific services. In essence, cost accounting techniques are a means of identifying the total cost of providing a particular service at a specific level and of making clear the interrelatedness of budgetary items.

One cost accounting technique is full costing, which includes both direct and indirect costs.[4] (Indirect costs include administrative support and overhead; overhead would include managerial salaries, employee benefits, financing, interest, and other related costs.) Only in the late 1990s did governments begin using full costing. The concept of full costing is consistent with the philosophy behind service-based budgets.

Initiating full costing for a specific level of service allows local governments to shift their focus from arbitrary cuts in expenditures, which result in cuts in services or programs, to reductions in cost, which result in the continued provision of services but at lower cost and therefore with less impact or quality. With full costing in place, elected officials can make informed financial decisions by relating expenditures to defined levels of service. Accordingly, if a budget cut is made, the officials will be aware of the reduced level of service that will result. Fully costed service-based information gives local elected officials a fuller picture of the services that the tax dollars are purchasing and allows them to make decisions to enhance, cut back, or shed services. Fully costed service-based information gives nonelected public servants a sense of clear direction and the freedom to exercise choice and expertise, and it gives elected officials true control over policy and level of service.

Full costing becomes particularly valuable in connection with issues around transfer pricing, user fees, and make/buy decisions. Although costing and pricing are distinct concepts, an understanding of full-cost information is very important to a pricing strategy, whether the pricing is internal or external.

Collecting full-cost information does, however, involve challenges. Direct costs related to a service may be easier to identify than fixed or ongoing costs. Utility costs for a fire station, for example, would have to be apportioned among the services delivered from the station, with some sort of allocation formula brought to bear. Possible formulas include taking a certain percentage of on-call volume, or using average length of call, or combining the two in some way. Allocations of salaries may also be a challenge. If staff is paid on an hourly basis, the payroll system may be able to allocate costs directly to the service, but if staff is paid on a biweekly basis, some allocation method is required. And some method of allocating downtime costs must be taken into consideration.

Full costing also requires a better understanding of cost attributes (i.e., type of cost: fixed, semifixed, and variable). The behavior of each type of cost must be considered, managed, and influenced over a period of time. For example, variable costs can be affected by decision makers in the short term, but fixed costs can be affected only over the longer term. What this means is that if a financial target of a 5 percent expenditure reduction is set but 75 percent of the departmental budget consists of fixed or semifixed costs, the 5 percent reduction is tantamount to reducing the remaining costs (the variable costs) by 20 percent. Education about these concepts and a better understanding of them at all levels of the organization would produce a better understanding of the cost effects of decisions.

Monitoring and reporting

For effective financial management to occur at all levels, monitoring must be conducted and various types of reports are required. Attest audits (see the sidebar below) of financial results in fire and rescue services are generally prepared annually, but a department that approaches its future with so distant a perspective on daily, weekly, and monthly events is assuming potential risks. One of the risks is the inability to monitor on a timely basis. Others are as follows:

Historical data become stale very quickly and may not accurately predict future events and occurrences.

Accounting relies heavily on estimation techniques, so the general ledger balances tend to be somewhat arbitrary.

Financial statements may suggest emerging problems, but they rarely reveal causes or solutions. To discover why business problems have occurred and what can be done to solve them, managers must look behind the financial statements.

Annual reports should therefore be supplemented by periodic reports, and both types should be accompanied by variance analysis (discussed below).

Periodic reporting

To make informed decisions about the organization's fiscal situation, management needs financial information more often than annually. Periodic reporting generally presents data for a month, a quarter, or the year to date, and the information it provides to operations management (at the fire and rescue services level) and to other local government stakeholders allows decisions affecting operations to be made before the fiscal year ends.

Definitions of accounting terms used in this chapter

Attest audits A controller or auditor attests to the validity of the revenue and expenditure figures or—in most fire departments—of the cost figures.

Estimation techniques Accounting must often rely heavily on estimation. Common methods of estimating when specific costs are unknown are to start with the previous year's budget and add increases in cost of living and potential increases in personnel, equip-ment, or apparatus. Accordingly, educated guesses are not unusual.

General ledger balances General ledger balances are reports established at needed time frames or on an ongoing basis to demonstrate the present, or actual, financial situation at a given time. These balances help indicate to managers whether they are on target—that is, whether their estimations are accurate to some degree (thus, whether they will have to modify their financial forecasts to any extent).

Periodic reporting might include

Some comparison of actual revenues and expenditures with budgeted revenues and expenditures

A link to performance targets

Projection of revenues and expenditures to the end of the fiscal year (and beyond)

Comparisons with spending in the previous fiscal year and with expected spending

An accompanying narrative (this is essential) explaining the trends and assumptions built into projections, and highlighting and explaining major variances

Graphic presentations, which are often easier to understand than financial statements and schedules.

Those components of interim reporting enable management to

Monitor the organization's financial position

Evaluate effectiveness, inasmuch as performance can be measured more effectively

Gain insight into anticipated financial activities (quite often projections are produced on a "best," "most likely," and "worst case" basis, allowing management to assess the financial risks to the organization; and from the point of view of local government as a whole, projections make it possible to choose between taking measures to avoid an overall deficit and applying for special appropriations, or transfers, between services and programs)

See how well the organization is doing

Evaluate incipient problems and take preventive action.

More generally, periodic reporting makes possible

Enhanced knowledge of spending patterns, historical trends, and general business operations

Ongoing knowledge of and confidence in the budget and budgeting process

Enhanced planning and thinking about their budgets by operational personnel (this helps the fire chief understand his or her accountability for management of the budget)

Increased accuracy and reliability of future forecasts

Ability to take proactive measures

Management of costing issues.

For a periodic report to be useful, it should have the characteristics of timeliness, relevance, understandability, and reliability:[5]

Timeliness The reports must be available on a timely basis so that operational personnel can take corrective actions if necessary. A good guideline is that information should be available at least as soon as it would have been if it had been gathered informally.

Relevance to user The reports must be tailored to meet the needs of the personnel using them—must highlight the data and information necessary for making specific operating decisions or monitoring key performance factors.

Understandability   The reports should be easily understood—should be formulated and formatted so that the relevant information can be readily extracted and grasped.

Reliability   Reliability is essential. Decisions will be based on this information, so it must be accurate and complete.

Figure 6–11 is an example of a periodic report.

Annual reporting

Annual financial reporting plays a major role in fulfilling the fire service's duty to be accountable to citizens, local elected officials, state or provincial regulators, investors or creditors such as bond-rating agencies, and analysts (see the sidebar on users of annual reports). Annual reporting is the source of the information that is used to justify collecting public resources and applying them to, or expending them for, particular purposes.

In annual reporting, all expenditures made in a year are summed up and assigned within an approved framework of accounts and categories. This report of annual totals is used primarily for comparing actual financial results with the legally adopted budget. The information is also used for assessing the department's financial condition and the effects of its operations. In other words, the annual totals should help users of the financial information evaluate the efficiency and effectiveness of operating results and should make the fire and rescue organization publicly accountable.

In particular, annual reports must provide information that is useful for those who want or need to do the following:[6]

WINNIPEG EMERGENCY RESPONSE SERVICE
FIRE SERVICE COMPONENT
STATEMENT OF OPERATIONS
Projected for the year ending December 31, 1999
as at June 30, 1999

	1999 Budget	1999 Actual	%	1998 Actual	%	1998 Budget
REVENUE						
User Fees						
Plan Review Fees	20,000	20,011	100%	19,210	98%	19,540
Fire Protection Services	112,000	94,576	84%	58,302	115%	50,774
Central File Property Searches	27,500	25,355	92%	25,950	92%	28,125
Government Grants	0	80,000	0%	0	0%	0
Transfer from Waterworks Fund	3,248,350	3,248,350	100%	3,345,507	93%	3,608,000
Other Revenue	0	55,976	0%	16,482	0%	0
Total Revenue	3,407,850	3,524,268	103%	3,465,451	93%	3,706,439
EXPENDITURES						
Operations						
Fire Fighting	54,635,074	54,721,581	100%	46,394,425	103%	44,991,112
Training Academy	972,087	969,646	100%	720,096	65%	1,103,498
Communications	1,488,573	1,493,314	100%	1,319,067	94%	1,408,025
Administration and Support						
Administration (Including Employee Benefits)	2,772,960	2,822,414	102%	9,099,566	103%	8,840,090
Fire Prevention	2,140,167	1,894,952	89%	1,270,115	61%	2,077,451
Emergency Mechanical Services	3,731,694	3,691,109	99%	3,058,252	99%	3,074,320
Special Programs	0	0	0%	0	0%	0
Debt and Finance Charges	3,177,354	3,177,354	100%	1,338,655	100%	1,338,655
Hydrant Rental	3,248,350	3,248,350	100%	3,608,000	100%	3,608,000
Total Expenditures	72,166,259	72,018,720	100%	66,808,176	101%	66,441,151
Deficit funded by appropriation from General Revenue Fund	-68,758,409	-68,494,452		-63,342,725		-62,734,712

Figure 6–11   Example of a periodic report.

Users of annual reports

The public, which provides a significant portion of the revenues and resources necessary for local government operations.

Elected officials, who are authorized to administer public financial affairs and resources and are accountable for their administration.

Regulators, who have regulatory authority over local government operations and financial affairs.

Investors, who provide financial resources to the local government.

Analysts, who provide information to the public and to special interest groups.

Know what the local government owes and owns

Assess the local government's long-term financial sustainability

Manage the department's assets and liabilities (or potential for risks)

Determine the affordability of programs and services

Compare spending in the current period with spending in previous periods, and compare current spending with the approved budget

Report performance, and benchmark (i.e., compare one's own department's processes or activities with those of another department whose processes or activities are considered to be a benchmark, or industry standard; benchmarking is discussed in detail in Chapter 10)

Demonstrate stewardship and accountability.

Ultimately, departmental annual reports will be integrated into the overall local government financial report. Also ultimately, local elected officials, administrative staff, and the general public will make financial decisions, such as those related to amalgamation of departments, downsizing, or the alternative delivery of services. Before they do, however, they will have to have financial information that is complete, accurate, and consistent and is received as such by all interested parties and jurisdictions.

Variance analysis

Variance analysis compares actual expenditures with budgeted expenditures, displays the difference in both dollar and percentage terms, and highlights and explains any differences that are significant. The explanations should be coordinated by the financial manager of the emergency fire and rescue organization but should be prepared by the operational personnel who are responsible for the areas of variation. These explanations constitute a key tool in the accountability process and are a valuable source of information about extraordinary events in the department.

There are cost variances and revenue variances, both of which are self-explanatory; volume variances, which may refer to an increase or decrease in the number of fires responded to or the number of fire inspections accomplished; and activity variances, which refer to an increase or shrinkage in activities such as community participation programs. These activities may not reflect a cost to the department per se but may come under the heading of a "public good"; for example, faster response times or an increased number of inspections may not cost a department anything but are certainly a "good" received by the public.

Managing financial information

Financial information is essentially an organizational resource to be safeguarded and managed like physical assets. Paramount in the management of information is the system in which the information is stored, manipulated, and accessed. (For a detailed discussion of fire service management information systems in general, see Chapter 14.)

An effective financial information system does the following:

Puts system tools directly into the hands of users

Trains the system's users

Meets users' needs

Presents information in new, accessible, and innovative ways

Ensures ongoing technical support

Converts new technologies into streamlined processes

Captures information usually only once, and as close to the source as possible

Focuses on service

Incorporates management information such as performance measures and statistical and costing data

Can be integrated with other applications.

Once a financial information system has been set up, it makes possible the safeguarding of departmental assets and the accurate reporting of financial results.

Financial information must meet the highest standards of integrity and accuracy, and controls should be in place to monitor the quality and collection of the information. Ensuring consistency is also important: in the recording, maintaining, and reporting of financial information, the underlying accounting must be consistent from transaction to transaction and from year to year, and any change in reporting principles should be disclosed. Finally, establishing usefulness is critical: when decisions are made about what information to report, two notions must be kept in mind—relevance and reasonableness.

Relevance has to do with whether the information is required by users. For example, when the user is an operating manager who is choosing between two courses of action, relevant information is information about the future financial implications of each of the two choices. The two choices would presumably affect financial resources differently, and the differences must be made clear. If there are no differences, that needs to be stated as well. (Financial information is not the only information a decision maker should consider. Financial factors should be supplemented by those usually referred to as qualitative— e.g., safety considerations.)

Reasonableness has to do with the value of collecting a specific type of financial information. A trade-off should be explored or a cost-benefit analysis made to determine whether the cost of monitoring, collecting, reporting, and analyzing certain information is justified. There are limits to what should be reported, and it is management's responsibility to weigh the value of financial information.

Financial risk management

The preceding section was about managing financial information—that is, managing the flow of normal financial information and controls. Although financial risk management is a component of financial information, it is treated separately here because risks of all sort (e.g., economic downturns, disasters, and unintended consequences of financial or operational decisions) must be considered and planned for.

Financial risk management is the process of making and implementing—at a reasonable cost—decisions to (1) minimize the negative effects that accidental losses may have on the organization, (2) protect the organization's assets, and (3) ensure the organization's ability to meet objectives. In essence, financial risk management is the process of assessing and controlling the risks (in terms of financial exposure) that are inherent in any operation. There are clear costs and benefits to be considered: increasing the department's control is often an expensive proposition, but relaxing control, although less expensive in the short term, may hold longer-term risks. The goal is to have the right balance between control and risk—to have effective control and an acceptable level of risk. Effective risk management provides reasonable assurance that the organization will achieve its objectives and that the level of residual risk of the organization's failing to meet its objectives is known and acceptable.

Fire and rescue organizations normally have one top priority, and that is safety: the safety of operational personnel performing their duties (for if these personnel are not safe, no one is); the safety (preservation) of departmental assets, which, like personnel, are exposed to serious risk; and the safety of the public (i.e., keeping the public safe from injury, loss of life, and loss of property). When the attention of a fire and rescue service is not on safety, the organization is exposed to risk. Moreover, the focus on safety must not be directed only at the front lines. Massive exposure can lie in many directions, both internal and external. Internally, risk relates to the elements of an organization that, when taken together, support people in their efforts to achieve the organization's objectives—elements such as the organization's resources, systems, processes, culture, structures, and tasks. Externally, managers must always bear in mind the power and perceptions of the local elected and appointed officials, who are influenced not only by budgets (debt and deficit) but also by interest or pressure groups, the media, and the general public. The perceptions of the local elected and appointed officials are often no more than assumptions, but if acted on, those assumptions have the potential for seriously jeopardizing a department's ability to function. Thus, chief officers have a dual task: they must attempt as much as possible to educate the powers that be about the effects of their decisions while simultaneously ensuring that their own iterations are not viewed as self-serving or empire building. In short, there is great risk in having financial decisions controlled by parties who are uneducated about the fire and rescue service.

Traditionally, the fire service has approached risk management by reducing its exposure to tort litigation and loss of financial resources. (For a discussion of fire service liability, see Chapter 13.) However, competent fiscal management also considers other areas of potential loss that can have significant, even disastrous, consequences, such as loss of physical and human resources through accident or deterioration; loss of mandate or program, which can threaten the organization's ability to realize its goals and objectives; loss of customer satisfaction and support, or what is known in the private sector as market share; loss of suppliers; reduction of budget; increased supplier costs; loss of public support as a result of actions, inaction, or unintended consequences that may flow from financial decision-making processes; and failure to realize or take advantage of opportunities. These are only examples. In fact, the areas of possible risk may be beyond anyone's capacity to enumerate.

How then can a fire and rescue organization establish a balance between control and risk and approach the analysis of negative outcomes sensibly, especially when the scope of potential risk is so vast that there is no such thing as either perfect or free control? The first step is to obtain knowledge of the working environment with a comprehensive SWOT analysis, determining internal strengths and weaknesses and external opportunities and threats (the same SWOT analysis that is conducted in connection with business planning). To establish the location and magnitude of risk associated with the working environment, one needs a comprehensive risk assessment study (usually from a consultant, for reasons discussed above in the section on budgeting). The risk assessment identifies key areas of hazard, and controls are designed to manage whatever risks are deemed unacceptable. To design, implement, and/or improve risk controls, managers must

Identify the risk (what?)

Pinpoint its source (where?)

Measure it (how much?)

Monitor and evaluate it.

Here, too, consultants may be helpful, but to provide true guidance they must have had significant experience in the field. A theoretical one-size-fits-all approach, though providing insight, will not satisfy the local need.

Managers also have to shift their own orientation in several respects. First, they need to shift from risk aversion to risk management. Risks are independent variables and can present themselves in a variety of ways. Simply avoiding risk does not allow managers to understand fully the nature of the working environment. Exposure to risks can ultimately have devastating consequences: It can culminate in considerable destruction of human and physical resources, completely nullifying any financial planning and budgeting effects. So it is better to know where risk is located and manage it than to be managed by it at some later date.

Second, managers need to shift their focus from the mechanisms of control to the goal of control. Most organizations are driven by the mechanisms—policies and processes that have been designed to control losses and increase resilience (see the discussion below of "hard" controls). However, if one focuses not on the mechanisms but on the goal, one can establish an organization-wide ethos of recognizing that risk exposure exists beyond the reach of policy. Instead of emphasizing the process, one manages risk on all fronts by managing the organization's general practices (see the discussion below of "soft" controls). On the whole, this shift from the mechanisms to the goal requires putting less emphasis on formal policy and more on strong leadership. Chiefs need to be strong enough to be willing to take chances, supported by those who empowered them in the first place (if administrators micromanage the fire chief, they might just as well fire him or her).

Third, managers need to balance risk taking (innovation and empowerment) with stewardship (governance and accountability).

The fourth way in which managers need to shift orientation is by understanding that risk represents both threats and opportunities. It is obvious that risk to organizational well-being constitutes a threat, but viewing risk solely in negative terms is to miss an opportunity that could affect an organization in positive ways. Missing an opportunity for positive action can also represent significant risk.

The remainder of this section discusses risk financing and risk control and then describes four models for analyzing and assessing risk.

Risk financing and risk control

Risk financing speaks to the concept of providing some sort of measure or insurance against negative financial effects on the organization. Such measures can take the form of reserve funds (many local governments have substantial financial reserves or expense budgets through which they can basically self-insure, i.e., retain risk internally); self- or third-party insurance (risk can be transferred to external life and property insurance companies or to hold-harmless agreements and waivers); transfer grants or relief from other levels of government; or well-designed training programs to prevent loss. Alternatively, one can do nothing at all (ignoring the presence of risk and hoping it will go away). Financing risk involves paying for losses that may or may not occur (in effect, paying to prevent risks from materializing: again, the steps taken to reduce risks entail some expense).

Risk controls are actions set in place which, once loss begins to occur, help to identify problem areas and prevent further damage to the organization. Total risk control is virtually impossible: as mentioned above, the nature of the services provided by the fire and rescue organization means that the number of active variables is infinite. Therefore, engaging in risk/loss prevention is more appropriate than trying to achieve total control.

Traditionally fire and rescue services have organized risk management, or risk control, by using fairly rigid processes, which are referred to as hard controls. Because hard controls consist of various rules, regulations, and policies, they are relatively easy to quantify and can provide an instant yardstick for measuring performance. A substantial degree of risk management can also be achieved with the application of soft, or informal, controls, but the difficulty of quantifying any tangible evidence that could relate directly to performance measures makes these types of controls hard to implement; in addition, implementation is often blocked by an organization's culture and values. For a list of hard and soft controls, see Figure 6–12.

Analyzing risk: Four risk management models

Decisions to reject or accept risk (i.e., to control it or choose not to control it) must be conscious. A risk that is taken unconsciously or inadvertently (or that cannot be measured) cannot be managed. Most significant risks can be analyzed in conjunction with one or more appropriate models. Both visually and conceptually, models help clarify risk and therefore can help educate people about potential exposures and areas of vulnerability; models can also identify options for controlling risk. Although knowledge is often gained from "lessons learned," the only way such knowledge will lead to better risk preparedness is if an enabling process is in place.

There are a number of risk management frameworks, or models, that represent systematic methods not only of identifying risks associated with the achievement of objectives but also of analyzing, assessing, treating, and monitoring risks and communicating information about them to the organization. Discussed here are four such models that indicate how a risk management process could work: the Planning-for-Risk Paradigm, the Control and Risk Self-

Figure 6–12 Hard and soft controls in managing risk.

Hard (or traditional) controls	Soft (or informal) controls
Regulations	Ethical values
Policies	Leadership
Procedures	Competence
Standards	Reward systems (not specifically wages)
Communication	Teamwork
Direct supervision	Vision
Duty segregation (i.e., appropriate staff assignment)	Mission
Physical security	
Clear objectives	
Performance measures	

Assessment (CRSA), the Community of Sponsoring Organizations (COSO) model, and the Liability Self-Assessment Checklist.

Organizations must view risk in terms of their own working environments and must choose models that fit. Organizations are beginning to realize that true understanding can come only from adopting multiple perspectives, making use of several tools, and using more than one model. Although every model mentioned here provides valuable insight, none stands alone. For a model that helps an organization make predictions, achieve effective balance and accountability, and ensure public confidence—in short, for one that fits the working environment—the organization may have to combine parts of several models, creating a hybrid to achieve a tailor-made organizational fit.

Planning-for-Risk Paradigm   Figure 6–13 depicts the cycle or process of planning for risk. The primary focus is on outcomes that are customer based. Meeting customers' needs and wants in a manner they find acceptable can considerably reduce risk.

The figure portrays two linkages, one between the results of environmental scanning (SWOT) and risk analysis, the other between strategic planning—achieving outcomes that can be measured—and the customer as citizen. Risk analysis can predict *likely* outcomes, but for the *desired* outcomes to be achieved, administrative and political policy decisions are needed. To identify the extent to which desired outcomes become *actual* outcomes, performance measures are necessary. The results of the exercise in performance measurement provide further understanding of the environment. Each critical area of the process is supported by the needs of citizens/customers. Thus, the focus is on needs-based outcomes.

Control and Risk Self-Assessment (CRSA)   At the beginning of the new millennium, organizations are facing continual change. To cope with the rapid pace of change, many of them have adopted the CRSA model as one of numerous tools for achieving effective risk control. CRSA uses teams of em-

Figure 6–13 Planning-for-Risk Paradigm.

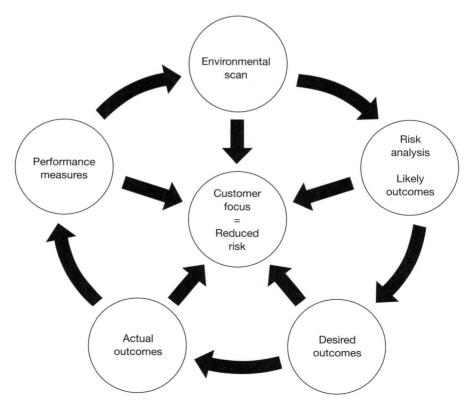

ployees working with their managers and a facilitator to identify the risks and controls that help or hurt their ability to achieve their organization's objectives. In addition, the teams develop an action plan to optimize control and achieve an acceptable level of risk.

A tool such as CRSA is useful because it allows managers and staff to

Better understand their shared responsibility and accountability for control

Directly analyze risks and controls related to achieving their objectives

Know what they have to do to improve control

Take action

Provide elected officials with the information they need in order to carry out their governmental responsibilities

Gain more assurance in general, and at less cost

Develop a common language about, and skill in, assessing risk and designing controls.

Community of Sponsoring Organizations (COSO) model   The COSO model depicted in Figure 6–14 was developed by major accounting and auditing professional organizations in both Canada and the United States. The five major components of the model—of the organization—are the environment, risk assessment, activities, information and communication, and monitoring. As the figure shows, activities are associated more with monitoring and information and communication, whereas risk assessment is associated more with the environment.

1. *Environment*   Because people are the core of any organization, their interaction with the environment in which they operate depends greatly on their individual attributes, including their integrity, ethical values, and competence.
2. *Risk assessment*   The organization must be aware of and must deal with the risks it faces. It must set risk management objectives that are integrated with all its functions and with its overall strategy. It must also establish mechanisms to identify, analyze, and manage risks.
3. *Activities*   To ensure that employees effectively undertake and complete the activities prescribed by management to address the risks that might prevent the organization from achieving its objectives, management must establish control policies and procedures.
4. *Information and communication*   Information and communication systems must be provided to enable the entire organization to capture and exchange the information it needs for conducting, managing, and controlling its operations.

Figure 6–14
The COSO model.

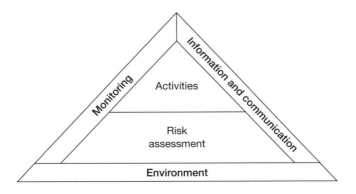

5. *Monitoring*   Monitoring provides feedback. For the organization to be able to react appropriately to change, organizational processes must be monitored by means of various performance measurement tools.

The Liability Self-Assessment Checklist   All individuals and organizations are exposed to potential legal liability (this subject is covered in detail in Chapter 13). Liability claims for failure to provide a "duty of care," or a "standard of care," can bring an organization to complete fiscal collapse. Traditionally, fire and rescue services have focused primarily on avoiding liability. To minimize exposure to litigation, fire and rescue service providers should fill out the Liability Self-Assessment Checklist (see Figure 6–15). Developed for Canadian

Figure 6–15 Liability Self-Assessment Checklist.

☐ Does your department have copies of all legislation, regulations, bylaws, codes, and standards that are relevant to your department's operations?

☐ Has your municipality passed a fire bylaw? If so, was it tailor-made to suit the particular needs of your department? Does it accurately reflect both the duties imposed on your members by provincial or state legislation and the discretionary powers actually exercised by your department?

☐ Do you know how policies in place at the time of an incident can afford a defense to a civil liability action?

☐ Does your department have written policies?

☐ Does your department have Standard Operating Procedures (SOPs) for the implementation of department policies? If so, were they tailor-made to suit the particular needs of your department?

☐ Is there a mechanism for the review of the SOPs on a regular basis to assess them and implement changes?

☐ Are members from the fire floor (i.e., the general firefighter population, the operational rank and file) involved in the development of department policies and the SOPs?

☐ Does your department provide instructional programs, either in-house or through an outside agency, to train department members in the operational standards required by the SOPs?

☐ Does your department have methods of recording and maintaining information that may be needed for defending a liability action or an occupational health and safety (OH&S [see Chapter 10 on U.S. OSHA]) prosecution?

☐ Does your department have a public information officer? Is he or she adequately trained to effectively deal with the media? Does your public information officer understand the legal liability implications and risks inherent in his or her duties?

☐ Do your firefighters, officers, and incident commanders customarily prepare written reports as soon as possible after a call (whether or not it was a false alarm)? Are the reports prepared in such a way as to make them useful as evidence in a legal action? Are they systematically retained?

☐ Does your department have mutual aid agreements with neighboring communities?

☐ Have your chief and senior officers met with neighboring municipalities and addressed problems of mutual aid, for example, incompatible equipment or emergency communications in the event of a disaster?

☐ Have your department's mutual aid agreements been reviewed for potential traps from a legal liability perspective?

☐ Have you developed a relationship with one or more lawyers who are knowledgeable in the fields of civil liability of fire services and OH&S liability and who can provide your department with the necessary guidance concerning your liability risks and potential and pending legal actions? Have you educated your lawyers respecting issues of particular concern to the fire service generally and to your department specifically? Have you reviewed your fire bylaw, SOPs, and fire service agreements with a lawyer knowledgeable about fire service liability?

☐ Do you understand the details of the liability insurance coverage covering your department? Do your department members understand their duties to the insurer and how the municipal liability insurance will respond in the event of a legal action against your municipality respecting the actions or omissions of your department?

If you answered either "no" or "I don't know" to any of the questions posed above, you have work to do.

departments by fire lawyer and consultant Terry-Dawn Hewitt, the checklist consists of a questionnaire about the department's activities, standards, processes, and policies, requiring yes and no answers; Hewitt maintains that answers such as "no" or "I don't know" indicate work to be done on the development of a risk management program.[7]

Asset management

To deliver services efficiently and effectively, a fire service has to manipulate various levers. These include information technology (discussed in Chapter 14), human resource planning (Chapter 5), performance measurement (Chapter 10), and asset management (the discussion of capital resource management in Chapter 7 complements the material in this section). Like information technology, human resource planning, and performance measurement, asset management

Is linked to fiscal management in a strategic manner (i.e., fire service managers must think strategically in terms of the cause-and-effect relationship between other departments' processes and their own)

Can have significant financial effects

Must be managed across the local government system and not only within distinct units.

Compared with many other local government departments, the fire and rescue organization (depending on its size and scale) manages physical assets that are very valuable. One engine (pumper truck), depending on how it is configured with equipment, can cost as much as $500,000 (in 2001 dollars), and one aerial ladder truck can cost more than $1 million. Apparatus, rescue and medical equipment, protective clothing, buildings, property, and so forth all represent an extensive financial commitment. To manage and properly account for this accumulation of physical assets, the organization should commit to an asset management plan, which should ensure that the overarching business plan considers the activities and costs related to asset acquisition, preservation, replacement, and disposal. An asset management plan is an integral component of risk management.

An asset management plan ensures not only that all the major assets used by the fire service or for which the fire service is responsible are properly recorded and valued, but also that forecasts of each asset's remaining life and replacement need are properly recorded. The plan should also touch on measures for preserving the life and reliability of assets in a cost-effective manner, disposing of assets that will not be required, and acquiring new assets as needed to conduct the organization's business.

An asset planning framework therefore has four main components: the organizational strategy relative to the delivery of emergency response services, asset planning and acquisition, asset preservation, and asset replacement/disposal (see Figure 6–16).

An assessment of a department's current portfolio of assets from the perspective of the department's public programs and services will identify additional needs as well as opportunities for disposal. Once the mix of existing and required assets is known, a local government can identify maintenance and protection programs to preserve assets and can then either develop strategies compatible with time frames for replacement or anticipate a period of anomalies. (Items are often disposed of by local governments rather than by departments because the former can hold auctions of a large quantity of items from several departments, making the disposal process much simpler and much more transparent to public scrutiny and audit.)

Fire and rescue service providers that have significant responsibilities for

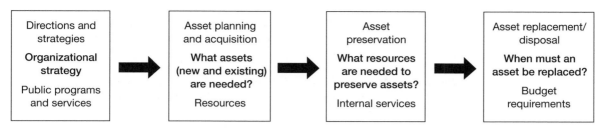

Directions and strategies		Asset planning and acquisition		Asset preservation		Asset replacement/ disposal
Organizational strategy	→	**What assets (new and existing) are needed?**	→	**What resources are needed to preserve assets?**	→	**When must an asset be replaced?**
Public programs and services		Resources		Internal services		Budget requirements

Note: The bottom line represents what must be considered when a statement is made about the top line. The bold-face center headings or questions indicate a process that flows from one box's boldface to the next.

Figure 6–16   Asset planning framework.

infrastructure may already have various systems in place to assess, preserve, and replace or dispose of physical assets. However, the financial requirements associated with the process are not always fully budgeted for and may not be obvious to decision makers. In such cases, the cost of services could be underestimated. An important first step in quantifying the need to protect and preserve assets is adopting systems that properly report and record the future effects of failing to invest in asset protection and preservation.

Funding mechanisms and sources of potential revenue

The funding for a fire and rescue program influences the amount of financial resources available. But "the funding issue is not one to be left solely to accountants and finance officers; it is a vital public policy issue that can literally mean life or death in the community."[8] Thus, governance and equity, and not simply issues of financing, play a major role in how a fire and rescue department is funded.

When funding for a service is considered, the following questions about that service need to be asked and answered:

Who should pay for the service?

Should the service be treated as insurance against community loss?

Could there be user fees?

Should fire and rescue services be offered by local government as a public good?

More broadly, should firefighters compete in the marketplace, assume revenue-generating roles not typically part of their job description, or step outside the collective agreement (i.e., perform work beyond what the labor-management contract calls for—work for which the union will require additional pay)? Initiatives to make any of that happen are normally fiercely opposed.

This section outlines a wide variety of funding mechanisms in use in the year 2001 and surveys possible future sources of revenue.

Funding mechanisms

The funding mechanisms listed below, the descriptions of which have been adapted from the Federal Emergency Management Agency's publication *Funding Alternatives for Fire and Emergency Services,* run the gamut from taxes to private sector sources.[9]

Taxes Inasmuch as the fire service is considered a public good, tax revenue —generated locally through property, sales, income, and transient taxes—may be set aside specifically for it.

Borrowing When a local jurisdiction is not allowed to issue bonds (the more conventional debt instruments) for purchasing capital equipment and facilities, it can use certificates of participation (COPs), a funding mechanism that is similar to general obligation bonds but that operates much like home mortgages.

Benefit assessment charges Benefit assessments are charges for services based on the estimated benefits the users are expected to derive from those services. Administered somewhat like property taxes, these charges factor in not only the size and type of property but also the "benefits" of being close to fire stations (reduced insurance, availability of special services, and so forth). These charges are a way to get around property-tax limitations and can make charges for fire protection more equitable.

Fees Fees range from small revenue producers to more lucrative ones. The former include permit fees for new construction, special events, and performance of hazardous activities (such as putting on fireworks displays, removing old underground fuel-storage facilities, or making explosives or highly flammable or toxic products); the latter include fees charged for emergency medical care and transport.

Contracts Fire and rescue departments are contracting out many of their services. For example, they may agree to provide all the fire and emergency medical care in neighboring jurisdictions, or selected services for parts of jurisdictions, or special services (such as training, HAZMAT response, and technical rescue) under contract or through user fees.

Cost sharing (partnering) Many departments are sharing costs, or partnering, to pay for new facilities or services. Cost sharing reduces the burden on each party, especially when the facilities or services are not used frequently (see Chapter 16).

Subscriptions Subscriptions, most commonly used for emergency medical service, are essentially a form of insurance in which households pay a fixed fee per year for the service if—and no matter how many times—they should need it during the year. Often the subscribers can then recover the fixed fees from medical or home owners insurance carriers. When nonsubscribers need service, they must pay the full amount each time.

Development impact fees New developments can be required to pay for their impact on capital expenditures (e.g., building and equipping new fire stations).

Federal and state programs Local fire and rescue agencies can obtain considerable funding from state and federal programs and grants. (Many states provide direct funding, grant aid, or low-interest loans for capital improvement projects.) The sources of such funding are varied. Departments can learn about them through their state fire marshal's office.

Private sector sources Public fire departments are increasingly turning to private donations by establishing nonprofit foundations. Volunteer fire and rescue services, especially, can often raise considerable funds from the private sector. The list of fund-raising and equipment-acquisition activities is endless. Often the local culture and context of each community will suggest appropriate types of activities.

Potential sources of revenue

The traditional view of the fire service is that it is a provider of emergency response only—waiting, like the military for war, for human crisis and tragedy. But in large communities, providing fire and rescue services is very costly, and fire and rescue organizations should note that avenues for generating revenue are available. The most plausible areas for revenue generation are the support services, such as public education sections, fire prevention and inspection departments, training academies, and mechanical (fleet maintenance) services.

1. Public education programs on preventing accidents and fires could be made available on a user-fee basis. These programs are now offered for free and in most cases are loosely organized. However, this type of service is in great demand, and many departments cannot keep up with the plethora of requests from various civic organizations. Yet printing five-color pamphlets and acquiring videotapes and programs for children's safety can be extremely costly. Some of these costs can be recovered through sponsorships, donations, and user fees. The object is not to make a profit but at least to cover the costs associated with the efforts. If fire and rescue organizations stopped this activity, several other organizations would fill the resulting void and they, too, would move at least to have their costs covered.

2. Requests for building safety inspections generated by property sales could also generate fee income. Law and real estate firms are continually seeking safety inspections of buildings and properties up for sale, charging the customer for the service. Fire prevention and inspection divisions by rights should receive the fees generated. Generally this service can be offered only by inspectors trained in the various building and fire codes that govern the sale, and this type of training requires the expenditure of considerable time and money.

3. Some emergency responses consume vast quantities of resources, including personnel and equipment. HAZMAT incidents may result in the complete destruction of very expensive biochemical proximity suits, breathing apparatus, and protective firefighting clothing (turn-out gear). The costs may be recovered through state or provincial programs, but more particularly the costs should be borne by the industry or individual responsible for the incident, whether the cause be improper transportation, processing, or packaging. This focus may yield insight into the range of opportunities that may be inherent in environmental projects: a department may be able to provide protective services other than emergency response.

4. Most fire departments respond normally to fire alarms, even when the alarms are from buildings with improperly installed or maintained alarm systems. Several buildings have hybrid systems that are prone to premature signal generation resulting in false alarms; responses to these false alarms often prevent much-needed manpower and apparatus from responding to genuine emergencies. For the owners of these buildings, having the local fire department respond—sometimes a dozen or more times during a twenty-four-hour period—might be easier than repairing or replacing the system at a cost of several hundreds of thousands of dollars. Departments could charge a user fee for each response beyond a predetermined acceptable number.

5. Many departments service their own self-contained breathing apparatus

(SCBA). But fire and rescue services are not the only users of such devices. Many industries and institutions are required to have these units on hand, with personnel adequately trained in their safe operation. These units require yearly inspections and servicing. Fire and rescue service providers that have certification for servicing their own SCBA can market this service to other users.

6. Most fire and rescue service providers have extensive training programs. The range of programs encompasses accredited firefighting, fire extinguisher training, paramedic skills, incident and human resource management skills, and various technical rescue programs, among many others. If a department has these capabilities, it is in a position to market its core competencies to industry in terms of training in first aid, accident and fire prevention, code and bylaw education, industrial and heavy rescue, industrial fire brigades, and so forth. These services can be brokered through the authority having jurisdiction; the authority would then gain a finder's fee and an incentive to help create public-private partnerships. If a modern simulator training complex is available, the surrounding localities can pay a rental fee to use it for live fire training on a cost-per-hour basis, including costs for material, equipment, and instructors.

7. Another not so common but creative approach is to rent out advertising space. A passing fire truck is virtually a large mobile billboard that will catch the eye of many, especially children. Of course, tact and a conservative approach would be essential.

8. Public-private partnerships are also possible. These are partnerships developed in alternative service delivery models whereby public entities partner with private industry to provide a much-needed private service, with each side performing its core competency. Often a department can offset the expense of mock-ups by partnering with a private entity. For example, airline passenger carriers must train their flight crews with basic first aid and fire extinguisher training, and providing the service locally is cheaper than shuttling people to a central training site. These companies may be more than interested in funding and constructing mock-ups for special training to meet federal transportation regulations. The fire department would affix the mock-ups permanently within the training facility and would also provide maintenance. Both air crews and firefighters could use them for aircraft firefighting techniques. Training (which could be held jointly) would be provided by fire department instructors. The carriers would pay a fee for use of the facility without having to maintain one themselves and would cover the costs of instructors and material. Firefighters and public education programs could also make extensive use of the mock-ups, so both savings and revenue would be generated.

9. Large fire services require fleet maintenance capabilities, either contracted for or provided internally. These mechanical services, especially in the area of diesel and heavy equipment, may also prove to be marketable.

10. Large fire and rescue organizations require extensive equipment for communications and logging radio traffic. A system that could service many departments through a trunking network (see Chapter 15) could be shared with other departments or agencies. Trunking has the capability of allowing privacy, with a large number of users using state-of-the-art technology that is upgradable. Other departments or private sector partners could either share costs or pay a fee for time used.

11. To achieve economies of scale and effectiveness, regional dispatching could prove to have a considerable advantage over traditional dispatch models. Costs for the system can be borne by several departments. In

terms of patient transport, regional dispatching can incorporate linkages to various medical centers or hospitals that practice specific types of medicine. If a "bed registry," too, is incorporated into the system, patients with specific medical problems can be transported to the nearest facility that has both available bed space and the appropriate specialized medical treatment.

For most of the examples listed above, potential benefits outweigh the risks. Because the infrastructure and personnel are already in place, there would be little financial effect. As a matter of fact, the fire service has an edge on the competition because it would be dealing in its core competency area and would be saving up to 28 percent of what the set-up costs would be for a private sector organization wishing to offer the same service.[10] Fire departments receive several requests each year for services that could be revenue generating, but often the requested service cannot legally begin to generate revenue unless changes are made in local, state, or provincial law.

The opportunities to generate revenue are certainly available. Taking advantage of them will require adopting a hybrid form of the private sector's raison d'être—making a profit, or at least a public-private version of making a profit (i.e., providing some recovery to the taxpayer). Once critical mass is achieved (i.e., once the entire department is looking for opportunities to generate revenue), the local fire station might have many other opportunities to develop revenues, a percentage of which could be turned back into the department budget as an incentive to other stations to implement other opportunities.

Final thoughts

Fiscal management does not happen in isolation but is part of a larger framework of organizational planning, management, and performance. Strategic operational choices have major financial effects, and the goals and strategies for delivering services must be balanced with the goal of sound financial management.

Financial stewardship includes setting financial management goals and implementing practices in order to

Develop strategies for strengthening the organization's financial position

Develop and deliver financial information that is appropriate for decision making

Make visible the costs of delivering individual programs and outcomes, thereby facilitating cultural and structural change and enhanced accountability within the organization

Integrate financial effects with operational decision making, organizational planning, and strategic direction

Manage financial risks and exposures.

Fiscal management also includes a sound regime for managing expenditures: alternative strategies of delivering services are examined, core competency services are analyzed, and strategies for generating new revenue are weighed and evaluated.

Finally, fiscal management focuses on information for decision making. Among the concepts that underlie information for decision making are budgeting, full costing, monitoring and reporting, managing financial information, managing the financial risks and exposures of the fire and rescue services organization, managing assets, and examining funding mechanisms and potential sources of revenue.

1 Council of the City of Winnipeg, *Plan Winnipeg . . . Toward 2010* (City of Winnipeg, 1993).

2 Henry Mintzberg, *The Rise and Fall of Strategic Planning* (New York: The Free Press, 1994), 118.

3 The discussion of the line-item budget is largely taken from Douglas Ayers and Leonard G. Marks, "Budgeting, Finance, and Cost Containment," in *Managing Fire Services,* 2nd ed., ed. Ronny J. Coleman and John A. Granito (Washington, D.C.: International City Management Association, 1988), 194–221.

4 This discussion of full costing is largely taken from Ayers and Marks, "Budgeting, Finance, and Cost Containment."

5 Audit Department, "Review of the Controllership Function," an internal document (City of Winnipeg, January 1993).

6 Chartered Accountants of Canada / Public Sector Accounting and Auditing Board (PSAAB), *An Illustrative Guide to Municipal Accounting and Financial Reporting* (Toronto, Canada: PSAAB, 1997).

7 Terry-Dawn Hewitt, *Fire Loss Litigation in Canada* (Scarborough, Ontario: Carswell, 1997), chap. 5, pp. 27–28.

8 Federal Emergency Management Agency (FEMA), *Funding Alternatives for Fire and Emergency Services* (Washington, D.C.: Government Printing Office, 1993), 1-2.

9 Adapted from FEMA, *Funding Alternatives for Fire and Emergency Services,* 1-2 to 1-5.

10 William D. Eggers and John O'Leary, *Revolution at the Roots* (New York: The Free Press, 1994), 111.

7 Capital resource management

This chapter provides local government managers with the information they need in order to manage fire department capital resources professionally. Capital resources are the equipment, vehicles, and facilities that enable firefighters to deliver service to their customers. For many communities, the equipment and vehicles used by the fire department in doing its work can be among the most costly expenditures of their type, but the cost of fire and rescue facilities is often small compared with the costs involved in providing other municipal services: the costs of public service facilities such as roads and wastewater treatment plants can easily overshadow the cost of a new fire station. However, very few public facilities are more integrated into the fabric of a neighborhood than the local fire station. It has been said that two of the most difficult tasks faced by local government managers are opening a new fire station and closing an existing one.

Valid generalizations about capital resource management are very hard to make because fire and rescue departments differ, sometimes significantly, in the services they deliver to their communities and in the means of delivery. The profile of emergency service delivery in each community is a function of history, finance, politics, standards, personalities, and community expectations. Thus, the information presented here does not always apply in full to the specific situation of every fire department in the United States and Canada, much less every fire department around the world. But by focusing on the processes used to procure, maintain, account for, and replace capital resources, the discussion should help most fire and rescue departments manage these resources. (The chapter assumes that the fire department has a role, whether small or large, in the delivery of emergency medical service [EMS]. Accordingly, the information presented here encompasses EMS-related procurement, maintenance, and replacement.)

The emphasis in much of this discussion is on accommodating the legitimate needs of the user of the equipment, vehicle, or facility—the person who delivers the actual service. In fire and rescue departments, that person is the firefighter, the inspector, the educator, the staff person, or the manager who has direct contact with the customer. The job of a support person, such as someone who provides equipment, apparatus, and facilities, is to provide front-line workers with the tools they need to do their jobs. Accommodating the needs of the person on the front line is the reason that support services exist.

The first section defines capital resources for the purposes of this chapter. The subsequent three sections discuss the procurement of, respectively, capital equipment, emergency vehicles, and capital facilities. Because procurement is closely tied to the decision to replace a capital resource, the factors that contribute to such a decision are included in the three discussions. Specific purchasing procedures, however, are not detailed because the actual methods a community uses to procure capital items largely depend on local laws, ordinances, and operating procedures. The three sections on procurement are followed by one on maintenance and accountability and then by a brief conclusion.

Capital resources defined

There is little doubt that a piece of fire apparatus or a fire station meets any standard definition of a "capital" resource, but the definition of the equipment that qualifies as capital varies widely from jurisdiction to jurisdiction. Some communities define capital equipment as any item costing more than $100 and having a service life longer than one year, whereas others use a higher purchase cost and longer service life for the definition. In this chapter, the term *capital equipment* refers only to the most expensive individual items of capital equipment as well as to tools, such as hose, that individually have low unit prices but collectively represent a significant cost. More specifically, this chapter defines the three kinds of capital resources as follows:

1. *Fire and EMS equipment*   Firefighters use a very broad array of tools and equipment to deliver fire protection and EMS. Most of these tools are relatively inexpensive (unit prices below $200) and are not discussed in this chapter. The equipment that is addressed here includes such items such as hydraulic rescue tools, defibrillators, hose, self-contained breathing apparatus (SCBA), and power tools such as saws.
2. *Emergency vehicles*   Only the specialized fire and emergency medical vehicles used for delivering emergency response services to the community are discussed here: apparatus (pumpers, ladders, heavy rescues, quints, all of which are defined in the accompanying sidebar and are discussed in some detail in Chapter 4); EMS vehicles (squads, ambulances); and emergency support vehicles (command, aircraft, and specialty vehicles) (see Figure 7–1). All of these are included in most of the generally

Figure 7–1   Fire department emergency vehicles: (a) A pumper (engine), equipped with a water tank, pump, ground ladder, and hose, makes hydrant and sprinkler/standpipe connections at a hotel fire; (b) A ladder (truck), with its aerial ladder raised; (c) A quint, combining the features of a pumper and a ladder; (d) A heavy rescue carrying vehicle extraction equipment, rescue rope, portable lighting, firefighting tools, and firefighters specially trained in special rescue activities; (e) An airport rescue firefighting (ARFF) apparatus, equipped with large water tanks and firefighting foam systems to fight fires involving aircraft.

accepted definitions of capital resources. Not addressed here are other capital vehicles, such as sedans, vans, and pickups, that are not unique to the fire and rescue department.

3. *Emergency service and support facilities*   Fire stations are the basic facility from which fire, emergency medical, and hazardous material (HAZMAT) services are delivered. Although some communities have experimented with emergency medical systems that deploy ambulances to

---

Fire and rescue vehicles

Pumper (engine)   A pumper is the type of fire apparatus most commonly operated by a fire department. It carries a water tank, pump, ground ladders, hose, and other fire and EMS equipment. The main mission of the firefighters who staff this type of apparatus is to secure a water supply—for example, by laying a hose line from a fire hydrant to the fire—and to put water on the fire. A pumper may also be referred to as an *engine*, a *squad*, or a *wagon*.[1]

Ladder (truck)   A ladder is a large firefighting vehicle that incorporates an aerial device, such as an aerial ladder, tower ladder, or platform. The vehicle carries equipment that is used for firefighting, forcible entry into buildings, and ventilation; it also carries other support equipment. The main mission of the firefighters who staff this type of apparatus is search and rescue; provision of access for firefighters into structures; removal of smoke and hot gases from structures; and use of the aerial device for access, rescue, and firefighting. Many ladder companies also provide other rescue services, such as the extrication of car crash victims. Ladders may also be referred to as

trucks, aerials, towers, sticks, bobtails, and *hook and ladders.*

Quint   A quint is a combination of pumper and ladder, although the full capabilities of these two types of vehicles cannot be completely accommodated in one vehicle. Quints incorporate a water tank, hose, pump, ground ladders, and an aerial device, and may be used as ladders or as pumpers in many situations.

Heavy rescue   A heavy rescue is a large firefighting vehicle that carries rescue equipment and firefighters but usually no appreciable water supply or large ladder. Rescue company firefighters (heavy rescues are called "rescue companies") are highly skilled in firefighting and rescue and may be considered the specialists of their department. Many rescue companies also provide technical rescue capability, such as dive rescue, heavy rescue for lifting heavy objects, and other services. The number of firefighters assigned to a heavy rescue is usually higher than the number assigned to a pumper or a ladder. Rescues may also be referred to as *squads* or *tactical units.*

[1] *Squad* is used in different communities to mean different things.

d

e

various positions in the service area on the basis of computer models (such deployment is called *system status management*), most fire and emergency medical systems provide service from fixed locations, such as fire stations. Addressed in this chapter are fixed service delivery facilities (e.g., fire stations, combined fire/EMS facilities, and EMS base stations) but not administrative facilities, unless the latter are co-located with service delivery facilities. Administrative facilities are not specific to the emergency response service, and adequate information on planning and operating them can be found in architectural and planning texts.

Procurement of capital equipment

Fire department equipment is used under the most extreme circumstances imaginable. Tools must work well in extreme heat and extreme cold, in situations of low visibility, in extremely wet and extremely dry environments, and in atmospheres contaminated with toxins. Equipment that may work perfectly well for most home and business uses will not survive the rigorous use it will receive at the hands of firefighters working under emergency response conditions.

In addition, all fire and EMS equipment requires an extremely high degree of dependability. Firefighters can ill afford saws that will not cut, hydraulic spreaders that will not spread, or defibrillators that will not deliver a shock. Failure of these devices in the field can have drastic consequences. The importance of this fact is hard to overstate. These tools literally make the difference between life and death for firefighters and the customers they are serving. Moreover, when an equipment failure affects the outcome of an emergency, significant civil liability is possible.

The following steps are discussed in this section: establishing the need for the purchase, assessing the existing equipment, complying with standards, seeking input from local and other users of the equipment, weighing costs (not only the cost to purchase but also the cost over the entire life of the equipment, the cost of standardization and of training in the absence of standardization, and the cost of—or savings from—vendor support), evaluating the safety of the equipment to be purchased, and considering possible ways of funding the purchase.

Establishing the need for purchase or replacement

The first step in any planned procurement process for equipment is establishing the need for the purchase. When a needed piece of equipment has been lost, stolen, or destroyed, a formal process that establishes need is unnecessary; the need is obvious. The need is also obvious when a new unit or program is activated and requires equipment. But in other cases, establishing the need is more difficult. Some items of fire and EMS equipment, such as hose adapters, will last for decades before wearing out or becoming obsolete, whereas others, such as defibrillators, are overtaken by obsolescence within a few years.

One important source of data for decisions about replacement is properly kept equipment maintenance records. Equally important are the observations of the firefighters who use the equipment. Their feedback, reflecting hands-on experience, can help managers identify specific pieces of equipment that have proven unreliable; or the users may identify trends that might lead fire department management to recommend the replacement of a piece of equipment on a department-wide basis. In regard to obsolescence, information on the state of the art in equipment is readily available from trade publications, seminars, direct mailings, and—of course—fire equipment dealers.

Assessing existing equipment

Once the need to replace has been established, an examination of the positive and negative aspects of the equipment being replaced is often very useful. Maintenance records should be examined for recurring problems that can be eliminated when the new equipment is specified. Here, too, the users should be consulted on changes that can be made to the new equipment to improve its usefulness and on the things that should not be changed. Two important considerations are the weight and size of the new equipment. A new defibrillator that is twice the weight of the old one is not likely to strike the user as a change for the better, regardless of any new features it might have.

Complying with standards

Increasingly in the United States, Canada, and the European Union, standards exist that establish minimum performance, construction, and certification norms for fire and EMS equipment. In many cases, compliance with these standards is completely voluntary. For example, standards produced by the National Fire Protection Association (NFPA) do not generally carry the force of law. In contrast, in the United States, Food and Drug Administration (FDA) standards governing medical devices and National Institute for Occupational Safety and Health (NIOSH) certification of SCBA are mandated by law.

Local government managers and fire chiefs who choose to purchase equipment that is not in compliance with voluntary or mandatory standards assume a higher level of potential liability and risk. Even though voluntary standards carry no compliance requirement, they have been used in litigation to establish a level of care for fire and emergency medical services. There are situations in which managers may choose to take exception to a standard. In these situations, at the time the decision is taken to ignore a component of a standard, managers should document the reasoning behind the decision and should file the documentation properly, thus possibly gaining some measure of protection if the decision is questioned in the future.

Seeking input from local and other users

The actual user of the equipment—the person who will be expected to put the tool to use once it is received—should continue to have a voice in the purchasing process. In some cases the way to gather user input may be as simple as visiting the fire stations where the existing tool is in use, discussing the replacement with the firefighters there, and providing the firefighters with information on the items whose purchase is being planned. For more expensive purchases or for purchases of critical safety equipment such as SCBA, a committee made up of fire department users, managers, and administrators should be consulted. For the largest purchases, an ad hoc committee of users and managers should be formed to research the products available in the market, decide what is best for the community on the basis of the usefulness of the products offered and their cost, and recommend appropriate replacement equipment to upper management. All members of the committee should be free to express their opinions without fear of recrimination or retribution; otherwise, discussions may be inhibited.

When the purchase of new or replacement equipment is contemplated, there is no point in reinventing the wheel. Other fire departments and users can provide very valuable information, and it is common for firefighters to compare notes about the performance of equipment. Other departments should be consulted about their experience with a particular brand or model of equipment, with maintenance, with parts availability, and with support from the manufacturer. Very often the equipment manufacturer will, if asked, supply the names of other fire departments that use a piece of fire equipment. One should keep in mind, however, that the list is being supplied by the person who is trying to sell the equipment.

A source of information that is tapped less often is users from outside the fire service. An excellent source of information about the reliability of a chain saw under heavy use would be a lumberjack. Likewise, information on the durability and reliability of an SCBA would probably be available from a heavy-duty user, such as an asbestos removal contractor or a hazardous-waste cleanup company. Too often these sources of information are ignored.

NFPA standards and the standards-making process   The National Fire Protection Association (NFPA), a nonprofit educational and standards development organization, produces consensus standards for use by the fire service. (On NFPA standards, see also Chapter 13.) NFPA standards exist or are under development for almost every piece of fire equipment, including hose, nozzles, hydraulic rescue tools, SCBA, and ground ladders. The proper development of NFPA standards depends on the quantity and quality of input provided to the standards-making process. Participation in this process can take several forms.

First, fire service and local government personnel are encouraged to participate actively as members of NFPA technical committees, if they can. Such participation typically requires attending an average of one to two meetings per year somewhere in the United States or Canada. Expenses for participation are the responsibility of the committee member or his or her sponsoring agency.

Second, those who are unable to participate as committee members have ample opportunity to propose new or existing standards and to comment on documents proposed for adoption. NFPA regulations require that every proposal and comment submitted on a given standard be addressed and an answer published. The vehicles for these discussions are a Report on Proposals and a Report on Comments, both of which are available from NFPA either in print or on the organization's Web site (www.nfpa.org). (Also available on the Web site is information about the NFPA standards development process and a listing of the standards published to date.)

Finally, there is also an opportunity to address the issues of a standard at the technical committee report sessions, where a standard is presented for action by NFPA's members. These sessions are held every May and November in conjunction with multifaceted NFPA meetings (in addition to action on standards, there are educational sessions and exhibits by vendors).

NFPA works very hard to maintain an appropriate balance on its committees: committee members include representatives of user groups, manufacturers, regulatory organizations, and others. However, it is not uncommon for meetings of committees related to fire service equipment to be attended by a high percentage of manufacturers; and at the same time, it is often difficult for fire service members to attend, given budget and travel restrictions. The access provided during the proposal and comment phases of standards development is intended to level the playing field for the various vested interests.

By whatever method, fire service input to the standards-making process is critical. The quality, affordability, and safety of all types of equipment hangs in the balance.

Weighing costs

The initial purchase price is only one cost that should be considered. Others are the cost of the equipment over its lifetime of service, expenses related to standardization (or its lack) and the need for training, and vendor support over the long term.

Life cycle costs   Fire departments that are considering the cost of new or replacement equipment should give some thought to the total cost of the equipment—both the initial cost and the cost of keeping the unit in service for its expected service life. Life cycle costs consist of the original purchase price,

---

Life cycle costs   The Bugtussle Heights Fire Department has completed a two-year process and is now about to select a new SCBA for the department. Two bids have been received from reputable manufacturers. The SCBA committee has determined that each SCBA meets the department's specifications and that each would be a good, safe unit for Bugtussle Heights. Twenty units are to be purchased.

After much research, the SCBA committee has determined that the new SCBA will have a ten-year life span. The committee has also determined, in advance of the bid, that the parts of the SCBA that are most often replaced are the facepiece, the shoulder straps, and the cylinder retention system.

SCBA #1   SCBA #1 has been offered at a unit cost of $2,500, with a 10 percent discount off the list price for parts and with free initial and annual training for the firefighters who maintain and repair Bugtussle Height's SCBAs. The manufacturer recommends that SCBA

#1 units be checked by a technician three times a year and that an overhaul be performed every three years. Parts for the overhaul cost a total of $200 after the discount has been applied. The standard package of replacement parts outlined by the SCBA committee has a total cost of $1,500.

SCBA #2   SCBA #2 has been offered at no charge, with a 20 percent discount off the list price for parts. Initial training is free for Bugtussle Height's SCBA maintenance team, and annual recertification training is offered for a flat fee of $300 per year. The manufacturer recommends that SCBA #2 units be checked by a technician twice a year and that an overhaul be completed once a year. Parts for the overhaul cost a total of $500 after the discount has been applied. The standard package of replacement parts outlined by the SCBA committee has a total cost of $2,500.

A life cycle cost comparison of the purchase, with all cost factors taken into account, is as follows:

	SCBA #1 ($)	SCBA #2 ($)
Initial cost per unit	2,500	0
Initial training	0	0
Annual recertification training (eight-year service life, unit cost based on twenty units)	0	120
SCBA checks, labor only, at $40 per hour, one hour per check	1,200	800
Overhauls, three hours labor per unit plus parts	960	5,580
Standard replacement parts list	1,500	2,500
Total life cycle cost per unit	6,160	9,000

If all other factors were equal, SCBA #1 would be the better buy despite the much lower initial price of SCBA #2.

---

any applicable sales tax, and the cost of parts and labor for repairs and preventive maintenance. Some unscrupulous equipment vendor may offer its product at a deep discount only to charge high prices for parts in the future. When life cycle costs are considered, the competing equipment that had a higher initial price may be a better value.

Standardization and training costs   Fire and EMS equipment is used in time-sensitive, high-stress situations. Establishing familiarity and practicing with equipment in advance of the emergency will make the firefighter more efficient in these situations. It is incumbent on the fire department to provide equipment operation training for anyone who is expected to use a tool. Standardization on one piece of equipment minimizes the need for training and the associated expense. In some cases, it may be less expensive overall to pay a little more for a piece of equipment that firefighters are already familiar with than to save money on the purchase price of a new or modified tool only to spend funds later for training. (Standardization is also discussed below under "Evaluating Safety.")

Costs and vendor support   A consideration of costs should include the support that the equipment manufacturer and the local equipment distributor will provide after the sale. Before a purchase is completed, the procedure to be used for warranty repairs, as well as the process for ordering and receiving parts, should be clear to everyone involved.

The relationship between a fire department and the supplier of some types of equipment can be very long term, but the vendor is generally most attentive to the fire department at the time of the purchase. This is an excellent time to establish a contract with the vendor for the purchase of parts and services related to the equipment. For example, a component of a purchase agreement for defibrillators might be a five-year contract that provides a standard percentage discount off the manufacturer's suggested retail price for parts and a set hourly labor rate for nonwarranty work.

Evaluating safety

Firefighting itself is among the most hazardous of occupations, but fire and EMS equipment should not be hazardous to the health of firefighters. NFPA, FDA, and NIOSH standards and certifications provide some measure of protection by giving assurances that equipment has met those minimum safety standards. In addition, before purchase, each piece of equipment should be assessed for its effect on the safety of firefighters.

Certain critical pieces of fire and EMS equipment should be replaced on a systemwide basis at one time rather than incrementally. Two examples of equipment that fit this description are SCBA and defibrillators.

SCBA provide safe breathing air in hazardous atmospheres and are used in situations that are defined as immediately dangerous to life and health (see Figure 7–2). Accordingly, their importance to the firefighter cannot be overstated. Each fire department should use only one type and model of SCBA (or SCBA that are extremely close in configuration and operation) so that firefighters are required to remember only one set of emergency operating instructions. This precaution ensures that if things go wrong in an emergency situation, when the firefighter is already under extreme stress from the emergency, he or she will not be forced to remember which type of SCBA is in use and what the proper emergency procedures are for that brand or model. Extreme emergencies involving the SCBA are rare but when they do happen, knowing and immediately performing emergency operations can mean the difference between life and death for the firefighter.

Defibrillators allow trained firefighters to read heart rhythms and deliver electrical shock to convert abnormal rhythms to normal (see Chapter 1). Using only one make or model of a defibrillator (or units that are extremely close in configuration and operation) will simplify training and ensure that all firefighters are familiar with the unit being used. Unlike SCBA emergencies, heart attacks and trauma are not rare, but they still require the firefighter to work with great speed and skill. The patient (the customer) should not have to wait for the firefighter to recall which defibrillator is in use and how it is operated. This knowledge should be instinctive, and the provision of a standard piece of equipment ensures that there are no delays caused by unfamiliarity with the equipment. Standard units also simplify the stocking of supplies, since only one type of pad and one type of leads (wires) have to be stocked.

Considering various funding sources

Funding sources for fire and rescue services vary widely from community to community, but the most common source of funding for fire and EMS equipment is the community's operating (noncapital) budget. Depending on local laws and procedures, funds for major purchases can be rolled from one fiscal year into the next so that sufficient funds accumulate. Some states, such as Florida, have statewide grant funds that can be used for the purchase of specific EMS equipment. Major purchases that cannot or should not be incrementally implemented, such as the replacement of a department's SCBA inventory, should be considered for bond program funding or lease purchase (defined in the next section). Often civic organizations, businesses, local foundations, or individuals are willing to provide certain types of equipment that a fire department needs but cannot afford. One example of private funding is the grass-

Figure 7–2 (Left) With a pressurized tank containing air that is fed into a facepiece, SCBA provide firefighters with clean air to breathe in hazardous atmospheres. (Right) Plano (Texas) firefighters doing a search with SCBA and rope guideline.

roots efforts that have purchased infrared cameras for local fire departments. (By allowing firefighters to see through smoke, these cameras speed up rescue and firefighting activities.)

Procurement of emergency vehicles

The primary mission of fire apparatus and emergency vehicles is to provide service to the customers (citizens and visitors) within the community, and the maintenance and reliability of these vehicles are critical for service delivery. But these vehicles are more than a means of conveyance. They are also a source of pride to citizens as well as to the firefighters who use them. They are the most visible symbol of the fire and rescue department.

The procurement of apparatus and emergency vehicles involves the same steps as the procurement of equipment, except that with vehicles, the development of specifications is of particular concern and so is obsolescence.

Establishing the need for purchase or replacement

The need to purchase a new vehicle for a new fire station or for a new program is fairly easy to establish. The decision about when to replace a vehicle is much more difficult. Emergency vehicles, especially engines (pumpers) and trucks (ladders), are extremely expensive pieces of equipment, and no matter how large the community, the cost is significant. Thus, managers should keep the vehicle in service as long as possible (to get the maximum benefit from it) while at the same time bearing in mind that all emergency vehicles require an extremely high degree of reliability.

Traditionally pumpers were retained in service up to fifteen years and ladder trucks up to as many as twenty years. Changes in the fire apparatus industry and in the fire service itself have pushed that convention in both directions: on the one hand, new apparatus is capable of longer service life than apparatus manufactured in the past, but on the other hand, the introduction of EMS has dramatically raised activity levels for many fire departments. And even in departments where the wear and tear on fire apparatus is at lower levels, new technology makes older apparatus obsolete before it wears out. In the past, a pumper or ladder with more than 100,000 miles on the odometer was unheard of. Modern apparatus reaches this milestone regularly.

Comparing fire department fleets with other fleets is difficult. One readily available indicator of use is mileage. Over-the-road trucks, eighteen-wheelers, can have service lives that last over 1 million miles. Local service delivery trucks, buses, and refuse vehicles can have service lives that extend into the hundreds of thousands of miles. So why cannot fire apparatus and other emergency vehicles last that long? The answer lies in three fundamental differences between fire department fleets and these other fleets.

First, a large percentage of the road miles placed on fire and emergency vehicles are incurred when the vehicle is responding to emergencies. Any emergency response requires repeated cycles of rapid acceleration and deceleration, hard turns, and quick stops—a type of use that places extreme demands on a vehicle. In addition, for fire apparatus engaged in pumping and/or aerial operations, long periods of stationary operations at high rpm are common.

The second difference between fire and rescue department fleets and other fleets is the need for reliability. Although with a refuse truck, a failure to start is not unimportant (especially to people with their trash on the curb), the effect of that failure can be addressed by assigning another vehicle in the same yard to perform the broken vehicle's duty or by making some other accommodation. The worst thing that happens is that the trash stays on the curb a little longer.

In the United States and Canada, if a fire truck or an ambulance fails to start, there is almost never another similarly equipped vehicle sitting next to it that can be rapidly deployed. In those two countries, the general practice is for fire and rescue departments to deploy a thin layer of emergency response resources in a large number of locations around the community. In Europe and other places around the world, in contrast, the number of fire stations present in the community is small, but multiple resources are concentrated in these stations. Compare Berlin with Houston, for example: the Berlin Fire Brigade protects more than 4 million people spread over 560 square miles with 37 fire stations, whereas the Houston Fire Department protects just under 2 million residents spread over 618 square miles with 85 fire stations.

In the U.S. deployment model, very few of the numerous fire stations have multiple response units of the same type. If the primary unit fails to start or is unable to function for some other reason, backup can be sent quickly from the next-closest fire department facility, but the travel distance from the other station can add minutes to the response. In fire and EMS situations, it is not an overdramatization to say that these additional minutes can be the difference between life and death.

Departments that house all their response resources in one location, as is the case for many volunteer and smaller career fire departments, are less affected by the failure of a unit to start because another vehicle is probably available and equipped to act in the first vehicle's place. Once a piece of equipment is at the scene of the emergency, its failure affects all fire departments to the same degree, regardless of their deployment methodology.

The third difference between fire and rescue department fleets and other fleets is that fire apparatus are fully loaded at all times, with vehicle components constantly bearing their maximum load. Over-the-road trucks, delivery trucks, refuse vehicles, and buses spend a significant part of their service life below maximum load. Suspension systems, driveline and power systems, and brakes are more taxed by full than by partial loads. This constant extreme use shortens the service lives of components on fire apparatus compared with components on vehicles that are used differently.

There is no national standard governing or making recommendations for the replacement of emergency vehicles. The decision is left to each locality and represents a balancing of numerous factors: fire department activity levels, maintenance cost and history, individual vehicle reliability, funding availability, technological changes, firefighter safety, and vehicle use. As mentioned above, fire apparatus must be replaced before it becomes unreliable but must be held in service for as long as possible to maximize the benefit of the large initial investment.

The purchase of fire apparatus should be defined in a local replacement plan: fire department managers and firefighters, fleet maintenance managers and technicians, and local government managers should meet and develop a long-term plan for the replacement of fire apparatus and emergency vehicles. Three successful replacement plans are outlined in the sidebar on the next page. The variety of well-thought-out solutions shows that there is no one way to structure a long-term fleet replacement plan, but unless some plan exists and is implemented, the department will eventually face an accumulation of unreliable emergency vehicles and the associated effect on the budget of a large vehicle-purchase package. (On asset management, including replacement, see Chapter 6.)

Assessing existing vehicles

As described above for fire equipment, examination of the positive and negative aspects of current apparatus and emergency vehicles forms a solid basis for

Three successful vehicle replacement plans The communities of Plano (Texas), Phoenix (Arizona), and Clifton Park (New York) have different but well-thought-out solutions to the problem of planning for the replacement of regular apparatus and emergency vehicles.

Plano, Texas Plano Fire-Rescue provides fire and emergency medical services to the 225,000 residents of Plano (near Dallas) from ten fire stations distributed over seventy square miles. In conjunction with the city's fleet maintenance department, fire department management established an expected service life for every vehicle type in the fleet. Expected replacement costs were also developed. The replacement cost for a piece of apparatus was divided by the expected service life of the apparatus, and an annual replacement cost was derived. Each year, the department budgets this amount for each apparatus covered by the plan, and the funds are deposited in an interest-bearing holding account. When the apparatus reaches the end of its expected service life, the funds should be available to replace it. The final decision on the need to replace an individual piece of apparatus takes into consideration its condition, its reliability, and the cost of maintaining it.

Phoenix, Arizona The Phoenix Fire Department provides fire and emergency medical services to 1.3 million residents from forty-six fire stations distributed over 478 square miles. The department found that its fleet of engines (pumpers) was deteriorating to the point that keeping all engine companies in service each day was difficult. In the previous seven

years, only two pumpers a year had been replaced on average. After analyzing the cost of maintenance and the reliability of the aging pumpers, management determined that this type of apparatus should be replaced when it had accumulated 150,000 miles. A large spreadsheet was developed that first estimated the annual accrual of miles on every pumper in the fleet over a period of ten years and then analyzed the cost and consequences of several replacement plans. In the end, the decision was made that the best way to keep the fleet healthy while also controlling costs was to replace five pumpers per year.

Clifton Park, New York The Clifton Park Volunteer Fire Department provides fire and rescue services to a suburban fire district located fifteen miles north of Albany. The department operates a heavy rescue, a ladder tower, and three pumper/tankers. The district is home to an estimated twenty thousand people in fifteen square miles. In the early 1980s the fire district commissioned a comprehensive analysis of the department's resources, including apparatus. A component of the final report was a recommended replacement time frame for each piece of fire apparatus. Replacements were spaced to allow the district to accumulate funding in advance and avoid getting into a situation in which all the department's apparatus would need to be replaced at the same time. Using the plan as a template, the district began saving funds in sufficient amounts to make the plan a reality. As of late 1999, four of the five major pieces of apparatus had been replaced.

---

developing specifications for a vehicle's replacement. Maintenance records can provide key information, as can input from the users of the vehicle.

Complying with standards

A great deal of information about specifications can be gathered from a review of current standards for fire apparatus and emergency equipment. NFPA manages the development of—and publishes—voluntary standards on many types of fire apparatus, including pumpers, ladders, tankers, wildland firefighting vehicles, and airport rescue firefighting (ARFF) vehicles. These standards do not usually have any regulatory force (although in some states, such as Texas, they may be adopted on a statewide basis) but are considered generally accepted industry standards. These are minimum standards, and using them as a basis for the development of any purchase specification is prudent.

Two standards that do have regulatory force are the General Services Administration's (GSA's) Triple-K standard related to the construction and performance of ambulances, and the Federal Aviation Administration's (FAA's) advisory circular that sets minimum standards for the construction and performance capability of ARFF vehicles.

KKK-A-1822, or the Triple-K ambulance standard, is used as a basis for most state EMS ambulance certification requirements. Ambulances that do not meet this standard generally cannot be licensed or permitted for use. The January 2002 edition of this specification is titled KKK-A-1822D, Ambulance, Emergency Medical Care Surface Vehicle–2310–FSS.[1] (At the time of this writing, the "E" edition of this document was scheduled for release sometime in 2002.)

The FAA's specification for all ARFF vehicles is AC150/5220-10C, Guide Specification for Water/Foam Aircraft Rescue and Firefighting Vehicles (February 2002).[2] If the vehicle is to be funded fully or partly by the FAA, it will have to meet this standard. If FAA funding is not to be used to purchase an ARFF vehicle, the advisory circular provides valuable information for developing a purchase specification and is considered an industry-acceptable standard.

Seeking input from local and other users

Involving local users with the specification and purchase of a new emergency vehicle is extremely important. Users are the people who will operate this vehicle in the course of their work, and their practical perspective on the vehicle's capabilities and features will prove very valuable. Many fire departments establish either standing or ad hoc apparatus committees to bring together the interests of users, management, and maintenance personnel in developing specifications (which are discussed in detail in the next subsection and under "Costs and Vendor Support"). In volunteer departments or departments serving small to moderate-sized communities, the fire chief or the fire district may appoint an apparatus committee. The committee's function is usually to research the needs of the department and the community, develop purchase specifications, and manage and track the apparatus throughout the design, construction, and delivery process. In larger fire departments where direct access to all users is difficult, user surveys are an excellent means of gathering information and input.

As with purchases of equipment, information related to other departments' experience with the apparatus and vehicles should be solicited. This information can help a local fire and rescue department avoid mistakes already made by others and develop an improved product for local use.

Developing specifications

The development of performance or construction specifications for the purchase of emergency vehicles is highly recommended and, in many communities, may even be required by local purchasing rules. The specifications should be open enough to allow manufacturers to address the needs of the purchaser in different ways with engineered solutions, yet restrictive enough to protect the purchaser from an inferior product. Draft or suggested specifications are available from most manufacturers; along with the appropriate standard, they can provide a basis for a purchase specification.

After the contract for construction of a piece of apparatus has been executed but before construction starts, the manufacturer and representatives of the fire department should meet and discuss the specification in detail. If possible, this meeting should be held at the apparatus manufacturer's production facility, where immediate access to engineers, managers, and production experts is possible.

Because there are relatively few manufacturers of fire apparatus and emergency vehicles, chances are that the apparatus being built for a community will not be constructed within or near that community. Thus, a final inspection of the apparatus before it leaves the manufacturer's facility is a good investment of time and resources. Problems with the apparatus that are discovered at the plant can be rapidly addressed by manufacturer's staff who are familiar with the vehicle. Once the vehicle leaves the factory, getting service becomes more difficult and may lead to long delays before the new unit can be deployed. Final inspection trips should be conducted by fire department members and others who are very familiar with the original purchase specifications and with any changes that were made during the design and construction process.

Weighing costs

As with capital equipment, one should consider not only the initial outlay but also costs over the whole life cycle, costs relating to standardization and training, and vendor support.

Life cycle costs　Fire service and fire apparatus publications often feature advertisements from manufacturers selling new fire apparatus at extremely low prices. These apparatus very often meet the minimum national standards and may be suitable for use in low-activity areas, but they are not generally constructed or equipped for use in communities that place severe demands on their apparatus. Missing are the shiny touches (such as chrome) and the optional systems (such as air conditioning) that are present on many pieces of vehicular fire equipment; also missing are some features—such as supplemental braking devices—that may extend the life of the apparatus, minimize maintenance costs, or improve firefighter safety.

When a department is developing specifications and comparing proposals from different manufacturers, it should give thought to the costs of operating and maintaining the vehicle. The addition of a heavy-duty drive train component may extend the life of a vehicle or reduce maintenance costs for the life of the vehicle. A minimal initial investment can help reduce ongoing costs throughout the life of the apparatus or emergency vehicle.

Standardization and training costs　Because of the long service lives of emergency vehicles, it is difficult to provide units that have standard ways of storing and using equipment and standard operational methods. But to the extent possible, fire apparatus and other emergency vehicles should have standard layouts, and the equipment stored in a particular location should be similar from unit to unit. Standardization in storage and layout will minimize time spent searching for a piece of equipment by firefighters who are unfamiliar with the exact layout of a unit from another location or who work in different locations from day to day. Operational standardization, too, is important; the need for additional training can be minimized if pumps and aerial devices have similar operational controls and characteristics. Achieving operational standardization is complicated, however, by advancements in technology that improve operational control and capability and by variations from manufacturer to manufacturer.

Costs and vendor support The fire apparatus and ambulance manufacturing industries have a long history of very old and reliable companies failing and new companies being developed, becoming successful, and then failing. The survival of any one apparatus manufacturer cannot be absolutely guaranteed for the life of the warranty, much less the service life of the vehicle. Fire departments and local government managers can take several steps to minimize this risk.

First, they can develop a good purchase specification. It should be based on local needs and requirements, national standards, and the experiences of those inside and outside the local fire and rescue department. A well-thought-out purchase specification can go a long way toward providing a vehicle that will serve the community and perhaps outlast those who created it.

Second, to the extent possible, a department should not use apparatus components that are handmade or bought on special order: later in the life of the vehicle, these parts and components will become scarce or impossible to procure. In addition, whenever possible, it is best to use components and configurations that are not unique to the fire service. If a component is in general use in the trucking industry, it will probably be available when needed in the future. If a department has a mission-critical component that may be unavailable in the future, it should purchase a spare one.

Third, the department should get an "as-built" electrical diagram of every vehicle. Electrical problems are one of the most common afflictions of fire apparatus and emergency vehicles—and among the most time-consuming and difficult problems to solve. The diagram will be expensive, probably costing in the thousands of dollars, but it will pay dividends over the life of the vehicle. Any changes made after the vehicle is placed in service should be documented on this diagram to keep it current, so it can help speed up the diagnosis of problems.

Finally, the department should require the provision of high-quality service manuals. The purchase specification should require documentation for the servicing and use of every major component of the vehicle.

Evaluating safety and obsolescence

The safety of firefighters and of the people who live their lives around fire and rescue vehicles should be central to the purchasing process. In most parts of the United States if not in most of the world, laws grant special permission or allowances to the operators of emergency vehicles responding to a call. In many cases the operators are allowed to proceed at speeds above the posted speed limit, to drive in opposing lanes of traffic, to proceed through red traffic signals and stop signs without coming to a full stop, and to engage in other high-risk driving behavior. Since these activities occur on every emergency response, they present some of the highest liability and life safety risks to the fire and rescue department. Every year, approximately 10 percent of the firefighters killed in the line of duty die while en route to or from an emergency. And firefighters are not the only ones at risk. In vehicle collisions involving fire apparatus and civilian vehicles, the driver and occupants of the civilian vehicle almost always suffer worse consequences than the firefighters.

Risks encountered in responding to an emergency rescue call can be minimized by vehicle operator training, response procedures, and traffic preemption devices. But although these risk management procedures are monumentally important, they are outside the scope of this chapter.

Other ways of minimizing the risks encountered during an emergency response, however, can be addressed here. NFPA, FAA, and GSA standards directly affect the safety of fire apparatus, ARFF vehicles, and ambulances, and these standards should be used as the basis for any purchase specification. They lie behind a number of positive safety changes in the fire apparatus industry, among which are noise attenuation, emergency-light conspicuity, and requirements for fully enclosed passenger compartments and for minimum load ratings of aerial ladders.

But the same changes that improve safety may also hasten obsolescence. In the 1990s, fire apparatus and other emergency vehicles changed in many ways, and many of these changes not only improved the safety of firefighters but also accelerated the obsolescence of existing apparatus. For example, aerial ladder standards at the beginning of the twenty-first century set minimum weight capacity capabilities for aerial ladders, improving the stability and therefore the safety of the ladders. Yet many older ladders were not capable of meeting these minimums and were not as stable as the newer equipment. These older ladders began to be removed from service and replaced by new, more advanced devices offering more operational capability and higher levels of safety for firefighters.

Another example of a change that both improves safety and accelerates obsolescence is the addition of compressed air foam systems (CAFS) to fire engines (pumpers). These systems introduce air and foam concentrate into the hose stream and have been found to increase firefighting efficiency and limit water damage. The systems are not inexpensive—most cost more than $25,000—but retrofitting many existing pumpers with them is impossible. Thus, the desire to add CAFS capability to firefighting apparatus has accelerated the replacement of some apparatus.

Considering various funding sources

Apparatus and emergency vehicles are funded by a variety of mechanisms, including the operating budget, capital purchases through bonds, lease-purchase arrangements, sinking funds, and leasing. Larger communities may be capable of funding the replacement of apparatus and emergency vehicles as a recurring cost in their annual budgets. Some communities choose to fund apparatus through voter-approved bond issues. With lease-purchase arrangements, communities can pay for purchases in much the same way that many people buy their family cars—that is, by making monthly or annual payments and paying interest for the use of the funds.

Sinking funds, which some communities have developed, are a pay-as-you-go means of replacing apparatus and vehicles. In these communities, replacing vehicles is viewed as a process rather than an event. Sinking funds are specially dedicated funds that are based on a replacement plan for apparatus and emergency vehicles. Every vehicle in the fleet is assigned a service life and a replacement cost estimate. The service life is based on the replacement plan, and the cost estimate accounts for inflation and projected cost increases. That cost is broken down into payments that are based either on the passage of time (payments made monthly, quarterly, or annually) or on vehicle use (payments by the mile or by the hour). The payments are deposited into an account, where they accumulate until it is time to fund the purchase of replacement apparatus and other vehicles. Depending on local laws and regulations, these accounts may or may not be capable of earning interest as a hedge against inflation. The accounts provide funding for replacements only, not for additions to the fleet. Fleet additions are usually paid for by some other funding source, and after the additions are bought, contributions are made to the sinking fund to pay for their eventual replacement.

The replacement plan must also make some accommodation for vehicles that are destroyed or rendered useless before their planned service life has expired. Either the plan itself (i.e., the sinking fund) may absorb such unscheduled expenses or another source of revenue may be called on to fund the replacement of destroyed and damaged vehicles. These other sources may be, for example, insurance, funds recovered from the responsible party, or the operating or capital budget.

One possible shortcoming of sinking funds is that they eventually reach a significant size and may therefore become the object of attention when fiscal conditions send local government managers in search of sources of quick cash. In some cases, funds have been withdrawn from sinking funds on the understanding that the withdrawals will be replaced when the economy turns upward again. But despite everyone's best intentions, these replacements cannot always be made. Although some local charters or government bylaws do not allow funds of any kind to be insulated from any legal use determined by the local governing body, steps should be taken to shield these funds from well-intentioned raids that will impair the funds' ability to function as intended. The other side of the equation may come into play as well: the fire chief who wants to purchase a 200-foot ladder when the plan contemplated only a 100-foot ladder may need to go somewhere outside the sinking fund to find the monies to pay for the difference in cost.

A late 1990s addition to the apparatus replacement landscape is the leasing of fire apparatus. The terms of the lease agreement are similar to those for the lease of a car. Payments are based on the difference between the original purchase price and an estimate of the residual value of the apparatus at the end of the lease period, at which time the department surrenders the apparatus and returns it to the vendor. Some leases contain a provision that allows for the purchase of the apparatus at a set price at the end of the lease, if desired. Positive aspects of lease arrangements include lower initial costs, regular replacement of apparatus, and, if a piece of equipment presents trouble, the ability to dispose of it in a shorter period of time. Negative aspects include the need to return or purchase the vehicle at the end of the lease period and the associated need either to find funding for a purchase or to arrange another lease.

Procurement of capital facilities

Fire department capital facilities consist mainly of fire stations, which are exposed to some of the most intense and demanding uses of any public facility. Career stations are occupied literally around the clock, and volunteer stations are occupied for significant amounts of time each week. In addition, many fire stations contain meeting rooms and rooms for other public uses. These capital facilities must not only accommodate the severe uses to which they are put but also be capable of serving for decades.

Establishing the need to replace an existing station and procuring a replacement are closely related actions, and both actions—closing an existing fire station and siting a new or replacement facility—are among the most contentious issues that public sector managers can address. Fire stations are an integral part of the fabric of the community they serve. They are constants in a changing world. Once a fire station is constructed, it may serve at that very spot for more than one hundred years. Firefighters assigned to a fire station identify very closely with the residents of "their" area (often called a company's first-due area), and they feel strongly about their duty to serve their area. In turn, the citizens living in proximity to an existing station often have strong feelings about the need to retain the station in its existing location. Faced with a station's closure or relocation, the neighbors may express concerns about levels of service and the fate of "our firefighters" and, most especially, about the response to their emergencies and the fate of the building that is vacated. When a new station is to be constructed, members of the new community are generally very happy about the prospect of having firefighters nearby but are concerned about the effect a fire station will have on their neighborhood in terms of traffic, noise, and light. For all these reasons, caution and a deliberative decision-making process are called for in any decision to close or relocate a fire station or open a new one.

The key to preventing community distrust and anger when a decision is made to close, relocate, or construct a fire station is communication. If the need to change fire station deployment is explained to the community truthfully and early, the decision will probably find more support than if the news is delivered in the morning paper.

The need to open a new fire station or relocate an existing one should be based on a fire station deployment plan that takes into account shifts in population, annexation of additional areas into a jurisdiction, and other factors. The deployment plan is often part of an overall master plan for a fire department or a community—a massive planning effort that can set the tone for fire department deployment for decades. This chapter does not discuss the master planning effort but does examine not only the decision to remodel or relocate an existing fire station but also some components of the process used to site and construct a new fire station. The final decision on remodeling or replacing an existing facility does not follow any formula. Local government managers must take all the factors discussed here into consideration before making their decision. (Also discussed here are fire station specifications and related matters.)

The actual decision to remodel or replace an existing fire station is based on the following:

The condition and serviceability of the existing station—that is, the physical condition of the facility itself and of its major systems, and the ability of the station to serve the current and anticipated needs of the community as they relate to the services to be provided from the station

The availability and acceptability of other sites

The availability of funding

Closing or opening a fire station The process of closing and/or opening a fire station can be a public relations nightmare. Local government and fire service officials need to be prepared for the fact that regardless of how citizens feel about the department itself, their views on the proximity of fire stations may be quite varied and may be expressed quite vociferously.

The officials of a small community in the southwestern United States had planned for years to close an undersized and poorly placed fire station. When funds finally became available, the matter became news when it was placed on the city council agenda. Two groups of citizens asked to be heard at the council meeting.

One was citizens from the quiet old neighborhood that had hosted the station since the 1920s. They were outraged that the city would consider moving the facility. They pointed out that their neighborhood had many aging structures and was in a renaissance mode, with many young families moving into the area. The group also complained that instead of being sold, the historic old structure should be remodeled and used for its intended purpose. The group was loud and well organized and did not take comfort in mere verbal assurances from the fire department that the new facility, to be located about 0.7 mile away, would provide very adequate protection within the specified norms for the city.

The other group of citizens asking to be heard represented the new, upscale neighborhood that was located a short

Other factors, such as the level of political and community interest in the siting process.

Physical condition and serviceability

The physical condition of the facility can be assessed by fire department staff, other government workers, or contractors. In a large or extremely talented fire department, this review could be conducted entirely in-house, but most departments will need to rely on the expertise of other agencies or contractors for some or most of the review. The review must include assessments of (1) the physical condition of the structure and its major systems, (2) the station's livability from the point of view of its occupants and visitors, and (3) the station's deployment and service delivery capability.

Structure and major systems This is the part of the assessment that is most often out of the fire department's ability to provide. Professional building maintenance and engineering expertise can be secured through the public works or facility maintenance functions of many jurisdictions. Another source of this type of expertise is private sector engineering firms. The review needs to address the physical condition of the structural components of the station (floors, bearing walls, roof); the operability of the building's systems (heat, air conditioning, water, gas, wastewater, steam, communications); and compliance with local, state, and national codes. Although in many cases compliance with codes is not required until the building is modified, the local jurisdiction may choose to comply with codes at any time. For example, a community may desire to make its buildings more accessible to people with physical handicaps (see the sidebar on standards and accommodation on the next page). This part of the review should include an estimate of the cost of resolving any identified problems and an overall professional recommendation about the decision to remodel or replace.

---

distance from the intended site of the new fire station. This group of citizens made it clear that they liked the fire department and thought the service the department provided was good and extremely important. However, they did not want a fire station near their neighborhood. It was certain to be noisy, smelly, too bright, too large, and in general a blight on property values. They invoked the diesel smoke, the noise of sirens, and the perceived threat that speeding fire apparatus posed to children playing in the area. Although they wanted a fire station as close as possible, they did not want it close enough to impinge on their environment.

The debate went on for months and even became an election issue. As a result of the turmoil, the inadequate old station was superficially remodeled and remained in service. Expansion of the city boundaries, however, was limited by the fact that adequate fire services were not readily available in one particular direction.

When asked later how he might have approached the matter differently, the fire chief made it clear that he had felt unprepared. Missing from his defense were critical data—specific and scientifically supportable data on response areas and on the environmental impact of a fire station. Certainly the emotional issues will always be a consideration, but good, supportable information will often help allay the fears of well-meaning citizens.

Occupant and visitor livability   Occupant and visitor livability is the part of the assessment that is most often within the fire department's ability to provide. Nobody understands the weaknesses and strengths of a building better than its occupants and those who visit it.

The occupants should be solicited for input about the station's comfort and capability. For example, should an individual dorm room be provided for each on-duty firefighter rather than the large bunk rooms that were standard in the past? Is there a need to provide space for physical fitness equipment, such as stationary bikes and treadmills, in response to an increased emphasis on firefighter wellness? Is there a need to provide more separation between the station's living areas and its apparatus storage areas in order to address concerns about safety and health? In addition, the increased role played by many fire departments in providing EMS may generate a requirement for an additional storage room or a designated space where equipment and clothing can be decontaminated.

The needs of station occupants who are not members of the fire department must also be addressed. Many fire stations serve as meeting places for community groups and as local contact points for other services. For example, many communities in Texas have regulations (partly as a means of revenue collection) that require trash to be contained in an approved bag, and the approved trash bags are sold through the local fire stations. Another example is blood pressure checks, which on-duty firefighters often provide. Thus, the public's access to the facility must be addressed.

Deployment and service delivery capability   A major part of the decision to remodel or replace a station is the ability of the existing facility to support fire department deployment. Fire apparatus has grown in size over time, and an older station may not be able to house new apparatus, especially aerial apparatus. Fire departments that provide emergency ambulance service may need additional space to house ambulances and staff. In addition, shifts in population or in emergency incident loads may require additional staffing and equipment in an area that did not need it in the past. Although many of these concerns will have been addressed in the development of the fire station deployment plan mentioned above, consideration must also be given to the ability of the

---

Standards and accommodation   New fire stations are required to accommodate both men and women, including those with disabilities, and the assessment of an existing station must keep these new requirements in mind.

Many fire departments, if not most, now have both male and female members. But the need to accommodate both sexes in fire stations is relatively new, and most older fire stations were built to accommodate only men. Accommodating women in a fire station generally involves converting or adding restroom and locker room facilities for women. Except in smaller stations where space is at a premium, these accommoda-

tions can generally be made without too much difficulty.

The Americans with Disabilities Act (ADA) has also affected assessments of fire stations, for the need to accommodate persons with disabilities in fire department facilities was not given much consideration when stations were designed in the past. Even if applied only minimally, the ADA requires that the public access areas of a fire station be designed and configured to accommodate people with physical disabilities. Fire stations equipped with elevators, once an unimaginable building component for a fire station, are becoming more common.

existing site—both the building's internal space and the land available—to accommodate needed functions and to the availability (or nonavailability) of acceptable alternative sites.

Acceptability of other sites

Consideration should be given to the size of the lot or land that is secured to site a new or replacement fire station. The general location of the site will be driven by the department's deployment plan, but the exact site chosen should be large enough to accommodate the anticipated uses of the station now and far into the future. Placing a fire station on a postage stamp–sized lot will save money in the short term but will limit that site's future usefulness.

Funding and community interest

When possible, fire station sites in developing areas should be purchased before the wave of construction begins, even if funding for the station's construction is not available at that particular time. The sites for these future stations should be supplied with signs, as large as local ordinances permit, that announce "Future Site of Fire Station Number XX." These signs inform home and commercial buyers that a fire station will eventually be their neighbor and may lessen the force of any future NIMBY ("not in my back yard") movement.

Specifications, working with architects, and safety

Fire stations are unique in needing to keep living and sleeping quarters very close to apparatus storage areas and in experiencing so high a level of use. Thus, some architects working on fire station designs will be learning as they go. A fire department that prepares a standard fire station specification, similar to an apparatus specification, and provides it to the architect at the beginning of the process will be giving very useful help that will eliminate a lot of rework and will therefore speed up the design process. The station specification should (1) set out the number of firefighters to occupy the station, (2) describe living arrangements, (3) provide rough estimates of square footage uses for each activity, and (4) describe the standard features and fixtures that are expected but may be unfamiliar to architects (e.g., those that address NFPA standards on infectious disease control or safety issues related to diesel exhaust management).

The specification should give primary consideration to firefighter safety: the provision of proper walking surfaces, minimization (when possible) of the use of stairs and fire poles, infection control and hazardous-waste disposal, diesel exhaust management, proper lighting, and safe movement of apparatus. These issues are very familiar to members of the fire service but need to be effectively communicated to architects (as well as to public works officials, upper government managers, and customers).

Excellent examples of the type of specification discussed here have been developed by the Fairfax County, Virginia, Fire and Rescue Department; the Miami-Dade, Florida, Fire Rescue Department; and the Phoenix, Arizona, Fire Department. A body of literature, mainly in the form of journal articles, gives guidance on station design. And an excellent resource on safety in the design of fire stations is a free publication prepared by the U.S. Fire Administration titled *Safety and Health Considerations for the Design of Fire and Emergency Medical Services Stations.*[3]

Maintenance and accountability

Once the fire department's capital equipment, emergency vehicles, and facilities are procured, they need to be maintained so that their readiness is preserved and a long service life ensured. This section provides maintenance recommendations and suggestions for managing accountability for these capital assets.

For capital equipment

The information in this section does not provide guidance on such details of equipment maintenance and accountability as the recommended frequency for testing ladders. Instead it provides information for public sector managers on overall maintenance and accountability programs, the effect of these programs on delivery of services, sources of information, and general guidelines for managers.

As mentioned above, firefighters use a very broad array of tools in performing their work. At one extreme, some of these tools have not changed in a hundred years and generally do not require much maintenance beyond routine lubrication and painting. At the other extreme, some tools are so complex that many fire and rescue departments choose to have maintenance performed by outside vendors or by the manufacturer of the tool. Examples of this type of complex tool are the cardiac monitor/defibrillator used by paramedics and the automatic external defibrillators used by other firefighters (see Chapter 1). Such equipment is routinely maintained and repaired by the manufacturer or a manufacturer-authorized service center. Very few fire and rescue departments have the expertise, inventory, or inclination to fully maintain this type of equipment.

Maintenance   In two respects, maintenance requirements for fire equipment differ from those generally applicable in every industry. First, given the emergency circumstances in which fire equipment is used, extremely high rates of reliability are necessary, as mentioned above. An SCBA, for example, needs to have the highest level of reliability because its correct functioning literally means the difference between life and death for the firefighter. Similarly with a cardiac monitor/defibrillator: its correct operation—every time—is critical to the survival of cardiac customers. For such equipment, therefore, periodic tests are a vital part of an adequate maintenance program. SCBA and defibrillators, for example, should be checked by career firefighters at the beginning of each shift to ensure reliability. In volunteer departments, equipment checks should be performed on a regular basis—at least weekly—to ensure readiness. In addition to periodic checks by the user, many items of fire and EMS equipment must be checked periodically by technicians trained in maintaining them. These checks are discussed below (see "A Support Function").

The second respect in which equipment maintenance is different in the fire service from that in other industries is the role of inventory, given the fire department's need to plan and be prepared for both natural and man-made disasters (see sidebar on the next page). Accordingly, inventory levels for fire equipment (spare equipment that is on hand to temporarily replace equipment that is broken or in the maintenance cycle) and for parts for that equipment are often maintained at higher levels than the casual observer might think appropriate.

Maintenance of fire department equipment generally involves the active participation of at least four players: the firefighter, a support function of the fire department, the manufacturer, and NFPA. An overall maintenance plan that involves all four of these players, and any others as required on the local level, provides a good basis for equipment readiness.

Civil disturbances, terrorism, and strategic reserves The disabling disasters and civil disturbances—not to mention the attacks by domestic and international terrorists—of the 1990s and the opening years of the twenty-first century have served as a reminder that fire departments need to maintain a strategic reserve of equipment for these situations, however infrequent. The civil disturbances in Los Angeles in 1992 left that city's fire department with missing and damaged fire equipment and apparatus that had to be immediately replaced to ensure continued service to the community. The terrorist attack on New York City's World Trade Center on September 11, 2001, led to the destruction of a huge amount of fire equipment and apparatus and to the deaths of 343 fire service personnel. Proper prior planning by the New York City Fire Department allowed spare and reserve apparatus and equipment to be rapidly placed in service. The arrival of international terrorism in the United States, succeeding the riots in Los Angeles and the bombing of the Alfred P. Murrah Federal Building in Oklahoma City in 1995, calls for strategic reserves to be reevaluated.

The firefighter Firefighters routinely perform daily, weekly, and monthly checks of equipment as prescribed by policies developed within each department and by the maintenance plan. As mentioned above, in career departments the operation of equipment is generally checked at shift change; in volunteer departments, during weekly training days/nights. Firefighters also perform more detailed checks at a lower frequency, generally weekly or monthly.

A support function The support function of the fire and rescue department performs maintenance beyond the minor maintenance performed by firefighters; it also repairs broken or damaged equipment and manages the department's inventory of tools and parts. This support function may be provided in a number of ways, depending on the size of the department, the range of the equipment to be maintained, and local considerations. One way is to have the function provided by fire department members working in a fire department support operation or by firefighters assigned to fire stations who are trained and equipped to perform maintenance. A second way, and one used by many fire departments, is to employ firefighters or civilians whose sole function is to provide equipment maintenance and repair. Third, still other departments develop "specialties" for their stations and provide these stations with the necessary training, tools, equipment, and parts (see the sidebar on the next page). A fourth option is to contract with outside vendors to provide such services, although the use of outside contractors does not relieve the fire department of all maintenance responsibilities. Program management and such details as equipment collection and delivery to the vendor still need to be addressed.

The manufacturer Equipment manufacturers are an excellent source—most often the only source—of maintenance information. The manufacturer's literature that comes with fire equipment needs to be retained and held in a reference library for use in the development of maintenance plans and for general reference. Manufacturers of some pieces of fire equipment, such as SCBA and hydraulic rescue tools, provide maintenance schools and certifications for their equipment. These programs often cost little or nothing. Manufacturers may also provide service for their equipment.

NFPA NFPA publishes standards for the maintenance of fire equipment items such as ground ladders and hose. These standards provide information on maintenance frequency, testing, maintenance methods, records retention, and prac-

Support service without support staff The Poudre Fire Authority serves Fort Collins, Colorado, and the surrounding Poudre Valley Fire Protection District. The department operates nine career and three volunteer fire stations with a total of 149 career and 40 volunteer members, protecting 235 square miles and a population of 145,000. When the department found itself without sufficient resources to devote full-time staff to many support services, Chief John Mulligan initiated an imaginative system of specialty fire stations to perform emergency and support duties. One station specializes in HAZMAT incident response (along with responses to its regular fire and EMS call load), and another specializes in the maintenance and repair of safety equipment such as SCBA. Each station has some specialty that contributes to the strength of the organization.

---

tices for specific classes of equipment. For example, NFPA 1962, Standard for the Care, Use, and Service Testing of Fire Hose Including Couplings and Nozzles (1998 edition), prescribes testing of hose and nozzles, record keeping, and testing procedures. Other NFPA standards are in place or under development to guide the maintenance of ladders and protective clothing. Although NFPA standards do not carry the force of law, they are often referenced by manufacturers and are considered industry standards of care for equipment.

Accountability To manage their inventories, fire departments should have equipment accountability systems in place. The basis of these systems should be any local asset-inventory reporting requirements and whatever system is used for record keeping for equipment maintenance. Each piece of equipment should be marked to identify its proper owner or assignment. These markings may include retroreflective stickers containing the name of the fire department and the name or number of the station or unit to which the tool is assigned; or they may include inventory numbers that are painted on or tamped into the equipment, or bar codes that are chemically etched into the metal. Advances made in bar coding systems during the 1990s can simplify and automate many labor-intensive inventory-related activities.

A system should also be in place to report and document the absence (due to loss or theft) of a piece of equipment. Because fire equipment is most often purchased with public funding, an accurate and timely accounting for the location and use of all equipment is called for. When equipment is lost, stolen, or destroyed in the course of its life, proper documentation must exist to ensure the integrity of the accountability system and to provide a basis for requesting replacement equipment.

For emergency vehicles

The same basic concerns and cast of players that relate to fire equipment relate to emergency vehicles. The basic concern is that extremely high levels of reliability for the vehicle and its systems are required if service is to be delivered effectively. The cast of players consists of firefighters, who perform routine maintenance and checks; the fire department support function, which manages more complex or involved maintenance and repair; manufacturers, who provide support; and NFPA standards, which address periodic testing and maintenance of vehicle components, such as aerial ladders and pumps.

Unlike equipment maintenance and repair, however, vehicle maintenance and repair are very often performed by a division of the larger governmental body, such as a city or county fleet management function. In these situations, the fire department support function coordinates service and the movements of vehi-

cles. A large number of fire departments, however, perform their own maintenance, with civilian or uniformed members of the department providing the
service.

Maintaining adequate reserve vehicles and an adequate parts inventory is
more costly than in the analogous case of fire equipment. Reserve vehicles are
needed to ensure that a service-ready vehicle is present to replace a vehicle
that is unavailable because it is in maintenance, has broken down, or is being
tested. The term *reserve* is actually a misnomer, for it is used throughout the
fire and rescue service to describe a vehicle that is not permanently assigned
to front-line duty but may be regularly called upon to serve in that capacity.
The number of vehicles required to maintain an adequate reserve depends entirely on the size of the fire department fleet, the level of activity the department
experiences, cycle time for the maintenance and repair of vehicles, the overall
health and age of the fleet, and other local considerations. The Insurance Services Office (ISO), still considered by some to be the authority for fire department evaluation, recommends one reserve pumper for every eight pumpers
(or portion thereof) needed in service and one reserve ladder, or aerial, for
every eight ladders (or portion thereof) needed in service.

The importance of regular vehicle checks cannot be overstated. In career departments, daily operational checks of apparatus are the norm, usually performed
by the oncoming shift at shift change. In volunteer departments, regular checks
often occur on weekly training nights or on some other regular basis. Because
of the high level of reliability that is expected of fire apparatus, catching a failure
during a regular check may mean preventing a failure in delivering service.

Accountability for vehicles may be more or less of a challenge than accountability for equipment. Although a fire engine is harder to lose than an ax, it
must be accounted for in the same way: as prescribed by local asset-tracking
rules and as tracked for maintenance record keeping. Collisions involving fire
department vehicles should be well documented, and when the damage created
in these collisions is assessed, the impact of the collision on fire department–
related components of the vehicle needs to be included. For example, if an
aerial ladder is involved in a collision with another vehicle, the body of the
truck may have received damage that a local body shop can adequately assess,
but if a component of the aerial system, such as an outrigger (or jack), is
involved, the services of an engineer employed or authorized by the aerial
manufacturer may have to be secured so that any negative impact on the aerial
system may be competently evaluated.

For capital facilities

Facility maintenance and accountability involve mostly the same concerns and
cast of characters that have already been discussed. Reliability is a concern
with facilities: critical systems within the fire station, such as heat, water, sewer,
gas, and air conditioning, need to work without fail. And standard everyday
station maintenance is almost always provided by firefighters, although some
communities use other government workers (such as parks workers) or contractors to perform landscape maintenance. Many volunteer fire departments
employ or contract with maintenance workers to handle day-to-day chores.

What is different about capital facilities, though, is that fire stations are
among the most heavily used of government buildings, as mentioned above.
They are occupied around-the-clock or for significant periods each month. In
particular, volunteer fire department stations are very often the focus of many
non-fire-department functions. Moreover, career fire stations are now emulating
volunteer fire stations in providing community rooms (as many volunteer stations have done for years) to integrate the fire station more closely into the
community. These rooms can be used for meetings of local home owners as-

sociations or of Boy Scouts and Girl Scouts, and for other social functions. In the normal course of use in a fire station, things will break and wear out, so planning in advance for the eventuality will make everyone's life pleasanter.

Provisions should be made to enable emergency repairs to be performed at any time: contracts and/or after-hours contact information should be in place before the service is needed. The availability of this information will allow the fire department to have contact with maintenance and repair providers after hours and on holidays. Although the average home could make it through a weekend with no hot water, for example, a fire station could not. Unless fire-fighters can cook, clean, and maintain personal hygiene (e.g., take showers), the fire station will not remain functional.

Certainly, much of the information needed to manage facilities properly is not unique to the fire service. An annual operational assessment of all fire department facilities by a qualified individual will prevent system failures by identifying problems before they become failures. Preventive maintenance on such systems as heating and air conditioning can dramatically extend the lives of the systems.

Very few fire departments provide all their own facility maintenance services (beyond taking care of chores and minor maintenance). Most departments do not usually employ construction workers and the like who do remodeling, electrical work, plumbing, and other trade work. Rather, departments contract out some services or have another governmental agency perform the work. An individual or a position within the department should be identified as the fire department's facility manager. In smaller organizations, this role can be adequately performed by a single individual; in larger organizations, a staff may be called for.

Many governments carry or list their facilities as assets, and in these cases local rules governing annual or periodic reporting must be followed, as with equipment and apparatus. Although fire stations do not get up and move on their own—do not get lost or stolen—improvements or remodeling since the previous reporting period should be detailed in the current period's report.

Conclusion

The fire service's customers demand that the fire service be good stewards of their money. They also demand that the tools, apparatus, and facilities used to provide fire and emergency medical services work when they are needed. In the future a still higher level of scrutiny by the public and the press can be expected, focusing on matters that might once have been considered too mundane or insignificant to warrant close attention—matters such as capital resources. This scrutiny will certainly have a strong effect on capital resource management. A structured maintenance program for capital equipment, vehicles, and facilities ensures that funds are spent wisely and that these essential resources are available when needed.

Technology, too, promises to have a major effect on capital resource management. Already the computerization of records and inventories has made the fire and rescue service more accountable and efficient, and the application of technology in tracking equipment, operating fire apparatus, managing facilities, and maintaining all three types of capital resources can be expected to have a like effect.

1   This standard is available for a nominal charge ($20.00 in 2002) from GSA. To confirm price and availability, contact the GSA Specification Section by telephone at (202) 708-5082, by fax at (202) 619-8985, or by mail at Federal Supply Services, Specification Section, 470 L'Enfant Plaza, Suite 8100, Washington, DC 20407.

2   This standard is available at no charge from the FAA. Contact the FAA online at www.faa.gov/arp/150acs.htm or by fax at (301) 386-5394.

3   U.S. Fire Administration, *Safety and Health Considerations for the Design of Fire and Emergency Medical Services Stations* (Emmitsburg, Md.: USFA, 1997).

Part three:
Improving
resources

Leading and managing

The fire service has always been viewed very positively by taxpayers and elected officials, but at the beginning of the twenty-first century it faces increasing competition for limited dollars. Although a competing fire department is unlikely to open a station across the street and drive the first organization out of business with a half-price sale, more and more fire and rescue services are being reminded that they have competitors. Police services, road improvement projects, community development and rehabilitation—these are some of the many diverse projects and services local governments can fund, but there is not enough money to fund them all.

Many people understand competition in terms of a Burger King opening up across from a McDonald's, and the concept is the same if the competition arises within the public sector and if funding rather than customer patronage is at stake. A number of fire service organizations, therefore, have touted the value of transferring private industry principles to public sector management and have realized that there are always opportunities for improving service delivery. They have been able to compete by modifying traditional fire service cultures in the direction of service and quality management and by approaching leadership in a new way. Their crucial role in homeland security helps emphasize the importance of their service.

In fact, the need to be increasingly competitive in an environment in which the demands on the fire services are changing more and more rapidly has caused a shift in fire service attitudes toward leadership. In the past, fire chiefs closely guarded their leadership authority, but in the new millennium, chiefs are finding it necessary to distribute the leadership responsibility more broadly. Future organizational responsiveness and effectiveness will depend on the cultivation of leadership skills throughout the organization.

Broad-based leadership—extending beyond fire chiefs and others in formal leadership and managerial positions—is the best predictor of the success or failure of an organization. Although an organization may be influenced by environment, culture, technology, and many other factors, when these factors are held constant, organizations succeed or fail on the basis of the quality of their leadership: organizations that teach leadership skills to all employees have more flexibility and a higher capacity for changing to meet market needs.[1]

Many fire departments, either independently or under the direction of their local governments, have implemented the concept of broad-based leadership by devising new programs. Unfortunately, the word *program* often has negative connotations, for managers often charge ahead with programs that are based on new ideas before the ideas have been sufficiently examined. In addition, programs are often introduced by managers who have the best intentions but who fail to consult those who would be most affected, fail to follow up on the progress of those affected, or fail to follow through on initial commitments. Skeptics in fire and rescue departments know to watch for signs that new initiatives are merely management fads.

To minimize skepticism about the new concept of broad-based leadership, leaders must model the performance they expect from their departments. They will be more effective if their own knowledge of the issues involved in leading and managing fire services is enhanced. This chapter examines management (leadership) concepts both in general and from the specific perspective of fire service organizations. Definitions of management and leadership are given first, followed by an outline of what management theorists have concluded are best management practices. Then leadership training is discussed: the personal skills necessary for leadership, and ways of using the concepts of leadership throughout an organization. The next subject is the delegation of tasks to individuals and teams: broad-based leadership (the diffusion of leadership throughout an organization) requires that employees be empowered both individually and as members of teams so that they can engage actively in the organization's growth. Leadership is then viewed in the context of organizational culture: what is organizational culture, what is involved in addressing cultural issues, and above all, how can a culture be shaped and changed? Finally, because leadership within the fire service organization is complemented by the relationship between the fire chief and the local government manager, this relationship is explored from the viewpoint of both parties.

One can define leadership in a fire service organization by answering certain basic questions, but answering them unsystematically can be like trying to fit together the scattered pieces of a jigsaw puzzle (see Figure 8–1). In the absence of systemwide planning and effective communication, members of the department may see the departmental mission, goals, and culture—all of which are critical aspects of leadership—as separate initiatives instead of as interlocking pieces that already form a single picture.

Figure 8–1
Leadership: Puzzle
in pieces.

Management and leadership defined

Management is a set of processes that can keep a complicated system of people and technology running smoothly. The most important aspects of management include planning, budgeting, organizing, staffing, controlling, and problem solving. Leadership is a set of processes that creates organizations in the first place or adapts them to significantly changing circumstances. Leadership defines what the future should look like, aligns people with that vision, and inspires them to make it happen despite the obstacles.[2]

People incorrectly compartmentalize the activities of managing and leading, assuming that managers manage, leaders lead, and everyone else just works. Certainly, organizations typically develop a chain of command that formally assigns management responsibilities to particular individuals; doing so is seen as necessary to the running of many organizations. And the fire service, given the necessarily autocratic nature of emergency scene management, is particularly good at developing these hierarchies.

But neither management nor leadership should be limited to a small segment of an organization. The employees at the top of the hierarchy (those in management positions) are not the only employees who can—or should—engage in the activities of managing or leading. Every employee should have the capacity and be given the opportunity to engage in managing and leading at some level within the organization. Every employee has a particular area of responsibility as determined by the needs of the organization, and it is at this level, within this sphere (or circle) of influence, that the employee should be responsible and accountable for using management and leadership skills. A sphere of influence might be equipment, a truck, or a company, battalion, or department (see Figure 8–2). In the sphere of influence in which firefighters, for example, operate, they are responsible individually for the maintenance of their own equipment and are responsible jointly for the activities of their company.

Understanding the scope of activities for which leadership skills can be used is an integral element of organizational development. Introducing shared leadership responsibilities at multiple levels in an organization requires senior managers not only to establish accountability for responsibilities at specific levels of the department but also to communicate their expectations clearly.

Employees can participate in managing by providing input on how a specific job should be done. Front-line staff, for example, best understand the equipment, technology, or systems used in the department and may have some of

Figure 8–2
Circles, or spheres, of influence.

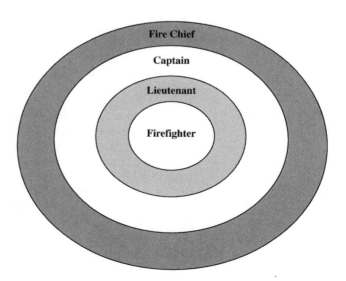

the best ideas about how to improve services or how best to use equipment to do the job. By expressing their ideas or, better yet, acting on them, front-line staff are being effective leaders in contributing to the overall management of the organization.

Best practices in management (leadership)

The practices considered "best" for managing and leading at the beginning of the twenty-first century (and espoused in this chapter) grew out of decades of evolving management theory. Ranging from Frederick Winslow Taylor (whose *Principles of Scientific Management* was published in 1911 and became controversial in the 1920s) to W. Edwards Deming (whose ideas of quality management were prominent in the 1950s and 1960s) and Stephen R. Covey (touting principle-centered leadership in the 1990s),[3] theorists have had their own views about which management techniques are most appropriate, and the differences in these views reflect changing models of the work environment. The early theories were based on the assumption that profit is the sole goal for an organization and that employee interests and motivations as well as customer service are irrelevant. More recent theories have been based on two premises: the first is that employees seek to do a job well but the systems within the organization are most often what prevents them from doing so, and the second is that the underlying values within an organization influence its every action.

More particularly, theories of management at the beginning of the twenty-first century focus on dispersed leadership, an overriding vision of the future, alignment with an underlying set of values and principles, and a need to respond to an ever-changing market. With the accelerating growth of technology and changes in citizens' expectations, organizations that do not continually adjust to changing needs will fail.

All modern management theories (i.e., beginning with Taylor), although they take different approaches, have several important components in common: focusing on the customer, continuing to improve the organization, measuring performance, managing change, and centering on principle.

Focusing on the customer

Customer service is not an original concept, and an attempt to tie quality management to a focus on customer service must begin by acknowledging that fire department members have always valued community and customer service and have had years of experience and technical training in satisfactorily fulfilling the service's emergency response mission. Nevertheless, when experience and technical expertise are paired with professional ego, they can interfere with successful customer service: people who view themselves as "the experts" are tempted to pay only lip service to customer feedback.

Being focused on the customer involves more than providing quality customer service. It means defining business around citizens' needs—in other words, being flexible enough to redesign products as the community's needs and expectations change. More broadly, it means being both able and willing to change, recognizing that future success in the fire service depends on matching services with citizens' evolving needs. As the public becomes increasingly sophisticated, citizens expect and critically evaluate services they once considered novel. The same community that once marveled over the new rescue tool the Jaws of Life now expects its local fire and rescue department to routinely provide the most sophisticated of rescue and medical services.

Evolution of management theories

Believing that profit was the organization's sole goal, early management theory (so-called scientific management) focused on the rational and mechanistic aspects of organizations. The key duty of management was to develop organizational structures to promote success (defined as profit). Accordingly, managers focused on the internal functioning of systems and procedures. Frederick Winslow Taylor, whose management theory dominated the debate in the 1920s, conducted time and motion studies in his search for the most efficient processes for doing a job.

After 1930, the focus of management theory shifted from mechanical processes to social constructs, or employee behavior. The famous Hawthorne experiments came from this era: experimenters altered light levels in electrical wiring rooms of a Western Electric plant in Hawthorne, New Jersey, to test whether light affected job performance. They found that as light levels were altered, performance improved, regardless of whether brightness was increased or diminished. These experiments demonstrated that interactions with employees (i.e., attentions paid to employees) could affect production, regardless of the precise nature of the interactions (in this case, regardless of whether brightness increased or decreased).

By 1960, theorists of management recognized that successful businesses gave consideration to external factors. Rejecting the importance of the social component of organizations, theorists focused explicitly on mechanistic ways in which organizations could react to changing external forces.

In 1970, a new theory (management by objectives) arose that recognized the changing nature of the organizational environment, postulating that all aspects of organizations—vision, mission, goals, objectives, and market demands—are constantly in flux and that the role of managers, therefore, is to guide organizations in a general direction. Experimentation was deliberately carried on throughout the organization, and those experiments that were successful led to innovation and change: managers focused organizational resources in the direction pointed to by the successful experiments.

In the mid-1980s a new theory of management (dispersed leadership) began to emerge. The previous decade's theorists had enshrined unpredictability; their successors searched for a foundation of certainty and predictability beneath the ever-changing character of organizations. These theorists of the mid-1980s found the key to successful organizations in effective leadership at all levels of the organization. Successful organizations possessed, in addition to dispersed leadership, an overriding vision of where they should be headed, and that vision was consistent with (aligned with) an underlying set of values and principles.

In the early twenty-first century, the concerns of the mid-1980s remain central but have been augmented by a sharp awareness of the ever-changing market.

Continually improving the organization

Another component of modern theories of effective management is the importance of continually improving the organization. Just as customers' needs are not static, the organization's way of operating should not be static either. Organizations are able to succeed by constantly improving not only their delivery of services to the customer but also their own procedures.

To identify ways in which they can improve in a changing environment—

that is, to learn to compete—fire service organizations should nondefensively evaluate their procedures. Leaders must encourage department members not only to identify problems candidly but also to propose improvements. When the penalty is greater for trying and failing than for not trying, organizations discourage innovation and encourage complacency. Without innovation, organizations risk losing their future competitive viability.[4]

Measuring performance

Improving an organization means knowing what needs to be improved. In addition to expecting department members to identify problems, managers can use performance measures to evaluate an organization's performance (see Chapter 10).

For fire service organizations to be competitive, they must be willing to evaluate themselves as others evaluate them and to do so without taking refuge in the belief that as public safety agencies, they deserve to be held to different standards. Using the evaluation tools of quality management—customer surveys, evaluation cards, comparative performance measures, and benchmarking with best practices in the industry—can lead to new methods of problem solving as well as to new techniques of gathering, analyzing, and displaying information. These new methods and techniques will enable management to track performance, identify opportunities, and learn the underlying causes of problems.

Managing change

Central to the three components of quality management discussed above is the need to compete by changing. To do this successfully, organizations must move out of their comfort zones and align services with community needs. So the fire service leader must spend sufficient time and energy scanning the environment for changes that may affect the organization, preparing for an appropriate reaction, and then communicating the need for adjustment to an organization that, by job design, may have a more narrow field of vision. The leadership challenge is to identify what an effective fire department will look like in the future and establish a steady course toward the envisioned future. On the one hand, firefighters cannot define the business the department is in on the basis of the missions that have the most appeal or provide the most immediate gratification. On the other hand, a fire chief cannot impose his or her will on the department. Leaders must lead their organizations toward a future that they envision in different terms from the present. The measure of leadership and departmental success must be the extent to which changing community needs within a dynamic environment are satisfied.

Centering on principle

Success rarely comes without compromise, but an effective leadership vision of the future should be tied to the organization's core principles. At the scene of an emergency, the incident commander may adjust tactics to achieve the desired results, but his or her strategy will remain constant because it is based on core principles. In leading an organization, management may change its plans, but its principles must remain consistent because they are based on the organization's core values.

An organization can *focus* on a variety of different concerns—for example, customer service, employee satisfaction, stakeholder satisfaction, profit, or market share—but will *center* on one thing: the organization's primary concern.

That is the bedrock of the organization. An organization centered on profit, for example, will serve customers only to the extent that those customers generate profit, and employees will produce only those goods that are profitable. An organization centered on principle will live by the core values of mutual respect, integrity, and honesty, and those values should be the basis of every action taken.

Organizations aligned by commitment to principle will focus on other concerns (employees, customers, stakeholders, market share) only as they relate to the core values. Employees and customers will be treated in a manner that is consistent with the organization's values. This is not to say that the other concerns are irrelevant; an organization cannot function without employees, for example, and it has no reason to function unless customers and citizens are satisfied. But whereas an organization should focus on these concerns, it should not be centered on them.

Leadership training: Who benefits and what is it?

Management (i.e., people in supervisory positions) comprises all people in an organization who are formally responsible for the actions of other employees —all people who have formal authority for deciding how a job should be done. In the fire and rescue services, management positions can include the fire chief, battalion chief, company officers, staff officers, and nonsworn civilian personnel. People in management positions are also responsible for leading—for deciding which jobs should be done to ensure that an organization fulfills its overall goals and objectives.

Leading can be done much more easily if management personnel are trained in the techniques of leadership and have a clear understanding of how to use leadership skills. For example, the Arlington (Texas) Fire Department developed a leadership contract to establish shared expectations for leaders in the organization, to emphasize and reinforce critical leadership priorities, and to increase leadership accountability (see Figure 8–3).

An organization will also benefit from having nonmanagement personnel learn and practice leadership skills. Many members of the fire and rescue service are not classified as "management" and may not formally supervise anyone in the organization, but they are responsible for carrying out decisions. Knowing leadership skills will allow them to implement policies more effectively and could enable these informal leaders to exercise their influence more productively and positively.

All employees should be able to step back and examine their actions from a broader perspective—that of the effect their actions will have on the company, battalion, department, or organization. Without this broader perspective, employees can become so immersed in the specifics of their daily activities that they lose sight of why they are doing what they are doing. They start to look solely at how the job affects them personally, paying no attention to how the job affects anyone else, including co-workers and customers. Stepping back to look at the broader purpose and implications of a job will help employees understand how their jobs are related to the functioning of the department and the city or county organization. This understanding may provide insight into changes the organization might have to make to increase its effectiveness.

Firefighters, for example, can become so involved in the specific tactics of fighting fires that they do not consider how the public perceives their actions. One fire department found that while focusing on suppressing fires, it was not addressing the concerns of residents adjacent to emergency scenes. The department did not talk with residents about potential dangers to surrounding houses or dangers to people from toxic chemicals in the fire. By stepping back, the department realized that a necessary part of ensuring public safety is providing information to people at emergency scenes. The department established a community service sector as a component of its incident command system, with the function of answering questions and helping residents cope with emergencies.

Although organizations that use leadership skills appropriately will benefit greatly from engaging employees in leadership training, it would be counterproductive to expect all employees, even when trained, to excel at leadership. Every individual has a unique potential for growth. Some have less aptitude

AFD Leadership Contract

In serving the members of the department and in being part of a business that serves the community, much is required of the leaders of the Arlington Fire Department. However, much is also given. High expectations will be placed on us – from those we serve and from each other. The following is a contract of what can be expected of the Fire Chief and what the Fire Chief will expect of each department leader.

Expectations of the Fire Chief	Expectations of Department Leaders
▪ To follow through; to be consistent in his vision for this organization and to do what he says he's going to do.	▪ To communicate with the Fire Chief and the Assistant Chiefs.
▪ To hold himself and all department leaders accountable to department members.	▪ To communicate with department members.
▪ To tell the truth.	▪ To knowledgeably answer questions about where we are going.
▪ To build our organization's reputation nationally and locally, and to use that reputation in service to our department and our community.	▪ To cross traditional barriers to coordinate and cooperate with each other.
▪ To build our credibility and to use that credibility in service to our department and our community.	▪ To model respectful communications and support between sworn and non-sworn members.
▪ To be accessible.	▪ To take input and respectful criticism and to encourage a climate of candor.
▪ To make honest mistakes and to admit to them.	▪ To focus on our Medical Program as part of our expanded mission.
▪ To take input and respectful criticism and to encourage a climate of candor.	▪ To encourage community involvement and customer commitment.
▪ To stand his ground.	▪ To support the department's vision and to be positive, progressive role models, confident in our future.

Figure 8–3   Leadership contract of the Arlington (Texas) Fire Department.

for leadership than others do, just as not everyone can be a basketball legend like Michael Jordan no matter how hard he (or she) trains. Individual aptitude determines how much improvement additional training will yield. Everyone will benefit from training, but in different ways. Organizations should understand this concept so that they do not have exaggerated and unrealistic expectations of leadership training.

Organizations can realistically expect employees who have participated in leadership training to be more proactive in problem solving, more responsible in their own actions, and more appreciative of the benefits of teamwork. Although these employees may not go on to become the next fire chief, their daily activities throughout the organization will certainly demonstrate the benefits of the training.

It would also be counterproductive for organizations to look on leadership as a corporate tool that can be handed out to employees like department-issued uniforms. Leadership principles, or habits, must be cultivated in each individual, and the process takes time and effort because people may have to learn new ways of approaching their jobs. In fact, leadership training is an ongoing process of sharpening the personal skills necessary for an employee to operate effectively within his or her sphere of influence.

Leadership training begins with the recognition that the attributes of successful leaders cannot be taught but that the habits of mind can be. Successful leaders are described as having a variety of attributes that make them successful, including inspiration, dedication, intelligence, motivation, competence, and creativity. But how does one teach inspiration or dedication? Rather than focusing on specific character traits, therefore, leadership training follows the lead of Stephen R. Covey's *The Seven Habits of Highly Effective People* and considers the processes, or habits, that successful leaders use as their personal operating procedures:[5]

Being proactive
Beginning with the end in mind
Putting first things first
Thinking win/win
Seeking to understand
"Synergizing"
Sharpening the saw.

Be proactive　The person should shape the job, not vice versa. To be proactive, one must take responsibility for one's actions. People tend to react to situations, allowing the situations to shape their actions. Proactivity, in contrast, means understanding that one's actions affect the circumstances and that one is in control of how one acts in any given situation.

Firefighters at an incident site are by nature proactive. They will not say there is nothing they can do about a fire and then sit down and watch a house burn. Fire departments have an arsenal of strategies and techniques for suppressing fires and minimizing risk to surrounding buildings and people.

The same attitude should hold true when one is dealing with organizational issues. A fire department should not just accept that the local government may not be able to fund a particular project. The department can find out why the project is not funded and adjust its strategy accordingly. (Perhaps the program does not meet local goals or objectives, or the timing may be wrong.)

Begin with the end in mind　When working on a task, one should start by thinking about the final product: what should the task produce? Clear objectives help people focus their activities on a goal. As a task progresses, goals may shift, but it is necessary to have a goal—some goal—at which to aim.

Put first things first   Trivial matters often get in the way of more important projects. As trivial issues arise, they drain attention and energy from the larger and more significant issues. To prevent this from happening, one should think about exactly which issues are the important ones and should then focus on those issues first. Of course, choosing between issues may be difficult. For example, what is most important to a fire department? Is it being prepared to suppress fires as they occur, or is it educating the public so that fires are prevented?

Think win/win   There is no reason for anyone to have to lose when a decision is made. If a decision causes members of the fire team to think they are losing, the negative feelings engendered can be detrimental to the organization as a whole.

Win/win decision making focuses on developing consensus among all involved parties. Decisions that are based on open and honest discussions are much easier to accept. Including employee input in a decision-making process whenever possible will greatly increase the likelihood that no employees feel they are losing.

But it is not always possible or advisable for decisions to be based on staff discussions and consensus. At times the fire chief should make decisions that staff may not like. In those cases, however, the decision still does not have to be perceived as a "losing" situation by staff. The key is for the fire chief to be honest with staff about the reasons for a decision.

Seek first to understand, then to be understood   Understanding what other people say starts with empathy. Empathy is listening to what others are saying from their point of view rather than from one's own. Not surprisingly, people tend to listen from their own perspective, which is based on their own experiences. But the speaker will not have the same perspective or experiences as the listener. To understand truly what another person is saying, one should try to put oneself in the speaker's shoes and see the situation from the speaker's perspective, assuming the speaker's knowledge and frame of reference. Doing so will build the other person's trust in the relationship.

Once one understands, it is time to be understood.

Synergize   "Synergizing" means accomplishing tasks by pooling the talents of several people rather than relying on one person. Could one firefighter put out a huge blaze by himself or herself? When people work together in a trusting environment, they are more willing to share ideas and suggestions. The final decision, emerging from honest discussion and evaluation of shared ideas, will be far more powerful than anything that any of the members could have thought of or done alone.

Sharpen the saw   "Sharpening the saw" simply means keeping all aspects of one's life healthy and in good order. Just as the body requires regular exercise, so does the mind.

Delegation of tasks to individuals

Part of teaching employees leadership skills is giving them opportunities to use the skills they have learned. This means assigning them tasks and empowering them to carry out those tasks—in other words, delegating. "A task is an assignment to produce a specified outcome (including quantity and quality) within a targeted completion time, with allocated resources and methods and within prescribed limits (policies, procedures, rules, regulations, etc.)."[6]

Delegation requires managers to find the proper balance between authority and leadership skills: employees who are given too much authority before they have the necessary leadership skills will not succeed, and employees with too much leadership skill and too little authority will not feel challenged. Leadership skills and authority should be inseparable: without authority, an employee has no scope for exercising leadership skills, and without leadership skills, the employee is unable to use authority effectively.

What empowerment is   One of the most misunderstood terms in the worlds of business and public employment today is *empowerment*. Failure to communicate what the term means can leave employees disgruntled and disillusioned. Every organization has stories about a project team that spent months on a project, only to have a manager reject or amend the team's recommendations. These stories of pseudo-empowerment reinforce what employees suspected all along: that employee participation receives only lip service. For a leader to be credible, there has to be clear communication of expectations, criteria, and boundaries when tasks are delegated or committees formed.

An important leadership principle in any fire service organization is to involve employees as members of teams. As in any dynamic organization, fire departments have multiple ongoing tasks that provide many opportunities to involve team members in defining the future. Such involvement is a critical part of communicating and building trust, and leaders who fail to communicate face a high-stakes risk of losing credibility.

For a team to be empowered, the members must be challenged to find creative solutions to problems—to search not for the first right answer but for the best right answer. However, in an organization with limited resources, asking for the best right answer does not mean sending a team down a rabbit hole. It means telling the team up front what the potential for funding support may be, and speaking openly about how the project fits with department-wide priorities. Empowerment encourages team members to be

creative, and effective empowerment ensures that committees are aligned with departmental values and priorities. The point is not to control, to dictate, or to stifle innovation but to focus the organization's limited resources of time, energy, and dollars on priority needs. The objective is to maximize success, maintain trust, and preserve leaders' credibility.

Empowerment does not mean democracy. It does not mean that every decision is a popularity contest or that a "good" boss should implement every suggestion for change simply because the suggestion is the result of a committee process. It does not mean there will no longer be occasions when decision making—with a limited opportunity for input—is required. Empowerment does not alter the fact that an organization's leaders maintain authority not as a privilege of rank but because their positions demand that they be responsible and accountable.

In contrast, empowerment *does* mean reinforcing a fundamental team concept: an organization can be strengthened if it draws on the best that each of its members can contribute toward improving the organization. Empowerment means asking for input—and really listening. It means treating people with respect and, when they have invested their time in a project, providing honest feedback. It also means encouraging a wide variety of opinions and challenging the status quo.

To be effective, empowerment must also hold team members accountable: they cannot use their input to advance personal agendas but must evaluate options solely in terms of the best interests of the organization.

Leaders must also be careful to delegate tasks to employees in such a way that the difficulty of the task matches the employee's skill level. A model of worker behavior in the year 2000 suggests that workers want to do a job that maximizes their potential.[7] In addition, the employee must be given control over the necessary resources. Otherwise, he or she will be dissatisfied and will not be able to complete the task successfully. In such situations, leaders may find it necessary to give additional authority to employees. Finally, the process of delegation should remain unbiased. That is, tasks should not be delegated carelessly or unfairly. If employees think tasks are assigned unfairly, they may resent leaders.

Besides helping workers maximize their potential, delegation is an excellent educational tool. Employees may be assigned specific tasks with which they would otherwise never have been involved. When one officer is responsible for hiring procedures, for example, a different employee may be assigned the task of developing a standardized procedure for hiring, and the assignment will provide an opportunity for the second employee to become involved in the hiring process. As this example shows, however, delegation involves a potential danger. When tasks are shifted between employees, the person who originally had the task may feel punished. The other employee may also feel uncomfortable about taking the job away from someone else. To resolve this tension, a leader needs to communicate with both employees clearly and honestly. When employees are told a job is reassigned to provide someone with a learning opportunity, they are less resistant than when they are allowed to think the reassignment is a punishment for the first employee.

Delegation of duties is also an excellent tool for making organizations more responsive to the market. Response time can be speeded up if individual employees are given the authority to respond on particular issues without having to go through the chain of command. For example, employees may be given the duty of purchasing equipment for a station without unnecessarily involving administrative and managerial personnel. Such an arrangement can streamline equipment acquisition and maintain the responsiveness of the entire department.

As a department grows larger, maintaining responsiveness requires that duties be delegated to numerous employees. But dispersed delegation runs the risk that consistency of service will be lost and that not all consumers will be treated equitably. This potential for inconsistency within the organization is something all employees should be aware of at all times. The solution may include greater frequency of communications, written or oral, to keep all key employees aware of current circumstances and precedents.

Even as leaders delegate more tasks to employees, employees, in turn, must be able to accept more accountability. Part of the trade-off in delegation is that when the leader grants the employee the necessary authority, the employee accepts responsibility for the assigned task.

Leaders must also remember that as more authority is delegated, it may be abused. Abuse of authority or power, even extending to the misappropriation of public funds or property, can be a problem at all levels of an organization. Before organizations can begin to delegate authority, therefore, they must address the underlying issue of trust.

In an organization based on principle, the values of honesty, trust, and ethics are important aspects of daily activity. This means that interviews with potential employees will take into consideration not only applicants' skills but also their character. Skills are necessary but not sufficient. Personal character—the traits of trustworthiness, honesty, motivation, integrity—becomes the defining criterion for successful applicants. Many people can pass entry-level exams and training to become firefighters, but only those with character will help a values-based organization grow and prosper.

Delegation of tasks to teams

Tasks may be delegated either to individuals or to teams. Teams serve many different functions in organizations: there are special project teams that exist for a short time to address one specific problem, permanent teams that are part of an organization, and everything in between. Using teams is natural for fire services because traditional fire suppression requires fire companies to work as teams both at an emergency scene and at the station.

Getting a team started

One of the first steps in establishing a team is selecting its members. Traditionally a manager picked staff to serve on a team. In some situations this may still be necessary, but depending on the nature of the team's objectives, other ways of selecting a team's members may also be used. If self-selection would bring together a more motivated group of people, volunteers could be sought. If the team will comprise representatives of various units of the organization, the manager or supervisor of each unit should choose that unit's representative.

Initially teams should spend time having the members get to know one another. Since they will be working together, team members will have to feel comfortable enough to speak freely. Because every member of the team will be expected to contribute to discussions, team-building exercises to encourage cooperation may be helpful. Some authorities suggest that the first few meetings should be devoted entirely to team-building exercises.[8]

One strategy for team building is to have the team develop a statement of purpose, possibly by creating a team mission statement. Like an organization, a team should be guided by explicit values in its efforts to accomplish its stated goals. Another strategy for bringing team members together is to clarify individual roles, authority, and accountability. If all members are aware of their appropriate roles, the risk of any one member's overstepping his or her proper role on the team will be greatly reduced.

If there is conflict between team members, those issues should be sorted out early in the life of the team. Further, any limitations on the team's scope or authority or on the implementation of its recommendations should be explained early on.

Finally, every team needs a leader; groups are most effective when someone guides discussion and helps organize meetings. That does not necessarily mean having one specific person as the leader. Team members can alternate taking the leadership role at meetings so that no one member will feel that his or her role is any more important than other team members' roles.

Optionally, the team may also benefit from having a facilitator—an impartial observer who can help guide discussions while indicating to team members when they have done something that might hurt the group as a whole (e.g., when they have broken the rules, spoken negatively of other team members, etc.). When a team is working to build trust, it may be difficult for one member to tell another directly that the latter has acted inappropriately. During a brainstorming session, for example, one member may start critiquing ideas, and although another member may find it difficult to say something, a facilitator can remind members to wait until all ideas are expressed before critiquing any of them. Using a facilitator to enforce rules may reduce potential conflict between team members over rules. Either an outside facilitator can be hired to ensure impartiality, or members of the team could alternate serving as facilitator.

But the first step in developing effective teamwork begins even before a team is set up: the first step is to work on leadership skills with every employee.

All employees are potential members of a team, and knowledge of leadership skills will help them contribute more to their teams. As a result, the teams will be able to function better and will be more responsive to changing demands.

Empowering a team

For leaders to truly empower employees, they must delegate leadership and decision making down to the lowest level possible. Employees are often closest to the problem and have the most information, and as such can often make the best decision. The second component of empowerment, and the one most often overlooked, is equipping followers with the resources, knowledge, and skills necessary to make good decisions.[9]

Teams can have many different levels of authority and can be empowered in several areas. Levels of authority can range from having specific tasks with set criteria as guidelines to having much more leeway in how the team accomplishes its assigned tasks. Areas in which employees can be empowered include

Identifying the problem
Solving the problem
Setting goals
Planning changes
Implementing the plan
Managing the changes that may occur
Performing human resource functions.

These areas are not specific to teams. Any organization can empower individual employees at any level in any area; however, this range of areas is mentioned here because it offers insight into the types of tasks that can be given to teams. It should be pointed out that only fully autonomous teams perform human resource functions, and studies have shown that these teams require at least three years to become successful (if they succeed at all). Studies suggest that semiautonomous teams—those with responsibility for all functions except human resource concerns—will have the greatest success.

Teams have often failed in local government because managers have neglected to identify the intended level of empowerment and have not understood the key factors required for success. Figure 8–4 can help managers in this regard. It diagrams the differing levels of authority and responsibility that teams can assume over their processes, depending on the charge made to the team or on variables within the team's decision-making process itself. The continuum is from a directive work environment to a fully empowered, autonomous working team. ("Suggestion systems" means that the team makes recommendations or suggestions to management as opposed to being able to proceed with implementation. "Success factors" refers to the characteristics of the organization that should be present if the team is to be successful.)

Guidelines for successful teams

Successful teams generally exhibit similar behaviors, as follows:[10]

They set clear goals.

They establish an improvement plan.

They establish ground rules; in particular, they have well-defined procedures for making decisions.

They seek good data.

The members have clearly defined roles.

The members communicate clearly with each other.

		Levels of empowerment				
	Traditional	Involvement			Empowerment	
	Directive	Suggestion systems	Problem solving	Participative decision making	Semiautonomous teams	Fully autonomous teams
Key characteristics	Managers manage, workers work Hierarchical organizational structure	Ideas submitted to management Management usually fixes problem and implements suggested solutions Suggestion systems Focus groups Communication survey	Groups of 6–12 people who problem solve together Meet approximately once a week Outside of normal work activities (parallel organization) Quality circles	Collaboration on operational decisions Integrated with the way work gets done Supervisor and manager still have final work and carry most weight	Responsible for quality, productivity, and total workstation All necessary information, authority, and decision making in hands of team Supervisor as facilitator Span of control Operational results focused	Team responsible for all supervision and support functions No supervision Split between human resource focus and operational results focus
Type of empowerment						
Problem ID	No	Yes	Yes	Yes	Yes	Yes
Problem solving	No	No	Yes	Yes	Yes	Yes
Goal setting	No	No	No	Yes	Yes	Yes
Planning change	No	No	No	Yes	Yes	Yes
Implementation	No	No	No	No	Yes	Yes
Managing change	No	No	No	No	Yes	Yes
Performing HR functions	No	No	No	No	No	Yes
Success factors	Stable and loyal workforce	Timely feedback on suggestions/on ideas/on what will be done with identified problems Recognition for ideas Avoidance of bureaucratic review process	Members and leaders require training in problem solving, communication, and meeting management skills Formalized procedures Must be relevant to the work of the group Activity must connect to operational goal system Activity must be recognized and rewarded	Team members and managers require training in the skills of facilitating or conducting meetings Project's goals assumed to be measurable Recognition and reward for demonstrated results	Team members and managers require training in the skills of facilitating or conducting meetings and in human resource functions Team structures need to be developed, documented, and used to create the team's mission and goals, articulate the roles of team members, and establish process for team meetings *Gradual* assumption of decision-making authority Supervisor becomes coach and trainer and has an equal voice on the team except in a few areas	Stable business with few or no changes in product, process, or equipment
Documented field study results	In control group studies, significantly less effective than empowerment strategies	Most suggestion systems have low effectiveness The best have a 48-hour turnaround for feedback	Mixed results: A third fail to meet expectations within one year. Very few are in existence after five years	Increases in productivity and quality 10–30%	Improvements in productivity, quality, and cycle time (time span before a job/task repeats itself) 30–60% Continuous improvements at 10–15% per year after installation	Mixed results: Most control group studies have shown that fully autonomous teams fail or take three or more years to become successful.

Figure 8–4   Empowerment continuum for teams.

All the members participate and are *actively* involved in discussions.

The members are aware of group process.

Setting clear goals   Before a team is formed, there should be identifiable objectives for it to meet. Goals can be anything from figuring out how to have more interaction with the public to developing a complete restructuring of the organization. Part of setting clear goals is establishing a time period for the life of the team. There is no ideal time limit; some teams are formed to meet for only a short time, whereas others—formed with some time limit commensurate with the issue they are dealing with—become permanent.

Establishing an improvement plan   An improvement plan outlines what a team will need if it is to do its job effectively. Early in its existence, the team should spend time planning strategy. This will help the team determine what resources it will need in the course of performing its job. The plan will also outline a schedule for completing tasks. The plan is not a static document and should be reevaluated periodically and adjusted on the basis of any new developments or further insights into the team's mission.

Establishing ground rules   All teams have ground rules, explicit or not. It is healthier for a team to discuss the ground rules so that they can be openly established and agreed upon by all team members at the outset.

In particular, the team should take time to consider how decisions will be made. Methods of making decisions include (among many others) using decision mapping, a decision hierarchy (the fishbone diagram—see Figure 8–5 and the accompanying sidebar; see also the detailed discussion of fishbone diagrams under "Determining the Causes of Poor Performance and Eliminating Them" in Chapter 10), a decision tree, or a decision matrix. The team must also decide whether decisions will be made by consensus or by majority vote.

Seeking good data   The group should actively seek good data on which to base its decisions. By collecting data, the team can arrive at a better-informed decision: collecting data can slow the decision-making process enough to prevent members from jumping to hasty conclusions before they have considered enough information.

The team should also keep in mind that no data are infallible. Data can be interpreted to mean many different things. The key is to collect as many data as possible (within a realistic time frame) so as to develop a more rounded picture.

Defining roles clearly   From the outset, all members of the team should clearly understand their specific duties, tasks, authority, and accountability for the team's performance. The team should try to delegate responsibilities so that all members can use their talents.

Duties and tasks can be the responsibility of a single team member, can be shared, or can be rotated. Whatever the division of tasks, it should be clearly understood by all team members.

Figure 8–5
Sample fishbone diagram.

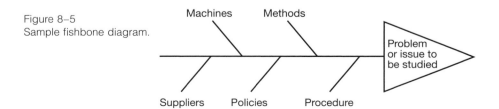

Communicating clearly For discussions to be effective, people need to communicate clearly. Suggestions on how to do this include the following:[11]

Speak with directness
Speak succinctly
Listen actively to other team members
Avoid interrupting others
Share information.

What is a fishbone diagram? A fishbone diagram is an analytic tool that provides a systematic way of looking at effects and at the causes that create or contribute to those effects.

Why use it? A fishbone diagram is used to identify, explore, and graphically display possible causes of a problem so that one can discover the root causes.

When should it be used? A team should use the fishbone diagram when it

Needs to study a problem or issue to determine a root cause

Wants to study all the possible reasons a process is beginning to have difficulties, problems, or breakdowns

Needs to identify areas for data collection

Wants to study why a process is not performing properly or producing the desired results.

What does it do? A fishbone diagram

Enables a team to focus on the substance of the problem

Creates a snapshot of the team's collective knowledge of and consensus about the problem

Directs the team's attention to causes, not symptoms.

How do I construct it?

1. Draw the fishbone diagram (see sample diagram on page at left).
2. Write the problem or issue to be studied in the "head of the fish."
3. Label each "bone of the fish." The major categories typically used are

    The four M's: *M*ethods, *M*achines, *M*aterials, *M*anpower

The four P's: *P*lace, *P*rocedure, *P*eople, *P*olicies
The four S's: *S*urroundings, *S*uppliers, *S*ystems, *S*kills.

Note: You may use any of the categories suggested, combine them in any fashion, or make up your own. The categories are to help you organize your ideas.

4. Use an idea-generating technique (e.g., brainstorming) to identify the factors within each category that may be affecting the problem or issue and/or the effect being studied. For each category, the team should ask, for example, "What are the machine (equipment) issues affecting/causing . . . ?"
5. Repeat this procedure, in turn, with each factor under the category to produce subfactors. Continue asking, "Why is this happening?" and put additional segments under each factor and subsequently under each subfactor.
6. Continue until you no longer get useful information as you ask, "Why is this happening?"
7. After team members agree that an adequate amount of detail has been provided under each major category, analyze the results of the fishbone. Do this by looking for items that appear in more than one category. These become the "most likely causes."
8. For all items identified as the "most likely causes," the team should reach consensus on listing them in priority order, with the first item being the "most probable cause."

Source: Adapted with permission from John Rogers, *Decision Solutions: Decision Facilitation Guidebook* (Greenwood Village, Colo.: CH2M HILL Companies, 1997), part 2, 39–42.

Participating actively in discussions   *All* team members should be *actively* involved in discussions. For a team to be able to consider the widest range of ideas, it needs input from every member. Any member who consistently fails to contribute is not strengthening the team. Active involvement may mean initiating discussions, helping to keep other team members on task, or clarifying what one has heard other team members say.

Being aware of group process   Each member of the team should be aware of how the team functions as a group. This means being aware of both verbal and nonverbal methods of communication and of the communications process as a whole. Group members should discuss their perceptions of the process—its strong points, possible problems, and ways to improve it.

Building effective teams in the fire service

To develop an effective team in a fire and rescue department, a leader needs to take into consideration the fact that the department consists of various broad categories of employees (e.g., firefighters, apparatus operators, administrative staff, emergency medical service personnel, and management personnel). The interactions between employees in different categories will bear heavily on a team's ultimate effectiveness. Certainly, external customers should see the fire department as a single agency speaking with a single voice. On a day-to-day basis, cross-functional cooperation is what building a team is all about. The types of categories that will require the greatest attention are sworn and nonsworn employees and employees in operations and in staff positions.

Teams with sworn and nonsworn members   The dialogue about sworn and nonsworn is old and often heated, with passionate and committed advocates for each perspective. (For an explanation of the terms, see the sidebar "Sworn and Nonsworn Personnel.") Under the term *civilianization,* positions formerly filled by sworn firefighters have been converted to nonsworn status. From one perspective, civilianization has meant a reduction in the number of positions; a loss of some variety in work assignments; a loss of promotional opportunities; and a loss of the fire service experience, insight, and affiliation that are perceived as necessary for doing key jobs successfully in the fire department. From another perspective, civilianization has provided the opportunity to maintain or increase the number of highly compensated fire professionals, as positions in which sworn status is not required are filled by lower-salaried, nonsworn people. Further, civilianization has provided the organization with an opportunity to strengthen itself by hiring professionals in specific disciplines. There are some jobs that require a fire service background, but in the case of other jobs, hiring sworn personnel is a luxury that is neither practical nor affordable. Still other positions may be strengthened and enhanced by specific technical or professional skills that are not widely available within the existing sworn personnel pool.

A successful fire service depends on special skills and abilities. In many cases, civilian professionals hired from outside the organization will make a strong contribution to the department's effectiveness. But whether sworn or nonsworn personnel are matched with a department position, every department employee—from battalion chief to office administrative assistant—shares a responsibility to identify with the mission of the organization. Although all

Sworn and nonsworn personnel In this chapter, the terms *sworn* and *nonsworn* are used to differentiate between commissioned or certified firefighters and civilian employees. Other pairs of terms sometimes used for the same purpose are *commissioned* and *civilian,* and *uniformed* and *nonuniformed.* None of the pairs is used exclusively in all jurisdictions.

Sworn is a reference to the oath of office that is usually associated with a position as firefighter. Sworn positions include both staff and line positions. Staff positions filled with sworn personnel include (1) those for which a background and certification in fire protection are considered essential, and (2) those that civil service law or contract

specifies are to be filled by sworn individuals.

Nonsworn refers to positions in which firefighter certification is not a requirement. Assignments may range from administrative support positions through maintenance positions to professional positions in the areas of finance, planning, and engineering.

There is a significant amount of variance from jurisdiction to jurisdiction in the division between sworn and nonsworn. For example, many departments use sworn personnel in dispatch and fire protection bureau assignments, whereas other departments use civilian professionals for those same assignments.

positions do not require sworn status or fire service background, all do require a fundamental respect for the fire service.

Basic to developing a respectful, cooperative environment is maintaining respectful communication. Firefighters are the internal customers of most of a fire department's support activities, and respect for them as customers should be evident in communication. An organization's support team and nonsworn professionals cannot be too busy to consider how they are communicating and cannot suggest through their actions that firefighters are not valued. But neither can a fire service organization be successful if it creates an environment in which nonsworn personnel cannot succeed. It is important that bias not be allowed to create an environment in which every action by nonsworn personnel is suspect and every communication subject to critical evaluation.

When asked how best to integrate civilian fire protection engineers into the fire department, one manager who has tried responded, "There is some uniform/civilian friction and a lack of fire service respect for civilian engineers." A civilian fire protection engineer provided a more personal perspective: "I was made to feel like a second-class employee."[12] Combining both personnel groups on a single team is inherently problematic. For example, it is very tempting for nonsworn employee groups to make compensation comparisons with their sworn peers. Yet the groups are generally evaluated and compensated on the basis of very dissimilar markets. With a fire service background and sworn status comes a pay scale that is driven by the field firefighter serving the community in a frequently hazardous environment.

Despite the fact that the sworn or nonsworn status of existing or proposed positions may be controlled by labor contract or local civil service personnel policy, using both employee groups on a single team requires active team management. The successful team must extend its valuing of diversity well beyond sex and cultural background to include sworn and nonsworn personnel and (as discussed below) those who are assigned to all divisions.

Teams with operations and staff members Not only sworn and nonsworn personnel but also divisions and sections within a fire department must work together if the organization is to be successful. Although most fire service organizations represent themselves as professional teams, all members of which are equally important to effective service delivery, there remains a wide chasm between the desirability of staff assignments and that of field assignments. Shift (field) positions are generally viewed as conferring a distinct personal advantage over the traditional forty-hour-per-week assignment.

Work assignments have an obvious effect on morale and productivity, and work assignments that are seen as less desirable (i.e., staff assignments) may lead to high turnover in staff technical positions. High turnover in any position means high training costs and loss of valuable experience. High turnover in management positions can also result in inconsistent leadership, ineffective long-range planning, and limited institutional memory.[13]

Although firefighters may resist the conversion of many dispatch, training, and fire positions (i.e., staff positions) to nonsworn status, developing and maintaining staff assignment policies for sworn personnel is an ongoing problem in many fire and rescue departments. Balancing a desire for consistency (associated with having a credible assignments policy) with the flexibility necessary to accommodate a dynamic organization is frequently a challenge. Efforts to increase the incentives associated with staff assignments are difficult to "sell" to the local government manager who questions the logic of proposing pay incentives to induce someone to work forty hours per week with weekends off instead of a fifty-six-hour shift. And because staff employees are fewer in number, they may often be underrepresented by employee bargaining groups when benefits are being negotiated.

Furthermore, training programs to develop and adequately prepare an employee to function effectively in a specialized staff assignment are very limited. Thus, many departments are in the situation of spending up to six months training new firefighters before releasing them to a highly supervised field company, but when these firefighters are reassigned to staff positions that, by contrast, might include a work environment that is unsupervised, the only orientation they receive may be a two-week overlap with a predecessor.

The fire and rescue service can fulfill its expanded mission only with the coordinated efforts of both staff and field divisions. Management's challenge is to lead all divisions to work together as equal partners. Introducing a continuing process to build effective teamwork between staff and field positions may include efforts to

Model support for staff positions

Expand cadet training programs to introduce new department members to a broadened department mission

Communicate the importance of staff experience for career progression

Develop recruiting brochures and procedures that introduce prospective applicants to all positions

Improve the quality and consistency of staff training and orientation

Conduct a thorough job analysis, and evaluate options to break down traditional staff descriptions and division barriers to create new jobs that balance job duties seen as desirable with those seen as less desirable

Increase communication to educate personnel about the work that takes place in staff divisions

Introduce short-term internships so that personnel can be exposed to staff divisions without undergoing more than limited personal disruption

Increase staff and field partnerships, making sure that both are represented on committees and in problem-solving groups.

Organizational culture

The same process that can be used to build effective teamwork between staff and field positions may also be used to modify the department's existing culture. Every organization has a culture, whether that culture has been deliberately cultivated or has unintentionally evolved. The culture is the shared values, beliefs, and underlying assumptions of the organization's members. As employees interact with each other, with customers, and with other agencies, the organization develops a unique attitude—a unique way of delivering its services. This attitude and style are the organization's culture. "[Organizational culture] must be understood as an active, living phenomenon through which people jointly create and recreate the worlds in which they live."[14]

Culture is one of the four components of an organization that need to be in alignment. The other three are the marketplace, the organization's strategy, and the organization's leadership style. For local governments, the marketplace is the expectations and desires of stakeholders, citizens, and customers. Strategy is a composite of the vision, mission, and goals the organization has developed in response to the market. Culture represents the organization's capabilities of implementing the strategy. Leadership style is what the organization uses to drive the strategy and shape the culture. This section focuses on culture, but to ensure that all the components are in alignment, leaders need to spend time evaluating the conditions in the organization that are related to each.

Culture is no more static than an organization is. Organizations evolve, and as they do, their values, beliefs, and underlying assumptions—their cultures—may change. Change is natural and normal. But although change may be natural, changes in the culture will not necessarily produce the culture that is best for the organization and compatible with its needs. The culture may no longer be responsive to the community's expectations or to the organization's own strategy, management philosophy, or leadership style.

Culture can drift out of alignment with management or the community because of changes inside or outside the organization. The impetus for cultural change can be either subtle (e.g., changes in the ages and backgrounds of the workforce) or dramatic (e.g., significant cutbacks in funding or the assumption of an enhanced level of emergency medical service). In either case, the leader may see that the organization needs to address these changes, whether inside or outside the organization, in ways that may require alterations in the culture.

The alignment of the four components is best analyzed in the budget process, which brings all the components together in creating the document that will serve as the operational plan for the next year (or for the duration of the budget). The allocation of funds to various projects determines how the organization will address community needs—the expectations of customers/citizens. If a fire department espouses a primary goal of developing prevention programs yet allocates most of its attention and resources in the budget process to updating suppression equipment, there may be a misalignment within the department between culture and strategy.

The budget process also indicates how the various departments of the whole local government work together. Traditionally a local government budget process is thought of as adversarial, with every department competing for funding against every other department. The fire department competes against the police department, both compete against streets and drainage, and all four compete against the library. If the local government as a whole espouses values of cooperation and teamwork, however, a competitive budget process demonstrates serious misalignment. When the basic values are cooperation and teamwork, proper alignment is demonstrated by a budget process in which the various departments work together to develop a budget in which each department has the maximum amount of funding for its needs, given the financial constraints of the entire organization. In such a process, all departments consider the needs of the organization as a whole and of its customers. As a result, some departments may even accept reduced funding to help an important program in another department.

Although this description of the budget process focuses on the entire local government of which the fire department is one part, the same principle holds true for a fire department's internal budgetary process. The budgetary interaction among various divisions within a fire and rescue department demonstrates the true nature of all interactions within the department. If the budgetary interactions do not match the department's culture, values, or strategy, a misalignment exists and the organization should attempt to realign itself.

Cultural types

There are four general types of organizational culture: administrative, developmental, integrative, and production.

Administrative cultures Organizations with administrative cultures tend to have set bureaucracies with rigid rules and procedures that control employee behavior and processes. These organizations favor permanence and stability. The most widespread example of an organization with an administrative culture is the government agency.

Developmental cultures Developmental organizations are entrepreneurial and visionary. To enhance their entrepreneurial aspect, these organizations favor creativity and flexibility. Policies and procedures are empowering for employees. Examples of developmental organizations in the private sector are advertising or marketing organizations, and within local government, convention and visitors bureaus and economic development organizations.

Integrative cultures Integrative organizations focus on long-term relationships with suppliers and vendors. Integrative organizations accomplish work through teams, and they value trust and cohesive relationships. Again, policies and procedures are written to empower employees. Integrative cultures produce educational efforts and can contribute to intensive ongoing fire prevention efforts. An integrative culture is fundamental to community-based fire and life safety programs.

Production cultures Production organizations focus on results. These organizations are rational, with a bias toward action. As in administrative organizations, policies and procedures control employee behavior and processes. Examples of production-oriented organizations are emergency responders, such as fire suppression units. Other organizations that are commonly production based include manufacturing businesses and some local governments.

Addressing cultural issues

One difficulty the leader may have in addressing cultural issues is that problems may not necessarily seem to be problems of culture. That is, the presenting issue may, instead, seem to be one of climate (what people perceive when they look at how an organization functions). However, issues of climate may in fact reflect underlying cultural issues, or they may reflect external factors. If a problem in the climate of an organization indicates problems either in the culture or in the external environment, simply trying to fix a problem in the climate would be a mistake. In such a case the focus should remain on the underlying cultural considerations or on the external factors.

For example, a fire chief institutes a new program to have firefighters spend most of their time on educational programs for the public rather than on suppression activities. Despite the new policy, the chief finds that most firefighters are avoiding the new duties. By focusing strictly on the climate (the fact that firefighters are not engaging in the appropriate activities), the fire chief may conclude, incorrectly, that there is a problem with discipline or morale. But if the fire chief looks at the deeper cultural issues, he or she may find that the firefighters are operating within a production culture, whereas the new policy reflects a developmental culture. In this case, the cultural discontinuity is the underlying cause of the tension firefighters are experiencing—a tension they ease by avoiding the new duties.

But a problem that is superficially one of climate will not always be rooted in the culture. Sometimes stresses that are manifested in the climate will be caused by external factors. Thus, to diagnose a cultural problem could be premature. Before leaders attempt any intervention, they should ensure that the problems they see are in fact reflections of cultural problems. In the situation described above, for example, it may be that the reason firefighters are reluctant to engage in educational programs is that the public is unwilling to respond to their efforts. In this case the underlying culture is still sound, and the problem is a result of external factors. If the fire chief automatically undertakes cultural interventions to motivate firefighters to engage in educational programs, he or she will only be creating more stress for the firefighters. Rather, the chief should create or seek other opportunities for the firefighters to be successful and should wait for external factors to change before engaging in educational programs.

Before beginning cultural interventions, in other words, the chief must eliminate any alternative explanations of problems visible in the climate of the department.

Components of culture

To differentiate between true cultural problems and problems that are the result of external factors, one needs to understand organizational culture in more detail.

All organizational cultures have ten components that may change over time: autonomy, tolerance for change, communication, internal organizing, performance reward, external coping, identity, conflict, control, and corporate optimism (see the sidebar on the next page). An organization's behavior in each of these categories determines its culture.

Each of the components can be thought of as a continuum. Depending on the type of organization and its needs, the tolerance for change, for example, could fall anywhere between extremely tolerant and extremely intolerant. There is no preconceived notion of an ideal place on the continuum. Some organizations may be healthier with some intolerance for change, whereas others may require an extremely high tolerance for change. To determine where the organization should be on each continuum, the organization should review its values and the needs of its community and then determine what cultural qualities will best enable it to meet the various demands it faces.

Because so many components of culture can vary independently of one another, changes in culture may be difficult to track. Moreover, a change in culture

---

The ten components of organizational culture

Autonomy: Preference for clear definition of tasks and performance.

Tolerance for change: Preference for a high willingness to change when a reason or broad direction is given.

Communication: Preference for more formal communication on a regular basis rather than for communication through informal networks.

Internal organizing: Preference for greater participation by staff in setting goals.

Performance reward: Preference for having individuals meet short-term targets or goals.

External coping: Preference for a more integrated, relationship-building approach to external interests.

Identity: Preference for emphasizing achievement based on objective measures.

Conflict: Preference for resolving conflict by negotiation on established objectives.

Control: Preference for an approach that uses predetermined requirements to produce outcomes.

Corporate optimism: Preference for performance that is based on individual results rather than on informal networks of established relationships.

---

does not necessarily mean a sudden shift in the type of culture. The culture may continue to be administrative, for example, but lose some of its orientation toward control.

Subcultures

Complicating the situation is the fact that cultures contain subcultures. Organizations often operate in various market situations simultaneously, and local governments have a variety of divisions that serve different functions to meet different community needs. To operate most effectively, each division may require a different culture. Within the fire service, for example, hazardous material (HAZMAT) technicians, fire prevention educators, and dispatchers are different specializations or service delivery points and may have their own cultures. To manage the department most effectively, the fire chief must understand each of them.

One of the principal issues connected with subcultures is the service delivery point or assignment. As discussed above, most fire and rescue departments rotate personnel through field and staff assignments. However, it may be more economical for HAZMAT team members with higher-level certifications to remain in the field.[15] But if the HAZMAT team is managed under different policies, an impression of inequity may be created and tensions may arise among the different groups of firefighters. Tension may also exist between firefighters and support personnel. In the public's eyes firefighters have a great deal of prestige, and support staff has less. As a result, support staff may feel unappreciated.

In successful organizations, leaders understand the issue of different subcultures within the organization. They understand that different subcultures are necessary for different service delivery points and that interactions between the various subcultures will affect other parts of the organization. Successful leaders will recognize the particular different needs of the various subcultures and will adapt their managerial styles accordingly.

The growth of cultural "literacy"   In dealing with different cultures within an organization, one may find it helpful to consider various ways in which people interact with a culture that is different from their own. Such interactions may evolve over time: just as people grow in intellectual skills, from concrete to abstract thinking, so attitudes and approaches to other cultures can grow. What follows is an outline of the growth process of cultural thinking.

Our way is their way.

Their way is different, it's wrong.

Our way is "X," their way is "Y."

Both our way and their way have strengths and weaknesses.

Cultural synergy: We can learn from them, and they can learn from us.

Cultural flexibility: We can bridge differences during our interactions by adjusting our behaviors.

Cultural literacy: With this partner, we can bridge in this way; with that partner, we can bridge in another way.

Cultural mediation: We can prevent conflict and, where it is already present, can defuse it, keep it from escalating, and resolve it.

Source: Wendy Hall, *Managing Cultures: Making Strategic Relationships Work* (New York: John Wiley & Sons, 1995), 22, 31. From handouts prepared by the Innes Strategy Group in Auckland, New Zealand. Reproduced with permission.

In addition, managers should try to foster within their own organizations the culture of the overall organization (the local government) into which each of the subcultures (service delivery points) is integrated. Because of the special nature of local government, it is important that teamwork and cooperation be promoted throughout the organization. Managers at the top of the organization and at the tops of departments must model this cooperative approach. The surest way to minimize the effectiveness of a part of the organization is to disregard its subculture. Saying that all the subcultures of an organization need to be respected does not mean that the entire organization will necessarily have one culture; rather, the entire organization will have a home culture that embraces each subculture and allows all of them to function effectively without detracting from one another.

Strategies for changing a culture

Changing an organization's culture is a difficult and long-term process. The end result is never certain, and people tend to avoid uncertainty whenever possible: however problematic the current conditions may be, people fear that change may make them worse. To compensate for the necessary uncertainty and to reduce it, the organization needs a careful strategy for implementing change. Figure 8–6 is the blueprint that the Arlington (Texas) Fire Department (AFD) developed to detail its plans for repositioning the organization so as to best achieve its vision. The blueprint is an outline for changing an organization's culture. The AFD's change management model depends on leadership principles (symbolized by the bulldozer) to overcome the obstacles (symbolized by the brick wall).

The key to changing an organization's culture is having a vision for the future of the organization, sharing that vision with the entire organization, and developing a culture that is consistent with the vision. The vision must be as much substance as rhetoric. People are far more likely to accept a vision for the future if they understand that it is realistic and that the values espoused in it are sincerely meant to affect action.

Figure 8–6   Arlington (Texas) Fire Department leadership blueprint: Outline for changing an organization's culture.

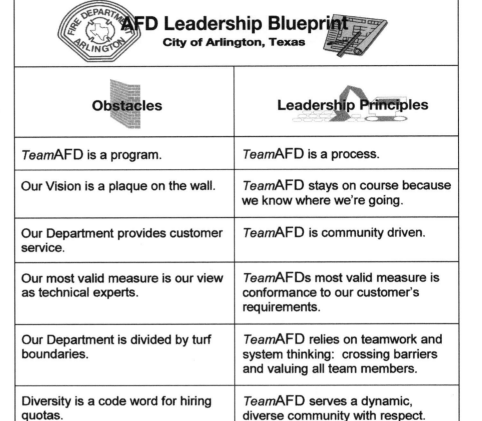

Obstacles	Leadership Principles
*Team*AFD is a program.	*Team*AFD is a process.
Our Vision is a plaque on the wall.	*Team*AFD stays on course because we know where we're going.
Our Department provides customer service.	*Team*AFD is community driven.
Our most valid measure is our view as technical experts.	*Team*AFDs most valid measure is conformance to our customer's requirements.
Our Department is divided by turf boundaries.	*Team*AFD relies on teamwork and system thinking: crossing barriers and valuing all team members.
Diversity is a code word for hiring quotas.	*Team*AFD serves a dynamic, diverse community with respect.
"They" do whatever they want without including us.	*Team*AFD includes team members aligned with the Department's goals, objectives, and values.
Our Department operates with Policies and SOPs that are not regularly reviewed and revised.	*Team*AFD depends on non-defensive evaluation.

As organizations develop a vision for the future—a direction, or strategy—and seek language to communicate their vision, terms such as *mission, vision,* and *values* may come to be used interchangeably. However, there are subtle but important distinctions among them: *mission* is the business of an organization, *vision* is the direction of an organization, and *values* are what define the character of an organization. The distinctions are illustrated by Figures 8–7 and 8–8. One is a values statement created in the year 2000 by the employees of the Huntsville, Texas, local government following employee training in values awareness. This values statement forms the basis of the Huntsville local government's processes for evaluating personnel and selecting new employees. The other figure is Huntsville's vision statement and mission statement, which are the filter through which all the local government's programs and activities are reviewed.

Figure 8–7 Employee values statement, Huntsville, Texas.

VALUES STATEMENT

Public service is our business and our goal. We believe in commitment - not just to our job, but to our faith, our beliefs, and our family. Our pride in our work and the organization compels us to a high degree of professionalism.

Honesty in all our actions;

United in our commitment to ensure a safe work environment, fair wages and benefits, and opportunities for advancement;

Nurture an environment of cooperation between the City and its citizens,

Teamwork depending on one another to improve the quality of life;

Service excellence provided at every level in an efficient and economical manner;

Vision of an enriched future enhanced by encouraging skills, talents, and potential of our employees through training, opportunity, and recognition;

Integrity demonstrated in the treatment of our coworkers and those we serve and protect;

Leadership through communication in a responsive manner while maintaining a high degree of professionalism;

Loyalty to our faith, our beliefs and our families;

Embrace the diversity of our employees as a strength of our organization

Figure 8–8 Vision and mission statements, Huntsville, Texas.

VISION

Our Vision for the City of Huntsville is to have a community that is beautiful, historic, culturally diverse, affordable, safe and well planned with great opportunity for our citizens.

MISSION

In order to maintain and enhance the quality of life and the achievement of our vision, the City of Huntsville provides, facilitates and regulates services, facilities and infrastructure for citizens, customers, visitors, businesses and state agencies, in a friendly, efficient, fair, honest and competent manner with quality and forethought.

Creating or amending a mission statement

One technique that can be used to institute change is to create or amend a mission statement. A mission statement outlines and institutionalizes an organization's goals and values, and it is these that guide the organization's actions. Even as the environment changes, as the fire service industry evolves, as the number and complexity of services grow, as budgets adjust to changing economic cycles, and as elected and appointed officials change, values remain constant. Values are the common denominator that all members of an organization may support. They are the standard by which policies and decisions should be measured. Successful organizations choose their core values deliberately.

The process of adopting a mission statement directs staff's attention to the values the organization desires to live by and the goals it desires to attain. Adopting a mission statement can therefore constitute the beginning of a process of implementing change: When an organization actively attempts to live up to a mission statement, it may have to make changes. And employees may be more willing to work toward changes when they are shown a vision for the future, which the mission statement represents, and when (as mentioned above) they understand that the vision is realistic and is sincerely meant to affect action.

The first step in creating a new mission statement may be to review the existing one and decide whether it is still valid. Does it mention the organization's changing, broadened mission? Does it reflect the organization's priorities? For example, is the organization in the emergency response business while doing some building inspections on the side, or is it in the emergency prevention business while being staffed with professionals who are also trained to respond to emergencies if they occur? Management theorists have suggested that organizations ask themselves the question, "What business am I in?" This question may seem simple, but answering it may create some confusion. For example, identifying the business of a *fire* department could reveal that more than half the department's transactions involve *emergency medical service*. Or a department may say its most important business is fire *prevention* but dedicate most of its resources to fire *suppression*.

An organization may introduce into the mission statement a statement of values that identifies the organization's commitment—the manner in which the organization chooses to address its mission.

What follows are practical suggestions for creating a mission statement:[16]

Involve the entire organization in the writing process in order to give the statement immediate legitimacy and authority.

Have the wording and tone reflect the organization's culture and personality, and do not misrepresent the organization. Some organizations use straightforward prose, for example, and others use more poetic language. Either approach is legitimate if it truly reflects the culture of the organization.

Consider using outsiders for their special perspectives. Outsiders may have insights that insiders inevitably lack because they are too close to the organization.

Keep the mission statement succinct and brief—no more than a few short sentences or paragraphs. Longer statements will be a distraction, giving a less forceful definition of mission.

Make the statement specific enough to generate objectives and programs but broad enough to stand the test of time.

Use "results" terminology—language that focuses on end results, not on the methods of achieving those results.

Be operational. That is, use the mission statement as a basis for judging organizational priorities and operations and employee progress.

Make the completed mission statement highly visible so that employees are reminded of it daily.

Figure 8–9 is the mission statement developed by the Arlington (Texas) Fire Department. This mission statement is the filter through which all the department's programs and activities are reviewed.

Arlington Fire Department Mission Statement

To provide to the citizens and visitors of Arlington an effective, well-trained team of professionals to protect their lives and property through fire prevention and education, emergency medical/fire suppression/rescue services and Emergency Management.

Figure 8–9   Mission statement of the Arlington (Texas) Fire Department.

Using the hiring process

Another technique to use in implementing change is to adjust the hiring process. As prospective employees are interviewed, the values and goals toward which the organization is moving should be emphasized. When new employees are hired because of their consistency with these values, changes toward those goals will be easier to make.

It is also possible to hire a new fire chief or other management personnel from outside the department. Outside personnel can offer a new, unbiased perspective on operations within a department. They may be able to see problems that people who are already in the department have either ignored or accepted as part of the job. Bringing in outside personnel presents complications, however. People within the department may feel resentment toward the new person, who "doesn't understand how things are done around here." And no doubt some existing staff members will be disappointed that they did not get the position. Accordingly, the outside person's efforts to institute change may meet resistance. The resistance will not be insurmountable, but when outside people are brought into an organization to make changes, care must be taken.

Dealing with resistance

Regardless of whether the attempt to implement change is made by people brought in from outside or by existing leadership, employees will not always accept change willingly. As mentioned above, every change is associated with a certain level of stress because it brings uncertainty. As the change becomes more unpredictable and less controlled, stress levels rise. Heightened stress can lead to health problems, irritability, and other negative side effects. Stress may also reduce job performance. As job-related stress increases, employees may begin to act against the organization. They may compromise themselves and the organization with acts of omission and with both administrative and criminal acts of commission. They may also develop a sense that, in compensation for their work, they are entitled to local government–provided goods or services without having to pay for them.

In the short term, the easiest way to deal with employees' resistance would be to force them to accept the changes whether they like it or not. In the long term, however, these employees' resentment and frustration would erode the foundation of the entire department. But there are various other strategies for implementing changes in an organization, and the one to use depends on the particular situation of a given organization. Some organizations need to follow a rigidly structured procedure, whereas others may need to base changes on more subtle persuasion. The time frame for change may also vary. In other words, there is no set formula for making changes within an organization.

Middle managers may prove to be most resistant to change, especially when the change will take responsibilities away from them. But even when managers do lose some responsibilities in a change process, they will find many more duties to replace the old responsibilities. When the new duties are as important if not more so, managers will be satisfied with the change. Clear communication of this element of the change process—that is, of the shift from old responsibilities to new ones—will alleviate managers' fears of the process. The most successful process of implementing change will in fact include middle managers in the decision.

Opposition to change does not have to be fact based. The rumor mill is an important aspect of resistance. When a fire department introduces policies with the intention of changing the culture, rumors about the intended goals of the change may fly. As people talk about their perceptions and apprehensions, misconceptions may get blown out of proportion. Soon employees are opposed to the change because of something they heard that has nothing to do with reality. The only way to combat the rumor mill is to actively promote clear and honest communication throughout the organization.

Effective communication is vital to the success of an organization in any circumstance, but especially during times of change. Talking about the future will help employees feel they are a part of that future and have a role in it. When employees feel they are a part of the process and have ownership in it, they are more likely to be supportive.

Establishing a decision-making process for implementing change

Although all change, for better or worse, causes stress, the stress is particularly detrimental when people perceive that they have no control over what is causing it. At such times they may express resistance to the decision-making process that is leading to change and is causing them to experience stress.

An especially useful way to create a sense of predictability within a process of change is to establish a consistent process for making decisions. The consistent process will help employees gain a sense of control over the uncertainties that lie ahead and will therefore reduce resistance to the change itself.

Basically, the decision-making process can be thought of as the use of leadership skills throughout the organization. This process involves several steps, each of which should be completed before the next step is initiated (see Figure 8–10). If, for example, the group involved in the process has difficulty with the fourth step (collecting valued information), the second step (framing the problem that is being dealt with) may have to be redone to yield terms that are more easily studied.

Establishing leadership and developing commitment
Any change process, or even a decision-making process, needs an individual or group of people to act as leaders. Organizational leaders, such as the fire chief, are ultimately responsible for driving the change process. This means that initially they may have to do the organizing (getting a group together) and the motivating (bringing

Figure 8–10
Decision-making
process.

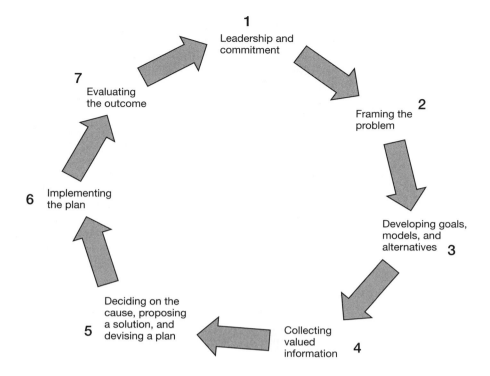

the group to see the task at hand as important), but it does not mean that they should retain all leadership responsibilities throughout the process. If the fire chief retains all authority, the team becomes useless.

As the change/decision-making team takes shape, more of its members should share in leadership responsibilities. Spreading the leadership responsibilities around will help ensure commitment to the process within the group. And if the group is not committed to the decision-making process, time should be spent cultivating that commitment; otherwise, the decision the group develops will not be viable.

For example, a particular fire station has statistically longer response times than any other station in the department. Statistical response time is the average response time for all emergency calls from a station over a period of time, and prompt response time is essential to fighting fires effectively because the difference of a few minutes can be the difference between a building saved and a building totally lost. The fire chief may decide to organize a team to determine the cause of the below-average performance and to propose potential remedies. He or she would first need to designate the team's members. They may be either appointed or allowed to volunteer.

When the team first meets, the fire chief is responsible for providing its members with the necessary information about the station and motivating them to want to improve the station's performance.

Framing the (secondary) problem   It is the group, and not the chief, that should determine exactly what problem gives rise to the poor performance. (Poor performance is the primary, or presenting, problem, and its cause is the secondary problem.) The group should analyze this secondary problem in terms of organizational objectives and values. Determining the secondary problem and relating it to the organization's objectives and values will narrow the focus, reducing the amount of time spent collecting ultimately unneeded data and discussing irrelevant alternatives.

In the example given, the presenting problem is that a particular fire station has statistically longer response times than any other station in the department, and the first task of the team is to determine the secondary problem—the cause of the poor response time. Perhaps the secondary problem is the station's location, or it may be equipment readiness, or there may be a blockage en route to the fire scene that is beyond the control of the firefighters. In this example, the presenting problem (subnormal response times) is fairly straightforward, and the possible causes (secondary problems) are framed in terms of efficiency or external constraints rather than morale or technology. Morale is an individual internal motivational issue and beyond the scope of any team. Similarly, deficiencies in technology most often require input and "fixes" also beyond the scope of any team. Thus, although morale or technology may be a contributory cause, the team should stay focused on achieving such departmental objectives as efficiency, public safety, and rapid response times. Maintaining that focus will enable the team to concentrate on the task at hand.

Developing goals, models, and alternatives   The group also has to decide what it hopes to achieve. By starting with discussions of the desired end result, the group can develop models and ideas about how best to obtain that result. In this case, the goal for the team will probably be to improve the station's statistical response time to make it equivalent to that of other fire stations in the department. Goals may not always be so straightforward, but whatever goal is chosen by the team, it will be the basis for creating models to identify alternatives and potential solutions. Before team members have much information, they should try to develop several models that might identify or explain the problem—in this case, the key factors lowering the station's statistical response times.

Collecting valued information   Before any possible decision can be developed, data are necessary. As more relevant information is acquired, the group can be more confident about its final decision.

The information collected should pertain to the model(s) the team has already created. The information may be based on more rigorous evaluation of the station's procedures, simulations of emergency procedures, staff interviews, or any other information collection techniques that team members might consider valuable in determining the cause of the slow response time.

Models may suggest three possible causes of the problem, as mentioned above: the station's location, the readiness of equipment, or a blockage en route to the fire scene that is beyond the control of the firefighters. At first the team members may not know which of the three is the true cause, but as they collect more data, they will find more support for one of these possible causes over the other two.

Deciding on the cause of the problem, proposing a solution, and devising a plan   On the basis of the best data available, a decision as to the cause of the slow response time needs to be made. There is no set decision-making formula for choosing the right cause, but with careful deliberation and discussion of how each alternative will work in light of the information collected, the group should be able to reach a rational decision. The group will then be able to take the next two steps: proposing a solution and devising a plan for putting the solution into effect—a plan that all team members can support.

In considering a plan for solving the problem (i.e., a plan for addressing the cause of poor response time), the team should evaluate the risks to be faced once the plan is implemented. Will implementation result in more stress for the firefighters? Will they be put at greater risk in unsafe conditions? Will the risk of lawsuits increase? Will operating costs increase?

The plan should mention any tasks that will have to be done and who will do them; it should also mention potential barriers to implementation, with suggestions for alternative activities. The more explicit the plan, the better understanding the staff will have of its purpose. The plan should also address how to ensure staff acceptance. Finally, it should contain provisions for gathering feedback on progress. Feedback will be important in evaluating the plan's success.

Implementing the plan   Both the decision about the cause of the problem and the proposed strategy for dealing with it (i.e., the implementation plan) need to be clearly disseminated throughout the organization. In particular, staff members at the affected station should be prepared for the necessary changes; preparation may include training sessions or additional staff meetings.

Evaluating the outcome   Once a plan has been formulated and implemented, the actual results should be compared with the intended results. Was the statistical response time for the station reduced? If not, the team will have to review its decision-making process and alter either the plan or its implementation until the goal is met. For example, perhaps the members interpreted some information incorrectly, or maybe the selected model was flawed. The team will have to repeat the steps discussed above until the station's statistical response time is reduced. But if the goal has been met, it is time to look for new problems and goals and to initiate another decision-making process that is based on the last one.

It is also important to realize that although a process for decision making is necessary, it is not sufficient. A process will provide a consistent and predictable framework within which to make decisions, but it will not offer any understanding of the issues involved as the team works toward its decision as to the cause of the problem. For that understanding, one must again discuss values. Organizational and individual preferences and ideas are based on values. Understanding a person's underlying values allows one to understand why that person supports a particular position. An analysis of individuals' values will assist with understanding of the issues and will ensure that the ultimate decisions are centered on the organization's values.

Relationship between the fire chief and the local government manager

For the most part, this chapter has been about leadership and management *within* a department. But fire service leaders cannot succeed only by directing their leadership skills toward their own departments. They must also look outward—toward the political process as a whole (see Chapter 3) and toward their relationship with their own city or county manager.

All public officials, not only fire chiefs, are charged with doing their part to make their communities safe and livable. But although local government managers share many objectives with fire chiefs, differences in perspective can inhibit communication. In addition, both fire chiefs and local government officials are very human, and like everyone else, for the sake of efficiency they may form opinions on the basis of limited experiences and paint entire professions with a broad brush.

Local government managers may view fire chiefs as inflexible or may assume that their scope of interests and concerns is limited. Fire chiefs may see local government managers as transient, searching for short-term wins. For both fire chiefs and local government managers, meeting changing needs and maintaining successful peer relationships with the other are a challenge. Some fire chiefs and local government managers, however, have built and maintained very effective working partnerships. A peer relationship between local government managers and fire chiefs can be built if questions are asked that test understanding and alignment.

In particular, local government managers, concerned about the "traditional" fire service, may wonder whether their fire chiefs have a vision for the future of the fire service. If chiefs are asked, "On what does the future of the fire service depend?" they should be prepared to respond. And if the question is not asked directly, they should be prepared to volunteer their ideas about what their community's fire service ought to look like in the future and why.

The fire chief's perspective

Most fire chiefs sincerely want to be heard, respected, trusted, and treated as professional peers. Fire chiefs have dedicated their careers to a specific technical discipline. They do not want someone to evaluate, label, or dismiss them on the basis of their uniform or occupation.

Local government managers should be mindful of the situation in which they may put their fire chiefs. Chiefs have been asked to position the department for the future by looking beyond the parochial needs of their own departments and developing interdepartmental systems to serve the community. City/county managers have asked for analyses of bureaucratic structures, with management layers eliminated or consolidated to become more efficient and responsive. Managers have asked for budgets framed by affordability, with reductions in funding. But as chiefs reposition their departments, appropriately questioning existing assumptions, they must not compromise the safety of the community or of their firefighters. The fire chief has to make difficult choices, balancing a commitment to being a responsible, responsive member of the manager's team with a desire to maintain an effective organization while managing an increasingly anxious workforce.

For fire service leaders to stand for safety seems fundamental, and on consensus issues—those on which the population at large is in general agreement—it is comparatively easy to believe in truth and to want the best for the people in an organization. The real test of ethical leadership may come when a leader must stand alone on difficult issues. For example, balancing code compliance with legitimate business concerns may present fire service leaders with an ethical challenge. Another example involves the fire chief's position within the context of local government as a whole. In that context, an understanding of the sensitive political issues in a dynamic government and community environment is fundamental to leadership success (see Chapter 3). A leader should be able both to identify multiple solutions and to modify a position when additional information is provided. But adopting a position solely because it is politically popular, or changing a position as a result of inappropriate pressure, can be an abdication of leadership. A credible leader is defined by the ability to balance the two extremes in search of a personal and professional ethical standard.

The local government manager's perspective

From the point of view of the city or county manager, the key to a successful working relationship with the fire chief is the chief's credibility. Fire chiefs can improve their credibility with local government managers by avoiding a self-righteous communications style and remembering that they are not the only ones concerned about community safety; managers share this commitment and responsibility.

Credibility begins by telling the truth without a "spin," having one's facts straight, nondefensively evaluating systems and structures, and candidly responding to questions. Credibility means giving the manager the same assistance the chief expects from his or her own staff: multiple options with a thorough analysis of the alternatives.

Participating more in the public policy debate by providing factual data is also important. For instance, the manager expects the fire chief to be forthcoming about the effect that fire department staffing and other budgetary decisions (station locations, new equipment, and so forth) will have on insurance rates paid by home owners. The manager's aim is to seek an equitable balance among the community's fire rating, insurance rates paid, and expenditures; and data from the fire chief can help in that regard. Each budgetary decision relating to the fire and rescue service will affect the financial burden that every citizen and property owner bears in supporting local government services, and the manager's goal is to ensure that this financial burden produces the necessary services but is neither excessive nor unwarranted.

In addition, the fire chief should remember that in the context of local government, the fire and rescue service represents the expenditure of a relatively large amount of money. More important, however, is the fact that the staffing of a fire service organization is different from that of other city or county departments. This traditional difference—twenty-four-hour, or overnight, shifts in the fire service—necessitates a different method of calculating overtime, standard workweek, holiday pay, and budget expenditures. Consequently, comparisons made by other employee groups may create conflict. Moreover, as technology evolves in the areas of fire suppression equipment and fire/smoke detection and in the building and trades industry, the manager expects the fire service to stay up-to-date.

Although much is said about fire prevention, too often suppression consumes a larger portion of the fire service budget (this is partly because of tradition and partly because of staff orientation). The manager expects a chief to be creative in finding ways of bridging the gap between suppression and prevention—ways of strengthening education about fire prevention, in partnership with the building and trades community. Fire chiefs are expected to be creative in using firefighters to carry out an expanded view of fire prevention so as to meet broader local government objectives. This use of firefighters could include code enforcement activities as well as emergency preparedness, education, and prevention efforts; through pre-fire and emergency response planning, it could also include identifying hazards that confront the community. (For details on fire prevention, see Chapter 12.)

Finally, as fire service evolves into emergency medical response, the manager expects the chief to see his or her role in a broader context of community health. The emergency response program must be integrated closely into, and coordinated with, community health services as a whole to ensure adequate and equitable delivery of overall comprehensive health services within the community.

Conclusion

The fire and rescue service is experiencing tremendous internal and external pressures to meet expanding demands. The public expects an ever-greater variety of services, local governments expect increasing effectiveness and efficiency, and staff expect an increasingly high-quality work environment.

These demands can be met when the department develops a vision for the future and works toward that future with open and honest teamwork. The foun-

Figure 8–11   The Arlington (Texas) Fire
Department developed this graphic to
illustrate the leadership puzzle completed.

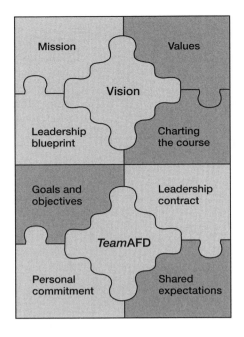

dation for the future starts with leadership training for all employees. Effective leadership at all levels of the fire service is essential to ensure the department's ability to meet expanding demands while offering the most appropriate, effective, and economical services.

As the department develops leadership skills at every level, all the pieces of the organizational puzzle will fit together (see Figure 8–11). The critical leadership elements are developing a vision, defining a mission, establishing goals, and aligning an organization's culture with key values. If these elements have been combined with systemwide planning, structured teamwork, and effective communication, the result will be a dynamic, healthy organization that is prepared to adapt to a competitive future.

1   Noel M. Tichy, *The Leadership Engine* (New York: HarperBusiness, 1997), 190.

2   John P. Kotter, *Leading Change* (Cambridge: Harvard Business School Press, 1996), 25.

3   Frederick Winslow Taylor, *The Principles of Scientific Management* (New York: Harper 1911; reprint Engineering and Management Press, Norcross, Ga., 1998); W. Edwards Deming, *Out of the Crises* (Cambridge: Massachusetts Institute of Technology, 1986); Stephen R. Covey, *Principle-Centered Leadership* (New York: Simon & Schuster, 1991).

4   Robin Paulsgrove, "Evaluating Our Services," *NFPA Journal* 90 (May/June 1996): 49.

5   This entire discussion of processes or habits, including their names, is based on Stephen R. Covey, *The Seven Habits of Highly Effective People* (New York: Simon & Schuster, 1989).

6   Elliott Jaques, "Glossary," *Requisite Organization: A Total System for Effective Managerial Organization and Managerial Leadership for the 21st Century* (Arlington, Va.: Cason Hall & Co., 1997), 13.

7   Ibid., 14.

8   Kathleen D. Ryan and Daniel K. Oestreich, *Driving Fear out of the Workplace* (San Francisco: Jossey-Bass, 1991), 235.

9   Richard L. Hughes, Robert C. Ginnett, and Gordon J. Curphy, *Leadership: Enhancing the Lessons of Experience,* 3rd ed. (Boston: Irwin/McGraw-Hill, 1999), 593.

10   Adapted from Peter R. Scholtes, Brian L. Joiner, and Barbara J. Streibel, *The Team Handbook* (Madison, Wis.: Joiner Group, 1988), 6–10 through 6–22.

11   Ibid., 6–13, 6–14.

12   Quoted in Robin Paulsgrove, "Recruiting and Retaining Fire Department FPEs," *NFPA Journal* 87 (January/February 1993): 60.

13   Robin Paulsgrove, "Take This Job and Love It," *Fire Chief* 36 (August 1992): 48–53.

14   Gareth Morgan, *Images of Organization* (Thousand Oaks, Calif.: Sage, 1997), 141.

15   Paulsgrove, "Take This Job," 31.

16   Adapted from E. B. Knauft, Renee A. Berger, and Sandra T. Gray, *Profiles of Excellence: Achieving Success in the Nonprofit Sector* (San Francisco: Jossey-Bass, 1991), 120; Patricia Jones and Larry Kahaner, *Say It and Live It: The 50 Corporate Mission Statements That Hit the Mark* (New York: Currency-Doubleday, 1995), 264–267; and John Carver, *Boards That Make a Difference* (San Francisco: Jossey-Bass, 1990), 65–67.

Training for fire and emergency response services

In almost every industry, training or education is necessary at some or all levels of operation if a job is to be safely and effectively completed. The level of training or education required to perform a given set of tasks varies with the tasks and the personnel assigned to them. The level may also vary with the organization's depth of commitment to excellence, high quality of service or products, and safety.

The fire and emergency response services have a long history of delivering high-quality service to their communities and therefore of placing a high value on training and continuing education for their employees. But it is not just the striving for high-quality service delivery that should drive the training and education programs of a fire department (regardless of its size or status as career or volunteer). Another important reason for training is to help ensure the safety of fire and rescue personnel. The health and well-being of emergency responders, which is important in all aspects of organizational operation, is generally regarded as the single most important reason to train.

In the last two decades of the twentieth century, major changes in protective equipment, safety-oriented procedures, and training significantly improved the safety record of the fire service. In many respects continued emphasis on safety is mandated, but it is also good policy. In emphasizing the importance of safety, the organization is meeting both its moral obligation to protect its workers and its financial obligation to the local jurisdiction to manage its resources wisely, as well as following through on its commitment to its citizen-customers.

The terms *training* and *education* have been used here without any explanation. Although their exact meanings are much debated by educators, the definitions guiding the use of the two terms in this chapter are as follows:

Education is the process of delivering essentially academic knowledge. Adult education is generally delivered in traditional and nontraditional settings by institutions of higher learning and is part of a program of study that leads to a degree or certification granted by an accredited degree-granting institution.

Training is the process of delivering essentially vocational skills and knowledge. Training is delivered through either traditional or nontraditional modalities by a broad spectrum of institutions and generally results in the achievement of a certain training objective, which may or may not be part of a program of study leading to a certificate. Certification is a measure of competence vouched for by an entity that is licensed or accredited to issue the certification.

Although on paper the distinction between training and education seems clear-cut, in reality it is not, and organizations regularly ignore the boundaries between the two. In the fire and rescue service, innovation to meet customer needs will mean that the lines of demarcation between training and education remain blurred, for both are necessary if the goals are to be achieved.

This chapter discusses the elements of a successful training process; the elements of the training program itself; and the necessary facilities and personnel, along with sources of assistance.

Elements of a successful training process

Successful training requires paying particular attention to five elements of the training process:

Planning for the training

Ensuring its safety

Meeting national, state, and local training standards and requirements

Recognizing and responding to the training needs of the particular department (i.e., using the "training-in-context" approach)

Thinking carefully about formats for delivering the training.

Planning

Planning is an important part of the training process. To be effective, planning should involve management, labor, training personnel, and any appropriate external experts. The latter may include vocational training specialists, regional or state fire training personnel, and others who can contribute special skills or knowledge to the planning process.

Planning for a fire service training program should start with the recognition of departmental goals and objectives. The next step is building on them to develop specific training objectives. The plan should also identify the resources necessary to achieve the objectives; it should have benchmarks; and it should undergo regular evaluation and revision. Overall, the plan (and the document formalizing it) should reflect the realistic capabilities of the organization, and it should be available for all within the organization to review at their convenience as often as necessary.

It is particularly important, as part of the regular evaluation, to provide a customer feedback mechanism for the plan and for the training program (the customer in this case being everyone in the training program). Many programs suffer when those being trained are not afforded an easy, continuing, and informal way to provide feedback. Open input from all involved will help those in charge evaluate the plan (and the organization) in terms of the stated objectives. It will also allow all concerned to continually update their perspectives. Formal and organized student/trainee feedback will also be useful, particularly for evaluating the plan and the training delivery process.

Safety

Safety is paramount in any fire and rescue activity, especially in the training environment. Successful training programs have to recognize two important aspects of safety. First, the overall mission requires that all participants be trained continually in safe methods of accomplishing their tasks. But if learned safety behaviors are not continually reinforced, people will invariably compromise them. Accordingly, initial and subsequent training must contain the safety elements for the given subject every time the subject is taught. Second, training must be conducted safely. Because the emergency services typically operate in dangerous environments, they must practice in similar or simulated situations. Unfortunately, each year tragic training-related deaths and injuries occur in generally preventable circumstances. The major contributing causes of these incidents include improper student/instructor ratios and well-meaning efforts to make training scenarios too realistic.

In the mid-1980s several interested national fire service organizations asked the National Fire Protection Association (NFPA) to develop standards addressing the growing number of training accidents. The standards that emerged provide a blueprint for the safety policies and procedures of training agencies and fire departments. NFPA 1500, Standard on Fire Department Occupational Health and Safety Program (2002 edition), is the enabling document that outlines a comprehensive safety program for fire departments and in some states or provinces is the law. The following other standards were also developed by NFPA's Fire Service Training Committee:

NFPA 1401, Recommended Practice for Fire Service Training Reports and Records (2001 edition)

NFPA 1402, Guide to Building Fire Service Training Centers (2002 edition)

NFPA 1403, Standard on Live Fire Training Evolutions [an evolution is a segment of a fire ground operation] (2002 edition)

NFPA 1451, Standard for a Fire Service Vehicle Operations Training Program (2002 edition).

Additional resources are available from the International Society of Fire Service Instructors and the Fire Department Safety Officers Association. These organizations and many of their state affiliates concentrate on helping their members achieve training that is both high in quality and safe.

Standards and requirements

External mandates are often a primary determinant of training content. Departments providing emergency medical service (EMS), for example, often find that a large percentage of their resources are required for initial and continuing education to meet local and state medical requirements. Various federal, state, and local authorities that regulate other aspects of the services offered by a fire department also specify requirements for certain levels of competence. Typical of these other requirements are

Defined hazardous materials (HAZMAT) training, required by the federal government

Firefighter training, required by the state or province

Driver/operator training, required by an insurance carrier

Specific training for airport firefighters, required by the federal government.

Although they may not be mandated, several NFPA standards detail minimum job performance for various fire service positions. NFPA's performance standards are adopted as requirements by many jurisdictions, and even where not specifically adopted, they effectively serve as guidelines. Among the applicable standards are

NFPA 1001, Standard for Fire Fighter Professional Qualifications (1997 edition)

NFPA 1002, Standard for Fire Apparatus Driver/Operator Professional Qualifications (1998 edition)

NFPA 1003, Standard for Airport Fire Fighter Professional Qualifications (2000 edition)

NFPA 1006, Standard for Rescue Technician Professional Qualifications (2000 edition)

NFPA 1021, Standard for Fire Officer Professional Qualifications (1997 edition)

NFPA 1031, Standard for Professional Qualifications for Fire Inspector and Plan Examiner (1998 edition)

NFPA 1033, Standard for Professional Qualifications for Fire Investigator (1998 edition)

NFPA 1035, Standard for Professional Qualifications for Public Fire and Life Safety Educator (2000 edition)

NFPA 1041, Standard for Fire Service Instructor Professional Qualifications (2002 edition)

NFPA 1051, Standard for Wildland Fire Fighter Professional Qualifications (2002 edition)

NFPA 1061, Standard for Professional Qualifications for Public Safety Telecommunicator (2002 edition)

NFPA 1071, Standard for Emergency Vehicle Technician Professional Qualifications (2000 edition).

Some states and provinces use either variations of these standards or standards they have generated themselves.

Generally, when standards are used to specify job performance requirements, a system of evaluation and certification testing is also used. A number of commercial entities provide instruments to test both the skills and the knowledge specified by the standards. And many states and provinces provide the testing process and tools through an agency that has been legally authorized to provide them. These certification processes, in turn, may be accredited by the International Fire Service Accreditation Congress. Accreditation reasonably ensures that the certification process is conducted in a manner that is fair, open, and relevant and accords with the applicable standards.

Training-in-context

NFPA standards are national consensus documents that attempt to serve a broad range of fire services, but training to the standards must necessarily take place in the context of the needs and resources of a given community. The concept of training-in-context gained popularity during the 1980s and 1990s.

Essentially developed by the state of Montana, where it has been widely implemented, the concept has been adopted and adapted by several other states and jurisdictions as well. Specifically, training-in-context uses the available time and resources to focus on the needs of the department, recognizing that national standards may require skills and knowledge in areas that may not be applicable to rural firefighters. Further, training-in-context recognizes that a department may not own the type of fire apparatus or equipment assumed by the standard.

In lieu of using the prescribed training, therefore, the Montana process takes carefully designed tactical problems and incorporates as many elements of the training standard as possible into a given drill. The exercises are carefully conducted, available equipment is used, and staff simulate realistic local scenarios. Coaching is a significant part of the activity, as are the use of sound instructional methodology and a high level of safety consciousness. Lecture and demonstration stress the teaching and learning objectives and are followed by practice, for reinforcement.

In many fire departments, training-in-context may not be necessary, but in small communities with limited resources, it is particularly applicable and effective.

Training-in-context: How it works

Vince Lombardi said, "Practice doesn't make perfect; perfect practice makes perfect."

This describes the approach taken by the Frenchtown Rural Fire District in Frenchtown, Montana. Training-in-context is a major element of the department's training program and has served the department well. Support comes from Montana State University's Fire Service Training division, but the teaching is done primarily by in-house instructors.

Training-in-context consists of four steps:

1. The operation is explained.
2. The expected product is illustrated.
3. The candidates are coached as they practice, aiming for a perfect product. The practice includes repetitions to master the sequence of necessary actions, and repetitions to master the technical skills needed.
4. The candidate's "perfect product," after coached practice, is evaluated.

During the explanation of the operation, the instructor demonstrates the need for training by referring to operational needs, often drawing from actual past incidents. Taped reproductions of the expected product—the perfect process—are then used to show the candidates the goal. Objectives are then identified and rehearsed mentally, and in sequence, to condition the candidates for the application of technical skills. The skills are then rehearsed physically, one at a time and in sequence, until each candidate can reproduce an example of the expected product within an acceptable time frame. At this point the candidates are ready to be evaluated: can they go through a perfect process, meeting the predetermined standard?

It is also important to note that operationally, firefighters work as part of a crew under the direct supervision of a crew leader. Each candidate must understand and be able to demonstrate the objectives for each role in a given tactic. Throughout the process, therefore, the team concept is emphasized as critical to expected outcomes. Putting the emphasis (for crews and apparatus) on response readiness serves the organization by instilling in its members a sense of responsibility. The message is, "We are our brother's or sister's keeper."

The Frenchtown Rural Fire District uses the training-in-context approach throughout the myriad of services it provides. If there is a down side, it is that the training is labor-intensive. It takes a lot of supplies and a lot of experienced individuals to maximize the candidates' experiences. However, when members get to do more, the department's retention of members is better and so is the members' retention of knowledge and skills critical to the services the department provides.

The Frenchtown Rural Fire District provides structural and wildland fire suppression and prevention, advanced life support and basic life support transporting and nontransporting emergency medical services, all phases of specialized rescue, and hazardous materials mitigation. The district encompasses more than one hundred square miles and has eight stations and over seventy (volunteer) members.

Formats for delivering training

The technology used in educating people and even the psychology of education are constantly under study. Like the rest of the high-tech world, audiovisual techniques and equipment are changing so fast that most instructors have trouble keeping up. And scholars continue to seek the most effective ways not only to educate people but also to measure effectiveness.

Any training program must therefore be aware of the scope of instructional methodologies available to the teaching team. Formats for delivery may include

Traditional lecture plus note taking for abstract material

Demonstration for scientific principles or particular skills

Traditional self-study for a broad range of topics

Interactive computer self-study for a broad range of topics

Hands-on practice for purely motor skills

Simulation for strategic and tactical decision making.

In terms of the instructor's skills development and the facilities, planning for use of the best (i.e., most appropriate) instructional methodology will ultimately make the training program more effective and more economical. Each of the formats listed can be varied in ways that make the proper approach affordable even to the smallest fire department. Shared facilities, community assets such as schools and churches, and some creativity generally make it possible to identify a place and some equipment to help make the program work. Moreover, classes in instructional methodology and other subjects important to fire service instructors are generally available from the state or provincial agency responsible for fire service training. Such classes are also generally available through a state or regional vocational education school.

Proper preparation for any educational presentation is essential. Instructional staff should have access to the skills and tools that will allow them to prepare the curriculum materials they will need. Although course materials may well be commercially available, instructors will have to be completely familiar with them and will generally want to modify them to meet the needs of a particular department or setting. The necessary training in developing course outlines and delivering classes is specified by NFPA 1041, Standard for Fire Service Instructor Professional Qualifications.

One aspect of the instructional methodology used is evaluating the training for effectiveness. Planning should therefore include consideration and adoption of evaluation strategies for the range of subjects taught. When certification levels are either mandated or offered on a voluntary basis by a state or provincial agency or by others, the evaluation process will generally be well established and outside the control of the local fire service. However, when certification does not exist or the topic is not a certification subject or activity, evaluation still has to take place so that the effectiveness of the teaching/learning process can be measured.

Elements of the training program itself

Training programs can be simple or complex, depending to a great extent on the size and needs of an organization. However, all programs require certain elements if they are to be successful and meet applicable laws and standards. These elements are

Training for incoming personnel

In-service training

Staff development

Learning from incidents

Training for special operations

Training records.

Training for incoming personnel

In essentially all fire departments, basic training for incoming personnel is a major concern and commitment. Training programs must be designed to provide a standard level of competence for those employees or volunteers who are about to fill a given position (in most cases, that of firefighter). In many jurisdictions, incoming personnel will be required to meet the skill level of either Firefighter I or Firefighter I and II, as described in NFPA 1001, Standard for Fire Fighter Professional Qualifications. Specialized training in policies and procedures for the given jurisdiction are also part of the initial training. And if the department offers emergency medical services, the basic training covers first responder or emergency medical technician (EMT) training.

Some communities require incoming personnel to have certain credentials before they are employed. Requirements for a Firefighter I certificate, an EMT certificate, or both are not unusual, especially in urban areas where such preemployment training may be easily accessible to large numbers of people.

However, when preemployment certificates are required, it is a good idea for the employer to be in close touch with the preemployment training community. It is critical for the employer to be certain that the community colleges, states,

---

Training together   Like many counties in the United States and provinces in Canada, Tippecanoe County, Indiana, has a number of medium-size and small volunteer and career fire departments. Since none of the volunteer fire departments has an extensive full-time staff or extensive financial resources, the burden of training new recruits to meet local and state standards used to weigh heavily. Then, under the leadership of an active countywide firefighters association, the training dilemma was approached collectively.

In recognition that neither the full amount of time nor the complete expertise required to instruct new firefighters was resident in any one department, a training committee was established. Each department was responsible for designating a training coordinator, who not only coordinates schedules for his or her department but also contributes to the instructional process. Furthermore, at least one representative from each department has to achieve and maintain the state's certified-instructor status.

For each multiweek training class, an overall coordinator is selected. The coordinator designates the instructor for the various sessions and sees that the proper records are executed and main-

tained. Class sessions are held at various facilities throughout the county on agreed-upon evenings and weekends. Final testing for certification is accomplished in compliance with the state's requirements.

The net result is that a difficult problem faced by a set of small fire departments has been solved. The departments are now able to process new recruits in whatever number might be needed by pooling enough recruits from various departments to form a class of the proper size. The cost, in both dollars and volunteer time, of training a recruit has diminished for each department. The quality of training and the enthusiasm of the trainees have increased dramatically, for the training is completed in a timely manner and the rewards of certification flow quickly.

A side benefit to this process has been the need to ensure that all fire departments are operating with a new degree of uniformity. Command systems and general tactical approaches have been aligned to make training as well as joint operations easier.

This is a simple approach that takes few resources but yields substantial benefits.

or other agencies doing the training are covering the desired topics and testing the students in a high-quality and comprehensive manner. The amount of training done by the hiring entity is inversely proportional to the amount of training required in advance. However, the responsibility to field a properly trained team remains the employer's.

Turning a would-be firefighter into a properly certified Firefighter/EMT ready for an initial operational assignment is a substantial task. The methodology and time frame used in doing so vary widely among organizations and need to reflect any state requirements. Some training agencies require a certain number of hours, whereas others offer much of the cognitive training as take-home work or work to be done at the computer. However, the critical factor in determining the level of competence is a thorough knowledge- and skills-based testing effort. Because such tests are difficult and expensive to develop and administer, most departments use a standard, validated process developed by a fully accredited testing agency. Very often, testing services will be offered by an agency of a state or provincial government or by a local community college.

One critical and continuing debate centering on the training of recruit firefighters involves the question of when they are ready to respond to incidents. In many volunteer, small-community fire departments, new personnel may be added in very small numbers; thus, the concept of a "recruit class" for training is not applicable. Some of these fire departments simply spread the initial training over months of training sessions—and thus have uncertified personnel for many months after initial hiring or membership.

NFPA 1001, Standard for Fire Fighter Professional Qualifications, certainly implies (although it does not state) that firefighters should complete the requirements for Firefighter I before responding to calls. The dilemma arises when personnel moving through the training process are also responding to calls.

The state of Washington has implemented a somewhat different concept. The state has developed a list of critical skills and packaged them into a training program designed specifically to be taught before a recruit is assigned to any response duty. Thus, the state can certify a firefighter for the conditional levels of response training even as the person's more extensive training continues.

In-service training

The fire and rescue service enjoys an excellent reputation for in-service training. Training is traditionally thought of as taking place during every shift for the career service and at a defined time each month for noncareer operations. However, many organizations overlook the need to augment that regular, routine training with a well-planned and well-executed program of in-service training.

The modern fire department, in addition to fulfilling the requirements that certain certifications have for continuing education, needs to provide directed and documented in-service training on a myriad of subjects. Doing so will enable the department to address skills degradation, advances in technology, expansion of services, changes in policy, and many other topics.

Planning and delivering an in-service training program can be a substantial task. To ensure that all needs are being addressed and to increase the level of "buy in" from all areas, the planning phase should involve representatives from throughout the organization. This phase should consider the following questions, among others:

What subjects should training cover? A needs analysis should focus on
  Critical skills and knowledge that are used infrequently
  High-consequence skills and procedures

Input from incident experience
Continuing education required for certifications
Mandated training
Departmental goals and objectives.

How can schedules of trainers and trainees be managed?
What alternative ways of delivering the training are there?
What outside resources are available and affordable?
What restrictions are imposed by labor contracts?

Providing in-service training to very busy response units, whether career or volunteer, can be challenging. Not only may all units have a class interrupted if they remain in service, but very busy fire companies may also have literally no good training time available in the normal work setting. In these cases, units may have to be removed from service even to cover the simplest of subjects. Although declaring units out of service for training is undesirable, it is every bit as important as taking them out of service for response to incidents or for maintenance. Declaring units out of service for training implies that the vacated response district will be covered to the best of the organization's ability.

In-service training resources abound. Video subscriptions and online training programs are available on a broad range of topics. More than fifty publishers provide materials to help train fire and emergency responders, and some even provide books specifically geared to in-service drills and exercises.

However, in-service training means more than sending a video to every station to watch or assigning personnel to view a subscription program. In-service training is a planned and executed process that is ongoing and addresses very specific needs. To stop training implies that the trainee is "fully trained," but everyone can benefit from additional training.

Staff development

Fire and emergency response managers continually point to the lack of high-quality staff-type development programs—opportunities for employees and volunteers to grow—as a significant problem in their organizations. That the lack still remains well after it has been recognized attests to the difficulty in designing and implementing a good staff development program.

Fire departments need to create such programs. Training resources are well spent if expended in this area—and a good program requires much investment in time and money. The ever-increasing demands on fire and emergency response managers will continue to put a premium not only on good leadership and basic management skills (see Chapter 8) but also on sound problem-solving skills and the ability to manage multiple functions.

Good staff development programs do not rely principally on internal resources. Instead, they make use of higher-education offerings, state and national fire academy programs, and training opportunities made available by the private sector. In this training, diversity is important to quality. Providing a broad scope of input will expose future leaders and managers to various approaches and philosophies in both public and private sector settings.

Like most aspects of departmental training, a staff development program should be grounded on an open planning process. The items to consider (in all aspects of departmental training, but especially in this one) include

Applicability and accessibility of the program

Prerequisites

Time and travel constraints

Access to learning resources (both print and nonprint)

Financial resources for tuition, travel, lectures, and so forth

Resource sharing with other fire service and non–fire service entities

Equivalency of various forms of education and training.

Many departments have added a formal mentoring program to staff development training. It is important that potential leaders learn not only from external sources but also from the people who currently lead within the organization. In many cases informal mentoring takes place without prompting, but a formal process ensures that everyone has access to the officers.

Certainly, college degrees in management, public or business administration, fire service administration, or other related areas will go a long way toward developing the skills necessary for officers. Some fire departments even require a degree for certain levels of promotion. But there are always local issues and policies that make a supplementary departmental program necessary.

The content of staff development training programs is very important and requires careful planning. Many resources describe management training; and NFPA 1021, Standard for Fire Officer Professional Qualifications, identifies the job performance standards for several levels of fire officers.

In the late 1990s, the International Association of Fire Chiefs developed a certification program for chief officers in the fire service. This program, adapted from a Canadian program, specifies a significant number of educational and experiential benchmarks that must be achieved. If certification is to be awarded, the candidate must submit substantial documentation to a certification board for evaluation. This program is not an educational delivery project but is designed to evaluate an individual on the basis of education received from other sources and level of personal experience. However, the program's requirements can serve as a guide in the planning of staff development programs.

One of the most popular and highly acclaimed programs of the National Fire Academy (NFA) is its Executive Fire Officer (EFO) program. This comprehensive staff development program provides a multiyear learning experience for enrollees, with work both at home and on the NFA campus in Emmitsburg, Maryland. Candidates must meet certain prerequisites, and space in this challenging program is always limited. Designation as an EFO graduate is often a requirement or a preference in lateral-entry chief officer recruiting.

Whatever the source of the education and training, each fire and rescue organization has an obligation to the community to provide high-quality leadership. Grooming those within the department to manage effectively not only addresses that obligation at the particular time but also provides an investment in future leadership.

Learning from incidents

Another form of training is the formal process of learning from experience. Nearly every fire department conducts some type of critique process after major incidents. However, only a small percentage of departments have in place a policy describing the process and the "afterlife" of critiques. Yet these exercises are of little value unless the lessons learned are documented, integrated into training and practice, and evaluated again.

Post-incident evaluations (PIEs) should be governed by a written policy. Done properly, a PIE can be a very high quality training tool that will enhance customer service and personnel safety. Done improperly, the sessions can be threatening, hurtful, and of little technical merit. When a policy for PIEs is being developed, the following points (among others) should be considered:

Participation should be broad and the input process inclusive.

Adequate materials (audiovisual, written, etc.) should be prepared.

The environment and process should be nonthreatening.

The time frame for each element should be defined.

A record should be made of the session and its conclusions.

A follow-up process for applying the lessons learned should be established.

Probably the most critical failure of PIEs is the failure to assimilate the lessons learned into the department's training and operations even though doing so is, after all, the reason to conduct PIEs. Although it is essential to make sure that lessons from incidents are integrated into the training program, it is even more critical to ensure that they become part of policy and that the policy is carried out by all concerned.

The incident scene is the most realistic training that any organization can experience. Failure to scrutinize operations at the scene carefully and positively is indeed a training opportunity missed.

Training for special operations

The aspects of training that are most expensive and difficult to develop and deliver include the training that is designed for the special operation areas in fire and emergency response services. These areas include HAZMAT handling, technical rescue services, responses to weapons of mass destruction, and advanced emergency medical skills. Federal, state, and local laws may mandate training in these highly technical areas. But even if training is not mandated, keeping skills and knowledge up to high levels in these high-risk and low-frequency response categories is extremely important.

The expense of training in specialty operation areas can be considerable. In many cases the instructional expertise and materials will not be resident in a department or even nearby. Although state or provincial training agencies may offer the specific training, significant fees may be involved, and the delay may be long if demand is high. Very often personnel will have to be sent to a remote location for training, and this requirement generates travel and coverage costs.

Because specialty training can consume such a large percentage of a training budget, the overall training plan should include this element in detail. Some of the factors to be considered in planning are

Availability and accessibility of training (e.g., are training programs offered by our county?)

Accessibility of specialized learning resources (e.g., can we receive instruction via closed-circuit television?)

Frequency of required recertification

Evaluation for skills degradation

Travel and coverage costs

Public and private sector training sources

Training with other jurisdictions

Electronic and other nontraditional delivery.

Some specialized training is motivated by standards that may or may not be adopted as law. Documents such as NFPA 472, Standard for Professional Competence of Responders to Hazardous Materials Incidents (2002 edition), and NFPA 1006, Standard for Rescue Technician Professional Qualifications, will be of great assistance in determining the content of a training curriculum. Other topical areas lack specific performance criteria, but most specialty-area training topics are addressed by either a public sector document or a publication from one of the more than fifty publishers in the fire and emergency field.

Training records

Record keeping is not a type of training but a function that is important to all training plans. The importance of maintaining thorough records in the area of employee (career or volunteer) training cannot be overemphasized.

The evolution of computer-based systems has been a breath of fresh air in the area of training records. A myriad of good training record systems is available in the marketplace for very affordable prices. Regardless of the size of the fire department or the kind of computer hardware it has, a training database program is available. For the technologically inclined, a simple database can be developed from standard software programs.

Because training records should reflect training given and received, one important factor cannot be overlooked when computer-based record systems are used. There must be some process, either within the software or in a parallel paper-based system, to register the acknowledgment (signature) of both the trainer and the trainee. Many court decisions have upheld the importance of the dual acknowledgment.

The records for a given trainee should reflect more than just the simple titles of courses or sessions taken. Many courtrooms have also confirmed the need to list some level of detail as to the course/session content. For instance, if an evening training session were covering HAZMAT awareness, the department would be wise to list the table of contents from the course material or at least to reference the title of any commercially available curriculum being used.

High-quality training records not only provide legal reference in disputes but also form the basis of a training history for every employee. Using good records, the training officer can easily schedule timely recertifications, required continuing education, and annual skill evaluations. Further, by examining groups of employees, he or she can readily discern gaps in the teaching of certain skills and knowledge.

Finally, good-quality training records that substantiate the level and quality of training are required by insurance rating services and by fire service accrediting authorities. The records also may form the basis for individual applications for certification and/or for reviews by promotional boards.

Training facilities, personnel, and sources of assistance

Without resources, a training program will exist only on paper. For a department to carry out its plan and meet the statutory, service, and moral requirements for training, it must have—or at least must have access to—the necessary facilities and personnel. (Assistance in accessing these resources is available through a number of channels.)

Over the years, fire and rescue departments have done an admirable job of working together to provide resources that are needed for a broad spectrum of activities. Mutual aid (see Chapter 16) is a common example. Cooperation in the field of training is essential and limits the burden on each organization of meeting what may seem like a sizable responsibility.

Fire service training centers

A fire and rescue service training center can consist, at one extreme, of a mowed field with some utility poles on which to practice ladder evolutions or, at the other extreme, of a multimillion-dollar metropolitan academy. Certainly most fire departments cannot afford, nor do they need, a training center to teach all the skills and knowledge required by firefighters. However, they do need access to certain facilities that may be available through state/provincial or regional fire training academies. These facilities consist of

A building, a set of buildings, and/or props that allow firefighters to practice and be tested on all the nonburn skills referred to in NFPA 1001, Standard for Fire Fighter Professional Qualifications.

A building that will allow firefighters to be trained and tested effectively and safely in all the live burn skills referred to in NFPA 1001 (see Figure 9–1). Although buildings scheduled for demolition are a tempting substitute for actual burn chambers, using them for this purpose is fraught with difficulty. Burn structures should meet the requirements of NFPA 1403, Standard on Live Fire Training Evolutions, which clearly specifies the structural needs for the burn building—needs that evolved from tragic experiences over the years in non-engineered burn buildings—and not all buildings scheduled for demolition meet these requirements.

A flammable liquids burn pit to teach and test the flammable liquid firefighting skills specified in NFPA 1001. This facility needs to meet the environmental regulations applicable in a given area. In some cases, meeting the regulations may mean substituting a gaseous fuel for a liquid fuel to simulate a liquid fuel fire.

A water supply source, either pressurized or available from draft, to supply fire suppression water for all training evolutions. Local environmental regulations may require that this water be collected and either processed through an approved treatment plant or recycled.

A properly equipped classroom area that includes restrooms.

Safety and rehabilitation equipment, such as a safety shower, an eye-wash fountain, a drinking fountain, and a refreshment area.

Although many state/provincial and metropolitan training centers go well beyond the items discussed here, these represent the basic facilities needed by a center. The types of buildings and props will vary with the desired frequency

Figure 9–1 Conducting live burn drills at the Phoenix (Arizona) Training Academy burn tower.

of use and size of simulations. For instance, a training academy for a large metropolitan county may need a multistory training tower to simulate the high-rise building scenarios that exist in the community. In addition, a very busy academy may need an extensive set of structures to accommodate large, frequent classes.

Training centers that teach specialty topics will need additional physical facilities. For instance, a center that serves an airport fire department will probably need a flammable liquid prop large enough to meet the size requirements set by the Federal Aviation Administration, the agency that regulates aviation fire protection. Centers that teach HAZMAT technicians, rescue technicians, and so forth will need the props specific to those classes. Some of these props may be very large and expensive, whereas others can be constructed at very low cost.

One of the major concerns of those who develop and operate fire and emergency response training centers is the environmental impact of the center. Strict regulations apply to these centers, especially to the ones that use flammable liquids. Design firms should consult with the applicable environmental enforce-

---

Regional training in Charlotte, North Carolina   The Charlotte (North Carolina) Fire Department, with 867 firefighters and officers as of 2002, is the largest paid fire department in the state; and among the eighteen fire departments in Mecklenburg County, it is the only paid department. The entire Mecklenburg fire community is so closely knit that the chiefs of eight of the volunteer departments, and some members of all seventeen volunteer departments, are also Charlotte firefighters. Charlotte firefighters who live in counties other than Mecklenburg are active in their local volunteer departments as well. Thus, the decision of the Charlotte Fire Training Academy to become a regional training facility was only natural.

With a staff of eight, however, the Training Academy by itself could not meet the ongoing training needs for a department as large as Charlotte's, let alone the additional needs of all the other departments in the county. The solution was a partnership with the North Carolina Department of Community Colleges and its two local branches, Central Piedmont Community College in Charlotte and Gaston Community College in Gastonia. The community colleges provide (and pay) instructors who are certified by the North Carolina Fire and Rescue Commission (Fire/Rescue) and the North Carolina Office of Emergency Medical Services

(Office of EMS) in the specialties they are teaching; the colleges also provide class materials approved by the appropriate officials of those two agencies. The Training Academy provides classroom space and equipment and has the right to approve the choice of instructors. Most of the instructors are members of the Charlotte Fire Department.

In classes sponsored by or through the community college system, tuition fees are waived for active firefighters and other public safety personnel. Charlotte firefighters have first choice of classes, but classes are open to other firefighters, paid and volunteer, throughout the seven-county region. Introductory classes leading to first-time certifications are open, as are recertification and continuing education classes in all areas of expertise.

Fire/Rescue and the Office of EMS set the requirements (which are the same for paid and volunteer firefighters) for certifications for emergency responders: standards are in place for recruit firefighters (based on NFPA 1001), emergency rescue technicians, hazardous materials (HAZMAT) operations, emergency medical technicians (EMTs), and paramedics.

Charlotte's recruit training is a nineteen-week program covering twenty-three

ment agency at every step of the way. Air pollution and surface and ground-water pollution must all be considered.

Finally, there is always a concern about the location of a fire training center in relation to its neighbors. Except for the centers that routinely burn flammable liquids, most facilities will produce little or no smoke beyond the immediate area of the burn building. However, there are typically issues of the noise that arises in the evening and at night—the times when the volunteer fire service commonly trains. A key to neighborhood acceptance is involving adjacent owners in the planning phases for any initial construction or significant expansion. Videotapes of working centers from other jurisdictions are often helpful in demonstrating the low impact on neighbors. In addition, the liberal use of natural screening is encouraged.

There are a number of quality vendors of skills buildings, flammable liquid burn simulators, and burn buildings, among other props. These vendors offer a wide variety of sizes and other options to meet the needs of nearly any fire department. They can be accessed through Web sites; in addition, state/provincial training agencies can provide referrals.

---

topics (including avoidance of harassment—a city requirement—and response to terrorist incidents) and leading to certification as a Firefighter II, HAZMAT operations, and rescue technician. The recruit program has attracted new hires from paid fire departments in smaller cities in the region. These departments typically need fewer than five new firefighters at any one time, so sending them to Charlotte for their initial training is cost-effective. Charlotte usually runs two or three recruit classes for fifteen to twenty annually, and adding a couple of recruits from other departments is not a problem. Many recruits already hold EMT certification when they are hired, so they do not have to take EMT in the recruit program. Those who are not EMTs are required to acquire certification within a year of their date of hire. Classes are available at the academy or at the two community college campuses in the area.

Since 1990, the Charlotte Fire Department has required completion of Officer Candidate School (OCS) I for promotion to captain and OCS II for promotion to battalion chief. The OSC courses are taught through the community college system, and several also count toward the Associate in Applied Science (AAS) degree in fire technology offered by both of the community colleges in the area.[1]

The regional concept is feasible because the Charlotte Training Academy has delivery agency status. Essential to keeping this status is proper record keeping with good software; training records are subject to audit at any time. The Training Academy must be able to show Fire/Rescue 150 hours of in-service training for any member. In addition, the academy must have the equipment that is on the Fire/Rescue list: a training tower, a drafting facility, hose, ladders, SCBA, and so forth.

The training partnership has been an excellent deal for the Charlotte Fire Department, the community college system, and firefighters throughout North Carolina. It keeps training costs at a reasonable level while providing up-to-date continuing education for emergency responders, whether career or volunteer.

[1] Fire service professionals in North Carolina are excited about the bachelor's degree program in Fire Safety Engineering Technology that was started at the University of North Carolina at Charlotte in the fall of 1999. This program is designed to allow emergency services personnel with the AAS degree to continue their education and earn a bachelor's degree. Creation of the degree program is due to the perseverance of area fire chiefs and university officials in seeking funding to meet the long-standing need for a bachelor's program for fire and emergency services personnel to match programs for law enforcement personnel.

Source: Sally Young, Charlotte Fire Department planner.

Overland Park Fire Training Center

The Overland Park (Kansas) Fire Department (OPFD) is a nonprofit, incorporated, combination department comprising 110 uniformed responders in five stations, twenty staff personnel, and twenty-five fire and emergency medical service volunteers. Overland Park, a suburb of Kansas City, covers about sixty-eight square miles. Occupancy is mostly residential, office, commercial, and retail, but does include a little rural and light industrial. The OPFD responds to slightly more than ten thousand calls per year.

In 1992, the department started looking at an area in the middle of its rapidly expanding response district as a location for building a training center. At the same time, the Sprint Corporation, with its worldwide headquarters in Johnson County, Kansas, was looking for a site to build its technical Academy of Excellence. The OPFD and the City of Overland Park approached Sprint with a package deal. The city would build a fire training center that had provisions for Sprint. Sprint, in turn, would agree to a ten-year lease agreement with the option to renew for another ten years. Sprint's acceptance of this proposal opened the door to a creative and innovative $4.5 million financing package, ultimately resulting in savings to the taxpayers of Overland Park.

Planning started in 1993 with tours of fire training centers all over the country; construction was completed in late 1995.

The Overland Park Fire Training Center covers twelve acres and consists of a classroom building, a technical training/maintenance facility with showers, a five-story fire training tower, a trench and a confined-space rescue area, and vehicle extrication and vehicle fire training areas.

The classroom facility's twenty-two thousand square feet have room for Sprint's classrooms, technical training labs, and offices. Four classrooms incorporate state-of-the-art audiovisuals to enhance adult learning.

The classroom building also contains a microwave television station that broadcasts to all five fire stations and the department's administrative offices. This distance learning capability makes it possible for training to be held simultaneously for all on-duty personnel in all areas of responsibility. The studio is equipped with professional lighting and a set design borrowed from a local news station. Studio cameras are all fitted with TelePrompTers.

The technical training and maintenance facility allows fire apparatus to be driven into the classroom, placed on hydraulic lifts, and lifted into the air for in-depth pump training. Much-needed men's and women's shower facilities are located here as well. The building also fulfills multiple roles: there are two bays for vehicle maintenance, a room for maintenance of self-contained breathing apparatus, and storage space.

The fire training tower is a computer-controlled clean-burn facility with three live fire props representing a bedroom, a kitchen, and a living room with fire flashover simulation. Although fires are created with natural gas, smoke is light hydraulic oil based. The smoke produced is irritating but nontoxic.

The confined space training area has a forty-five-foot-long concrete trench with a graduated depth going from four feet to eight feet. The two underground confined space vaults can be accessed either horizontally from the trench through a thirty-six-inch conduit or vertically through manholes. A thirty-inch sloped conduit connects the shallow (six-foot) vault to the deep (twenty-foot) vault. Simulated electrical switch boxes enable lockout/tag-out procedures to be practiced.

Four vehicle extrication pits are separated by jersey barriers to simulate various road widths and surfaces. Close by stands a home-made vehicle fire trainer. An old propane truck was anchored to the ground and piped for propane. A movable control valve station can create fires to involve the engine compartment, cab, propane tank valves (with a pop-off valve that can be activated separately), or a unique fuel spill fire. Two five-by-ten-by-one-foot steel pools were sunk into the ground, one under and one beside the truck, where a saddle tank would be located. These were also piped for propane. The tanks are kept filled with water, and when the propane bubbling up through it is ignited, a realistic fuel spill scenario is created.

The propane truck is a favorite of the many local agencies and organizations that use the Overland Park Fire Training Center on a regular basis. Contractual agreements have been entered into with Johnson County Community College's Fire Service Training Corporation, Roco Rescue, the U.S. Air Force, Wolf Creek Nuclear Operating Corporation, Kansas City Power and Light, and Allied Signal. Contracts run the gamut from simple use of the facility to formal training programs designed to cus-

tomer specifications and conducted by OPFD employees. Many more area departments from both sides of the state line pay up to $5,000 per year to use the center. Various agencies lease classroom and meeting rooms on a regular basis. Caterers find the small kitchen an ideal base of operations for lunch or dinner functions. Revenue generated from customers provides the city of Overland Park with $250,000–$300,000 each year.

Future plans for the training center include acquisition of another twelve acres, to be developed jointly with the Overland Park Police Department. A flammable liquids and compressed gases fire training area, tactical assault village, and emergency driving pad are just some of the things planned for the expansion. In addition, finishing the classroom building's ten-thousand-square-foot basement will make available more classrooms and a fitness room.

The fire academy of all academies In the mid-1990s, the U.S. Department of Defense (DOD) developed the largest and busiest fire academy in the world. Located at Goodfellow Air Force Base near San Angelo, Texas, the facility cost more than $50 million to build and serves the basic and advanced fire service training needs of all branches of the U.S. military.

The numbers and statistics associated with this marvelous facility dwarf those of other fire training academies. This facility includes many state-of-the-art props, simulators, and classrooms as well as the environmental and support facilities necessary to keep the operation moving. For instance, there is a separate building just to maintain the more than seventy-five pieces of fire apparatus assigned to the facility. And a separate building and contractor are on site just to build and maintain the many training props. There are large- and small-frame aircraft fire training

areas as well as fire investigation mock-ups. There is also a groundwater recovery system, as required by federal environmental regulations.

Included are a large residence hall and dining facility for the hundreds of students on site at any given time. It has sometimes been necessary to operate two and even three training shifts a day to meet the demand for trained personnel. The instructional and support staff (military and civilian) number well above 150.

Few if any organizations would need a facility like the DOD academy. However, all who plan to construct a facility —or even a prop—can benefit from the experience that the military have gained in their intensive effort to find the best solution. They willingly share their experiences, good and bad, and serve the rest of the fire training world as a quasi-research institution.

Critical to the design of any training facility is a knowledgeable, experienced design firm or individual. Relatively few firms have the experience needed to understand the stresses on burn buildings and burn pits. Requesting a level of experience in either the main design firm or a consulting firm is worthwhile.

Some very specialized types of training are available at only one or a few sites in the United States and Canada. Examples are training for Amtrak passenger railcar extrication, rail tank car incidents, large-frame aircraft fires, and shipboard fires. State/provincial training agencies will either have direct access to these special facilities or be able to refer fire departments to them.

Taking the training to the troops

Oklahoma State University Fire Service Training (FST) serves Oklahoma's more-than-nine-hundred fire departments with training and certification services from its base facility six miles west of Stillwater in north-central Oklahoma. FST's management had long recognized that it was difficult for a vast majority of firefighters to travel the great distances necessary to attend training or testing sessions at the base facility. This was especially true because a large proportion of Oklahoma's firefighters are volunteer and the state is large in land area.

To address this customer need, FST worked with the other fire service organizations in the state, interested communities, and cooperating vocational-technical schools to develop several regional training centers. The original plan was to make the travel distance no more than eighty miles from any community in the state to a center. The effort started with grass-roots supporters at each proposed location contacting the legislature and the governor's office. The project enjoyed very good support at all levels, and funding started with one or two of the eleven proposed sites being funded annually. At all sites, in-kind or real dollar participation was necessary and was interpreted by the legislature as a key indicator of local interest. (Each site had a price tag of $350,000–$450,000.)

Each of the sites consists of approximately three to five acres of land, a commercially prefabricated two-story burn building, a constructed skills building, a water supply, a water retention dike, and security fencing. The centers do not include any flammable liquid training facilities because of the costs associated with the environmental protection requirements. Flammable liquid burn facilities are located at the base facility near Stillwater and at four military facilities within the state.

The regional centers are all located adjacent to very high quality classroom (with restroom) facilities and are typically operated by a vocational-technical school or a fire department.

In addition to the regional training centers, FST staff designed and constructed a skills trailer that could be delivered on demand to any fire department in the state. The trailer, which looks a bit like a maze of scaffolding with windows, door frames, and stairways, has a workstation that will test all the nonburn skills required by NFPA 1001, Standard for Fire Fighter Professional Qualifications.

The regional training centers and mobile skills trailer represent FST's commitment to delivering training to the customers in lieu of expecting the customers to make sacrifices to come to the training. The large amount of funding that might have gone into an extensive bricks-and-mortar centralized academy has instead been invested in the regionalization effort. The centers provide a safe and consistent environment for both the training and the testing functions. As funds from local sources become available, some of the centers will probably grow to include specialized props.

The partnership among communities, FST, and the vocational-technical schools resulted in a win/win solution for the internal and external customers of Oklahoma's fire services.

Staff resources for training

In training, the most important and expensive resource is personnel. The quality of the leadership and execution of the training functions of a fire and emergency response agency can be the major determinant of a program's success or failure. There are many examples of training programs that failed because those assigned to the training function were the "sick, lame, and lazy."

Measurable job performance standards for training personnel are stated in the provisions of NFPA 1041, Standard for Fire Service Instructor Professional Qualifications. This document describes skills needed by four levels of training officer, ranging from basic class delivery skills to management of the training function. What it does not specify or measure are the important traits of enthusiasm and a gift for instructing and mentoring. The upper-level job performance standards described in NFPA 1041 are akin to those met by someone with advanced training in educational methodology and/or a college degree in education.

In most organizations, the training officer is not responsible for delivering all the training. Indeed, NFPA 1021, Standard for Fire Officer Professional Qualifications, specifies that each Level I fire officer should also be a Level I fire instructor. As implied, most departments will use their midlevel officers to deliver in-service training to small work groups. This is generally accomplished with the use of a schedule, a curriculum, and materials provided by a designated

---

The Charlotte Fire Department's Training Division   The main work of the Charlotte (North Carolina) Fire Department's Training Division is keeping certifications current. Each fire company is scheduled to attend one four- or eight-hour class per month at the Training Academy, but this is only the beginning of ongoing educational efforts. A portion of the required emergency medical service continuing education is delivered by videotape in the stations, with individuals completing the questionnaire that accompanies the tape and returning it to the Training Division. A portion of HAZMAT continuing education is delivered in the same way. The Training Division also schedules the dive team and HAZMAT technician continuing education; each of these specialties requires seven hours of training quarterly.

Company officers are required to hold training classes with their personnel in the station and are allowed to base the content on their assessment of the needs of the fire company. In addition, battalion chiefs may direct fire companies to hold training sessions in areas where the chiefs have identified problems. All training hours are recorded on the training record and are submitted to the Training Division monthly for entry into the training records system. In this way, the department maintains a clear and permanent record of what its personnel have accomplished.

Fire personnel are also required to maintain appropriate standards of physical fitness, based on age and gender, in order to stay on the job. Basic exercise equipment is provided in each station to ensure that firefighters have the opportunity to meet the standards. The physical fitness qualifying test is given annually, and those who fail to pass are immediately assigned to the Training Division for intense remedial work until they are able to pass.

The Training Division also conducts company evaluations annually. The division's captains design a series of drills for companies to perform, and the drills are sent to the stations so that companies have time to practice. When the companies come to the Training Academy for the evaluation, they are graded on their performance, and the Training Division's captains use the results to design the emphases for the next year's training programs.

Source: Sally Young, Charlotte Fire Department planner.

training officer or staff. Clearly, some company-level officers will do better as instructors than others, depending on their skills and motivation. However, if the job requirements include providing training and if that function is properly evaluated and reinforced, the use of line officers as instructors typically works very well.

In both the career and the volunteer fire service, mandatory or voluntary rotation of some personnel assigned to the training function is very common. Rotation allows fire officers to share their field skills with others in training and then return to the field periodically to sharpen those skills. It also works to prevent burnout of individuals and to provide a variety of personal styles in the training area.

In summary, the quality of training, as of most functions, is directly attributable to the quality of staff assigned. Highly motivated, enthusiastic, and well-trained people will deliver training that will make a difference to the department and to its internal and external customers.

Sources of assistance

The resources that can help local governments meet their fire and emergency response training responsibilities run the gamut from state or provincial agencies to internships, and they represent both the government and the private sector.

State and provincial agencies   Each state in the United States and each province in Canada has an agency that is responsible for providing fire and emergency training. These agencies vary widely in funding and capabilities but are generally able to deliver a menu of training classes for fire departments. And they will have access to national-level programs that under some circumstances can be delivered locally.

Most of the state/provincial agencies are affiliated with a college or university or are in the office of a state fire marshal (or provincial fire commissioner). Others are part of a state public safety or insurance department. Depending on the course and the agency's funding, the training services may or may not be free.

In some states or provinces, the agencies are responsible not only for delivering training but also for doing certification testing. In others, a separate agency is responsible for adopting performance standards and for testing and certifying emergency response personnel. The testing and certifying functions (but not the training function) are subject to a voluntary accreditation procedure conducted by the International Fire Service Accreditation Congress (IFSAC), the National Board on Fire Service Professional Qualifications, or both. The IFSAC is a peer group function (i.e., members of the fire service formulate requirements) and, in addition, accredits fire-related degree-granting programs at colleges and universities. (This aspect of the congress's work is discussed in more detail below.) The National Board is operated by several national fire service organizations and confines itself to certification programs.

State and provincial fire training organizations are closely aligned with one another through the North American Fire Training Directors Association. This organization works with the U.S. and Canadian national governments to maintain high standards and to further the cause of emergency service training.

Federal training resources   In the United States, although there are undoubtedly a myriad of small federal grants, programs, and so forth that fire departments could access for help with training, the primary federal government resource for fire and emergency service training is based in the Federal Emergency Management Agency (FEMA). FEMA is responsible for the operation of the U.S. Fire Administration (USFA) and its National Fire Academy (NFA) and for the operation of the Emergency Management Institute (EMI). Campus functions of these organizations are located at the National Emergency Training Center in Emmitsburg, Maryland.

NFA and EMI are large agencies with broad missions in the area of training. The former was created in the mid-1970s by the Fire Prevention and Control Act and offers a wide variety of training courses, delivered both in Emmitsburg and at remote locations, specifically for fire departments. It works closely with state fire training agencies and metropolitan fire departments to coordinate the development and delivery of training.

EMI also offers a huge variety of resident and remote-delivery courses, but the focus of these courses is the breadth of the emergency management field. EMI's state partners are the training and exercise officers for each of the state emergency management agencies. In addition, EMI works very closely with colleges and universities in developing and delivering programs in emergency management.

NFA and EMI jointly operate an extensive Learning Resource Center at the Emmitsburg facility. This comprehensive library is accessible not only to on-campus students but also, through interlibrary loans and Internet connections, to all emergency service providers.

Other specialized federal programs with significant funding for training exist in the National Highway Traffic Safety Administration (emergency medical training), the Department of Justice (antiterrorism training), and the Federal Aviation Administration (aircraft firefighting and rescue training).

Although the Canadian system of government is much less centralized, that country's federal government does work with the provincial fire commissioners to coordinate training efforts and standards. Some specialized programs similar to those mentioned above for the United States exist through Canadian federal agencies. In addition, the Canadian government has devoted significant resources to help with training in fighting fires at marine facilities and on shipboard.

Associations   There are several associations that focus their attention on issues and efforts involving fire and emergency training. Among them are

International Society of Fire Service Instructors   As its title implies, this organization is a professional association for fire service instructors. It issues some publications and offers several professional development conferences and seminars each year. It also sponsors a reference and referral service. Dues are required for membership.

National Fire Protection Association (NFPA)   A primary mission of this public advocacy organization is developing voluntary consensus standards. However, NFPA also publishes several fire service-related training titles and offers a number of professional development sessions and an extensive reference service. Dues are charged for membership, which is open to anyone.

International Fire Service Training Association   This association is an advisory group to Fire Protection Publications, a division of Oklahoma State University. Membership is by invitation, with participants meeting to review and validate a variety of fire training manuals published and sold by the university.

International Association of Fire Fighters   This labor union, an affiliate of the AFL/CIO, represents a large majority of the career firefighters in the United States and Canada. It offers a number of training programs and resources, primarily in the area of firefighter health and safety. Membership is limited to paid, career fire personnel.

International Association of Fire Chiefs   This national professional organization for fire chiefs offers some training materials and programs, most of which focus on management and leadership. Membership is limited to chief-level officers in any fire department, and dues are charged.

In nearly every state and province there are membership organizations for fire chiefs, fire instructors, fire investigators, and firefighters. These organizations, which offer training sessions, training materials, or both, serve a large number of people from many fire departments; thus, their programs achieve economies of scale.

Private sector companies   Certain private sector companies serve fire and emergency response training needs in specific subjects. For instance, some insurance companies that specialize in covering fire departments offer training that is related to firefighter health and safety and to vehicle safety. Thus, a fire department may want to ask its insurance carrier if courses and materials are available either free or for a nominal fee.

Several for-profit companies and private individuals offer training on a contract basis. Many of them focus on technical rescue or hazardous materials. Fire service publications and the Internet can provide information on how to get in touch with these companies and individuals.

Colleges and universities   Since the 1970s the number of high-quality fire-related degree-granting programs in U.S. and Canadian colleges and universities has grown dramatically. As of 2001, many community colleges and a number of full-service universities offered associate and baccalaureate degrees in fire science, fire administration, fire protection technology, and related areas. One long-standing program at Oklahoma State University offers a degree in fire protection and safety engineering technology, and another at the University of Maryland offers a degree in fire protection engineering.

A number of institutions have begun offering graduate degrees in subjects related to fire service management.

Many of the college-level programs are now available via distance learning. The technology allows the programs to be taken at home or at work, with little or no on-campus time required.

As mentioned above, the development of undergraduate and graduate programs in emergency management is encouraged and supported by EMI. Many of these programs are available via distance learning or in more traditional settings that have been adapted to accommodate a fully employed student body.

Unfortunately, the quality and content of the college-level programs in areas related to fire and emergency services vary widely. In an effort to address this matter, the IFSAC has developed a comprehensive accreditation process for degree-granting programs. The IFSAC process is patterned after the processes of other national accreditors of programs in other higher education specialties. Some schools have taken advantage of the IFSAC process, but a large number of programs choose to function without any level of industry oversight.

Internships   Other opportunities for pre-service and in-service training, including internships and exchange programs, are available for chiefs, other fire service managers, and aspiring firefighters. But although other professions within local government require or strongly recommend participation in such activities, the fire and emergency response services have not widely used them.

Interning involves bringing in potential department candidates for a period of time, usually four to twelve months, and allowing them to work in the organization to gain experience with and insight into the fire service. Another form of internship that has been used effectively is assigning an existing member for a defined period of time to an area to which that member is not normally assigned.

Some organizations have developed cadet programs for preemployment situations. These programs provide high school students or others with the opportunity to work with the department in low-risk environments and receive on-the-job training. Such programs are win/win situations in that both the potential employee and the employer can view each other in the work setting.

Conclusion

The customers of today's fire and emergency response service expect high-quality service from a trained organization. They also expect and demand an ever-expanding range of services. These factors in combination, and the increasing demands placed on the fire service by legal requirements, impose a tremendous burden on the training function of a fire department. Given the limited time and resources available, departments must take advantage of all opportunities to train effectively and efficiently. Using a wide range of resources and sharing those resources with like agencies are central to achieving the level of professionalism that customers demand.

10 Performance measurement and organizational improvement

In theory, improving the performance of a fire and rescue organization is simple. It requires only three basic things: that the organization

Have a clear picture of where it wants to go (i.e., of its desired state), which requires the organization not only to understand what its mission is in the broader context of the governing body's strategic plan but also to have a departmental strategic plan setting forth the programs, activities, and processes necessary for achieving the desired state

Set realistic goals and objectives for an implementation plan

Put the implementation plan into practice, and measure performance with respect to the required programs, activities, and processes in order to close the gap between existing performance and the desired state.

But although simple in theory, improving organizational performance is in fact a complex process that entails a number of stages. First, strategic planning, which is a vital component of organizational improvement, should draw on the perspectives of all stakeholders: management, labor (career and volunteer alike), citizens, and the business community. Second, after a strategic plan is developed, performance measurement tools must be developed, and doing so (after identifying the goals and objectives of performance measurement) also involves many people, this time from different levels within the organization. Third, the organization must collect and then analyze the necessary data and report the findings. Fourth, the organization must investigate and evaluate reasons for high or low performance levels and use the findings to consider needed changes. Finally, after a department has established the existence of performance gaps, explained them, and considered changes, it must develop strategies, goals, and objectives for changing performance and must then implement and evaluate the strategies.

Performance measurement captures data about programs, activities, and processes, and displays the data in fairly standardized ways that are useful for managing programs to their peak performance. It identifies the causes of gaps in performance and explains the effect that additional budgetary expenditures or reductions will have on achieving performance goals and objectives. Performance measurement tools have been used to significantly improve how government agencies in general, and fire and rescue departments in particular, set and refine goals and achieve results.

One may well ask what makes performance measurement such a powerful agent for change and why all that work is worth doing. Simply put, what gets measured gets done. If a fire and rescue department measures the right things and regularly and accurately reports the results to managers and first-line supervisors, the people in a position to make needed changes will be aware of what is happening and will be able to take steps to affect it. But if the wrong things are measured and reported—or, worse yet, if nothing is reported—managers and supervisors will not have the information they need to make performance-optimizing adjustments.

Indeed, the hardest aspect of performance measurement is measuring the right things in the right way. Fire and rescue departments have measured many activities for many years, but often the items measured have not been related to the performance of core business functions or have not described the results (outcomes) of the activities. For example, a significant amount of staff time and energy has been spent recording and reporting the number of feet of hose and ladders used at fires, even though that information has not been particularly useful to anyone.

Measuring what really matters

Maximizes the benefit to the department by allowing scarce resources to be used in the most productive way possible

Gives managers a sense of where the organization, work unit, or individual is in relation to performance expectations

Allows managers and work-team leaders to focus their time and efforts where they are most needed to improve performance

Provides information for budget justifications in language that budget developers, reviewers, and policy makers understand and use, giving the organization a chance to compete effectively for limited budget dollars

Provides important input into internal performance and quality improvement processes.

This chapter presents work done in the 1990s and the early years of the twenty-first century in using performance measurement to improve organizational performance generally and process performance in particular. The chapter begins by (1) reviewing two sets of established criteria against which fire and rescue departments are often measured, and (2) surveying four broad-based efforts to establish performance measurement criteria. The subsequent sections are on modeling the use of performance measurement to identify and resolve performance problems, especially at the process level (with particular attention paid to process mapping as a tool for measuring processes); using performance measurement in benchmarking, most notably in the "service efforts and accomplishments" (SEA) reports; presenting performance data; following up the results of data analysis to determine the causes of poor performance; using performance measurement in results-based budgeting; and avoiding pitfalls.

Setting the stage

Work in the area of performance measurement has been going on since the 1940s. In 1943 Clarence Ridley (executive director of the International City Managers' Association) and Herbert Simon published a book suggesting ways for governments to measure their municipal activities.[1] A half century later, Alan Ehrenhalt made the case that performance measurement in government operations had been around for a long time.[2] He noted that the desire to improve performance measurement had been the common link among certain management and budget strategies used since at least 1960:

The planning, programming, budgeting system (PPBS) introduced in the 1960s

Zero-based budgeting (ZBB), which emerged in the 1970s

Management by objectives (MBO), which became popular in the 1980s

Benchmarking and performance measurement in the 1990s.

Since about 1950, a significant body of research in quality assurance and quality improvement has developed. Initially that research was directed at the private, for-profit business sector, but the performance measurement and benchmarking efforts of the 1990s attempted to apply the research to the public sector. Most of these efforts reflect an increased concern on the part of citizens and elected governing bodies to know what the expenditure of tax money is producing for the community. This heightened concern has led to increased reporting of "meaningful information about the services being provided—including, for example, information about efficiency, quality, and the results achieved."[3]

By the year 2000, two methods of measuring fire and rescue departments against established criteria were in widespread use. One, the Insurance Services Office's rating system, has a specific, narrowly focused purpose and is therefore of limited applicability. The other is an accreditation process, one component of which is a self-assessment.

Insurance Services Office

The Insurance Services Office (ISO) is an independent, private organization that publishes the Fire Suppression Rating Schedule, which contains rating criteria for grading jurisdictions; insurance companies use the grades in setting fire insurance rates.[4] To determine a community's rating on a scale of 1 to 10 (with 10 "representing less than the minimum recognized protection" and 1 representing the best),[5] ISO evaluates many factors, some of which come under fire and rescue department control.

An emphatic word of caution is needed here. Although for years fire and rescue departments have treated ISO ratings as bestowing "bragging rights," the ratings are not necessarily a valid tool for comparing departments in terms of whether they provide their communities with the most effective or efficient service, nor is it valid to say that a community with a rating of 3 somehow has a worse department than a community with a rating of 2 or 1. ISO rating schedules should not be used for any purpose other than the one for which they were created: "to review the available public fire suppression facilities, and to develop a Public Protection Classification for fire insurance rating purposes." All that the schedule does is measure "the major elements of a city's fire suppression system," turning these measurements into a number from 1 to 10. The schedule does not go beyond that: it "is a fire insurance rating tool, and is not intended to analyze all aspects of a comprehensive public fire protection program. It should not be used for purposes other than insurance rating."[6]

In its practical application, the rating schedule is a tool used for assessing the insurance rate charged in a specific community on a specific property. Generally, the better the rating schedule classification, the lower the insurance premium charged. Although one cannot say with certainty what the effect of an improved rating schedule classification might be in a specific community, improvements in the classification in communities with ratings between 10 and 5 tend to result in lower insurance premiums for residential properties. Improvements when the community has ratings better than 5 can result in lower premiums on commercial and industrial properties but will usually have only a negligible effect on premiums for residential properties. Before community and fire department leaders invest significant monies in improving the rating schedule classification number, they should undertake a cost-benefit analysis to see if improving the number will make economic sense.

To receive a rating better than 10, a department must meet the following minimum criteria:

Be organized on a permanent basis under state law, have one person in charge, and serve an area with definite boundaries

Have sufficient membership to ensure the response of at least four members (including the chief) to structure fires

Conduct two hours of training every two months for active members

Have alarm facilities and arrangements to ensure that there is no delay in receiving alarms and dispatching resources

Have at least one piece of apparatus that meets the general requirements of National Fire Protection Association (NFPA) 1901, Standard for Automotive Fire Apparatus (1999 edition)

House the apparatus to provide protection from the weather.[7]

For jurisdictions that have *both* a public water system capable of delivering, in addition to maximum daily consumption, 250 gallons per minute (GPM) at a fire location *and* a pumper with a capacity of 250 GPM or more at 150 pounds per square inch (psi), the rating system evaluates (1) the relative strength of the community's dispatch capability, (2) the department's engine and truck capabilities and related resources, and (3) the community's water supply. In all cases, the needed fire flow for selected properties in the service area has to be available. (Details on the evaluation criteria for the three capabilities appear in the sidebar in Chapter 4 on page 136.) Jurisdictions without *either* domestic water systems capable of delivering 250 GPM fire flow for two hours in addition to the maximum daily consumption *or* a pumper with a capacity of at least 250 GPM at 150 psi are rated according to separate criteria.

Under the rating system, it is possible to earn credit for the ability to shuttle water to a fire location in quantities that can sustain the needed fire flow even though all or some of the jurisdiction does not have a domestic water system.

Accreditation by the Commission on Fire Accreditation International

The International Association of Fire Chiefs, in conjunction with the International City/County Management Association (ICMA), has developed an accreditation process for fire and rescue organizations. The process is a self-evaluation that an organization goes through by measuring itself against criteria within ten categories prescribed by the Commission on Fire Accreditation International (CFAI).[8] When the organization believes it meets the criteria, an independent evaluation team visits it and audits the results. (For more details, see the sidebar in Chapter 1 on "Third-Party Assessment," page 10.)

Self-assessment and accreditation provide fire agencies with opportunities to develop both baseline and benchmarking information. Thus, the accreditation process helps agencies define their levels of service. Furthermore, as is implied by the motto of the process ("Continuous Improvement through Self-Assessment"), self-assessment is not a one-time event but an evolving iterative process. The process often leads fire agencies to develop products that run the gamut from strategic plans to short-term plans of action to support documents for day-to-day operations. (To help fire agencies continue with the improvement process, the CFAI produces documents, references, and training materials.)

Establishing performance measurement criteria: Broad-based efforts

During the last decade of the twentieth century, several projects were undertaken to establish more-usable criteria for performance measurements. The projects described here were undertaken by the Governmental Accounting Standards Board (GASB), which produced a research report; ICMA (in conjunction with the Urban Institute), which set up the Performance Measurement Consortium (now the Center for Performance Measurement); and the Phoenix (Arizona) Fire Department, whose endeavor is known as FireDAP. Also described here are the annual meetings of the Fire Department Planners Consortium, where the focus is on performance improvement.

The Governmental Accounting Standards Board

The GASB of the Financial Accounting Foundation studied the use of performance measurements by state and local governments. (GASB has not issued any standards with regard to performance measurement.) The study's results were presented in the GASB research report *Service Efforts and Accomplishments Reporting: Its Time Has Come,* which establishes five categories of measurement: input indicators, output indicators, outcome indicators, efficiency (and cost-effectiveness) indicators, and explanatory information.[9] Each of these categories takes a slightly different approach to fire department operations and provides a slightly different perspective not only on what the community is putting its money toward but also—and more importantly—on the results of that expenditure. Definitions of the categories, or performance indicators, appear in Figure 10–1. These indicators provide a framework within which fire and rescue organizations can look at—and make some sense of—the data they are capturing.

Input indicators   Inputs measure the monetary and nonmonetary resources expended or consumed to produce outputs of the department's activities. Obviously a basic measure of monetary input is the dollars expended for fire department functions. Likewise, a way of measuring nonmonetary inputs is to use the number of staff hours expended in performing services. For yearly comparisons, the staff hours of effort devoted to a function are normally expressed as full-time equivalent positions (FTEs); for shorter durations, the actual number of hours is used.

Many organizations already report both the number of staff assigned to various divisions and the costs associated with those divisions' activities. However, organizations often use staff from one program area to perform activities in

Figure 10–1 Types of performance indicators.

Category	Definition
Input indicators	These are designed to report the amount of resources, either financial or other (especially personnel), that have been used for a specific service or program.
Output indicators	These report the units produced or the services provided by a service or program.
Outcome indicators	These are designed to report the results (including quality) of the service.
Efficiency (and cost-effectiveness) indicators	These are defined as indicators that measure the cost (whether in dollars or employee hours) per unit of output or outcome.
Explanatory information	This includes a variety of information about the environment and other factors that might affect an organization's performance.

other program areas (e.g., fire suppression unit staff may also respond to medical emergencies, perform fire inspections, or conduct public fire education programs). To allocate the costs correctly, an organization should track the amount of time spent on various program activities.

A word of caution is appropriate here. When data are collected and reported as suggested above, inexperienced analysts could conclude—incorrectly—that a shift in program activities would result in cost savings proportional to the FTEs affected. If, for example, 20 percent of the field operations program dollars (or the same percentage of the program's FTEs) is allocated to performing fire inspections, an inexperienced analyst might presume that moving the inspections somewhere else could save 20 percent of the fire suppression budget. But this logic is flawed because it ignores two critical points. First, shifting the fire inspection workload to another agency usually means adding additional FTEs at the receiving civilian agency, and even though civilians usually work for a lower compensation package than firefighters, funding is still required and reduces the apparent initial savings. Second, firefighters perform these inspection duties while they are on standby for emergency response. In other words, they perform inspections as an ancillary duty, but whether the inspections are performed or not, the firefighters are still needed to respond to emergencies. The primary reason for fire suppression positions is to respond to and control emergencies. Thus, the reduction in monies with the consequent 20 percent reduction in field operations staff might well have a drastic negative effect on operational effectiveness at emergency incidents. The perceived "go-away" cost savings of moving the inspections activity function might therefore be nonexistent or actually end up as a cost increase.

Output indicators   Output measures count the number of activities produced as a result of the expenditures: for example, the number of incidents responded to, the number of inspections performed, the number of violations detected, the number of car safety seats checked, and the number of training programs given.

Outcome indicators   The most important and most difficult measures to capture are outcomes, for they address the effect that the program, process, or activity has had. Macrolevel outcomes for fire prevention and suppression activities are the deaths, injuries, and dollar losses from fires that the community experiences. (On intermediate measures, see the discussion below of the ICMA Center for Performance Measurement.)

Efficiency (and cost-effectiveness) indicators   Efficiency measures for fire department programs can be expressed in two ways: as unit costs (input dollars divided by output or outcome) or as units of output or outcome per input (output or outcome divided by either costs or some other measure, such as FTEs). Cost-effectiveness measures are determined by dividing the cost of either output or outcome by the number of units of output or outcome.

Efficiency measures for outputs might include the operating cost per incident, per capita protected, per $1 million of property value protected, or per inspection. Cost-effectiveness measures for outcomes might include the operating cost per fire code violation corrected or per fires extinguished within fifteen minutes.

Historically, departments have done a very good job of counting inputs and outputs, and some departments have developed good cost-effectiveness and efficiency measures. But fewer departments seem to have been able to measure outcomes in a meaningful way, or to link outcome measurement with resources and accurately gauge how changes in resources or business practices affect outcomes.

Explanatory information Explanatory information should be included whenever necessary to draw attention to variations from expected results in data displays or to changes in measurement results that are caused by modifications in the way data are defined or collected or by the removal or addition of data elements. Footnotes should connect the explanatory notes to the relevant data elements.

The ICMA Center for Performance Measurement

ICMA has been a leader in developing practical uses for performance measurement. In 1994, in conjunction with the Urban Institute, ICMA initiated a project to bring together working managers from cities and counties with populations of 200,000 or more to develop useful comparative measures for critical services. Originally called the ICMA Performance Measurement Consortium, the project later came to be called the ICMA Center for Performance Measurement; and as of the beginning of the twenty-first century, 130 cities and counties of all population sizes were participating in the program, tracking their fire data and comparing them against both the data of other communities and time-series data for their own jurisdictions. (For updated information, see http://icma.org/performance.)

The four areas selected for study were fire, police, neighborhood services, and support services. (Neighborhood services included code enforcement, highway maintenance, housing, parks and recreation, libraries, and refuse collection. Support services included facilities management, fleet management, human resources, information technology, purchasing, and risk management.) A fifth area—youth services—was added subsequently. Harry Hatry of the Urban Institute, who served as a project consultant to advise on the development of performance measurement categories, offered the definitions that are listed in Figure 10–2. The definitions that the project used for performance measurement types differed slightly from the GASB recommendations and provided examples. A new measurement called *intermediate outcome* was added and is explained below.

Representatives from participating fire and rescue departments (initially there

Figure 10–2 Definitions of ICMA performance measurement categories.

Category	Definition
Input	A count of the resources (money, people, FTEs[a]) devoted to the activity measured
Output	The number of things produced as a result of the efforts (e.g., incidents responded to or inspections performed)
Output efficiency	Inputs/outputs (e.g., the cost per inspection or the number of inspections per inspector FTE)
Outcome efficiency	Inputs/outcomes (e.g., serious violations corrected per inspector FTE)
Outcome	The results of the effort (including quality) (e.g., reduction in the number of fires or in fire dollar loss at inspected properties as a result of the inspection program)
Intermediate outcome	Factors expected to directly result in a change in outcome (e.g., emergency vehicle response time and the number of structure fires that reach flashover)

[a]FTEs = full-time equivalent positions.

were forty) began meeting in 1994 to discuss and select measures. During the group's first several meetings, the participants were trained in performance measurement and began the process of identifying meaningful measures for their study area. The group identified the critical functions that should be covered in its efforts—fire suppression, emergency medical service (EMS), fire prevention, and public education—and began the laborious process of developing recommended measures and defining them. It quickly became clear that the group would also have to collect community descriptors so that users of the data would be able to discern the presence of significant differences (if any) among jurisdictions.

The fire group spent a significant amount of time developing definitions of all the data elements. For each function, the group created templates of measures and agreed-upon definitions. Figures 10–3 and 10–4 are sample pages from the templates (one on residential-structure fire incidents and one on re-

---

ICMA Center for Performance Measurement (CPM)
FY 2001 Fire Services and EMS Template

Jurisdiction Name: _____   **State:** _____

The data collection period is for FY 2001, so use the fiscal year that ends in calendar year 2001.

RESIDENTIAL STRUCTURE FIRE INCIDENTS: ONE- AND TWO- FAMILY DWELLING STRUCTURES

Residential one- and two-family dwelling structures are defined as private dwellings and duplexes each occupied by members of a single family group, with total sleeping accommodations for not more than 20 people and rooms rented to not more than two outsiders per unit. Row houses, townhouses, garden apartments, and other similar units shall be counted here if there are only two units. A mobile home and a travel trailer not in transit and used as a dwelling should be counted. (All NFIRS 4 fixed property classifications 410-419.)

59. Residential structure fire incidents: one- and two- family dwelling structures				
See general instructions on page 21	1. Number of incidents (Do not double count incidents)	Not available	2. Of these, how many had an automatic sprinkler system?	Not available
a. Fire was out on arrival	#		#	
b. Flamespread was confined to the room of origin	#			
c. Flamespread was confined to the structure of origin	#			
d. Flamespread was beyond the structure of origin	#			
e. Undetermined extent of flamespread	#			
f. Total number of residential structure fire incidents: one- and two- family dwelling structures	**Computer calculated (sum of parts a-e)**			
g. Total number of residential structure fire incidents: one- and two- family dwelling structures[1]	#			
h. Incidents with fire out on arrival as percent of total residential one-and two-family dwelling structure fire incidents.	Computer calculated			
i. Incidents with flamespread confined to room of origin as percent of total residential one-and two-family dwelling structure fire incidents.	Computer calculated			
j. Incidents with flamespread confined to the structure of origin as percent of total residential one-and two-family dwelling structure fire incidents.	Computer calculated			
k. Incidents with flamespread beyond the structure of origin as percent of total residential one-and two-family dwelling structure fire incidents.	Computer calculated			
l. Incidents with undetermined extent of flamespread as percent of total residential one-and two-family dwelling structure fire incidents.	Computer calculated			
[1] If you are unable to provide the detail in parts a-e, but you are able to provide the total number of structure fire incidents in this category, please do so here.				

Figure 10–3   Sample template page, FY 2000 fire services and EMS, ICMA Center for Performance Measurement: Residential structure fire incidents.

Figure 10–4 Sample template page, FY 2000 fire services and EMS, ICMA Center for Performance Measurement: Response time for fire calls.

ICMA Center for Performance Measurement (CPM)
FY 2001 Fire Services and EMS Template

Jurisdiction Name: _____ **State:** _____

The data collection period is for FY 2001, so use the fiscal year that ends in calendar year 2001.

RESPONSE TIME FOR FIRE CALLS

Even if you are completing other sections, please provide all information requested. Please do NOT write "same" or refer to a previous page.

Name of person completing this section: _____

Telephone: _____ **Fax:** _____ **E-mail:** _____

*NOTE: This template is also available in a **convenient electronic format**. If you haven't had the opportunity to try the electronic version, please contact your primary coordinator or ICMA for more details*

↓ MODIFIED INSTRUCTIONS ↓

For Questions 139-143:
INCLUDE
- All calls dispatched to fire suppression staff, regardless of the priorities they were assigned
- All fire calls dispatched, including those that eventually were determined to be false alarms
- All fire calls dispatched for medical assistance or other non-fire incident response from fire suppression staff

EXCLUDE calls for EMS (whether based in a fire or EMS department). This information is requested in a separate section.

DEFINITIONS:
Emergency calls
INCLUDE all calls dispatched as emergency calls (lights and sirens), regardless of traffic or weather conditions that may be encountered en route.
EXCLUDE those calls that are downgraded from emergency to non-emergency <u>prior</u> to engine arrival due to: 1) false alarm, 2) fire having already been extinguished.

Arrival on the scene refers to the first responding unit on the scene.

"__ minutes and under"
INCLUDE
- Responses up to and including that number of minutes
- Turnout time as one component of overall response time

EXCLUDE responses in that number of minutes plus any seconds (e.g., a call responded to in 5 minutes, 1 second or 5 minutes, 59 seconds would not be considered to have been responded to in 5 minutes and under.)

↓ MODIFIED INSTRUCTIONS ↓

74. Average Public Safety Answering Point (PSAP) processing time _____ seconds ☐ Not available

DEFINITION
PSAP processing time
- The average time it takes to transfer a **911 call** from the point at which it is **answered** at the Public Safety Answering Point (PSAP) to the point where the fire/EMS call taker answers the call.
- If the PSAP call taker is the fire dispatcher, then enter "0," and report time in Question number 140 (the first question below).
- If 911 calls are first answered by the sheriff's or police department and then transferred to fire/EMS, enter the time from when that department answered the call to when it is transferred to fire.

75. What is the average time from *call entry* (when the fire/EMS call taker answers the call) to the conclusion of dispatch?

_____ seconds ☐ Not available

76. What percentage of total fire calls have a response time of 5 minutes and under from *call entry* (when the fire/EMS call taker answers the call) to arrival on the scene?
    a. Total calls _____ % ☐ Not available
    b. Emergency calls _____ % ☐ Not available
    c. Non-emergency calls _____ % ☐ Not available

77. What percentage of calls have a response time of 8 minutes and under from *call entry* (when the fire/EMS call taker answers the call) to arrival on the scene?
    a. Total calls _____ % ☐ Not available
    b. Emergency calls _____ % ☐ Not available
    c. Non-emergency calls _____ % ☐ Not available

↓ MODIFIED QUESTION ↓

78. What percentage of calls have a response time of 5 minutes and under from conclusion of *dispatch* to arrival on the scene?

NOTE: Response time of 8 minutes and under represents total from 0 to 8 minutes. Thus, this percentage should include and be greater than all calls responded to in 5 minutes and under (per previous question).

    a. Total calls _____ % ☐ Not available
    b. Emergency calls _____ % ☐ Not available
    c. Non-emergency calls _____ % ☐ Not available

79. Comments: List comments and their question numbers below. Do not send attachments or write in the margins. Information on attachments or written in margins will not be entered in the database and, therefore, will not be reviewed during data analysis.

Question #	Comment

sponse time for fire calls). The templates helped the departments identify what data had already been collected and where they resided; determine how to collect what was not already collected; and begin the process of collection and recording.

The data collection and reporting process was iterative: the first two cycles of quarterly collection and reporting served as a test of the templates and the measures. Revisions were made on the basis of the departments' experiences. A number of jurisdictions found that data were available and could be reported as requested with little effort, but others found that some portion of the data collected by their organizations did not exactly meet the definitions decided on by the group. This finding generated various organizational efforts to try to reorganize and analyze the data so that they could be reported to meet the agreed-upon definitions. Finally, some jurisdictions that participated in the project had difficulty collecting and reporting a large portion of the data. That learning process, clearly highlighting significant areas for improvement, was very beneficial to the representatives and leaders of departments in that last group of jurisdictions, suggesting that much internal work had to be done before the organizations could participate meaningfully in the project.

Early in the process of developing outcome measures, the fire group encountered a significant problem. Although reductions in the number of deaths and injuries and in the size of dollar losses from fire are desired outcomes of fire department prevention and response activities, in many communities the low frequency with which death, injury, and (to a lesser degree) dollar loss occur makes it difficult to measure changes from year to year. Many smaller jurisdictions experience few fires each year and perhaps a fire death only once every few years or even every few decades. Thus it was decided to concentrate on intermediate measures to track progress on factors that were believed to directly affect fire loss or other outcome measures.

Some intermediate measures are response times for all the components of the system's response process. Response times are intermediate outcomes because the expectation is that the faster the appropriate emergency units arrive on the scene, the more positive their effect will be in terms of limiting the damage caused by the incident. The presumption is that if properly trained and equipped emergency responders are dispatched, arrive, and deploy at the emergency more quickly, the specific actions they will be able to take will mitigate the negative consequences of the event. As a result the level of deaths, injuries, and fire losses should be lower than what it would have been if response times had been longer. By tracking response times and their critical subcomponents, an organization can begin to see the effects of changes in the response process more quickly and can begin to judge whether these changes are having the desired results. (Response times are discussed in much more detail below.)

Fire Department Analysis Project (FireDAP)

In the early 1990s the Phoenix (Arizona) Fire Department, in conjunction with NFPA's Urban Fire Forum, undertook the Fire Department Analysis Project (FireDAP), whose purpose was to develop a standard methodology that departments could use to evaluate their operations. The background research resulted in standard operational performance criteria that establish, and monitor the achievements of, standard milestones for the incident mitigation process. For a residential structure fire (the first of four modules produced), the methodology starts with a description of the expected outcomes and then identifies key indicators that should be accomplished, and the requirements that should be met, to achieve the desired outcomes.

The products of the research are a document, a videotape, and a workbook. The document and videotape describe the research process and its results, and explain the logistics and techniques for successfully resolving residential fires. The workbook explains the details of a residential-structure fire-operation scenario that is based on the research results.

The other three modules explain, respectively, unit tasks and command operations at a three-alarm structure fire in a commercial occupancy, the procedures and task assignments of responding units on a medical code, and the policies and techniques for parking apparatus safely at emergency incidents. All four modules, complete with documents, videotapes, and workbooks, are available from the Phoenix Fire Department.

Fire Department Planners Consortium

The Fire Department Planners Consortium meets once a year for several days to discuss issues and opportunities that departments face in trying to improve their operational safety and effectiveness. Topics range from innovative service-improvement techniques to the effect of (and reactions to) external influences, such as changes to Occupational Safety and Health Administration regulations (see Chapter 13), court decisions affecting the application of the Fair Labor Standards Act, or other federal requirements.

Departmental representatives demonstrate and share real-world examples of tools and techniques that others can then take back to their own organizations. For attendees who are involved in measuring, evaluating, and improving fire department performance, the interaction with others who are similarly involved provides an invaluable networking opportunity. Information on the consortium can be obtained from the planning officer of the Phoenix Fire Department or from fire departments in most major metropolitan areas.

Modeling the use of performance measurement

As noted above, a significant body of research and literature has been geared toward improving the quality of organizational performance both in business and in government. One way to begin improving performance is to measure it. In business literature, the topic of performance measurement is generally handled under the larger headings of "total quality management" and "continuous process improvement" (the latter is discussed below). Public sector literature addresses performance measurement as the critical first step in effectively using either benchmarking or results-based budgeting to improve organizational performance. (On budgeting, see Chapter 6.)

Geary A. Rummler and Alan P. Brache have developed a model for assessing business-sector organizations and improving performance that is directly applicable to fire and rescue organizations. They view an organization as a system, one of whose key components is the "control mechanism—management."[10] Viewing the organization as a system makes it possible to understand better the relationships among the various components and the ways in which changes in one part may affect the operations of other parts. Rummler and Brache identify three levels of performance in organizations and three performance needs that are necessary at all three levels. The three levels of performance are the organization, the process, and the job/performer. The three performance needs are goals, design, and management.

The organizational level is concerned with the basic functions of the organization and its relationship to the external world; the organization's outputs are produced through work processes that involve contributions from many different organizational units. The process level is concerned with meeting both the customer's and the organization's requirements for products and services. The job/performer level involves the individuals who perform and manage the processes to create products and services. Each of the levels should be evaluated on the quality and effectiveness of its goals, design, and management.

When the three performance levels and the three performance needs are combined into a matrix, the result is nine performance variables, as shown in Figure 10–5. This matrix offers a framework that organizations can use to target areas for organizational improvement.

In the areas of all nine variables, Rummler and Brache strongly emphasize performance measurement—its development and effective use—as a means of control. (See Figure 10–6 for their list of "truths about measurement.") "Performance measures provide the latticework of the [organizational] system. A Three Levels measurement system provides a window on more than just results. By monitoring and improving those factors that influence results, managers are able to cause a more systematic improvement and to understand what's needed to implement change."[11]

The measures selected should provide managers with the basis on which to communicate not only performance expectations but also feedback that identifies performance successes and gaps. In addition, the measures selected should inform individual employees specifically about what is expected of them while allowing self-evaluation (as well as feedback from managers). Rummler and Brache argue that it is critical to measure the right things and that what turns performance measurement data into "intelligent action" (i.e., improved performance) is the management process, or the control mechanism.[12]

The rest of this section outlines performance measurement at each of the

Figure 10–5 Rummler and Brache's nine performance variables.

The three levels of performance	The three performance needs		
	Goals	Design	Management
Organizational level	Organizational goals	Organizational design	Organizational management
Process level	Process goals	Process design	Process management
Job/performer level	Job/performer goals	Job/performer design	Job/performer management

Figure 10–6 Truths about measurement.

Without measurement, performance isn't being managed.

Without measurement, one cannot specifically identify, describe and set priorities on problems.

Without measurement, people cannot fully understand what is expected of them.

Without measurement, people cannot be sure whether their performance is on or off track.

Without measurement, there cannot be an objective, equitable basis for rewards (such as raises, bonuses, promotions) or punishments (such as disciplinary action, downgrading, dismissal).

Without measurement, there are no triggers for performance improvement actions.

Without measurement, management is a set of uneducated guesses.

three levels; the next section elaborates on the details of performance measurement at the process level, where the potential for improvement is greatest.

Organizational-level performance measures

Organizational goals (like organizational strategies and objectives) are usually found in the strategic plans of the jurisdiction and the department. Because these goals are usually very broad and general, the performance measures that would indicate progress toward accomplishment need to be macrolevel. An example of an organizational goal might be to "employ innovative methods to maintain effective fire and rescue response times as population and density grow."[13] An appropriate intermediate outcome measure of system performance would be one that identified the overall system response time and could be compared for changes from one reporting period to the next.

The term *organizational design* refers to how the organization is structured into divisions or functional groups and where work is performed to accomplish the organization's mission. Performance measures for this area are a little more abstract than the measures for organizational goals. They might address the outcome, effectiveness, or efficiency of the structural design, or of the culture, or of the interaction among the individual components. They might enable one to evaluate several alternative placements for the performance of a critical function, or they might be used to estimate the effect of a proposal to consolidate or separate functions or divisions. For example, an organizational design question might be "where in the organization is it best to perform the building/construction plan review function for fire protection purposes?" The decision as to where the function should be performed in the local government's organization structure—for example, by the fire marshal or by the building official—might benefit from an evaluation of measurements of (1) the quality of the reviews performed of the fire protection system plans, (2) the quality of the reviews performed of the building construction plans, and (3) fire loss caused by fire protection or building defects.

Measures of organizational management might address, at the macrolevel, key management tasks or specific management issues. When employee morale is a management issue, for example, one measure might be the frequency with which disruptive, significant personnel actions (grievances) occur and the amount of staff time spent dealing with them. Other possible organizational management measures that might be addressed are the timeliness and quality of management decisions (did these decisions have the expected results?).

Process-level performance measures

In the case of the fire and rescue service, process goals and priorities for emergency response to fires generally include protecting life, protecting the environment, stabilizing the incident, and conserving property. Measuring progress toward achieving these goals involves ensuring that the process is producing results based on and directly meeting customers' needs.

Outcome measures of process goals might include losses incurred, stage or size of the emergency when control occurs, time to achieve each goal and the sequence in which they are achieved, customer complaints filed, and the rates of customer satisfaction with the results of the process. If the process is to achieve a positive result, the process goals must be acceptable from the customer's perspective.

Process design involves establishing the sequence of steps to be performed and the flow of tasks and activities among various work groups or individuals. Measures of process design include the time to accomplish a component task or activity, the quality of the product of the task or activity, variance in the performance of the task or activity, and variance in the result of the process compared with the result of alternative designs for the same process.

Measuring process management requires that process measurement systems be developed and established, ensuring that accurate and complete data are captured, reported, analyzed, and interpreted in a timely fashion to target problems of variance. Solutions to these problems of variance might involve training staff, redesigning the steps of the process, or reengineering the available tools and equipment used to perform the tasks so as to improve performance. Outcome measures of process management might include measurements of process variance, improvements in process efficiency, improvements in error rates, and so forth.

Job/performer-level performance measures

Measures for job/performer performance as it relates to individual or work-team performance are also critical. Immediate supervisors should be held accountable for individual and work-team performance and should be able to use process or activity performance measures (discussed in detail in the next section) to identify whether the team is performing adequately. When there is a variance from the expected performance, the supervisor must evaluate each member's performance or contribution to the team effort and identify any individual performance problems that exist.

Some problems are obvious, such as when a pump operator fails to charge an attack line on time. That kind of performance error immediately stops the firefighting crew's activity, which stays stopped until the problem is corrected. Other performance problems are less obvious. Thus, changes in performance measures need to be tracked over time. These tracked changes indicate to the supervisor where to concentrate attention to identify the performance issues, practices, and individuals that might be causing the changes. Some useful measurement tools (e.g., Pareto charts and run charts) and their applications are discussed later in the chapter.

Creating performance measures at the process level

Process-level performance measurement and analysis generally lead to the greatest amount of improvement in outcomes and efficiency. Thus, this section first explores the need for measuring process and then highlights process mapping—a specific technique for devising and analyzing process performance measures.

The need for process performance measurement

To improve business operations—that is, to improve how processes work—George Robson advocates using "continuous process improvement."[14] He explains how to use judgmental and analytical problem-solving techniques to improve processes and gives detailed instructions on accomplishing process flow diagramming, analytical data charting, and control charting. He measures the performance of a process in order to let the process tell him—tell managers—what is happening. In his scheme, critical data are gathered at set points in the process to provide feedback to those who perform and manage the process, ensuring that they understand what is happening and can keep the process operating at full capacity. Process steps that do not add value should be eliminated. For the process to be efficient, variables such as cycle time, cost, and conformance to control limits (specifications) must be measured.

Robson advises readers and managers to focus on the process's activity rather than its output. Focusing on activity reduces variation in the product at the earliest possible point, whereas waiting until the end to inspect for variance is too late: by then the damage is already done. To Robson, the need to focus on the activity is even more valid in a service setting than in a manufacturing setting. "In non-manufacturing processes such as those found in service type industries, focusing on the process is even more critical. Why? Because if the process steps are not well defined, clearly explained, and totally understood, the process becomes very 'people dependent'. When that occurs, you have a high probability that process output cannot be accurately predicted which leads to process variation. And, that's exactly what you want to avoid."[15]

Fire departments are in an industry that provides services to its customers. To ensure that the services provided meet the customers' needs, departments must pay attention to the details of processes (how the critical tasks are performed—i.e., the manner in which services are provided). The Rummler and Brache model of measuring the goals, the design, and the management of processes performance offers a way for fire departments to meet performance standards and minimize the variations between, for example, one company's way of performing a task and other companies' ways, or between one shift's way and other shifts' ways. Anyone who does not think such comparisons between units are necessary should consider how often one hears something like "when we operate on incidents together, it seems as if we are from [insert the number of stations/battalions/districts/shifts here] separate fire departments."

Some people claim, "We can't plan for or measure firefighting because no two fires are alike." In reality, though, most fires are substantially the same. True, there is some variation in where a fire starts within a structure, where it has spread to by the time the fire department arrives, and whether there is anyone needing rescue. That variation is the reason the Incident Management System (IMS) was developed. The IMS is a method of bringing consistency to the process of assessing the situation upon arrival, planning a course of action, and implementing that action plan, or managing the process.

Once the specific nature of the situation has been determined and the plan of action has been set (the incident commander orders standard tactical assignments—search, fire attack, vertical ventilation—to meet the needs of the particular incident), the responding companies execute the assignments. And firefighting process managers must ensure that each company's crew operates within the IMS and can execute the standard tactical assignments correctly and within the process limits (with respect to time and safety) set for each. Measuring the ability of responding crews to perform *before* the emergency is a necessary step toward ensuring consistent performance *during* emergency incidents.

As of the start of the twenty-first century, too little of the performance measurement work for fire departments has focused on measures at the process level. Each separate program or major activity for the fire and rescue department should develop and diagram its own internal chronological work flows and measures for critical tasks and activities. EMS systems typically do this: The physician serving as the system's medical director establishes medical protocols that identify specific requirements for the performance of advanced life support procedures by paramedics in the field. Usually a formal system is in place to review and evaluate whether the protocols were followed, whether they worked, and, if not, what changes are needed in either the protocol or the performance of teams or individuals. An equivalent process of developing specific process-performance protocols and improving quality should be instituted by the "fire doctor" (the fire chief) for fire suppression, HAZMAT activities, technical rescue, basic life support activities, fire inspection activities, 911 call receipt and dispatch processes, and every other critical activity or process in which the department is engaged. The FireDAP program mentioned above is an example of work in this area.

Another example is the firefighter certification program used in Montana. That state's fire training organization has developed a training and certification program based on standard tactical assignments performed by crews in a real-world setting. The scenarios are designed to meet both the requirements of NFPA 1001, Standard for Fire Fighter Professional Qualifications (1997 edition), and the operational needs of the firefighters in the field operating under an IMS.

To do performance measurement at the process level, the emergency response function should report performance measures for each significant component of a process, depending on how the service is delivered. If the department has separate tactical units (engine, truck, heavy rescue, or ambulance/medic companies), stations, and/or shifts, the data should be collected by each tactical unit and then combined into station-, shift-, and division-level information that fits the needs of the organization. If the organization has multiple stations that make up geographic battalions or districts, the data should be reported at the lowest level (unit, station, etc.) that performs the activity and should then be aggregated at the battalion and division level. Why is it important to do this? The only way to identify clearly where the variance is occurring is to separate out the data to the significant level for each process—in this case, the level of the tactical unit, station, shift, or battalion.

Process mapping

Each critical process should be mapped out, and the mapping should identify the chronological steps that must be completed to achieve the desired result. The process map can take any number of forms, from a list of sequential activities to a process flowchart of how the task should be performed. Several worthwhile examples of process maps can be found in the booklet "A Leadership Guide to Quality Improvement for Emergency Medical Services (EMS) Systems," published by the National Highway Traffic Safety Administration of the U.S. Department of Transportation.[16]

The flow of activities for emergency incidents contains ten critical time points (discussed in more detail in connection with Figure 10–7 below):

A. Incident occurs.
B. Incident is detected.
C. Incident is reported (911 rings).
D. Call is processed.
E. Call is dispatched.
F. Unit(s) respond(s).
G. Unit(s) arrive(s).
H. Unit(s) begin(s) work.
I. Incident is under control.
J. Incident ends.

When deciding what emergency response time measures to collect, the department should recognize that identifying and attempting to track all the components that make up the response process is critical, even if some of the components are not under the department's control. The only way to represent accurately how the service is provided to the customer is to record and report response time (and other significant measures) *from the customer's perspective.*

The customer is not concerned with who operates the 911 center or how the call gets processed. The customer calls 911 to activate emergency response, period. Customers start their response time "expectation clock" when they pick up the phone and dial. Fire and rescue departments should start their clocks at the earliest possible point: when the 911 phone begins to ring.

Using the customer-based definition means that the collection of data on fire and rescue system response times should begin with the beginning of the emergency itself. Unfortunately, usually no accurate record of the time can be made until the response system is activated by someone's dialing 911 to call the public safety answering point (PSAP). But although performance in the areas of detection and notification cannot be accurately recorded, it can be inferred from analysis over time of the number of fires that have spread beyond the area or room of origin before response units arrive. Information about the times of occurrence and notification can also be gathered from witnesses.

In many jurisdictions the fire department does not control the 911 call receipt process or the dispatch process. In those jurisdictions, the fire department should work with the PSAP manager to specify what performance measures and performance standards are expected. The fire department is the PSAP's internal customer and depends on the timely processing and/or dispatch of emergency calls in order to meet its own customers' expectations. The fire department cannot ensure good service unless all the components that make up the service provide performance measurements.

For specific types of incidents, the variables within each segment should be more detailed. For example, for an EMS call, the deploy- and control-time intervals should be subdivided to capture other critical times, such as "at patient," "patient extricated," "patient transported," "at hospital," and "available for another call."

In selecting the precise points at which the measurements will start and stop, a department should consider when in the process delays might occur and what effect these delays might have on each starting and stopping point. For example, if the start of the clock for "call received in communications" is defined as when the telephone is answered rather than when it starts to ring, the definition does not necessarily allow accurate capturing of the "ring time," nor does it allow a determination of how long the customer had to wait for the telephone to be answered.

Using a process mapping system, an agency can assign responsibilities, develop measures for each interval, and address strategies for improving each interval either independently or in groupings that make sense. For example, overall system performance is the responsibility of the chief of the department. This performance is indicated in Figure 10–7, which charts out the incident

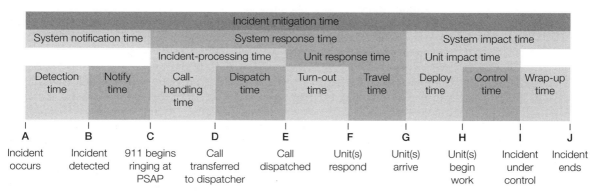

Figure 10–7   Overall system performance: Sample emergency incident response time line and response intervals.

mitigation time. Incident mitigation time comprises three combinations of intervals: system notification time (points A to C), system response time (points C to G), and system impact time (points G to J). As an indicator of overall system performance, these macrolevel performance factors can be reported regularly to the city or county manager, the local elected body, and citizens.

How the call receipt and dispatch functions are conducted will determine who is responsible for the call-handling time interval (points C to D) and the dispatch time interval (points D to E). For example, if the PSAP is handled by a separate agency that processes (handles) the 911 call and then transfers information to the fire department for dispatch, the PSAP manager is responsible for the call-handling time component of system response time. The fire department dispatch center manager is then responsible only for the dispatch time component. When the PSAP answers 911 and, upon learning that the caller requires fire response, transfers the caller to the fire department for processing (handling) as well as for subsequent dispatch, the call-handling interval (C to D) needs to be divided into two components: the initial answer at the PSAP until transfer, and the subsequent answer and data gathering by the fire department before dispatch.

A field unit commander (e.g., an engine company officer) is responsible for the unit response time component (points E to G) and the unit impact time component (points G to I) for his or her unit. Field unit commanders should be held accountable for their assigned crews' ability to turn out rapidly and safely, travel to incidents, deploy themselves and their equipment, and operate at the scene of emergencies.

For each standard tactical assignment to be performed by response crews, a process map should be prepared. It should specify in what sequence the steps are performed, who does what, and what tools are used. Figure 10–8 presents a sample—a process map for vertical ventilation. This process map will become the basis for (1) the teaching and evaluation of standard training evolutions (tactical scenarios or assignments) during recruit and certification training, (2) periodic evaluations of crew performance, and (3) the assessment of actual on-scene performance during postincident analysis.

Battalion or district commanders are responsible, within their assigned geographical or functional areas, for the system response time (points C to G on Figure 10–7) of response resources and for the system impact time (points G to J)—that is, for coordinating the activities of multiple response units to quickly achieve positive outcomes at incidents. For example, the district chief might be made responsible for developing a battalion management plan to focus on the problem within the residential community of above-average times for accessing the system (time line points A–C). Analysis might show that district personnel need to direct their efforts at smoke detectors, either having them installed or having the batteries replaced to ensure that smoke detectors in residential properties are operational.

At a more detailed level, a company might have a higher-than-expected unit response time. The station officer would be made responsible for developing a station management plan, the goal of which would be to reduce the station's unit response time. The officer would look at the two components of the time line that are under his or her direct control: turn-out time and unit travel time. Closer examination might reveal one potential reason for the high response time—the fact that to perform physical fitness training each day, the company travels to the extreme dead end of its first-due area (i.e., the area within which it is the first company due at a fire). In this case, reengineering the work environment to provide adequate physical fitness facilities closer to the center of the company's response district may have a significant and positive effect on the unit's travel time. Similarly, changing the work process by analyzing the time of day at which calls are occurring and then scheduling the physical

Tasks	Primary responsibilities	Officer activity	F/f 1 activity	F/f 2 activity
		Observe conditions Complete task Ensure crew safety	Back up f/f 2 Saw operator	Sound roof Back up saw operator Clear opening
1	Receive and echo tactical order	Listen to radio Echo tactical order back to command		
2	Give task order to crew	Tell crew assignment and location	Acknowledge order	Acknowledge order
3	Collect tools and transport them to task area	Monitor crew performance and radio	Carry ladder butt, saw	Carry ladder tip, sounding hook
4	Establish ladder access to roof	Observe conditions Monitor crew performance and radio	Heel ladder, tie off	Raise and set ladder
5	Don facepiece and climb to roof with tools	Don facepiece Second up ladder Monitor crew performance and radio	Don facepiece Foot ladder while others climb Third up ladder with tools	Don facepiece First up ladder with tools
6	Sound roof	Ensure f/f 2 sounds roof Monitor crew performance and radio		Sound roof before stepping off Hold ladder tip
7	Select cut location and proceed to cut area	Select cut location and communicate to crew Walk only where sounded Monitor crew performance and radio	Back up f/f 2 while sounding, walk only where sounded	Sound path to cut area and entire cut work area, walk only where sounded
8	Make inspection cut	Select cut location Monitor crew performance and radio	Start saw, cut inspection opening	Back up saw operator
9	Decide whether to proceed	Decide based on conditions in inspection opening Communicate decision to crew	Acknowledge receipt of decision	Acknowledge receipt of decision
10	Make cut	Observe conditions Monitor crew performance and radio	Cut 4' x 8' opening with louvered panels	Back up saw operator
11	Clear hole	Observe conditions Monitor crew performance and radio	Back up f/f 2 while clearing	Clear hole of cut wood and Sheetrock below
12	Radio status to command	Radio command that vent hole is cut and crew is exiting roof		
13	Exit roof	Move to ladder, walk only where sounded, hold ladder tip while others climb Monitor crew performance and radio Climb down ladder third	Back up sounder Move to ladder, walk only where sounded Climb down ladder second with tools	Sound roof, move to ladder Climb down ladder first with tools Foot ladder when down
14	Report status to command	Radio command that crew is clear of roof and ready for reassignment		

Figure 10–8 Sample process map of vertical ventilation tasks (assumes a crew of three on scene and wearing personal protective equipment, including self-contained breathing apparatus except for facepiece).

fitness training at the time of lowest probability for a call may also have a positive effect.

Figure 10–9 presents guidelines for improving response time performance on the basis of the interval during which the time spent is excessive.

Benchmarking

Performance measurement makes benchmarking possible. Benchmarking means searching for and identifying best practices in organizations that perform functions either the same as, or similar to, the functions that one's own department performs, so that managers can then adapt or adopt the methods used by the best practitioners to improve the performance of the managers' own organizations. Richard Fischer defines the difference between performance measurement and benchmarking: performance measurement is "the determination of how effectively and efficiently (at the lowest cost) your jurisdiction is delivering the public service of interest" and is "the initial work done to specify and gather data on the criteria that account for the performance of a program or service. . . ."[17] Benchmarking is "the next step, which is taken to discover what those [departments] identified as having best practices are doing that you are not doing." Benchmarking, Fischer argues, is the reason to do performance measurement. He calls performance measurement a planning tool and benchmarking an improvement tool. One important form of benchmarking is service efforts and accomplishments (SEA) reporting. SEA reports compare critical performance measures with those of selected comparison jurisdictions.

Guidelines for benchmarking

William Gay, who has consulted and written extensively on benchmarking specifically for the fire and rescue service, provides a number of guidelines for benchmarking that are useful to anyone embarking on this process. He suggests that benchmarking is both a concept and a process, and he defines benchmarking as "a quest for best practices. It is a continuous process that leads to superior performance in fire and emergency medical services through the implementation of innovations."[18]

Detection time	Notify time	Call-handling time	Dispatch time	Turn-out time	Travel time	Deploy time	Control time	Wrap-up time
Citizen CPR	Citizen CPR	Technology changes: Enhanced 911	Technology changes: New computer-aided dispatch, new radio system	Duty crew at station	Review and modify procedure	Staff training	Provide needed staff early in incident	Provide relief crews
Automatic detection systems	Citizen 911 training	Staff training	Staff training	Station design modification	Improved road network and conditions	Review and modify procedure	Review and modify procedure	Rehab crews often
Neighbor-hood Watch	Automatic alarm no-tification systems	Review and modify procedure	Review and modify procedure	Review and modify procedure	Add more stations	Use new equipment and technology	Use new equipment and technology	Preserve area of origin early
Police patrols		Increase staffing levels	Increase staffing levels		Add more units at existing stations Staff training Traffic control preemption	Have more staff arrive at same time	Staff training	Review and modify procedure

Figure 10–9   Potential methods of reducing time intervals between key points.

Gay proposes a nine-step process that he illustrates as a benchmark spiral of progress (see Figure 10–10). The first spiral, or phase, contains five steps and is based on good performance measurement. A department works through the process of (1) deciding what to benchmark, (2) selecting benchmark partners (i.e., identifying comparables), (3) collecting data, (4) determining performance gaps, and (5) communicating the results.

Gay suggests that in selecting benchmark partners, a department should look at three levels. First, it should compare various fire companies or functional divisions within the department. Doing this not only allows a department to practice benchmarking before becoming involved with outside agencies but also creates the basis for establishing internal standards and performance goals.

Second, the department should find similar agencies with which to compare itself. This is a critical and difficult step (and is discussed in greater detail below). The jurisdiction to choose is the best of the comparable jurisdictions for the particular performance area the department is interested in. It is important to realize that a jurisdiction may excel in one aspect of service delivery but do poorly in others, so the department should not assume that all of the other jurisdiction's processes can be adapted or adopted.

The third level in seeking a benchmark partner is to identify agencies that are recognized as best-in-class jurisdictions of any size or type. Even though there may not be a close match in service descriptors, comparison with the performance of these recognized industry leaders is valuable and will often lead to the discovery of new and innovative approaches. This type of comparison is best done after a department has successfully benchmarked at the first two levels.

Gay's second spiral, or phase, involves designing and implementing changes and improvements that have been identified in the first phase. In this second phase, realistic improvement goals are set on the basis of the previous gap analysis, a plan of action is developed, and the actions are implemented and

Figure 10–10 Gay's nine-step process for benchmarking: Benchmarking spiral of progress.

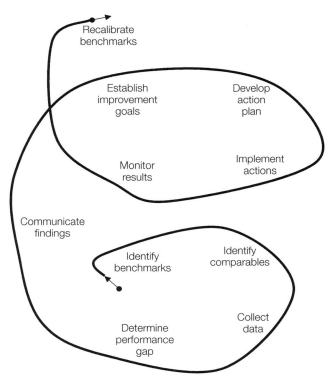

monitored for results. Finally, the benchmarks need to be recalibrated period-ically so that the department can take into account both the progress it has made toward its goals and the continually changing environment.

According to Gay, departments that participate in benchmarking will reap several benefits. They will

Develop a culture in which the changing world is understood

Identify and establish priorities among those agency processes and proce-dures that need improvement

Use others' experience to break down the "not-invented-here" barriers to improvement

Develop a commitment to continual improvement so as to meet and exceed citizens' expectations about the costs and quality of service

Add procedures, processes, and technologies that have proven effective in other jurisdictions

Share locally invented best practices with their benchmark partners.[19]

As mentioned above, it is important to find several like jurisdictions with which to compare one's organization, but doing so is easier said than done. Comparison departments should protect similar geographic areas, have com-parable resources, and provide similar services. If the comparison department does not perform similar services, benchmarking best practices against that department just because it is engaged in the same activities makes no sense. Some of the variables to be considered, especially in terms of size and type of services provided, are listed in Figure 10–11. Close attention should also be paid to how jurisdictions measure the performance of each service.

Figure 10–11   Variables of a departmental comparison.

Jurisdictions and organization	Size of area protected Population protected Demographics (age distribution, income) Budget Number of stations, uniformed members Type of members (career/volunteer/paid on-call/combination)	

Services provided	Fire
	  Structural
	    Pumper
	    Ladder truck
	    Heavy rescue squad
	    Rural water supply
	  Wildland
	  Aircraft rescue and firefighting
	    (ARFF)
	Emergency medical service
	  Basic life support
	  Advanced life support
	  Transport
	  No transport
	  Fire unit first response
	Hazardous materials
	  Cross-trained engine/truck staff
	  Basic containment team
	  Mitigation team
		Technical rescue
		  Cross-trained engine/truck
		    staff
		  Dedicated technical rescue teams
		    Confined space
		    Swift water
		    High angle
		    Urban search and rescue (USAR)
		Prevention activities
		  Fire inspections
		    Dedicated inspection staff
		    Company inspections
		  Fire investigations
		    Dedicated investigation staff
		    Shared investigation authority
		      (with police)
		  Public education programs
		    Dedicated staff
		    Company presentations

Types of buildings	Old buildings (balloon construction) Large-area buildings, industrial, high-rise	
Uses, processes in buildings	Residential, office, retail Industrial hazardous processes	

If exact matches are not available (and they rarely are), it is important to understand the significant differences and articulate how they will affect the comparison of performance measures. For example, response time is a common intermediate outcome measure, so understanding how the comparison jurisdictions measure response time for the services they share with one's own jurisdiction is critical: what are the component time intervals called, when is the "clock" started and stopped for each component, and so forth. A brief review of the size and type of service variables presented in Figure 10–11 indicates how confusing and difficult it may be to clarify all the significant differences between jurisdictions. Differences in how system performance is measured further complicate the comparing of jurisdictions.

Figures 10–12 and 10–13 present the findings of the Tricom Consortium, a group of three fire and rescue departments that joined forces to benchmark and develop a common time line (see the sidebar on pages 314–316). Originally there was quite a difference in what the jurisdictions called the component intervals of response time. Similarly, there was a difference in when they started the clock: the three 911 centers and call-taking and dispatch processes were not operated in the same way. These differences complicated the attempt to compare previous years' data and created a situation in which, if meaningful cross-jurisdictional benchmarking were to occur, at least one of the three departments would have to change its way of capturing and reporting data.

Is it really important to worry about whether the partner jurisdictions are similar? A hypothetical example will answer that question. One jurisdiction is trying to compare the performance of its fire companies with that of the fire companies in another jurisdiction. The two communities are similar in size and makeup (square miles, number of stations, number of personnel, and type of service providers [career]) and in number of fire incidents (450). However, the subject jurisdiction performs not only the response to fire incidents but also fire company first response on emergency medical calls (2,000 per year) and company-based inspections and public education activities (500 per year); the comparison department does not. Unless these differences are understood, the difference in function makes for an improper comparison that may produce inaccurate and misleading conclusions (see Table 10–1 on page 317).

Figure 10–12
Translation table, Tricom emergency response time line terminology.

Prince William County (Virginia)	Howard County (Maryland)	Charlotte, North Carolina
Action time	Launch time	Turn-out time
Alarm time	911 call receipt	Alarm time
Dispatch time	Alert time	Dispatch time
Stabilize time	Under control	Control time

Figure 10–13   Incident time line, Tricom Consortium.

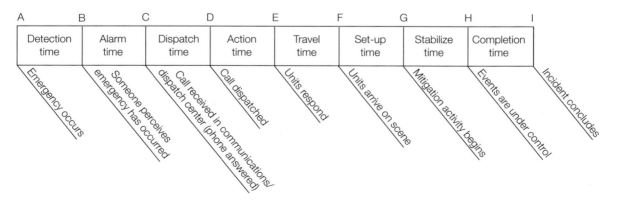

Interim report of the Tricom Consortium

Representatives from the Charlotte (North Carolina) Fire Department, the Howard County (Maryland) Fire and Rescue, and the Prince William County (Virginia) Fire and Rescue Department assembled to address the issues of benchmarking and performance measures as these issues apply to the fire and rescue industry. They began meeting in early 1998 and have continued to refine their efforts at benchmarking.

What did we set out to accomplish?

A. Define commonly useful measures with agreed-upon definitions.
B. Develop a comparison model that could be used between jurisdictions that are dissimilar (in an effort to normalize the process).
C. Define measures for fire department activities that are nontraditional from a service and quality measure standpoint (e.g., administrative services).

What did we get done?

We defined some common organizational demographic and output measures that will enable us to identify how we are similar and where we are dissimilar. These data will be useful in determining why there might be variances in the performance of the organizations.

Comparison organizational and demographic data

Population related
Average age of population (median age)
Total population (derive population per square mile
Daytime versus nighttime population (coming in/going out)
School-age population
Senior age population
Ethnicity/percentage of minority population(s)
Median income
Average household income
Average education level
Percentage of population with health insurance (third-party payers)
  Percentage with Medicare
  Percentage with Medicaid

Assessable tax base
Average age of buildings
Median age of all structures
Percentage assessable base commercial
Percentage assessable base residential

Number of structures
  Number residential
  Number commercial
  Number agricultural
Number of square feet of nonresidential structure
Number of miles of interstate highway

Budget
Total reporting jurisdiction spending budget (derive fire department budget as percentage of total budget)
Total fire department spending budget (derive fire department budget as percentage of total budget)
Sources of funding for jurisdiction budget (narrative)
Sources of funding for fire department budget (narrative)
Funding received by volunteer departments through local government: Are there other funding sources? Y/N, list

Political structure
Elected bodies and administrative structure

Fire/Rescue Department
Number of stations
Number of engines
Number of ambulances
Number of incidents where patients were transported
  Number of patients transported
Total number of incidents
  Fire (total and broken down by 901 Use Codes)
  Medical
  Hazardous materials
  All other types
Number/percentage of certifications
Number of volunteers
  Operational
  Administrative
Number of paid employees
  Uniform/sworn
  Civilian/support

Miscellaneous
Automatic external defibrillators per 100,000 population
Number of hospitals (patient-receiving centers) in reporting jurisdiction

The group developed a Customer Outcome Model to guide development of measures of emergency response service:

Customers expect the department to:
  Come quick
  Solve my problem
  Be nice
  Stay safe
  Be well managed

The group defined and organized specific measures, including definitions, to address each area of the Customer Outcome Model.

Come quick
Number of stations
Square miles of jurisdiction
Population served
In 90% of the incidents we will arrive within
  xx minutes and *yy* seconds (calculation
  based on all emergency indicators)

Solve my problem
Fire dollar loss
Fire dollar loss as a percentage of assessed
  value (Note: If a jurisdiction does not do a
  fire loss estimate on all fires, it should report the percentage of those reported
  fires for which an estimate is done.)
Fire deaths (per 100,000 population served)
Fire injuries (per 100,000 population served)
In 90% of emergency medical service (EMS)
  incidents we will spend fewer than *xx*
  minutes and *yy* seconds on the scene
  (calculation based on all EMS incidents)
Number of advanced life support (ALS) providers (per 100,000)
Number of basic life support (BLS) providers (per 100,000)
Number of EMS units (per 100,000)

Be nice
Does the agency employ a mechanism to
  routinely measure customer satisfaction?
  Y/N
Percentage of reported customers satisfied

Stay safe
Number of reported (workers' comp) per-
    sonnel injuries—all incidents
  (per 1,000 incidents)
  (per 100 employees)
Number of reported exposures to communi-
    cable diseases
  (per 1,000 incidents)
  (per 100 employees)
Number of lost work hours due to injury
  (per 1,000 incidents)
  (per 100 employees)
Dollar loss due to injury
  (as a percentage of adopted expenditure
    budget)
  (per 1,000 incidents)
  (per 100 employees)
Number of vehicle accidents reported during the reporting period

Be well managed
Cost per capita
Cost per incident
Fire and rescue expenditure budget as a
  percentage of jurisdiction operating
  budget excluding schools
Dollar loss due to injuries as a percentage
  of adopted expenditure budget

Additional work was devoted to developing measures for numerous functions
and activities:

Budget development
Budget implementation

Purchasing
Accounting
Payroll
Finance
Planning
Human resource management
Information systems/geographic infor-
  mation systems/records
Office systems (clerical)
Logistics: facilities/apparatus
Public information
Legislation

In addition, the group defined specific
  activities that would be considered
  as "administration":

Public education
Number of public education programs
Number of participants in public education
  programs
Number of full-time positions devoted to
  public education (F/T FTEs)
Expenditure budget dedicated to public education (derive public education budget
  as a percentage of total department
  spending budget)
Hours of public education completed (derive
  public education hours as a percentage
  of total department personnel hours)
Percentage of population trained in CPR
Number of incidents of out-of-hospital cardiac arrest
Number of episodes of bystander CPR (derive percentage of cardiac arrest incidents with bystander CPR)

Community service
Hours of community service activities
Number of community service activities and
  events
Number of constituent contacts

Health, safety, and fitness
Number of personnel injuries (per 100
    personnel)
  On scene
  In station
  During physical training
  (Refer to NFPA and IAFF?)
Percentage of workday allotted to physical
  training
Dollar loss due to injuries
Work-time lost due to injuries (report hours)
Do you have a spending budget devoted to
  health, safety, and/or fitness? Y/N
Dollars devoted to health, safety, and fitness
  (derive percentage of budget devoted)
Number of confirmed occupational illnesses
Number of firefighter fatalities
Number of motor vehicle accidents
  In reverse
  At incidents
  Involving overhead doors

continued

continued

Emergency related
Non-emergency related
Derive: per 100 personnel
    per 100 incidents
    per 100 unit responses
Dollar loss due to motor vehicle accidents
Dollar loss due to preventable motor vehicle
    accidents (could the fire/rescue driver
    have prevented it?)   Y/N
Do you have an employee member safety
    committee?   Y/N
Do you provide physicals for employees?
    Y/N
Do you comply with NFPA 1582 [Standard
    on Medical Requirements for Fire Fight-
    ers and Information for Fire Department
    Physicians, 2000 edition]?   Y/N
Do you have a safety officer?   Y/N
Do you have a risk management
    plan?   Y/N
Percentage compliance with NFPA 1500
    [Standard on Fire Department Occupa-
    tional Safety and Health Program, 2002
    edition]   Y/N

Planning
Do you have a planning function/section?
    Y/N
Number of full-time positions devoted to
    planning
    Uniform
    Civilian
Do you have a plan?   Y/N
Duration of plan (years)
Frequency of revision of plan (in years)
Has the plan been approved by the appro-
    priate authority having jurisdiction?   Y/N

Is your plan published (has it been copied
    and distributed)?   Y/N
Is the plan used as a working tool?   Y/N

Human resources (HR)
Number of HR functions performed by
    Fire and Rescue
    Government HR
    Contractor
Do you have an HR function/section?   Y/N
Number of full-time positions assigned to HR
Vacancy rate (needs definition of
    calculation)
Attrition rate (turnover) exclusive of retire-
    ments (needs definition of calculation)
Number of retirements
Number of medical retirements
Number of grievances
Number of volunteers
Volunteer attrition rate (needs definition of
    calculation)
Average length of service of volunteers
Do you have a volunteer LOSAP (length of
    service award program)?   Y/N
Are you under a mandated affirmative action
    plan?   Y/N
Number of employees
    Males/females
    Protected class
    Civilian/uniform (sworn)

Finally, we experimented with ratios of
demographics that would enable the
weighting of measures for comparing
dissimilar jurisdictions.

Source: Adapted with permission from Dorothea St. John, Tricom Consortium, Prince William County, Va., February 1998.

If one looks at the cost per fire incident response, the subject department appears to be significantly more expensive per fire incident response (by $445) than the comparison department. But a comparison of the cost per total incident response shows that the subject department is much more productive inasmuch as it responds to 2000 emergency medical incidents in addition to the 450 fires: the difference in cost per incident thus shifts dramatically in the subject department's favor, with the comparison department costing $2,288 more per incident. This margin grows to $2,380 if one looks at the cost of total activities: incident response, inspection activities, and public education combined.

Good benchmarking should lead to analysis at a much more detailed level than that provided in the simple example just discussed. Department program managers can identify other departments that are performing better than they are in a functional area or a process and can investigate the reasons the others' performances are better. By examining "best practices" at the process level of those superior-performing organizations, a manager can identify factors that suggest changes worth considering. If a companion jurisdiction's elapsed interval between arrival time and patient transported is significantly lower than the subject jurisdiction's, all aspects of the operation should be investigated to determine why. The manager should evaluate whether it makes sense to adapt or adopt some or all of the companion jurisdiction's practices to improve his or her own department's performance.

Table 10–1
Comparison of similar
jurisdictions.

	Budget ($000)	No. FTEs[a]	Fire incident responses		All incident responses		All activities[b]		Total activities per FTE[c]
			No.	Cost per response	No.	Cost per response	No.	Cost per response	
Subject department	$1,500	22	450	$3,333	2,450	$600	2,950	$508	134
Comparison department	$1,300	24	450	$2,888	450	$2,888	450	$2,888	19

[a]Full-time equivalent positions. [b]Incidents + inspections + public education programs performed.
[c]Number of all activities divided by number of FTEs.

Service efforts and accomplishments reporting

Local government policy makers are using the GASB measurement categories discussed earlier to develop service efforts and accomplishments (SEA) reports (see Figure 10–14). These reports make macrolevel snapshot comparisons of critical governmental functions across similar jurisdictions and are therefore a form of benchmarking. Figure 10–15 shows some sample pages from a 2000–01 SEA report from Portland, Oregon, which has been using SEA reports for a number of years. The side-by-side comparison of critical data for the jurisdictions being compared shows areas of strength and weakness and provides guidance for policy makers and departmental management. The fire and rescue department is often one of the first agencies in a jurisdiction targeted for the

Figure 10–14 GASB
categories of indicators
for service efforts and
accomplishments.

A. Indicators of service efforts
   1. Inputs—dollar costs of the service period
      a. In "current" dollars
      b. In "constant" dollars—that is, adjusted for price-level changes
   2. Inputs—Amounts of *non*monetary resources expended, especially the amount of work time expended during the period (for the service). These might be expressed in such units as full-time-equivalent years or employee-hours.
B. Indicators of service accomplishments
   1. Outputs—amount of workload accomplished
   2. Outcomes—a numeric indicator of program results. This category includes indicators of service quality (such as timeliness), effectiveness, and the amount or proportion of "need" that is (or is not) being served.
C. Indicators that relate service efforts to service accomplishments
   (These can also be labeled efficiency indicators, which for the purposes of this report include both input/output and input/outcome indicators.)
   1. Amount of input related to (divided by) amount of *output*. "Input" can be any of the variations included under Section A, and "output" refers to B.1, not B.2.
   2. Amount of input related to (divided by) amount of *outcomes* or *results*. Again, "input" can be any of the variations noted in Section A. "Outcome" refers only to B.2, not B.1.
   3. Productivity (or efficiency) *indexes*. These traditionally have been used in reporting national productivity trends. Indexes are calculated by relating the ratio of productivity in the current year to that of a preselected base year. These indexes have the advantage that the productivity ratios for different activities for services, or across services, can be combined by weighting each ratio by the amount of input for each activity.
D. Explanatory information
   This is a term used to cover a variety of information relevant to a service that helps users understand the performance of the SEA indicators and factors affecting an organization's performance. The explanatory information should be grouped into two categories:
   1. Elements substantially outside the control of the public agency, such as demographic characteristics
   2. Elements over which the agency has significant control, such as staffing patterns.

CHAPTER 1   FIRE, RESCUE AND EMERGENCY SERVICES

SERVICE MISSION

The mission of Portland Fire, Rescue and Emergency Services is to promote a safe environment for all protected areas, to respond to fire, medical, and other emergencies, and to provide related services to benefit the public.

The Bureau's primary goals are:

- to reduce the frequency and severity of fire, medical and hazardous materials emergencies through prevention efforts, such as education, investigations, enforcement programs and arson prosecution assistance

- to minimize suffering, loss of life, and property from fires, hazardous materials, medical and other emergencies through emergency response programs

- to ensure preparedness and safety through training, disaster planning, and emergency management programs and to provide all divisions with a high level of planning information and activities

- to provide leadership and coordination that encourages Community–Fire and Rescue partnerships that result in City and Bureau mission and goal accomplishments

- to effectively manage the resources and support necessary for Portland Fire, Rescue and Emergency Services to accomplish its mission

SPENDING AND STAFFING

Total Fire & Rescue operating expenditures, adjusted for inflation, have declined over the past five years, while capital spending has jumped:

- over the last five years, emergency service spending is down 8 percent, while prevention spending is up 8 percent

- operating costs per capita have dropped by 8 percent

- capital spending increased dramatically due to fire station construction and rehabilitation funded by a $53.8 million facilities bond approved by voters in 1998

The number of staff has returned to about what it was 5 years ago. Compared with 10 years ago, total staff has decreased but average on-duty emergency staff has increased.

FIGURE 3   FIRE BUDGETS PER CAPITA AND ON-DUTY EMERGENCY STAFF PER 100,000 RESIDENTS: PORTLAND AND SIX OTHER CITIES

Charlotte	37
Sacramento	33
Kansas City	42
Denver	35
Portland	31
Seattle	36
Cincinnati	55

Operating costs

City's contribution to sworn pension

SOURCE: FY 2000-01 and CY 2000 budgets and CAFRs

Compared with other cities, Portland spends slightly more on fire and rescue services due to the "pay-as-you-go" pension system established by City Charter. If pension costs are excluded, Portland is below the average of the other cities.

	City population	Operating expenditures (in millions/constant '00-01 dollars)					Capital expenditures * (in millions)	Total staff (FTEs)	Average on-duty emergency staffing	No. of emergency vehicles**	Operating costs per capita
		Emergency	Prevention	Other	Sworn ret./ disab.	Total					
FY 1996-97	503,000	$48.9	$4.8	$11.2	$25.6	$90.5	$2.2	746	167	61	$180
FY 1997-98	508,500	$47.1	$4.2	$10.4	$26.5	$88.2	$1.7	704	163	61	$173
FY 1998-99	509,610	$45.5	$5.4	$10.2	$27.0	$88.1	$2.6	729	163	59	$173
FY 1999-00	512,395	$45.2	$5.3	$10.4	$26.7	$87.5	$1.8	730	167	59	$171
FY 2000-01	531,600	$44.9	$5.2	$10.6	$27.6	$88.3	$7.3	743	165	61	$166
change over last 5 years:	+6%	-8%	+8%	-5%	+8%	-2%	+232%	0%	-1%	0%	-8%
change over last 10 years:	+17%	-3%	+6%	-	+13%	-	-	-2%	4%	-	-

* General Fund CIP, plus facilities construction bond expenditures starting in FY 1998-99

** Front-line fire engines, trucks, squads and other emergency response apparatus

Figure 10–15   Sample pages from the Portland (Oregon) Fire Department SEA 2000–01 report.

WORKLOAD

The total number of incidents the Bureau responds to continues to increase:

- the number of medical incidents has risen steadily

- the number of fires has fluctuated – it is slightly higher than five years ago, but less than ten years ago

- total incidents per on-duty firefighter is 8 percent higher than five years ago, and 33 percent higher than ten years ago

The Bureau did more than 17,000 inspections last year. They estimate that there are over 35,000 inspectable occupancies in the City.

The total number of structural fires in inspectable occupancies was not available due to lack of detail on multi-family fires. However, new data is being collected and will be available next year.

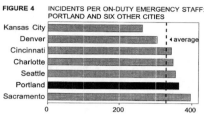

FIGURE 4   INCIDENTS PER ON-DUTY EMERGENCY STAFF: PORTLAND AND SIX OTHER CITIES

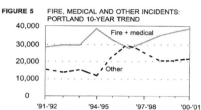

FIGURE 5   FIRE, MEDICAL AND OTHER INCIDENTS: PORTLAND 10-YEAR TREND

	Incidents				Incidents/ on-duty staff	No. of occupancies *	Structural fires, by occupancy type *				Code enforcement	
	Fire	Medical	Other	TOTAL		Inspectable / non-inspectable	Inspectable	Non-inspectable	Multi-family	TOTAL	Inspec-tions**	Re-inspections
FY 1996-97	2,738	24,630	28,568	55,936	335	- / -	-	-	-	998	-	-
FY 1997-98	2,527	27,880	27,076	57,483	353	- / -	-	-	-	878	-	-
FY 1998-99	2,658	32,090	20,562	55,310	339	- / -	-	-	-	807	17,279	8,294
FY 1999-00	2,881	34,285	20,422	57,588	345	- / -	302	478	184	964	21,015	11,642
FY 2000-01	2,790	36,202	20,660	59,652	362	34,792 (total)	270	448	207	925	17,629	11,370
change over last 5 years:	+2%	+47%	-28%	+7%	+8%	-	-	-	-	-7%	-	-
change over last 10 years:	-11%	+45%	+34%	+37%	+33%	-	-	-	-	-18%	-	-

* "Inspectable" occupancies are all commercial and public occupancies; "non-inspectable" occupancies are 1- and 2-family residences. However, "multi-family" occupancies include *both* inspectable (common areas) *and* non-inspectable areas (individual units).

** Includes scheduled and unscheduled inspections.

RESULTS

Fire safety has shown steady improvement over the past ten years:

- total fires per 1,000 residents are down 24 percent

- structural fires per 1,000 residents are down 30 percent

- Portland's structural fire rate is lower than the average of the comparison cities

Fire property loss occasionally rises dramatically due to unusual, single fires. However, fire loss, as well as civilian lives lost, shows a decline over the five and ten year periods.

Response time performance continues to fall short of the Bureau's goal: only 38 percent of fire responses and 40 percent of medical responses were within 4 minutes last year.

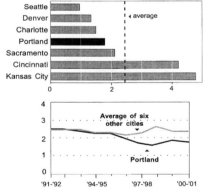

FIGURE 6   STRUCTURAL FIRES PER 1,000 RESIDENTS: PORTLAND AND SIX OTHER CITIES

SOURCE: Fire Bureau records and auditor survey of other cities

	Fires/ 1,000 residents		Fire property loss		Lives lost/ 100,000 residents	Response times within 4 mins.**	
	Structural	Total	Per capita (constant dollars)	% of value of property		Fire	Medical
FY 1996-97	1.98	5.44	$48	.56%	2.2	43%	46%
FY 1997-98	1.73	4.97	$38	.48%	1.6	43%	46%
FY 1998-99	1.58	5.22	$42	.40%	0.6	37%	41%
FY 1999-00	1.88	5.62	$73	.24%	1.2	41%	43%
FY 2000-01	1.74	5.25	$41	.14%	1.3	38%	40%
GOAL	-	-	< $49 *	<.36 *	<1.1 *	90%	90%
change over last 5 years:	-12%	-3%	-15%	-75%	-41%	-5%	-6%
change over last 10 years:	-30%	-24%	-37%	-74%	-35%	-	-

* no more than 97% of prior 3 years' average   ** includes both travel **and** turnout time

Multijurisdictional efforts The experience of the ICMA Center for Performance Measurement and the SEA report initiatives have generated efforts by local departments to meet with one another and develop performance measurement tools for SEA reporting and benchmarking. Organizations making these efforts have identified similar organizations within their regions of the country and have entered into alliances to meet periodically, exchange their performance measurements, and evaluate their underlying business processes. Although this effort is relatively new as of the beginning of the twenty-first century, it is showing promise as a way for departments to share knowledge and experience relative to performance measurement and benchmarking, ultimately improving their own operations. One such effort is described in the sidebar on the Tricom Consortium.

development of an SEA report because its dollar expenditures are such a large percentage of an overall jurisdictional budget. SEA reports give citizens, elected officials, and senior government and department executives comparison data on a few critical areas to highlight how well each department is doing relative to others like it.

In the SEA process, usually the jurisdiction's auditor or staff collects data from preselected comparison jurisdictions each year. (For each targeted service, the items compared often include measures of efficiency, effectiveness, and outcome.) It is imperative that the fire and rescue organization be involved from the beginning in selecting the comparison jurisdictions. A jurisdiction selected without fire and rescue involvement may be an incredibly close match for the purpose of comparing either finances or such services as police or social services but not be a close match at all for fire and rescue.

This circumstance poses a problem for fire departments because in SEA reporting, the desired result is to use measures to compare like services, and when the organizations or services do not match, the report must include explanations of differences that affect the measures. But the explanation is made in footnotes, which readers of the report may not take the time to read. If the numbers displayed make one's jurisdiction seem to be underperforming, SEA report users who do not read the explanations may reach the conclusion that the department is in fact underperforming even though the variance in performance has a rational explanation. (It is also possible that comparison jurisdictions are exceptionally high performers and that a department that therefore seems to be underperforming is nonetheless performing at a relatively high level.)

Presenting performance data to enhance their usefulness

Collecting data on performance is one thing; organizing the data for presentation is another. Data are not very useful until they are presented in some kind of organized way. In *How Effective Are Your Community Services?* Harry P. Hatry and colleagues provide a number of examples illustrating how data can be used to highlight the effectiveness of fire protection functions.[20] Their material, which deals only with fire protection, offers information about measures and data collection procedures that are linked to several areas: loss minimization, prevention, suppression, and citizen satisfaction. However, they caution against taking citizen-satisfaction survey results too seriously: "Citizen satisfaction measures . . . tend to reveal little since most citizens love their fire fighters; anything short of top ratings should be taken as dire warnings here."[21]

Figure 10–16   Eleven suggestions for improving the usefulness of information.

1. When reviewing services and programs, explicitly address service quality and outcomes.
2. Ask program managers to set targets for each performance indicator. Assess progress regularly against these targets.
3. Provide performance data in a timely manner.
4. For each indicator, calculate key breakouts of data.
5. Include indicators of both "intermediate" outcomes and "end" outcomes in the performance measurement process, and clearly identify both types of indicators.
6. Ask programs to provide explanatory information with each performance report.
7. In agency training programs, routinely provide supervisors and managers with information on performance measurement and its uses.
8. When feasible, incorporate outcome-related performance requirements into contracts.
9. Consider including information on service quality and outcome progress as part of the performance appraisal process for internal employees, especially supervisors and managers.
10. Use information on service quality outcomes in formulating and justifying budgets.
11. Finally, do not expect outcome information to indicate the causes of the outcomes.

In another publication, Hatry, Craig Gerhart, and Martha Marshall offer public managers eleven specific suggestions to enhance the usefulness of performance data (see Figure 10–16).[22] These suggestions are based primarily on the authors' experience in Prince William County, Virginia, and deal with the following: the need to continually use (and reinforce the importance of) performance measures in program evaluations; data collection and reporting issues, such as timeliness, ease of collection, and disaggregation of the data; the need to explain not only changes (or the lack of changes) in measures but also external influences that were beyond the control of the reporting agency; the need to provide supervisors and managers with ongoing training in performance measurement and its uses; and suggestions for specific uses of outcome data.

Outcome data might be useful as performance specifications in contracts, as the core of progress reports in performance appraisals for internal employees, and as the basis for formulating and justifying budget requests; but the authors warn against expecting the outcome data to identify the reasons for a change in performance. The data indicate only that a change has taken place. Determining *why* it took place is the responsibility of the program and process managers (and is the subject of the next section).

The rest of this section looks in depth at three specific ways of displaying process data to help the numbers make sense and to aid in meaningful interpretation. The alternatives discussed here are the Pareto chart, the run chart, and the histogram.[23] When these three tools are used to display process data, a large number of data points begin to make sense and the analyst can identify meaningful patterns that indicate a special cause at work in the process. This cause must be identified. Again, the tools do not explain why the effect is there but merely reveal that it exists and that further study is needed.

The Pareto chart

A Pareto chart displays data in a series of bars arranged in descending height from left to right. The name comes from the Pareto Principle, which states that a small number of causes account for most of the problems. The display of data in this way breaks a big problem into small pieces, identifies the most significant factors contributing to the problem, and shows which areas are likely to respond most to changes and therefore which uses of limited resources are likely to be most productive.

An example is a situation in which there are delays in system response time. The data captured indicate that the delays are generated in several areas of the response process, as listed in Table 10–2. To prepare a Pareto chart for this or any other situation, one first orders the data elements from largest to smallest (see Table 10–3) and then places them into a Pareto chart, as in Figure 10–17. The *X* axis is the categories and the *Y* axis is the number of occurrences.

Table 10–2 Count of response time delays by point of occurrence.	Number of occurrences
Call-handling time	5
Dispatch time	25
Turn-out time	16
Unit response time	4

Table 10–3 Ordered count of response time delays by point of occurrence.	Number of occurrences
Dispatch time	25
Turn-out time	16
Call-handling time	5
Unit response time	4

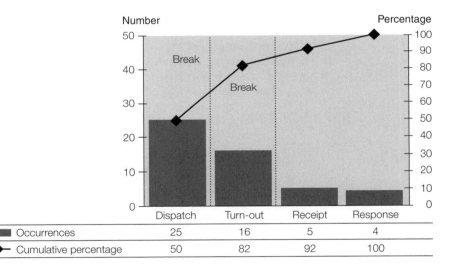

Figure 10–17   Pareto chart—System response time delays: Where delays are occurring.

	Dispatch	Turn-out	Receipt	Response
Occurrences	25	16	5	4
Cumulative percentage	50	82	92	100

In this case, two bars are significantly taller than the others. Both the dispatch segment and the turn-out segment of the process experienced a high number of delays. The cumulative percentage of the bar values is plotted as indicated by a single line. The first two bars, dispatch and turn-out, account for more than 80 percent of the total. The differences in bar heights between the first and second bars and between the second and third bars are much larger than the difference between the third and fourth bars. These dramatic differences in height are called the break points. The first break occurs after the dispatch bar;

the second, after the turn-out bar. Another way to spot the break is to note the break point(s) where the slope of the percentage line lessens significantly.

The objective of the analysis is to find the break points and focus attention on the factors to the left of them. If the reasons behind the delays in the two largest categories can be identified and corrected, 80 percent of the causes for delays, or variation in performance, can be eliminated. As mentioned above, Pareto charts allow one to focus one's efforts where they are likely to be most effective. If no break points are evident, one should evaluate other factors to see if a distinct pattern develops. For example, if all the process components have approximately the same number of delays, it might be useful to identify the length of delays in each category to focus one's primary efforts on reducing the delays in the category where they are longest.

The run chart

A run chart is a line graph that plots data points on process performance in chronological order. The data points can be measurements, counts, or percentages of process outputs. One uses the run chart to understand whether unusual variation exists in a process and, if so, to help identify what might be causing that unusual variation. One also uses the run chart to monitor process performance over time, and to communicate information about that performance to others.

Some variation in performance is expected. Unusual or excessive variation, however, must be brought under control before more sophisticated analysis can be performed to fine-tune the process performance. Run charts look for unusual variation as indicated by the existence of a trend, run, or cycle (defined below). Once statistical control of the process is achieved (i.e., once there is no trend, run, or cycle in at least 100 observations), additional analysis can be done.

To construct a run chart, one orders the data that have been captured from the process so that the range and median values can be determined. The median value for the process becomes the centerline of the graph, while the range is used to establish the Y axis. The X axis is the chronological time period represented by the data. If the process in question is the deployment time for a $1\frac{3}{4}''$ preconnected hand line from a pumper, data are collected for ten drills (see Table 10–4) and are ordered so that the range and centerline can be determined (see Table 10–5). The median value is 2.25, which becomes the

Table 10–4 Time to deploy 1¾″ preconnect.

Drill	1st	2nd	3rd	4th	5th	6th	7th	8th	9th	10th
Time	2.8	2.5	2.9	2.2	2.3	2.3	1.9	1.9	1.8	1.7

Table 10–5 Rank order of deployment times.

Rank order	Value
1	1.7
2	1.8
3	1.9
4	1.9
5	2.2
	Centerline (2.2 + 2.3)/2 = 2.25
6	2.3
7	2.3
8	2.5
9	2.8
10	2.9

centerline of the graph. All the data points are plotted in the order they were collected (see Figure 10–18).

As mentioned above, run chart analysis looks for unusual data-point variation that indicates the presence of special causes. The unusual variation itself can be for better or for worse, so its causes can be either positive or negative.

The three forms that an unusual variation may take are trends, runs, and cycles. A *trend* is a series of seven or more data points steadily increasing or decreasing with no change in direction. A repeating value stops the trend. When the run chart shows seven or more consecutive data points in a trend, the causes of the unusual variation must be investigated so that it can be understood. Figure 10–18 does not show a trend: the largest number of consecutive data points moving in one direction is two, between drills 8 and 10. If a trend were present, special causes would have to be investigated.

A *run* is present when two or more consecutive data points appear on the same side of the centerline. A run stops when a data point touches the centerline. If the process has not changed in any way, some variation above and below the line is expected. Thus, a run of nine or more consecutive data points on the same side of the centerline indicates a special cause, and the reasons for each run of nine or more data points should be investigated. The run chart in Figure 10–18 shows seven consecutive data points below the centerline starting with drill 4. If the eleventh and twelfth drills remain below the centerline, the causes for the run should be investigated.

A *cycle,* or repeating pattern of data points, is the third type of indicator of some special cause at work on the process. A cycle must occur eight times or more to be considered an indicator of a special cause. Figure 10–19 illustrates the pattern of a cycle.

Although the presence of a trend, a run, or a cycle indicates that there is a special cause (which must be investigated) for the unusual variation in the process, the absence of a trend, a run, or a cycle does not necessarily mean the process is without variation. Before one can say the process is in statistical control, the run chart should be done over a period of 100 observations without any signal of a special cause.

Once statistical control is achieved in a process, more sophisticated analysis can be conducted with the use of control charts, which establish upper and lower limits of the process specification and thereby enable the variations above and below those limits to be analyzed. Control charts are not addressed in more detail here, but the suggested readings for this chapter provide more information.

Figure 10–18   1¾" Run chart—Preconnect deployment: Time to deploy 1¾" preconnect, drills of Battalion 4.

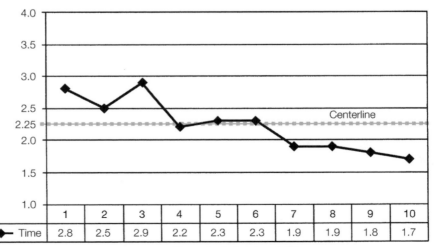

	1	2	3	4	5	6	7	8	9	10
Time	2.8	2.5	2.9	2.2	2.3	2.3	1.9	1.9	1.8	1.7

Chronological order of drills

Figure 10–19 Run chart showing a cycle pattern.

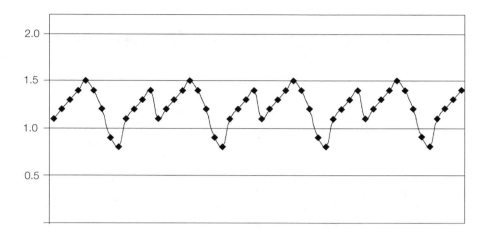

The histogram

A histogram is a vertical bar chart that displays the distribution of a set of data. It provides a snapshot of a process at a moment in time rather than the process's performance over time (as in the run chart). A histogram is used when one wants to summarize a large data set in graphical form, compare process performance with process limits, communicate information in a readily understandable format, and have a decision-making tool.

A histogram comprises vertical bars placed on the X axis. The X axis shows the scale for the values of the measurements. The bar's width represents the length of the interval represented by the bar. The bar's height is measured against the Y axis and represents the number of occurrences within the X axis interval. A legend is used to explain the source of the data. (Figure 10–20, which is discussed below, is a histogram.)

To construct a histogram, one does the following:

Count the number of data points to be displayed
Summarize the data points on a tally sheet
Compute the range
Determine the number of intervals to use
Compute the interval width
Determine the interval starting point
Plot the data
Add the title and legend.

Figure 10–20 Histogram of training times, Battalion 4.

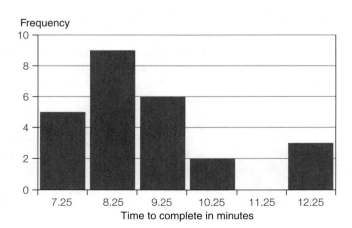

For example, a battalion chief has been given the data on crew performance for her assigned stations. The data were collected during the rotation of tactical unit crews to the fire academy for proficiency testing and captured the time that each crew took to complete the firefighting tactical exercise at the burn building. Of the twenty-five times that the drill was conducted, the time of completion ranged from a low of 7.25 minutes to a high of 12.75 minutes. The departmental standard for maximum time allowed is 10.25 minutes.

The first step in constructing a histogram is to count the number of data points; the second is to tally the data to determine the count of each data point and the range for the data (see Table 10–6).

Table 10–6   Count, tally, and range of training data.

Data point	Tally	
7.25	1	
7.75	2	Number of data points
8.0	2	25
8.25	2	Range
8.5	2	12.75 − 7.25 = 5.5
8.75	3	
9.0	2	
9.5	3	
9.75	3	
10.5	1	
10.75	1	
12.5	1	
12.75	2	
Total	25	

Next, one determines the number of intervals, or bars, that should be used to display the data on the histogram. Table 10–7 tells how to select the proper number on the basis of the number of data points in the sample.

Table 10–7 Determining the number of intervals.

Number of data points	Number of intervals to use
Under 50	5 to 7
50–90	6 to 10
100–250	7 to 12
More than 250	10 to 20

To determine the interval width, one divides the range by the number of intervals selected and rounds up to the next whole number. In this case, the range (5.5) is divided by 6 to equal 0.9, which is rounded up to 1. To determine the starting point for each interval, one begins with the lowest value—in this case, 7.25. This makes the intervals as shown in Table 10–8.

The data must now be plotted on the histogram (again, see Figure 10–20). The scale of the *X* axis is the previously determined intervals. The *Y* axis represents the frequency of observations in each interval. The bar height for each interval corresponds to the count of observations in each.

Table 10–8   Tally of measurements at the intervals selected.

Interval	Count
7.25–8.24	5
8.25–9.24	9
9.25–10.24	6
10.25–11.24	2
11.25–12.24	0
12.25–13.24	3

As mentioned above, histograms are graphical representations of summarized data. One can interpret histograms to determine whether performance meets expectations and what type of variation occurs during the performance period. From the distribution of the data, or groupings, one can tell whether the performance is within specification limits. In the histogram in Figure 10–20, the performances of most of the battalion units are grouped to the left of the maximum time allowed of 10.25 minutes, but several units exceeded the maximum time and are shown tailed off to the right.

A distribution that is relatively narrow and symmetrical shows little process variation. When the target performance is indicated on the histogram, the image gives an immediately comprehensible picture of how the process is performing (see Figure 10–21).

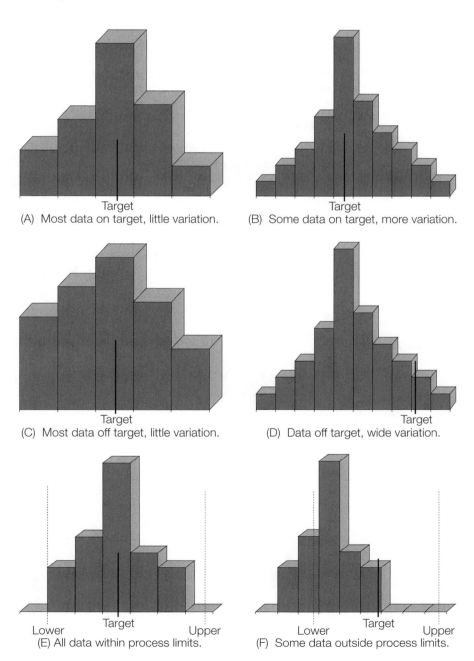

Figure 10–21
Histograms with target performances indicated.

(A) Most data on target, little variation.

(B) Some data on target, more variation.

(C) Most data off target, little variation.

(D) Data off target, wide variation.

(E) All data within process limits.

(F) Some data outside process limits.

Determining the causes of poor performance and eliminating them

As mentioned above, neither performance measures nor analysis explains why the performance problem exists. To discover the cause of the problem, one needs other tools. The fishbone cause-and-effect diagram (when completed, it resembles the skeleton of a fish) is particularly useful for this purpose.[24] With the fishbone, one divides the causes (there is generally more than one, and they are often interrelated) into groups, or categories. Grouping related causes allows one to evaluate the true part played by each. (For more on fishbone diagrams, see Chapter 8.)

To construct a fishbone cause-and-effect diagram, one does the following:

Develop a statement of the problem. Write it down on the right side of a piece of paper (the fish head). Draw a central arrow horizontally across the middle of the paper pointing to the statement of the problem (the fish skeleton backbone).

Brainstorm a list of potential causes of the problem. Write these on a separate piece of paper.

Review the list of causes and group them into major categories. Write the names of the categories as the main branches (fish bones) off the backbone.

On a separate piece of paper, list all causes under their appropriate categories. If necessary, revise or expand the original list.

Write each cause as a small branch of the line for the appropriate main category.

Figure 10–22 shows how a fishbone diagram might be used to identify the reason(s) a vehicle is getting poor gas mileage. The centerline points to the statement of the problem. Main branches lead to four categories of causes: methods, machinery, people, and materials. Specific causes are grouped under

Figure 10–22
Fishbone diagram.

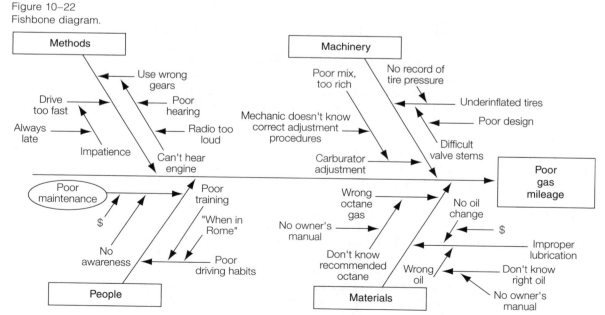

"Poor maintenance" is circled because measurements can perhaps be developed for it, and action taken. This cause should probably be investigated.

the appropriate major category. The problem-solving team's analysis of each variable will enable the team to identify the root causes of the problem and decide on priorities for those causes that should be pursued.

If one knows what the problems are and has discovered what is causing them, it is relatively easy to change performance. Performance problems usually turn out to be the result of an inadequate physical or psychological work environment, ineffective operating procedures, or failure to follow established procedures. When staff members fail to follow procedures, the reason is usually either that they have not learned the correct procedure or that they have deliberately chosen not to follow it. For performance problems not caused by deliberate acts, assessment of the problem and strategies for change generally focus on three areas: the work environment, operating procedures, and training.

1. *The work environment*   The work environment can be reengineered to eliminate the impediments, both physical and psychological, that have been identified. Reengineering may include changing or updating the tools and equipment available for performing the tasks. A task analysis of the process or an organizational/cultural analysis may be called for, depending on the severity of the problem. (Cultural analysis is discussed in detail in Chapter 8.)

2. *Operating procedures*   Operating procedures can be modified to take maximum advantage of the physical environment (tools and equipment, either existing or updated) and of staff capabilities.

3. *Training*   Staff can be trained, retrained, or coached in how to do the job.

Solutions to performance problems often involve some or all of the areas listed above. If analysis shows that neither the environment nor existing procedures need to be changed, the training solution is the only one applicable. (For more discussion of how to change performance, see Chapter 8.)

However, if the performance problem results from deliberate acts of omission or commission on the part of the member, a strategy for change must be developed that includes training or verification that the correct process steps are understood and that the importance of following the steps is also understood. The training must be followed by monitoring, coaching, and, if necessary, counseling and progressive discipline to correct the behavior.

Applying performance measurement in results-based budgeting

As mentioned at the beginning of this chapter, an important benefit of performance measurement is helping managers explain the effect of additional budgetary expenditures or reductions on achieving performance goals and objectives. The direct application of performance measurement in preparing and justifying budgets for specific programs or activities is called results-based (or outcome-based) budgeting.

In results-based budgeting, one develops budget requests by addressing specific community or organizational needs that have been identified by the community's strategic plan or the department's service improvement plan. To identify the areas needing improvement, one uses performance measures. One also uses performance measures to estimate the effect of the budget increases or decreases on closing the performance gap: the same properly crafted performance measures and thoughtful analysis that made clear where the problems were will also provide the means of analyzing the effect of any corrective changes.

For example, if the performance gap is in the system's or the unit's response times to emergencies, the budget request should propose solutions that will close the gap. The request should identify not only the cost of the solutions that are expected to improve service delivery but also the expected changes in the performance measures of the affected services. The clearer a department is about the specific improvements it expects, the more likely that the budget request will be approved.

Figure 10–23 is an extract from a results-based budget that speaks to converting a career medic unit from daytime-only staffing to twenty-four-hour-a-day staffing. This improvement involves adding two additional shifts of personnel for a total additional cost of $801,095. What is the community going to get for that increase in expenditures?

The budget document establishes a direct link to the county's strategic plan and provides background allowing the request to be understood in the context of that plan. The organization's mission statement shows how the department supports accomplishment of the strategic plan. The "major issues" section sets out the items of critical importance with respect to service delivery; the "FY 2000 budget additions" section contains narrative and data tables to clarify the need for, and effect of, the funding improvement. (The example in Figure 10–23 does not contain all the major issues or all the requests.)

The response-time improvements in the "service-level impacts" table show the expected improvements for important measures. The "FY 2000 base" column indicates what percentage the measure is expected to attain with no service improvement; the "FY 2000 adopted" column shows the percentage expected with the new funding level. The percentage of responses in Medic 3's first-due

Figure 10–23   Results-based budget justification for 24-hour medic unit staffing, Prince William County, Virginia.

Mission statement
The mission of the Department of Fire and Rescue is to provide quality fire, medical, emergency environmental, and support services for the community.

Major issues (partial)
Response time improvement   The Department of Fire and Rescue is working toward the FY 2001 strategic plan response time community outcomes of a 5% improvement in fire and basic life support (BLS) and 4% in advanced life support (ALS).

FY 2000 budget additions
24-hour medic unit—$801,095
Response time   The expansion of the existing medic unit at Dumfries from a daytime-only to a 24-hour/7-day-a-week (career-staffed) medic unit will have a significant effect on response times and coverage in this area. Dumfries is geographically remote from other stations with medic units that could provide ALS response assistance. This area is also geographically remote from the hospital, which heightens the need for prehospital ALS treatment. This unit will also provide regional coverage that will impact Montclair, Dale City, Woodbridge, and Coles. This unit will serve as support to the staffed medic unit assigned to Station 10 (Birchdale).
Emergency medical services (EMS) incidents   It is projected that 992 EMS incidents will be directly impacted during volunteer hours in the Dumfries Triangle and regional coverage response areas. This improvement will enhance delivery of BLS response times within 6.5 minutes and, more importantly, ALS response within 8 minutes.
Patient impact   843 of these patients will be treated and transported. 595 of these transports will be ALS patients. The figures and percentages shown below are for Dumfries Medic 3 only. These patients are expected to be treated for the following conditions:

Type of condition	Number of patients	Percentage of incidents
Medical emergencies (e.g., heart attack, stroke, asthma, and diabetes)	345	58
Trauma (e.g., car accidents, injuries from falls, burns)	202	34
Other (e.g., childbirth, poisonings, behavior emergencies)	48	8

areas that will meet the service delivery goal of advanced life support (ALS) within eight minutes is expected to increase more than 100 percent, rising from 35 percent to 75 percent. (For ALS response in high-density areas, the expected increase countywide is expected to be not quite 3 percent because the high-density area overall is so much larger than the first-due area overall.)

The importance of capturing and reporting good data (see Chapter 14) is evident. Good data give one the ability to show clear improvement in performance and to explain the effect of that improvement in human terms. In this example, the estimated call volume for the new unit is clearly stated; the types of emergencies the unit is expected to handle are presented; and the case is made that a total of 298 patients will receive lifesaving treatment. This information is important in enabling citizens, the governing body, and senior governmental officials to understand what they will be getting for the money they are being asked to spend. When everyone understands, everyone wins, including the fire and rescue department.

Avoiding the pitfalls of performance improvement and measurement

Efforts to improve performance require strong commitment, both formal and informal, by the organization's various leaders. If the fire and rescue chief is not committed, the efforts are likely to fail because subordinates will recognize

---

Medical intervention   Medical director estimates approximately 50% of our ALS responses fall into interventions that are immediately lifesaving, that result in a significantly better outcome than sickness and death, and that will shorten the critical disease stage that could result in death. This equates to 298 patients annually whom the proposed medic unit will treat to preserve the "chain of survival."

Strategic plan   This addition request is applicable to the public safety strategy goal and, more specifically, to the objective that "fire stations adequately respond to the needs of the community 24 hours per day." With the expansion of this existing daytime medic unit to a 24-hour medic unit, the county is ensuring that the needs of the community are adequately responded to 24 hours a day.

Desired community and program outcomes by 2001
Improve response time for ALS by 4%
Improve response time for BLS by 5%
Maintain citizen satisfaction with EMS at 97%

Service-level impacts	FY 2000 base, %	FY 2000 adopted, %
Improve ALS response time during volunteer hours in Medic 3 first due (90% target level)	35	75
Improve BLS response time during volunteer hours in Medic 3 first due (90% target level)	58	75
Improve ALS response time during volunteer hours in high-density areas (90% target level)	73	75
Improve BLS response time during volunteer hours in high-density areas (90% target level)	80	81

that the goal is not considered important. The same is true for the fire and rescue chief's boss. Likewise, if program and process managers are not involved and not committed to the effort, success is unlikely. In addition, both career and volunteer members of the organization should be involved in the process, for they are the people who will be capturing and reporting the basic performance data. If they do not understand the reasons for the effort—or, worse, if they oppose it—the likelihood of success is reduced. Similarly, process and activity team managers should be involved, for they are the people who must analyze the data and take corrective action depending on the results of the analysis. Unless everyone in the organization understands the purpose and effect of collecting the necessary information, there may be confusion and divisiveness. Unless support from the top is highly visible and consistent, the effort is likely to fail under the perceived weight of the additional workload.

For the data and analyses to be of high quality, the people capturing and analyzing the data must take the effort seriously and must have the requisite skills. The usefulness of performance measurement information is directly related both to the accuracy and completeness of the data collected and to the analytical skills of those interpreting the data. The data collected and the analyses performed become the bases of judgments about the effectiveness of programs and activities—about what is working and what is not. With complete and accurate data and sound analyses, the judgments are more likely to be good ones.

Finally, it is important not to be caught unawares when people—and there may be some—try to use the data and analyses against the organization. This attempt that may be made is not a legitimate reason for failing to collect the data and report the information. The positive gains in improving organizational performance and explaining what the community is getting for its money far outweigh any potential negative effects of high-quality collecting and reporting.

Summing up and looking ahead

Regardless of whether an organization is large or small, career or volunteer, performance measurement is a valuable tool in the effort to improve organizational performance. Performance measurement is the foundation for improving and monitoring an organization's programs, activities, and processes; it is the foundation for benchmarking with similar organizations to identify best practices and improve operations; and it is the key ingredient in results-based budgeting, enabling managers to explain how improved resources or new program initiatives will result in changed outcome measures. So although using performance measurement involves a substantial amount of work, the payoff is worth it.

One must ensure that the measures are tied to the goals and objectives of the jurisdiction's and department's strategic plans. One must also ensure that stakeholders are involved in developing the measures and that the things that get measured are the important things.

Measures should be developed at the levels of the organization, the process, and the job/performer and, at each level, for each of the three needs (goals, design, and management). The process-level work team will often obtain the most dramatic improvement. At every level (but especially that of the work team), supervisors and managers must have access to the performance measures and must use them to identify and correct unwanted variances in outcome.

In the future, as more jurisdictions learn how to use performance measurement, fire and rescue managers—whether career, combination, or volunteer—will be held increasingly accountable for their organization's performance or lack of it. Middle-level managers will have to become comfortable with and proficient at performance measurement, which cannot remain an activity of concern only to office staff. And work unit leaders will have to learn how to use quantitative measurement and analytical methods to describe the performance of their work units. In short, the successful fire and rescue manager of the decade 2001–2010 will be as proficient in developing and interpreting run charts and other quality assurance and improvement tools as in working with pre-fire plans. As a result, benchmarking will become the norm instead of the exception.

Learning how to measure performance, how to analyze the data obtained, and how to use the data and analyses to improve operational outcomes is the challenge facing all supervisors and managers in the fire and rescue service. There is much to be learned and much to be gained.

1   Clarence E. Ridley and Herbert A. Simon, *Measuring Municipal Activities: A Survey of Suggested Criteria for Appraising Administration* (Chicago: International City Managers' Association, 1943), cited in David N. Ammons, ed., *Accountability for Performance: Measurement and Monitoring in Local Government* (Washington, D.C.: International City/County Management Association, 1995), 1.

2   Alan Ehrenhalt, "Performance Budgeting, Thy Name Is . . . ," *Governing* 8 (November 1994): 9, cited in Ammons, ed., *Accountability for Performance,* 1–2.

3   Ammons, ed., *Accountability for Performance,* 1.

4   Insurance Services Office (ISO), *Fire Suppression Rating Schedule*, Edition 08-98 (New York: ISO, 1980, 1998).

5   Ibid., 1.

6   Ibid.

7   Ibid., 2.

8   The information here on the Commission on Fire Accreditation International is provided by Ronny J. Coleman, FiFireE, CFC, Chairman, and CFAI Board of Trustees.

9   Harry P. Hatry, James R. Fountain Jr., Lorraine Kremer, and Jonathan M. Sullivan, eds., *Service Efforts and Accomplishments Reporting: Its Time Has Come; An Overview* (Norwalk, Conn.: Governmental Accounting Standards Board, 1990).

10   Geary A. Rummler and Alan P. Brache, *Improving Performance: How to Manage the White Space on the Organization Chart* (San Francisco: Jossey-Bass, 1990), 10.

11   Ibid., 192.

12   Ibid., 193.

13   Prince William County, Virginia, 1995 Strategic Plan, 12.

14   George D. Robson, *Continuous Process Improvement: Simplifying Workflow Systems* (New York: The Free Press, 1991).

15   Ibid., 110.

16   National Highway Traffic Safety Administration, "A Leadership Guide to Quality Improvement for Emergency Medical Services (EMS) Systems" (Washington, D.C.: U.S. Department of Transportation, July 1997).

17   Richard Fischer, "An Overview of Performance Measurement," *Public Management* 76 (September 1994): S3–S4.

18   William G. Gay, "Benchmarking: Achieving Superior Performance in Fire and Emergency Medical Services," *MIS Report* (ICMA) 25 (February 1993): 6.

19   Ibid., 16.

20   Harry P. Hatry et al., *How Effective Are Your Community Services? Procedures for Measuring Their Quality*, 2nd ed. (Washington, D.C.: The Urban Institute and the International City/County Management Association, 1992), 93–94.

21   Ibid., 93.

22   Harry P. Hatry, Craig Gerhart, and Martha Marshall, "Eleven Ways to Make Performance Measurement More Useful to Public Managers," *Public Management* (September 1994): S15–S18.

23   Information in this section is adapted from *Handbook for Basic Process Improvement: Tools for Basic Process Improvement* (Washington, D.C.: Total Quality Leadership Office, U.S. Department of the Navy, 1992).

24   National Highway Traffic Safety Administration, "A Leadership Guide to Quality Improvement."

11 Health, wellness, and injury prevention

Health, wellness, and the prevention of injuries have become increasingly important management issues in local government. During the 1980s, there was growing recognition that health conditions (e.g., certain cancers and heart disease) were affecting the lives of firefighters around the country. At the same time, each year there were more than one hundred line-of-duty deaths from a variety of causes, but about 50 percent of them were from heart attacks or heat stress.[1]

To organizations such as the International Association of Fire Fighters, the International Association of Fire Chiefs, and the National Fire Protection Association (NFPA), the data indicated that firefighters were sustaining a relatively high risk of becoming sick or dying from occupational hazards. These findings produced much concern, which led fire chiefs and local government officials across the country to form committees to analyze the problem and produce recommendations aimed at reducing the number of deaths and injury-related incidents affecting firefighters. Those who were involved realized that the problem had two components: poor physical health and the absence of a comprehensive wellness program to provide adequate protection.

As used in this chapter, the terms *health* and *wellness* overlap a great deal. *Health* describes the state of the body, principally in terms of things that can be measured (e.g., blood pressure, height, weight) and the data generated from, for example, X-ray studies, blood and urine analyses, vision testing, and so forth. Although mental health, too, can be assessed, the results are more often qualitative or descriptive. *Wellness* includes health but extends beyond it and is best thought of in terms of fitness for certain specific activities. ("General" wellness can be thought of as fitness for living in general.) The difference between health and wellness is illustrated by the hypothetical example of an Olympic skier with a broken leg: this person can be considered healthy but is not particularly fit. Both health and wellness are influenced by factors such as occupational and environmental exposures, sex, age, genetic makeup, and lifestyle.

As concepts, both health and wellness are elusive, for they are hard to define with precision. After all, there is no unit of measurement for either of them. If

---

A definition of physical fitness
According to a position stand of the American College of Sports Medicine, "the term 'physical fitness' is composed of a variety of characteristics included in the broad categories of cardiorespiratory fitness, body composition including regional fat distribution, muscular strength and endurance, and flexibility. In this context, fitness is defined as the ability to perform moderate-to-vigorous levels of physical activity without undue fatigue and the capability of maintaining this capacity throughout life."[1]

[1]Michael L. Pollock et al., "The Recommended Quantity and Quality of Exercise for Developing and Maintaining Cardiorespiratory and Muscular Fitness, and Flexibility in Healthy Adults," *Medicine & Science in Sports & Exercise®* 30 (June 1998). Available at www.msse.org.

someone's state of health or wellness could be put as "73 health units" or "14 percent well," the two concepts would be easier to comprehend.

The third concept with which this chapter is concerned, *prevention of injuries,* also cannot be measured in units. But experience in a variety of occupational settings shows that workers who are healthy and fit, who are alert, contented, and trained, have lower accident rates and less-severe injuries than workers who are not. There is a close connection, therefore, between wellness and prevention of injuries.

Because the joint concept of health and wellness is becoming ever more complex, managers often prefer to study and deal with it in terms of one or more programs. (On starting a health and wellness program, see the accompanying sidebar.) The basic mission of a health and wellness program should be to preserve the operational strength of the organization by addressing the health (physical and mental) and fitness of the organization's human resources —the career and volunteer firefighters and the support staff. Today it is known that a healthy and fit workforce is both safer and more operationally effective; and reliable data may reveal that a healthy, fit workforce is also cost-effective. In addition, the natural spin-offs from health and wellness programs can be repackaged to have a very positive effect on the community. Many fire departments sponsor health-oriented educational activities and projects for their communities, including childhood immunization programs, urban survival, pool safety, and classes in cardiopulmonary resuscitation. The Phoenix (Arizona) Fire Department's program about personal safety touches on thirty-five different dangers to children.

For people in physically taxing occupations such as firefighting, the measurable objectives of a wellness program include such things as the achievement or maintenance of a healthy heart rate and blood pressure, an improvement in the blood lipid profile to lower the coronary risk ratio, a change (usually a lowering) in body fat composition, an increase in strength and flexibility, and an improvement in cardiovascular conditioning. Any wellness program, however, must also address the mental aspects of wellness.

The classic managerial approach to safety, or prevention of injuries, has also been to develop programs. And like wellness programs, safety (or injury-prevention) programs must consider the mental as well as physical aspects of the subject.

Safety is a learned behavior; people are not genetically either safe or unsafe. But by the time recruits enter a fire service program or a fire training academy, they have already had twenty-plus years of learned behavior involving—among other things—traffic situations; sports; the military; recreational activities; use of vehicles; use of tools and firearms; and exposure to disease, alcohol, and drugs. From a practical standpoint, therefore, safety training, or safety learning, is a career-long effort that covers both on-the-job and off-the-job situations. Hence all training programs must include safety as part of the curriculum.

Prevention-program reporting can be deceiving, for there is no direct way to prove how many accidents a program has actually prevented. Thus, if a report quantifies the number of accidents prevented, managers should look long and hard at the mathematical assumptions underlying the data.

Important health and medical concerns for firefighters

The demands of the firefighter's job are stressful, random in occurrence, and often physically challenging. Firefighters who are already mentally or physically exhausted from their response to a call may nonetheless have to respond to subsequent requests for emergency services before their shifts end. Given this situation, firefighters and their health and wellness programs will continue to have several important health and medical concerns in the twenty-first century.

Starting a health and wellness program Typically, the person or group appointed to manage a wellness program in a fire department is already interested in some areas of health and fitness and thus has the interest and knowledge to develop the basic elements necessary for starting a program. The fire chief's first step should be to identify this person (or group) and assign him or her the responsibility of managing the program. Care should be taken to make sure that the program is versatile enough to be attractive to as many department members as possible rather than being focused on the organizer's favorite activity. For instance, some people do not like to run or jog but can get the same fitness results from a brisk walk or other activity.

A departmental labor-management team can be used to gather information about personal needs, produce operating procedures, identify the equipment and facilities needed, and propose a plan to start (and maintain) a meaningful wellness program. The team must have representation from throughout the department and must gain all necessary approvals as it proceeds.

The program manager must have the responsibility of surveying the department's members about their specific needs, evaluating the resources available, establishing time frames, and identifying the issues of department members as a group. Maintaining confidentiality, making the program mandatory, and dealing with those who do not wish to participate are the kinds of group issues that can make or break the program.

Depending on the size of the department, this preliminary work could take considerable time and become somewhat complicated, especially with respect to personal issues. The program manager, fire chief, and departmental labor-management group, however, must stay focused on what the program can do for the majority of the members and the department; they must be careful not to focus on issues that affect only a few people, lest the program be undermined by lack of support from the membership as a whole.

Source: Thomas Healy, chief, Daisy Mountain Fire Department, Phoenix, Arizona.

Guidelines for a safety program
Safety is a mindset, a mental and intellectual state, a discipline. Safety programs should be designed and followed to

Reinforce and refine existing patterns of safe behavior

Teach new patterns of safe behavior

Practice techniques

Supplement safety concepts with physical activities, exercises, and/or drills to cause the safe behavior to become ingrained.

Serious injuries on trips to and from emergency incidents

Historically, one of the most dangerous parts of a fire call has been the ride—the trip to the incident and the trip back to the station. Burns, sprains, lacerations, and blunt trauma incurred during the two trips will account for a significant amount of what we can expect to continue seeing as part of the occupational risks of firefighting. As airline personnel used to admonish passengers upon arrival at the destination airport, "Thank you for flying with [Name of] Airlines. The most dangerous part of your journey will begin when you start to drive home from the airport."

Local government managers can approach fire department administrators to learn when, where, and under what conditions serious accidents have occurred and whether a safety program is in place that addresses such things as use of seat belts, availability and use of protective equipment, driving with flashing red lights and siren, and so forth.

Heat stress

Heat stress is the occupational disease of the firefighter. The body is a constant-temperature heat machine that, when subjected to a hot environment, requires continuous cooling. The cooling is accomplished almost entirely by the evaporation of sweat. For the cooling process to function efficiently, the body must have a supply of fluid (water) and certain electrolytes (principally sodium and potassium); it must also have some "free" surface area *from* which sweat can evaporate; and it must have air space (the drier the better) *into* which sweat can evaporate. The kidneys help manage this evaporative cooling process by sorting, saving, excreting, and filtering the fluids and electrolytes presented to them.

When the body is unable (for whatever reason) to achieve adequate cooling, a condition called *heat stress* develops. The body's core temperature starts to rise, and other body systems become affected. Without adequate cooling, the body's strength and reflexes deteriorate rapidly. If the heat stress continues, the body gives up—loses its ability to cope with heat. This condition, usually characterized by loss of consciousness and lack of sweating, is termed *heat stroke*. Heat stroke is a bona fide medical emergency.

The problem of classic heat-stress disease within the fire service has been well documented.[2] Encasing the body within a fully turned-out envelope of protective equipment (see Figure 11–1) effectively halts sweat evaporation—the principal process by which body temperature is regulated. The addition of physical activity accelerates the onset of symptoms (fatigue, syncope, cramps). Heat-stress disease itself is treatable, especially if detected early, but when an environment characterized by heat stress is coupled with hard physical work, the result can be acute exertional rhabdomyolysis (AER): small fragments resulting from the breakdown of muscle clog the kidneys' filtration system. AER can cause permanent kidney damage and kidney failure.

Cancer

When firefighters discuss the long-term occupational risks associated with their work, the question they most often ask is "Am I more at risk for developing cancer because of my job?"

Behind this question lies the presumption that firefighting entails exposure to chemical compounds that cause cancer (see, e.g., Figure 11–2). Chemical carcinogens can gain access to the body in several ways: by injection or penetration, via the respiratory tract (breathing), by direct contact with the skin or mucous membranes, or by ingestion. However, although many fire departments (as well as most individual firefighters) are now documenting the incidents of actual and potential exposure to chemical compounds, in most cases it is not known precisely what chemical compounds were encountered. Thus the exposure diary often cannot identify the compounds accurately. To complicate matters still further, researchers correlate the risk of cancer with the length of the exposure to and the concentration of the substance (i.e., parts per million or percentages). Firefighters simply cannot be expected to have this information. When individual records of exposure to unknown potential carcinogens are so often incomplete, it is virtually impossible to establish cause-and-effect relationships for cancer. In some states, therefore, firefighters' cancers are, by law, presumed to be job related.

Figure 11–1 (Top) A fully turned-out envelope of protective firefighting clothing. (Center) Firefighters decked out in full protective dress as well as self-contained breathing apparatus (SCBA), leaving no outlet for sweat evaporation. (Bottom) A firefighter encased in a hazardous materials (HAZMAT) "moon suit."

Figure 11–2   A dump site fire can put firefighters at risk for exposure to both airborne and soilborne carcinogens.

Furthermore, firefighters, like everyone else, are exposed to the "invisible" forces that have also been linked to cancer: X rays, for example. And we are all more or less at risk of developing cancer as a result of lifestyle (diet, drugs, use of tobacco, etc.), the state of our immune system (which is affected by everything from mental health to ingestion of antioxidants), and our genetic profile (sex, ethnicity, heredity).

No discussion of cancer would be complete without reference to tobacco. Very little need be said here about the use of smoking tobacco, which has been clearly shown to have carcinogenic effects and may have financial effects as well. In states, provinces, and countries that have presumptive heart-lung laws (laws according to which any firefighter's death or disability from heart or lung disease is presumed to be job related, even if the person used tobacco), smoking carries a financial liability. Alternatively, depending on either the restrictions placed on specific benefit plans or the content of legislation relating to occupational disabilities, firefighters could lose certain medical-related pension benefits if they smoke.

When smoking is banned or discouraged on the job, however, another problem may arise. In that situation, some occupational groups—firefighters among them—often succumb to the lure of smokeless (or spit) tobacco. The ingredients in spit tobacco are not listed on the containers, nor are the manufacturers required to affix warning labels (as they are for smoke tobacco), so the long-term effects of spit tobacco are not widely publicized. Nevertheless, the body of evidence about the harmful effects of spit tobacco—effects such as mouth and tongue cancer—is mounting.

In summary, no definitive evidence yet exists that firefighters have a greater risk of cancer than the general population. This lack of evidence that firefighting increases one's risk of cancer may be due to the fact that firefighters do not work exclusively at firefighting; they often have other, supplemental jobs, and these may involve exposure to carcinogens. Furthermore, people hired to be firefighters are presumably in better health than the general population. However, several precautions can be taken to substantially improve firefighters' chances for enjoying a healthy and extended retirement. These precautions consist of proper training, superior protective equipment, a competent administration and command structure, emphasis on healthier lifestyles, and support for monitoring and early detection programs.

Cancer checklist

Protect your lungs, dilute dangerous air, and wear and maintain your personal protective equipment (PPE) It is known that chemical carcinogens can enter the body in four ways (injection or penetration, breathing, direct contact with the skin or mucous membranes, or ingestion). It is also known that a fully turned-out firefighter is well protected: PPE, properly worn and maintained, is the key to that protection. The respiratory tract is the most vulnerable part of the body, so a department should consider diluting the concentration of pollutants at incidents by using fans. Potential exposure may also exist post-fire, especially during overhaul. (Post-fire refers to the period when firefighters are still on the premises of the incident but the fire has already been put out; overhaul refers to that part of the post-fire period when the scene is being cleaned up and the equipment —fans, etc.—is being removed and put back on the trucks.) During overhaul, the respiratory tract can be protected with self-contained breathing apparatus (SCBA) or filter masks. Diesel exhaust has been identified as a potential carcinogen, so firefighters should turn off the truck motors, if possible; not run truck motors in closed spaces; ventilate whenever possible; and if all else fails, wear SCBA.

Prevention—what you can do for yourself Smoking and diet are two risk factors for cancer. Grilled steak and burning houses have much in common, for both are potential carcinogens. Eating fruits and vegetables may exert a protective effect on the body; because of dietary variations among individuals, some nutritional experts recommend supplemental intake of the antioxidants, vitamins A (beta carotene), C, and E. (Getting the advice of a doctor is always a good precaution to take.) Research into the environmental and behavioral risk factors for cancer and, by implication, its prevention is ongoing. Studies have shown, however, that the immune systems of cheerful, happy people are generally stronger than those of dejected or depressed people.

Monitoring and early detection—what your department can do for you If it is presumed that firefighters are at increased risk because of their occupation and that they protect themselves with PPE and adopt lifestyles that help prevent malignancies, it makes sense for departments to establish monitoring programs designed to detect cancer early. Some specific examples of monitoring programs are prostate screening for men, PAP smears for women, and colon exams and melanoma screening for members of both sexes. Ideally these monitoring and early detection efforts will be woven into a comprehensive health program designed for the monitoring and early detection of all diseases and medical conditions, not just cancer. (See the section on "The Structure of a Comprehensive Health and Wellness Program for Front-Line Firefighters.")

Once disease is detected, treatment must be initiated immediately. Haste must be made, but deliberately enough to get the best medical opinions, the best facilities, and the best physicians.

Heart disease and stroke

The cardiovascular system is the main target of the contemporary wellness movement, the goal of which is to reduce the risk of a heart attack or stroke by modifying the so-called changeable risk factors (e.g., blood pressure, percentage of body fat, tolerance for exercise, blood lipid profile, and lifestyle). The contemporary wellness movement has also focused on decreasing or eliminating the use of tobacco, drugs, alcohol, and certain prescription medications —all of which are risk factors for heart disease and stroke—while encouraging education related to stress-reduction techniques and diet. These concerns are particularly relevant to firefighting, which is among the occupations with the largest number of heart attack deaths.[3]

Cardiovascular wellness is therefore absolutely essential to any general wellness program. The sources of specific information about it are almost limitless, and local government managers might want to become more familiar with the fundamentals—especially because so many states either have presumptive heart-lung laws (defined above) or are being urged to pass them. In jurisdictions with such laws, cardiovascular wellness could result in financial savings.

Mental health and the SAD (stress, alcohol, and drugs) diseases

Mental health is a major component of total wellness. In particular, stress is a mental condition that is said to be responsible for everything from depression to eating disorders, drug and alcohol problems, and anxiety.

Life has always been difficult, but each year it seems to become even more stressful for many people. In addition to the stress factors common to everyone, however, firefighters must cope with the need to always operate in a "cocked-and-ready" mode, often without normal patterns of sleep. And their stress levels are affected by what they see and do on the job.

Depression—which stress may exacerbate—is a feeling of intense sadness; it may follow a recent loss or other sad event but is out of proportion to that event and persists beyond an appropriate length of time. Depression can accompany other medical problems and is often mentioned as an underlying condition associated with suicide. Medically, there is mounting scientific evidence that depression can adversely affect the immune system. Often, however, depression can be successfully treated.

Drug and alcohol problems, too, may be exacerbated by stress. But although the magnitude of these two problems is staggering, treatment programs exist for them as well as for virtually every other addiction and addictive behavior. (Alcoholics Anonymous [AA], e.g., has worked well for many people addicted to alcohol, and for gamblers, there is Gamblers Anonymous.)

Dealing with stress Very few organizations outside of the military specifically train people to deal with the stress they can expect to encounter. One of the best of mental health support systems is built into the fire service, and that system is the close bond of collegiality and friendship that characterizes people who must work together as a team under stressful and potentially dangerous conditions. In certain circumstances, however, this support system is a disadvantage for the firefighter—for example, when it encloses him or her so effectively that the needed external treatment (such as professional counseling, medical treatment, or both) is either delayed or withheld. The aftermath of the terrorist attacks of September 11, 2001, will add a great deal of new information about the mental health aspects of firefighting.

Burnout People in highly stressful occupations (e.g., emergency medical service personnel) may develop a condition commonly referred to as *burnout*. Burnout is characterized by mild depression, loss of energy and appetite, and diminished interpersonal skills. Although the medical literature on whether burnout is a specific disease is controversial, local government managers can gain insight into a fire department by discussing the incidence of burnout with the department's administrators.

During the 1990s many public safety departments began using critical incident stress debriefing (CISD) teams, whose purpose is to provide emotional support by listening to, befriending, and counseling firefighters and their families in times of great emotional stress, both on and off the job. In some jurisdictions this function is extended to victims of fire, violence, and other disasters. If properly trained and managed, CISD teams can be of great service. Their debriefings should not, however, take precedence over (or be promoted as a substitute for) adequate sleep, good nutrition, and personal attention to one's own emotional and spiritual needs.

Mental health program checklist

Begin with a team and a plan   Start (or energize) your educational programs with respect to drugs, alcohol, and other addictions by focusing on the supervisory people. Teach them how to recognize addictive, self-destructive behavior and give them the network and tools to move people into treatment channels. Get some expert help. This is where a trained, dedicated physician can provide advice and guidance. And do not overlook or minimize the potential contribution that, for some people, clergy may make in this effort. Besides providing access to a physician, therefore, a department may arrange to make a chaplain's time available as well.

Be alert to the use of drugs and alcohol   Recognize, understand, and accept that in the United States, all use of drugs and alcohol in the workplace (except for a few prescription medications) is illegal and dangerous for everyone. If you have an employee assistance program, use it. If not, create one. Get Alcoholics Anonymous (AA) or another treatment program involved. If a problem of drug or alcohol abuse exists in your department, seek legal advice about the disciplinary and other options available to you.

Recognize inappropriate or destructive behavior   Pay attention to behavior that is destructive (to self or others) or that does not seem to fit the situation. Do not make light of such behavior or dismiss it, facilitate it, or escalate it. Above all, do not look the other way. Plan in advance how you are going to deal with inappropriate behavior. Remember: discipline alone does not resolve every case of inappropriate behavior.

Become more observant   Become more observant, especially of changes in attitude and/or participation in group events or discussions. Does the person's body language or conversation send a message of despair? Such a message may be a subtle plea for help.

Be ready to act   As of 1998, suicide was the eighth leading cause of death in the United States and accounted for 15 percent of deaths among people between the ages of 25 and 44.[1] If someone attempts or threatens to commit suicide, make absolutely certain that he or she is not left alone until the management of that person is formally turned over to a mental health professional capable of dealing with the situation.

Accept the fact that a price will have to be paid   Accept the fact that almost always a price has to be paid for relief of depression and removal of the person's concomitant dependence on drugs and alcohol. For some, loss of social status and of close friendships may become the price for sobriety: giving up drugs or alcohol may mean giving up one's former "drinking buddies" or avoiding friends whose social activities revolve around drugs. Some "friends" who use alcohol or drugs themselves may not support a person who has given these substances up; thus, the former abuser may be cut off from his or her former social circle. The person's supervisor may therefore have to deal with an employee who now feels lost, alone, or rejected; and the supervisor may have to encourage the employee to develop compensations for the loss.

[1] National Center for Health Statistics, *National Vital Statistics Reports* 48 (July 24, 2000): 26.

Sex-based medical issues

The integration of women into the fire service has led to some accommodations (e.g., in the shape and cut of uniforms, gloves, and shoes, and in the remodeling of stations to provide bathrooms and sleeping quarters for women). From the standpoint of health and wellness, the introduction of women into the ranks of firefighters has made it essential for health and wellness programs to provide sex-specific procedures and awareness. In the area of screening and early detection, examples such as the PAP test for cervical/uterine cancer and mammography for breast cancer come to mind. Screening technology for diseases of both sexes will continue to evolve.

A much more complicated workplace issue of women's health has to do with the potential for pregnancy. Every female firefighter in her childbearing years who has an intact reproductive system can potentially become pregnant. Since very early pregnancy is not always detected or detectable, there exists a temporal gray period when toxic, hazardous, or occupational exposures may affect a developing fetus. Once a pregnancy is ascertained, any accommodations, restrictions, or limitations with respect to duty assignments necessarily become a more individualized matter.

Local government managers should learn about policies and practices related specifically to female firefighters, especially those of childbearing age. Are the existing policies regarding pregnant firefighters realistic from the standpoint of health?

Infectious diseases and hazardous materials

Firefighters the world over will undoubtedly continue to work in hazardous and unfriendly environments. They will perform despite heat, noise, swift water, darkness, fatigue, and pain because they have been trained to deal with these problems—problems they can see or feel. Other occupational perils, however, cannot be readily seen or felt. These are the serious infectious diseases (human immunodeficiency virus [HIV], hepatitis B and C, tuberculosis, meningitis) and the silent toxins, gases, and radiation. The only remedy is constant

Figure 11–3   A HAZMAT identification placard.

vigilance and a comprehensive program of protection, monitoring, education, and training. (See also Chapter 13.)

In addition, firefighters—like everyone else—may have toxic or hazardous exposures when they are off the job. From the standpoint of screening and early detection, therefore, it is important to know what potential exposures could be associated with such things as a second job, recreational activities, hobbies, trips, and pets.

Health and wellness in relation to recruitment, selection, and basic training

Health and wellness activities have three main functions within the fire and rescue service: they play a role in the recruitment, selection, and basic training of firefighters; they make up ongoing programs for front-line firefighters; and they support community health education. The first two functions are discussed in this section and the next. For a discussion of health and wellness in relation to community education, see Chapter 12.

The customary objective of a fire department's recruitment and selection process is to recruit and select mentally and physically healthy, trainable people for entry into a formal instructional program. The recruitment and selection must be done within the framework of applicable laws, rules, and administrative regulations (see Chapter 5).

Historically, a number of occupations and professions have developed rigorous standards that individuals must meet in order to qualify for a position and then to retain it. In this regard, the fire service is similar to the military, the airline industry, the police, and other fields that have identifiable physical and training requirements. Sometimes these standards are reinforced by laws and ordinances. In the fire service, NFPA standards in the 1500 series have been developed through research and public comment and are an excellent starting point for discussion and action.

Hard and fast departmental rules and rigid physical standards are frequently challenged, however, so public safety administrators must balance two sets of responsibilities. On the one hand, they must abide by the legal definition of *qualified* as it applies to public safety applicants and trainees (as well as to firefighters and chiefs). On the other hand, they must ensure the safety and protection of citizens. Members of the public need to have confidence in the physical, technical, and emotional proficiency of the people responding to their emergencies (fires, traumas, etc.), just as they need to have confidence in flight crews when traveling on an airline, for example (but with respect to the fire service, members of the public have no choice as to who responds to their emergencies).

Accordingly, managers should learn whether the fire and rescue departments

---

Health and wellness in training recruits In addition to working in the classroom and learning basic firefighting techniques and the proper use of equipment, firefighter recruits usually spend a great deal of time in physical conditioning. Most moderate injuries incurred during training (e.g., shin splints, sprains, strains, contusions, and bruises) occur during physical conditioning or when the recruits are becoming familiar with the equipment. The more severe medical problems—for recruits, as for experienced firefighters—are related to heat stress, which is exacerbated by hard physical work. Some mental health problems may arise in connection with beginning a new career. Occasionally, previously masked problems of substance abuse may emerge.

Figure 11–4   Firefighter recruits warming up and working out to meet physical and training requirements.

Testing for physical performance and for trainability   In some jurisdictions the recruitment and selection process for firefighters is supplemented (or preceded) by pretest educational programs. Should pretesting and remedial programs also be considered for the physical performance part of the selection process? Can local organizations such as community colleges, the YMCA or YWCA, or sports teams be involved in the physical conditioning effort?

In addition, if capacity for training is the entry point, consider testing a recruit for the ability to be trained to perform the tasks of a firefighter. If the department's company officers are developed through internal promotions, the standard of trainability should be incorporated into the recruitment, testing, and selection process.

in their communities conduct systematic and repetitive proficiency testing (including testing in safety procedures) for applicants, trainees, and front-line firefighters alike. To continue the airline analogy: if a pilot or prospective pilot does not pass the "landing the airplane" test, cannot see the map book, cannot reach the pedals, or is too obese to fit into the pilot's seat, that person will not be allowed to pilot (or continue to pilot) a commercial aircraft.

Managers should learn about their own fire departments' standards for recruiting, selecting, and training and about the procedures for developing, enforcing, modifying, and revising these standards. They should, moreover, form a clear picture of their departments' expectations *before* having to make decisions.

The structure of a comprehensive health and wellness program for front-line firefighters

The initial description of a health and wellness program for front-line firefighters often centers on measurable elements (e.g., strength, in bench-press pounds; endurance, in time on the treadmill; percentage of body fat; and blood pressure). Unfortunately, much less attention is given to mental health and overall fitness. A comprehensive program must address not only health—physical and mental alike—but also wellness.

Enlightened fire administrators, union leaders, and local government managers are helping to educate the public safety community about the benefits of comprehensive wellness programs. A prime example of educating the public safety community is the IAFF/IAFC Wellness-Fitness Initiative introduced in 1998, developed and sponsored jointly by the International Association of Fire Fighters and the International Association of Fire Chiefs.[4] The Wellness-Fitness Initiative is a complete wellness program designed to fit the needs of firefighters and written by a committee on which both management and labor were represented.

For a health and wellness program to be effective, it must include eight fundamental structural elements, which must be linked: health baselines, periodic assessments, prevention programs, early detection, prompt and competent intervention, treatment, rehabilitation, and policies on return to work and alternative duty assignments. (The next section discusses the content of a comprehensive program.)

It is very important to note that medical records *must* be treated as confidential. Managers should make certain that the laws, customs, and conventions affecting access to medical records in the particular jurisdiction are being followed and that everyone is aware of the rules.

Health baseline A health baseline should be established for every member of the department. This is done with a physical examination, a medical and occupational history, and appropriate laboratory testing. In most departments this step will start during the selection process. The costs will vary with the depth and breadth of the examination, but comprehensive health baselines are very important and, as time goes on, will prove valuable for all concerned.

Periodic assessments Periodic assessments are used to detect any variation in the health status of the individual. A great deal of judgment is involved in achieving a happy medium between what is minimally needed for periodic assessments and what the departmental budget allows. This problem of bridging this gap between what is needed and what is affordable has been approached in a number of innovative ways: many departments use their own paramedics to help; medical doctors, physicians' assistants, and nurses sometimes volunteer, as do hospitals and clinics; and charitable organizations are occasionally willing to help financially.

Prevention programs   Prevention programs should be directed first at known exposure risks. Prevention can take several forms: a medicine, the use of specific techniques or equipment, or education. In the case of hepatitis B, for example, prevention takes all three forms. A vaccine is available, there are standard precautions to take with emergency medical service patients (see, e.g., Figure 11–5), there are specific techniques for disposing of contaminated materials, and a variety of educational opportunities exist. The more mundane aspects of protection that are intrinsic to the fire service should not be overlooked; among them are earplugs, gloves, self-contained breathing apparatus, face shields, and seat belts. Prevention programs for mental health, by their very nature (involving, e.g., invasion of privacy), receive much less emphasis. To help raise awareness of the problem, posters in the workplace can remind personnel that mental health is important and that counseling is available.

Early detection   Early detection is the basis of a truly effective health and wellness effort. Medically, early detection is achieved by means of screening exams or tests, which are commonly used to detect such things as cancers (of the prostate, testicle, breast, cervix, colon, skin); infectious diseases (HIV, hepatitis, tuberculosis); and enlargement or abnormalities of the thyroid, lymph nodes, and internal organs. Mental health issues, too, including depression and problems related to drugs and/or alcohol, may surface during the early detection health assessment.

Figure 11–5   For a paramedic, standard precautions include outfitting with protective mask, sleeves, and gloves.

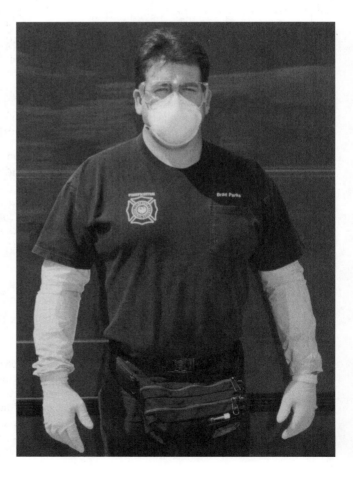

Prompt and competent intervention Prompt and competent intervention (the second adjective is as important as the first) is critical. The system must be geared to respond promptly when a firefighter is injured; has been exposed to a toxic, hazardous, or infectious substance; or is found to have a physical or mental problem.

Treatment A process or pathways must be in place beforehand to handle the commonly encountered or expected medical situations. In addition to treatment for physical problems, treatment programs (not necessarily cures) are available for virtually every addictive behavior problem as well as for depression, stress, and burnout.

Rehabilitation Rehabilitation—the process that continues after the initial treatment of most medical events—should be monitored. Larger departments should consider doing some of the commonly encountered rehabilitation (e.g., physical therapy) internally. If an employee assistance program is in place, it can do mental health monitoring. Monitoring the rehabilitation process makes good sense both fiscally and clinically. (Rehabilitation in a different sense— rehab at the scene of an emergency—is discussed below.)

The return to work Policies on return to work and alternative duty assignments involve some of the most difficult decisions the health and wellness staff must make. In most jurisdictions the official duty assignment is an administrative decision, but the recommendations of a medical or nursing professional are usually followed. It is absolutely essential to have in place a method or process of resolving medically based conflicts equitably. The arbitration model is often effective: each party selects a medical expert, and the two experts together select a third expert. The parties agree in advance to abide by the majority decision of the experts.

A related question involves the level of fitness that should be required or even expected of the more senior members of fire and rescue departments. In

---

Health and wellness program checklist

Agreement between labor and management Do labor and management agree on the process by which medical disputes are resolved? In health and wellness programs, this is a key point.

Medical control Definitive administrative control of the medical aspects of a program should rest with a licensed medical professional. The responsibility for ensuring the confidentiality of medical information also rests with the medical professional.

Ancillary staff In addition to having the services of a dedicated and licensed physician, a comprehensive program should have access to the services of a licensed or certified physiotherapist, exercise physiologist, registered nurse, physician's assistant, and dietitian.

Cost-effectiveness The harvest of such programs as prevention by early detection and screening will be proportional to the depth and breadth of the programs, which are proportional to the dollars spent.

Baselines At a minimum, everyone should have an age-based medical exam to establish baselines and comparative trends.

Incorporation into training Some aspect of health, wellness, and prevention of injuries should be incorporated into every company training session.

larger departments, where chiefs and other senior officers are not required to perform heavy physical tasks on the fire ground, their fitness levels may be geared more to the demands of a strictly administrative job. But in smaller departments, the chiefs and senior officers may be required to do actual fire-fighting. In this case, personal pride and the prospect of a healthy and vigorous retirement are probably better motivators than hard and fast (and sometimes unrealistic) mandates.

The content of the health and wellness program

A comprehensive health and wellness program will have components that address the following content areas: physical health; physical fitness; mental health (stress reduction); use of tobacco (smoke and smokeless); nutrition; environmental heat and cold; and physical fitness staff, equipment, and facilities.

Physical health: Annual examinations/evaluations

NFPA 1582, Standard on Medical Requirements for Fire Fighters and Information for Fire Department Physicians (2000 edition), outlines the cycle for performing annual physical examinations and evaluations and the components necessary for each.

The cost of performing annual physical examinations can significantly affect a department's budget. If funds cannot be allocated to start a program of annual physicals, the cost should become part of the fiscal planning process for the future. If budgeted funds are not available, many departments obtain grants or donations from civic groups or local labor organizations.

If funding simply is not available, a department can begin by maintaining annual records of vital signs, height, weight, and percentage of body fat. Over time these measurements of a firefighter's health can indicate to a physician—when funds become available for annual medical examinations—how that firefighter's health is evolving. However, departments should not rely on this method: almost half of line-of-duty deaths are heart related, and comprehensive heart-related testing and evaluation by a physician will be necessary if the health and wellness program is going to be successful in maintaining members' health.

Figure 11–6   The treadmill test is a routine part of a firefighter's annual physical examination.

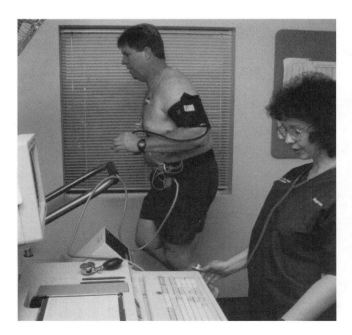

Physical fitness

When the health component has been addressed within the department, a physical fitness or skills evaluation of personnel can be conducted. This evaluation will indicate areas on which firefighters need to focus to protect their bodies from injury or disease. Higher levels of physical fitness, when combined with the other wellness components, enhance the body's ability to fight off a variety of conditions related to poor health. The program must offer assistance to firefighters in either maintaining or improving their physical fitness level. (On physical fitness staff, equipment, and facilities, see below.)

Mental health (stress reduction)

If the mental health (stress reduction) component of the program is lacking, nothing will be able to improve a department member's ability to remain healthy. Some medical experts have suggested that even cancer and heart disease might be tied to mental stress and the lack of stress management.

A high level of mental stress is endemic to firefighting. People choose to become firefighters because of their desire to help others, and they are therefore exposed to many negative life situations: they are called on to assist with assaults, shootings, stabbings, cardiac arrests, automotive crashes, technical rescues, and fires. These incidents can have lasting emotional after-effects on the care givers—who must nonetheless remain psychologically and emotionally stable and healthy throughout their careers if they are to enjoy their family, friends, and life in general. The unavoidable mental stress must therefore be appropriately managed.

Limited employee assistance programs (EAPs) appeared in the early 1980s and subsequently became full-family assistance programs. Fire department managers began realizing that for firefighters to remain healthy, an emphasis had to be placed on psychological and emotional wellness. This emphasis encompasses exercise, nutrition, stress management, and even family counseling. An EAP can give firefighters the tools to cope with the stresses from their work, thus preventing those stresses from interfering with the firefighters' home life. (CISD, discussed above, is a short-term debriefing process used after a traumatic incident; EAPs provide counseling to individuals and family members for general problem solving.)

Tobacco and nutrition

Campaigns to stop the use of tobacco in all forms and improve nutrition can be initiated through a departmental information and advisory program. Regarding tobacco, the American Lung Association and the National Cancer Society are able to provide posters and information that can be set out in the workplace. Using this material is the simplest, most effective way to begin a program with minimal funding. Nutrition programs can be initiated in the same way: if professional consultation cannot be funded, magazine articles can provide information to firefighters on how to reduce fat and make other improvements in their diet. The important thing is to get started at some level and build from there.

Heat, cold, and environmental stress management

When firefighters are engaged in emergency activities, they run the risk of becoming dehydrated in hot and cold weather alike. Maintaining hydration is extremely important because it is now known that even after incidents are

Figure 11–7 A post-fire rehabilitation sector.

completed, firefighters can become ill from problems (including cramping and kidney failure) associated with dehydration.

Emergency scene rehabilitation (rehab) programs are designed to bring fluid and food to the scene to rehydrate department members and restore their energy. Small departments can accomplish basic rehab by bringing an ice chest to the scene along with fluid-replacement drinks and nutrition bars. Large departments normally have dedicated resources available to set up a rehab sector. As the scene develops into a large-scale emergency operation, the need to provide the necessary resources for rehab services grows accordingly.

In hot climates, departments may use misting systems, fans, or both to provide a cool-down area for the rehab of members. When the weather is cold, dry blankets should be provided to keep members warm after their protective clothing is removed; consideration should also be given to providing heaters and enclosed rehab areas because clothing will be wet from water and activity, and if the situation is not monitored, cold-related injuries can occur.

When each firefighter enters the rehab area (whether enclosed or not), his or her vital signs should be taken and documented; they should then be monitored throughout the rehab process. If, after a period of time, the firefighter's vital signs do not stabilize, he or she should be transported to a hospital for evaluation by a physician. In the past, when there was no rehab area and proper hydration was not maintained, severely dehydrated firefighters had to be placed on dialysis until their kidneys began functioning again.

Physical fitness staff, equipment, and facilities

The larger the department, the more resources are typically available. There are frequently people on staff who can offer knowledge, tell of personal experience, and provide assistance. In some departments, the personnel include experts on health, fitness, and nutrition. Some of a department's members may also be able to construct fitness equipment in-house when the funding to purchase equipment is not available.

The program manager can also approach local fitness organizations, community colleges, or high schools to seek access to their expertise, equipment, and facilities. Or the community's cooperation may take the form of a donation —of equipment or money—to the fire department.

Fitness equipment can be elaborate or simple but must be durable and of high quality. The manager must remember that the program's focus is on maintaining a level of fitness to protect the body, not on building super athletes. The equipment should provide a full-body workout to maintain overall muscle tone. Multistation machines that include an area for chest, back, arms, and legs can easily fit into most rooms. Free weights consisting of barbells and dumbbells with benches are very popular but will require more room. Aerobic equipment such as stationary bikes or treadmills work best to provide aerobic exercise. Commercial-grade equipment is preferable because of the heavy use to which it will be subjected.

Vacant facilities used for storage or other purposes may be converted into wellness facilities. In some departments, old fire stations or maintenance buildings have been converted and are very efficient in their new function.

A state-of-the-art program

If money were no object and a fire department received approval to proceed with a state-of-the-art health and wellness program, what would be required?

The first step would still be to appoint a program manager. In small or large departments, this person should be someone with a vision of what would be necessary to build a program that would continue long after any particular manager was gone.

A model program would use a department physician to perform the annual physical examinations and other evaluations. If the department was large and had several hundred members—or if a few small departments joined together —a physician's assistant might be used to conduct the hands-on process, but a physician would still have to be available to oversee the examination results.

Physicians can work on a contract basis; contracting with a physician might have less effect on the budget than contracting with a company for physical examinations.

A department physician could provide several other services. One would be consulting firefighters about their exposure to infectious diseases and guiding them through the prescribed protocol. Another could be coaching department members on lifestyle changes necessary to improve wellness. A third could be analyzing statistical data to forecast the future needs of the health and wellness program and to monitor the status of department members. A fourth would be clearing firefighters for returning to work after illness or injury; the department physician would be familiar with the specific requirements of the job and would be reluctant to allow a member back too soon, perhaps to become reinjured.

Medical laboratories are available to contract with the health and wellness center for blood evaluations, X rays, and more intensive examinations as needed. These tests would be necessary for the physician to complete the examination process, but the combined cost of having a department physician and laboratory could be less than that of contracting with an outside company to perform the comprehensive examinations.

When a department is contracting for a physician and physician's assistant, it should consider including a medical assistant or nurse receptionist. This person will be invaluable in organizing physical examinations and administering the services offered by the health and wellness center. The department should also negotiate with a hospital that will work with it to manage the medical services contract. The department should make sure that the contract allows it to manage the people allocated in the contract. Managing the content of the contract is important because the department will have to set the hours of operation for services that will fit the department's shift scheduling. Hospitals usually include in the price of the contract the salaries of the people involved, malpractice insurance, and the administration of contract costs. Because of the size of the hospital, the malpractice insurance and administrative costs are usually at a group rate.

Actual facilities and equipment needed will depend on the size of the department and the design of the program.

Conclusion

Over time, managers of fire departments ask firefighters to expose themselves to a variety of hazards. Managers provide firefighters with a protective envelope of clothing, self-contained breathing apparatus, and the rest, but sometimes something gets neglected: the effects of the hazards on the person inside the envelope are not always monitored. The true asset to the department is the person inside, and that person is the focus of a health and wellness program.

1   National Fire Protection Association (NFPA), *Analysis Report on Firefighter Fatalities* (Quincy, Mass.: NFPA, August 1991), 52. Copyright © 1991. NFPA, Quincy, MA 02269.

2   See, e.g., J. E. Richardson and M. F. Capra, "Physiological Responses of Firefighters Wearing Level 3 Chemical Protective Suits while Working in Controlled Hot Environments," *Journal of Occupational Environmental Medicine* 43 (December 2001): 1064–1072; Denise L. Smith and Steven J. Petruzzello, "Selected Physiological and Psychological Responses to Live-Fire Drills in Different Configurations of Firefighting Gear," *Ergonomics* 41 (August 1998): 1141–1154; and B. L. Bennett et al., "Comparison of Two Cool Vests on Heat-Strain Reduction while Wearing a Firefighting Ensemble," *European Journal of Applied Physiology and Occupational Physiology* 70, no. 4 (1995): 322–328.

3   See, e.g., J. Paul Leigh and Ted R. Miller, "Job-Related Diseases and Occupations within a Large Workers' Compensation Data Set," *American Journal of Independent Medicine* 33 (March 1998): 197–211; and Bernard Choi, "A Technique to Re-Assess Epidemiologic Evidence in Light of the Healthy Worker Effect: The Case of Firefighting and Heart Disease," *Journal of Occupational Environmental Medicine* 42 (October 2000): 1021–1034.

4   See Dionne Walker, "IAFF/IAFC Push Test for Physical Ability" (April 2, 2001). Available at www.firehouse.com/news/2001/4/2_cpat.html.

Part four:
Prevention

12 Comprehensive prevention programs

Benjamin Franklin is credited with the aphorism "An ounce of prevention is worth a pound of cure." It is obvious to most people that preventing a problem is much more cost-effective than dealing with it after the fact, but few prevention efforts receive the resources and support they need if they are to be effective. Yet every nation has experienced disasters involving fire that have compelled its leaders to promote prevention to one degree or another. The 1903 fire at the Iroquois Theater in Chicago is one example: although the building was supposedly constructed to be fireproof, its contents and structure burned; 602 people died, and another 250 were injured. That disaster produced fire prevention solutions that remain part of fire codes and fire safety education efforts to this day. Fire officials and the other local decision makers who decide how much fire protection is necessary should know and apply these historical lessons when other people forget Benjamin Franklin's words.

This chapter covers the basic components of a comprehensive prevention program for modern fire departments. The major parts of such a program are engineering, enforcement, education, and investigation—functions that fire departments should address if they wish their prevention efforts to be effective. In passing, the chapter also describes two emerging trends for prevention programs: establishing community coalitions to support the prevention efforts, and expanding the prevention effort to cover losses and injuries from causes other than fire (e.g., falls by elderly people, bicycle mishaps, or drownings). Finally, the chapter includes a section on evaluating prevention programs and a section on staffing and funding options.

Comprehensive prevention: An overview

The term *comprehensive prevention* may be unfamiliar to many within the fire service or to other local decision makers with an interest in prevention. The term *prevention* is itself almost a misnomer. Typically it means preventing a problem before it occurs, but for the fire service it has traditionally described not only efforts to prevent fires from occurring but also efforts to mitigate them after the fact with built-in protection. All these prevention efforts have been traditionally limited to code enforcement and public education activities, with the emphasis usually placed on code enforcement programs. The broader term *comprehensive prevention* has evolved to mean the prevention of loss—not only from fire but also from a variety of emergencies on a community-wide basis. Preventing loss, like preventing fire, can mean preventing an incident before it occurs or mitigating its effect after it happens, and comprehensive efforts contain elements of both strategies.

Fire departments at the beginning of the twenty-first century no longer deal exclusively with fires but are called upon to deal with a wide variety of emergency incidents. Most calls handled by a modern fire department (for some departments, the figure is as high as 70 percent) are medical emergencies. Other emergencies to which fire and rescue departments respond are a variety of hazardous material (HAZMAT) incidents that are a threat to either public health or the environment or both. Drowning incidents, auto accidents, trench accidents, terrorist actions, and numerous other emergencies may also result in a call to the local fire department for help. Consequently, the prevention efforts in most fire departments are really efforts to control property damage and losses in human life from a variety of causes.

The building blocks for prevention

For each type of emergency, the building blocks for prevention (including mitigation) are essentially the same: engineering, enforcement, education, and investigation designed to reduce risk or actual loss. In practice, these four concepts are generally embodied in specific functional areas. For example, engineering principles are used in the function of reviewing plans of new construction so that fires or fire spread can be prevented: the review ensures that building features meet code requirements or that alternatives, such as fixed fire protection, are identified and included in the design before construction begins.

The enforcement function assumes a need for laws and regulations that govern construction and behavior and lead to reduced risk or loss. This assumption naturally calls for the development of such laws and regulations and for the ability to enforce them. Developing and enforcing the laws helps ensure an acceptable level of safety.

However, the world is a complex place, and not every emergency situation can be regulated with construction practices or laws. Many fire departments are finding that their most significant problems occur in family dwellings, where efforts to design or regulate safety clash with cultural values that give priority to personal privacy and rights. Thus, public education necessarily becomes a principal tool in ensuring safe behaviors that contribute to reducing risk and loss.

Underlying these loss control tools is the assumption that active investigation of the causes of emergencies will lead to better prevention efforts. Virtually every major fire code requirement can be traced to the lessons learned from past disasters and to the investigations that yielded those lessons. As a result, most departments pursue some type of investigation activity as part of their comprehensive prevention effort. And many are also actively involved in preventing arson-caused fires, so investigation programs usually address that issue as well.

Obstacles to prevention

The establishment of comprehensive prevention efforts is made more challenging by a number of factors: a shortage of resources, cultural biases that may be unpropitious, an increase in the size and cultural diversity of the population served, and an increase in potentially hazardous new technologies.

Most fire and rescue departments lack the resources to conduct prevention efforts on a large scale. Consequently, they are discovering that the only way to control losses effectively is to involve the community. Establishing coalitions with business and community groups has become more common and has proven to be very effective in inducing a local community to take charge of its own emergency problems.

Cultural biases also complicate the fire service's ability to establish comprehensive prevention programs. According to Dr. John Hall of the National Fire Protection Association (NFPA), the United States and Canada are still among the worst of the industrialized nations at controlling fire losses. A number of studies have examined why European and Asian nations tend to place more emphasis on prevention.[1] The studies found that in Europe and Asia, a long history with fire has produced a strong behavioral emphasis on safety, whereas the United States and Canada (and some other industrialized nations) still emphasize technology and believe that nature (and fire) can be controlled by external means. That belief, combined with a consumer culture that uses materials and discards them, may make U.S. and Canadian populations relatively apathetic about prevention, to which they might assign a low priority.

Another challenge to a comprehensive prevention effort is increases in population, which put greater demands on services of all types, including those a fire department provides. Growth of population means greater density of housing; and where fire can spread more quickly from one housing unit to others, greater prevention efforts are required. In addition, the stacking of living or working space in high-rise buildings creates problems that traditional fire department response normally cannot meet (see Figure 12–1).

As the population grows not only in number but also in cultural diversity, behavioral differences can further increase the demands on a fire department's resources. In many instances, immigrants who are unfamiliar with some heating or cooking appliances may misuse them. Prevention efforts for diverse populations require multicultural and multilingual programs that, in the past, few departments were prepared to produce.

Finally, the exponential growth of science and technology increases the pressure on fire departments to stay abreast of the hazards to the community that new technologies represent. The use of exotic chemicals and products increases the potential for HAZMAT emergencies that can threaten large portions of any community.

Generally speaking, the more complex (culturally and technologically) a community is, the more challenges it will face in establishing comprehensive prevention efforts. But whether small or large, communities must meet these challenges, and the way to do so effectively is to use the four basic loss control tools of engineering, enforcement, education, and investigation.

Figure 12–1 In 1993, the Louisville (Kentucky) Division of Fire conducted tests in cooperation with the National Institute of Standards and Technology to examine the capability of fire departments at high-rise building fires. The conclusion was that extinguishing fires in these structures may be beyond the resources of even the best-equipped and best-staffed fire departments.

Engineering programs: Reviewing construction and development plans

A department that includes an engineering component in its prevention program is taking advantage of engineering concepts to help ensure a safe level of construction and use. In other words, the department is making sure that construction and development plans are reviewed with an eye to fire and life safety issues. This review allows a fire department to engineer safety designs into the community, thus reducing the occurrence of fires (as well as the expense of providing fire protection after the fact) and improving public safety. One way of advocating cost-effective protection features during the construction plan review process is by seeking the installation of fire sprinkler systems. In general, the fire department's active involvement in the plan review process can ensure continuity between the construction and the use of a building and can give the department a different (and more cost-effective) view of protecting the public.

Plan review requires time, specialized training, and expertise in the fire, building, and mechanical codes. It also requires some understanding of the construction process and of the way in which issues (e.g., placement of fire department connections for building suppression systems) translate from a piece of paper to actual construction in the field. In addition, plan review requires coordinating the fire code with building, planning, transportation, and environmental codes. Another challenge is the need to pay special attention when alternative materials and methods are proposed as part of a performance-based safety objective (in lieu of prescriptive requirements). Finally, plan review presents specific legal issues that a fire department, when it is involved in the process, must be prepared to deal with.

Fire and life safety issues in relation to new construction

Before the plans are reviewed for other fire and life safety issues, the use of the building and its construction type must be reviewed for compliance with the building code. This determination is usually made by the building department, but because the interrelationship between use and construction type bears heavily on safety, the participation of the fire department is valuable. There must at least be very close coordination between the building department and the fire department.

It is important for plan reviewers and decision makers (elected officials, city and county managers, and fire chiefs) to understand that buildings are approved and constructed for certain uses and that no one set of construction requirements will suit all types of use, or occupancy. For example, the construction requirements for a public assembly occupancy (e.g., a concert hall) usually include more exits than do the requirements for a warehouse structure of the same square footage. Obviously, the reason for the difference is that the number of people per square foot is far greater in a structure where the public will assemble than in a warehouse, and all those people must be able to exit quickly in the event of an emergency.

This interrelationship between occupancy type, or use of the building, and its construction requirements is rooted in the disasters that have shaped the fire code. The fire service must understand this interrelationship fully and must be prepared to respond appropriately at the plan review stage. Parenthetically, the relationship between the building's construction and its occupancy (use) can be affected when new businesses try to locate in a building that was not designed to handle their safety needs. The incompatibility between the original construction and the new use is usually discovered by a fire inspector making regular rounds of his or her inspection district. Most businesspeople, after all, are focused on their own operational needs and either lack the safety expertise required for assessing their safety needs or overlook the matter in their haste to do business. If inspectors do not understand this relationship between the building construction and its use, they could miss unsafe situations that should be corrected.

In addition to proper emergency exiting, other fire and life safety features that typically concern fire departments in connection with new construction include fire department access, water supply for firefighting, and fixed fire protection features (e.g., fire sprinklers and alarms).

The plan review process is an opportunity to ensure that fire department vehicles can respond and position themselves effectively during an emergency, that water supply is adequate for handling a fire (in other words, the fire water-flow requirements have to be calculated), and that the number and placement of fire hydrants are adequate.

Although fire sprinklers are usually part of the building code rather than the fire code, fire departments have an active interest in their installation. Over time, sprinklers have proven to be effective in extinguishing a fire or at least controlling it until the fire department can respond. Consequently, fire sprinklers are now required in many types of buildings, but different types of buildings require different sprinkler systems, and some types of systems have special applications. For example, the dry sprinkler systems are for areas where water pipes might freeze; other systems are specially designed for use in homes. Sometimes fire sprinklers are required to be retrofitted when older buildings are remodeled and brought into compliance with more modern codes. It is often valuable, therefore, to have plan reviewers who are dedicated professionals and who understand the construction and hydraulics of sprinkler systems.

As mentioned above, exiting requirements are very important to the fire service because of incidents in the past when it was impossible to rescue large numbers of people who were trapped inside a burning building.

These and other fire and life safety issues are often reviewed by fire service personnel, or by another agency such as the building department, during the construction process. Whichever agency does the review, the fire service must understand—and other local decision makers should recognize—that the fire service has an active interest in the building construction process and therefore in having the plans reviewed from the perspective of fire and life safety issues. Whether the plans are actually reviewed by fire service personnel or not, these construction issues always enter into a fire department's consideration of the entire fire protection and loss control package that constitutes its fire protection capabilities.

Many fire departments have found it valuable to contract with (or hire) fire protection engineers to help them with the plan review process. Staying abreast of the changes in construction code requirements is challenging and often requires special expertise. In addition, because many private firms in the development industry are hiring their own engineers to provide technical reviews of the construction plans or to assist in design, a fire department has to be prepared to meet a technical review with an equal measure of expertise. If it does not, it may fail to note technical flaws and may miss important safety items during the review process. When the need for technical expertise is combined with the issue of coordinated or conflicting codes (discussed below), one can see how critical it is to have specialists and technical expertise in the plan review arena.

In addition to dealing with the general issues already discussed, plan reviewers must be able to handle the more specific problems associated with certain types of construction or of occupancy. One such type is hospitals; another involves expansion into wildland areas (see the next subsection).

Interrelationships and competition among codes

Because of the relationship between construction requirements and the intended use of a building, the codes relevant to each portion of a building's construction must be both promulgated and managed in a coordinated fashion (a change to one code may affect another code); and conflicting interests must be kept in balance. These codes are building, planning, transportation, environmental, and fire.

Building codes generally establish the prescriptive requirements in building construction for safety purposes. Building codes generally include separate code requirements for mechanical systems (heating and ventilation), plumbing, seismic stability, structural stability, and electrical safety. Mechanical systems are often of strategic value for smoke control, and electrical safety is obviously a major factor in fire prevention.

Planning codes usually delineate density and zoning requirements—issues that can directly affect the need for fire department emergency response capabilities. For example, the planning department will usually be the agency that decides whether housing can be built in a wildland area. It also determines housing densities and the location of business or manufacturing operations, all of which require specific fire department response capabilities. Furthermore, planning codes may be sources of intense community conflict: developers may want increased density within the codes to allow for more development, and local decision makers may desire increased density to prevent urban sprawl (a goal that has a natural citizen constituency within many communities), yet local property owners may want more green space and may resist increases in density for construction, particularly for housing.

Transportation codes cover road construction requirements, which can sometimes conflict with fire department goals for quick emergency response. Consequently, planning and transportation codes are where the requirements for adequate fire department access are sometimes addressed. Access in urban/ wildland areas is one example of the potential for problems to arise, as explained in the accompanying sidebar. Another example occurs when the desire to reduce traffic accidents leads to actions—such as reducing road widths or erecting speed bumps—that can create delays in emergency response. Both goals (reducing accidents and facilitating emergency access) are legitimate but are usually supported by different sectors of a community concerned about different types of problems.

Environmental codes may exist separately or be contained within broader codes that deal with sewage disposal, water supply, and water drainage. Environmental codes may conflict with the needs of the fire department in terms of the water supply. Fire departments have obvious concerns about water supply for firefighting purposes, but there might be, for example, a restriction on flowing water from fire hydrants because of water quality issues. Conflicts can also arise when fire departments attempt to deal with wildland issues of vegetation control, for vegetation is directly or indirectly connected both to environmental concerns and to water quality: environmentalists desire more trees and vegetation to protect water and air quality, whereas fire departments attempt to reduce fuel load in the event of wildfires, which can devastate communities, even in urban areas (see Figure 12–2). Consequently, some fire departments participate in environmental impact reviews to determine how fire hazards may be mitigated while environmental issues are being addressed.

Fire codes are generally designed to prevent fires from occurring and to minimize their effects once they have begun. Fire codes themselves are potentially problematic in that many of them allow alternative materials and methods to achieve a result equivalent to prescriptive code requirements (see the next subsection, "Performance-Based Codes"). For example, when a developer wishes to reduce either fire flow from hydrants or fire department access requirements, fire sprinklers are often accepted as an alternative method of providing adequate water for suppression. And new efforts to achieve performance objectives instead of meeting prescriptive code requirements provide even more opportunities for creatively crafted local solutions to construction problems. When such opportunities exist, it is advantageous to have fire department personnel involved in the plan review process, devising engineering solutions that

---

Problems posed by urban interface and intermix areas   Whatever other problems urban sprawl may present for a community trying to control its growth, sprawl also places demands on an urban fire department that the department may not be prepared to meet. One situation that puts particular pressure on fire departments is the expansion of urban areas into surrounding wildland areas with highly flammable vegetation (this expansion is called *urban interface* or *intermix*). Many urban departments are simply not prepared to fight wildland fires on a large scale. Under these circumstances, a fire department must identify ways to control fire losses in urban/wildland areas other than by fighting the fires: it must review for vegetation control and roofing material requirements.

Urban/wildland areas also require wider access (i.e., wider roads into and out of the community) so that people can escape while fire agencies are responding to the scene. In situations in which people escaping in automobiles meet responding fire crews, the streets should be wide enough to handle the extra traffic load. Furthermore, on-street parking presents a hazard in the same situation, and the fire department may want to prohibit it unless adequate off-street parking is not available.

But these various requirements are not neutral in their effects. They tend to generate conflicts between the needs of the fire department and the needs of other groups in the community, as the text explains.

Figure 12–2   A devastating wildfire erupted in Oakland, California, in 1991. It killed 25 people, destroyed 3,469 homes and apartment units, and damaged an estimated 1.5 billion dollars' worth of property.

can be balanced against emergency response capabilities (see Figure 12–3). An example of such a solution would be allowing fire sprinklers in a building in exchange for extended fire hydrant spacing or reduced fire department access.

The interrelationships among these various codes must be understood in the first instance by decision makers if plan review efforts are to take place not in isolation but in relation to a larger context—that of development. In addition, decision makers should not forget that codes and ordinances for construction are usually in place for a reason. Although pressure to streamline development procedures for local jurisdictions often leads decision makers to conclude that a one-size-fits-all kind of plan review process can be of great benefit to the community's economic vitality, attempting to lump codes and ordinances together in a quick review can cause vital safety issues to be missed in the plan review process. Consistency and efficiency are certainly legitimate goals, but those who are designing a municipal or county system for reviewing construction and development plans should approach their task cautiously.

As for the fire department, it needs to pay attention to its part in the larger community development process—the process in which competing interests within the community seek to use the codes to support their own values and goals. The conflicts that may arise may require advocacy, as the various interests are balanced for the collective good. A lack of advocacy for fire safety issues could eventually lead to disasters that capture the attention of the community and force it to ask why such a situation was not prevented.

Consequently, one of the challenges for fire departments in the plan review process is to be advocates for public safety while coordinating their efforts with the requirements of the other codes. Such a challenge requires a knowledge of other, related codes on the part of plan reviewers as well as a commitment to working as a team to resolve problems when all the conflicting interests have legitimate points of view.

Figure 12–3   A fire service professional reviews a set of plans for compliance with applicable fire and life safety codes. When confronted with a desire to deviate from required fire department access widths, he can accept alternative solutions, such as fire sprinklers that will reduce the need for quick response by larger fire suppression apparatus.

Performance-based codes

As already indicated, an important issue within the plan review process is the effort to streamline the development process by allowing performance goals to replace prescriptive requirements. These goals would allow alternative solutions

---

How to compare performance-based alternatives with prescriptive code requirements According to Martin Reiss, P.E., the current approach to accepting performance-based designs—having a third party validate the engineering methodologies used in the design—can be very difficult, even for a qualified engineer. This approach requires a range of reasonable assumptions about the tools used, including the fire modeling techniques and the computer programs involved in the evaluation. This approach also relies on the establishment of "typical" fire scenarios that establish a quantifiable level of fire safety. But establishing these quantifiable fire safety objectives is difficult. Mr. Reiss proposes, instead, the use of a "comparative approach":

To identify alternate designs to be considered acceptable, the expected risk-to-life value shall be equal to or less than the risk-to-life value of a building conforming with the regulations, and the fire-cost expectation for the alternative design shall be less than or equal to the value for the conforming building.

The calculated expected risk-to-life values for designs conforming with current regulatory requirements provide an estimate of current risk-to-life safety. These risk levels are assumed to be acceptable to the community.[1]

Mr. Reiss (and the authors he quotes) stipulates that the risk levels found in the more common prescriptive codes are acceptable because they have been in use for a long period of time and are widely adopted. This comparative approach therefore involves comparing an "equivalent design or feature to a design or features meeting the prescriptive code using the same engineering methodologies." In other words, "the desired level of fire safety would not be specifically articulated but would be considered achieved when an equivalent design meets or exceeds the performance of the pre-scriptive code design." In essence, the comparative approach creates a performance-based design process that does not require a definition of the desired level of fire safety.

Further,

There is [at present] little attention to reliability in design except for some of the more obvious needs, such as the requirement for stand-by power in fire alarm systems. It is [therefore] necessary to quantify the reliability of the different system elements before a cost-effective decision can be made on trade-offs and redundancy.

As the issues of reliability are quantified and can be included in the process with a high degree of confidence, they should be introduced into the prescriptive codes and standards process which would indicate how to achieve reliability in a system that delivers the performance required by code. Then, by using the "comparative approach" they will automatically be included in the "equivalent" design.

When the comparative approach is used, the development of separate performance-based codes with a defined level of fire safety is not necessary, since one can achieve the desired result by adding to the current prescriptive code the option of comparing an "equivalent" design with a prescriptive code–conforming design.

Mr. Reiss maintains that the benefit of using the comparative approach will be twofold: an enhanced level of cost-effective fire safety on a global basis, and a methodology for the use of performance-based codes that local jurisdictions will find easier to use.

[1] David Yung and Vaughan Beck, "Building Fire Safety Risk Analysis," in *The Society of Fire Protection Engineers Handbook of Fire Protection Engineering*, 2nd ed. (Quincy, Mass.: National Fire Protection Association [NFPA], 1995), 5-95 and 5-96.

Source: Adapted with permission from Martin H. Reiss, P.E., "Global Performance-Based Design: Is It the Solution?" (paper presented at the 1998 Pacific Rim Conference and Second International Conference on Performance-Based Codes and Fire Safety Design Methods, Maui, Hawaii, May 3–9, 1998).

and could be met by specific designs for construction and development. The purpose of this effort is to allow flexibility in construction practices without reducing the level of safety for building inhabitants. Some developers of buildings that would normally require fire sprinklers, for example, have sought to save time and money by offering, instead of sprinklers, design features that they estimate would provide the same level of life safety protection but without the installation of sprinklers.

As of the year 2001, model fire and building codes already incorporate a degree of performance design. Although these codes require certain specific safety features (e.g., fire sprinklers, smoke and fire separation between the floors of a building, and specific requirements for earthquake/seismic stability), they also allow alternative materials and methods that will achieve the same level of safety that prescriptive code requirements achieve.

To the extent that fire departments already have experience exchanging some protection features for others, performance code issues have represented an opportunity to look at local solutions from more than one viewpoint. However, the movement toward performance-based codes does present fire officials and local decision makers with additional challenges. As Fire Marshal Joseph M. Fleming of the Boston (Massachusetts) Fire Department has pointed out, "One of the problems that performance-based design creates for code officials is that it is harder for code officials to discover design flaws in designs that utilize performance design techniques."[2] These design techniques often involve computer modeling, which relies on assumptions that the local jurisdiction may not be able to evaluate because of a lack of expertise or technical proficiency. Fleming's recommendation is to challenge these modeling assumptions. Most of the computer models are still in their infancy and may have flaws that another design professional could identify. For that reason, he recommends that local officials require a third-party review by experts in the field to accurately determine if performance objectives will actually produce the desired safety results. Other departments have hired fire protection engineers as permanent staff to help evaluate performance-based designs.

Beyond computer modeling, performance-based design requires a level of expertise in engineering that most fire departments do not have at the start of the twenty-first century. Fire officials and local decision makers will therefore have to ensure that they can provide adequate scientific and engineering analysis to properly evaluate performance codes in the plan review process.

Legal issues in plan review

Whenever a government agency establishes requirements of any kind, legal issues invariably arise. It is impossible to totally protect an agency from the threat of a lawsuit, for people may file suit in court as they wish. Each agency responsible for fire protection should therefore be prepared to protect itself and to conduct its operations in a fashion that minimizes legal liability. Doing so will help the agency prevail in court. (For a discussion of fire department liability for negligence, see Chapter 13.)

The most important thing local decision makers can do is obtain expert legal advice to determine how they are affected by federal, state, and local statutes applicable to the adopting and managing of fire codes. That advice usually comes from a municipal, county, or special fire district's legal counsel hired specifically to provide such advice.

The legal issues most commonly connected with plan review concern the competence of the review itself and the justification for the government's requirements. Taking an individual's property rights by means of code requirements, without submitting to due process, can represent an enormous exposure to legal liability. For example, limiting someone's ability to build a structure but providing no kind of notification or appeals process could be considered a "taking" of value from the developer or property owner.

Jurisdictions that perform the plan review service should always be concerned about the qualifications of their employees who actually do the work. Any legal challenge to the accuracy of the work will ultimately come down to the ability of plan reviewers to perform their jobs skillfully. Technical training and certification are becoming more prevalent and in some jurisdictions may even be required. In addition, issues of inadequate information in the plan review process sometimes arise. For example, a reviewer may approve a developer's plans but overlook some code requirements. If the overlooked requirements are caught later and expense is involved in complying with the code after the fact, the developer may sue for damages.

There may also be legal challenges if the person performing the plan review tries to require features that are not included in applicable codes. Builders who find out they added safety features that are not actually required are usually upset, and justifiably so. If plans are approved that do not comply with the applicable code, almost certainly there will be some liability. Conversely, when safety features are clearly overlooked in the plan review process, an unsafe building may result, and if that building later burns and someone is injured in the fire, liability probably will exist for the jurisdiction that approved substandard construction practices.

Fire officials and local decision makers who are responsible for the plan review process must understand the limits within which they are allowed to operate. The best and most appropriate way to understand these limits is to obtain proper legal counsel with the appropriate expertise.

Enforcing codes and developing them

The second principal function of a comprehensive prevention program is enforcing fire and life safety codes (and helping to develop model codes). Enforcement is the mechanism used to obtain compliance with codes and laws during the construction process and afterward, when buildings are occupied. (Enforcement after construction can mean regulating people's behavior.)

Laws and codes developed with the best of intentions accomplish nothing if they are not followed. Most people will comply with laws and codes if they understand the need, but nowadays not everyone sees the same need for fire safety codes, even though each of the model codes is rooted in an actual past fire disaster, such as the fire on May 28, 1977, at the Beverly Hills Supper Club in Southgate, Kentucky, which killed 165 people, and the one at the MGM Grand Hotel in Las Vegas, Nevada, in 1980, which killed 85 people and injured another 600. Both of these fires, and others before and since, taught lessons about fire safety that have been incorporated into modern fire and building codes. As mentioned above, laws requiring smoke detectors and codes requiring fire sprinklers and adequate exiting in case of emergencies stem from these lessons. It is important, therefore, to ensure that everyone complies with the codes.

Codes are often paired with standards. In fact, codes are founded on sets of standards. For example, simply requiring fire sprinklers is not enough. Rather, the specific installation and hydraulic standards necessary to make sure the sprinklers will function properly have to be outlined as well. Thus, not only codes but also standards need to be enforced as part of a comprehensive prevention program.

Enforcing codes and standards means adopting them and administering them, and fire officials and local decision makers must understand the limits and the foundation of their authority to do precisely that. Administering codes requires identifying and drawing up an inventory of properties to be inspected, maintaining a database and a record-keeping system, training and selecting personnel, and managing the appeals process. (Evaluating the performance of enforcement personnel and the enforcement program is also necessary and is discussed in the section below on "Using Performance Measures to Evaluate Prevention Programs.") To understand the legal issues involved in adopting and managing a code enforcement program, those who administer the codes should obtain legal guidance about the extent of their authority, and about their liability, when enforcing fire codes.

The codes that have been adopted are based on model codes, and the process of developing model codes is ongoing. Fire officials should participate in this process as much as possible. In doing so, however, they must recognize that the globalization of codes and standards (a concomitant of the globalization of trade and commerce) will challenge their operations and their ability to influence code development.

The authority to enforce laws, codes, and standards

Usually the authority to administer laws, codes, and their underlying standards is passed down from the state. That is, the laws and codes relating to fire safety, which are adopted by local jurisdictions, usually exist either as part of a model fire code that has been adopted in a statewide version or as parts of specific state statutes.

Model codes are codes that are produced regionally, nationally, or internationally to provide the concepts and terminology on which modern code enforcement can be based. (They are explained more fully below.) In addition to the model codes, some states establish laws relating to fire reporting, smoke detectors, fire sprinklers, or fireworks, and many adopt a statewide version of a model fire code. But model fire code language is useless to a local jurisdiction unless it is legally adopted for that community (i.e., the state has to permit the local jurisdiction to adopt certain code provisions, and the jurisdiction then has to actually adopt the provisions that it wants to adopt). Fire officials and other decision makers must understand which level of authority belongs to the federal government, which to the state, and which to the local jurisdiction. Most codes have been in place for many years, so the underlying authority is taken for granted. But legal challenges may nonetheless arise; and for newly formed fire departments, the foundation of legal authority may not be clear. It is most important that fire officials obtain proper legal advice locally so that they will fully understand both the legal authority of the jurisdiction's code enforcement efforts and the limits of that authority.

Administration of the code enforcement process

Adopting the laws necessary to administer codes and standards is only the beginning of code enforcement. Administering the enforcement process effectively is critical, and one of the first issues local decision makers must address is how to do that. Administering the code enforcement process is often an art that requires sound judgment and open communication between those responsible for enforcement and those who are legally required to comply.

Not all fire departments have been given the authority to administer their jurisdiction's code enforcement activities. Philadelphia, for example, assigns fire hazard inspections to the city's Division of Licenses and Inspections. For fire departments that do administer code enforcement activities, policies are usually required that help guide the various personnel who are responsible for enforcement at different levels of the organization (e.g., fire marshal versus inspector). The distinction between law and policy for code officials is that laws and codes usually state the prescriptive requirements (e.g., what kinds of structures are required to have smoke alarms), whereas policies—much like standards—deal with the more specific how-to questions that arise during the daily administration of codes. For example, a law may state that a smoke alarm is required in every home; the standard may say where in the home the alarm should be placed and what type of alarm is appropriate; and the policy describes how that law will be enforced. More specifically, a policy may say that enforcers will gain compliance by issuing a specific form. And if resources are inadequate to ensure annual inspections for compliance, a policy may address the frequency of inspections or the way in which a self-inspection by building occupants could occur.

Policies establishing code administration practices can provide the consistency desired by the community and can offer guidelines to help enforcers administer codes equitably. After all, many codes require some interpretation as to their exact meaning, and some codes leave decisions about specific issues up to the local fire chief, as does the Uniform Fire Code (a model code), which stipulates that the chief may determine what constitutes an imminent fire hazard requiring drastic enforcement measures. Such discretionary authority is very broad in theory but is rarely exercised in practice because of practical political concerns. Any fire administrator who thinks that he or she is the final word in code enforcement is naive about the pressures that concerned citizens can bring to bear if they perceive what seems to them an abuse of power by fire officials or decision makers. Given the occasional need for interpretation and for the exercise of discretion, clear policies establishing code administration practices can be very advantageous. In addition, whenever discretion is exercised, it is wise to make sure first that political leaders will support the conclusions drawn by the direct supervisors of code enforcement personnel.

Policies may or may not have the same force as law; again, local jurisdictions

Figure 12–4 An inspector from the Phoenix (Arizona) Fire Department conducts an inspection as part of the department's Urban Services program.

should obtain legal advice about their authority to enforce policies as well as laws.

The steps in administering the code enforcement process are outlined in several publications, two of which are *Fire Inspection Management Guidelines* and *Conducting Fire Inspections.*[3] Among the issues discussed in these two books are identifying and inventorying properties to be inspected, maintaining a database and a record-keeping system, training and selecting inspectors, and managing appeals. (Also discussed there, although not here, is the matter of evaluating the performance of the personnel and program.)

Identifying and inventorying properties to be inspected   The goal of a code-enforcement inspection program is to ensure that business properties comply with appropriate fire safety codes, although inspections also provide an opportunity to make nonbinding fire and life safety recommendations. Ideally, every commercial property in a jurisdiction receives regular, systematic fire safety inspections. However, many jurisdictions do not normally put the ideal into practice, and local decision makers may be forced to prioritize their inspections. They may base their priorities on a statistical history of fire problems and on a list of potential problem occupancies—such as hospitals and schools—where the risk of death or loss is great although the likelihood of fires is small. Consequently, a prioritized inspection list may combine properties where fires are frequent with properties where the risk is great although occurrences are infrequent.

Maintaining a database and a record-keeping system   A database and a record-keeping system are very important aids in prioritizing inspections; they provide information on where fires are occurring and how often buildings are inspected. When a fire occurs, decision makers usually want to have some idea of when the building was last inspected (and what the inspector found) to see if there is a relationship between the hazards noted in the inspection and the cause of the fire. A good record-keeping system can therefore help improve prevention efforts by allowing officials to pinpoint the businesses that most commonly have fires and the hazards that most commonly lead to fires. A good record-keeping system is also important for legal purposes, as discussed below.

Usually hazards that have been identified are abated through some type of administrative or quasi-judicial system of code compliance. In some cases, court orders are actually sought to obtain compliance. Most jurisdictions allow thirty days for correcting simple hazards—those that do not pose an imminent threat to life safety. Most codes define an imminent threat loosely, and the judgment of local decision makers is required. An imminent threat usually exists when a fundamental fire safety feature has broken down and the breakdown threatens the safety of a structure's occupants. Typical examples include locked exits, shut-off fire sprinkler or alarm systems, and people placed in a hazardous area that was not designed for them. Finding people living in a building that was not designed for their safe exiting is most threatening to fire officials, who are concerned about residents' safety and about their own liability if they were to allow an unsafe practice to remain unabated. In these kinds of circumstances, a much shorter time to gain compliance is usually given. In extreme cases, a business may be closed until compliance is obtained.

Some hazards involve structural or mechanical problems that may require longer periods of time to be corrected. Under those circumstances, it is up to fire officials to determine an acceptable timetable for correcting the hazards.

Training and selecting inspectors   As indicated above, a major issue in administering code inspections is the need to ensure consistency. This need is partly addressed by policies and partly by the training and selection of inspectors. The codes can be complex, and inspectors who are more experienced are often better able to identify a multitude of code violations—whereupon occupants complain that previous inspectors did not find a specific hazard and so this other inspector must be "harassing" them. Consequently, inspector training and selection are critical for the effective management of code enforcement activities.

A variety of training programs for code enforcement personnel are available, as is certification for both familiarity with the code and experience doing inspections. Each of the model code organizations (see "Code Development" below) offers some type of training and certification program. And many jurisdictions are finding value in "certifying" their inspections by certifying their personnel and carefully administering their inspection process. For example, many jurisdictions include a checksheet for their inspectors so as to provide more consistency during the inspection (see Figure 12–5). And some use preinspection letters to notify businesses as to what common hazards will be looked

Figure 12–5 The Palm Beach Gardens (Florida) Fire Department's checksheet for inspections lists common hazards that inspectors should check for.

PALM BEACH GARDENS FIRE DEPARTMENT
10500 N. Military Trail, Palm Beach Gardens, FL 33410   Phone (561) 775-8260   Fax (561) 775-8269

FIRE SAFETY INSPECTION REPORT

Occupant:_____   Date:_____

Address:_____   Suite:_____   Phone No.:_____

Emergency Contact:_____   Title:_____   Phone No.:_____

( )	Means of Egress: ( ) obstructed ( ) locked ( ) improper locking device. Location(s):
( )	Emergency Lighting: ( ) inoperative ( ) not provided. Location(s):
( )	Illuminated Exit Sign: ( ) inoperative ( ) not provided ( ) battery back-up inoperative. Location(s):

( )	Fire Sprinkler System: ( ) required clearance (18 inches) not maintained for fire sprinkler heads
	   ( ) not monitored by fire alarm system ( ) no maintenance contract *NFPA 25*
	   Fire Department Connection: ( ) obstructed ( ) damaged ( ) missing caps
	   Fire Sprinkler Riser: ( ) valves not chained and/or locked ( ) spare heads not provided

( )	Fire Alarm System: ( ) non-functional ( ) no current inspection tag ( ) no central station monitoring
( )	Dangerous accumulation of waste or combustible material. Location(s):

( )	Fire Extinguisher(s): ( ) not provided ( ) not accessible ( ) not mounted ( ) requires maintenance
	   Minimum classification is 2A-10BC rated extinguisher inspected and tagged by a licensed technician
	   Location(s):

( )	Electrical Hazards: ( ) improper use of extension cord ( ) missing blanks in electrical panel
	   ( ) use of outlet multiplier ( ) combustible material too close to a heat producing appliance
	   ( ) electrical panel obstructed – *minimum 30" clearance* ( ) circuits not marked
	   Location(s):

( )	Address not visible from the roadway: ( ) front ( ) rear
( )	Knox Box: ( ) requires maintenance ( ) missing/improper keys
( )	
( )	
( )	
( )	

Authority: Chapter 38, Code of Ordinances, City of Palm Beach Gardens

( ) NO VIOLATIONS NOTED THIS DATE	**( ) FORWARD TO FIRE MARSHAL**
( ) ALL VIOLATIONS CORRECTED	**( ) FORWARD TO CODE ENFORCEMENT**

Your immediate attention is required on the above listed items. You have (14) days to correct any and all violations unless otherwise noted. Failure to correct violations on or before the re-inspection date will result in further action by the Fire Marshals office. Please contact the Fire Prevention Division of the Palm Beach Gardens Fire Department if you have any questions. (561) 775-8260.

Inspected by:_____, I.D. No.____, Date:_____ Occupant:_____

Re-inspected by:_____, I.D. No.____, Date:_____ Occupant:_____

Remarks:_____

White copy – Occupant   Yellow copy – Occupant after violations corrected   Pink copy – Fire Prevention

for during an inspection so that the business owners may prepare and become partners in creating a safe environment, rather than being merely passive recipients of enforcement actions that are imposed on them (see Figure 12–6).

Selecting the right kinds of people to work in a code enforcement program is just as important as training them properly, and can be difficult to do. Choosing enforcement personnel from among firefighters may be desirable because firefighters' experience with fire helps them refine code enforcement efforts. Firefighters are usually dedicated to fire safety and, because of their own experience, can be effective advocates when enforcing the code or persuading someone to comply. (Persuasion is often effective in gaining willing compliance before enforcement is necessary.) Unfortunately, many firefighters are reluctant to become enforcers because in that role they have to push people to do something the people may not want to do. Pushing people to act against their will contrasts strongly with the role firefighters usually play of being present to help in the event of an emergency. Consequently, some departments have used nonfirefighting personnel, or even volunteers, to conduct inspections.

Staffing patterns are discussed in more detail in the section on "Staffing and Funding Options for Prevention Programs," but decision makers should pay particular attention when selecting their code enforcement personnel. No one can cause problems for a fire official or local decision maker more quickly than a fire code inspector who is either inept or overly attracted to the role of enforcer.

Figure 12–6 Some jurisdictions (e.g., Portland, Oregon) are now sending out pre-inspection letters to allow building owners and managers to comply *before* an inspection is actually done. The idea is to achieve willing compliance from businesses that are otherwise ignorant of what is required by proper fire and life safety regulations.

CITY OF

PORTLAND, OREGON

FIRE PREVENTION DIVISION

Jim Francesconi, Commissioner of Public Utilities
Robert Wall, Chief
Jim Crawford, Fire Marshal
55 S.W. Ash Street
Portland, Oregon 97204-3590
(503) 823-3700
FAX (503) 823-3710

"YOUR SAFETY IS YOUR RESPONSIBILITY"

Dear Business Owner/Manager:

We're sending this letter to let you know that an Inspector will visit your occupancy soon to perform a regular routine fire prevention inspection. While the Inspector will look for compliance with all parts of the Fire Code, he/she will pay special attention to hazards/violations that are most common and that are most likely to cause fire damage to your business. A list of these hazards (and detailed explanation of each) is enclosed. We encourage you to correct these hazards and any other violations before the inspection. **Any hazards from this list that we find during the initial inspection will result in a fee of $10 per violation category.**

It is the Fire Marshal's responsibility to inspect all commercial structures in the City except one- and two-family residential units. The objective of these inspections is to reduce fire damage and loss of life. **The Fire Marshal's Office seeks willing compliance with the Fire Code.**

Upon completion of the inspection, our data base will be updated and **a bill for the inspection mailed to you.** There is a fee for each occupancy as listed on the enclosed "Fee Schedule." Most businesses can expect the initial bill after the first inspection. There are also fees that will be billed after a re-inspection if code violations are not corrected in a timely manner.

The fee-for-service aspect of this fire prevention program is new. It is the result of decisions by the City to recover costs of services that include private benefits. See "Background Information" for an explanation of this new program and information about your right to appeal.

If you have any questions before the inspection, or if you would find it convenient to schedule an appointment for the inspection, call 823-3700. Your call will be directed to the appropriate District Inspector.

Managing the appeals process   The final authority for fire code administration is usually some type of appeals board. Boards do not generally have the authority to eliminate code requirements, but they do have broad authority to determine equivalent forms of protection. A board may be created at the state level, as is the Massachusetts Fire Safety Commission, or at the local level. Members of these boards usually consist of architects, engineers, and design professionals from the community who have a working knowledge of the code but are not directly connected with the fire service. The purpose of these boards is to act as the final arbiter when the code requirements are subject to interpretation or when alternative materials and methods are being suggested for equivalent levels of fire and life safety protection. (The obvious example is when fire sprinklers are offered in lieu of other fire suppression water supplies.) However, appeals boards do not supplant the judicial system when the issue is one of legal interpretation or legal challenges.

Managing the appeals process means establishing some kind of review board (i.e., the appeals board itself) with specific authority for the task. It means processing appeals in a timely fashion and preparing board members and code management personnel to deal with decisions professionally and within the scope of their authority.

Code development: Model codes and globalization

Adopting laws, codes, and even policies implies not only that they will be administered effectively but also that the people involved in administering them have a responsibility to ensure that the codes and standards they use are up-to-date and in accord with modern fire safety practices. To meet this responsibility, decision makers at the local level must make a commitment to participate in the development of codes and standards. No one is a better advocate for high-quality codes, and no one better understands their effect on the community, than the people who administer them daily.

Not all fire departments can afford to participate in the development of model fire and life safety codes, but those that can afford to usually do. And their role is important: they help ensure that model codes are based on actual field experience in firefighting and inspection activities.

As of 2001, model code processes were conducted by (among other organizations) NFPA, the Building Officials and Code Administrators International (BOCA), the International Fire Code Institute (IFCI), the Southern Building Code Congress International (SBCCI), and the recently formed International Code Congress (ICC). All these organizations either have produced or are in the process of producing fire codes as models for adoption at the state and local levels. A model code set can include building, fire, plumbing, and mechanical codes.

Participation in the model code process usually involves becoming a member of the organization, traveling to its code development meetings, and voting on the language of the model code. In 2001 many code development organizations allowed input and proposals via the Internet, but voting still had to be done in person.

Scope of model codes   Some of these model codes represent the minimum standards for fire and life safety; local jurisdictions may exceed these minimums depending on the community's specific needs or desires. For example, some jurisdictions have adopted local ordinances that exceed their statewide requirements, as is the case with the fire sprinkler ordinance of Louisville, Kentucky. Kentucky's state code, like most state codes, applies to new construction only, but Louisville was able to demonstrate its inability to control high-rise fires with traditional firefighting means and was therefore able to adopt into law a requirement that fire sprinklers be placed in all commercial high-rise buildings. The requirement was retroactive, and it superseded previous building codes. Another example of exceeding a minimum standard is when a community requires that sprinklers be installed in all residential properties, not just in commercial structures or in one- and two-family homes.

Other codes, primarily building codes, are mini-max in their scope: they specify both the minimum and the maximum fire and life safety requirements and cannot be changed except by specific appeals or an amendment process.

Globalization of codes and standards   As fire officials or other decision makers participate in code development, they are exposed to an emerging trend that affects the process used by each of the model code organizations. Trade has become global, and trade agreements between nations have opened up economic opportunities for international companies, which desire consistency of code applications across international boundaries. Thus, there is a need for codes and standards (in all areas) that can be used in more than one nation. The first areas to feel this pressure have been product standards and construction practices, but other codes and standards are following suit. As the demand for uniform codes and standards increases, the participants in the process of adopting model language become more numerous and represent a wider range of national perspectives, histories regarding fire and life safety, scientific analyses, and views about how codes should be written. Many of these participants are from nations that cannot afford the protections taken for granted by people in more industrialized nations. Accordingly, views vary widely about how many safety features should be provided and what constitutes an acceptable level of risk.

To meet this challenge and to influence the code development process in an international arena, decision makers will have to bring to bear active participation, sound scientific and engineering techniques, and accurate data.

Legal issues in code enforcement

Like the plan review process, the enforcement strategies used by fire officials raise or may raise specific legal issues.

First, maintaining records and ensuring the completion of hazard abatement are important for legal purposes. In numerous court cases, local jurisdictions have been found liable because they failed to abate hazards that either had been or should have been identified.[4] Consequently, having an accurate record of inspections and hazard abatement may very well provide some protection from legal liability. Second, local authorities should be aware that entry to inspect a property is not granted automatically and may require some kind of administrative warrant from an appropriate court. Third, local jurisdictions may have some protection from liability for failing to inspect if they lack the resources to inspect.

To determine what level of protection from liability they may enjoy, fire officials and decision makers should obtain expert local legal counsel.

Educating the public about fire and life safety

Most fires and most fire-related deaths and other injuries occur where people live, for that is where the ability to enforce codes is severely restricted. A basic precept in the United States is that a person's home is his or her castle. Accordingly, fire and life safety codes have traditionally been much more lenient with regard to personal living space. One- and two-family dwellings and even individual apartment units enjoy protection from code enforcement activities.

But most fire deaths occur in residential properties, so public fire and life safety education should be one of the more important strategies of a comprehensive prevention program.

Many jurisdictions say that public education is a priority but in fact give it little support. However, more fire departments are coming to understand the value of public education and the effect it can have on their total protection and prevention effort. They are increasing their resources for this vital function and are seeing positive results.

A modern public education program that strives to reach the general public and change behavior in a number of ways consists of two very general approaches: bringing education into the schools and taking it directly to the public. Bringing fire education into the schools reflects the long-held belief that the way to produce lasting results is to reach young children, who will grow up to be safer adults. Going directly to the public with a variety of methods has the same basic goal: to increase knowledge and change behavior so that people are safer. But however public fire and life safety education programs are delivered, they tend to work best when they involve partner agencies that already have concerns about particular audiences.

Conducting a comprehensive public fire and life safety education program means providing true educational opportunities in a variety of settings. Whether in schools, at community meetings, or through marketing outlets, high-quality education must be age appropriate and in a form that will capture interest. It raises the public's level of consciousness about safety. But to be effective, education efforts must ultimately do more than raise consciousness: they must change the behavior of targeted populations to reduce the risk of, and the losses from, fire and various injuries.

Education in the schools

Schools are generally recognized as a critical part of any public education program. To be effective, however, fire and life safety education for children must go beyond simple presentations of what a firefighter looks like in protective gear. Showing schoolchildren what firefighters do has good public relations value, but the field of public fire and life safety education has become more sophisticated. It now includes well-designed educational activities that use firefighters or public education personnel to teach children directly by involving them in decision-making and learning exercises. Research indicates that stu-

Figure 12–7   A local firefighter visits an elementary school classroom.

dents who are actively involved in making decisions are more likely to remember educational messages and change their safety behaviors.

Fire and life safety education in the schools also includes preparing teachers' curricula, which serve as technical guides for the teachers' lessons. Preparing curricula for fire and life safety educational purposes is based on the simple principle that teachers are the best resource for providing education in the schools. The fire service accomplishes its prevention goals more effectively by helping teachers than by trying to replicate their role.

The fire department's own role in school programs is to support solid educational curricula with presentations that reinforce the safety consciousness achieved by children who have been exposed to a well-structured educational program. For example, presentations such as clown programs or puppet shows as well as other age-appropriate educational offerings can reinforce the proper messages for children. And a simple visit from the local firefighters can serve as a positive reinforcement mechanism for teachers to help them motivate children's learning, for children usually enjoy a visit from the fire department.

Children's fire safety house   Firefighters in Lincoln, Nebraska (as in many communities), have built a downsized mobile replica of a two-story house featuring a bedroom and a hallway on each floor. Their purpose is to teach fire safety to elementary school children. Firefighters conduct fire exit drills with the children inside the fire safety house using electronically operated smoke detectors, a nontoxic smoke machine, and red strobe lights to simulate a real house fire. A control room operated by one firefighter is located inside the fire safety house, which also contains the controls for the smoke machine as well as the piping system used in directing the smoke. The fire safety house is a successful and quite visible tool of the Lincoln Fire Department's commitment to fire education in the elementary school system. The program has helped heighten concern for the importance of fire safety—not only among children, but among adults in the community as well.

Source: John Huff, "Children's Fire Safety House," *Ideas in Action: A Guide to Local Government Innovation* 5 (fall 1999): PS-23.

Figure 12–8   The Tualatin Valley (Oregon) Fire and Rescue fire safety house.

Besides achieving a level of sophistication that truly teaches students proper messages and behaviors, and besides involving solid educational activities in which the students practice decision-making and learning exercises, activities for the schools must also be well tested, and there must be documentary evidence that the resources invested are actually producing something of value for the children and for the departments expending the resources. High-quality products like *Risk Watch*® (discussed below) and others have been tested, and the educational value of their material has been documented. Anything developed at the local or state level must not only meet the same standard of testing but also be in a form that teachers will find useful. Otherwise the materials will sit on the shelf.

Many local decision makers have also begun to understand that schools are under increasing pressure to improve their performance while reducing costs and that fire safety alone may not receive the priority it once did. Thus, many fire departments are expanding their public education efforts in schools to cover the prevention of other injuries besides those related to fires. In this way, fire departments are seeking to do more with less—to maximize their effect on children's safety behaviors while using limited resources.

One example of this new direction is the *Risk Watch*® curriculum developed by NFPA with contributions from the Lowe's Home Safety Council and with the technical support of leading safety organizations, such as the American Red Cross and the National Safe Kids Coalition. The curriculum covers eight basic injury-control topics (see Figure 12–9). Its underlying concept is that safety for schoolchildren is best promoted by a coalition approach; it presumes that the fire service, police, public health, and other agencies with an interest in public safety must cooperate to maximize their effect in schools already pressed for time and resources.

In fact, those pursuing effective educational strategies in schools will find that there are two national trends—one toward preventing all the injuries encountered by a modern fire and rescue service, the other toward establishing coalitions between the fire service and other organizations. The purpose of these coalitions is to raise the public's consciousness of, and level of concern for, safety by doing so *collectively*. Fire departments, police departments, public health agencies, safe-kids coalitions, the Red Cross, and others are beginning to become more effective partners in fire and life safety education.

Targeted public education programs

Educating children is only one major part of a comprehensive public education strategy. The other is to take the message directly to the general public, usually using one or more of the media. Because resources generally applied to public education programs are at a low level, the effort to reach the public outside the school system must commonly be prioritized and targeted.

To produce a true target audience, a fire department needs to analyze its data about the community's fire or injury problem and then decide which public education strategies are most appropriate for controlling those losses. Taking this approach usually leads to the conclusion that there are several other target audiences besides schoolchildren. National data from NFPA show that the other targets are usually elderly people, ethnic minorities, and economically depressed people.[5] In fact, the strongest correlating factor for fire losses is the income level of victims.

Targeted education programs are most effective when they are developed specifically for each target audience or target message. And for maximum ef-

Risk Watch® is a registered trademark of the National Fire Protection Association (NFPA), Quincy, MA 02269.

Figure 12–9 *Risk Watch*® logo and icons.

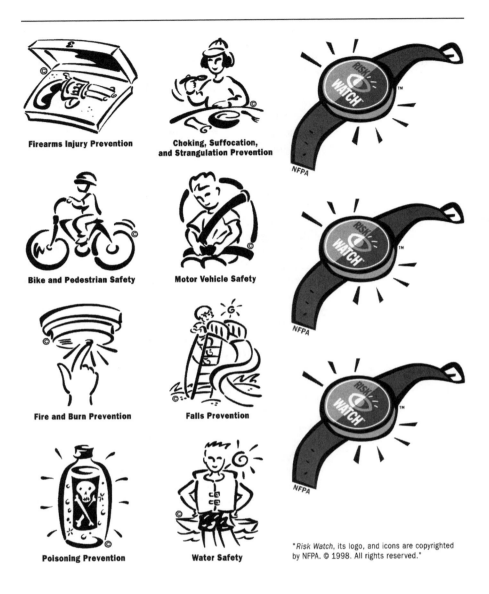

Firearms Injury Prevention

Choking, Suffocation, and Strangulation Prevention

Bike and Pedestrian Safety

Motor Vehicle Safety

Fire and Burn Prevention

Falls Prevention

Poisoning Prevention

Water Safety

"*Risk Watch*, its logo, and icons are copyrighted by NFPA. © 1998. All rights reserved."

fect, they are often combined with other prevention strategies. Portland, Oregon, for example, has a combination program designed specifically for elderly people that couples educational strategies with a low-cost sprinkler initiative. The program tests the concept of providing single fire-sprinkler heads for the location in the home where fires occur frequently (i.e., the kitchen). It also provides educational messages designed to produce positive behavioral changes (i.e., preventing kitchen and other fires from occurring). Partners in the program include the Multnomah Area Agency on Aging, the local Loaves and Fishes program, and other agencies active in providing services to elderly people.

As already mentioned, targeted education efforts extend beyond the typical educational setting and use modern marketing venues to reach people where they live. Radio, television, and newspapers all play a role in this marketing effort. Many fire departments have also had success using grassroots efforts, such as door-to-door canvassing, to get their message across. The use of specialized displays or home fire safety "trailers" to help demonstrate the value of fire sprinklers has become another popular way to provide education to certain segments of the community (see Figure 12–11). And many departments still provide specialized presentations to businesses or civic organizations, and participate in such large events as home and garden shows, to disseminate the fire and life safety message.

Other fire departments have targeted specific audiences or messages in connection with other issues. For example, juvenile firesetting is a specific fire problem that requires a multidisciplinary approach. Education is needed, of course, but families involved with firesetters need screening to determine the level of firesetting activity of the children; and sometimes psychological intervention is needed to keep the firesetting behavior from recurring.

Figure 12–10 A "Summer in the Parks" program in Portland, Oregon, where children in summer recreation programs were given special fire safety presentations.

Figure 12–11 A fire sprinkler demonstration trailer, used to demonstrate the effectiveness of fire sprinklers.

Program to control juvenile fire-setting The St. Paul (Minnesota) Fire Department takes a comprehensive approach to fire prevention. One element of this approach is a program designed specifically for youths, with special attention to juvenile firesetters.

Like many fire departments, St. Paul offers a screening service for juvenile firesetters to help determine the proper course of treatment for the child. Some youngsters are referred to professional counselors to receive treatment for emotional disturbances that manifest themselves in firesetting behavior. Oth-

ers, who have been determined to be "curiosity firesetters," receive educational intervention to prevent further firesetting behavior.

The foundation of the educational effort is "Footsteps to Fire Safety"—a school-based curriculum that teaches children to identify when fires are good or bad and to describe the outcome of fire play. One section, which has a first-aid component, tells children what to do in the event of a fire or burn.

This screening program helps St. Paul control juvenile firesetting.

Seasonal programs are designed to educate the community about fire problems just before the problems normally begin. Examples include programs that deal with heating fires or Christmas tree safety in the winter. Summer problems usually include outdoor cooking, fireworks around the Fourth of July, or wildfire hazards for urban/wildland interface zones. For example, the Los Angeles City Fire Department has developed specific public education programs during wildfire season. Some departments increase their prevention efforts around Halloween, when destructive activities traditionally increase. Many departments also take advantage of fire prevention week (always around October 9), when school and community attention is drawn to the subject, by increasing their education and other prevention efforts to coincide with the increase in public interest.

Some seasonal programs can be oriented more toward local problems. The Phoenix (Arizona) Fire Department, for example, has an excellent program oriented toward drowning incidents, which are a particular problem in the Phoenix area.

Opportunities for targeted educational programs are numerous, and excellent resources are available to local jurisdictions, which can produce their own programs or buy ready-made ones. The U.S. Fire Administration (USFA) maintains a resource guide on its Web page, and NFPA has an active education department, including a Center for High-Risk Outreach.[6] A special report by Rossomando and Associates outlines examples and step-by-step procedures for developing local programs that have the greatest chance of changing audience behaviors.[7]

Investigating fires

Fire investigation—the fourth major component of a comprehensive prevention program—is the basis on which the engineering and educational components are built. It is also a direct part of the enforcement component in the many fire departments where the fire investigation unit is responsible for arson determination and assistance in the prosecution of arson cases.

Most fire departments investigate fires to identify the area of origin and determine the probable cause so that future such events can be prevented. Sometimes the cause is readily evident, and responding fire officers can successfully conclude how a fire originated. Sometimes the cause is not so clear (see Figure 12–12).

Figure 12–12 Fire investigation activity.

Fires are also investigated to determine whether the crime of arson has been committed. If a crime is suspected, the nature of the investigation changes: its scope usually increases dramatically, law enforcement officials (the police and public prosecutors) become partners in the investigation, and interviewing witnesses becomes more difficult. (Arson investigations are discussed in more detail below.)

But even if a crime is not suspected, elements of an investigation may still involve outside interests. For example, most insurance companies routinely hire their own investigators to determine the cause of a fire. They do so to protect themselves from probable civil actions, such as subrogation suits between insurance companies or product manufacturers over who is responsible for paying for the damage: the manufacturer of the electrical appliance that caused the fire may be sued by the insurance carrier to recover expenses for the damages of the actual fire and for the investigation. Under these circumstances, private investigators hired by insurance companies may or may not agree with local authorities about the cause. And when a very expensive fire loss occurs, there are usually enough special interests with a stake in the financial loss to make the investigation complex and subject to scrutiny by many outside sources. These circumstances demand a high level of proficiency on the part of fire investigators, who must make a solid presentation, with scientific evidence, to support claims about cause. Accordingly, many fire departments are increasing their proficiency in fire investigation.

The causes of fire, of course, vary widely. Many fires are caused by some electrical malfunction. Carelessly discarded cigarettes are also a principal cause of fires and fire deaths. Many fires occur in the kitchen because of unsafe practices, such as leaving cooking unattended. Whatever the specific cause, the general cause is always that a source of heat comes into contact with something that will burn. And human behavior, whether it is deliberate or not, is almost always a significant factor in a fire's starting or spreading.

Whether a fire occurs because of unintentional events or is purposely set, certain investigative activities are basic. First is the actual physical investigation of the fire scene, beginning with observations about fire conditions made by those who arrive at the scene first: for example, certain characteristics of smoke or flame color can indicate causal factors. Second, during fire suppression, firefighters must preserve the scene of the fire as much as possible so that critical physical evidence will not be destroyed: examination of burn patterns can lead investigators to the area of origin, even in a badly damaged structure, and understanding how physical items in a structure react during a fire can lead to a determination of probable cause. For example, burn patterns of ordinary wood can help indicate whether accelerants were used to start a fire, and multiple points of origin indicate that a fire was deliberately set. Third, narrowing the cause further requires a good deal more scientific analysis and sophistication: providing evidence, say, that a fire occurred in a particular appliance may require some preliminary understanding of how the unit operates and may ultimately require a scientific analysis by a private laboratory.

Because it is the mission of a fire investigation program to determine cause effectively, those performing the investigation must be well trained in recognizing fire burn patterns and applying the science of investigative techniques to the physical characteristics of the many materials inside a fire scene. But training is not enough. Effective fire investigation efforts also require the equipment necessary to identify causes and to aid in the prosecution of crimes. For example, many fire investigations require laboratory reviews to corroborate the conclusion of an investigation. Many departments are also using accelerant detection dogs to help pinpoint and prosecute cases of arson (see Figure 12–13). Finally, investigators must also be trained to interview witnesses to the fire to help recreate the fire scenario.

Interviewing witnesses is particularly important when arson is suspected. In that case—when a crime is suspected that involves the entire criminal prosecution system, from police officers to prosecutors and judges—the investigator enters another realm of investigation technique. This realm involves preserving any evidence and establishing a chain of its possession so that the evidence can be used in any future court proceedings. This realm also involves using special interviewing procedures and documentation so that the conclusion will withstand legal scrutiny.

During arson investigations the relationship among investigators, the local police, and prosecutors is critical. A report prepared for the USFA by TriData

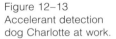
Figure 12–13
Accelerant detection
dog Charlotte at work.

Corporation concluded that because the activities of determining cause, investigating whether arson was involved, and developing a criminal or civil case occur in sequence, close coordination between fire and police agencies is particularly important.[8] In some cases, fire departments train and certify their fire investigators as police officers in order to control the investigation sequence in criminal cases more effectively.

Nationally produced guidelines for fire investigation—such as NFPA 921, Guide for Fire and Explosion Investigations (2001 edition); the International Fire Service Training Association's manuals on fire investigation; and the *Pocket Guide to Arson and Fire Investigation,* produced by the Factory Mutual System—can all help local decision makers design an investigation program that will sustain legal challenges and provide accurate information.[9]

The use of data from fire investigations

Another part of the fire investigation effort is compiling and analyzing data. This function can be conducted by investigators or analysts, and the data can be either statistical or anecdotal. Similarly, the analysis can be done either statistically on a large scale, with databases built over time, or anecdotally on specific fires. Both kinds of data and analysis are valuable to officials who design proactive prevention strategies.

Anecdotal evidence about human behavior and other contributing factors can be especially revealing. For example, the examination of a single fire can provide information that decision makers who are unfamiliar with the technical aspects of an investigation will understand. A thorough investigation might reveal that papers were left too near a portable heater, doors were left open (thereby allowing air to feed the fire), and wall coverings were flammable—three factors that contributed to the fire's start and rapid advance. Specific examples like these can bring the complex nature of investigations down to a simple level that laypeople can readily understand.

Nevertheless, long-range evaluation of loss data should be part of the goal of an accurate fire investigation program. Prevention strategies benefit from the historical perspective provided by a good investigation process that produces detailed and relevant data. Consequently, a record-keeping system for fire investigations is a critical long-term tool of comprehensive prevention efforts.

Legal issues in investigation

Local decision makers should be aware that conducting investigations produces its own set of potential legal liabilities, which usually include standard police rights and responsibilities about conducting criminal investigations. But for an unintentional fire, the right of entry could also become an issue. To protect themselves from legal challenges by ensuring quality control, local decision makers should be sure that investigators receive proper training and should establish clear-cut policies and procedures. And they should have local legal experts review their practices to ensure compliance with appropriate local, state, and federal requirements.

Using performance measures to evaluate prevention programs

The major parts of a comprehensive prevention program are the engineering, enforcement, education, and investigation activities that help reduce risk and loss within a community. One basic management issue underlying all these components must now be addressed. Specifically, local decision makers are asking how prevention efforts can be evaluated to ensure that these efforts are being managed effectively and efficiently. Even though most people accept the concept that preventing an incident is cheaper than dealing with it after the fact, local decision makers are facing more pressure to justify expenditures for every type of government service. Concerned taxpayers want to know what their tax dollars are producing and whether the services are managed efficiently.

Prevention programs are often the most difficult to evaluate. Performance measures are available, however, that indicate whether prevention programs are producing the desired results and are doing so efficiently.

The Governmental Accounting Standards Board has worked to produce evaluation measures that can be applied to fire department activities, although the board stipulates that comparing one jurisdiction with another is very difficult because the variables in jurisdictions are hard to match. The USFA, in conjunction with the California Polytechnic Institute, has also produced measures. The International City/County Management Association (ICMA), too, through its Center for Performance Measurement, is involved in measuring prevention activities and their outcomes. ICMA's measures include indicators connected with fire inspections, community risk reduction, and educational programs. Generally speaking, these indicators can be categorized as measures of workload, efficiency, and effectiveness and as steps toward the identification of best practices. (Chapter 10 discusses performance measurement in detail.)

Workload measures are those that document the amount of work performed. They cover topics such as the number of code enforcement inspections done per inspector and the number of presentations by the number of public educators. Efficiency measures are those that demonstrate whether something is done quickly and at the lowest possible cost. They cover the cost per inspection or the cost per public education presentation. Workload measures will demonstrate that employees are doing an adequate amount of work, and efficiency measures will provide some indication of how quickly things are being done and what they cost in relation to similar services, but effectiveness measures may produce the most solid results for local decision makers who are evaluating their department's prevention efforts. Effectiveness measures show the outcomes of specific prevention efforts and the relationship between these outcomes and the stated goals and objectives of the efforts. Effectiveness measures get at the heart of the question usually asked by concerned taxpayers: Why is this service in place and what is it providing us?

The most commonly used effectiveness measures measure educational gain, risk reduction, and loss reduction. Measuring educational gain means providing evidence that public fire and life safety education activities are (or are not) producing a desired learning result. A questionnaire asking about the practices of the recipients of an educational program before and after they are tested on the program can document whether the recipients are actually learning or are merely sitting through a presentation they will forget the next day.

One of the basic reasons for having a comprehensive prevention program is to reduce risk. Measuring risk reduction means documenting an increase (or lack of increase) in safety behaviors or a decrease (or its lack) in hazard-producing behaviors. For example, national statistics indicate that smoke detectors are effective in saving lives; therefore, documentation that the number of working smoke detectors in a community has increased can be evidence that the risk of dying in a fire is reduced. A compilation of hazards abated during fire inspections can also provide evidence that risks have been reduced: if hazards have been removed, risks have been reduced. Some jurisdictions offer voluntary inspections for private homes and, as a result, have demonstrated measurable reductions in home fire losses.

In fact, measuring risk reduction is a valuable part of a strategy for evaluating prevention programs because the indicators provided can be used to quantify the overall effectiveness of a prevention program. For example, a random sample survey of citizens in a community might indicate *how many* are practicing safe behaviors that lead toward a reduction in fire deaths or property loss: *how many* people have working smoke detectors and *how many* practice fire escape planning. Local decision makers can also quantify *how many* community fire hazards have been abated in a code enforcement inspection program. However, documenting changes that reduce risk does not necessarily mean there will be fewer fires.

Consequently, the ultimate performance measures will always be those that document loss reduction. Measuring the loss reduction that is due to prevention programs will provide the most evidence of positive results. That is the ultimate performance (or outcome) measure that, if favorable, justifies the expense of conducting prevention programs. However, local decision makers should be warned against leaping to conclusions based on short-term analyses of loss data. A change in activity can be caused by normal variations in any statistical analysis, so all the performance measures that look at effectiveness should be evaluated over a period of at least five years. Looking at loss reduction over a period of time can provide the best picture of whether a local jurisdiction's losses from fire are decreasing or not. And it is statistically more accurate to compare any jurisdiction with its own history than to compare it with another jurisdiction.

Staffing and funding options for prevention programs

Evaluating the performance of prevention programs leads local decision makers to examine their options for staffing and funding.

The variety of staffing and funding options seems endless. Local decision makers should routinely conduct surveys of best practices among other jurisdictions to get ideas about how to staff and fund their own prevention programs most effectively. Sometimes the best ideas come from a jurisdiction that is not comparable in size or population, so the people conducting these surveys should be cautioned against being overly restrictive.

Local decision makers should also understand that not every idea can work effectively in their own jurisdictions. Local politics, the strength of professional unions, and the needs of the particular community are all relevant factors when departments are deciding on the most appropriate mix of services and staffing for their own areas.

And finally, local decision makers should be cautioned against expecting too much of any one person. Expecting one person to do an adequate job of conducting a plan review of new construction, enforcing the fire code, conducting public fire and life safety presentations, and investigating fires is unrealistic and may result in a lack of expertise or attention—a lack that can create legal liabilities and ultimately doom prevention efforts. If a community's resources are limited, the type and scope of prevention programs conducted in that community must also be limited.

Staffing

There are a variety of staffing options for performing prevention activities of all types. Many jurisdictions, such as Seattle, Washington, use emergency response personnel to conduct all or part of their fire code inspections. This type of code enforcement activity is commonly called a "company inspection" because it uses fire and medical emergency crews (called "companies") to conduct the inspections. Many jurisdictions that use company inspections also certify their firefighting personnel through model code development organizations

The responsibilities of a fire marshal

The responsibilities of a fire marshal have expanded in recent years and will expand still more with the need to manage comprehensive prevention efforts. Traditionally, the fire marshal in most fire departments has been responsible for supervising the efforts of fire inspectors to make certain that businesses are complying with elements of the fire code. In some departments, the fire marshal is also responsible for fire investigation activities; in others the person is involved in reviewing plans for new construction to ensure fire code compliance; and in still others, the fire marshal has responsibility for the fire department's public education activities.

However, the role of fire marshal is expanding to include coordinating all these components of a comprehensive prevention effort. Some fire marshals, such as Steve Zaccard of St. Paul, Minnesota, are further expanding their responsibilities to include an all-injury approach to prevention efforts. Using programs like *Risk Watch*® and forming coalitions to support broader prevention efforts have become normal parts of their job.

The position of fire marshal can be extremely sensitive to the politics of local government. The fire code is subject to some interpretation, and the person responsible for its administration must have good judgment and tact. Pressure from the business community to lessen standards can be intense, and elected officials are often the first to hear complaints about a fire marshal who is—or is perceived to be—abusing his or her authority. These complaints put constant pressure on the person holding the position to perform in a consistent and tactful manner. Accordingly, it can be a high-pressure job with a great deal of responsibility, requiring technical expertise, the ability to manage diverse job functions, and the ability to perform well under pressure.

Personnel who aspire to the position of fire marshal will not receive the immediate gratification of fighting fires or helping an injured person at a medical emergency. However, those who choose to put their efforts into longer-term solutions to local fire and life safety problems will find it a rewarding career path.

to ensure that those personnel are knowledgeable enough to be able to conduct a thorough inspection. The Portland (Oregon) Fire Bureau uses a combination of regular inspectors (on a forty-hour workweek) and emergency response shift inspectors (on a fifty-three-hour workweek); the latter conduct code enforcement inspections during the day and respond as the fifth person on a firefighting apparatus at night.

Many departments use firefighters as inspectors, public educators, or investigators and promote them into a specialized unit to conduct their respective fire prevention programs. Other jurisdictions use personnel hired from outside the fire department and recruit for employees with specialized education and experience relevant to the tasks they will be assigned. Some volunteer departments (e.g., some departments in Nassau County, New York) also use volunteer inspectors. Whether a volunteer or a paid professional is used, training of personnel is critical.

Many fire departments are expanding their code enforcement options with self-inspection programs, in which businesses are asked to identify their own hazards and abate them voluntarily. Self-inspections are often the only substitute for prevention programs when departments lack the resources to inspect their commercial occupancies with any regularity. The Los Angeles and Los Angeles County Fire Departments have taken the concept of self-service to another level: they have programs that train citizens in how to protect their homes from wildland/urban interface fires.

Many businesses are inspected by a variety of local and federal safety agencies, including the Occupational Safety and Health Administration, and the working relationship between these various code enforcement organizations is a common subject of complaint by businesses. To achieve their prevention goals, therefore, some fire departments are coordinating efforts by the various agencies. The Houston (Texas) Fire Department developed a Tri-Ad inspection program that involves a partnership with the city's building department and the local Building Owners and Managers Association. The partnership allows the agencies to maximize their resources and limit complaints from the business community about multiple code enforcement inspections.

Funding

Funding options for prevention programs are somewhat limited. Many small departments rely on donations to keep their prevention and public safety education efforts alive. Most prevention programs are funded through local property taxes or sales taxes that support all the fire protection services in the jurisdiction. Still other departments charge fees for inspections on the grounds that business occupancies receive a higher level of fire protection inasmuch as they are inspected, for private homes are not usually within the scope of a fire code and cannot legally be inspected.

Many departments are starting to use technology to increase the efficiency—the cost-effectiveness—of their prevention efforts. The use of computers to compile databases is common; in addition, many departments are finding the use of handheld computers to be beneficial for activities such as code enforcement inspections.

Summary

Comprehensive prevention programs are a combination of four strategies designed to reduce risk or losses in any given community. The first strategy consists of engineered safety solutions: the plans for new construction are reviewed for fire department access, adequate water supply, and fixed fire protection systems. The second consists of enforcement efforts: well-designed fire inspections ensure compliance with a properly adopted and administered code enforcement program. The third consists of education activities that are well designed to reach children in school or any other targeted group. The fourth consists of an adequate fire investigation program that provides the information necessary for targeting prevention efforts appropriately and that includes efforts to help control the problem of arson in the community.

Comprehensive prevention programs can be conducted by specialized personnel, emergency response personnel, or even volunteers. These programs can involve any activity in which the public takes an active role to protect itself better (e.g., self-inspection programs for code enforcement, or neighborhood coalitions that go door-to-door with appropriate fire and life safety materials).

However comprehensive prevention programs are conducted, they are multifaceted, using the full variety of prevention strategies to work toward the common goal of prevention: fewer deaths and less loss.

The technological and legal issues that prevention personnel must deal with will become more complex in the future. Some of the emerging trends in prevention include greater emphasis on performance codes, the movement toward all-injury control, and the establishment of coalitions to promote fire and life safety. As *Fire Prevention 2000: Challenges and Solutions* emphasizes, if prevention efforts are to be successful, planning and partnerships with the community will be needed,[10] as will more professional development for fire prevention personnel. Furthermore, the limited nature of the community's resources could require the fire department to put ever-greater emphasis on prevention. Thus, prevention programs should be a vital part of any fire department's total fire and life safety protection package for its community.

1 Philip S. Schaenman, *International Concepts in Fire Protection: New Ideas from Europe* (Arlington, Va.: TriData Corporation, 1993), *International Concepts in Fire Protection: Practices from Japan, Hong Kong, Australia and New Zealand* (Arlington, Va.: TriData Corporation, 1985), and *Proving Public Fire Education Works* (Arlington, Va.: TriData Corporation, 1990).

2 Joseph M. Fleming, "A Code Official's View of Performance-Based Codes" (paper presented at the National Fire Protection Research Foundation symposium on fire suppression and detection research, Orlando, Fla., February 12–14, 1997).

3 *Fire Inspection Management Guidelines,* developed by the National Fire Protection Association (NFPA) and the Fire Marshals Association of North America, in cooperation with the U.S. Fire Administration (Quincy, Mass.: NFPA, 1982); and Deborah Shaw, ed., *Conducting Fire Inspections: A Guidebook for Field Use* (Quincy, Mass.: NFPA, 1989).

4 *Adams v. State (of Alaska),* 555 P. 2nd 235 (1976); *Coffey v. City of Milwaukee (Wisconsin),* 74 Wis. 2d 526, 247 N.W. 2d 132 (1976). See Appendix A of *Fire Inspection Management Guidelines.*

5 Marty Ahrens, *The U.S. Fire Problem Overview Report, Leading Causes and Other Patterns and Trends* (Quincy, Mass.: NFPA, 2000).

6 See USFA at www.usfa.fema.gov; NFPA, www.nfpa.org, and mailing address (1 Batterymarch Park, Quincy, MA 02269-9101) for programs; and Center for High-Risk Outreach, www.nfpa.org/Education/HighRiskOutreach/HighRiskOutreach.asp.

7 Christina Rossomando, *Reaching High Risk Groups: The Community-Based Fire Safety Program* (Alexandria, Va.: Rossomando and Associates, 1990).

8 TriData Corporation, *A View of Management in Fire Investigation Units,* vol. 1, and *A View of Management in Fire Investigation Units: Issues & Trends for the 90's,* vol. 2 (Arlington, Va.: TriData Corporation, 1990, 1992).

9 FM Global, *Pocket Guide to Arson and Fire Investigation,* 5th ed. (Johnston, R.I.: FM Global, 1990).

10 *Fire Prevention 2000: Challenges and Solutions* (Quincy, Mass.: Fire Marshals Association of North America and NFPA, 1998).

13 Regulations, standards, and issues of liability

Since the late 1960s and early 1970s, the development of regulations and standards (as well as of codes) and their use in everyday fire service activities has grown exponentially. The fire service uses regulations and standards to specify apparatus, protective clothing, and equipment; to maintain occupational health and safety; to develop public education programs; and to enhance the professionalism of the occupation.

In today's litigious world, the terms *codes, standards, rules,* and *regulations* are used synonymously, but in fact they represent different things and have different enforcement criteria. (This chapter highlights regulations and standards.) In the federal or state government, laws might be enacted that spell out what the rules and regulations are supposed to accomplish. A regulatory agency then promulgates and enforces the rules and regulations. An excellent example of a regulation is 29 CFR (Code of Federal Regulations) 1910.134, Respiratory Protection Regulations, which is enforced by the federal Occupational Safety and Health Administration (OSHA). In contrast to a regulation, which has the force of law, a code outlines an accepted engineering practice or dictates a set of objectives; an example is code 70 of the National Fire Protection Association (NFPA), the National Electrical Code, which is used as a guideline throughout the United States. A standard is neither a regulation nor a code but outlines a set of recommendations and is itself no more than a recommendation (unless it is also adopted legislatively, as discussed below).

Federal regulations are referenced in different NFPA standards, but NFPA is not an enforcement authority. Nor do NFPA codes and standards have the force of law unless a legislative body adopts them, at which time they may be enforced by some agency (but not by NFPA). NFPA codes and standards are referenced in court cases, regardless of whether the authority having jurisdiction has adopted them. If a fire department member or the jurisdiction is sued for negligence (criminal or civil), rules, regulations, codes, and standards may be used as evidence.

It is important for fire and rescue departments to know whether their authorities having jurisdiction have adopted specific codes and standards. It is also important that a fire and rescue department not recommend the adoption of a full set of codes (e.g., the NFPA Fire Codes, consisting of more than 320 codes and standards) without understanding the full implications of such adoption. If a city council, for example, adopted a full set of codes without knowing or being told the extent of the codes it was adopting, it would be exposing itself to the possibility of being sued in the future for negligence and damages because it had adopted a certain code but never enforced it. Certainly, recommending the adoption of a full code set is easier and may seem to be the right thing to do; but justifying the adoption of a specific code or standard, instead, is far wiser.

Codes, standards, and regulations are documents that are so intertwined in their legal language that users may have a hard time interpreting, enacting, adopting by reference (e.g., as part of a local ordinance), and enforcing them. The documents are not written to confuse or cloud the issues, nor are they written to inhibit people from using them. But users sometimes interpret them from one perspective and enforcement authorities from another, depending on which person or agency is doing the interpreting or enforcing. In some cases, interpretation of the regulations and standards has been the responsibility of the legal community. Since about 1998, the fire service community has been divided about the legal community's interpretive role, and some portion of the fire service has concluded that it would not use these documents. When sections of the fire service turn their backs on regulations, standards, and codes, however, the greatest impact is on the customer—the citizen who has made that call for service.

This chapter surveys the implications and impact of the regulations and standards that are of greatest general relevance to the fire service at the beginning of the twenty-first century and explains the liability of the fire service for negligent firefighting.

When one considers fire protection codes, one thinks of code enforcement, building construction, and related areas. Such codes go back at least as far as Hammurabi, the law-making Babylonian ruler who reigned from approximately 1792 to 1750 BC and is probably best remembered for the *Code of Hammurabi,* a statute based primarily on retaliation. The following decree is from the *Code of Hammurabi:* "In the case of collapse of a defective building, the architect is to be put to death if the owner is killed by accident; and the architect's son, if the owner's son loses his life."

Obviously, society no longer endorses Hammurabi's ancient law of retaliation but seeks instead to prevent accidents and the resulting loss of life and property. From this objective have evolved not only the rules and regulations that represent contemporary life safety and building codes but also standards for fire prevention, fire protection, and fire suppression—and for firefighter occupational health and safety. In fact, the two topics of health and safety, along with fire service organization and deployment, have been the primary motivation for the development of and revisions to codes, standards, and regulations.

Complying with codes, standards, and regulations is now a significant aspect of managing the fire service. Accordingly, fire service managers and their governing authorities need to keep abreast of these documents and need to know how to participate in the process of developing and reviewing them.

The origin of modern fire safety codes and standards Modern fire safety codes and standards trace their origins to the automatic sprinklers developed in the nineteenth century. From the beginning, sprinklers performed well as extinguishing devices but were installed in so many different ways that their reliability was uncertain.

In 1895, a small group of concerned citizens representing sprinkler and fire insurance interests gathered in Boston, Massachusetts, to discuss these inconsistencies. They knew that nine radically different standards for piping size and sprinkler spacing could be found within one hundred miles of the city.

This plumber's nightmare had to be resolved.

The group—which called itself the National Fire Protection Association—eventually created a standard for the uniform installation of sprinklers. This standard, which would become NFPA 13, Standard for the Installation of Sprinkler Systems, was NFPA's first fire safety document. Today NFPA maintains some three hundred fire safety codes and standards, and they are in widespread use around the world.

Adapted with permission from "Codes and Standards for a Safer World" (Quincy, Mass.: NFPA, n.d.), n.p.

In the United States, codes, standards, and regulations related to fire and rescue services are developed by federal government agencies and by organizations such as NFPA, the American National Standards Institute (ANSI), and the American Conference of Governmental Industrial Hygienists (ACGIH).

Some of the federal rules and regulations were initially intended for general industry use—for example, in construction or industrial firefighting—but over time they came to cover local fire services. The primary agency with which the fire service interacts is the Occupational Safety and Health Administration (OSHA) within the Department of Labor. Other agencies whose rules and regulations bear on the fire service are the National Institute for Occupational Safety and Health (NIOSH); Environmental Protection Agency (EPA); Centers for Disease Control and Prevention (CDC); Federal Emergency Management Agency; and Departments of Transportation, Justice, and Defense.

The regulations developed by federal OSHA (see the sidebar on federal and state OSHAs) often refer to the standards developed through consensus by NFPA, a nonprofit membership organization open to both individuals and organizations. OSHA has also cited NFPA standards in its enforcement procedures. In turn, NFPA has used OSHA rules and regulations as references in its standards, and OSHA personnel actively participate in the NFPA standards-making process by sitting on technical committees.

The next two sections of this chapter describe, respectively, the regulations of OSHA and those of NIOSH that are most relevant to the management of fire and rescue services. Regulations of EPA and the CDC are also mentioned. The subsequent section reviews the NFPA standards that are most widely adopted by communities; discussed in some detail are the legal considerations related to the NFPA standard on medical requirements for firefighters. The chapter concludes with an overview of the legal context within which regulations, standards, and codes are brought to bear in the courtroom: the liability of fire service organizations for negligent firefighting is explored.

Occupational Safety and Health Administration regulations

Congress created OSHA when it passed the Occupational Safety and Health Act of 1970 (29 U.S.C. 651 *et seq.*). The act made OSHA responsible for promulgating regulations to protect the health and safety of U.S. workers. As directed, OSHA adopted existing federal standards and national consensus standards that had been developed by various organizations, including NFPA, ANSI, and the ACGIH.

OSHA regulations deal with such issues as hearing conservation, respiratory protection, and infection control—issues of fundamental importance to fire and rescue services. "Studies have shown that fire-fighting functions require working at near-maximal heart rates for prolonged periods of time. . . . [Firefighters]

Federal and state OSHAs   The regulations issued by federal OSHA have been adopted by twenty-five states inasmuch as those states' legislatures have enacted federal OSHA by law. Any of these twenty-five states may also have its own state OSHA. The twenty-five states that have not adopted federal OSHA legislatively have their own state OSHAs or some semblance thereof. The twenty-five federal OSHA states are required to have a safety and health plan for all public employees, including fire department members. (The District of Columbia, not being a state, is not subject to this requirement.)

and emergency response personnel also are exposed to many toxic substances during their work. . . . Available data indicate that [firefighters] have increased risk for injuries, pulmonary disease, cardiovascular disease, cancer, and noise-induced hearing loss."[1] OSHA regulations may also deal with, for example, local government safety and health programs, risk management requirements for mandatory seat belt usage, and local government employee assistance programs.

Typically OSHA's and other federal agencies' rules and regulations are developed and revised through a comprehensive public review and hearing process in which the public is encouraged to participate. Hearings to receive public testimony are held in numerous locations, and written testimony is allowed if someone is unable to attend the hearings. Proposed revisions and information about hearings are published in the *Federal Register*.

As explained above in the sidebar on federal and state OSHAs, in some instances—that is, in states that have opted not to adopt (legislatively) the OSHA regulations for municipal brigades (i.e., fire departments)—federal OSHA may have no direct enforcement authority to ensure that state and local governments comply with its safety and health regulations, such as the OSHA fire brigade regulation for public employees. Industry, however, has no option.

But if federal OSHA has approved a state's safety and health plan, the state may opt to implement its own enforcement program. Section 18 of the Occupational Safety and Health Act requires that a state must provide satisfactory assurance that it will establish and maintain an effective and comprehensive occupational safety and health program for all public employees that is as effective as the program in the approved state plan covering private employees. OSHA has given those states in which an OSHA–state plan agreement is in effect six months from the publication date of the final OSHA regulation to adopt a comparable standard that is "at least as effective" as the OSHA standard. All fire departments (whether state, county, or local) in any of the states or territories where such an agreement is in effect therefore have the protection of the minimally acceptable safety and health standards promulgated by federal OSHA. Individual states may provide more stringent standards if they wish. As of 1998, twenty-five states and territories had state OSHA plans.[2]

Federal OSHA has also issued a set of rules and regulations that would allow for the development of a state plan applicable to, and enforceable for, public employees in states where an approved state plan for private employees does not yet exist. These rules and regulations—29 CFR 1956, State Plans for the Development and Enforcement of State Standards Applicable to State and Local Government Employees in States without Approved Private Employee Plans—set forth the requirement that if states without approved plans for private employees wish to receive federal financial support for public employee safety and health programs, they must develop a safety and health plan for public employees that meets the requirements of the plans in states whose plans have been approved.

When one considers the existing OSHA regulations and the protections they provide, the fact that public employees are covered under minimum acceptable standards as promulgated by federal OSHA becomes important. In states whose plans have been approved by federal OSHA, these standards are enforceable for all public firefighters.

The OSHA regulations that are widely used, interpreted, and enforced in the fire service are discussed below. They deal with hazardous waste and materials, respiratory protection, fire brigades (departments), bloodborne pathogens, hazard communication (employee right to know), and noise exposure and hearing protection.

Hazardous waste and materials (29 CFR 1910.120 and companion EPA regulation 40 CFR 311)

The development, implementation, and enforcement of 29 CFR 1910.120 and 40 CFR 311 are applicable to fire service personnel as emergency responders to hazardous materials (HAZMAT) incidents. These two regulations require minimal initial training at the operational level (see the sidebar on definitions of responder levels at HAZMAT incidents), with annual documented training thereafter. Personnel who are assigned to supervisory positions at incidents should be trained in the positions of incident commander, sector officer, HAZMAT safety officer, and other functional positions within an incident management system. A HAZMAT incident is the only kind of incident at which all personnel involved in it are required to use and be trained in the incident command system. (OSHA regulation 1910.120, enacted in 1986, specifically uses the name "incident command system." The incident command system is just one type of incident management system; the latter term is used in NFPA standards.) Also required are the proper training in and use of personal protective clothing and equipment, and annual medical evaluations for responders.

In the twenty-five OSHA-plan states, enforcement of the two regulations is the responsibility of federal OSHA. In the other twenty-five states, EPA is responsible for enforcement.

The two regulations are complemented by NFPA Standards 471 and 473. NFPA 471, Recommended Practice for Responding to Hazardous Materials Incidents (2002 edition), outlines the professional competencies in specific terms for both private and public sector employees who respond to HAZMAT incidents. NFPA 473, Standard for Competencies for EMS [emergency medical service] Personnel Responding to Hazardous Materials Incidents (2002 edition), likewise applies these criteria to public and private sector employees. If a jurisdiction uses a third-party EMS provider or has a third-service rescue crew/squad (a contractual ambulance service) that responds to these incidents, the personnel must be trained and able to operate within the jurisdiction's incident

---

Definitions of responder levels at HAZMAT incidents There are four levels of responder at HAZMAT incidents: awareness, operational, technician, and command.

Awareness level First responders at the awareness level are those who, in the course of their normal duties, can be the first on the scene of an emergency involving hazardous materials. They are expected to recognize the presence of hazardous materials, protect themselves, call for trained personnel, and secure the area.

Operational level First responders at the operational level are those who, as part of the initial response to the incident, respond to actual or potential releases of hazardous materials for the

purpose of protecting nearby persons, the environment, or property from the effects of the release. They should be trained to respond defensively to control the release from a safe distance and keep it from spreading.

Technician level HAZMAT technicians are those who respond to actual or potential releases of hazardous materials for the purpose of controlling the release. They are expected to use specialized chemical protective clothing and specialized control equipment.

Command level The incident commander is the person responsible for all decisions relating to management of the incident. This person is in charge of the incident site.

command system. If a fire service is providing emergency medical capabilities at incident scenes, it has probably addressed the issues dealt with by NFPA 473.

Respiratory protection (29 CFR 1910.134)

OSHA initially promulgated the respiratory protection regulation in the early 1970s to regulate the training, staffing, use, and medical evaluations of personnel assigned to use respiratory protection. With many revisions and clarifications, the regulation was reissued on January 8, 1998. It applies to both private and public employees. Other applicable standards that are referenced in the regulation are ANSI Z87.1, Practice for Occupational and Educational Eye and Face Protection; ANSI Z88.5, Practices for Respiratory Protection for the Fire Service; and ANSI/CGA [Compressed Gas Association] G7.1, Commodity Specification for Air.

Also referenced in this regulation are the following NFPA standards (titled here in accordance with their most current editions as of 2002): NFPA 1500, Standard on Fire Department Occupational Safety and Health Program (2002 edition) (discussed below); NFPA 1981, Standard on Open-Circuit Self-Contained Breathing Apparatus for Fire Fighters (2002 edition); NFPA 1404, Standard for Fire Service Respiratory Protection Training (2002 edition); and NFPA 600, Standard on Industrial Fire Brigades (2000 edition).

Certain issues connected with this regulation have heightened the fire service's awareness and use of it. These issues are (1) the wording of, and discussion about, the "two-in/two-out" section and its relationship with NFPA 1500; (2) the process for maintaining communication and accountability between the interior and exterior personnel; and (3) annual medical examinations and their compatibility with NFPA 1582. (NFPA 1582, Standard on Medical Requirements for Fire Fighters and Information for Fire Department Physicians [2000 edition], is discussed below.)

The first issue has probably changed many departments' practices regarding deployment and organization at an incident scene. The OSHA regulation is very clear about the assembly of four personnel and the establishment of personnel entering an atmosphere that is actually or potentially immediately dangerous to life and health. The issue was first discussed in the 1992 edition of NFPA 1500, and the discussion was revised and clarified in the 1997 edition. OSHA's revision was clearly aligned with the intent of NFPA 1500: that personnel at an incident scene should be deployed safely and efficiently.

The second issue concerns the tracking of personnel, or accountability. The OSHA regulation does not allow for radios to be used as tools for direct communication between personnel, unlike NFPA 1500, which does.

The last issue involves the use of and requirements for medical examinations for personnel required to wear respiratory protection. Medical requirements under the OSHA regulations are less restrictive than those contained in NFPA 1582. The OSHA regulations provide a template, or checklist, that needs to be completed by an occupational physician, and the requirements are limited. In both NFPA's statistical data and the NIOSH firefighter fatality investigation reports, however, someone's ability to work with respiratory protection equipment is directly correlated with that person's medical and physical conditions. OSHA does not address physical conditioning, whereas NFPA 1500 and 1582 do.

Fire brigades (29 CFR 1910.156)

Federal OSHA uses the term *fire brigade* to refer to both public and private fire departments. (In the United Kingdom, the term describes a municipal fire department.) NFPA, however, differentiates between fire departments (which have fire trucks and fire stations) and fire brigades (which do not). NFPA 600, Standard on Industrial Fire Brigades, covers health and safety issues for industrial fire brigades, whereas NFPA 1500 covers the same issues for industrial (among others) fire departments.

A major concern of industrial fire protection professionals is protecting their employees and property from the threat of fire in the workplace. In 1980 OSHA defined its requirements for fire brigades at industrial facilities.

In an attempt to establish levels of fire brigade function and to identify the training and safety requirements for each level, subpart L of the OSHA regulation defines two types of fire brigades: the incipient-stage category (basically, fighting small fires with fire extinguishers) and the interior structural brigade category (doing the same thing that local fire departments do). Industrial fire protection professionals have been wrestling with the need to categorize existing fire brigades as one of the two types.

In attempting to develop a state-of-the-art industrial fire brigade standard, NFPA's Technical Committee on Loss Prevention Procedures and Practices has followed OSHA's lead in setting requirements that depend on which definition a fire brigade meets—incipient stage or interior structural. This standard, NFPA 600, applies NFPA 1500 to the industrial fire service.

In many respects the needs of industrial fire brigades, including those that can be referred to as industrial fire departments, are far different from the needs of local government fire departments. But the primary difference between the two is that industrial fire brigades must deal only with conditions and hazards that exist within a given facility, generally one that is privately owned and operated. Although these site-specific hazards can and do represent the same degree of hazard to both industrial fire brigade members and local government firefighters, industrial fire brigade members are not usually concerned or expected to deal with hazards and emergencies beyond the boundaries of the facility served by the brigade.

It must also be remembered that at an industrial facility, a program of occupational safety and health has already been established for all personnel, including members of the fire brigade. Further, fire brigades constituted in accordance with the standard of this established program will almost certainly have a much more thorough knowledge of the buildings and facilities where they respond than will local government firefighters, who must respond to a significantly greater variety of buildings and facilities, many of which have unidentified and undisclosed hazards. A local government fire department, providing service to a very broad based jurisdiction, faces a multitude of potentially unknown factors at any given response. Factors that can hinder the effectiveness of any local government fire department and place firefighters at greater safety risk include such variables as property size and accessibility; building size, construction, and contents; manufacturing-process hazards; fixed fire-extinguishing systems and special agent availability; and the storage and use of solvents, oils, chemicals, or other hazardous materials.

Bloodborne pathogens (29 CFR 1910.1030)

In 1991 OSHA issued a regulation on bloodborne pathogens, outlining how firefighters, emergency medical technicians, and other health care workers are to be equipped and trained to protect themselves from these pathogens. The introductory text of the regulation outlines in great detail the rationale behind the development of this document. OSHA recognizes that bloodborne pathogens—including, among others, the hepatitis B virus (HBV) and the human immunodeficiency virus (HIV)—account for significant morbidity and mortality in the workplace. In the final text of the regulation OSHA estimates that "for every 1,000 workers with occupational exposure to blood or other potentially infectious material, between 83 and 113 will become infected with HBV over the course of their working lifetime because of occupational exposure to the virus."

This regulation relies on several mechanisms to protect workers: engineering controls, a risk management plan, personal protective clothing and equipment, training, an exposure-reporting process, and the offer of hepatitis vaccinations to all at-risk employees at no cost to them. Many fire departments have extended the vaccination process to other infectious and communicable diseases, such as flu, tuberculosis, and hepatitis C.

The primary issue here is worker protection. With over 70 percent of the fire departments in the United States providing EMS at some level and with those responses constituting 60–70 percent of those departments' total responses, care providers (EMS workers) are facing increased risk. NFPA 1581, Standard on Fire Department Infection Control Program (2000 edition) (discussed below), reinforces the requirements of the OSHA regulation. Protection of workers against bloodborne pathogens is a key component of a fire department's occupational safety and health program.

As of 2002, only six states did not have worker notification laws (laws requiring that workers who have been exposed to bloodborne pathogens be notified of their exposure). The six states were Alaska, Nevada, New Mexico, New York, South Dakota, and Vermont. Figure 13–1 lists the states that as of 1998 had laws allowing the testing of people to whose blood a firefighter or EMS worker had been exposed.

Hazard communication (employee right to know) (29 CFR 1910.1200)

OSHA's regulation on hazard communication requires that people responsible for the areas in which hazardous substances are stored shall be trained in the chemical and physical hazards of stored materials and of combinations of stored materials. The training is to include adequate coverage of other topics as listed in the regulation. Because fire service personnel respond to HAZMAT incidents, they fall under this regulation.

Material safety data sheets prepared in accordance with this regulation describe the composition of a material, its hazardous properties, mitigation of the hazard, and information about disposal of the material. Employers are required to provide the employee (firefighter) with access to the information contained in material safety data sheets for the types of materials or substances that may be used or stored in the workplace.

Many fire departments have met the training requirements of this regulation by incorporating the requirements from 29 CFR 1910.120 (see "Hazardous Waste and Materials" above) into the requirements of 29 CFR 1910.1200. The requirements of both these regulations are met when the community updates

Figure 13–1 States with laws allowing for testing of victims, 1998.

Arkansas	Illinois	Mississippi	Pennsylvania[a,c]
Colorado	Iowa	Montana[a,c]	Rhode Island[a]
Connecticut[a,b]	Louisiana[a]	Nebraska	Texas
Delaware	Maine[b]	New Mexico	Utah[c]
Florida	Maryland[c]	North Dakota[c,d]	Virginia
Hawaii	Michigan	Ohio[b]	Washington
Idaho[c]	Minnesota[c,d]	Oregon[c,d]	Wisconsin

Note: "Victim" designates any person to whose blood a firefighter or EMS technician has been exposed.
[a] Testing may be performed on any blood or bodily fluid previously drawn.
[b] A court order to require testing of the victim may be obtained.
[c] Informed consent from the victim is required.
[d] Consent is not required on deceased persons.

its comprehensive emergency management plan as required by Title III of the Superfund Amendments and Reauthorization Act (SARA) of 1986.

HAZMAT terminology defined   The term *hazardous material* is defined and described in many ways, depending on the nature of the problem being addressed and the purpose of the defining agency. The federal agencies involved, as well as state and local governments, have different purposes in regulating hazardous materials that, under certain circumstances, pose a risk to the public or the environment, and no single list or definition covers everything. This list touches on the major categories of hazardous substances.

Hazardous materials   The Department of Transportation (DOT) uses the term *hazardous materials* to cover eleven classes of hazards, some of which have subcategories, called "divisions." DOT regulations put hazardous substances and hazardous wastes into Class 9 (Miscellaneous Hazardous Materials). Both hazardous substances and hazardous wastes are regulated by the Environmental Protection Agency (EPA) if their inherent properties would not otherwise be covered (i.e., by other regulatory agencies, such as the Nuclear Regulatory Commission or the Department of Energy).

Hazardous substances   EPA uses the term *hazardous substances* for chemicals that, if released into the environment above a certain amount, must be reported; and depending on the threat to the environment, federal involvement in handling the incident can be authorized. A list of EPA-designated hazardous substances is published in 40 CFR 302, Table 302.4. OSHA uses the term *hazardous substance* to mean every chemical that is regulated by both DOT and EPA (see 29 CFR 1910.120, a regulation that resulted from Title I of the Superfund Amendments and Reauthorization Act [SARA] of 1986 and covers emergency response).

Extremely hazardous substances   EPA uses the term *extremely hazardous substances* for chemicals that must be reported to the appropriate authorities if released above the threshold reporting quantity. The list of extremely hazardous substances is published in Title III of SARA (40 CFR 355).

Toxic chemicals   EPA uses the term *toxic chemicals* for chemicals whose total emissions or releases must be reported annually by the owners and operators of certain facilities that manufacture, process, or otherwise use a listed toxic chemical. The list of toxic chemicals is published in Title III of SARA.

Hazardous wastes   EPA uses the term *hazardous wastes* for chemicals that are regulated under the Resource Conservation and Recovery Act (40 CFR 261.33). Hazardous wastes in transportation are regulated by DOT (49 CFR 170–179).

Hazardous chemicals   OSHA uses the term *hazardous chemicals* to denote any chemical that would be a risk to employees if they were exposed to it in the workplace. Hazardous chemicals cover a broader group of chemicals than the other chemical lists.

Dangerous goods   In Canadian transportation, hazardous materials are called "dangerous goods."

Highly hazardous chemicals   OSHA uses the term *highly hazardous chemicals* for chemicals that fall under the requirements of 29 CFR 1910.119, Process Safety Management of Highly Hazardous Chemicals. Highly hazardous chemicals are chemicals that possess toxic, reactive, flammable, or explosive properties. A list of covered substances is published in Appendix A of the OSHA rule (i.e., 29 CFR 1910.119).

Noise exposure and hearing protection (29 CFR 1910.135)

OSHA noise requirements as of the year 2002 specify a maximum permissible noise exposure level (PEL) of 90 dBA (A-weighted decibels) for an eight-hour duration, with higher levels allowed for shorter durations. This level is known as a time-weighted average sound level (TWA). When firefighters are exposed to different levels for different periods, the TWA must be calculated. To protect the worker when sound levels exceed the PEL, OSHA requires sufficient engineering controls, a hearing conservation program, or a combination of both.

The OSHA requirements are also included in NFPA 1500 as part of a hearing conservation program. Other NFPA standards, such as NFPA 1901, Standard for Automotive Fire Apparatus (1999 edition), and NFPA 1582, Standard on Medical Requirements for Fire Fighters and Information for Fire Department Physicians, also require noise-level engineering controls and audiometric testing as part of a hearing conservation program.

National Institute for Occupational Safety and Health rules and regulations

The National Institute for Occupational Safety and Health (NIOSH), an agency within the Department of Health and Human Services with offices across the country, has been actively involved in issues of fire service occupational health. Most fire service personnel need to be familiar with NIOSH's certification of respiratory protection equipment—specifically, self-contained breathing apparatus (SCBA) (42 CFR 84). This certification process, formerly carried out in conjunction with the Bureau of Mine Safety (which is now part of NIOSH), certifies that every SCBA unit meets the standards. When discussing SCBA as a primary component of the firefighter's personal protective equipment, buyers, users, and enforcers must understand that when a unit is approved under the NIOSH certification process, it is approved as a total unit with all the components. This understanding is also valid for particular NFPA standards, especially NFPA 1981, Standard on Open-Circuit Self-Contained Breathing Apparatus for Fire Fighters.

In the fall of 1997, Congress appropriated $2.5 million for NIOSH to establish a dedicated firefighter fatality investigation team that would be able to deploy anywhere in the United States or its territories to investigate and issue reports on the specifics of a fatality. NIOSH uses existing databases (NFPA's, the one maintained by the International Association of Fire Fighters, and the one maintained by the U.S. Fire Administration)[3] to help track short- and long-term trends in injuries, fatalities, and health-related exposures of firefighters, both career and volunteer (see Figures 13–2, 13–3, and 13–4). This effort is supported by all fire service organizations. Within its investigation division, NIOSH has set up a specific team to look at and track cardiac fatalities. NFPA statistics show that more than 50 percent of firefighter fatalities are caused by heart attacks and that 50 percent of those 50 percent occur to people with previously diagnosed heart-related problems.

NIOSH is also working closely with the CDC and the health-related professions in developing rules and regulations to protect workers from exposure to and transmission of infectious diseases.[4] With the fire service reporting that a majority of its responses continue to be related to EMS, the need for a proactive infection control policy and program is paramount; the need is paramount even in fire departments that do not provide EMS, because the incidents to which fire departments are called to respond—including domestic violence, hazardous materials/waste, and even routine structure fires—can potentially infect a fire department member. The person or persons appointed to fill the position of infection control officer need not be an officer, but someone must fill the po-

Figure 13–2 Number of on-duty firefighter deaths, 1977–2001.

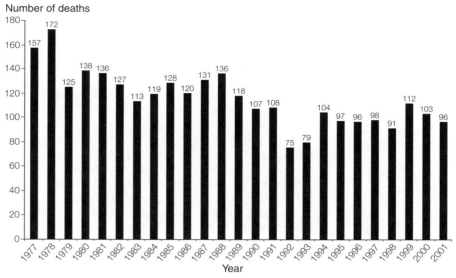

Number of deaths

Year

Note: According to a forthcoming report from NFPA, this figure is intended to reflect "the types of fatal situations that occur each year." Therefore, it does not include the firefighters who perished at the World Trade Center on September 11, 2001.

Figure 13–3 Number of on-duty firefighter deaths by age and cause of death (2001).

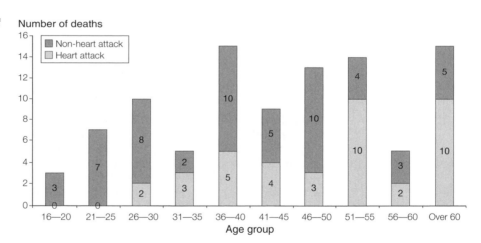

Number of deaths

Age group

Figure 13–4 Percentage of firefighter deaths by cause of injury (2001).

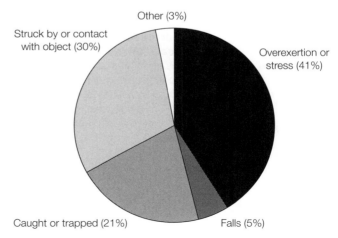

sition of designated officer as required in Public Law 101-381, The Ryan White Comprehensive AIDS Resources Emergency (CARE) Act of 1991.

National Fire Protection Association (NFPA) standards

The National Fire Protection Association (NFPA), founded in 1895 and based in Quincy, Massachusetts, is an international consensus standards-making organization accredited by ANSI (its documents carry the ANSI standard).

NFPA standards address issues affecting fire protection, fire prevention, public life safety education, and fire suppression, and the fire service has always taken an active interest in their use, adoption, and enforcement. As of the year 2002, NFPA has more than three hundred codes, standards, and recommended practices that are used internationally and are called the National Fire Codes.[5]

Typically NFPA standards are revised every three to five years. The revision process contains two public review processes, when the public may submit proposals and comments on an existing document or on revisions to an existing document.

NFPA staff provide support to technical committees, develop handbooks and workbooks, present papers at conferences and events, provide professional development classes, and field technical advisory service calls in their areas of expertise. Within the Public Fire Protection Division—examples of other divisions are engineering and data analysis—most staff members have an extensive fire service background, with the division's staff as a whole coming from many different types of fire departments and various geographical areas.

This section discusses only the fire protection standards that are most widely used and generate the greatest number of questions from NFPA fire service members: NFPA 1500, 1521, 1561, 1581, and 1582. In addition, the section touches briefly on groups of standards that deal with professional qualifications, training, professional clothing and equipment, apparatus, and hazardous materials.

The Technical Committee on Fire Service Occupational Safety and Health was responsible for developing the standards discussed here. In January 1997, NFPA's Standards Council divided the committee into two, one responsible for occupational safety and the other for occupational medicine and health. The Technical Committee on Fire Service Occupational Safety has responsibility for NFPA 1500, 1521, and 1561. The Technical Committee on Fire Service Occupational Medicine and Health has responsibility for NFPA 1581, 1582, 1583, and proposed 1584.

About the National Fire Protection Association (NFPA) NFPA's *National Fire Codes*®, adopted and enforced throughout the world, are administered by more than 220 technical committees on which sit approximately 6,100 volunteers. NFPA is a nonprofit membership organization with nearly seventy thousand members from seventy nations. Members represent business and industry, excluding insurance and fire equipment manufacturers and distributors (20 percent); health care facilities (11 percent); the fire service (24 percent); the insurance industry (6 percent); federal, state, and local governments (7 percent); architects and engineers (8 percent); fire equipment manufacturers and distributors (6 percent); trade and professional associations (2 percent); and other fields and disciplines (16 percent).

Adapted with permission from "Codes and Standards for a Safer World" (Quincy, Mass.: NFPA, n.d.), n.p.

Participating in the development of NFPA codes and standards It is incumbent on the parties who are affected by codes, standards, and regulations to understand and participate in the process of developing them. People can participate as individuals or through representative associations, such as ICMA, the National League of Cities, the National Association of Counties, the International Association of Fire Chiefs, the International Association of Fire Fighters, or the National Volunteer Fire Council.

Within NFPA, the development of codes and standards is a consensus-making process. Typically NFPA documents are revised every three to five years in a specific cycle, and anyone who wants to participate can do so. To submit proposals or comments on new or revised NFPA documents, one does not have to belong to NFPA or serve as a member of a technical committee.

Public proposals to change or revise a standard are submitted to NFPA electronically or on paper and are electronically logged in as they are received. The submitter of the proposal receives confirmation from NFPA that the proposal has been received.

A standards-making technical committee with responsibility for changing or revising the standard schedules a meeting to respond to the public's proposals. The committee has a series of options for responding: *accept, accept in part, accept in principle, accept in part and principle,* or *reject.* On any of these actions except "accept," the committee must report to the submitter in writing why it acted as it did. The committee members are then polled by letter on the actions they took (i.e., on the proposed revised document), and if the revision receives a two-thirds affir-

mative vote, it then moves forward in the process. The proposed document is put on NFPA's Web page, and copies (on paper, on floppy disk, or in CD format) are available free of charge. This proposed document is called an ROP (Report on Proposals).

A sixty-day window for public comment follows. Again, comments are received and logged in electronically, and the submitter receives confirmation of receipt. The committee schedules another meeting to respond to the comments. The possible actions on the comments are the same as those on the proposals, and each particular action taken is communicated, with an explanation, to the submitter. Again committee members are polled by mail, and the proposed document must achieve a two-thirds affirmative vote. A document that is so affirmed is called an ROC (Report on Comments) and is available in the same three formats.

The proposed document then comes to a vote of the NFPA membership at either the fall meeting in November or the annual meeting in May. On the floor at the meeting, many actions can take place, including motions by those who submitted proposals or comments but were not satisfied by the actions of the technical committee. The association membership can then either overturn the technical committee's decision and agree with the submitter or uphold the committee's actions. If the membership votes in favor of the document with or without amendments, the revised text moves forward to NFPA's Standards Council for adoption.

A submitter of a proposal or comment who does not agree with actions taken may appeal the decision first to the Standards Council and then up to NFPA's board of directors.

NFPA 1500, Standard on Fire Department Occupational Safety and Health Program

Development of NFPA 1500 began in the early 1980s, when a contingent of fire service leaders and experts in the field of occupational safety and health began developing document(s) whose effect would be to reduce the number of firefighter fatalities and injuries. The original goals of that group are still intact today as committee members, using NFPA and other major fire service organizations' data, continue to strive toward reducing those numbers.

The result was the first edition (in 1987) of NFPA 1500, Standard on a Fire Department Occupational Safety and Health Program. The standard was intended as an umbrella document under which specific standards would be developed to outline various components of a safety and health program. This intention was fulfilled with the development of five documents and the splitting of the technical committee into the two mentioned above. By 1997, when the third edition of the document was published, the number of firefighter fatalities and injuries had dropped dramatically.

Despite mostly small fluctuations, the number of firefighter fatalities has been steadily on the decline since 1988—except in 1994, when thirty-seven wildland firefighters lost their lives. (Again, as indicated by the note on Figure 13–2, this trend does not reflect the 340 firefighters who died on September 11, 2001.) This steady drop was due partly to safety consciousness on the part of fire service personnel, whose level of awareness of how to work safely in a dangerous occupation was raised by NFPA 1500. However, much work remains to be done. Several tragedies in 1995 and 1996 occurred when an incident management system (IMS) was not used, an accountability system was not in place, or protective equipment was either not worn or not activated.[6] In other words, safety cannot result from regulations or standards alone.

The third (1997) edition of this standard incorporated the fruit of significant work by members of the technical committee in the areas of risk management, training requirements for personnel who could be required to do wildland firefighting, and increased training in and awareness of the cleaning and disinfection of protective clothing and equipment. The committee spent considerable time and effort working on Chapter 6 of the standard, expanding the discussion of accountability and incident management, rehabilitation, and fire department operations that involve civil disturbances and/or terrorism. The committee also included text on facility safety (putting sample inspection sheets in the appendix) and on medical requirements. (These requirements were also updated in NFPA 1582, as discussed below.) The committee split the subject matter of employee assistance programs and critical incident stress into two chapters and expanded the material in the appendix to provide additional information on, or guidance about, the committee's intent. The third edition of NFPA 1500 serves as the parent document for all the fire service occupational safety and health documents, and it references numerous other NFPA standards that deal with this subject and contribute to firefighter safety.

NFPA 1521, Standard for Fire Department Safety Officer

NFPA adopted the first edition of the Standard for Fire Department Safety Officer in 1977. The second edition—a complete revision—was adopted in 1987. Both editions were identified as NFPA 1501. But in 1992, when another complete revision was adopted, the identifying number was changed to NFPA 1521 to fit into the numbering plan for all fire service occupational safety and health documents.

In the 1997 revision to what had become NFPA 1521, the committee focused on adding text to differentiate between the role of incident scene safety officer and that of health safety officer: numerous questions had arisen about the roles and responsibilities, qualifications, and training for each of these positions. As of 1994–1995 the National Fire Academy, with assistance from NFPA staff and members of the technical committee, had developed two courses for the fire service outlining the differences in these two positions and referencing the applicable requirements from within NFPA 1521. The courses provide an opportunity for the fire service to train personnel who have been designated for these positions.

The 1997 edition of NFPA 1521 includes sample forms to help with fire station inspections, and it shows how each of the two positions fits into a fire department's development of a risk management plan—a key component of any fire department's occupational safety and health program.

NFPA 1561, Standard on Emergency Services Incident Management System

One of the areas addressed in NFPA 1500 is a standard for fire departments to conduct emergency response operations with an effective IMS. Although op-

---

NFPA resources NFPA codes and standards are constantly reviewed by their respective technical committees to ensure that they are kept current with new fire protection knowledge and technologies. To keep the documents up to date, technical committees gather information using state-of-the-art resources, in addition to public input and the involvement of expert committee volunteers. Five examples of the resources used are discussed here.

To provide new information about the effectiveness and actual application of NFPA codes and standards, the NFPA Fire Investigations Department conducts on-site investigations of fires and related disasters that have occurred all around the world. After completing a thorough investigation of an incident site, the department publishes a comprehensive report that thoroughly analyzes the fire or explosion, focusing on how NFPA codes and standards were used, how effective these guidelines were during the event, and—when the codes and standards were not followed —how they might have provided additional protection.

The NFPA One-Stop Data Shop (OSDS) is the NFPA statistical data archive that publishes reports measuring the size and characteristics of particular fire problems. The data are from the U.S. Fire Administration's National Fire Incident Reporting System (NFIRS), the Fire Protection Research Foundation (FPRF), the NFPA Fire Investigations

Department, and various other fire data resources around the world. Data from the OSDS allow customized data to be compiled on specific hazards or safety issues, as requested by technical committees.

The FPRF conducts independent research on fire risk, new technologies, and fire strategies, and publishes research reports that serve the technical committees as primary resources. From time to time, technical committees directly ask for specific research on subjects relevant to them. The FPRF will determine whether the specific study has been done before and, if it has not, will help obtain the needed information from research, testing, consulting, or other institutions.

NFPA's Charles S. Morgan Technical Library contains the largest fire protection collection in the United States and one of the largest in the world. It has a comprehensive collection of more than 3,000 books, 6,500 technical reports, 200 periodicals, films, videocassettes, and NFPA-published archives dating from the association's founding in 1896.

The NFPA Web site, *http://www.nfpa. org,* provides direct support for the codes and standards process, including the online submission of proposals and comments.

Adapted with permission from "Codes and Standards for a Safer World" (Quincy, Mass.: NFPA, n.d.), n.p.

erational coordination and effectiveness are often considered to be the primary objectives of an IMS, the technical committee recognized the safety aspects of a functional command structure. The consequences of operating without an effective IMS have been documented in reports on deaths and injuries to firefighters.

When NFPA 1500 was being developed, several different incident management systems and many local variations were known to be in use. In the development of these systems, safety and health had not necessarily been identified as major concerns. The technical committee determined that, in addition to specifying the use of an IMS, it should establish performance criteria for the components of the system that would contribute directly toward safety and health objectives. Accordingly, the committee set to work developing a standard on incident management that would specifically address those concerns. NFPA 1561, adopted in 1990, was the result.

In developing this document, the committee examined several incident management systems that were in use in different fire departments and in related organizations. Committee members also met with representatives of departments that were successfully using one or another system, and with organizations that developed and provided training in recognized systems—systems of whose existence others were aware.

The committee concluded that many of the performance objectives of this standard could be met by the adoption of any one of the existing recognized systems. (Two such were the fire ground command system developed by the Phoenix [Arizona] Fire Department in 1974 and the incident command system developed by a group of fire service professionals in California in the early 1970s.) The committee also decided that some additional considerations might be necessary to address specific safety and health concerns, including the problem of maintaining accountability for members operating at the scene of an incident. The standard allows organizations to adopt or modify existing systems to suit local requirements and preferences, as long as they meet the performance objectives that are considered important for safety and health. Among these objectives are having an incident commander, a safety officer, a defined span of control, a defined strategy and tactics, a risk management plan, and a plan for the allocation of resources.

In short, because the majority of existing systems were observed to be more similar than different, with the greatest variations being terminological (the components themselves were similar), the overall opinion of the committee was that it would be more beneficial to have every fire department adopt a suitable system than to create one specific system and suggest that every organization adopt it. Most of the existing recognized systems should be able to conform to the standard with few, if any, modifications.

The technical committee believed that this document emphasized the essential considerations for safety and health in incident management systems and would lead the fire service to use such systems in managing all emergency incidents. The goal will be reached when effective incident management is routinely practiced for all types of situations.

During the revision process of this document, the technical committee revisited areas that had been looked at in the initial development of NFPA 1561: accountability, use of rapid intervention crews for rescue of members, interagency cooperation, and the realization that incident management includes more than fire ground operations. The second (1995) edition expanded the discussion of these areas to reflect the mainstream use of an IMS.

As the roles and responsibilities of the fire service expand, it is in fact critical for the health and safety of fire department members that an IMS be used. Furthermore, because the actions or inactions of other agencies with which the department responds and works affect fire department members directly, those other agencies must also be properly trained to use the system—that is, whichever IMS is the one being used.

NFPA 1581, Standard on Fire Department Infection Control Program

NFPA 1581 was developed to address infection control practices. These practices are necessary for persons providing emergency medical care, persons who come in contact with potentially infectious victims, and other persons in both emergency and nonemergency settings. The standard was developed to be compatible with guidelines and regulations from the CDC and NIOSH that apply to public safety and emergency response personnel. (See the section above on NIOSH rules and regulations.)

NFPA 1581 was approved in 1992. In the 1997 revision, members of the technical committee addressed numerous items dealing with decontamination, separation of equipment, location(s) where equipment can be stored, and the overall concept of a safe and healthy work environment. The appendix of the 1997 revision includes sample infection control policy statements, programs, and exposure forms. The revision also references the federal regulations, guidelines, and informative publications that appeared after the first edition of the standard had been published.

NFPA 1582, Standard on Medical Requirements for Fire Fighters and Information for Fire Department Physicians

In 1988 a joint task force of members representing the Technical Committee on Fire Service Occupational Safety and Health and the Technical Committee on Fire Fighter Professional Qualifications began addressing medical requirements for firefighters. In 1990, a standing subcommittee on Medical/Physical Requirements for Fire Fighters was created under the Fire Service Occupational Safety and Health Committee and given responsibility for developing NFPA 1582.

Published in 1990, NFPA 1582 created two categories of medical conditions, Categories A and B. Category A represents conditions that, if they exist in the candidate or current firefighter, will not allow this person to perform firefighting operations. Conditions in Category B, in contrast, must be evaluated on a case-by-case basis so that the fire department physician can determine whether the medical condition in a particular candidate or current firefighter will prevent that person from performing firefighting operations. Chapter 3 of the standard describes the actual medical conditions that make up the two categories. Chapter 2 addresses medical evaluations, medical examinations, record keeping, and confidentiality. The appendix contains extensive advisory and informational material for fire department administrators and fire department physicians on how to use and implement the standard.

In revising NFPA 1582 in 1995, the technical committee wanted to update five critical areas: hearing, vision, and cardiac, neurological, and metabolic conditions. The committee then moved some of the previous Category A medical conditions into Category B and enhanced some of the remaining Category A material (i.e., material on conditions that would prohibit an individual from being hired or from continuing as a structural firefighter). In addition, the committee added (1) explanatory material on medical conditions whose categories were changed (e.g., a number of cardiac conditions, diabetic conditions, seizure disorders, asthma, and therapeutic anticoagulation); (2) further information about requirements under the Americans with Disabilities Act; (3) explanatory material for both fire department administrators and fire department physicians;

and (4) sample physician checklist forms. Currently (2002) this technical committee is working on the 2003 edition, which will focus on the candidate being hired as a firefighter and will incorporate text adopted by the International Association of Fire Fighters and the International Association of Fire Chiefs into an incumbents' occupational medical program. This proactive approach allows for screening before hire and then an ongoing medical and wellness program for incumbents.

Legal considerations in applying NFPA 1582　When the determination is made whether to accept an application (or, for an already hired firefighter, whether to continue that person's employment), basing the decision on medical or physical performance evaluations has legal implications. Thus, the authority with jurisdiction may wish to consult counsel before making an adverse employment decision based on NFPA 1582. This sidebar discusses legal issues relating to (1) persons with handicaps or disabilities, (2) antidiscrimination laws, (3) protected classes, and (4) pregnancy and reproduction.

Individuals with handicaps or disabilities　The Rehabilitation Act of 1973, as amended, 29 U.S.C. 791 *et seq.*, and its implementing regulations prohibit discrimination against those with handicaps or disabilities under any program receiving financial assistance from the federal government. The Americans with Disabilities Act of 1990, 42 U.S.C. § 12101 *et seq.*, also prohibits employment discrimination by certain private employers against individuals with disabilities. In addition, many states have enacted legislation prohibiting discrimination against those with handicaps or disabilities. These laws prevent the exclusion, denial of benefits, refusal to hire or promote, or other discriminatory conduct against an individual based on a handicap or disability when the individual involved can, with or without reasonable accommodation, perform the essential functions of the job without creating undue hardship for the employer or program involved. These issues should be kept in mind when NFPA 1582 is applied.

The medical requirements of the 1992 edition of NFPA 1582 were developed and found to be job related by a subcommittee comprising medical doctors, physiological specialists, and fire service professionals, who processed the requirements through the NFPA consensus standards-making system. Changes for the 2000 edition were proposed by a task group with similar expertise. The standard provides that, to the extent feasible, decisions concerning those with medical ailments, handicaps, or disabilities be made after case-by-case medical evaluations. Thus, most medical conditions have been assigned to Category B (see the discussion in the text of Categories A and B).

The medical requirements in the 2000 edition of the standard were revised on the basis of the critical core firefighting functions mentioned in Appendix C of the standard. It is recognized that some firefighting functions and tasks can vary from location to location because of differences in department size, functional and organizational differences, geography, level of urbanization, equipment used, and other factors. Therefore, it is the responsibility of each individual fire department to document, through job analysis, that the critical core firefighting functions performed in the local jurisdiction are substantially similar to those mentioned in Appendix C.

A wide variety of job-analysis techniques are available to document the essential functions of the job of firefighter. At a minimum, any technique used should be current, be in writing, and meet the provisions of the Americans with Disabilities Act (29 CFR 1630.2(n)(3)). Job descriptions should focus on critical and important work behaviors and specific tasks and func-

Other standards

Other NFPA standards relevant to safety and health deal with professional qualifications, training, protective clothing and equipment, apparatus, and hazardous materials.

Professional qualification standards   The NFPA standards on professional

---

tions. The frequency and/or duration of task performance and the consequences of failure to perform the task should be specified. The working conditions and environmental hazards in which the work is performed should be described.

The job description (examples can be found in Appendix E of the standard) should be made available to the fire service physician for use during the preplacement medical examination, when the determination of the medical suitability of individual applicants for firefighter will be made.

Antidiscrimination laws   The user of NFPA 1582 should be aware that, although courts are likely to give considerable weight to the existence of a nationally recognized standard such as NFPA 1582 (e.g., *Miller v. Sioux Gateway Fire Department,* 497 N.W.2d 838 (1993)), reliance on the standard alone may not be sufficient to withstand a challenge under federal and state antidiscrimination laws. Even in the case of Category A medical conditions, courts can still require additional expert evidence concerning an individual candidate's or firefighter's inability to perform the essential functions of the job. Until the courts provide further guidance in this developing area of law, some uncertainty as to the degree and nature of the evidence required to establish compliance with the antidiscrimination laws will remain.

Individuals who are members of protected classes (race, sex, color, religion, or national origin)   Title VII of the Civil Rights Act of 1964, as amended, 42 U.S.C. 2000e, and implementing regulations of the Equal Employment Opportunity Commission (EEOC) pro-

hibit discrimination in employment on the basis of race, sex, color, religion, or national origin (i.e., protected classes).[1] Additionally, many states, cities, and localities have adopted similar legislation. Generally, physical performance or other requirements that result in "adverse impact" on members of a protected class (e.g., women) are required to be validated through a study that accords with EEOC guidelines, if such requirements are to be relied on when employment decisions are made. Under EEOC guidelines, a study validating employment standards in one jurisdiction can be transportable to a second jurisdiction (and therefore used instead of the second jurisdiction's conducting a separate study). However, specific preconditions must be met in this regard, and the authority having jurisdiction should seek the advice of counsel before relying on a "transported" validation study.

Pregnancy and reproduction   Federal regulations as well as the decisions of many courts (including the U.S. Supreme Court in *International Union et al. v. Johnson Controls, Inc.,* 499 U.S. 187, 111 S.Ct. 1196 (1991)) have interpreted the requirements of Title VII with respect to pregnancy and reproduction. The authority having jurisdiction should seek the advice of counsel in resolving specific questions concerning these requirements as well as others that state or local laws may impose.

[1]Under Title VII, *employer* is defined generally to mean a person with "15 or more employees for each working day in each of 20 or more calendar weeks in the current or preceding calendar year" (see 42 U.S.C. 2000e). Several federal jurisdictions have held that unpaid volunteers are not considered to be "employees" under Title VII.

qualifications, written as job performance requirements, provides a minimum set of standards for various positions within the fire service. Some departments have used the NFPA standards for basic training, promotional exams, or assessment centers. In most departments, however, each standard stands alone for the specific position (e.g., firefighter, fire inspector, public life safety educator, fire instructor). Many training agencies base their training curricula on the NFPA professional qualification standards.

Many jurisdictions have required that their personnel be certified to certain standards, and the agencies providing the certification are accredited by either the National Board on Fire Service Professional Qualifications or the International Fire Service Accreditation Congress. Certification should not be confused with documented training, however. It simply provides an additional level of validation.

Training standards   Training standards cover issues ranging from specific training programs (e.g., in using SCBA) to live fire training in a structure that was either acquired or manufactured for the purpose. Instructors have the time and resources to properly plan for drills and exercises, so there is no reason for the training environment to be unsafe. The standards state that training shall be provided for all members before they are assigned to specific functions or job assignments and that members shall not be put in positions for which they are not trained: no on-the-job training. The emergency incident scene is no place for training firefighters. Safety is instilled in the training environment and is carried over to operations at actual incident scenes.

Protective clothing and equipment standards   NFPA 1500 requires the use of protective equipment, and the standards on protective clothing and equipment provide the specifications and testing requirements for the development and certification of such gear. These standards also require third-party certification of the clothing and/or equipment.

The Technical Correlating Committee oversees this group of standards and has recommended the development of additional documents on the selection, care, maintenance, and retirement of protective clothing and equipment. The committee also works with the technical committees of the International Standards Organization on compatibility issues in terms of the use of both organizations' standards in the international firefighting community.

Apparatus standards   The apparatus standards cover automotive fire apparatus, with chapters specifically on engines, aerial ladders, command vehicles, rescues, and special services. The chapters on vehicle engines, drivetrains, and chassis are common for all vehicles. The technical committee has also developed a document specific to wildland firefighting. One of the issues most discussed by fire chiefs is whether to rehabilitate the current apparatus or buy a new one. The technical committee has developed a document to help chiefs make that decision. The committee has also developed a vehicle maintenance document to help chiefs put together a cost-effective, comprehensive maintenance program for their apparatus.

The safety of personnel riding and responding on apparatus has been highlighted in past NFPA annual firefighter fatality studies and continues to be a major safety problem.

Hazardous material standards   For a discussion of NFPA standards on hazardous materials, see the commentary above on applicable OSHA regulations.

The liability of fire service organizations for negligent firefighting*

In 1955, a large quantity of gasoline was spilled onto a city street in Lawrence, Kansas, during the removal of gasoline storage tanks from a gas station. The local fire department was notified and quickly arrived at the scene. To determine the extent of the problem, the fire chief who was supervising the scene instructed a firefighter to touch a cigarette lighter to the ground. Not surprisingly a conflagration ensued, destroying several automobiles. In the lawsuit that followed, the court refused to hold the town liable for the action of its fire chief.[7]

This case and many others from that period reflect the traditional view that local governments were not liable for their failure to provide effective fire protection. Indeed, even extreme carelessness in fighting fires would not give rise to liability. At the beginning of the twenty-first century, however, in firefighting as in most other fields, the historical limitations on legal liability are eroding and theories of liability are expanding. Fire service legal liability must now necessarily concern the fire service.

This section describes the general principles that are used in analyzing the legal liability of fire service organizations for negligence in conducting firefighting activities. (The modern fire service encounters many other potential types of legal liability, but they are not treated here—e.g., negligent inspection or automobile negligence. Also not treated here are issues of employment law —e.g., worker's compensation, wrongful termination of employment, and the expanding field of antidiscrimination law.)[8] The law in the area of negligent firefighting is not uniform but is governed largely by state and local laws and therefore varies from jurisdiction to jurisdiction. Accordingly, the liabilities of an individual firefighting organization can be determined only by reference to the specific law in its jurisdiction.

For convenience, this discussion generally uses the terms *fire service organization* or *local government* in referring to the entity that may bear liability for negligent firefighting. However, the actual party named in a lawsuit alleging negligent firefighting will vary depending on how the fire service is organized in the particular locale. Most frequently, fire departments are branches of local government, and when a lawsuit is brought, it is the city or town that is named in the suit and that is responsible for paying any judgment. In other cases, the responsible party may be an independent fire district or a county.

The law of negligence in the context of firefighting

In any endeavor, and particularly in one as fraught with danger and uncertainty as firefighting, things can go wrong. Fires sometimes cause deaths and injuries despite the best efforts of the fire service. Property may be damaged, not only by the fire but also by the activity of firefighting itself. A tactical decision made in the midst of impending disaster may, in hindsight, turn out to have been terribly wrong. Bad outcomes alone, however, do not make the fire service liable.

The principal theory of liability used in lawsuits for personal injury and property damage is what is known in the law as negligence. (Sometimes other theories of liability are used in suits against the fire service—alleging, e.g., some discriminatory action or deliberate misconduct—but they are beyond the scope of this chapter.) The law of negligence does not hold a person liable for

*This section was written by Maureen Brodoff, associate general counsel of NFPA, and was adapted from an article that originally appeared in Arthur E. Cote, ed., *Fire Protection Handbook®: NFPA Codes, Standards and Recommended Practices*, 18th ed. (Quincy, Mass.: NFPA, 1997). *Fire Protection Handbook®* is a registered trademark of NFPA, Quincy, MA 02269.

any damage that results from his or her actions but only for damage that results from some act of carelessness in circumstances in which the actor had some duty to act with reasonable care. This principle can be understood by way of an illustration from an actual case involving allegations of negligent firefighting.

In 1978 in the city of Lowell, Massachusetts, five brick buildings were destroyed by a fire that started on the sixth floor of one of the buildings.[9] This building had a working sprinkler system and, indeed, in the initial stages of the fire the system worked properly. But the firefighters who responded to the fire chose to use the available water source to operate hoses, reducing water pressure in the sprinkler system—in effect, turning it off. There was evidence that good firefighting practice would have been to rely on the building's sprinkler system to fight the fire rather than to divert the water from the system to fight the fire with hoses. There was also evidence that the sprinkler system, if allowed to operate, would have put out the fire or contained it until it could have been put out by manual means. Instead, because firefighters chose in effect to shut off the sprinkler system, the fire eventually engulfed and destroyed five buildings.

This case presents the four essential elements of a firefighting negligence case. First, under the law all persons generally have a duty, once they undertake to act, to do so with reasonable care. Although (as discussed below) there is some controversy about whether firefighters owe such a duty of care, in this case it was conceded that, once the firefighters undertook to fight the fire, they had a duty to do so with reasonable care.

Second, the firefighters breached their duty to act with reasonable care. In lay terms, this simply means that they acted carelessly in fulfilling their duty to fight the fire. Reasonable care in the context of firefighting means that level of care which the reasonably prudent firefighter would use in similar circumstances. Since the evidence in the case showed that proper firefighting practice would have been to leave the sprinklers on, turning them off is viewed in the eyes of the law as negligent.

Third, the firefighters' breach of their duty to reasonably fight the fire caused the destruction of the buildings. The evidence shows that, if the sprinklers had been allowed to function, the fire would have been contained. In other words, the firefighters were the legal cause of the destruction of the buildings because, first, that destruction would not have occurred had the sprinkler system been left on and, second, the consequences of shutting it off were reasonably foreseeable.

Fourth and last, the firefighters' negligence resulted in damages. In this case, the damages roughly equaled the value of the destroyed buildings and their contents.

This case of the turned-off sprinkler is a good example of what any case of negligence has to prove in order to be successful—that is, the existence of a duty of care, the breach of that duty, causation, and damages. It is important to remember, however, that this is but one example of what can be alleged as negligent firefighting. The types of negligence that can be alleged in the firefighting context are infinite. Areas of potential liability include fire suppression activities, tactics and strategies, the emergency response system, operation of fire service vehicles,[10] maintenance of hydrants and the water supply, and maintenance of firefighting equipment.

Actual cases that have been brought illustrate the variety of claims that can arise. In an Indiana case, for example, it was alleged that a fire service organization was negligent in failing to maintain a sufficient number of firefighters for the equipment that the organization intended to use.[11] In the same case it was also alleged that there was negligence in the organization's failure to supervise and train its firefighters in controlling and extinguishing fires under the conditions encountered in a particular fire. In an Alabama case, negligence was claimed in a fire department's failure to respond to a house fire because the driver of the truck had gone home sick.[12] In a Maryland case, negligence was alleged in the failure to properly control and extinguish a brushfire that eventually reignited and caused a second fire in which a warehouse was destroyed.[13] And in a Massachusetts case, it was alleged that firefighters were negligent inasmuch as they fought a fire burning at the rear of a house by spraying water on the front of the house, where there was no fire.[14]

In a particularly dramatic Alaska case, liability was alleged and found for negligent failure to rescue a person stranded on an upper floor of a burning building. The rescue failed because the ladder used in the attempt was too short to reach the victim's window. Although the court said this fact alone did not constitute negligence, the firefighters had failed to use other commonsense methods of rescue that were available as alternatives. In particular, the court was deeply disturbed that spectators who had obtained an extension ladder long enough to reach the victim—and had raised the ladder and started to extend it—were ordered by a fire official to get away from the building and were driven off by fire hoses when they refused to obey.[15]

These illustrations would seem to indicate that liability exists around every corner. Although allegations of negligence are easily made, however, not all negligence claims result in a finding that the fire service was liable. There are two broad reasons tending against findings of fire service liability for negligent firefighting.

The first is that allegations of negligence are generally more difficult to prove in firefighting cases than in the typical negligence case. In the typical negligence case, a party is accused of creating a dangerous situation that resulted in injury. In the typical firefighter negligence case, the dangerous situation—that is, the fire—already exists when firefighters enter the picture. A plaintiff, therefore, is usually in a position of having to prove that the firefighters either worsened or failed to mitigate a harm that they had not caused. This is a difficult task, especially because the unpredictability and destructive power of fire in general often make it hard for someone to say with any assurance that some other course of action not taken by the firefighters would have yielded a better result. Thus, as the Alaska case described above vividly shows, liability is most often found in the extreme case when the conduct of the firefighters is viewed as foolhardy or outrageous.

The second reason tending against findings of fire service liability for negligent firefighting has even greater impact. As discussed above, a case of negligence is made by proving that an individual or group, in acting carelessly, violated a duty to act with reasonable care and thereby caused damage. If firefighting were strictly a private enterprise, carried out by and for the benefit of private parties, such proof would be all that was required to entitle the injured party to hold the fire service organization liable to pay for all of his or her damages.

But firefighting is not a private enterprise. It is generally a governmental function carried out by cities, towns, and other governmental units for the benefit of the public. Because of this, the fire service is the beneficiary of an elaborate body of law that has been developed to shield the government from liability even when it has acted negligently. This law of governmental immunity greatly complicates the question of whether and when a fire service organization can be held liable for damages caused by negligent firefighting.

The doctrine of governmental immunity and its counterweight

At one time, the doctrine of governmental immunity fully protected governments from lawsuits aimed at governmental functions. Under this doctrine, the government as "sovereign" could do no wrong and could not be sued. In the case of firefighting activities, this meant that no matter how negligent a fire department might be or how much damage to life or property its negligence might cause, the local government whose firefighting had caused the damage could not be sued.[16]

The doctrine of governmental immunity left individuals who had suffered injuries—not just in the firefighting context but also as a result of other government activities—no remedy. As might be expected, over the years the injustice that the doctrine often seemed to impose led to much criticism of the doctrine and calls for its reform.

Beginning in the 1970s, the federal government and the states began—either through court decisions or, more often, through the passage of legislation—to severely limit the absolute immunity that governmental entities had enjoyed. The most common type of legislation, now in existence in some form in most states as well as in the federal government, is generally known as a *tort claims act*. Each state's tort claims act is different, but for the most part, the acts provide that public employers are liable for injury caused by their negligence in the same manner and to the same extent that a private individual is.[17] There are important qualifications, however, that provide the fire service with significant protections against liability.

Legal protections for the fire service

The tort claims acts provide the fire service with certain protections. These consist of (1) limits on the amount of damages a government can be required to pay, (2) exemptions aimed specifically at the fire service, and (3) the discretionary-functions exception. In addition to the protections in these acts, there is the public-duty rule (to which there are, however, exceptions), which offers further protection from negligence liability.

Limits on the amount of damages   Although in many cases government entities can now be held liable for their negligence just as a private individual can, tort claims acts place rather stringent limits on the amount of damages the government can be required to pay. In Massachusetts, for example, the amount of liability that a local government can be required to pay if found negligent is limited to $100,000 per claimant. Frequently there is an overall cap so that no matter how many claimants, the total damages awardable for fire department negligence in any one incident cannot exceed a given amount. Vermont, for example, has a limit of $250,000 per claimant with a maximum aggregate liability of $1,000,000 to all claimants arising out of any given occurrence; Maryland has a limit of $200,000 per claimant with an overall cap of $500,000 per occurrence.[18] A few states provide lower maximum damages for property damage than for personal injury.[19] Finally, punitive damages—that is, damages designed to punish the wrongdoer rather than to compensate the injured party—are generally forbidden.[20]

These various limits on liability are significant protections for fire service organizations because they cap damages at an amount that may frequently represent only a small fraction of the damages actually awarded by a jury. In the area of fire suppression in particular, where mistakes can result in millions of dollars of personal injury and property damage, the tort claims acts provide a great deal of protection against potentially huge damage awards.

Exceptions aimed specifically at firefighting and related activities   Several state tort claims acts have exceptions that specifically retain governmental immunity for firefighting and related activities. North Dakota, for example, retains governmental immunity for failure to provide adequate fire prevention personnel or equipment, except if gross negligence can be proven. Illinois retains governmental immunity for any injury caused by the failure to suppress or contain a fire or while fighting a fire. Kansas and Texas retain immunity for the failure to provide, or for the inadequate provision of, fire protection.[21]

There are also other types of exceptions that relate to the fire service. Alaska specifically retains governmental immunity for the performance of duties "in connection with an enhanced 911 emergency system" and for the performance of duties upon the request of or by agreement with the state "to meet emergency public safety requirements."[22] Some states retain immunity for claims relating to the provision of or failure to provide emergency services.[23] Many states specifically retain immunity for the failure to make an inspection or for the making of an inadequate or negligent inspection.[24]

The discretionary-functions exception In addition to the exceptions in some states expressly relating to firefighting and related activities, in most state tort claims acts another type of exception exists that provides significant protection for the fire service. This is known as the *discretionary-functions* exception, and it requires some explanation.

Although the lawmakers of the various states, in passing tort claims acts, wished to make it possible for citizens to obtain compensation for injuries caused by governmental entities, they were reluctant to abolish immunity for all governmental activities. They were concerned that lawsuits might be used to second-guess every governmental policy decision and that the constant fear of lawsuits could severely hamper the ability of local government officials to govern and to freely exercise the discretion of their office. To address these concerns, lawmakers created an exception in the tort claims acts that preserved governmental immunity for "discretionary functions."

The typical discretionary-functions exception merely states that the tort claims act and its abolition of governmental immunity do not apply to any claim based upon a public employee's performance or failure to perform a "discretionary function."[25] What is a discretionary function and what does it mean in the context of firefighting? Many legal battles have been fought over that question.

The main problem has been determining the breadth of the discretionary-functions exception; taken literally, the exception could be quite broad indeed. In its essence, the word *discretion* implies the exercise of judgment, and therefore a literal interpretation of the discretionary-function exception might lead to the conclusion that all conduct involving the exercise of judgment is immune from negligence liability. In addition, because virtually all firefighting activities involve the exercise of judgment even if only in relation to minor details, one might conclude that all firefighting activities are immune from suit. This, however, is not the case.

Courts have generally rejected a too-literal reading of the term *discretionary function*. They have felt that granting immunity to all acts that involve some exercise of judgment would, in effect, immunize all governmental activity and therefore defeat the whole purpose of the tort claims acts, which was, after all, to abolish complete immunity. Courts have therefore looked to the purpose of the discretionary-functions exception, which, as discussed above, was really only to protect conduct involving the kinds of broad public policy and planning judgments that governmental actors need to be able to exercise without the constant threat of being sued. In keeping with this purpose, most courts have tended to find immunity not for all discretionary conduct but only for conduct that involves "policy making or planning."[26]

In the context of firefighting, what does this mean? The decisions are far from clear and vary widely in how they treat particular fire service activities. Nevertheless, certain themes emerge.

First, there are aspects of fire service decision making that have an obvious basis in planning or policy making. These are administrative policy decisions involving the overall structure and makeup of the fire department, the training and equipping of firefighters, and the allocation of limited firefighting resources within the community. They include decisions about the number and location of fire stations, the amount and type of equipment to purchase, the size of the firefighting staff, the type and extent of firefighter training, the number and location of hydrants, and the adequacy of the water supply.

When lawsuits blame these types of administrative policy decisions for bringing about injury or death, they are frequently dismissed on the basis of the discretionary-functions exception. For example, a claim that firefighters were unable to suppress a fire because the nearest fire station was too far away to make timely firefighting possible would generally fail because decisions about where to locate a fire station, even if patently unreasonable, are protected from liability under the discretionary-functions exception.

Of course, some courts are more stringent in applying the exception than others. Many courts, for example, will view any broad administrative-level policy decision as categorically immune from liability without any inquiry into the thought processes of the decision makers. Other courts, however, will require that the fire service organization, in order to claim immunity, present evidence showing that the decision makers actually went through a weighing of policy choices. In a case alleging that firefighters had not been supplied with a particular type of rescue equipment that would have prevented an injury, such a court would, for example, require that the fire service organization show that its failure to provide such equipment was the result of a conscious policy-making decision involving the balancing of competing interests, rather than the result of a simple failure to consider whether the equipment was needed.[27]

It is clear, therefore, that administrative decisions are generally covered and immune from suit, at least when they involve a conscious weighing of policy considerations. What about operational decisions made in the course of fighting a particular fire? Some have argued, for example, that the initial decision to fight a fire is discretionary but that all the subsequent actions in actually fighting the fire are not. Under this view, almost all actual fire suppression activities on the fire ground would fall outside the discretionary-functions exception and would therefore be subject to potential liability.

This point of view, however, has mostly been rejected. Although many— indeed, even most—decisions taken in the course of firefighting do not involve policy or planning considerations, not all decisions made at the operational level fall outside the discretionary-functions exception. The courts have found that some decisions made on the fire ground do involve broad public policy choices protected by governmental immunity.

To determine whether a particular operational decision constitutes a discretionary function, courts generally look not at the particular action but at the reasons for it. An illustration is the case described above in which the firefighters turned off an operating sprinkler system in an unoccupied building because they wanted to fight the fire with hoses. Their decision to turn off the sprinkler system was negligent in that good firefighting practice would, in those circumstances, have dictated using the sprinkler system to extinguish the fire. The decision to shut off the sprinkler system also did not involve any policy or planning considerations because the firefighters simply made a careless decision about how best to fight the fire.

In slightly different circumstances, however, the decision to shut off a sprinkler system could easily involve a significant policy choice. Suppose, for example, that the firefighters had decided to shut off the sprinkler system in the unoccupied building not merely to deploy hoses but also to divert the water

supplying the sprinkler to fight a fire in a neighboring building that was occupied. The decision to sacrifice the unoccupied building in order to devote
limited firefighting resources to saving lives next door clearly would involve
policy choices about the relative value of property and human life. Thus, even
if the decision to shut off the sprinkler system were ultimately shown to have
been negligent in that the occupied building could have been saved without
diverting water from the sprinkler system, the decision would have been
grounded in an important policy choice, and many courts would rule that it
was immune from liability under the discretionary-functions exception.[28]

In sum, although court decisions in this area vary widely from jurisdiction
to jurisdiction, it can be said that the discretionary-functions exception provides
immunity to the fire service from liability for most broad administrative-level
decision making and for many operational-level decisions as well. Although
the discretionary-functions exception is far from comprehensive and is less than
certain in any individual case, it still provides the fire service with substantial
protection from liability.

The public-duty rule (and exceptions to it)   So far, the liability for negligent
firefighting, although complicated, can be summarized quite simply. Initially
the doctrine of governmental immunity completely protected firefighting operations from liability, even if a fire was fought negligently. In the early twenty-
first century, however, fire service organizations can in some circumstances be
successfully sued for negligence. The extent to which they can be sued is
limited in most jurisdictions by the tort claims acts and the court decisions
interpreting them. In general, through the discretionary-functions exception and
other exceptions aimed at protecting fire and emergency services, those acts
will entirely immunize fire service organizations for some activities. But where
these acts do abolish immunity, they still provide a cap on damages that can
be won against a fire service organization.

If the law preferred simplicity, even of a relative kind, the story might end
here. There is, however, one more important twist to this story. That twist is
known as the *public-duty rule*.

Although state legislatures have abolished governmental immunity and permitted local governments to be sued in many situations, courts have continued
to be sympathetic to the problems of cities and towns and to their difficulty in
paying even the limited awards permitted by the tort claims acts. Particularly
in the area of fire and other public protective services, some courts have expressed the fear that imposing even limited liability for negligence could place
a crushing burden on local governments, especially in busy urban areas. As
one judge pointed out, in extreme circumstances—such as the Los Angeles
riots of 1992, when there were hundreds of fires and severe obstacles to effective firefighting—the potential costs of liability could be catastrophic.[29] This
fear has led some courts to develop a judge-made rule to shield the fire service
and other public protective services such as police and inspection. This public-
duty rule offers an immunity from negligence liability that goes far beyond the
limited immunity retained in the tort claims acts.

Under the public-duty rule, firefighting and other public protective services
are viewed as an obligation that governments owe not to any particular individual but to the public as a whole. On the basis of this view, the public-duty
rule holds (somewhat paradoxically) that because firefighting is for the benefit
of all, it is in effect for the benefit of no one in particular. Under the rule,
therefore, no individual can seek damages for injuries caused by negligent
firefighting because, in essence, the fire service owes no duty to any particular
individual to act reasonably.

What is the effect of the public-duty rule? Its greatest impact is at the operational level of firefighting. As shown above, the immunity offered by most state tort claims acts under the discretionary-functions exception is quite limited, and most decisions made on the fire ground can give rise to potential liability unless they can be said to involve public policy choices. In the states that follow the public-duty rule, however,[30] decisions made on the fire ground become largely immune, and any firefighting activity—even if negligent and even if devoid of public policy implications—cannot give rise to liability.

It would seem that fire service organizations in states following the public-duty rule have nothing to fear from lawsuits claiming negligent firefighting. This is largely true. However, every rule including this one has its limitations and exceptions.

First, courts that follow the public-duty rule limit its protections to the suppression of fires not caused by the fire department itself. Thus, if a fire department negligently caused a fire during a fire training exercise or some other activity not related to fire suppression, the public-duty rule would offer no protection. Second, a few courts would not apply the public-duty rule to protect firefighters in cases in which they aggravated an existing fire as opposed to merely failing to suppress it.[31] These courts, for example, would provide complete immunity when firefighters negligently failed to put out an existing fire because they aimed hoses at the wrong part of the building. They would, however, permit liability when firefighters took some action that actively made matters worse, such as turning off an operating sprinkler system that, left alone, would have contained the fire.

Finally, there is an exception to the public-duty rule known as the *special-relationship exception*. It holds that, even though firefighting and other protective services are viewed in general as an obligation owed only to the public at large, a fire or other protective service organization can by words or actions in a particular case create a special duty to particular private parties.

How does a fire service organization create for itself this special duty to private parties for which it may incur liability? Application of the special-relationship exception has been complicated and often inconsistent, and in practice courts have been very reluctant to apply it to hold the fire service liable.[32] It seems clear that a fire department does not create a special duty to an individual property owner merely by responding to the owner's call for assistance and fighting the fire on the property.[33] To expose a fire department to liability under this exception, firefighters would probably have to do one of two things: offer a special service or protection to an individual that was not available to the general public, or induce an individual, through specific assurances of assistance or safety, to put himself or herself in danger.

Apart from the potential liability opened up by the limitations and exceptions to the public-duty rule, there is yet another reason why fire service organizations in states that observe the public-duty rule should not rest with complete ease. The public-duty rule has been widely criticized as fundamentally inconsistent with the tort claims acts because the rule creates immunity where legislatures have sought to remove it. The trend, therefore, has been to abolish the rule, and many states have done so.[34]

But again, a number of states still recognize the public-duty rule. And in at least one state (Massachusetts) after a court abolished the rule, the legislature revived it by incorporating it into the state tort claims act.[35] It is safe to say, therefore, that in many states the public-duty rule still offers fire service organizations a large measure of immunity.

Liability issues: Summary

As the foregoing discussion reveals, the degree to which the fire service may be exposed to liability for negligent firefighting depends to a large extent on the law of the state in which the fire department is located. Although all states have abolished to one degree or another total governmental immunity from negligence lawsuits, the amount of remaining protection varies from one jurisdiction to another. In all states, however, it is important to remember that even in the absence of complete immunity, significant protections are still offered the fire service. Although the principles defy easy summarization, in general the following can be said:

1. In virtually all states, fire departments will be protected from suits criticizing broad administrative policy decisions of fire department and local government administrators. Thus, suits claiming injuries resulting from bad policy decisions about the placement or number of fire stations, the size of fire department staffs, or the adequacy of funding for fire department activities will generally be prohibited under the discretionary-functions exception or similar legal principles contained in the tort claims acts of most states.

2. In the majority of states, fire departments will generally be liable for injuries for negligent firefighting when the claims are based on bad operational decisions made on the fire ground about how to fight a particular fire. But if those decisions involve public policy choices, fire departments will sometimes be protected under the discretionary-functions exception.

3. In the minority of states that still follow the public-duty rule, fire departments will be protected from negligence suits, even those involving operational decisions, unless the department or its employees has by word or deed created a "special duty" toward an injured party beyond the duty owed to the public as a whole.

The trend has been to hold firefighters to a duty to exercise reasonable care in the conduct of firefighting operations and to hold fire departments liable when firefighters have acted negligently. This trend, however, is far from total. As the above discussion shows, limited immunity still exists both in the discretionary-functions exception and in the persistence of the public-duty rule; the latter, despite much criticism, remains in force in many states. In addition, the caps on damages that exist in all states will continue to soften the impact of negligence cases on the fire service. The explosion of liability that occurred in all areas of the law has therefore had only limited effect on the fire service.

Back to the future

Many readers will remember the movie called *Back to the Future,* in which a character went back in time to attempt to change the future as he saw it unfolding in front of him. The connection to the fire service is this: the primary mission of the fire service has always been to protect lives, and although that will not change, what has changed is how the fire service deploys and operates to fulfill its multifaceted mission. In addition to fire suppression, the fire service now provides EMS, technical operations, community-based risk management, community life safety education, and so on. The fire service has seized the opportunities presented to it and has made the most of them.

Rules, regulations, codes, and standards will continue to be developed and promulgated. Fire administrators and the authorities to whom they report need to understand these documents, participate in developing them, and use them to improve the professionalism of the fire service and strengthen the services it provides.

In the not-too-distant future, standards will probably be developed for a growing array of services provided by the modern fire service. In addition, cooperative agreements between public and private service providers will continue to grow. And the community will want to be more involved in how risks are measured against benefits. What the fire service becomes will depend on what risk the community is willing to accept.

As the number of fires continues to decrease, the community will ask, "What does the fire department do for me?" The answer—highlighted in the aftermath of the terrorist attacks at the World Trade Center and the Pentagon and the related plane crash in Somerset County, Pennsylvania, on September 11, 2001 —is that its personnel are willing to serve to protect their neighbors and friends and are willing to risk everything when necessary. Accordingly, the protection, health, and safety of fire service personnel are the manager's first priority, and the proactive manager will use the codes, standards, rules, and regulations as the basis for ensuring that protection, health, and safety.

1 NFPA 1582, Standard on Medical Requirements for Fire Fighters and Information for Fire Department Physicians (2000 edition), Appendix B, 1.2–1.4.

2 The states and territories that had state OSHA plans as of 1998 are Alaska, Arizona, California, Connecticut, Hawaii, Indiana, Iowa, Kentucky, Maryland, Michigan, Minnesota, Nevada, New Mexico, New York, North Carolina, Oregon, Puerto Rico, South Carolina, Tennessee, Utah, Vermont, Virgin Islands, Virginia, Washington, and Wyoming. In California, Connecticut, and New York, the plans apply only to state and local government employees.

3 NFPA has tracked firefighter fatalities since 1980, issuing statistical reports and case studies each July.

4 The CDC has expended considerable effort to develop a training curriculum and guidelines for emergency workers, and EPA has also prepared a guide for emergency workers. The CDC materials are *A Curriculum Guide for Public-Safety and Emergency-Response Workers: Prevention of Transmission of Human Immunodeficiency Virus and Hepatitis B Virus,* DHHS (NIOSH) Publication No. 89-108 (February 1989); *Guidelines for Handwashing and Hospital Environmental Control, 1985* (DHHS, 1985); W. W. Williams, "Guidelines for Infection Control in Hospital Personnel," *Infection Control* 4 (suppl.) (July 1983): 326–349; and "Guidelines for Prevention of Transmission of Human Immunodeficiency Virus and Hepatitis B Virus to Health-Care and Public-Safety Workers: A Response to P.L. 100-607, The Health Omnibus Programs Extension Act of 1988," *Morbidity and Mortality Weekly Report* 38 (S-6), June 23, 1989, pp. 3–37. The EPA's material is *EPA Guide for Infectious Waste Management,* NTIS No. PB 86-199130 (Office of Solid Waste, 1986).

5 The National Fire Codes are produced in hard copy as a set, in pamphlet form individually, and in an electronic version.

6 NFPA regularly investigates some of these incidents and publishes its reports in a series called *Fire Investigations: Fire Fighter Fatality Reports* (part of the publications referred to in note 3).

7 *Perkins v. City of Lawrence,* 281 P.2d 1077 (Kan. 1955).

8 Works designed for the lay reader on these and other legal issues relating to the fire service include Timothy Callahan, *Fire Service and the Law,* 2nd ed. (Quincy, Mass.: NFPA, 1987); Thomas D. Schneid, *Fire Law: The Liabilities and Rights of the Fire Service* (New York: Van Nostrand Reinhold, 1995); and Nancy Grant and David Hoover, *Fire Service Administration* (Quincy, Mass.: NFPA, 1994).

9 The fact pattern used for this illustration is drawn from the Massachusetts case of *Harry Stoller & Co. v. Lowell,* 412 Mass. 139 (1992).

10 The law involving the operation of fire service vehicles presents something of a special case because many states have laws aimed specifically at limiting liability for the operation of emergency and fire service vehicles. These statutes vary from state to state. Indiana, for example, provides immunity for the operation of fire service vehicles only when the operator of the vehicle is an employee of the fire service organization and only in the case of authorized emergency vehicles (see Indiana Code § 9-4-1(d)). Other states have additional requirements, such as that emergency sirens or lights be activated.

11 See *City of Hammond v. Cataldi,* 449 N.2d 1184 (Ind. App. 3d Dist. 1983).

12 See *Williams v. City of Tuscumbia,* 426 So.2d 824 (Ala. 1983).

13 See *Utica Mut. v. Gaithersburg–Washington Grove,* 455 A.2d 987 (Md. App. 1983).

14 See *Cryan v. Ware,* 413 Mass. 452, 469 (1992).

15 See *City of Fairbanks v. Schaible,* 375 P.2d 201, 206 (Alaska 1962).

16 Although in most cases a fire department is clearly part of the government and is entitled to sovereign immunity, some cases are not so clear-cut because fire departments can be organized in a variety of ways—for example, as a department of a local government, as an independent corporation receiving varying degrees of funding from a local government, as a fire district, and so forth. In determining whether —and, if so, to what degree—a fire service organization may enjoy immunity from liability for negligence, one needs to know what type of organization it is and how that organizational form is viewed by applicable case law and statutes. Thus, for example, in one case a court found that a volunteer fire department which was formed as an independent corporation; owned its own property, buildings, and equipment; paid its own nonvolunteer staff; and enacted its own rules and regulations was not sufficiently controlled by the municipal government it served to be considered a governmental entity entitled to any governmental immunity (see *Utica Mut. v. Gaithersburg–Washington Grove*). Because governmental immunity is not completely abolished by tort claims acts (i.e., legislation limiting absolute governmental immunity—see discussion in text) and the protections of governmental immunity still exist except to the degree that a tort claims act decrees, it remains important for fire service organizations to

know whether they are covered by governmental immunity.

17 It is important to note that the various state tort claims acts vary significantly. A few, for example, abolish the governmental immunity only of the state and not of local governments (see Vt. Stat. Ann. tit. 12, §§ 5601–5605; Haw. Rev. Stat. § 662-2, *et seq.*). In other states, the degree to which governmental immunity is abolished depends, at least to some degree, on whether the governmental unit has liability insurance that covers the alleged claims (see, e.g., Colo. Rev. Stat. § 24-10-104; N.C. Gen. Stat. § 160A-485; Vt. Stat. Ann. tit. 12 § 560(f) and tit. 29, § 1403; Wyo. Stat. § 1-39-118(b)). In addition, not all states have adopted the general approach taken by the tort claims acts described here. Some states, for example, rather than enacting a general abolition of immunity together with various exceptions and qualifications, have instead abolished immunity for specific types of governmental activities (see, e.g., Del. Code Ann. tit. 10, § 4012 [abolishing immunity only for certain designated activities, including the operation of a motor vehicle and the maintenance of public buildings]). The importance of consulting individual state laws to determine the scope of immunity, therefore, cannot be overemphasized.

18 See Vt. Stat. Ann. tit. 12 § 5601(b); Md. Cts. & Jud. Proc. § 5-403(a).

19 See, e.g., Or. Rev. Stat. § 30.270; N.M. Stat. Ann. § 41-4-19.

20 See, e.g., Mass. Gen. L. ch. 258, § 2; Minn. Stat. Ann. § 466.04.

21 See N.D. Cent. Code § 32-12.1-03(3); Ill. Rev. Stat. ch. 85, § 5-102, 5-103; Kan. Stat. Ann. § 75-6104(n); and Tex. Civ. Prac. & Rem. Code Ann. § 101.055(3).

22 See Alaska Stat. §§ 09.65.070(d)(6) and (d)(5).

23 See, e.g., Iowa Code § 613A.4; Tex. Civ. Prac. & Rem. Code Ann. § 101.055(2).

24 See, e.g., Kan. Stat. Ann. § 75-6104(k).

25 See, e.g., Mass. Gen. Laws ch. 258, § 10(b).

26 See, e.g., *King v. Seattle,* 84 Wash. 2d 239, 525 P.2d 228, 233 (1974); *Keopf v. County of York,* 198 Neb. 67, 251 N.W.2d 866, 870 (1977); *Johnson v. State,*

69 Cal. 2d 782, 788, 447 P.2d 352 (1968); *Harry Stoller & Co. v. Lowell.*

27 As examples of the differing approaches used by courts, compare *City of Hammond v. Cataldi,* 449 N.E.2d 1184 (Ind. App. 3 Dist. 193), with *Waldorf v. Shuta,* 896 F.2d 723, 728–730 (3d Cir. 1990).

28 See, e.g., *Dahlheimer v. City of Dayton,* 441 N.W.2d 534, 538–539 (Minn. 1989).

29 See *Cryan v. Ware,* 455.

30 See, e.g., *Shore v. Stonington,* 187 Conn. 147 (1982); *Randall v. Fairmont City Police Department,* 186 W. Va. 336 (1991). A 1993 case identified the states that follow the traditional public-duty rule as California, Connecticut, Hawaii, Illinois, Indiana, Kansas, Maryland, Michigan, Minnesota, Missouri, Nevada, New Hampshire, New York, North Carolina, Ohio, Pennsylvania, Rhode Island, South Carolina, Utah, Washington, and West Virginia; see *Jean W. v. Commonwealth,* 414 Mass. 496, 518 n. 1 (1993) (O'Connor, J., concurring).

31 See *Cryan v. Ware,* supra, at 452.

32 Contrast, e.g., the markedly different treatment the court gave police and firefighters, respectively, in *Cryan v. Ware,* supra, at 452, and *Irwin v. Ware,* 392 Mass. 745 (1993).

33 See, e.g., *Commerce & Indus. Ins. Co. v. City of Toledo,* 543 N.E.2d 1188 (Ohio 1989). But see *Ziegler v. City of Millbrook,* 514 So.2d 1275 (Alabama 1987).

34 See *Adams v. State,* 555 P.2d 235 (Alaska 1976); *Leake v. Cain,* 720 P.2d 152, 158–159 (Colo. 1986); *Adam v. State,* 380 N.W.2d 716, 724 (Iowa 1986); *Maple v. Omaha,* 222 Neb. 293, 301 (1986); *Schear v. County Commissioners,* 101 N.M. 671 (1984); *Coffey v. Milwaukee,* 74 Wis. 2d 526 (1976); *DeWald v. State,* 719 P.2d 643, 653 (Wyo. 1986); *Ryan v. State,* 134 Ariz. 308, 310 (1982); *Commercial Carrier Corp. v. Indian River County,* 371 So. 2d 1010, 1015–1016 (Fla. 1979); *Brennen v. Eugene,* 285 Or. 401, 407 (1979).

35 See Mass. Gen. L. ch. 258, § 10, as amended by 1993 Stat. Ch. 495, § 57.

Part five: Managing support services

14 Information management

Fire and rescue service managers must have accurate information. They need it to make decisions, and they also need it to explain and defend their decisions to local government managers, budget directors, the media, and citizens. Like other agencies and public interest groups, the fire service must be prepared to make the case for its priorities. In addition, good information and proper use of it helps managers do the best possible job of reducing fires and related losses and providing the best emergency response service with the resources available.

Because the range of problems facing fire departments today is formidable and the range of activities they engage in is broad, the amount of information managers have to assimilate is huge. Even the smallest department can have any of ten thousand chemicals spilled at its door, can fall victim to arson, must deal with a variety of medical emergencies, and must account for hundreds of different tools and supplies. No one can remember it all, and in fact no one has to.

This chapter outlines the basic principles of how to design and maintain a management information system (MIS)—a system for storing and processing data (which are the raw material for the information needed by managers). Written for the fire service manager who may have only minimal familiarity with computers, the chapter explains what management information systems and data are and what the National Fire Incident Reporting System is. The chapter also lists the data elements of some common fire service database systems; lays out some of the uses of data; discusses the importance of ensuring data quality, analyzing data, and presenting information effectively; and ends by looking at management issues involved in designing and purchasing an MIS.

The discussion applies to fire departments of all sizes and types. Even though the size of the MIS and its degree of computerization may vary, as may the sophistication of the data analysis, the basic principles and considerations are similar for all departments.

Data and management information systems: What are they?

Webster's defines the word *data* as "factual information used as a basis for reasoning, discussion, or calculation." The items of factual information that are the basic component of a data collection system are called data *elements*—for example, incident number, incident date, and incident time. When data elements having to do with a single occurrence or incident are collected and brought together, the analyst or interpreter can form a picture of the situation and of the steps taken to mitigate it. When these data elements are further collected into common groupings, or *databases*, analysts are then able to form an even clearer picture of incidents that have similar characteristics.

Databases may be constructed to describe the following general categories, among others: fire dispatch, fire incidents, hazardous material (HAZMAT) incidents, fire prevention and inspections, tactical inspections, fire hydrant maintenance, emergency medical service (EMS) patients, geographic information, 911, and vehicle location. In addition, databases may be organized, indexed, and interconnected by a common relationship. When this is done, analysts can create an even more refined picture.

As the raw material for the information needed by managers, data have to be stored and processed. Systems that do this—usually using computers—are called *management information systems.* Sometimes the term refers to simple computerized systems that store separate files of data from which the desired information can be retrieved. More commonly the term refers to systems of greater complexity that allow data from several files to be manipulated and intermixed or relationally connected (i.e., organized by a common relationship, such as address, census tract, or any other administrative or geographic area). A more advanced MIS may use computer models to help with decision making and may incorporate the logic and information of experts in the form of "expert systems" that imitate highly experienced advisers. Often the MIS is a collection of many programs that set up files, maintain files, provide specialized analysis, and govern output report formats. This kind of MIS may consist of more than a hundred separate programs or several large programs that work together under an executive computer program. The system may be designed to be user-friendly so that people with little training can interact with it directly, or it may be designed so that only programmers/analysts or specialists trained in the use of the system can use it, or it may be designed so that both types of users may use it but often for different purposes.

In short, the fire chief has choices as to the type and capabilities of the department's MIS. The system can be manual or computerized and, if computerized, can be at any level of complexity and cost. The chief can store information in a simple set of paper ("hard copy") files or can use computers to store and retrieve data for analysis. The chief who is so inclined can even use expert systems to support management decisions.

The National Fire Incident Reporting System

The need for the fire service to collect data was realized and identified in 1973 with the publication of *America Burning* (see also Chapter 1), which recommended "that a national fire data system be established to provide a continuing review and analysis of the entire fire problem."[1] This and other recommendations in *America Burning* led to the creation of the U.S. Fire Administration (USFA), the agency that evaluates the nation's fire problem. One of the duties of the USFA is to provide for a nationwide exchange of standardized information pertaining to fire and life safety; another is to have the capability of collecting, storing, retrieving, and disseminating data.

Early efforts to collect data varied throughout the country. The National Fire Protection Association (NFPA) Pamphlet 901 system in the mid-1970s, using an early version of the National Fire Incident Reporting System (NFIRS), was initially tested by California, Maryland, New York, Ohio, and Oregon. In 1975 the NFIRS program started with an NFIRS Users Conference. NFIRS software version 1, developed by the National Fire Prevention and Control Administration (predecessor of the USFA), was used in Minnesota, Missouri, and South Dakota. Version 2 of the software was completed between 1976 and 1978, development of version 3 began in 1979, and development of version 4 began in 1985. Version 4.1 was implemented in 1990 and includes the HAZMAT module.

In January 1999, NFIRS version 5.0 was implemented as the new national standard for fire incident reporting. This version was the culmination of a long review process that began in 1988; input was received from more than two hundred fire departments, NFPA, the Consumer Product Safety Commission, the International Association of Fire Chiefs, the International Association of Fire Fighters, the National Association of State Fire Marshals, the National

Highway Traffic Safety Administration, and the National Volunteer Fire Council.

The most significant changes in this new version were a simplified coding structure, a modular construction, and, most important, an "all-incident" reporting system. What makes this last feature so significant is that at the beginning of the twenty-first century the fire service is not in just the "fire business." Rather, it provides its communities with many types of services, including EMS, HAZMAT response, and technical rescue (see Chapter 4 in particular).

NFIRS version 5.0 allows for the collection and comparison of information gathered by the reporting fire departments at several levels (national, state, and local) and in many jurisdictions. Because of its modular design, additional modules can be added to meet the changing needs of the fire service.

NFIRS 5.0 takes advantage of two new technologies: the Internet and JAVA (a programming language designed for use with Internet browsers). The Internet allows fire incident data to be transferred more quickly to the state agencies responsible for collection, and they, in turn, forward the data to the USFA's national database. (The plan is to have the National Fire Database eventually accessible only on the Internet.) The JAVA language was selected because it is platform independent: it will run under several operating systems (Microsoft Windows 95/98/ME, Microsoft Windows NT/2000/XP, Mac Operating System, LINUX, and UNIX).

Without the Internet and the ability to use it to transfer data files more quickly, data collection would lag approximately two years behind the current collection year. This lag would severely hinder the decision-making process. The increased use of personal computers throughout the fire service has given new meaning to interoperability and encourages the quick transfer of data files.

With NFIRS version 5.0 used as the standard, records will contain the data elements listed in the sidebar on the next page.

Data elements of selected fire service database systems

This section lists the data elements for the following database systems: computer-aided dispatch (CAD), EMS patients, fire inspections and tactical information, fire hydrants, and personnel records.

Computer-aided dispatch

An especially critical system within the fire and rescue department is CAD (see Chapter 15). This system should interrogate other systems that may provide useful information to emergency operations personnel. Such interrogation could involve data from global positioning satellite/automated vehicle location systems, special location information, fire hydrant maintenance systems, tactical information systems, and geographic information systems. By gathering information from these databases, the CAD system can dispatch the closest available unit and provide field personnel with vital information. Any CAD system must also be able to pass data elements to the incident reporting system, thereby eliminating the need to reenter data—an activity with the potential for introducing errors.

At a minimum, the CAD system should record the following data elements for purposes of dispatch:

Incident number

Date and time the call was received

Date and time the incident was dispatched

Data elements for use with NFIRS version 5.0

Basic incidents
Incident number
Incident date and time
Location of the emergency
Type of incident
Action taken (up to three)
Aid given or received (mutual aid or automatic aid [see Chapter 16])
Times for the following: alarm, on location, control, last unit cleared
Shift working and number of alarms
Resources used (apparatus and personnel for these categories: suppression, EMS, other)
Casualties (fire and civilian)
Property use
Property owner
Person or entity involved in the incident (owner, occupant, etc.)

Fires
Property details
On-site materials or products
Ignition details, including cause
Factors contributing to ignition
Human factors contributing to ignition
Equipment involved

Fire suppression factors
Mobile property

Structure fires
Building data (structure type, status, height, ground-floor area)
Fire origin (location, spread, damage, factors contributing to flame spread)
Detector data (presence, type, power supply, effectiveness)
Automatic extinguishment equipment (presence, type, operation, effectiveness, reason for failure)

Civilian casualties
Casualty personal data
Cause of injury
Human factors contributing to injury
Nonhuman factors contributing to injury
Activity when injured
Location at time of injury
Primary symptom and area of body injured

Firefighter casualties
Firefighter personal data
Primary symptom, cause, object involved, area of body injured, factor contributing
Location where injury occurred

Location of emergency: address, street name, street type (e.g., dead end, divided road, etc.), cross street

Type of incident (i.e., fire or medical emergency)

Medical self-help provided to caller by dispatch

Phone number of the party making the emergency call

911 data supplied by the local phone company (calling phone number, address, etc.)

Any comments that were supplied by the caller (e.g., description of the situation, location within a building, name of building)

Assignments (e.g., units assigned, date and time assigned)

Times for the following occurrences: assignment, en route, on location, clear

Identity of the first-arriving unit or company, date, and time

Identity of the first-arriving engine company, date, and time

Identity of the first-arriving chief, date, and time

If vehicle location data are used for dispatching the closest unit, unit location at date and time of dispatch.

If protective equipment contributed to injury, equipment involved and type of failure

EMS

Time arrived at patient
Symptom or provider assessment
Personal data (age, race, sex, ethnicity)
Body site of injury
Type of injury
Procedures used (aid provided)
Equipment involved
Cardiac arrest data
Level of provider care
Patient status and disposition

HAZMAT

Chemical identification
Container data (type, capacity, release state)
Released-area data (population density, area affected, area evacuated, persons and buildings evacuated)
Cause data (cause, factors contributing, factors affecting mitigation)
Equipment involved
Mobile property involved
Disposition

Wildland fires

Location specifications
Fire cause, human factors, suppression factors, heat source, mobile property, equipment involved
Weather data
Property data (buildings ignited, buildings threatened, acres burned, crops burned)
Property management
Fuel model data
Person involved
Fire behavior data

Apparatus or personnel

Apparatus identification
Apparatus type
Date and time of dispatch, arrival, clear
Action taken by unit
Personnel identification number
Action taken by each person

Departmental demographics

Fire department name, address, phone number, fax number, e-mail address, and Federal Information Processing Standard (FIPS) code
Number of stations
Number of career firefighters, volunteer firefighters, firefighters paid per call

Emergency medical service patients

For many fire departments, information on EMS patients can be as important as incident data, but unfortunately as of the year 2001 there is no nationally recognized standard for patient data. Each state and/or jurisdiction's medical director is responsible for each jurisdiction's control of these data requirements. The listing of EMS patient data in the sidebar above is an attempt to identify a minimal set of data. For departments that charge patients for services rendered, that listing contains the data necessary for minimal billing, whether by the incident or by a cost itemization. A more detailed list of EMS data elements is as follows:

Incident number

Date and time the call was received

Date and time the incident was dispatched

Location where service was rendered

Type of medical emergency

Medical self-help provided to caller by dispatch

Patient's medical history

Medication history

Primary symptom

Aid provided

Drugs provided

Pulse, blood pressure, and respiratory rate, and date and time of each

Cardiac data

Obstetric data

Fee assessment (where the charging of fees is permitted), including the accounting data necessary to comply with auditors' requirements.

Fire inspection, site orientation, and the tactical information that stems from them

A tactical information system should contain planning data helpful to the emergency operations personnel while they are en route to the scene of the emergency. It should store structure or occupant information that may or may not be obvious to the first-arriving company officer, and it should contain information about the storage of hazardous materials, the location and description of fire alarm and fire extinguishment systems and specific reset/testing instructions, the location and description of other types of potential dangers, the presence and location of any people who are physically impaired, and so forth. For departments whose CAD systems interface with mobile data computers (MDCs) installed in the emergency vehicles, field personnel can receive vital tactical information while en route. For departments that do not have MDCs, this information can be printed ahead of time and stored in a loose-leaf notebook. (In this instance, terminals may be either intelligent workstations/computers or dumb workstations able to perform only specific tasks. *Mobile* implies that the device is communicating in real time with a central host computer. Most MDCs communicate with the host computer via radio transmissions.) Some departments have facsimile (fax) receivers in stations, to which brief site-specific data are sent for "tear and go" response help (i.e., tear it off the printer and go get on the engine, truck, or other vehicle).

The following is a list of possible tactical information data elements:

Structure address

Building name, alternative names

Building owner(s)/representative: name, mailing address, and phone number

Building owner's emergency contact: name and phone number

Building characteristics (e.g., height in stories, ground-floor area, construction type [truss construction, etc.], date of construction, date of last remodel)

Business name, phone number, and hours

Business emergency contact: name and phone number (and alternative name and phone number)

Type of business

Location of the closest fire hydrants in all four directions

Location of standpipe connections

Drawings (e.g., floor plans, when appropriate; HAZMAT locations; locations of invalids)

Plans/methods to gain entry while minimizing damage

Security codes, etc.

For structures with multiple occupancies: similar information about the different occupants

Hazardous materials: identity, description, location, and guideline number

Tactically significant problems: identity, description, and location

Invalids living in structure or visiting: special needs or assistance (identity, description, location)

Underground storage tanks: location, tank capacity, date installed, date of last inspection

Permits required for special equipment, materials storage, etc.

Inspection history: date of last inspection, violations found in last inspection, date of next-to-last inspection, violations found in next-to-last inspection, next scheduled inspection date

HAZMAT response data

Court cases pending

Fee assessment (where the charging of fees is permitted), including the accounting data necessary to comply with auditors' requirements

Complaint history: date, type, and resolution

Fire protection features: standpipe types and locations, sprinklers, detectors

Alarm system description and history.

Fire hydrants

A fire hydrant system is used to collect data about the condition and status of each hydrant. This information can and should be shared with fire suppression/emergency operations personnel. For departments with CAD systems that interface with MDCs installed in the emergency vehicles, responding crews can receive real-time hydrant status information while en route.

A hydrant system should contain all the following data elements, even though not all the information would be provided to responding units:

Location of hydrant (hydrant "A"): street address

Next-closest hydrant: direction, distance from hydrant A

Make and model of hydrant A

Outlet type

Color code identifier: water main size, pressure, flow

Date of last test

Current repair status, date of last status change.

Personnel records

All departments keep some data about their current and past personnel. In particular, exposure records are an important means of tracking exposure history to hazardous or toxic materials and to potentially contaminated body fluids. The most important aspect of personnel data is security: privacy should not be violated.

A typical personnel record system can include the following:

Individual employee data: training history (physical fitness levels, firefighter certification levels, EMS certification levels, training scheduling), medical history, exposure history, personal data, and education history

Personnel rosters: current assignment, previous assignments

Work scheduling: workdays, shift planning, vacation planning, staffing levels

Work history.

Uses of data, including identification of a department's fire problem

Once all the databases discussed above (and any others that a department may be using) are created, organized, and populated, they can be used as summarized in the sidebar that presents a bird's-eye view of data uses. And if those databases are then grouped and organized by a common relationship (e.g., by address or census tract), they are capable of generating information that is useful for doing the following:

Dispatching the proper type and amount of equipment to the correct location

Analyzing the relationship between incidents that occurred and resources (e.g., engines, trucks, and personnel) dispatched

Developing annual budgets

Analyzing and modeling the placement of facilities or individual resources in relation to time of day, day of week, traffic patterns, etc.

Summarizing and analyzing annual activity.

Information generated by databases that are organized by common relationships may also be useful in connection with

Changes to the building codes

Changes to the fire protection codes

Departmental operation standards

Departmental personnel safety standards

Departmental training standards

Apparatus and equipment maintenance policies

Equipment standards and geographical analysis for long-range planning and forecasting

Common measurements of productivity, 911 call analysis (911 call analysis gives one view of the department's workload)

Specialized studies

Legal responses

Public relations.

In planning annual budgets, for example, fire service managers can use summaries of relevant data to justify expected expenses and to prevent unwarranted cuts in personnel and purchases of equipment. Or managers can use summarized incident data for identifying the seriousness of the fire problem and the range of demands on the local fire and rescue department.

More particularly, every department can identify its fire problem by analyz-

Bird's-eye view of uses of data

Fire incident data can be used for summarizing activity by incident type and for calculating response times, time out of service, dollar loss, and so forth.

Company resource data can be used to calculate staffing statistics, total time on scene, action performed by company, and so forth.

Fire service injury data can be used to study injuries and develop safety standards and equipment standards.

Fire hydrant data can be used to verify the serviceability of fire hydrants and to track maintenance problems by hydrant type.

Vehicle maintenance records can be used to identify problems early so that preventive maintenance can reduce the cost of some repairs.

Tactical information can be used to identify structures and occupancies that present a tactical problem or a hazard for fire service personnel: fire service personnel can receive this information while they are en route to an incident.

911 data can be used to summarize calls and identify the times when call volumes are highest.

Emergency medical patient data can be used to analyze patient care protocols (for fire departments that provide local ambulance service).

Vehicle location data provided by global positioning satellites (see Chapter 15) can be used to analyze and predict the travel times to each and every incident dispatched.

ing the "what," "where," "who," "when," and "why" questions about its fires, casualties, and losses. Strangely, however, this rich array of incident data elements—which is at the heart of many aspects of prevention, suppression, and other public service programs—is largely underutilized. To be sure, by the time most officers rise to the position of chief they are familiar with and have learned to make use of a wide range of management data (albeit not necessarily within the context of a formal MIS): personnel information, training schedules, shift scheduling, inspection scheduling, hydrant maintenance scheduling, and other day-to-day operational issues. And it would seem natural to assume that the category of fire incident data would be among them. Yet experience shows that it is not. Although officers generate incident data for most of their careers, this class of management information reports, which provides a usable picture of local hazards and risks, remains underutilized.

There are perhaps two main reasons for the underutilization. First, many of the details now recorded about incidents are relatively ambiguous and complex. This may be because NFIRS version 4.1 attempted to use a single data element for the answers to more than one question—a technique that can create ambiguity. (The form often requires officers to "force" answers into the system. Thus, either better instructions and education for officers or a better design of the system is needed.) Second, because the details of incidents are most useful in guiding prevention programs and other public service programs, their usefulness for identifying an actual or potential fire problem may not have been recognized locally.

For a department that wishes to identify its fire problem by analyzing its fire incidents, some of the necessary questions and the elements needed to answer them are presented here.

What type of property burned? Specify structures (by type of construction, number of stories, etc.), vehicles (cars, trucks, trains, planes, etc.), outdoor materials (forest, grass, brush, etc.), other.

What type of occupancy? Specify residential, stores and offices, institutions, schools, places of public assembly, industrial facilities, storage, vacant, under construction, other.

Where did the fire occur? Specify census tract or area, and whether central business district or residential or commercial neighborhood.

Who suffered losses? Specify owners and occupants (e.g., residents, shoppers, people sleeping, etc.), with dollar loss; civilian casualties; firefighter casualties.

When did the fire occur? Specify time of day, day of week, month, year.

Why did the fire, casualty, or loss occur? Specify cause, contributing factors, human factors, automatic detection equipment, automatic extinguishment system.

What environmental factors affected the fire? Specify temperature, humidity, etc.

Why did the fire spread? Specify contributing material and factors (open doors, clutter, flammable interior furnishings, etc.).

Other information is also needed:

Suppression factors: long response time, special problems

Use of data by a small fire department   In a relatively small fire department, collecting data and predicting trends can be difficult because statistical samplings are small. The St. Matthews Fire Protection District in Louisville, Kentucky, regularly reviews the data it collects, with an eye toward finding unpredictable deviations. It has used these data—and these deviations—in a number of ways.

In one year, for example, the district noticed an unusually high number of malicious false alarms; furthermore, they were not in any particular neighborhood but across the whole district. After carefully considering any factors that might have tainted the data, fire officers instituted an extensive education campaign in the area's schools. The results were dramatic: over the next year, malicious false alarms decreased by 60 percent.

In another year, the data were used to address what seemed to be a steady increase in the number of fire alarm system malfunctions. Again, a program was developed to educate building owners and area contractors about improving the maintenance and use of automated fire alarm systems.

The district has assigned the specific duty of monitoring the collection and analysis of data to two of its officers. In addition to working with the raw numbers collected by the district, the two officers make presentations and receive questions that might be addressed through data collection.

To date, most of the conclusions drawn from the analysis of the St. Matthews Fire Protection District's data have driven public education programs. However, the district is now sharing its data with other area fire departments through its Web site postings; the hope is that sharing will make it possible to have better statistical samplings in the future.

Casualty circumstances: activity at time of injury, condition before injury

Extent of the loss: direct property loss, extent of damage, number of buildings

Indirect losses: person-days lost from work, person-days displaced from home or business

Use of resources: incident type (i.e., fire, nonfire), property use at time of incident (was there an unreported change of occupancy? e.g., the local garage owner may have rented the empty tailor shop to store his tires and batteries without reporting the new use).

Data and cooperation between the fire and planning departments   A growing city in the upper Midwest collects a good bit of data through its computer-aided dispatch system as well as through its long-term and committed use of the National Fire Incident Reporting System (NFIRS). Working with a very progressive planning department, the fire department identified some potential uses for its data that were not necessarily traditional.

The community was in a constant process of reviewing and modifying its subdivision ordinance. In this process, the fire and planning departments identified some questions that could be addressed by comparisons of the fire department's data with demographic information from other sources. Among the questions were these:

Are there definable relationships between subdivision covenants and fire loss or emergency medical impact?

Are there definable relationships between the size of homes and the demand for advanced life support services?

Do retention/detention ponds for surface-water drainage affect the frequency or severity of calls for fire services?

The answer to all these questions was yes. For instance, when the subdivision covenants permitted in-ground swimming pools, calls for service increased. Similarly, when houses were required to have a large percentage of brick on their exterior, the percentage of property loss went down. When covenants prohibited combustible roofs, fire loss (predictably) decreased.

The trend in the demand for advanced life support services was subtle and might be difficult to substantiate. The hypothesis, however, was that homes with higher value tended to be occupied by slightly older citizens. Accordingly, the likelihood of heart attacks and strokes in neighborhoods with more-expensive homes seemed to be higher, whereas the overall incidence of emergency medical calls was lower.

Finally, this community had a serious soil percolation problem that required subdividers to provide substantial ponds to hold surface-water runoff from developed land. The data indicated (although the statistical basis was not huge) a trend in drownings or near-drownings that required special and substantial resources from the fire department.

Although this type of information may not directly affect the placement of emergency service resources in a community, it does help to predict trends in service demand as planners look at the short- and long-term development of a community. Fire and emergency medical services are part of the system that responds to demands created as a result of the socioeconomic makeup of a community. Both demographic and response data play an important part in predicting what services will be needed as a community grows or changes.

Finally, proper use of good statistics can help managers identify potential problems, develop public education programs, and build a positive image of the fire department (see the sidebars on pages 432 and 433). During the first decade of the twenty-first century, the idea of advertising the services provided by the fire department may be implemented as a way of improving the relationship between the citizens and fire department management. (Although communities love their firefighters, fire department budgets are often less warmly received.)

Data quality, analysis, and presentation

If the data that are captured are not of high quality, the information produced and the conclusions drawn will be neither accurate nor meaningful. In themselves, data are not meaningful; rather, they must be analyzed, and the analyses of various databases can help managers make a number of important decisions. In addition, how the information is presented plays a major role in how effectively it communicates.

Ensuring the quality of the data

Data living in a database are subject to the principle enunciated by the old adage, "Garbage in, garbage out." *Garbage* refers to useless, inaccurate, or unhelpful data, and eliminating it is what is meant by *ensuring the quality of the data.* Garbage can be introduced in three ways: the data that firefighters input can be inaccurate or incomplete, every incident can be forced to fit a category, or the data collection system may be too complex. Ensuring that data are of high quality means ensuring that the database in question is a true and accurate representation of the situation being recorded. The database should be void of both contextual errors and relational errors. (A contextual error, e.g., reports the wrong type of occupancy. A relational error might indicate a lack of advanced life support transport capability when in fact only basic life support transport was necessary.)

The only way to verify data quality is to look with a jaundiced eye at the reports generated from a database. The manager can create cross-tabulation reports against the database and look for anomalies inconsistent with previous values in the reported cells. When an anomaly is found, a little research into the data entry process will help one determine whether the anomaly is a deliberate attempt to bypass the coding system (either by omission or commission) or is the first appearance of a new situation. Another way to find anomalies is to search for data extremes, or outliers (values that are outside the normal range, either high or low)—for example, a dollar loss greater than $9,999,999.

Analyzing the data

Given the databases mentioned above, it is obvious that the fire and rescue service collects a tremendous amount of data. Reports generated from these databases should provide insight into the daily, weekly, monthly, and annual activities of the fire department. It is understood that somewhere the number of incidents and average response time will be reported, but a fire department's list of needed reports does not always include those that reflect the numbers and types of incidents by day of the week, hour of the day, or month of the year.

More generally, there are at least four good reasons for fire service managers to look more closely at their data: first, to gain insights into the pressures that various types of incidents place on the fire department; second, to improve the allocation of resources to correspond to the demands of the jurisdiction; third, to identify training needs necessary for meeting these demands; and fourth, to identify potential problems with equipment or vehicles before the problems become real issues.

For example, an improved allocation of resources (the second reason for looking more closely at the data) can result from a statistical analysis of emergency medical calls: the analysis can show the effect of adding an additional ambulance unit in the field, and it can also show the best place to berth this new unit. An increase in the number of units by one, if that one is placed correctly, can reduce the average response time from 5 minutes to 3.5 minutes. This reduction would mean better medical coverage across the jurisdiction.

The same type of analysis can help determine the correct locations for fire stations. A change in, or the growth of, a jurisdiction may affect the department's overall response to a specific geographical area. Accordingly, a decision can be made to build either a new additional fire station or (if the existing station is old enough) a new replacement station.

The third reason for analyzing the data, as mentioned above, is to identify training needs. Traditionally the training curriculum centers on firefighting. However, an analysis of current incident data may indicate that changing the curriculum to include first-responder medical training, vehicle extrication, basic HAZMAT training, or even areas not previously identified may be warranted.

To do these analyses, one does not have to be a professional certified statistician, but a little basic understanding of statistical processes can be very useful, improving the quality and acceptability of one's information. Many instructional books are available in the marketplace, including one produced by the USFA and titled *Fire Data Analysis Handbook.*[2] A basic guide to statistical analysis, it was written specifically for use by fire service personnel; fire service examples are used throughout. And several statistical software programs are available; two of the more popular are SPSS and SAS.

Table 14–1 (produced with Microsoft Word 97) is a sample list of the types of calls for one year in raw numbers and percentages, describing the demand for service for the year. The data in this example are derived from NFIRS version 4.0. (Data collected using the NFIRS version 5.0 standard became available in late 2001.)

Once a few tables have been prepared, questions will immediately arise as to why certain numbers are large or small. These initial questions will suggest still others. The additional questions and their answers will form much of the basis for planning and evaluating the fire protection—and overall protection —for the community.

Sometimes, as in the case of Table 14–1, the data are so numerous that a graphic presentation is needed before their implications can be understood. Figure 14–1 takes the percentages that are listed in the table and puts them into a bar chart, which indicates at first glance that more detailed research is needed in the areas of rescue and false calls. But even in the form of a bar chart, the information is too detailed to be absorbed. Accordingly, Figure 14–2 displays a summary of those same data in a pie chart—a form that is clearly more usable. The pie chart makes it obvious that the bulk of this department's work entails providing EMS to the community. Further analysis of the data should enable the department to determine the percentage of first-responder incidents, the levels of emergency service needs, the types of aid provided, and so forth.

Table 14–2 is a summary of false-alarm data (malicious false alarms, alarm systems that malfunction, and other) from 1983 to 1998. A quick look at the table reveals a growing problem with alarm systems that malfunction, but by looking a little more carefully, an analyst can determine that both malicious false alarms and other false alarms are also increasing. Figure 14–3 presents the same information in an easily readable and digestible format.

Table 14–1   Sample incident breakdown in a given year.

Incident	Number	Percentage
Not-transmitted calls	2,499	2.7
Fire, insufficient information	17	*
Structure fires	2,060	2.2
Mobile structure fires	17	*
Mobile fire, in structure	116	0.1
Mobile fire, outside structure	2,490	2.7
Fire in trees, brush, grass	1,156	1.3
Refuse fire outside	1,906	2.1
Other outside fires	99,122	0.1
Fire, not classified	1,760	1.9
Steam rupture	99,934	*
Air, gas rupture	229	0.3
Process vessel explosion	4	*
Munitions explosion	209	0.2
Excessive heat, no ignition	74	0.1
Rupture, not classified	3	*
Rescue call, insufficient information	36	*
Major accidents	17,066	18.5
Assist ambulance	31,711	34.4
Lock-in	99,592	0.6
Person lost	16	*
People trapped, caught, buried	99,243	0.3
Drowning, potential drowning	24	*
Electrocution	99,995	*
Rescue call, not classified	108	0.1
Condition, insufficient information	76	0.1
Flammable gas/liquid condition	1,030	1.1
Toxic condition	91	0.1
Radioactive condition	8	*
Arcing, shorted equipment	1,947	2.1
Oil burner, delayed ignition	1	*
Minor vehicle accident, no injury	2,179	2.4
Explosive present	1	*
Attempted burning, illegal action	72	0.1
Condition not classified	60	0.1
Service calls, insufficient information	65	0.1
Person in distress	2,285	2.5
Water problem	702	0.8
Smoke, odor removal	4,917	5.3
Animal problem	70	0.1
Public service assistance	268	0.3
Unauthorized burning	20	*
Cover assignment, fill-in	7	*
Service calls, not classified	222	0.2
Good-intent call, insufficient information	1,246	1.4
Incident cleared prior to arrival	590	0.6
Wrong address	84	0.1
Controlled burning	18	*
Vicinity alarm	115	0.1
Steam mistaken for smoke	266	0.3
EMS call, patient left scene	42	0.1
Good intent, not classified	1,382	1.5
False call, insufficient information	679	0.7
Malicious false alarm	2,773	3.0
Bomb scare, no bomb	39	*
System malfunction	9,246	10.0
Unintentional false alarm	1,342	1.5
False call, not classified	240	0.3
Natural disaster, insufficient information	0	0.0
Earthquake	0	0.0
Flood	6	*
Wind storm	5	*
Lightning strike	13	*
Natural disaster, not classified	1	*
Citizen complaint	36	*
Situation not classified	50	0.1
Total incidents	92,192	

*Less than 0.05 percent.

Situation found

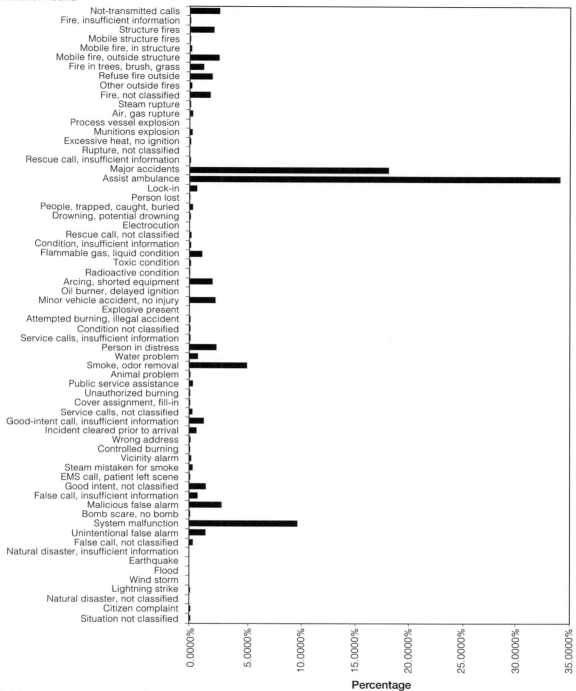

Note: Percentages are based on a total of 92,192 incidents.

Figure 14–1   Sample
incident breakdown in a
given year, bar chart.

Figure 14–2   Sample incident summary, pie chart.

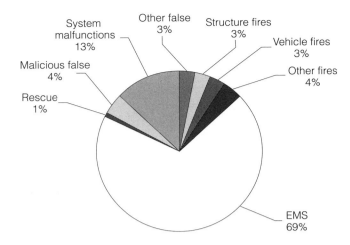

Table 14–2   Sample summary of false-alarm data.

Year	Malicious false	System malfunction	Other false
1983	1,843	2,439	874
1984	2,116	3,398	910
1985	2,465	4,614	835
1986	2,798	5,428	1,156
1987	2,607	5,138	841
1988	2,511	5,330	1,196
1989	2,585	6,187	1,107
1990	2,557	5,965	1,063
1991	2,494	7,030	1,284
1992	2,559	8,131	1,474
1993	2,633	8,066	1,726
1994	2,671	8,233	1,836
1995	2,540	9,080	2,005
1996	2,906	9,141	2,222
1997	2,812	9,246	2,261
1998	3,070	9,526	2,539

Figure 14–3   Sample chart of false-alarm growth.

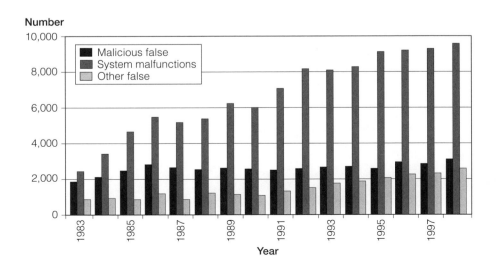

Presenting the information

Data analysis results in information that can be presented in many formats: textual recommendations, histograms (see Chapter 10), charts (bar, column, line, pie, dot), maps, or any combination of these. A decision on how to break out the data most meaningfully must be based on analytical skills and an understanding of the community. When information is assembled, it can become an annual report describing the department's activity and accomplishments. The annual report can be made up of both monthly reports (which graphically display the occurrence of, e.g., incendiary fires, car fires, or structure fires) and special reports (which could help with the search for patterns). Because locations of the incidents being reported will be displayed on a map of the local jurisdiction, over time the annual reports may indicate a pattern of fires. When assembling data into a report format, one should remember that a picture (histogram, chart, or map) can be worth a thousand words.

The presentation of data can also be used for cross-departmental comparisons. Figure 14–4 is a graphic presentation of the incident activity for the Baltimore County (Maryland) Fire Department, and Figure 14–5 is a graphic presentation of the incident activity for the Dallas (Texas) Fire Department. What conclusions can be drawn from a comparison of the two charts? (Both charts were produced with Software Publishing Company's Harvard Graphics.)

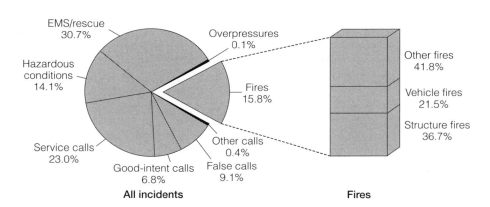

Figure 14–4 Sample incident activity, metropolitan county department.

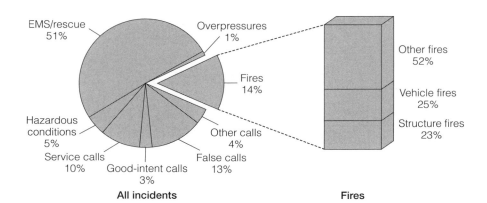

Figure 14–5 Sample incident activity, metropolitan city department.

Before drawing conclusions, one must ask certain questions, most obviously (in this case) about the disparities between the two departments' activities related to EMS and service calls. The following questions about definition should be asked:

How does each department categorize incidents?

Do different jurisdictional organizations dictate different definitions?

Does one geographic region use different definitions from another?

When information from one's own department is compared with information from other departments similar in size, area served, and population served, the chief must ask some of the following questions:

What is the call-processing time and how do I compare with other departments?

What is my turn-out time? What is my total response time? How is my response time? Is my response time better in some areas than in others?

How many structure fires are there in my jurisdiction? What are the causes of these fires?

How many vehicle fires? When are they occurring? Where are they occurring?

Should I expect the occurrence of specific types of incidents to be related to specific weather conditions? If yes, how can I best use my limited resources?

How many calls are false alarms? How many are system malfunctions? Are these false alarms seasonal? Are these false alarms weather-related?

What incident types predominate?

Where are my resources being used? When are my resources being used? How long are my resources being used per incident? Will better training or different training bring the figure down?

What can I do to get more from my current resources?

Do I have any problems that need immediate attention?

Designing and purchasing management information systems

Management issues in designing and purchasing an MIS include how the data are to be organized, who the users of the system will be, what the security requirements are, whether software should be bought off the shelf or be custom written, whether outsourcing should be used, what the proper acquisition steps are, and what computer hardware should be bought.

Organization of the data

Before data are organized, two major viewpoints should be considered: the potential user's and the programmer's. Accordingly, as a system is being designed, a dialogue must occur between the fire chief and the programmers. Often the user specifies needs first and then lets the programmer design the organization of information. The programmer may ask detailed questions about how the data will be used and how frequently.

Users of the system

Who will use the system directly and who will use it indirectly? Of the many users of fire department information, direct users include the fire chief, assistant and battalion chiefs, other departmental officers, the local government manager and staff, the local government legislative body, and other local government departments. Indirect users of the data may include the local media, the insurance industry, the state fire marshal, the USFA, the Consumer Product Safety Commission, and the public. Some users may have to use the system more frequently than other users. In addition, fire department analysts must have direct access to the data files for quality assurance, but secondary users will have access to the data only after the data have been quality checked. Managers and local media may have access only at the summary level rather than at the record level. It is important to identify these different types of users and the different ways in which they will be interacting with the system.

Security requirements

The answer to who is allowed access to the data will depend on the types of data and the local jurisdiction's open-records laws. To protect patient confidentiality, records that deal with EMS provided by paramedics should be very restricted. To follow the guidelines used for all criminal investigations, fire investigation records should be very restricted. To meet state requirements, records describing juvenile firesetters or juvenile suspects must be highly protected. Personnel data will, in part, be held as confidential. Some portions of the data on buildings should be considered confidential because they describe alarm systems, HAZMAT storage locations, and the presence and location of invalids living in the occupancy. Hydrant records and incident records from the CAD system may be available to anyone upon request. For online records, security should be set up with the following permissions: read only, add, change, delete, special update (outside of normal time frame), print option, password required, specific day of week, time of day.

Software: Off the shelf or custom written?

What are the pros and cons of buying software off the shelf as opposed to using custom-written software?

Off-the-shelf software Off-the-shelf software is available to perform many noncritical tasks, such as creating reports from databases and from spreadsheets, and to facilitate computer mapping, cross-tabulations, and statistical analysis. When looking at off-the-shelf products, one should remember that these products are useful only when the instructions are kept simple and the data requirements are neither complicated nor restrictive.

The office suite of products (such as Microsoft Office 2000 and Corel WordPerfect Office 2000) offers a wide variety of programs that many fire departments use. This suite includes a word processor; a spreadsheet package; a database package (such as Access, Dbase, FoxPro, Oracle, SQL, and Sybase), which can help the user organize and index data to make them more easily accessible; and a presentation software package.

Most of the report-writing software available (e.g., Crystal Reports, Hummingbird, or any of the SQL products) will work with database files and supports query by example. ("Query by example" is a query language that is supported in some form by most databases and helps the user construct queries; some databases refer to query by example as "Wizards.") This type of software is excellent for both standard periodic (weekly, monthly, and annual) and ad hoc reports.

Computer mapping programs are an excellent way to display information graphically. For most types of data, a spatial representation of raw data produces a better analytical tool.

Figure 14–6 is a map used to identify an area with potentially high response times (the stars identify intersections where traffic is heavy). This map was produced with MapInfo Professional; Arcinfo, GIS Atlas, and Intergraph are some of the other currently available mapping programs. This same general technique can be used for studying the occurrence of structure fires, car fires, assist-ambulance calls, alarm system malfunctions, or similar situations. Computer mapping programs that depict the demand for services can also be used for analyzing and locating fire department facilities.

One of the next-most-important tools for data analysis is the cross-tabulation, a product that will produce very good multidimensional cross-tabulation reports from flat files, hierarchical files (files containing different data records that must be processed in a predefined order), and Oracle/SQL databases. Not only will it produce tables but it also has options that enable it to produce reproduction-ready reports. Moreover, once a record is laid out and the data elements defined, the table request can be very simple. The following is an example of the kind of statement—the actual syntax—that was used to produce Table 14–3 (which was produced by the product TPL Tables from QQQ Software Inc.): "Table One: count then loss, situation then total." This request produces a report formatted so that column one contains a frequency count, column two contains a dollar loss figure, and each row identifies a type of incident. The finished table or report is ready for reproduction in any larger report.

Cross-tabulation programs can be used for determining how many incidents occurred on each day of the week, during each hour of the day, or during each month of the year. When the raw numbers are too overwhelming, a basic understanding of statistics is very important. For instance, average response time—used as a common measure of productivity—can be made more meaningful when it is compared with the median response time.

Another very important issue to keep in mind when buying off-the-shelf software is the need for (and availability and cost of) training. The fire and

Figure 14–6 Computer map showing area with potentially high response times.

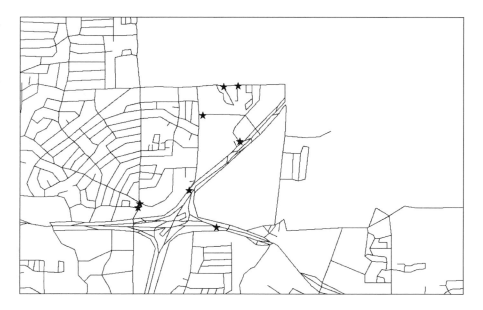

Table 14–3   Metropolitan fire departments, percentage of each type of fire, 1993.

Metropolitan fire department	Percentage of department activity							
	Structure fires	Outside structure fires	Vehicle fires	Trees, brushfires	Refuse fires	Explosions, no fire	Outside spill w/fire	Other fires
Austin	25.93	1.51	25.19	28.04	17.94	0.18	0.20	1.02
Baltimore City	39.72	4.29	16.76	9.89	28.50	0.47	0.13	0.24
Baltimore County	22.36	6.45	21.05	25.01	23.37	0.25	0.39	1.12
Boston	35.97	1.58	16.78	14.21	31.29	0.03	0.03	0.11
California Department of Forestry	15.33	4.30	19.34	43.59	15.67	—	—	1.76
Chicago	22.14	0.09	29.94	2.68	43.60	0.18	0.11	1.27
Cleveland	27.65	0.97	33.81	4.96	32.61	—	—	—
Columbus	28.50	10.70	23.97	5.91	30.45	0.24	0.10	0.12
Dallas	24.64	1.41	25.92	19.69	27.17	0.82	—	0.34
Denver	26.74	4.33	19.79	7.97	39.87	0.60	0.19	0.51
Detroit	44.30	0.96	23.85	2.64	28.03	0.12	0.05	0.04
El Paso	15.39	3.49	17.81	38.29	23.75	0.21	0.35	0.72
Ft. Worth	23.28	4.40	26.13	20.89	22.02	0.99	0.66	1.62
Houston	40.27	1.73	27.18	8.91	21.77	0.05	0.08	—
Jacksonville	31.83	0.75	22.79	19.98	23.77	0.13	0.07	0.68
Los Angeles City	21.10	1.51	32.96	11.29	33.02	—	—	0.12
Los Angeles County	21.82	4.15	32.30	19.08	21.86	—	—	0.78
Monroe County	41.50	1.28	21.45	10.66	22.37	0.41	0.23	2.12
Nashville	57.44	2.15	39.80	0.22	0.31	0.08	—	—
New Orleans	35.10	1.49	29.81	5.67	23.97	—	0.06	3.91
Oklahoma City	24.19	3.02	22.77	32.69	16.91	—	—	0.43
Phoenix	13.73	3.51	16.79	35.64	29.89	0.08	0.14	0.24
Prince George's County	33.10	5.34	28.71	20.93	11.54	0.15	—	0.23
San Antonio	18.47	2.11	20.10	30.27	28.05	0.22	0.18	0.59
San Diego	32.70	1.77	18.44	14.78	30.25	0.10	—	1.96
San Francisco	30.19	—	27.90	18.29	19.81	0.03	—	3.78
San Jose	40.29	5.57	24.93	11.57	15.65	—	—	1.99
Seattle	34.97	4.01	27.63	6.74	22.69	0.21	—	3.75
Washington, D.C.	17.58	1.42	25.70	13.20	39.89	0.41	0.45	1.35

— Data not available.

Note: More recent data will not be available until the conversion to NFIRS 5.0 has been completed.

rescue service spends a great deal of time on training, not just for rookies but also for the more experienced firefighters and (as far as computer support is concerned) for civilian members of the department. Most training classes provide some additional techniques for achieving better results. Moreover, as new versions of operating systems and applications software are released, more training will be necessary.

Custom-written software   Custom-written software can have advantages over off-the-shelf products if the department has the funds for contracting out or the in-house personnel to design, document, write, test, and implement the system. The greatest advantage of custom-written software is that as the department's needs change, the software can be modified to accommodate the new policies, whereas when off-the-shelf software is used, departmental policy must conform to the software's design rather than vice versa. The greatest disadvantage is that the modification process may require a long time for programming, testing, and implementation. Another disadvantage may be the cost of a custom-written code.

Outsourcing: Good or bad?

Outsourcing is the strategic use of outside resources to perform activities traditionally handled by internal staff and internal resources. Before deciding to outsource, a department should always address the following five factors because they have cross-functional implications:

Cost of providing the service

Quality level of the service provided

Effect on the organization's culture

Ways of measuring the results

Ways of managing the service provider.

Important issues relative to outsourcing are as follows:

If other systems must be integrated, can the vendor provide the necessary connectivity? Who accepts accountability for interface problems?

Can the vendor always respond in a timely manner regardless of the contractual agreement?

If the vendor's business should fail, what protection or recourse is available to the local fire department (what happens to the source code and its ownership, and how can the department gain access to it)?

In the case of custom-written code, who owns it?

Acquisition issues

When preparing to outsource or contract for custom-written software, a department should take the following steps:

Define in a general way its expectations of the system.

Identify the data elements that will be necessary for reaching the desired goals.

Study the data elements: will the coding scheme produce the answers to only one question?

Analyze the relationship between the data elements and the respective codes to determine any relational edits necessary for producing the desired goals.

Determine the implementation time lines and establish the necessary milestones.

Define the acceptance testing procedures to be followed.

Never make partial payments for products or work that has not been completed. When the product or work passes the acceptance test and has been proven to work as advertised, then pay for it. Spending less than the full amount on a product that does not do the job and for which a full refund cannot be obtained has not really saved the department a nickel.

The process of defining and specifying will take a lot of time, so managers should not be in a hurry. They should remember that the old adage still applies: "Garbage in, garbage out."

Computer hardware, present and future

In the early twenty-first century, the computer industry is progressing so fast that most equipment is obsolete within three years and unusable within six years. The overall cost of personal computers has come down so that in 1999 a 550-megahertz (MHz) Pentium II processor with 128 megabytes (Mb) of RAM (random access memory), 6.4-gigabyte (Gb) hard disk drive, 3.5-Mb floppy drive, accelerated graphics port video, tape backup, and keyboard with monitor was available for around $1,700. In 2002, for approximately the same price, the computer is configured with a 2.2-gigahertz (GHz) Pentium 4 processor (or faster), 256 (or more) Mb of RAM, 40.0 Gb (or larger) hard disk drive, and so forth. In some cases, it may be just as easy to use a laptop computer with a docking station. One should purchase the fastest computer with the largest hard drive (30.0 Gb or more), the most RAM (256 Mb or more), the largest screen size, and the longest warranty period (twenty-four months or more).

Before this book is in readers' hands, the 1999 crop of 32-bit processors will have been replaced by the 64-bit processors. This technology will add much greater computing power to desktops and servers. Video displays will be moving from the CRT monitors to the newer thin, flat, LCD screens. Network technology will continue to grow in both speed and capacity, using hardwire, wireless, and fiber-optic technology. The standard speeds in the year 2002 are either 10 Mb per second or 100 Mb per second, but the future will bring speeds in excess of 1 Gb per second. Locally owned microwave systems, cable television systems, satellite systems, and the local telephone system can be used to provide network connectivity that may be cheaper than what the local cable company can provide.

In 1999 Microsoft, the dominant operating software vendor in the industry, stated that its future operating system would be Windows NT-based and that further development of Windows 95/98/ME would be limited in order to simplify future enhancements to the operating systems. This new system is called Windows XP.

The LINUX operating system is becoming very popular because of its price and performance. Some of the large computer manufacturers are now providing it as an option for an operating system.

Computer hardware will continue to change as the central processing units become faster, from the 750 MHz of 1999 to speeds in excess of 3 GHz, while the internal bus speeds will increase from the maximum of 100 MHz in 1999 to 500 MHz or faster. Hard drives will become larger and cheaper per gigabyte, so that the 36.0-Gb drives considered large in 1999 will be considered small, and the norm will be 100 Gb or larger.

In addition, the digital video disk (DVD) technology will provide larger capacities, from the current 650-Mb standard to a 4-Gb or greater standard. These new DVDs can be used to back up data from the hard drives.

3D accelerated video graphics cards with new protocols will allow greater speed and the capacity to handle both 2D and 3D animated graphics. Display monitors built to the DVD standard will provide better image definition. Large-sized monitors will be built around either picture tubes or large-sized LCD screens.

The use of the Internet will continue to expand, providing that the backbone infrastructure between the major common carriers can be expanded to handle the higher demand. If the government continues to support the Internet, the common carriers that provide the backbone can support the higher capacity throughput needed to handle the increased demand. The Internet will continue to be a dominant influence in both business and personal life.

Conclusion

This chapter has provided a glimpse into the world of computers and data management, sketching out various possibilities for using technology in the fire and rescue service. The fire and rescue service, now and in the future, should view technology as a tool that will help it fulfill its mission of protecting citizens. To ensure that the protection provided to citizens is as good as it possibly can be, the fire service must approach technology proactively.

1   The National Commission on Fire Prevention and Control, *America Burning* (Washington, D.C., 1973), 9.

2   Tom McEwen, with Catherine A. Miller, *Fire Data Analysis Handbook* (Washington, D.C.: Federal Emergency Management Association, U.S. Fire Administration, n.d.).

15 Communication systems and emergency response centers

One of the main foundations of all strategic and tactical operations is communication between people. Whether in the factory, in the state capital, or on the battlefield, communication—the transmission of a message from one person or group to another—serves to set objectives, determine approaches, transmit orders, and report facts and accomplishments. Except when direct face-to-face dialogue takes place, most of this interchange uses some form of technological communications system. The message may be transmitted on a system that is part of a wired data or voice network or it may be sent over the airwaves via radio, but in either case, problems with communications can corrupt plans and interfere with actions. Accordingly, managers at all levels—especially in organizations that expect to be effective in the twenty-first century—must incorporate communications management into their programs.

Any manager, above all one engaged in such mission- and time-critical activities as public safety and emergency response, must make it a priority to understand clearly the types of systems involved and the limitations imposed by technology. The manager must ensure that emergency operation communications are reliable. Failing to do so may increase either safety problems or risk exposure and may result in additional deaths, injuries, and destruction.

Technology is not the only possible source of communication problems. Communication is an exchange of words and ideas between two people or locations, and the originator of the communication must ensure that the receiver actually understands the message as the originator intended. Failing to do so will compromise activities and endanger personnel and citizens.

Good communication operations, however, will not eliminate the need for critical decision making on the part of people in leadership positions. No matter how information is transmitted, it will always have to be reviewed and acted upon by individuals and staffs. An extreme example is the situation British leaders faced during World War II after they had intercepted and broken German codes. Learning that the Germans were planning a Luftwaffe attack on the city of Coventry—an attack that would inflict tremendous numbers of civilian casualties—they made the anguished decision not to risk revealing that they had intercepted and broken the codes.

In this chapter, communication is considered first as a process of transferring information from one person to another. The process has several points of potential failure, which can be identified and preventive steps taken. The technology of communications is discussed next: wireless communication of voice, data, and images; communication of the location of a person or vehicle; computer-aided dispatch; and geographic information systems. Then come sections on issues involving telephones (cellular, 911 systems, and 311 systems); the communications system infrastructure; the communications center itself (staffing, role, and joint facilities); planning, acquisition, and policies and procedures; and topical issues involving cost. The conclusion touches on aspects of future technology about which there is general agreement.

Clear and unclear messages, good and poor communications management　History, including recent history, reveals many examples of critical communication failures that dramatically affected outcomes. Similarly, successful communication operations have also had a major effect on operations.

An example of an unclear message was the one that sent the British Cavalry Light Brigade into the mouths of Russian cannon in the "Valley of Death" during the Crimean War. "Advance and take the enemy cannon" was confusing when the Russians had multiple and geographically separate artillery locations. In contrast, the message given to the Germans by the commanding officer of the Allies' Bastogne garrison during the Battle of the Bulge in World War II was succinct and unmistakable. "Nuts" clearly rejected the German's surrender demand and could not be misunderstood.

Another situation in which a critical communications failure dramatically affected an outcome occurred during the U.S. Civil War: a horse-borne message with significant information that might have affected the outcome of the Gettysburg campaign failed to reach General Robert E. Lee. And more than a century later, operational communication breakdowns in the 1990s were evident at several incidents where firefighters died.

An example of both poor and good communications management—poor on the part of the Imperial Japanese Navy, good on the part of the United States—was the shooting down of Admiral Yamamoto's aircraft during World War II. Moreover, the entire course of World War II was affected by the Allies' interception of Axis communications.

Interpersonal communication: Managing points of possible failure

The heart of communication system technologies is the transmission of information from one individual and group to another. Because this transmission is subject to problems and failure at several points, the public safety manager must be able to manage the transmission process successfully. It is important to examine how people frame and interpret information, remembering that the most basic form of communication—the basis for all exchange of information—is face-to-face dialogue.

Sending and receiving

When individuals exchange information, the process consists of one person deciding what needs to be said and framing the information for transmission, using terms the recipient should understand. The originator then utters the information as the recipient listens and begins to interpret it. If a reply is required, the recipient goes through the same process as the originator.

The first problem that may exist is that the recipient may not be interested in the issue. People receiving messages tend to decide very early in the transmission if the message involves a need to know or an "impact on me," and if they conclude it does not, they will begin thinking about other things.

The next possible problem is the choice of words used for conveying the message. Information presented in a manner that a recipient cannot understand or interpret will result in a lack of action or the wrong action. The words chosen must be simple and related to the message—but not too simple. If it becomes apparent early in the message that a reply is needed, the recipient will begin to think about and develop a response before receiving and interpreting the balance of the message and might miss critical information.

What both of those problems have in common is that they may lead to the recipient's not focusing on the message and its critical components, with the result that information can be misinterpreted or missed. After all, when people participate in a conversation, they do not need to use the full capacity of their thought process but can allow their minds to think about other matters.

Training that teaches people to focus on incoming information is called interpersonal communications training. It tries to eliminate the problems discussed above. Without such training, success in the transmission of information depends on individual variations in listening techniques—a third area of possible problems. People can be active listeners or passive listeners, and the difference will affect how they receive information.

Active listening is critical to emergency operations. Active listeners focus on the incoming information and listen to the entire message before consciously beginning to develop a response. Passive listeners, in contrast, allow the incoming information to come in without disrupting their other activities, and very early in the process they begin thinking about a reply. They are usually ready to reply as the speaker ends. If a passive listener is the speaker, he or she may become upset while the active listener takes time to formulate a response to the original message. In this case the speaker often ends up questioning whether the other person has received or understood the original message.

Because of its critical nature, the interpersonal communications process must be successfully managed. For this among other reasons, interpersonal communication has been a focus of programs developed and delivered by the National Fire Academy and other higher-level programs. Action to ensure that basic issues of communication do not compromise operations and safety is of the utmost importance.

For the manager who must deal with these issues, what are some of the options? Several may require the manager to reach beyond the emergency organization. Some managers may be reluctant to do so, especially if doing so can be misinterpreted as indicating that the manager should have resolved the problem earlier. Yet failure to reach beyond the organization if that is necessary may increase the liability exposure.

The first option is one for larger departments, which may wish to develop an internal capability to train personnel in communication issues. The trainers can be sent to programs that will give them the skills to present the necessary information in terms to which an emergency-oriented audience will be receptive. These programs to train the trainers may be offered through local colleges that have fire- or emergency-related degree programs.

Other options are available to departments of all sizes. For medium to small agencies, college programs may offer the only approach to training personnel in communication issues unless the agency is located in a community where a company has a regional or central training program. In those communities, companies that offer such programs to business and industry may agree to offer training to emergency organizations. Or larger industries, such as public utilities, may offer places in their internal training programs to emergency personnel.

Because the subject matter in these training programs is not oriented toward emergency services, a manager may face the obstacle of convincing responders that the material is pertinent to their needs. They can be persuaded if the manager points out to them how misunderstandings can occur in emergency communications.

Jargon and codes

Another obstacle to clear emergency communications can be the use of agency- or discipline-specific jargon. Each profession develops its own short-hand for use by people in the business, and fire and rescue services are no exception.

Several instructors at the Emergency Management Institute and the National Fire Academy use a simple but clear example of how jargon can affect emergency operations.[1] A class is asked, "What happens when you say, 'Charge the line'?" Then the class is asked if it makes a difference whether the person saying it is a police officer, a firefighter, or an electric utility lineworker.

When the person issuing the order and the person receiving it are of the same discipline, the instinctive reactions of the members of each service are relied on. The police commander expects the police officers to advance rapidly, the fire service leader wants to see hose lines fill with water, and the utility crew chief expects the circuit to be energized. Each order is shorthand within the profession.

Does it make a difference if the receiving person is of a different discipline from the transmitting person? What might happen if the order to charge the line were passed down the chain of command from a fire service person to an electrical utility subordinate? What safety issues would be raised if this order were misinterpreted or acted on by different disciplines simultaneously? Might the advancing police walk into an area being wet down as the circuit is being energized?

This issue has major implications for liaison officers and personnel operating in a unified command system. The use of jargon can cause more than delay in operations.

Another form of the problem of jargon arises when communication systems use numeric codes instead of a natural language. When all radio transmissions had to be entered into a written log, the codes were introduced as a form of dispatcher shorthand. Dispatchers then began to use them in actual transmissions to field units. This use was often formalized in written procedures. Often people mistakenly believed that the Federal Communications Commission (FCC) required the use of these codes, or signals.

Errors can occur when codes are used, generally in systems in which the dispatcher also gives the time over the radio as part of operational communications. This kind of error occurs especially from 10–00 to 10–59 in systems using "10" codes (codes that substitute numbers for commonly used phrases; e.g., "10–4" means "I understand and will comply"). Because 10–40 can be interpreted as 10:40, an operational message can be confused with the time.

Giving the time over the air began before the development of accurate court-acceptable time-recording systems (i.e., systems whose records can be used as evidence in a lawsuit involving, e.g., response times). Often the practice of giving the time over the air was codified into written policy, and the policy has not been updated to reflect newer technology.

In the well-equipped communication centers of the twenty-first century there is no need to use codes, because transmissions are recorded and the FCC no longer requires written station logs. There is also no need to use on-air time to announce the hour over the radio system.

These simple examples show that in planning sessions, the communications manager must be an advocate for both clear language and the absence of jargon. These examples also demonstrate the need for routinely updating existing procedures to ensure that all activity supports field operations and incorporates the benefits of new technology.

Technology of communications

Fire and emergency service managers must become familiar at the very least with technology that is being sold to the general public because this technology sets public expectations. When people can accurately find their positions in coastal waters or can call for assistance from their cars, they expect public safety services to be equally adept. In addition, effectiveness and efficiency are closely tied to technological advances. The microchip and computerization itself are proof that the fire and rescue service must use technological advances to keep up with the changing challenges of protecting communities.

Mobile radio communication

Public safety agencies pioneered the use of mobile radio communication as we know it. Putting radios in patrol cars and fire engines increased efficiency, safety, and productivity; thus, agencies deployed radio systems before businesses did. Public safety radio communications began with one-way voice dispatch.

Transmission of the spoken word is fundamental to command-and-control activities, and radio systems transmit the words of a message, but they often do even more. They often transmit, as well, other carriers of meaning such as inflection, emphasis, and background noise. These enable the receiver to recognize the speaker and to draw inferences.

Initially, mobile radio systems used analog transmission, and the signal was transmitted as an analog waveform. Such transmissions were normally restricted to the frequency range of 300 to 3,000 hertz (Hz), about the same as telephone calls. This range provides reasonable speech quality without using excessive spectrum, and it was within the capability of the technology of that era.

As the twenty-first century begins, the most commonly used analog technology is frequency modulation (FM) in 25-kilohertz (kHz) bandwidths. As compared with previous amplitude modulation (AM) systems, the FM bandwidth helps protect the voice signal from noise and interference. Analog FM signals can be received easily on scanners and monitors. This has both negative and positive effects. On the one hand, criminals can eavesdrop on public safety communications. On the other hand, public safety agencies can use scanners to monitor the communications of other agencies to learn when assistance is needed. Scanners provide one of the most widely used forms of interoperability between systems on different channels.

Although analog transmissions were originally hard to encode in a manner that provided a high degree of security from monitoring by eavesdroppers, modern technology now allows far more robust analog scrambling (rendering transmissions unintelligible except to authorized listeners). The process of scrambling is known as *encryption.*

Analog mobile radio has often been used to carry signals other than voice. An example is tone alert paging, which is often used to alert volunteer or part-time departments or staff officers. Or it may be used to "tone" (activate, or turn on, a radio receiver by sending one or more coded tones) or digitally

---

Analog and digital   "Analog" is data processing on a continuous meter, like a clock. "Digital" is data processing by digits, like a car radio, where you can get number 101.1, for example, but not 101.2, because when you push the button, the number that comes up next is 101.3.

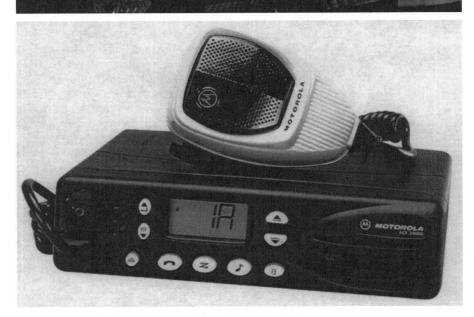

Figure 15–1   A firefighter uses a mobile radio system that is mounted in the fire engine.

control remote equipment and security systems. These tones or other types of signals can be used to turn on lights or open doors at stations.

Voice transmission is increasingly making the transition from analog to digital. In the digital environment, the speaker's analog voice is converted into a series of data elements. After the data bits are received by the recipient's radio, they are converted back into voice for presentation over the radio speaker to listeners. The device used to convert the analog voice waveform to a numeric representation is called a *vocoder,* shorthand for Voice-Coder.

Speech quality varies among different vocoders. Typically, those that transmit more digital bits generally produce better speech quality. Not until the late 1990s could affordable high-quality digital speech be implemented in land mobile radio. By the year 2000 many agencies were beginning to implement or consider digital systems. One advantage of digital voice transmission is security. Digital signals can be encrypted to prevent interception far more easily, reliably, and effectively than analog signals can.

Almost all public service personnel use voice-based radio communications to communicate from the field with their dispatchers and to communicate with their co-workers in the field. Vehicles are equipped with radios, and most response staff members are also equipped with portable radio units. Radio voice communication improves the responsiveness and effectiveness of public safety operations and increases the safety of field personnel.

These public safety communication systems normally operate using variations of two methods: *repeater* and *simplex.* A typical repeater transmission system uses two frequencies, one for communications from the mobile units to the base station and the other for transmissions from the base station to the mobile units. Repeater operation is found most often in bands above 406 megahertz (MHz), where frequencies are commonly paired, although when system managers have been able to license pairs of frequencies below 406 MHz, many systems use repeater operations in those frequencies.

In repeater systems, messages from one field unit to another must be relayed by the base station. This procedure ensures a more guaranteed reception by the field unit because the more powerful signal is used. Repeater operation is normally used for day-to-day operations, for dispatcher control of mobile units, and for communications over a wide area.

Some repeater systems do not repeat all of the mobile transmissions and send only communications from the dispatcher out on the base-to-mobile frequency. Other repeater systems allow simultaneous transmissions by the field unit and the base station, much like what happens with a telephone call. Simultaneous transmission is most often seen in the ultrahigh frequency channels used for emergency medical service communications between prehospital personnel and hospital staff. In most cases, however, the dispatcher will not hear field units while transmitting on the base station system.

The simplex method relies on direct unit-to-unit communications. Here one field unit transmits the signal and another field unit receives it. The message is not repeated by the base station system. This method is most common on bands below 406 MHz, where frequencies are usually not paired.

The simplex method is most commonly used by operations or tactical groups working in a small area and needing to coordinate with one another, but a number of wide-area and statewide systems use it as well. Many of the older radios systems that are still in use are simplex in nature. In addition, simplex operations may be used in a repeater-based system—for example, when units need to coordinate their actions at a fire, in a hostage situation, or in a situation involving the release of hazardous materials.

Significantly more efficient in the use of both spectrum and radio transmitter infrastructure is a technology called *trunking.* Trunked radio systems operate using a pool of frequencies, which are assigned to conversations one call at a time via computerized control systems. Trunking technology is more complex and more costly, but because of its advantages, it is often used by larger public safety organizations. (Trunking is explained in greater detail in the accompanying sidebar.)

Another approach to improved spectrum efficiency is the use of narrowband analog modulation. Although narrowband techniques had long been used in other applications, the engineering challenges of matching them to mobile communication channels were not overcome in commercially available products until the late 1990s.

Bandwidths: Historical background

Originally radio systems were developed to use AM because the technology of the first half of the twentieth century could easily achieve this form of modulation. But just listening to the AM band on a car or portable radio shows the technical issues and problems of this band. AM radio is very noisy compared with the other bands. It is affected by solar radiation more easily than other methods of modulation are and therefore has a tendency to carry for very long distances after dark.

During World War II, the Allied powers developed radar and other new technologies. Of the technologies that were rapidly deployed, one was FM radio. This provided a clearer and quieter transmission that was less affected by engine noise. In addition, new vacuum technology allowed the development of smaller and sometimes portable radio units.

How trunking works   Trunking uses computerized control to apply a concept that the telephone industry has used for years in managing local telephone service.

Nontrunked channels are like a series of one-lane highways laid out parallel to one another. Radio traffic is initiated by a party at one end of a single-lane channel. That party places a call to the recipient at the other end. No other traffic should use the channel until the recipient sends an answer back in the other direction. Yet other traffic does use the channel, causing co-channel interference.

Often this happens when one party cannot hear the other, a situation that is especially possible when one of the co-channel users is using a portable radio. The various users' radio traffic on these single channels can become intermixed, and people may miss transmissions meant for them. People have to wait for their own transmissions to be acknowledged. In a conventional system with five single channels, for example, if this waiting is happening on all five channels, only five sets of radio transmissions may tie up all the channels.

Trunking unites these single channels into a limited-access highway. Here the computers choose the channel that is to be used for individual components of the overall exchange of information. This control allows multiple messages to be intermingled on the highway. Messages that move to the recipient can switch from channel to channel just as cars move from lane to lane on a highway when spaces open up. Channels do not have to stay idle while people wait for a reply. The computer decides which channels to use for replies and which to make available to the next radio with which someone is trying to transmit. Just as the addition of only one extra lane to a four-lane highway increases the throughput of the highway by more than 20 percent, trunking allows more communication than a regular system does on the same number of channels.

As members of the military returned from the war and took up jobs in the public sector, they knew the benefits that radio communications would have in emergency tactical operations. Between the late 1940s and the mid-1960s, therefore, the use of radio expanded among public service agencies. Throughout the same period, manufacturers were able to improve radios so that the FCC —as the arbiter of radio issues for all nonfederal organizations—could make more radio spectrum available.

In 1967, the FCC doubled the number of available frequencies when it mandated that instead of being assigned in 50-kHz spreads, they be narrowed to 25-kHz bands. And as new technology allowed the use of shorter and shorter wave frequencies, other new, higher-frequency bandwidths were opened up. However, technological expansion was matched by ever-greater demand for wireless devices. Given this demand and the fact that radio is an area governed by international treaty, before long every new group of frequencies had been allocated to one user or another.

Significant battles were fought over the few remaining open bandwidths. Arguments between commercial broadcasters and public safety officials erupted over the use of television channels. Advocates of high-definition television affirmed their need for more allocations.

As technology expanded and microcircuits replaced transistors, new applications that needed more frequencies came into being. Two examples are wireless data transmission and cellular telephones. This need for frequencies forced the FCC to demand more efficient use of them. Proposals were made to continue to narrow down the bandwidth required for a channel. Some of these proposals were implemented as new and high channels were opened up.

Trunking (mentioned above) was one of the successfully implemented proposals. When the FCC responded to Congress with a public-safety-only allocation of 800-MHz frequencies, trunking was adopted as the standard.

But even with the additional channels made available and the benefits of trunking, demands for wireless data and other new technologies have increased the consumption of channels. The FCC has chosen to consider reallocating existing channels and applying new technologies, such as narrowbanding and trunking, to channels that were originally assigned to older methods of operation. This concept, called *re-farming,* would give existing licensees a certain amount of time to convert to new equipment. Many governmental agencies have protested against this approach because of the cost of replacing much, if not all, of the equipment in service. These protests have led the FCC to extend its review of the concept of re-farming.

The FCC is grappling with the fact that the radio spectrum is a finite resource. Much of the new radio bandwidth made available in the late 1990s came from federal and military allocations. Newer and higher frequencies—a traditional source of additional channels—are not available because they are already allocated and in use for microwave and satellite radio systems. In fact, the entire currently available spectrum is allocated.

Fire and rescue service managers must realize that the need to provide for better and more reliable public safety communications directly competes with all the new demand for wireless systems. The public safety sector will have to establish coalitions with other groups that can help it achieve public safety allocations. To do this, it must be willing to relinquish existing frequencies.

For example, some public safety channels are underused because previous mobile low-band systems were converted to point-to-point use as agencies deployed repeater-based very high frequency (VHF) or ultrahigh frequency (UHF) systems. One has only to listen to low-band business frequencies and hear the inordinate amount of traffic on them to realize that the possibility of releasing some underused public safety channels to the private sector could be part of a

Coping instead of competing As the demand for radio communication frequencies increases dramatically, many fire and rescue service providers are finding it difficult to obtain this resource. In an effort to cope with the problem (and not from a desire to compete with the demand for mobile telephones), some fire departments are now making extensive use of cellular/digital mobile phone technology.

For many years a majority of fire departments used radio channels directly to hospitals to make rather lengthy patient condition reports from the field. Other departments used radio channels directly to the fire dispatch center and then a landline telephone patch from the dispatch center to a given hospital. Both technologies effectively occupied available radio channels for long periods of time. Attacking this problem by seeking more radio channels complicated the process for the users and was generally not successful, because of radio spectrum management limitations.

As of the year 2000, a number of departments were using cellular/digital

phone technology and systems to get around the problem. With the explosive growth of this technology throughout the United States, it simply becomes easier to join the trend rather than fight it. In many cases, emergency medical crews are now using commercially available mobile phones to communicate with hospitals. The technology is every bit as good as radio technology, and antenna coverage is often better. A side benefit is an increased level of privacy for patients inasmuch as it is a bit harder for the general public to monitor mobile telephone calls than to monitor fire radio traffic.

In addition, many fire departments are using mobile telephones to conduct a fair amount of their nonessential and administrative communications. The advances in technology and the relatively low costs of using government contract rates or even franchise-required rates make this an effective and extremely convenient way to work. A side benefit is protection of valuable emergency radio channels through controlled, critical use.

---

coalition effort to gain either more appropriate public safety frequencies or the financial resources for full system conversion.

Figure 15–2 lists selected FCC frequency allocations in 1999. It illustrates the fragmentation of channels and the range of powerful interests competing for frequencies.

Communicating data

The demand for data communication capabilities has increased as the use of computers has expanded and their costs have dropped. In the office, data transmission by computer modems and facsimile (fax) machines has become commonplace. The public safety radio services have similar needs for data communications, especially because the data radio systems used by most public safety systems are based on technologies that date from 1980 or before.

Use of data communication Public safety services have used data to varying degrees since about 1970, first with short-status data and since the late 1990s with file data (both are defined below). The increasing availability and falling costs of mobile and portable data terminals have dramatically increased their use in public safety wireless applications. (Mobile terminals are in vehicles; portable terminals are handheld.)

Short-status data often convey voice shorthand, such as the common "10"

Figure 15–2 Selected 1999 FCC frequency allocations (MHz) and uses.

MHZ range	Use
118.0000–137.0000	Aeronautical AM
138.0000–144.0000	Federal government
144.0000–148.0000	Amateur radio (two meters)
148.0000–150.8000	Federal government
150.8150–150.9650	Auto emergency
150.9950–151.4750	Public safety
151.4900–151.4950	Special industrial
151.6250–151.9550	Business radio service
151.9850	Telephone maintenance radio service
152.0075	Special emergency radio service paging
152.0300–152.2400	Common carrier (mobile telephones/paging) base
152.2700–152.4800	Taxi radio service/business radio service
152.5100–152.8100	Common carrier (mobile telephones/paging) base
152.8400	Paging
152.8700–153.0350	Special industrial/remote broadcast/motion pictures
153.0500–153.3950	Remote broadcast/manufacturers/forest products/ petroleum
153.4100–153.7250	Power radio service
153.7400–154.4450	Public safety
154.4600–154.4900	Special industrial/power/local government
154.5150–154.6250	Business radio service
154.5850	Petroleum (oil spill)
154.6500–156.2400	Public safety
156.2750–157.4250	VHF maritime
157.4500	Special emergency radio service (paging)
157.4700–157.5150	Auto emergency radio service
157.5300–157.7100	Taxi/business radio service
157.7400	Paging
157.7700–158.0700	Common carrier (mobile telephones/paging) mobiles
158.1000	Paging
158.1300–158.2650	Power/petroleum/forest products
158.2800–158.4600	Petroleum/forest products/manufacturers
158.4900–158.6700	Common carrier (mobile telephones/paging) mobiles
158.7000	Paging
158.7300–159.4650	Public safety
159.4800	Petroleum (oil spill)
159.4950–160.2000	Motor carrier radio service

codes discussed above. A typical application conveys unit status, such as available, en route, at scene, or out of service. Emergency medical, fire, and law enforcement agencies use these status systems to reduce or eliminate noncritical traffic on the voice radio systems.

File-type data include what is commonly known as *data dispatch:* information on assignments is directly conveyed between a dispatch computer and a data terminal in the vehicle. These vehicle terminals, or computers, are usually capable of sending the preset short-status changes messages. Other file-transfer applications from data terminal–equipped users include direct access to information from state motor vehicle departments and the transmission of building plans and information to fire agencies.

As of the year 2000, data communication capabilities were being used in public safety for such purposes as digital dispatch and checking computer databases for information. The flow of information is asymmetric, with more data flowing to the field unit than from it.

Technology of data communication   Many of the early public safety data communication systems used circuitry much like telephone modems to create voice-like signals that could not only carry the data but also travel over the analog

voice paths of the public safety radio communication systems. Such hybrid systems were widely used during the middle to late 1990s.

As the 1990s ended, manufacturers began to provide radio systems that were fully digital and could carry data directly on the radio channel. Transmitting high-speed data reliably on mobile radio channels—compared with transmitting via wire, cable, microwave, fiber-optic, or other similar carrier—is an enormous engineering challenge.

The contrast between transmitting voice and transmitting data is significant in terms of reliability. Voice transmission is generally thought of as a real-time event, one that takes place while the speaker is talking. The goal in transmitting speech is to achieve as much reliability as possible in real time. The transmission of data (defined as nonvoice) generally lacks the real-time constraint of the transmission of voice. Thus, the goal in transmitting data is not to deliver as reliable a signal as possible in real time but to deliver 100 percent error-free data in as little time as possible.

Encryption—scrambling—is as relevant to data transmission as it is to voice. Although data are not intended to be converted into meaningful speech, the goal of data encryption is to prevent an unintended recipient from being able to convert the data back into their original form.

Typically, data communication in the year 2000 is done either with an analog modem, which transmits data signals over the voice communications radio link, or with another radio in the vehicle. Fire officials do not normally carry portable data terminals when they are outside the vehicle and therefore can normally use only a handheld radio for communication.

Communicating images

Images constitute a special category of data: data that represent a picture. Whereas voice transmission has the natural duration of the message as it is being spoken and the transmission of other data has the natural length of the message or file, the transmission of an image has no such inherent definition.

In the public safety service as in the broader economy, the use of wire-line-based fax transmission and similar image technologies has increased rapidly. The inexpensive digital storage or digital video camera developed in the late

1990s will cause the use of image services, too, to expand rapidly. Emergency medical providers want the ability to transmit images of the injured from paramedic units back to trauma centers or hospitals for better diagnosis and prearrival treatment. Fire agencies want the ability to transmit building plans and copies of permits and other data for better fire prevention and protection.

Still images include snapshots—for example, snapshots of accidents and crime scenes and a wide variety of other images. Modern digital cameras can take a picture and generate a data file containing a digital description of the scene photographed. This file can then be transmitted over existing communication pathways and either displayed on computer monitors or printed out. Therefore, public safety service providers have the option of putting in place still-image transfer capabilities.

At the same time, use of image transmission to and from the field in public safety is limited. Communication systems that support the necessary communications and all the ancillary equipment are available in the marketplace but not yet widely used. This situation is expected to change markedly by about 2010 or 2015.

Image transmission to the field will allow the dispatcher to send high-resolution diagrams of buildings and charts showing storage of hazardous materials to fire units at the scene of an incident. Still-image transmission from the field will allow fire and arson investigators to transmit photographs and fingerprints of suspects back to the office for processing, inspection by other officers, and comparison with information in databases.

Images will probably be transmitted as data files, with the use of file transfer protocols similar to those used in the transmission of other files. In most situations, one would expect image communications to be able to tolerate some delay as long as the delay does not affect field operations.

The electronic communication of moving images is television, or video. At

Figure 15–4 A firefighter uses a portable radio to communicate with other personnel during an incident.

the beginning of the twenty-first century, video is used in public safety primarily for the surveillance of crime scenes and highways. Video cameras are also used to record some arrests and activities at crime and fire scenes.

The use of wireless video systems in public safety has been limited, primarily because of cost and because radio spectrum over which to implement these systems is not available. There is only a single video channel for public safety video transmission, and it is shared with other radio services. State and local transportation agencies, however, have implemented wireless video systems to monitor traffic flow and detect collisions and hazards on roadways in congested metropolitan areas. If there were interfaces between the responsible agencies, these "smart-highway" systems could provide information to emergency responders.

Video images, like still images, can be ranked by the quality of the image. At one extreme, limited black-and-white slow-scan surveillance can be achieved in analog on a standard voice bandwidth channel. At the other extreme, broadcast-quality color requires a bandwidth of several megabits per second. High-definition television requirements are even greater. Public safety agencies have expressed varied operational requirements for video systems.

Video images are normally transmitted by analog modulation. Full-motion, high-quality video is normally carried on wideband channels (several megahertz), but only very limited spectrum is available to state and local agencies. Slow-scan video technology allows television pictures to be sent over a narrowband channel, with one picture sent every few seconds. Although slow-scan technology is not appropriate for situations involving rapid movement, it can be quite useful for monitoring traffic, weather, secured areas, and so forth.

The fire service has used full-motion video in some areas, primarily to monitor wildland fire scenes from air units, providing emergency command centers with real-time video. The lack of public safety spectrum, however, has often required state and local fire agencies to enlist Amateur Radio Service licensees to provide the needed channels.

As video camera technology continues to improve, the use of video is expected to grow greatly. One can foresee portable radio units with built-in video cameras. Transmission of images from these cameras back to central locations, such as mobile command units, could be quite helpful in the management of major incidents. Applications pairing the infrared technology of the year 2000 with video may well be developed so that a commander outside a building can see what hose teams inside are experiencing.

Affordable digital video cameras and affordable digital compression can be expected to substantially increase the demand for public safety video communications. Although recorded video will satisfy many video communication needs, such as use during postincident critiques or training sessions, the need for real-time recorded video communication will expand, and with it the need for public safety access to radio spectrum.

Communicating position location

After radio, another new technology has been finding its way from the military to the civilian sector: position location. Public safety agencies have long struggled with the problem of identifying the location of vehicles and personnel. A variety of techniques and systems have been tried over the years, with the federal government funding research into such systems in the late 1960s and early 1970s. As of the year 2000 there were several systems for obtaining such location information. Each has its strengths and weaknesses. Discussed below, they are

Satellite navigation systems (GPS and GLONASS)

The LORAN-C terrestrial navigation system

The licensed location monitoring service

Dead-reckoning systems

Signpost systems

Inertial navigation systems.

All the systems except the FCC's location monitoring service provide location information at the vehicle or at the portable unit. For such information to be used with computer-aided dispatch (CAD, discussed in the next section), it must be transmitted from the mobile unit to the control point (thus, the mobile unit must have a data communications capability). CAD systems can use the location, once it is known, to identify additional hazards or other risks to the responders.

Many applications of location technology are being implemented, ranging from real-time ambulance service dispatch management to hazardous material tracking systems. Many of these applications are paired with CAD systems to allow for the dispatch of the closest response unit. Most of these applications are based on the Global Positioning System (GPS), but cellular-based systems and personal communication systems are being set up or designed to locate people who call 911 centers, to allow better identification of the calling party. Emergency locator units are being used at sea or in wilderness treks.

Satellite navigation systems   The most widely known and most widely available position location systems are the satellite navigation systems, the best known of which are the GPS and the Global Navigation Satellite System (GLONASS). The U.S. Department of Defense operates the GPS, and the Russian Federation operates the somewhat similar GLONASS. This discussion focuses on the GPS, but in many respects similar comments could be made about the GLONASS.

The heart of the GPS is a constellation of twenty-four satellites in medium Earth orbit that continuously broadcast the time and satellite location. A system that receives a signal from four of these satellites can calculate its location to within about 100 meters. In the year 2000, consumer units are available that can use up to twelve satellites to calculate location and elevation. GPS receivers are offered in the consumer market for less than $200.

The GPS can provide location estimates that are accurate to within ten meters. Although they can provide signals to a ship or an airplane, they were not designed to provide a signal capable of penetrating a building or to operate optimally in urban canyons or heavily forested areas. In such areas, therefore, the GPS must be augmented by other technologies. In some applications, better reliability or better accuracy may be provided by a terrestrial system that processes signals from both GPS and GLONASS satellites.

LORAN-C   LORAN-C is an older radio navigation system that was developed for marine navigation. As a maritime system, it covers the coast of the United States, although in some areas of the country its coverage extends inland. Its future maintenance is uncertain.

Location monitoring service   What is now known as the *location monitoring service* was created in the 1970s when the FCC allocated spectrum for what was then known as the *automatic vehicle monitoring service*. One firm is providing commercial service in several larger cities, using multiple sites to measure the time of arrival of wideband pulses from a vehicle and then solving for the vehicle's location. Teletrac provides better coverage in urban areas than the GPS does. It does not require augmentation by dead-reckoning or inertial navigation systems.

Dead-reckoning systems   Dead-reckoning systems provide another way to derive location information. A computer system in a vehicle can count the number of rotations of the tires and thus estimate how far the vehicle has gone. The system can detect vehicle turns by using differences in the rotation of the left- and right-side wheels. Antilock braking systems already require wheel rotation sensors. When this information is combined with compass headings and a map database, the vehicle's location can be reliably calculated even if the vehicle has traveled a substantial distance. Systems that record this type of information are used in the trucking industry to evaluate driver performance.

Dead-reckoning systems do tend to lose track of the vehicle's location over time. To correct for this, either the user can update the location manually or another system can be used to update the dead-reckoning system's location estimate. The GPS is an excellent candidate to do such updating. Dead reckoning can be used for a few blocks until the vehicle drives into the open and reacquires the satellites, which then update its location.

Signpost systems   Signpost systems involve the use of low-power, short-range transmitters that send messages describing their own location. Each location so described is called a *signpost*. As a vehicle passes each of these signposts, it receives an update of its location. This technology requires a substantial investment in infrastructure. Signpost systems can be used to complement dead-reckoning technology.

Inertial navigation systems   Inertial navigation systems process data from acceleration sensors to estimate the path of a vehicle. Such systems, which were still expensive in the year 2000, work like dead-reckoning systems in that their location estimates must be updated from time to time.

Commercial mobile radio services such as cellular telephone or personal communication systems have the potential to provide location information of varying resolution. For example, cellular systems know which cell is serving the mobile or portable unit. Some personal communication systems also calculate fairly accurate range estimates and can combine the information from range estimates and cell locations to give more precise location estimates.

Computer-aided dispatch

Public safety managers' choice of the term *computer-aided dispatch* (CAD) may have been misguided because the choice has had unfortunate consequences: either CAD was integrated into overall governmental computer operations or else the assigned staff understood computer issues but not public safety dispatch needs.

The first CAD systems to be deployed were developed in one of two ways. Some were developed for law enforcement during the 1970s, with then-available Law Enforcement Assistance Administration funding, and were then adapted for fire and emergency medical service (EMS) use, running on dedicated processors. Others were developed in-house and were run on existing governmental computer systems. This second kind was seen by many fire and EMS managers as not meeting the needs of their agencies, and stories circulated of fire/EMS dispatch slowing down as water bills, tax notices, or payroll were run.

In the 1980s and early 1990s, as software and computer design improved, the experiences and lessons of the early CAD efforts could be incorporated. With the deployment of initial mobile data systems in the 1980s and the release of the GPS to civilian use, CAD systems could be created that would support field decision making.

Early CAD systems took incident location data that had been manually entered by a dispatcher and recommended a response. A dispatcher entered and maintained the status of available units, using radio transmissions from the field.

Newer systems have made it possible to transfer responsibility for status changes to the field units when those units are equipped with simple data status units, mobile data terminals, or mobile computers. With this transfer of responsibility, airtime that had been taken by routine changes in status has been freed up for critical communications. The transfer can also free up dispatcher time, allowing dispatchers to spend more time monitoring field operations or to provide support services, such as placing telephone calls, more expeditiously.

In addition, newer CAD systems can interface with enhanced 911 systems (systems that show the location of the caller) and with governmental computer systems. This interfacing allows access to vast amounts of information that, if properly managed, can be of assistance to emergency responders. Information about location-specific hazards or about previous activity at an address, for example, can improve responder safety.

Emergency service managers, however, must consider carefully what data should be made available. Assessed value and market value, for example, may be of use to investigators and fire marshals but are almost certainly not of use to fire suppression or EMS units. Merely having the ability to move data from one location to another is not in itself sufficient reason for moving it.

Geographic information systems

One of the systems that CAD can interface with is the new geographic information system (GIS) that is being implemented in many governments. This technology allows various data to be presented in graphical form tied to maps of the community. The information is of value to emergency planners but can also be helpful during an incident. A GIS allows a staff person, such as a telecommunicator, to create a circle one mile in radius around a factory site and feed the telephone numbers of all residences in that area to an automated telephone calling system, which can then provide evacuation information and instructions to the population at risk.

A GIS can also be integrated with enhanced 911 systems: when the location of the caller is overlaid with road closure information, emergency responders can be routed more efficiently. When a GIS and CAD are tied to occupancy data, they can identify locations that may be higher-priority exposures, depending on the nature of the incident. Often floor plans and staging areas that were developed before the incident can be integrated into a GIS and transmitted to graphic printers in command vehicles or to cellular fax machines.

Issues involving telephones (cellular, 911, and 311 systems)

The rapid expansion in the number of cellular telephones and their widespread use, as well as the installation of 911 systems throughout the nation and the growth of 311 systems, present challenges to emergency service organizations.

Fire service use of cellular telephones

From the early days of radio usage, people wanted a private wireless equivalent of the business and home telephone system. Initially the FCC authorized some frequencies for mobile telephone usage. These VHF high-band channels required the user to contact a telephone company operator to place the call to the other telephone location—a way of proceeding that is very similar to what is done in the maritime telephone service used in many areas of the world. Problems included the limited number of frequencies available and the fact that anyone with a radio monitor could receive the messages; in addition, neighboring systems would interfere with each other.

When more frequencies became available for wireless use, maritime interests moved to satellite-based telephone systems, and the telephone industry joined with the radio community to provide an equivalent service for people on land. To ensure maximum use of frequencies, the FCC placed several restrictions on satellite-based phones, including a very low limit on the power of mobile and handheld units and dynamic management of frequencies and trunking.

A demonstration project of what would become the cellular telephone network was developed and tested in the Chicago area. Many of the technological capabilities later deployed in public safety trunked radio systems were first tested during this project.

The FCC also authorized the landline telephone providers to provide cellular telephone service in their franchise areas. In most areas of the country the commission then awarded licenses to a second provider, chosen on the basis of lotteries and auctions. The purpose was to ensure competition, which was supposed to keep prices down.

Cellular telephones have provided a somewhat secure means of communication for field responders. They allow communications from the scene of an emergency without tying up a channel or talk group. Such communications may include calls to technical experts during hazardous material incidents, calls to responders' own families during extended emergencies, and so forth.

By the year 2000, cellular telephones had become common as prices have dropped from over $2,000.00 to $0.99 per unit and airtime costs have dropped commensurately. With widespread use, however, systems can become overwhelmed when multiple customers try to access them simultaneously. This happens especially during emergencies, when the public and the media are all trying to use cellular telephones in or near the incident location.

Some benefits from cellular telephones are not obvious without research. As a wireless technology, cellular has extended personal communications into parks and other areas where wired systems do not reach. In addition, cellular companies have the ability to assign priority to certain telephones. The carrier can set either a preempt or a next-available-circuit access level. After discussion, public safety cellular phones can be given one of these priorities, and public safety managers must be clear on which priority the carrier has agreed to.

Some carriers maintain caches of extra telephones that can be deployed to emergency sites. Some also maintain cellular telephone transmitter sites in wheeled or skid-loaded enclosures, which are sometimes referred to as COWs, or *C*ell sites *O*n *W*heels. When the wired telephone system has suffered major damage, COWs can be deployed to the affected area to provide service for responders or the public.

Mobile command units can be equipped with both cellular and satellite telephones, and both of these can be equipped to provide either fax or data transmission services.

911 systems

Legislation funding 911 was passed in many states in the 1990s, allowing 911 systems in communities in those states to be implemented or upgraded. The most significant part of the upgrading was the 911 enhanced capability, which allows the display of calling-party information rather than of the name of the originating central office, as was the case in most earlier 911 systems.

Calling-party information consists of two components: the automatic number identification (ANI) and the automatic location information (ALI). ANI provides the calling-party number to the telecommunicator in the 911 center. Using ANI, the telephone system can also provide ALI by querying a 911 address database. ALI gives the dispatcher the address of the calling telephone.

An early problem in the processing of 911 calls was caused by boundary differences: the service boundaries of telephone company central switching offices do not often coincide with the boundaries of government jurisdictions. Thus, many dispatchers in early 911 systems had to contend with calls from citizens not located in their jurisdictions or with the fact that calls from citizens who were located in their jurisdictions might be answered by a neighboring community's 911 system. Responders often saw this lack of boundary alignment as slowing down the processing of the critical initial call.

In contrast, the 911 enhanced capability permits the use of what is called selective routing: a routing code is assigned to each address in the community, and the telephone system uses the code to ensure that the right call reaches the correct public safety answering point.

Although the implementation of 911 enhanced systems has improved service to citizens, the explosion of cellular telephones has created a major problem for 911 centers. Cellular telephones are not tied to particular locations, because users move around. With some modification to the 911 systems, ANI can be provided. Moreover, it is possible to provide—in an *xy* format similar to latitude and longitude—a location for a cellular telephone. If the 911 system has a GIS or some other form of mapping, this location can be displayed to the dispatcher. But even nongraphical systems can determine the location and the correct response if the CAD system's address files are keyed to an *xy* system.

In 1999, between 20 percent and 35 percent of all calls came into 911 via cellular phones. Solving the problem of locating calling phones must therefore be a priority for all public safety managers. Field response agency managers must work with the 911 center managers to ensure that a solution is implemented.

The FCC provided several ways for public safety agencies to require the cellular companies to provide location-based information about their callers, but the FCC also allowed the cellular companies to recover the associated costs from the requesting government or agency. The companies have stated that there is no way to determine costs until the solutions are implemented. Most cellular companies have also argued that their service and customers are exempt from the surcharges on wire-line-based telephones. Many public safety agency officials have been reluctant to absorb unknown costs without any supplemental funding.

In the meantime, as of the late 1990s, more than 66 million cellular telephones had been sold. In some areas, cellular phones are being advertised as the replacement for the wire-line telephone in the home or office.

Another (and similar) problem is to determine the caller's location when the 911 call comes from a telephone located in an office on a campus or in a high-rise building served by a private telephone system or switch. Companies often provide service to multiple locations in a metropolitan region from a telephone switch located in another state. This situation has led to calls that give just a street address for a ten-story building or just the main office location of an organization with sixteen geographically separate offices.

Soon 911 service will also be affected by what is called *number portability* (an aspect of the developing competition to provide local telephone service). Number portability allows a person who moves to retain the same phone number. Initially the portability will be only within local service areas, but eventually it will spread to anywhere within an area code and finally to anywhere in the nation. By the year 2010, emergency units on the West Coast, for example, will be responding to an emergency caller who has an East Coast call-back number. Managers must be aware of these issues and, as the relevant services are implemented, must train response and planning personnel so that they will not be surprised when encountering such situations.

Another 911 issue is public expectations. Much as the television show *Emergency!* stimulated the spread of prehospital emergency medical systems, television shows such as *Rescue 911* helped convince the public and elected officials that 911 was needed. But the shows also portrayed an artificial world where people rarely died if they called 911, operators saved lives over the telephone and were rarely overloaded by multiple calls, units responded very quickly and never got lost, and there were no interagency problems.

Television portrayed the best possible world, and the public took it for the norm. But as many well-publicized cases gradually revealed, the norm was very different across the United States. Often 911 operators were untrained, improperly supervised, and poorly equipped. Some citizens called them irresponsible and dangerous. There were even calls for citizens to bypass 911 and contact agencies directly.

Often the real problem was a lack of sufficient field resources for all the calls, with 911 and the operators taking the blame for issues totally beyond the control of the communications and 911 system. To the public, 911 constituted the entire public safety system. The public was unaware of the actual decentralized system of independent agencies and limited resources for police, fire, and EMS. Solutions were demanded; some were found in training, organization, and technology.

Another issue for 911 arose when many cities, on implementing the 911 system, discontinued their previous seven-digit emergency telephone numbers and told citizens to call 911 if they needed any public safety service whatsoever. As a result, many nonemergency calls came into the 911 system. Even when the callers just wanted information, the incident had to be "dispatched" by radio to a responder because the dispatchers were not authorized to do anything else. Thus began what has sometimes been called "the tyranny of 911." Primarily affecting law enforcement, this situation was seen as producing never-ending 911 responses. Fire and EMS managers saw 911 systems, advertised as the citizens' lifeline, become clogged.

The end result of creation of the 911 system is that communications center managers have had to deal with pressures created by sometimes unmanageable workloads, reduced funding, and higher public expectations. One solution has been to adopt business concepts, such as "continuous improvement," that focus on improving items incrementally. Another solution has been to plan for quantum leaps forward in major projects. Both solutions are more effective if upper management is consistent in supporting program managers and staff.

311—An alternative?

Frustration over the clogging of 911 led to the development of an alternative system that used the number 311. Deployed initially in Baltimore, the 311 system has a cadre of light-duty police officers answering the 311 calls. If they cannot handle the issue, they can transfer the call to the police department district stations, which are staffed on a twenty-four-hour basis, or to the emergency dispatch. At any time, if the officer determines there is a need, the call can be transferred to 911. With 311, a major part of the previous 911 call load in Baltimore has been removed from the emergency system.

Several other communities with the same problem have adopted 311, and it is generally producing the same positive results. The federal government has embraced the concept and is urging more communities to adopt 311. In some communities, however, 311 is seen as a potential disaster. Areas with multi-jurisdictional centers do not have either the light-duty force or the stations staffed twenty-four hours to handle these calls. The same dispatchers who handle 911 would have to handle 311 but without the benefit of 911 location technology (i.e., the enhanced capability discussed above).

Furthermore, some public safety managers are troubled by the idea of letting citizens decide what is or is not an emergency. These managers think 311 dilutes the present system and makes it worse, not better. They believe that citizens should stay focused on calling 911 and that the 911 center should "triage" the calls, using common sense and keeping history and liability in mind. They think the citizen may not understand that being locked out of one's home or car—albeit a situation requiring help—is not considered a true emergency by call takers and emergency response providers.

In some communities, when 911 was implemented the existing seven-digit numbers were kept in service, and citizens were told to use 911 for emergencies and the seven-digit numbers for nonemergencies. As a result, some calls that should have come in over 911 did not, as citizens used their own criteria for what was or was not an emergency. But 911 did not get overloaded: citizens generally routed emergency calls to 911 and nonemergency calls to the seven-digit number.

As the twenty-first century begins, the story of 311 and its alternatives is not yet finished. Managers must evaluate the 911 center's handling of calls and must participate in the decision making on whether to use 311. Some communities will benefit from 311 and others will not. The fire and rescue service must be part of the process of providing this vital community service.

Communications system infrastructure

Managers who are responsible for communication systems that support fire, EMS, and other emergency responses must be concerned about the infrastructure underlying those systems: the towers, transmitters, and generators; the 911 system; and the communications center. This often complex combination of intertwined systems is never really visible to citizens or elected and appointed decision makers, but it requires much attention and maintenance because infrastructure failures can often disrupt or halt emergency operations.

Towers, transmitters, and receivers

Most communication systems consist of one or more locations with towers, transmitters, and receivers. The same sites also have buildings, outside cabinets, generators, lighting, and other ancillary devices. Although some towers are placed in buildings, most are generally on out-of-the-way hilltop or mountain-top sites.

These facilities are not routinely staffed, and provision must be made for access at all times of year for emergency repairs and routine inspections. Towers must be inspected and painted as required by Federal Aviation Administration rules. Sites should be provided with alarm systems that sound the alert when there is unauthorized intrusion or a failure of tower lighting or of generator start-up.

Remote sites must be linked to the communications center. This is done with leased telephone company cable, microwave, or other point-to-point radio systems. These interfaces must be designed to withstand the various major natural hazards that face the particular community. The high winds of a hurricane, for example, can damage or destroy microwave dishes without doing any damage at all to underground fiber-optic cable. An earthquake, in contrast, may sever underground fiber-optic cable without causing more than minimal damage to microwave towers if these are properly located and designed. Each hazard must be assessed during the implementation of a system, and alternatives must be developed. They may include diverse routing of fiber-optic lines or multiple microwave paths.

Even with multiple pathways back to the communications center, the prudent manager will assume that at some time some remote sites will be lost. At those times, reliable public safety communications must be ensured. The way to do this is to ensure that the loss of one site does not cause a total loss of communications. Design criteria should be used that result in the degradation of service from portable access to mobile access in the area served by the damaged site. To create this, the manager ensures that there is overlapping coverage from other transmitter sites in the system. Another possibility for preventing a total loss of communications is to develop a rapid-replacement program through the use of transportable temporary towers and trailer-based radio transmitters and generators.

In the case of an areawide disaster affecting the communications infrastructure, managers must be prepared to handle disruptions and damage in the communications system with their own resources for the first few days. They must remember that other vital services, including federal, hospital, and state radio systems, will be competing for repair services and replacement equipment in the event of such a major emergency. There are anecdotal reports of vendors accepting the effect of penalty clauses built into public radio maintenance contracts because the private sector was willing to pay ten to fifteen times as much for immediate service.

The 911 system

Another area of infrastructure concern is the 911 system. Many of the 911 systems that have been put in place have single points of failure, and failure of the single point can cause the whole 911 system to collapse. Managers should conduct the equivalent of a process safety analysis to see where the risk exists. For example, when a single central office is used as the 911 tandem office, all the 911 lines from the various end central offices are concentrated in one location. Or 911 trunks may be routed from multiple 911 tandem offices via the central office local to the 911 public safety answering point (PSAP). Or all the 911 circuits within the 911 PSAP may be concentrated in one set of switching and processing equipment.

The 911 manager must ensure that the 911 system has the same level of redundancy as the telephone network that we use in our everyday lives. The telephone network is inherently redundant for all lines but the one linking our own location to the local central office. From there to the central office serving the person we are calling, the system uses multiple pathways to ensure that calls go through. The 911 system should be equally redundant.

In addition, the manager must ensure that the 911 system has priority in restoration efforts. There is a national priority system for telephone-related restoration of service. To set what will be fixed first, the system uses a code applied to the records of the customer, and telephone companies have no choice but to restore designated customers first. If a 911 system has not been designated a priority, repairs will wait until service to all priority customers has been restored. To ensure that mission-critical telephone services are designated for priority restoration, 911 managers, along with emergency operations center managers and officials of agencies with emergency missions, must work with telephone company personnel. There is an additional cost for this service, but it must be viewed as an essential cost of doing business.

The National Communications System (NCS), a federal agency that works with state government and industry partners, is responsible for the management of the Telephone Service Priority (TSP) program. Local agency officials should contact the NCS if they cannot identify the state's contact person for TSP.

The communications center

Probably the most important infrastructure component is the communications center itself. Here all the parts of the system come together. However redundant the components and however diverse the routing, the communications center is potentially a single point of failure. Although backup facilities usually exist, few communities can afford a fully redundant communications center that can pick up the workload on a moment's notice.

Thus, the design and planning of the communications center must recognize the concept of "hardening" the facility. Hardening is a complex process and can result in additional costs that must be "sold" to the final decision makers. The presentation must establish the vital and irreplaceable nature of the facility and the personnel who operate it.

Issues to address include the fact that the facility may be attacked, that it should not be exposed to the results of a chemical release, and that it must be able to operate for a defined time with no outside support. Operating with no outside support creates the need for items such as multiple emergency generators and fuel or other systems for heating and air conditioning that do not depend solely on outside power.

Substantial investments may be needed in the area of fire detection and protection above what is needed for an ordinary government office building. For example, firewall ratings must be beyond what is required by code. And the floor above the center must be thicker. To protect a facility that should not have to be evacuated, specialized suppression and detection systems will be necessary.

Multiple points of entry for utilities should be considered. Electrical and telephone circuits serving consoles should be both redundant and diversely routed. Uninterrupted power sources should be used on every critical system. Even these systems should serve only part of the facility so that any single failure will activate a backup system, and the failure of the backup will disable only a small part of the system.

Hardening and redundancy of communication systems are among the most basic of the mitigation activities that should occur. Of the many lifelines in the community, the one most critical to emergency operations is communications.

Communications center: Staffing, role, and joint facilities

Despite all the equipment and no matter how hardened or redundant the communications system, the reliability of the entire operation comes down to the people who operate it—the call takers, dispatchers, and telecommunicators who staff the 911 and public safety communication centers. They are the most critical component of public safety systems, and their institutional affiliation and hiring and training are central. It is also important that the role of the communications center be clearly defined and understood. Finally, establishing a joint center may be a cost-effective option.

Staffing: Institutional affiliation

Historically, in most communities dispatchers began as combination radio operators and clerks. Some were civilians, but a number of them were members of the actual emergency staff. Many of the larger pioneering systems were able to have staff dedicated just to radio operations. By the late 1950s and early

1960s, most urban or town communities had fire and police dispatchers operating in separate locations.

In suburban, rural, or frontier areas, more individualized methods were often used. Some communities had "fire phones" in the homes or businesses of members of the department. Sometimes these locations were equipped with radios and could dispatch the volunteer fire department or contact the sheriff's deputy if necessary. In other cases, the call taker had to go to a central location to use the radio.

Some few areas had developed regional or countywide centers, but often these did not serve the entire community. And even the national professional groups that were coordinating frequency assignments were divided into law enforcement and fire-oriented groups. When 911 was assigned as a dedicated nationwide emergency access number, the complexion of public safety communications was about to change. Also about to change were the average citizen's expectations of public safety communications and 911 systems.

Because approximately 85 percent of incoming telephone calls are related to law enforcement, many communities assigned the responsibility for answering 911 to the police communications system. Although this decision provided a relatively low-cost solution, problems often arose because the workload that 911 created had been underestimated and because many suburban and rural communities were undergoing the massive expansion of the 1970s (so that a relatively small number of police officers were facing growing workloads) at the same time that large cities were suffering from economic loss and loss of population.

Staffing: Hiring and training

Key in the operation of the center is the selection of the right group of employees. Public safety officials often raise the issue of just adopting the same screening methods that field agencies use. This issue is usually brought up in connection with psychological screening. But although screening is a valid tool, field personnel–type screening may not be the right tool for a communications job. The communications center is not the street environment of the responder. Rather, telecommunicators do not see the incident and therefore have a radically different impression of what is happening. A fire chief once told of turning the command post vehicle so that the window did not look out on the fire, and he described how that simple action changed his thought patterns about the event. This must be taken into account when personnel are screened. So must the fact that telecommunicators often move on as new calls come in and rarely get the closure experienced by field forces, who see the patient delivered to the hospital or the arsonist arrested.

The foundation of service in the communications and 911 center is the initial training of telecommunicators. Training available for dispatch personnel expanded between 1985 and 2000. All of the professional organizations offer strong, job-validated courses in a number of subjects. Most of these courses have gotten longer as the complexities of communication operations have increased. Classroom training is supplemented by simulation training on consoles like the one the successful candidate will be expected to operate. Critical components of basic training are time on the job under the direct supervision of a coach and "ride-along" programs with field forces.

In addition, many "train-the-trainer" programs are available to allow agencies to develop internal programs. Often major industries are willing to allow telecommunicators to attend their training programs. Such arrangements can help emergency service telecommunicators develop an understanding that public safety communication centers are customer service agencies with many different customer bases.

Qualifications for dispatch personnel In the late 1990s, at the urging of a number of professional groups and individuals, the National Fire Protection Association (NFPA) agreed to develop a standard that would define minimum qualifications for public safety dispatch personnel. That standard—NFPA 1061, Standard for Professional Qualifications for Public Safety Telecommunicator (2002 edition) —spells out in measurable terms the job performance requirements for several levels of public safety telecommunicators. Developed by an NFPA committee of experts from the fire, emergency medical, law enforcement, and communication fields, the standard is revised at least every five years. The revision process allows frequent input from any interested party.

Armed with the standard, a number of state and local governments are developing written and practical tests that people will have to pass to become certified as public safety telecommunicators. Both management and labor have welcomed this increased level of professionalism.

Telecommunicators are encouraged to attend courses of the National Fire Academy and the Emergency Management Institute. A varied in-service training program may also include attendance at conferences and out-of-town courses. But the real need is to revisit the items that were part of basic training and are not regularly used in everyday operations. Examples include bomb threat procedures and aircraft crash policies. The best way to revisit these items is with drills, exercises, and other event-modeling activities. There must be sufficient staff to allow groups of telecommunicators to meet four to six times per year for daylong drills.

There must in fact be sufficient staff on duty in the 911/public safety communications center to handle the normal workload while being prepared for the sudden extraordinary emergency. This means that when a telecommunicator leaves a console to take a break or have a meal, sufficient relief staff is available so that a supervisor does not have to stop supervising to operate the console. People often ask what the extra employees will be doing when every console is staffed. Participating in in-service training, modeling possible response situations, reviewing rarely used procedures, handling tours, and verifying resource information—adequate staffing of the communications center enables all these activities to take place, improving the center's operational capability.

Communications center staff must also be an integral part of all field exercises. One reason is to enable the telecommunicator's side of the emergency event to be covered by the exercise; the other reason is to enable telecommunicators to observe field operations. The objectives of the exercises and drills should be put in writing so that areas identified in other emergencies as problems can be tested.

Role of the communications center

For this integration of communications center staff with field operations to occur, the role of the 911/public safety communications center must be clearly defined and accepted. A few 911 centers simply take the calls and route the callers to the responsible agency's communications center. Some 911 centers take the calls and refer them to dispatch centers. Other communication centers are responsible for taking and dispatching the calls, while still other facilities not only take and dispatch the calls but also are responsible for providing support to responders. Then there are centers that are responsible for the entire incident, from initial call to termination.

Often the type of system is not well understood by people in daily contact with it, let alone by the general public. When the situation is complicated by the use of procedures and practices that are not explained to either the public or responders, feelings of distrust and uneasiness about the system can arise. It is essential that managers provide the public and responders with sufficient education so that they understand the role and limitations of the public safety communications system. This education must reflect conscious and deliberate decision making about the role the center plays in the public safety system.

Too often, the role filled by the 911/communications center has evolved without any explicit analysis of the community's needs and expectations. And often an influx of residents from other areas of the country will change the public's expectations. The resulting disconnect can produce not only questions about, but also fears of, the system.

One key role played by the communications center (and the system) is to be the coordination and control network for the community during times of major emergency. To fill this role, the center and system must be solidly linked to the community's emergency operations center (EOC). The easiest way to create this link is to locate the two facilities adjacent to each other.

Telecommunicators have many skills that can be of value during EOC operations. They can staff the EOC message or public information lines. They can support the public information officer. They can help with situation assessment. (Other roles for communications center staff at large-incident command posts are discussed later in this chapter in the section "Emergency Response Operations: Policies and Procedures.") When the EOC and communications center are side by side in the same building, the communications system can integrate smoothly with supplemental systems (e.g., amateur radio networks and federal and state communication systems).

Joint facilities

A way to reduce costs and improve the professionalism of the communications system is to create a joint center. In the early twenty-first century's climate of cost reduction and privatization in government, many people believe that communications is an area where privatization should occur. Often public safety agencies see the creation of a joint facility as a last-ditch option.

Joint facilities are not without problems, however. The agencies will always feel that the communication operations should be part of the appropriate responder agency. People in responder agencies will feel that they have lost control of a key part of their agency's response capability. In addition, police officers and fire department personnel may still think the joint center works for their own departments only. Finally, the argument will always be made that the joint center should either come under a public safety agency to ensure appropriate management—or be split up.

How can the turf wars over joint communications be controlled? One way is to create oversight committees with members from each of the agencies served and from the public. The purpose of the committees is to address issues and concerns about the communications system. The committees are encouraged to find solutions, not just discuss the problem endlessly or assign blame. The principle of consensus can be applied to ensure that issues are resolved in a fashion that benefits all users and the public.

Another way to control turf wars is to use comment cards for complaints, comments, and compliments directed at all agencies, including the communications system. Any responder who has a complaint or comment about communication issues sends it to his or her supervisor, and it works its way up the chain of command. This process allows the agency heads to manage problems jointly and relay compliments.

Another option that may prove helpful is to permanently station liaison officers from operating departments in the joint center. Managers must be careful to ensure that the liaison officers work with the center's manager without disrupting operations and do not interfere in the center's chain of command.

To help build consensus, agencies can be allowed to provide input on training. In this way the field units and communications center can educate each other in the intricacies of their own jobs. The working relationship can also be reinforced with ride-along programs and tours of duty in the communications center. For field representatives and communications system personnel to be able to express their own concerns and hear the other group's concerns and questions, monthly meetings between the two groups can be held.

There will still be occasional problems that the oversight committees will not solve. With any real problem, the elected officials retain the final say because they are the FCC licensee and control the funding. Accordingly, there must be protocols for presenting both sides of the issue to the elected officials or their designee. Without such a system, an increasing number of individuals and agencies will come to lose confidence in the communications system.

Setting up a joint center by merging existing operations will require an intensive planning process, but to avoid problems, the leadership issue will have

---

A governance model for a joint communications center   There are many models for governing joint communication centers, all with advantages and disadvantages. One such model is used in Champaign County, Illinois. A single emergency communications center serves more than thirty—or nearly all—fire, emergency medical, and law enforcement agencies in this county with a population approaching 175,000. The center, known as the Metropolitan Computer-Aided Dispatch Center (METCAD), evolved from a joint police center for three agencies in the late 1970s to its current multifunction, multijurisdictional purpose.

METCAD's governance model uses two tiers of boards to maintain accountability to the public and operational control for the user agencies. Primary responsibility for METCAD's financial and policy interests is in the hands of its Governing Board. The members of this board are the mayors of the two largest cities, their city managers/administrators, an elected county official, and a senior official from the University of Illinois. This board meets infrequently to establish a budget, set the funding formula for user agencies, and determine major policy direction. The actual ad-

ministrative responsibility and functions for METCAD are handled by the city of Champaign, the largest user of the center.

The Operations Board is the second tier of governance. This group consists of fire and police chiefs from Champaign, Urbana, and the University of Illinois, as well as the chief deputy from the Champaign County sheriff's office. In addition, a representative is elected from the rural fire service organizations and the small-town police agencies. The METCAD administrator is an ex officio member. The Operations Board meets regularly to address operational policy, procedures, and problems. It also works with the METCAD administration to propose a budget and address nearly any issue. The position of chair of this board rotates among its members.

Although there will always be problems and issues that challenge large, joint communications centers, a well-established and functional governance model will help the participants resolve the problems in a systematic manner. Full representation by all interests without domination by any is critical.

to be settled early on. Generally the new management system should be in place so that it can be involved in the planning.

An announcement should be made that on a certain day, the new communications manager will assume control of the police, fire, emergency medical, and other systems involved. Every possible effort should be made to let communications personnel know that they are part of a new organization. Newsletters and one-on-one meetings can accomplish this. The police, fire, and EMS chiefs must demonstrate their clear-cut support for the joint center.

The best opportunity for establishing a joint facility is when a new facility is implemented. The new facility can provide a clean break with the past. It can include, besides the communication consoles, a training room, a break room, administrative offices, locker rooms, showers, sleeping space, and physical fitness facilities.

Planning, acquisition, and policies and procedures

To ensure that the best possible communication systems support the emergency and nonemergency activities under their responsibility, fire and rescue service managers must take clear-cut action: they must analyze system needs in detail; create long-term development plans to be presented for approval to the authorities having jurisdiction; and develop and present budgetary justifications of the project.

After the project is approved—and it will be one of the larger capital projects for any local or state government—all the manager's skills will be needed to ensure its successful completion. Project management will be a vital part of the installation of any new system. Opportunities for cost sharing or joint ventures will have to be evaluated and implemented, if appropriate. Life-cycle costing—identifying maintenance and operating costs over the expected life span of the equipment—will be necessary for developing understanding of total long-term costs among the governmental financial managers who will become involved in such a large project.

After a good system is in place, operational procedures must be established to ensure that responders use it properly. Policies and procedures must be given to personnel and must be followed up with training and exercise programs. Many organizations fail to practice how to use one of the most expensive systems with which they will provide service to the citizens of their communities.

Finally, communications system failures, frequently brought up as part of post-event critiques, are often identified but then left alone because of complexity and cost or because they are the responsibility of another agency. Such lack of action can later expose the fire and rescue service manager to liability if a communications failure is determined to be the cause of injury, damage, or death. Sometimes the deficiencies caused by a poorly performing communications system are not readily apparent and cannot be identified without a detailed analysis, which may require the use of outside agencies or consultants. Sometimes internal quality assurance efforts can be used to pinpoint the deficiencies.

Planning for communications

A critical component of any communications system is planning. In the planning process the manager must ensure that the needs of the public, responder agencies, and employees will be met in such a way that service is delivered efficiently. This goal requires that the field units have input into the process.

How the planning process is managed will depend on the position of the communications function in the government. If communications operates as a

Making communications a priority concern Elected officials are responsible for so many programs that they often do not see public safety communication systems as a priority. They believe such systems are a very specialized area that citizens do not worry about. They are astonished at the costs involved. Often they think this area does not require any special skills beyond those of a receptionist or switchboard operator. Sometimes they do not understand the complex nature of the public safety communications system as it operates every day.

The first and possibly most critical way for a public safety manager to counter these attitudes is to call attention to problems in the 911 system, if these are apparent, and point out that if the problems are allowed to continue, a liability may exist. Events around the country during the 1990s sensitized the U.S. public and press to the operations and deficiencies of 911 systems; almost everyone can recount a 911 horror story from some other community. These events identified certain areas of concern, and if the same areas of concern exist in one's own system, similar kinds of events can occur in that system.

A second way to counter the possibly dismissive attitude of elected officials is to undertake public education efforts that explain and build support for the system. Surveys of citizens' concerns about their public safety communication systems often make clear that the public and officials simply do not understand the system.

A third way is for the responder community to express public support for improvements in the communications system. These agencies, especially fire, emergency medical, and hazardous materials mitigation organizations, remain respected by the public. When they speak on issues, the public will respond.

Last, the voice of the people can be used to build the case that public safety communications are a critical issue for government managers and elected officials. Members of the public who have interacted with the communications system have made statements and written letters, and both the good and the bad aspects of the system can be documented. This is a source that appointed and elected decision makers will respect.

division or subpart of a fire department or is organized as a separate local or regional agency, the organizational issues will determine who the participants in the planning process will be and which issues will take precedence.

Although the questions of who participates and what issues take precedence may complicate planning, the planning process itself will generally be the same regardless of those matters. It should focus on identifying the needs and then developing the most appropriate path forward. The lead person in the planning process must remember that the technical knowledge of most participants is neither recent nor as extensive as is required. The first part of the process, therefore, may have to be training to ensure the participants' understanding.

Planning must start with a written needs assessment that is accepted by all the parties involved: elected officials (from multiple jurisdictions, if the system is a regional one), appointed officials, responder groups, and the public. For this level of consensus to be achieved, additional advisory groups may have to be developed.

After the written needs assessment is accepted and the planning group is organized, the planners will have to collect the information necessary for appropriately depicting the existing situation. They can do this with surveys (see Figure 15–5), field visits, technical tests, analyses of maintenance reports, and interviews with field personnel. To eliminate any inaccuracies caused by miss-

Confusion in the use of terms The cellular telephone market is spending a tremendous amount of advertising time to promote the benefits of digital communications over analog. This mass advertising has led to some confusion about what the differences between digital and analog mean for the public safety sector, especially because manufacturers of public safety radio equipment have also promoted one technology over the other. The terms are being thrown out with little, if any, explanation of what the differences between the two technologies are.

Public safety communication managers must be able to decipher the terms and explain them to decision makers and others who have no need to become technical experts. Often the manufacturer's sales force has no real understanding of the terms and technology. When the sales force's lack of understanding is combined with system managers' lack of knowledge, the potential exists for missteps in the expenditure of large sums of public money.

ing data elements or misinterpretation of single elements, they will have to analyze and interpret this information in context. Their analysis of the base information will have to be conducted in a manner that makes it impossible for anyone to claim that the information is being manipulated to control the eventual outcome. Here independent review committees or consultants can be of assistance. These precautions can assure the officials responsible for committing public funds that the need is real and that options have been reviewed.

Part of determining the existing situation is identifying the system's weak areas. To do this, the planners must interview all agencies that use the system. Staff must then analyze these weak areas to determine which ones can be eliminated by the use of new technology or systems. Field testing should be carried out to confirm the interview reports.

Once the base status of the communications system is established, a review of possible options is needed. For each option, the review should specify how it will address the problem areas identified earlier and should identify both the capital acquisition costs and the maintenance and operating costs over the expected life span of the equipment.

Also of concern will be additional costs of personnel and training that the operating agency will have to absorb. Many modern systems come with support requirements that are not at first apparent to people outside the vendor community. As elected and appointed officials decide to commit the funding required, they need to know all involved costs.

During the planning process, managers must also ensure that areas of possible cost savings are identified and analyzed and that a recommendation as to their feasibility is made. Nothing can derail a project faster than the decision makers' belief that all options for lower costs have not been put before them. Even if these options involve items that run counter to the culture and position of the agency responsible for the communications system, they must be discussed.

Once the options have been reviewed, a final path forward has been identified, and funds have been committed, the planning group will need to develop an implementation process and plan. The plan will outline the broad project management issues and will propose solutions.

Acquisition issues

A major part of the career of any communications system manager will be managing the communications acquisition process. Public safety communica-

Figure 15–5   Field
survey.

Person being interviewed _____

Address _____

Town _____ Zip code _____

Telephone _____

Position/title _____

Years of experience _____

Interviewer _____

Radio system _____

Frequencies _____

_____

Radio type _____

Manufacturer _____

Antenna system _____

Problem _____

_____

Comments _____

_____

_____

Resolution/outcome _____

_____

Manager's approval _____

Add additional sheets for narrative

tion systems are very expensive. Many public officials will never be involved with activities that spend as much public money as major communication projects do.

The written needs assessment should have established a potential path forward and identified any priority items or systems. The acquisition process should evaluate which systems can be implemented more quickly than others and should then examine how the newer systems will be integrated into existing operations and what the effect on operations will be. Often the simple path forward described in the needs assessment cannot be achieved because of system complexity or delivery dates.

Developing specifications   Key to the acquisition process is the development of specifications. These detail the requirements the vendor has to meet to satisfy the technical requirements of the project. To develop these specifications, the project's acquisition manager has to ensure the technical aspects of the acquisition process.

For technical requirements to be met, research is central. A reliable method of researching technical matters is to issue a Request for Information (RFI), to which interested vendors respond by providing information about their own company's approach to the subject of the request. Companies will provide the information that is publicly available; it will be well organized rather than redundant and confusing, as material collected at trade shows often is.

Applicable state law and local ordinances will determine whether an agency can use an RFI or a Request for Proposal (RFP) as opposed to the more traditional Request for Bids. As of the year 2000, some states still restricted the flexibility of local governments, prohibiting them from using acquisition methods that are common practice in other states or the federal government. The responsible manager must be fully aware of what methods are not only permitted but also acceptable to the elected officials and general public.

The information acquired from responses to the RFI or from other research is used to outline the necessary technical requirements (or specifications) of the new system. If bids will be solicited, the specifications will set benchmarks against which the delivered equipment or systems will be tested. If an RFP will be issued, the specifications can set overall performance levels that will have to be achieved.

In setting overall performance levels, public safety managers must be realistic. Public safety personnel will say that the system must perform 100 percent of the time in 100 percent of the service area in 100 percent of the attempted communications. Radio system experts will say that technology allows a 90–90–90 percent capability. This discrepancy often produces a vigorous debate. The manager must ensure that both sides are using terms in the same way and that discussions between engineers and users do not become so embroiled in the question of coverage (performance) that other questions are overlooked.

Managers must be very careful about the criteria used to measure coverage. Often a simple item, such as the height at which portable radios will be used (head height or belt height), can cause major differences in the complexity of the design. In trunked systems, a change in height can increase the number of transmitter sites needed by a factor of 50 to 60 percent. (Moreover, the comment that users use portables close to their heads overlooks the fact that personnel are often operating on their knees—at the equivalent of belt level.)

Reviewing vendors' responses   After the specifications are written, they will be released for responses from vendors. These responses will have to be reviewed for conformance with the specification requirements. Each item in the specifications must be matched to a corresponding part of the response. Often this matching will be hard to achieve because even if the government agency has issued a mandatory format, vendors will have a standard bid or proposal respond format. Vendors deal with so many procurements in a year that they cannot match every local requirement. Local officials must be pragmatic enough to realize this and deal with it.

The components of the specifications must be ranked in importance, and some form of scoring mechanism must be used to evaluate the response. The scoring format must be defensible, and the methodology used to apply the format must be justifiable. If a vendor thinks it was unfairly not chosen, the scoring format and methodology may end up in court or may be questioned even if the vendor chooses not to go to court. If the RFP method is used, scoring can be a major issue. One way to defuse this issue is to include in the public procurement documents a description of the scoring mechanism and methodology, if the law allows.

An integral part of the acceptance process, before payment is made, is technical testing of the new system. A formal process of testing should be a mandatory part of the procurement. One method is to use an independent testing agency. This would be at the expense of the agency managing the procurement, however, and the added cost has often been a deterrent to this form of testing. The only other ways to conduct technical testing are to use the vendor's technical staff, to use local communications technology companies, or to develop a major technical capability within the government.

Each of these options creates risk. Using the vendor's staff raises the problem of lack of objectivity. As for local companies, they may either be affiliated with the vendor in some way or be totally unfamiliar with the methodology involved. Developing an up-to-date capability inside government is costly and probably inadvisable unless the capability will have an ongoing role beyond the life of the particular procurement.

Using consultants One way to acquire the necessary technical knowledge is to use consultants. Here the manager must be aware of the background of the consultant and associates. After large vendors downsized their staffs, many personnel formed consulting firms. Such firms are not independent, however, because the consultant is familiar with only one approach, and that one is the approach of only one vendor. A way to determine the independence of a consultant is to review previous projects to see if a preponderance of projects ended up with one vendor.

Reference checks are a vital part of choosing a consultant. Although many states allow single-source contracting in the case of professional services, using a competitive process is preferable because it eliminates most complaints that the process is skewed one way or another.

The consultant's role in the acquisition process will depend on the technical knowledge of the communications staff. If the staff's knowledge is general or somewhat out-of-date, the consultant can provide the knowledge base of what is possible with current technology. If the staff's knowledge is nontechnical, the consultant can provide the engineering expertise to correctly describe the items required in the acquisition documents. Often consultants can help assess system needs because they are familiar with problems that have occurred in similar systems elsewhere. Finally, since consultants will soon be gone, they can be the focus for public debate and anger about the new system.

Specialist consultants can be useful when communities must submit their tower and facility plans for approval at planning or zoning hearings. The consultants can provide support at the hearings on issues such as tower safety, electromagnetic radiation, and television interference. Even communities where planning or zoning hearings are not required may find it beneficial to hold public hearings at which the experts are available to answer questions from the public.

Consultants can also help deal with the frequency coordination groups and the FCC on license applications. The FCC designated certain trade associations to act for it in the preliminary licensing process. The two associations that public safety officials will deal with most often are the Association of Public Safety Communications Officers and the International Municipal Signal Association. The former is responsible for coordinating law enforcement frequencies and public safety frequencies as designated by the FCC. The latter, in cooperation with the International Association of Fire Chiefs, handles fire frequencies as assigned by the FCC. As the FCC manages the spectrum and adjusts to new technology and the worldwide allocation of frequencies, the process of coordinating frequencies changes. Managers who are preparing for a major project must remain familiar with the mechanism applicable to new projects.

Emergency response operations: Policies and procedures

All the planning and acquisitions result in a system that receives the citizen's call and dispatches help. The communications system should support the responders if the technical infrastructure exists and the telecommunicators are qualified and trained—and if the correct policies and procedures are in place.

Policies should clearly set out what is expected of telecommunicators and responders. Everyone should be trained in the procedures to be used, and the procedures that are not used daily should be the subject of further training and drill. The items covered in the training should range from the mundane to the complex. Examples of the mundane are whether to use the unit identifier first in a transmission or to use the identifier of the party to whom the message will be directed, or what is the correct method for providing first-arriving-unit reports. An example of the complex is the procedure to be followed for requesting out-of-area mutual aid.

Communication managers should not hesitate to suggest techniques that will make it easier to follow procedures. One such technique is attaching sample summaries of first-in reports to the dashboard of apparatus by putting them in a cardholder. Making the samples very visible allows the reporting personnel to follow the required format consistently.

Use of emergency vehicle privileges   One area that needs to be clearly understood is what constitutes an emergency and when apparatus should use emergency vehicle privileges. Some state laws limit this privilege, especially for ambulances. The telecommunicator must obtain and convey sufficient information to allow unit commanders to understand whether they should proceed under emergency conditions. Requests for service for the following purposes or incidents could constitute grounds for a nonemergency response:

Provision of service at another fire station (called a transfer or a relocation or a cover-up assignment)

Assistance to police

Assistance with personnel (e.g., to help carry a heavy patient downstairs)

Fuel spill that is not endangering anything

Undetermined nature (sometimes called "undetermined origin")

People locked out of buildings or cars (with no risk to life)

Activation of carbon monoxide detector (with no symptoms indicated)

Wires down (with no structural involvement; i.e., no building fire, just street sparking)

Ambulance response to fires (if no report of injury or person trapped)

Rubbish/dumpster fire that is not endangering a building.

In the following cases, the first apparatus could respond using emergency privileges, whereas additional apparatus would respond under nonemergency conditions:

Alarm bells/smoke detectors/automatic alarms (no fire or smoke indicated)

Gas leak, or odor of gas outside

Grass- or brushfires (not threatening a structure)

Children locked in a car or room

Searches for missing persons

Downed wires arcing (no structural involvement).

Again, the information flow must be complete enough to support decision making by the responders. Telecommunicators as much as drivers and officers must be informed about the risks of emergency response.

Major emergencies   Major emergencies should require the use of large-incident command posts. At these locations, communications center personnel can play several roles. One location where they can be deployed is the communications unit within the logistics section. This is a technical support unit responsible for ensuring that radio equipment on the scene continues to operate; it provides replacement batteries, radios, and repair services. (If large caches of spare equipment are maintained for major disasters, however, inventory control becomes an issue.)

Other locations where telecommunicators could be deployed are the command post, the resource status unit, and the staging area. Deployment of telecommunicators at those locations would free response officials to manage their own assigned activities rather than performing actions that others can do better. Logging and tracking units is something telecommunicators do every day.

To ensure that telecommunicators can respond to the scene, some communities have developed field response programs. One benefit of these programs is that the communications system can be relieved of a lot of the responsibility for the incident and can return to its basic mission of community protection. Again, this requires a clear consensus on the role of the communications system and center.

Topical issues: Costs and coordination

The evolution of personal computers has given upper management in government a sense of how rapidly the world of technology is changing and how short the life cycles are. Nevertheless, public safety managers will still have to continually express the need to reserve funds for communication upgrades. And if the system is one that serves multiple agencies, managers will have to ensure that improvements in a local agency's technology do not cause a corresponding degradation in the overall communications system. This has happened when an agency has deployed an item such as mobile computers but the overall system lacked channel capacity to support the increased amount of data transmission. Cooperation and coordination are essential. (On other aspects of coordination, see the sidebar "Integrating Systems, Lowering Barriers.")

Another issue is operating costs. As governments try to reduce costs or concentrate on basic mandated services, the question of who is really responsible for public safety operations arises. It can arise, for example, when the system

Integrating systems, lowering barriers Emergency response managers must be advocates for the interface or integration of the normally disconnected information systems that make up government computer services. They must also be prepared to push for the elimination of hurdles raised by out-of-date or inappropriate procedures and rules. An example: information safeguards that were put in place to protect the identity of HIV, AIDS, and other public health patients have been extended to other areas regulated by public health agencies, such as restaurants (the names of owners) or environmental inspections (the results). The reason for extending the safeguards was merely to provide uniformity of policy and to simplify staff training. The result, however, is that a simple matter of putting an owner's name in the property record of a location requires a second visit by fire and rescue personnel to obtain information that another governmental agency has already collected.

Information systems must not only be integrated; they must also be able to share critical and potentially life-saving information. In some areas, for example, police officers are precluded by law from informing fire officials that intelligence work has identified the location of a "meth" lab or an illicit weapons storage facility, even if the fire and rescue services are responding to a working fire in the same building. The barriers that create this risk to responder safety must be removed. To ensure that appropriate changes are made to state and federal law when necessary, fire and rescue agencies must work through their elected officials and their professional trade organizations.

is operated by a county or regional government that does not have a response role.

One method used to raise revenue for communication systems is to put 911 surcharges on telephones or engage in cost sharing with user agencies. Another possible method is to begin leasing space on publicly owned radio towers. This approach may serve to defuse the problem faced by operators of supplemental technology, such as cellular telephone or wireless data companies, as they try to build their own systems: using existing towers is more attractive than trying to get approval to build at new locations. The public manager will have to walk a fine line between asking so much in lease charges that the companies may move on and being viewed as having sold out the public trust by asking too little. This again is an area where a consultant may be of assistance.

When these two methods are used, people may ask if the system is operating as efficiently as possible, and they may wonder if the manager did not unnecessarily overbuild the public system. Programmatic audits or reviews by panels of citizens can be used to answer these questions.

Sometimes the question of whether the private sector could do things better or more cheaply is asked. With private companies now operating round-the-clock help centers for the computer industry or problem-taking centers for the public utility industry, some people think the need for publicly operated public safety systems has passed.

Several attempts at large-scale privatization of communication centers have been made. Some have succeeded and others have failed. The public safety communications manager faced with questions about privatization must be willing to confront the issue head-on and prove, as have many other public agencies, that the agency can deliver the service better and more cheaply than anyone else. Ignoring the issue because one feels that public safety is sacrosanct is to ignore the many successful examples of privatization in every area of the public safety world.

Certainly cost savings must be identified and implemented unless they compromise efficient and safe operation. Often these cost savings can be attained only with the deployment of new technology. Upper management and the public must be convinced that a short-term expense can prevent long-term increases in costs—that money spent on mobile data systems today, for example, can prevent the hiring of more telecommunicators over the next five to ten years.

Conclusion

In the year 2010, a great many communication issues will be dealt with by a technology that, as of the year 2000, had not yet emerged from the research labs. However, several aspects of future technology are fairly well agreed on, regardless of the eventual specifics.

Technology is constantly improving radio spectrum efficiency. These improvements will allow newer equipment to operate on even narrower frequencies and will thus increase the number of usable frequencies. The increase will allow growth to be absorbed within the existing range of frequencies. But before the benefits of such high-spectrum efficiency can be realized, existing equipment will have to be withdrawn from service; thus, the need for high-cost major systems will probably continue for some time.

Digital technology will be key in the future. Most of the bandwidth-efficient methods used at the beginning of the twenty-first century plan on a digital signal format. Digital is essential to data transmission and appears to be superior for secure communications technology.

Nevertheless, a vast investment has been made in the already existing analog voice communications technology, which meets agency needs as of the year 2000 and will last for a long time. Analog equipment with ten- to twenty-year lifetimes will continue to be installed for several more years. Consequently, for the foreseeable future the public safety community will operate with a mix of analog and digital equipment, while the business community will continue to press for more allocations for business and consumer use, keeping the pressure on public agencies to continue moving rapidly to digital equipment. Public safety agencies will remain sensitive to these pressures.

Trunking will become increasingly prevalent, as the technology for trunking control is deployed and used in what are known as conventional systems. Refarming (the application of new technologies to channels originally assigned to older methods of operation) will allow the use of trunking on conventional frequencies. Again, before the new technology can be implemented, the existing equipment base will have to be withdrawn.

Improvement in non-voice-related technology, such as data and video, will be propelled by dramatic improvements in computer technology. It is quite conceivable that in 2010, computer efficiency may be more important than voice radio spectrum efficiency. Imaging and video technology will be widely used.

Fire and rescue service managers must work with elected and appointed officials to ensure that the communications system serving the emergency responder is as effective and reliable as it can be. At the same time, personnel within the system must understand its limitations and must not expect it to exceed its capabilities.

1   This example is provided by Lt. Sean Carr, Philadelphia Police Department; Lt. John Kane, Sacramento Police Department; and Deputy Commissioner Phillip McLaughlin (Ret.), Philadelphia Fire Department.

16 Intergovernmental cooperation

Intergovernmental cooperation agreements have become increasingly common among fire and rescue services. Based on the premise that all participants benefit in equal degree, these agreements make good sense and are good policy. They have numerous advantages, and their disadvantages can usually be controlled or neutralized by careful thought and planning.

This chapter covers the basic reasons for fire service cooperation, the main types of cooperative efforts, services covered other than fire suppression, the planning process, and the maintenance of cooperative efforts.

Basic reasons for fire service cooperation

Generally, before organizations arrange assistance to meet their goals and objectives, they look for one or more compelling reasons to do so. Although some organizations may be "force marched" into cooperative agreements, most modern managers examine the potential value of the undertaking. And fire service managers have a wealth of past experience to draw on when doing so because mutual aid and its variants have existed for many years in many forms. The first step in a process of developing an effective system of cooperation, therefore, is determining why these arrangements are good or bad for a given community. The factors to be considered are economic, social, political, tactical, and deployment related.

Economic factors

Many fire departments enter into cooperative agreements to address economic issues. Although not necessarily the only reason for a department to enter into such an agreement, the economic reason is often the most compelling one. Economic factors may relate to limited resources and/or protection of regional economic assets.

Limited resources Few fire departments are able to provide resources for all foreseeable emergencies in their community, and most local governments have to balance their affordable resources against an acceptable level of risk. When incidents occur that are not within the capability of those balanced resources, communities resort to neighboring jurisdictions for equipment, materials, and/or staffing to supplement their own. Thus, the receiving community has avoided the need to maintain the extra level of resources required for the unusual incident.

Depending on the nature of the cooperative agreement, incremental costs may be associated with the aid received. However, in well-planned programs those costs will be weighed in advance against the costs of maintaining the resources within the community.

Typically there are several communities that would enjoy the economic benefit of an agreement and would therefore be interested in no-cost or low-cost arrangements. These agreements, commonly referred to as *mutual aid* or *automatic aid,* depending on their provisions, are the most common forms of cooperation in the U.S. fire service. (Both forms are defined below under "Types of Cooperative Efforts.")

The premise on which these agreements are built is that all cooperators will achieve their balancing of resources and risk with enough resources left among all the communities together to handle unusual incidents. The assistance may take the form merely of requesting or providing more of a common resource, or it may be a conscious effort to have community A provide one type of item while community B provides another. Or an emergency response resource may be exchanged for a nonemergency service or even a service unrelated to the fire service (e.g., animal control). In any case, the economic gain from sharing resources can be very substantial.

Protection of regional economic assets   Another important economic reason to cooperate is the need to protect an economic resource that is important to several communities, if not an entire region. Very often large industrial complexes locate in a given community that may not be able to address certain emergencies unique to the industry. Cooperation, even if only for a single facility, may be necessary to maintain the viability of the industry and therefore its economic contribution to the community at large.

A common practice in luring industry to a community includes abating property taxes that may well be the source of funding for the fire and rescue service. The abatement assumes that the large increase in employment and commerce will generate enough economic activity to offset the need to tax the asset itself. Very often, however, the increased economic activity is regionwide and not just within the host community. In such a case, a multicommunity cooperative arrangement for providing fire and rescue services to a large asset, to protect the contribution of that asset and to help the host community with its unusually heavy response burden, makes good sense.

Social factors

Communities are social entities that may differ greatly from nearby or adjacent communities. Often, these social (and socioeconomic) differences will weigh in a decision about cooperation for fire and rescue services. Issues raised by socioeconomic disparities and by the special demands of "target" populations are sometimes hard to address and may end up as reasons for certain factions to support or resist cooperation among fire services. (Fire and emergency medical services operate within very specific socioeconomic contexts, a fact that local governments sometimes forget.)

Sharing resources For many years, three adjacent communities in the greater Chicago area have agreed to share ladder company services. The long-term agreement is simple: it funds the single ladder truck needed to provide good service to all three communities and provides for its common use. Officially the ladder truck and the personnel to operate it are owned and employed by a single community, the one that is the logical choice geographically. The agreement explains the training requirements, the equipment complement, and even a replacement schedule. Funds used to operate the shared resource are accounted for separately by the host community. The funding formula uses the comparative ladder service demand for the previous year for 80 percent of the total and the relative population of each community for the other 20 percent.

Disparate socioeconomic conditions   One aspect of the social environment of a community that generally has a large effect on the community's demand for emergency response services and perhaps an equally large effect on its ability to provide those services is the socioeconomic level of its citizens. When the socioeconomic level is low and the demand for services outdistances resources, one logical alternative is to seek cooperative arrangements with adjacent service providers. Doing so, however, may raise difficult issues.

For a relatively well-off community, entering into a cooperative agreement to help provide protection for a poorly financed community next door may not —on the surface—be very attractive to the local government. The economically depressed community may not be able to provide nearly as much assistance as its partners: there are sometimes large differences in the staffing of fire companies, in the quality of equipment, and in the frequency and severity of incidents. Thus, the concept of "mutual" becomes meaningless. Unless all these factors are weighed during the drafting of an agreement, they will probably become issues in its implementation.

Fortunately, many relatively well-off communities have approached the issue of cooperating with socioeconomically disadvantaged communities in a positive way, believing that the interests of all communities are served when the resources and concerns of an entire region are brought to bear on social issues. The problems that create social ills in a community do not generally respect political boundaries, and even if they do, substandard buildings and high crime and fire rates in one community often affect the prosperity and values of an adjacent community.

Poor and affluent communities, working together, have found good reason to cooperate. The benefits of open cooperation despite disparate socioeconomic conditions are community stabilization, increased experience for inactive fire companies, and the general well-being of the greater community.

Large target populations   Some regions contain communities with large populations that use emergency response services extensively, beyond what a normal, balanced population would use. These populations, called *target* populations, may create a service demand that quickly outstrips the capabilities of a community's tax base and thus its emergency response resources. An example is a community with an economically sound but elderly population, such as many areas of Florida.

The special demands of target populations are usually very powerful in motivating a fire and rescue service to seek cooperation from surrounding communities. But although the surrounding communities generally are very willing to cooperate, some local governments whose communities do not have the target population imbalance may balk at the lack of mutuality. However, as with socioeconomically depressed areas, the economic influence of the target population (poor or affluent) is usually significant enough to an entire region to promote the concept of cooperation.

Political factors

Local governments are political entities with political agendas. Given this reality, it is not uncommon for an intergovernmental agreement—or the lack of one—to be influenced by some political issue, such as the relationship between a central city and its suburbs, issues of territory and annexation, or payments by protected public facilities.

The relationship between a central city and its suburbs   The issues and disputes that arise between central cities and suburban communities are often a roadblock to good cooperation. Suburban communities are sometimes perceived to have incorporated merely to block—or incorporation has the effect of blocking —the growth of the central city. Or central cities may be large enough and equipped with enough overall resources to feel that they do not need cooperation. Or career fire and rescue personnel in a central city may decline to work with noncareer forces from smaller communities.

Although any or all of these issues need to be addressed in any agreement, many urban areas have come to realize that there is truly a need for comprehensive cooperation. Even very large fire departments have experienced reductions in resources that cause them to need occasional assistance. Again, the prevailing influence seems to be a valuing of the economic and social well-being of the greater community.

Issues of territory and annexation　Issues among governments that relate to boundaries and annexation can be reasons for, or obstacles to, good cooperation. Unincorporated areas that may be future annexation areas for a community are often protected by small fire departments of their own or by fire departments of other cities. Government officials in the communities adjacent to the unincorporated areas may be extremely reluctant to extend any form of city service (e.g., fire services) to the area in question. The disparate level of services can be a motivator for annexation but often it fails in this role, strengthening the position of the smaller fire department and creating emotional barriers to cooperation in later years.

Many forward-looking communities are now using potential annexation as a reason to cooperate. Demonstrating goodwill toward an adjacent unincorporated area seems to be a positive approach to persuading people to annex. However, the issues are not always clear, and the economic stakes are sometimes very high. As always, before developing an agreement to cooperate, a department must weigh the advantages and disadvantages for all parties.

Payments by protected public facilities　The cooperation of fire departments for the protection of a major public facility is very common and usually uncontroversial. Large universities, government complexes, hospitals, and correctional facilities can represent a challenge well beyond the resources of a single host jurisdiction. In these cases, cooperative agreements are essential for the collective good of the people and for the safety of fire service personnel.

One obstacle to reaching agreement in this seemingly clear-cut situation may be the funding of certain resources for the host community. It is not uncommon for a university or prison to provide some cash or in-kind payment to the primary provider of fire protection, nor is it totally uncommon in these cases for a cooperating agency to request payment if it responds to the facility or is even prepared to do so. The decisions about sharing or not sharing the funds received from the institution may well enter into any final agreement.

Tactical factors

The tactical needs of modern fire services are complex, costly, and often based on mandates from regulatory agencies. The use of cooperative agreements to address these very special technical issues is the only realistic way that a vast majority of fire departments can comply. This section focuses on special-response teams and shared companies and equipment, but the general subject is also discussed further on in connection with "Services Covered Other Than Fire Suppression."

Special-response teams　One of the most compelling reasons to enter into cooperative arrangements with other fire service agencies is to share responsibilities for special response activities. Duplicated efforts to own and operate teams

Cooperation in protecting public facilities Two midwestern cities share a boundary with each other and with a major university. In the late 1990s the university closed the career fire department it had operated for many years and asked the two cities to provide a full range of fire and EMS. The university and the two cities entered into a long-term agreement for those services to be provided without regard for city boundaries and with the two cities giving full mutual aid to each other. As a function of the agreement, the university paid a substantial sum annually to the two cities, proportioned on the basis of university floor space within each of them. The agreement also called for the university to construct a new fire station on campus for one of the cities.

The agreement is working very well: the university and the cities have high-quality fire and emergency response service, both cities receive additional resources, and the university saves significant amounts of money.

---

for responses to technical rescue problems as well as hazardous materials (HAZMAT) incidents and fire investigations are incredibly wasteful.

Teams organized on a wide-area basis using cooperative agreements are a very cost-effective way to address special problems, and there are literally hundreds of examples of these cooperative efforts throughout the United States and Canada in both urban and rural areas. Models that use a single department as a provider or assemble staff from several departments to respond are working very well. In the latter case—special-team situations—the cooperation agreement probably covers issues involving training, dispatch, and response. In addition, because response is often so infrequent, a successful program must address the problem of skills degradation. Most agreements include provisions for purchasing and maintaining the specialized equipment necessary to operate the team.

In a few cases, grants or other types of state or federal assistance are available to support the teams. However, as with other cooperative agreements, obligations may go with that funding. These obligations may include responding to incidents at an extended distance; supporting other teams; and having to demonstrate accountability for inventory, training, and finances.

Shared companies and/or equipment Much less common than sharing a responsibility is the true sharing of a resource. The most frequent example of this approach to cooperation is an unincorporated area's purchase of equipment or hiring of staff that it then assigns to an adjacent fire department. The adjacent department has full rights to use the equipment and/or staff as it sees fit, but it also accepts the obligation to handle situations in the unincorporated area.

The advantage to this approach is that areas that probably do not need completely separate fire departments do not have to form them. This approach also affords the host fire department a source of additional equipment and/or staffing that its tax base would normally not support.

A common scenario for sharing apparatus involves ladders or elevating platform devices. Adjacent suburban or small communities often have only a limited need for these very expensive vehicles; the need may be driven by one or a few significant life hazards and/or the desire to receive appropriate credit from the Insurance Services Office (ISO) for ladder company services (see Chapter 10 for an explanation of ISO credits). When distances permit, it may be very advantageous either for adjacent communities to share the purchase price of the vehicle and assign it at the most logical station or for one community to contract for ladder services from an adjacent community.

The ISO will generally give full or nearly full credit to communities that rely on one of these arrangements, as long as response is within the defined limitations as set by the ISO. (The ISO rates communities and assigns them a fire defense classification number, then publishes a rate for structures within the rated community.)

Deployment-related factors

From the perspective of customer service, probably the best reason for cooperating with another agency is to improve the deployment of limited resources. Because political boundaries are often irregular and changeable, deployment for emergency response can get very complicated and often redundant (i.e., two stations may be very close together but in adjacent communities).

For many years, fire departments have subscribed to the belief that the closest emergency response unit should be the first unit dispatched to an incident. Recognizing that the closest fire station may well not be in the community having actual jurisdiction, some companies enter into "closest-company" cooperation agreements. Critical to the success of this type of agreement is the need for the participating departments to train and operate together regularly. In this model, sometimes referred to as a *boundary melt*, the parties to the agreement should also make strong commitments that allow across-boundary command and control as well as consistent operating policies. (See the sections on "Automatic Aid" and "Functional Consolidation" below.)

Types of cooperative efforts

The list of types of cooperative agreements is long and still growing; there is much innovation among fire departments and communities, and undoubtedly great new ways of working together to achieve cost-effective customer service will emerge. This chapter, however, covers only the main existing types: mutual aid, automatic aid, functional consolidation, and broad-scope multiagency agreements.

Mutual aid

Although the term *mutual aid* has been widely used to refer to nearly all forms of cooperative effort in the emergency response realm, it also describes the single most common type of cooperative effort among fire service entities. The key thing to remember about mutual aid is that it implies "as needed." The term is used here to specify assistance *requested during an incident or activity* because of observable, suspected, or possible conditions that would require that aid.

Communities that enter into mutual aid agreements may, and probably should, plan in detail for the geographic areas and target hazards of their communities. Advance planning will eliminate the need for either the requesting incident manager or the providing agency to engage in guesswork at the time of an incident. Of course, the nature of an incident may very well dictate the type of request/response that occurs.

Mutual aid is generally used in the context of responses to emergencies, but the aid referred to may be broader and may not require emergency response. For example, very often mutual aid fire and/or emergency medical service (EMS) companies are asked to move into a jurisdiction merely to cover general areas of a community left unprotected because of a large incident or concurrent multiple incidents. Or mutual aid may be requested to assist with fire prevention efforts at a large civic event, such as a sporting event or exposition.

A word of caution is in order when cooperative agreements involve career and volunteer personnel assisting each other. Sadly, there are still areas where career fire services will not call on volunteer or paid on-call firefighters, even though there is an agreement and the volunteer or paid on-call firefighters are much closer than other resources. In fact, there are even union contracts that preclude or severely limit cooperative agreements with noncareer departments. Requiring the participants in an agreement to meet certain standards of quality and competence is sound practice, but the argument can be made that method of compensation should not be a basis for exclusion.

The purpose of mutual aid should always be to help a community meet its customer service goals through quality service. The two issues that arise most frequently in connection with mutual aid agreements are the mutuality of the aid and compensation for service.

The concept of "mutual"   Mutuality is fundamental to mutual aid. As the term implies, mutual aid is considered to be an agreement, written or implicit, between agencies that have some potential for providing benefit to each other. This does not mean that the organizations have to be of the same size or type, nor does it mean that they must have the same types of resources to offer. It does, however, suggest that each player will be able to help the other with a resource deemed valuable by both.

One of the major downfalls of mutual aid agreements is the lack of attention to mutuality. If one entity gives all the aid and receives none, economic and political pressures may come to bear on the system, with negative results. Mutual aid should be designed to benefit all its participants, with every cooperator offering and receiving either actual or financial aid.

Compensation for service   Mutual aid agreements need to address not only the sharing of tangible resources but also any compensation issues that may be logical or might emerge from operations. Some agreements recognize that there is a potential imbalance of resources and that the community giving aid may need some in-kind or financial compensation. For example, some communities choose to balance the books at the end of a fiscal year: a community that has received much more mutual aid than it has delivered may pay some compensation to the community that has provided the aid. These funds may help cover a number of costs associated with providing the assistance.

Participants may also recognize a need to address the costs of a service

---

Mutuality when resources are unequal   A large midwestern city has grown to completely surround several very small incorporated cities. One of these smaller communities is an area of extremely expensive homes. The small community operates its own career fire department with limited staffing and equipment and relies on a regularly used mutual aid arrangement with the large city for additional basic fire suppression resources.

When the attempt was being made to balance the needs of both agencies, it became obvious that the small fire department could offer literally nothing that the larger city routinely needed. However, it was determined that the small community could provide valuable assistance in combating the wildland fires the plague the larger community. Accordingly, the small community obtained and staffed a wildland company that the large city regularly uses.

Mutuality is well served in this arrangement even though the resources and actual equipment of the two participants are vastly different.

imbalance up-front. In these cases, one community may make an ongoing, predetermined payment to another just to address the imbalance.

Finally, all parties should understand which costs during an incident are the responsibility of each party. Disputes after the fact are often damaging to ongoing relationships. (Compensation is also discussed below under "The Planning Process.")

Automatic aid

Although the term *automatic aid* is sometimes used interchangeably with *mutual aid*, automatic aid has traditionally had a separate and distinct meaning. Automatic aid refers to the response of neighboring resources as part of an initial dispatch and in accordance with a predetermined plan. This approach relieves the responding fire officers of the burden of calling for an initial round of aid. Automatic aid is generally part of a response based on the closest-company concept or the specific needs of a target hazard. Some cooperation agreements embrace the concept of automatic aid for every response, whereas others use it only for certain defined areas or target hazards.

Functional consolidation

Functional consolidation, which may take many different forms, is a consolidation of certain functions within two or more jurisdictions. This type of cooperation has gained momentum as pressure on local governments to explore service delivery alternatives has increased. There is significant evidence that for the vast majority of communities in the United States and Canada, some form of functional consolidation will make good economic sense. In fact, Canadian municipalities have been very active in reducing redundant costs and services with functional consolidations and, in some cases, total amalgamation of fire services among adjacent communities (see the sidebar below).

Functional consolidations can range from very simple agreements for sharing single resources to complex agreements for combining the entire operations of two or more fire departments. No matter how a cooperative agreement is legally drawn or financially addressed, it can be considered a functional consolidation if all parties are empowered to act fully and completely for whichever jurisdiction is affected by a given incident or situation. But even while cooperating functionally, the participants retain their legal and political identities.

In the emergency response mode, functional consolidation generally expands on the closest-company concept. A functionally combined operation will obligate the closest command unit to assume the command role regardless of po-

---

A large, successful amalgamation
The amalgamation of fire services in the greater Toronto (Ontario) area in the mid-1990s brought about one of the largest functional consolidations in many years. More than a decade earlier, law enforcement and emergency medical services had been amalgamated. However, the fire services and their labor organizations had resisted consolidating several large, self-standing fire departments.

Public pressure and the increasing financial burden of independent municipal operations finally brought all parties to the negotiating table. The resulting amalgamation created a single administration and unified all functioning subunits without the need for any layoffs or sacrifice of service.

litical jurisdiction and will empower the person in command to request resources from any of the cooperating jurisdictions and to obligate any of the communities as if he or she were their own employee.

Alternatively, functional consolidation may be confined to a single aspect of operations—very often, dispatching. Consolidated dispatch functions often combine police, fire, and EMS dispatching within one political subdivision with the same functions from other jurisdictions. Again, functionally consolidated dispatch will be empowered to act on behalf of its sponsoring entities individually and collectively.

Broad scope and multiagency agreements

Many forward-looking local governments have chosen to enter, with other units of government, into agreements that serve as umbrellas for a myriad of public safety activities. This approach allows the participants a great deal of flexibility and speeds up the process of negotiating the provisions of new cooperative efforts. Master agreements for cooperation lay out the mechanisms for administering the cooperative efforts and the legal expectations of all concerned.

Important to the success of broad-scope master agreements, as well as of smaller-scope agreements, is the governance of the cooperative effort. Both the process and the players involved in this governance need to be representative of the spectrum of the political landscape and of the technical expertise that is needed. Many communities have resorted to a tiered system of governance that provides for a policy board of elected or appointed officials at the top of the leadership pyramid. Subordinate to this group is often a technical policy group made up of public safety agency heads. Keeping the roles of these groups in balance is important to the success of any agreement and to the quality of services offered within its framework.

Services covered other than fire suppression

Besides fire suppression, other services—both emergency and nonemergency—may be subjects of cooperative agreements. In fact, cooperation initiatives for nonemergency response activities have multiplied substantially since the taxpayer revolts of the 1980s. Communities have expanded their highly successful assistance agreements to cover such activities as code enforcement, fire and life safety education, fire investigation, and other program areas where

---

An umbrella agreement Several adjacent communities in California have developed a joint-powers master agreement that sets the tone and the funding formula for cooperation in any area. Specifically, the master agreement states what positions are responsible for serving on the master governing board and what interests are to be represented on subgoverning boards for specific functions. Finally, the master agreement describes a basic funding formula based on population and geography, but it also recognizes that service demands in certain disciplines may differ and require negotiable funding agreements.

For the fire services, the existence of a master agreement allows negotiations on cooperative agreements to focus solely on operational issues because the governance arrangement has been essentially predetermined. The funding is worked out quickly, within the formula, all parties recognizing that socioeconomic conditions within one of the partner cities will generate more demand for service.

cooperation may be mutually beneficial. Nearly every area of a fire department's operational and support activity is common to adjacent departments, and many areas are common to other functions within the same jurisdiction. Sharing resources or consolidating these functions makes good business sense and often improves customer service.

Emergency medical service

The primary delivery service of many fire departments is now extensive EMS, and providers have developed a number of important ways to cooperate. This discussion identifies only a few of them.

Public-private partnerships have worked well in many areas. They usually come about after an EMS system matures and managers recognize that there are places for both the public and private sector in certain provider roles.

Simple mutual aid agreements, automatic aid agreements, and functional consolidation are all models that have worked for EMS in various communities. Because delivery of EMS is cost- and labor-intensive, managers will want to pay particular attention to the division of responsibilities and to the relationship between income and expenses. Key to the success of any of the models is good management oversight. A governance panel can help to address profit versus nonprofit issues in general. All the stakeholders in a given system should be represented, if not actually present, on the governing body.

Inspection and code enforcement

With some notable exceptions, cooperation in the area of fire inspection and code enforcement has been slow to evolve. Differences in adopted codes from community to community, political decisions regarding enforcement, and legal issues all create barriers for this activity. In addition, the inspection and code enforcement function may well be considered a service to developers (inasmuch as inspection and code enforcement are prerequisites to getting permits) that is part of one jurisdiction's competition with another: when the adopted codes and/or the enforcement policies of adjacent communities differ, developers may choose to wield the siting of economic development projects as a bargaining chip in negotiation with these communities. Although consolidated code enforcement would probably eliminate the possibility of this competition, such consolidation can easily become a casualty in a very high stakes political process.

However, efforts to cooperatively inspect and enforce fire and building codes have been very successful. In addition to reducing expenditures, they generally level the playing field in the battle to lure business and industry from one community to another. The net result of consistency in enforcement has long been a reduction in fire and life safety hazards as well as a generally happier constituency (both developers and citizens).

Public fire and life safety education

Sharing resources for public fire and life safety education is becoming very common, especially when the cooperating communities are significantly different in size. The fact that fire and life safety efforts often involve volunteers from the community as a whole makes the sharing of human resources more credible. Cooperating agencies for fire and life safety efforts may well include non-fire service entities, such as social services, schools, and hospitals.

Sharing resources for public fire and life safety education A rural Oklahoma community of 12,000 is the only city with a population above 1,500 in a very large county. Because the career fire department in the city could not afford a full-time public fire and life safety educator, it assigned the duties to a firefighter who worked on the project with great dedication, but only in his spare time.

As in many rural counties, fire death and injury rates in that city were higher than the national average, and the entire community was serious about wanting to address this problem.

All the fire services and school districts in the county entered into an agreement with the county government and the city to provide a countywide, dedicated position. Funds to pay for the position came from a tax voted on and approved by the citizens. The project is operated under an intergovernmental agreement among several cities, several school districts, and the county government. Volunteer resources from the participating fire departments and schools continue to support the project, in partnership with the full-time employee.

Fire investigation services

Few small fire departments can afford the luxury of a dedicated or even part-time fire investigator. This extremely important position requires specialized and ongoing training for determining the causes and origins of fires and for helping law enforcement personnel identify and prosecute arsonists. Equally important is training for properly determining the causes of accidental fires and incidents that result in death, injury, and/or major loss of property.

Many communities' dependence on each other's resources takes the form of arson task forces. These cooperative efforts have been encouraged and even partly funded by state and federal agencies in the battle against the significant arson problem. Even in the absence of a task force, it makes good sense to share this resource to avoid costs and ensure adequate activity to prevent the degradation of skills.

Connection with the community

Many fire departments have taken the approach that it is important to serve their customers by connecting them to other community resources as needed. In urban areas especially, designated response teams or on-call individuals are used to help citizens, thus freeing up emergency response units more quickly. The net result of this approach is usually happier customers, who are connected with a social service or other agency that can deal with their problems in a more focused way than the fire service can.

An interjurisdictional approach to community connecting makes good sense. The problems do not respect political boundaries, and the service agencies are generally designed to serve a broad area, one larger than a single jurisdiction. This cost-effective approach is truly focused on providing better customer service to all citizens.

Health and fitness facilities and services

With evolving standards and a new emphasis on firefighter health and fitness, a number of communities have cooperated to provide high-quality exercise facilities and comprehensive occupational health services. In fact, this has become a common area for functional, if not actual, consolidation. With strong

Connecting with the community   In the greater Phoenix (Arizona) area, a significant effort has been made to connect the fire services with community needs. This process is an integral part of the mutual aid/automatic aid system.

Special teams are assigned to relieve responding fire, police, and EMS units in caring for customers whose loved ones have been killed or injured. Another group is responsible for assessing and referring elderly or disabled persons to the appropriate social service agencies. Still another group escorts noncombative intoxicated individuals to the detoxification center.

All these functions draw on both volunteers and career people in several cooperating communities, and they serve all the involved communities, not just their own. Dispatch is accomplished by the centralized fire dispatch function. Costs are shared through funding formulas.

support from both management and labor, and few issues to block success, cooperative efforts in this area speak to longer, healthier, more productive, and more rewarding careers.

Moreover, as workplace health and fitness become issues for other government employees, some fire service organizations have expanded their cooperative efforts to include sharing the costs of exercise facilities, rehabilitation services, and medical services for law enforcement and public works employees from their own units of government as well as others.

Emergency medical service direction

Many communities have joined together in selecting and compensating the professional oversight that is required of most EMS delivery systems. Because trauma centers and/or hospitals often serve areas that contain several EMS delivery agencies, it may even be mandated that a single person or single set of physicians be used. In any case, all communities that cooperate to obtain this very important service generally achieve an economy of scale.

Purchasing

One of the most common forms of cooperation among governments is joint purchasing. When larger quantities of expensive, specialized equipment can be specified, bid, and purchased, economies of scale are often very significant. To be successful, the pooling of resources for common purchasing requires an agreement with firm understandings and with commitments to complete the purchases.

The primary obstacle to the success of joint purchasing agreements for the fire and emergency response services has been some departments' unwillingness to compromise on differences of specifications. A process that uses national standards as a basis for specifications and then requires the participant representatives to achieve final consensus has resulted in the long-term success of some joint purchasing programs.

Finally, it should be noted that joint purchasing agreements are not restricted to cooperating agencies in proximity to each other. Several successful efforts at the joint purchasing of fire apparatus have been undertaken among cities in several states. Although the distance is greater, the principles are the same.

Recruitment and testing

Another area of increasing cooperation is that of career/volunteer recruiting and testing. This extremely expensive undertaking is a necessary part of a fair and open hiring process. Given that the requirements for positions in most fire departments are completely or nearly identical, it makes good sense for departments to join forces in the effort to find the best-qualified individuals. It also makes good sense from the applicants' point of view. For several decades, a fire service position has been a valuable commodity, sought by many qualified individuals; with large numbers of people testing for a few jobs, applicants often end up taking the same (or nearly the same) test in several different communities.

Joining other departments in recruiting, testing, and establishing a hiring list is good customer service (the customer being the applicant). Although subtle differences may exist between one city's requirements and another's, it is extremely cost-effective to address those differences and join forces in taking the steps that ultimately provide high-quality employees.

Training together

With the escalating cost of training and training facilities, there is also a move toward cooperative training efforts and academies. In this area, given the cost of infrastructure needed and the breadth of subject matter, the economies of scale are substantial. Additionally, environmental regulations and training safety standards have all but eliminated the burning of acquired structures (e.g., donated houses) in favor of using controlled training simulators (i.e., buildings designed for live fire training).

Multiagency agreements that provide for training facilities and personnel have become very common. It is also very common for a local vocational technical school or a local community college to be a major participant in these agreements. Combining the technical expertise of fire service trainers and the facilities and educational expertise of adult educators has been highly successful.

Besides producing the obvious economies of scale, joint training also pays dividends in sustaining the cooperation. Training is among the most important elements for ensuring the success of a cooperative agreement. Training toward tactical compatibility helps tear down walls between organizations. Whether the walls are based on career/volunteer issues or just reflect a classic "them and us" mentality, they need to be addressed. With guiding policies in place, multijurisdictional training will build confidence in the capabilities of each agency, define areas for improvement, and strengthen the command system. To

---

A public-private cooperative training effort   In Tempe, Arizona, the city and a regional electric utility company have jointly constructed a highly functional training facility. The fire chief recognized that the electric utility had significant training needs for its employees in the areas of industrial fire brigade operations, confined-space entry, and HAZMAT emergencies. He further recognized that the utility owned some significant open space that was conveniently located near the center of the city.

With all partners cooperating, a highly functional and architecturally pleasing emergency service training center was developed on the utility's property. The city and the utility share training space, instructor resources, and operational costs.

the extent that joint training reinforces tactical compatibility, the operational environment becomes safer for those who operate within it.

Also worth mentioning is the importance of training all potential incident managers in a consistent way. Making sure that a single system is used and then using that system extensively in a joint training mode will create a safer setting for operations and probably make it possible to iron out any compatibility issues before they cause serious confusion.

Maintenance operations

A number of communities have developed cooperative arrangements for the maintenance of emergency response equipment and, in some cases, the maintenance of a much broader scope of municipal equipment. As long as these efforts have remained oriented toward customer service, they have generally been successful. The dilemma faced by most local governments is whether to support a maintenance facility—either singular or joint—or to outsource vehicle and equipment maintenance. There is evidence that the success or failure of a joint facility is to some extent determined by the fire department.

Applying the principles of good customer service is extremely important to the success of these maintenance agreements. The cooperating agencies will soon tire of bad service and repeat maintenance visits, just as citizens do when dealing with a private maintenance shop. Fire departments have high expectations for the reliability of their equipment, and although this may well be the driving force behind developing a joint shop, it can just as well cause the shop's demise.

Administrative services

Increasingly, administrative services for cooperating fire departments are being shared. Generally this is part of a functional consolidation, but sometimes it is done purely to economize in the administrative area. Fire department administrations are generally part of a larger local government, however, so it is often difficult to combine administrative functions. Procedures may be subtly different, and organizational charts are rarely the same in any two cities.

When the difficulties of a cooperative administrative services agreement can be overcome, significant savings are likely. Administrative salaries and costs are often viewed as necessary overhead in relation to the delivery of quality service, and to the extent that those costs can be diminished or better controlled, the direct service budget can be increased or the revenue source adjusted downward.

Internal local government projects and problems

Well-managed local governments often use a team approach to managing projects and difficult problems. When they do, local governmental functions often share resources in a way that contributes to solving the problem and/or improving the cost-effectiveness of government services. To enjoy the logical sharing of community resources, fire and emergency service managers need to be an active part of intragovernmental teams.

The list of services for potential sharing within a local government is long. In addition to the standard financial, management, legal, and personnel services, it includes (but is not limited to) the items listed below, which often are performed at the department level:

Clerical services

Information services (computers)

Maintenance services (vehicles, radios, buildings, etc.)

Code enforcement inspections (combined health and fire)

Occupational health, fitness, and rehabilitation services

Public information and education services

Community relations activities.

Not all government services in a community are necessarily offered by the city or county government. Very often education, certain utilities, and parks and recreation operate independently. However, building alliances with the entities that provide such services is integral to a proper sharing of resources.

Fire department managers need to be team players, not only to take advantage of the potential for shared resources but also to be a positive influence in local government and among their counterparts in other departments.

The planning process

As communities approach the subject of cooperation to address fire and emergency service concerns, it is important to plan carefully. If planning is done properly, it identifies the items that must be addressed by policy makers and that will form the basis of an agreement.

As might be expected, the planning process is not complicated but requires high-quality input from a broad spectrum of sources. Fire service officials will undoubtedly provide much of the information, but it may be necessary to seek supplemental expertise by using a consultant who is familiar with successful approaches to the community's particular problems. In addition, communities should always gauge their citizens' expectations of fire and rescue services.

This section looks at four steps in the planning process: establishing goals and objectives, identifying resources, correlating communication capabilities, and focusing on the elements of an agreement.

Establishing goals and objectives

Goals are the broad aims of the agreement, such as "To provide quality fire service to the citizens of all communities in a safe and effective manner." Objectives are the more detailed statements about how the goals will be achieved. An example of an objective is "To provide the initial engine company response to 95 percent of all communities within 3.5 minutes travel time, at 85 percent of incidents."

Setting goals and objectives in relation to issues of cooperation means dealing with three kinds of goals: economic, performance, and fire insurance classification.

Economic goals   Any cooperation agreement must address the financial capabilities and goals of the cooperating agencies. Some of the considerations worth reviewing are as follows:

The cost of providing service to other communities as a function of the agreement.   This financial effect may be a major concern, particularly if there is going to be an imbalance in the number of calls. Setting a goal in this area may help identify the potential effect as well as set a benchmark at which some supplementing funding from one participant to another might be activated.

The costs avoided by receiving services from other communities.   However, care should be taken to ensure that the reasons for cost avoidance, the statistics used to support those reasons, and the cost figures attributed to those reasons are all realistic. Bad data may provide the basis for attacks on the agreement, either initially or when the agreement is reviewed in relation to the original data.

The impact (or potential impact) of the agreement on the per capita cost of fire and rescue services.   Cost impact could be expressed as a function of any number of other service/performance indicators. Setting financial goals as functions of other indicators establishes a link between the financial and performance goals of an agreement.

Performance goals   Any cooperative initiative needs to have a set of performance goals against which its effectiveness can be judged. This is particularly important when the cooperation is linked to important public services and the financial goals of a community. It is important that the measuring period for a response goal be stated for all to understand. In many cases, statistically significant data will not be generated until an agreement has been in use for some time.

A number of service and performance indicators are described in Chapter 10, but three of the more common areas of performance measurement are described here:

In most cases, communities will set emergency response goals that are based on a measurable response time over a percentage of the area to be covered and in a percentage of call volume. For instance, an agreement may call for mutual aid companies to respond upon request within ten minutes to 80 percent of a community and to do so 90 percent of the times when they are called. Variations abound, but the principle of a measurable response goal is widely used.

More abstract yet very important goals may be desirable in lieu of, or along with, a response goal. Measurables such as fire loss, fire deaths and injuries, and cost/loss index are valuable ways to judge a community's fire and rescue services in general and an agreement for cooperation in particular. Again, it may be some time before these items can be properly measured.

Communities may want to include a customer satisfaction element in their goals for an agreement. Citizens are great judges of quality of service, and to the extent that a cooperative effort affects quality of service (one way or another), stating expectations and then measuring them may be worthwhile.

Fire insurance classification goals   Many jurisdictions will be concerned about the potential impact of an agreement on their insurance industry fire defense capability rating. This numerical rating scale is commonly assigned by the Insurance Services Office (ISO) (see Chapters 1, 4, and 10) and will clearly be affected by cooperative agreements. Although most communities will be concerned about any negative impact, ISO generally views cooperative agreements very positively within the context of its grading schedule. In the few circumstances in which an agreement would pledge resources either over a large area or with great frequency, the agreement could have a negative impact on the rating.

In any case, ISO is generally very willing to help communities plan their goals for response and quantify the impact of the alternatives.

Identifying resources

A planning process includes the identification of resources by all parties. It is important not only to enumerate the resources but also, in the case of response units, to consider their deployment. For a comprehensive cooperation agreement, resources may include many aspects of local government facilities, personnel, and even financial capabilities. One of the most compelling reasons to cooperate is to avoid unnecessarily redundant resources and thus achieve the attendant economies. Discussed here are equipment, deployment locations, personnel, and other resources.

Equipment For most agencies, identifying equipment resources is relatively easy. Fire services routinely inventory their equipment and maintain good lists. However, the process should involve more than just listing response apparatus and equipment and should extend to the compatibility of equipment. Early cooperative agreements between fire departments were complicated by differences in hose threads and sizes. Although for the most part that matter has been addressed nationally, many issues of compatibility still remain. A lack of compatibility should not be a reason to avoid cooperation but should be part of the planning, to ensure that cooperation can function smoothly.

Very large differences in the equipment capabilities of potentially cooperating entities can be a significant issue. Some agreements call for participants to have a minimum pumping capacity per vehicle, a minimum complement of equipment, or similar baseline standards. This statement of minimums will often assist an underequipped fire department in its quest to improve its level of equipment.

Deployment locations Another common reason for cooperative agreements is covering inadequately deployed resources (i.e., improperly spaced stations or staffing or both). In the planning process, therefore, it is critical to look at the deployment locations of staff and equipment in the emergency response realm. Deployment locations can materially affect response times, minimum resource standards, and operational safety procedures.

Many communities turn to automatic aid agreements to protect growth areas within their corporate boundaries or to address an extremely remote set of properties. In these cases, the community is generally relying on fire stations and personnel that are deployed in another jurisdiction but are better able to serve the area in question. This approach works well as long as there is a recognition that a mutual benefit has to accrue in terms of either response or financial considerations.

In some cases, new and/or growing communities will plan development with the expectation of using shared resources. Although this approach reflects excellent use of taxpayer funds, it depends on two or more governing bodies' living up to a plan.

Personnel resources The most important resource in any cooperative agreement is personnel. Most failures of cooperative efforts can be directly linked to issues that relate to actual or perceived problems with the people involved in the system.

The balance of personnel resources among the cooperators is critical. Agreements that neither call for a specific number of responders nor address the fact that the number may differ from jurisdiction to jurisdiction are likely to fail. Particularly with suburban volunteer fire departments, the personnel resource may vary widely from daytime hours to evening hours. An agency requesting assistance from this type of operation should know well in advance that the response will be materially different depending on time of day. To the extent that all parties are aware of this situation and are able to develop supplemental sources of staffing, the relationship can and should be successful.

Meeting federal, state, and/or local mandates for safe numbers of personnel at an incident scene is a major motivator for cooperation. In many small communities with career fire departments, automatic aid agreements are being used to meet the mandates at all incidents, not just catastrophic events. In some places this approach has been contentious because communities that have chosen to meet the mandated safety requirements on a single company are resisting agreements that have them responding to their neighbors primarily so the neighbors can meet the minimum mandates. Of course, a system built on this imbalance is destined for difficulty, for the goals of the agreement may not seem to be shared.

Probably the greatest obstacle to workable cooperation, especially in urban environments, is the matter of career firefighter staffing in one community and volunteer (or paid on-call) staffing in an adjacent community. Whether real or perceived, the differences in capabilities have prevented many cooperative agreements from evolving. It is not uncommon for the use of volunteer fire companies in a mutual-aid agreement to be a labor-management issue in a city with an all-career fire department. Conversely, volunteer fire services often will call more-distant fire companies to avoid requesting career firefighters who, it is thought, will not cooperate. Although this unfortunate situation persists, departments in many places have reached good understandings, and cooperation is routine.

Other resources   As mentioned above, a cooperation plan may identify resources other than traditional emergency response equipment and staffing. Community service agencies, public works departments, EMS, and emergency management staff are but a few of the other categories of resources that should be considered and addressed in the planning for cooperation.

Correlating communication capabilities

Communications compatibility in the context of a cooperation agreement is absolutely essential. The technical nature of today's public safety communication systems requires that this matter be thoroughly addressed from both policy and technical viewpoints. This discussion mentions compatibility in terms of radios, radio procedure, dispatch, operations, incident management, and administration.

Radio compatibility   The ability of all responding agencies, not just fire services, to communicate with one another is essential. Addressing this matter may be costly. One way to address it may be to work with the technology involved; another may be to use a unified command approach (fire, police, EMS, other). Even if incompatible technologies make radio communications impossible, the face-to-face nature of a unified command will allow information to be shared quickly and effectively.

Radio procedure compatibility   Reaching consensus on radio language and other procedures is crucial to good communications and safety. Cooperating entities sometimes struggle with these matters, but the struggle is seldom based on substance and is more likely to be based on tradition. Use of old coded language (i.e., the "10" codes—see Chapter 15) should be discouraged in favor of plain language.

Dispatch compatibility   When cooperating entities are not dispatched from the same center, it is important that the dispatch centers involved coordinate their work. Good coordination is essential for knowing the whereabouts and availability of response units. Interfaces among the dispatch/status computers in adjacent dispatch centers are very effective and seem to be growing in number.

Operational compatibility To suggest a change in the tactical approach to handling an incident may be close to heresy for some of the fire service. The service is made up of very proud men and women who have studied hard and learned from experience. However, for any cooperative agreement to work, agreement on certain tactical issues is necessary. For instance, it would be tactically wrong to approach a rural fire with one fire department using a water-tanker shuttle process while other responding units opt not to do so. The firefighters might be able to adapt to the tactical discrepancy, but the effectiveness of the customer service would be seriously diminished. Other tactical issues might include size of the work team, approaches to smoke ventilation, hose sizes and coupling thread compatibility, command procedures and process, and firefighter safety and rehabilitation procedures.

Planning and training together in preparation for tactical activities is essential. To achieve safe and effective tactics, the cooperating departments can address incompatible approaches and work out compromises.

Incident management compatibility Although most fire and rescue services are required to have an incident management system in place, there are often subtle differences among the various systems that may require an effort toward correlation. Addressing these issues in the planning stage is important to the success of a cooperative effort and ultimately to the safety of the fire service personnel involved.

Administrative compatibility Administrative needs do not disappear in a large-scale incident. Indeed, they multiply, and large-scale incidents at which mutual aid is used may require a significant amount of administrative work and follow-up. Recognizing that possibility in the planning stages is important. If administrative needs are not properly addressed by the agreement, the consequences may be that many hours are consumed after the fact. Most cooperative agreements need to address the paper flow and accountability for large expenditures under emergency situations. Some jurisdictions may have emergency purchasing clauses, whereas others may not. Likewise, the accounting process neces-

---

Resolving issues of command The fire chiefs in a large metropolitan area had functioned under a very loose mutual aid agreement for many years. There was little formal coordination and the command systems used ranged widely, even though all the chiefs had been trained in basically the same system. When incidents occurred, there were many complaints that the smaller communities did not know what they were doing or that the larger communities moved in and took over the incident. Command issues were eroding the very basis for cooperation.

Progressive individuals in the area wanted the issue resolved and proposed a series of meetings to seek consensus on every aspect of the inci-

dent command system. The meetings were occasionally long and difficult, but they yielded a workable system that was totally accepted. The side benefit was a strengthening of the automatic and mutual aid aspects of this massive system in many areas of the relationship besides command.

Determining who is in charge is not something that should be left to fate. A high-quality cooperative system will define the command function in terms of who and how so that personalities are of little concern. Training together for command, and operating within the parameters of a well-defined system, will erase most jurisdictional issues and provide a safe environment for operating units.

sary to be sure that vendors are paid is important to the good public image of local government and to compliance with the law.

Focusing on the elements of an agreement

Some long-term, successful mutual aid projects are based on a handshake. However, most responsible managers in local government will prefer a comprehensive, written agreement to make all understandings clear and concise. As discussed above, the agreement to cooperate in the realm of fire and rescue services may be a function of a larger, more comprehensive intergovernmental agreement, but more often it is self-standing and addresses at least most of the following areas: goals and objectives, specific resources, compensation, operational and commodity costs, insurance and liability, compliance with the law, sustaining provisions, and termination provisions.

Goals and objectives The agreement should clearly state both the mutual goals and objectives of the signing parties and any goals or objectives that are not mutual but are understood by both parties. For instance, it may be the goal of one party to provide a third engine company to all structure fires. Another signatory may not need that service but will be compensated either financially or in-kind for providing the service.

Specific resources If the agreement is to cover a certain type of specific resource, that resource should be described in detail. For instance, "Party A agrees to provide hazardous material response to party B with vehicles, equipment, and trained staffing capable of delivering Level A services as described by the National Fire Protection Association (NFPA)." When the resource is clearly identified along with a standard of expectation, both parties will fully understand the response required.

As mentioned above, some agreements may specify the minimum agreed-upon staffing, apparatus, and other resources to be available at a given time. This is generally done to ensure that an imbalance of resources does not occur after the agreement is executed. In career fire services, it is not uncommon for a cooperation agreement to specify the number of fire service personnel that must respond to a call for assistance. However, this is usually expressed as a minimum, for daily staffing levels may vary within a certain range. Although staffing minimums are less common in agreements involving volunteer fire departments, staffing remains a consideration in order to ensure that the assistance is generally going to be equal in all directions.

Compensation If compensation is to be part of a cooperative arrangement, it should be clearly stated and defined. Variables that may play a role in determining compensation (e.g., numbers of responses, durations of responses, specific resources) must be clearly defined. For instance, is a response truly a response if the unit leaves its station but is returned before arriving at the scene of the call? Fixed levels of compensation are, of course, much easier to handle in an agreement than contingent levels are.

Particularly in cases in which the provision of EMS is an issue for cooperation, agreements generally address the question of which agency will bill for services and which will receive the revenue when out-of-community resources are used.

Operational and commodity costs Nearly all agreements will need to spell out who is to pay for what basic operational costs and commodities used at an incident. Basic operational costs include such items as insurance, salaries, mechanical wear on equipment, and other costs associated with operations that are not particular to a specific incident. Commodities are more closely aligned with a given response and might include overtime, food, equipment broken at a scene, and firefighting chemicals. The issues of operational and commodity costs routinely arise as a result of doing business and should therefore be addressed, and responsibilities understood, by all signers.

Insurance and liability   The matter of insurance and the expectation of liability must be addressed in an agreement. Most jurisdictions' legal officers will see to these provisions without being asked.

In many U.S. states and Canadian provinces, legislation has been passed that provides definitive responsibilities for liability and tort immunity. These laws may also take the guesswork out of establishing which parties pay for what commodities and who is responsible for workers' compensation coverage at all times. Whenever an agreement is being crafted, any mandatory provisions must be addressed.

Nearly all cooperative agreements should include some standard indemnification and/or hold-harmless language. Of course, the courts will ultimately decide the most difficult of these issues, taking into consideration the language of the agreement as well as the law in a specific matter.

Compliance with the law   Although the concept is simple and the assumption is basic, an agreement should nonetheless spell out the requirement that all parties obey the law. When local government empowers others to act for it on certain occasions, there needs to be a clear and explicit requirement and expectation that applicable laws will be upheld.

Sustaining provisions   As in all agreements, the term must be spelled out. Some mutual aid agreements automatically renew annually. Although this is desirable, it is also desirable to have a clause that causes some formal action to be taken to review the provisions periodically. Without some attention, agreements will soon become outdated in either a minor clause or a major provision. Calling for an annual review by specific officials is an approach that makes obsolescence much less likely.

Termination provisions   Cooperative agreements must acknowledge that change does occur and that there might be a need to terminate the agreement. Termination provisions should enable any of the signatories to withdraw from the agreement in a manner that is least disruptive to all parties. There are few guidelines for termination clauses, but common sense and applicable law should steer this provision.

The maintenance of cooperative efforts

Once a cooperative agreement has been established to the advantage of all parties, ensuring its success and longevity takes planning and effort. Typically, local government officials will have worked diligently to craft the agreement, and they will have to continue working—to carry out all aspects of it, to address any issues that arise, and to conduct the governance as specified in it and evaluate all the efforts. If the agreement is properly drawn up, it should provide the framework for success, but making it work will remain the responsibility of the parties.

Governance groups and process

Agreements for cooperation necessarily have to specify who is responsible for administering the agreement and what process will be used. These provisions vary widely. However, it is extremely important to the success of a cooperative effort that two areas be addressed regularly.

First, the policy makers for the signatories need to meet and confer on a scheduled basis. If these meetings do nothing else, they will ensure that the basis for cooperation still exists. Economic fluctuations, annexation/boundary issues, changes in the ranks of elected or appointed officials, and a host of other variables can affect a fire and emergency service agreement at the policy level. Open communication among the policy makers will keep many of these issues from affecting the agreement even when other areas of intergovernmental relationships may be strained.

Second, it is extremely important for the leadership of the fire service and other service provider agencies to communicate regularly. It is at the departmental policy level that most issues of operational compatibility are resolved. Again, regular meetings are important as "wellness" checks for the cooperative effort. Fire chiefs may also want to facilitate meetings at staff levels to discuss compatibility issues among the cooperating organizations.

Evaluation

Key to the continued success of any cooperative effort is evaluation. The performance of an agreement should be evaluated regularly against the stated goals and objectives at both the policy level and the operational level. Requiring a formal evaluation meeting may be the best way to ensure that evaluation is accomplished on a scheduled basis.

Evaluation implies that a need for improvement may be identified. If it is identified, all the parties have to be prepared to make adjustments within the bounds of the agreement to address progress toward goals and objectives. Evaluation also implies that certain elements of the agreement may have to be renegotiated and rewritten. These are not problems but, instead, opportunities to make the cooperative effort work for all parties and contribute to the safety and well-being of the communities.

Summary

Cooperation among fire and rescue service providers makes good sense, especially in terms of the safety of the providers, the quality of customer service delivered, and the economics of local government. Progressive leaders have long used carefully crafted agreements to define the goals and objectives of cooperation and to design systems that will achieve those goals and objectives. Helping each other in a well-defined and regularly evaluated framework is a good idea for almost any jurisdiction. Overlooking the possible advantages of cooperation is generally bad policy for a unit of government and for that government's citizens.

Further reading and resources

This guide to further reading and resources is highly selective and represents informed judgments about basic materials of managerial interest in the proliferating area of fire and rescue services. It is intended to supplement the material cited in the endnotes to individual chapters in this book with a selection of basic books and research reports on the many specific subjects within fire and rescue services management. The guide is arranged by chapter for the convenience of the reader, although some items will of course apply to several of the many functional divisions of the text. Such references will, therefore, be shown in each applicable chapter.

To help readers supplement the materials set out in the chapter listings of this guide, the following synopsis identifies some of the standard reference sources and information available in journals, yearbooks, and association publications with application generally to the fire and rescue services management field.

A fundamental reference source for statistics of concern to fire and rescue service managers is the *Statistical Abstract of the United States,* published annually by the U.S. Bureau of the Census and obtainable from the U.S. Government Printing Office, Washington, DC 20402, or through any U.S. Department of Commerce district office. The annual appendix titled *Guide to Sources of Statistics* is an invaluable guide to the many specialized statistical reference sources applicable to the fire and rescue service. *The Municipal Year Book,* published annually by the International City/County Management Association in Washington, D.C., is an authoritative reference source containing detailed guides to further sources of information—organizations as well as bibliographic materials—in local government management, including fire and rescue services. *The Fire Protection Handbook®,* published by the National Fire Protection Association (NFPA), Quincy, Massachusetts (and revised about every five years), contains data on loss of life and property from fire, informa-

tion on the behavior of materials under fire conditions, and many other facts on changes in fire protection techniques, systems, and equipment.

Several specialized fire service organizations have been described throughout this book. The major organizations presented immediately below are sources for a large variety of useful information about fire and rescue services management in general. Shown for each organization are name, address, Web site, and a short description of services; regarding the Web sites, readers should understand that these are subject to change and are correct at the time of publication. Next is a list of periodicals and other publications that are of value as continuing reference and information sources. The balance of this guide consists of additional references listed by chapters; this listing—mostly books—emphasizes general works that are deemed helpful for students and practitioners.

Associations and organizations

Association of Public Safety Communications Officers—International (APCO International), 2040 South Ridgewood Avenue, South Daytona Beach, FL 32119-8437; www.apcointl.org. The world's oldest and largest not-for-profit professional organization dedicated to the enhancement of public safety communications, APCO International publishes the magazine *Public Safety Communications* as well as numerous books and brochures.

Commission on Fire Accreditation International (CFAI), 4500 Southgate Place, Suite 100, Chantilly, VA 20151; www.cfainet.org. CFAI was formed under a trust agreement to ensure the continuous quality and improvement within the fire and emergency services through the support of the CFAI and the Commission for Chief Fire Officer Designation. CFAI grants accreditation to fire and emergency service agencies upon the successful completion of an in-depth self-assessment and on-site evaluation.

Congressional Fire Services Institute (CFSI), 900 Second Street, N.E., Suite 303, Washington, DC 20002; www.cfsi.org. CFSI works with more than forty-five national fire service organizations to educate members of Congress on the important issues and challenges that face first responders, such as threats of terrorism, aging apparatus, and reduced funding.

Federal Emergency Management Agency (FEMA), 500 C Street, S.W., Washington, DC 20472; www.fema.gov. An independent federal agency, FEMA was created in 1979 to respond to the full range of disasters and emergencies through a comprehensive, risk-based emergency management program of mitigation, preparedness, response, and recovery. Includes the U.S. Fire Administration.

Fire Apparatus Manufacturers' Association (FAMA), P.O. Box 397, Lynnfield, MA 01940-0397; www.fama.org. FAMA works to enhance the quality of the fire apparatus industry and emergency service community through the manufacture and sale of safe, efficient fire apparatus and equipment.

Fire Department Safety Officers Association (FDSOA), P.O. Box 149, Ashland, MA 01721-0149; www.fdsoa.org. Through its numerous educational seminars and publications, including a newsletter, *Health and Safety for Fire and Emergency Services Personnel,* FDSOA promotes safety standards and practices in the fire, rescue, and emergency services community.

Fire Protection Publications (FPP), Oklahoma State University, 930 N. Willis, Stillwater, OK 74078; www.ifsta.org. FPP develops and publishes training materials for fire and emergency service, including the *Speaking of Fire* newsletter. It also serves as headquarters for the International Fire Service Training Association (IFSTA), an advisory group, and is the publisher of the IFSTA manual.

Insurance Services Office (ISO), 545 Washington Boulevard, Jersey City, NJ 07310-1686; www.iso.com. ISO is an independent statistical, rating, and advisory organization that publishes the Fire Suppression Rating Schedule, which contains rating criteria for grading jurisdictions; insurance companies use the grades in setting fire insurance rates. The ISO rates communities and assigns them a fire defense classification number, then publishes a rate for structures within the rated community.

International Association of Arson Investigators (IAAI), 12770 Boenker Road, St. Louis,

MO 63044; www.firearson.com. Working in cooperation with other associations and law enforcement agencies to prevent and suppress the crime of arson, IAAI provides the latest information and technology in the field through annual and regional seminars, administration of the Certified Fire Investigator program, and publication of *The Fire and Arson Investigator.*

International Association of Black Professional Fire Fighters (IABPFF), 8700 Central Avenue, Suite 306, Landover, MD 20785; www.iabpff.org. The IABPFF seeks to create a liaison among African-American firefighters across the nation and to promote interracial progress throughout the fire service.

International Association of Fire Chiefs (IAFC), 4025 Fair Ridge Drive, Suite 300, Fairfax, VA 22033-2868; www.ichiefs.org. The IAFC publishes a variety of informational and educational materials about fire protection, including *IAFC On Scene,* a newsletter, and *International Connections* magazine.

International Association of Fire Fighters (IAFF), 1750 New York Avenue, N.W., Washington, DC 20006-5395; www.iaff.org. This labor union, an affiliate of the AFL-CIO, represents a large majority of firefighters in the United States and Canada and offers numerous training programs and resources, primarily in the area of firefighter health and safety. The IAFF publishes the magazine *International Fire Fighter.* The "Death and Injury Report," published in one issue annually, attracts national interest.

International City/County Management Association (ICMA), 777 N. Capitol Street, N.E., Washington, DC 20002; www.icma.org. ICMA publishes *The Municipal Year Book.* Fire service management topics are covered frequently in ICMA reports.

International Fire Service Accreditation Congress (IFSAC), 1700 W. Tyler, Oklahoma State University, Stillwater, OK 74078-8075; www.ifsac.org. The IFSAC is a peer group function (i.e., members of the fire service formulate requirements) and, in addition, accredits fire-related degree-granting programs at colleges and universities.

International Fire Service Training Association (IFSTA), Fire Protection Publications, Oklahoma State University, 930 N. Willis, Stillwater, OK 74078; www.ifsta.org. IFSTA develops and validates a complete series of training manuals published by FPP pertaining to all aspects of fire and rescue service.

International Municipal Signal Association (IMSA), P.O. Box 539, 165 East Union Street, Newark, NY 14513-0539; www.imsasafety. org. The leading international resource for information, education, and certification for public safety, IMSA publishes study guides, manuals, and the *IMSA Journal.*

International Society of Fire Service Instructors (ISFSI), P.O. Box 2320, Stafford, VA 22555; www.isfsi.org. ISFSI conducts seminars on fire service education and the training of instructors; sponsors a reference and referral service; and issues numerous publications, including *Rural Firefighting Operations.*

National Board on Fire Service Professional Qualifications (NBFSPQ), P.O. Box 690632, Quincy, MA 02269; bsd.npqs.win.net. By accrediting organizations that certify uniform members of public fire departments, both career and volunteer, the NBFSPQ has established an internationally recognized means of acknowledging professional achievement in the fire service and related fields.

The National Fire Protection Association (NFPA), Batterymarch Park, Quincy, MA 02269-9101; www.nfpa.org. NFPA publishes numerous codes, standards, recommended practices, public education programs (e.g., *Risk Watch®*, *Learn Not to Burn®*, and *Remembering When*), and manuals in all areas of fire protection; the *Fire Protection Handbook®*; *NFPA Journal* (the membership magazine); and various books, as well as educational and audiovisual materials. NFPA includes the International Fire Marshals Association (IFMA), which publishes *IFMA Quarterly* to provide timely information to the fire prevention, public fire, educational, and fire investigation community.

National Institute for Occupational Safety and Health (NIOSH), Hubert H. Humphrey Building, 200 Independence Avenue, S.W., Room 715H, Washington, DC 20201; www.cdc.gov/niosh/homepage.html. Part of the Centers for Disease Control and Prevention (CDC), NIOSH is responsible for conducting research on the full scope of occupational disease and injury; for investigating potentially hazardous working conditions; for recommending and disseminating information on preventing workplace disease, injury, and disability; and for providing training to occupational safety and health professionals.

National Volunteer Fire Council (NVFC), 1050 17th Street, N.W., Suite 490, Washington, DC 20036; www.nvfc.org. A nonprofit membership association representing the interests of volunteer fire, rescue, and emergency medical services, the NVFC provides information regarding legislation, standards, and regulatory issues.

Public Entity Risk Institute (PERI), 11350 Random Hills Road, #210, Fairfax, VA 22030; www.riskinstitute.org. PERI serves public, private, and nonprofit organizations as a resource for the practical enhancement of risk management. Its clearinghouse provides links to hundreds of resources in risk management, disaster management, and environmental liability management.

Public Technology, Inc. (PTI), 1301 Pennsylvania Avenue, N.W., Washington, DC 20004; www.pti.org. PTI researches and publishes technical solutions to widespread and urgent problems facing local governments.

U.S. Fire Administration (USFA), 16825 South Seton Avenue, Emmitsburg, MD 21727; www.usfa.fema.gov. An arm of the Federal Emergency Management Agency (FEMA), the USFA publishes numerous reports and brochures on public education. Within the USFA is the National Fire Academy.

U.S. Occupational Safety and Health Administration (OSHA), U.S. Department of Labor, 200 Constitution Avenue, N.W., Washington, DC 20210; www.osha.gov. To protect the health and well-being of America's workers, OSHA establishes protective standards, enforces those standards, and reaches out to employers and employees through technical assistance and consultation programs.

Women in the Fire Service, Inc. (WFSI), P.O. Box 5446, Madison, WI 53705; www.wfsi. org. WFSI publishes a wide array of print and video resources of interest to women in the fire service, as well as *FireWork* (a news bulletin) and a quarterly journal.

Periodicals and journals

In addition to the association journals, fire and rescue service periodicals on general topics include the following: *Fire Chief* (301 N. Michigan Avenue, Chicago, IL 60601); *Firehouse,* published by Cygnus Business Media, Inc. (445 Broad Hollow Road, Melville, NY 11747); *Fire Engineering* (21-00 Route 208 South, Fair Lawn, NJ 07410); *American Fire Journal* (9072 E. Artesia Boulevard, No. 7, Bellflower, CA 90706-6299); and *Journal of Emergency Medical Services* and *FireRescue Magazine* (P.O. Box 2789, Carlsbad, CA 92018). There are many different periodicals on special subjects—for example, arson investigation, communications, and labor relations; some of these are cited in the endnotes to the appropriate chapters. Those cited, and other special periodicals, can be obtained from the appropriate organizations.

Other resources

FIREDOC, at the National Institute of Standards and Technology (NIST), is the online bibliographic database of the 55,000 holdings in the Fire Research Information Services (FRIS) collection. www.bfrl.nist.gov/fris.

1 Modern fire protection, emergency medical, and rescue services

Clawson, Jeff J., and Kate Boyd Dernocoeur. *Principles of Emergency Medical Dispatch.* 2nd ed. Salt Lake City, Utah: National/International Academy of Emergency Medical Dispatch, 1998.

Gargan, James B. *Trench Rescue.* Bowie, Md.: Robert J. Brady Company, 1982.

Kuehl, Alexander E., ed. *Prehospital Systems and Medical Oversight.* 2nd ed. St. Louis, Mo.: Mosby-Year Book, 1994.

Limmer, Daniel, and Michael Grill. *Fire Service First Responder.* Upper Saddle River, N.J.: Brady/Prentice Hall Health, 2000.

Moore, Ronald E. *Vehicle Rescue and Extrication.* St. Louis, Mo.: Mosby-Year Book, 1991.

Ray, Slim. *Swiftwater Rescue.* Asheville, N.C.: CFS Press, 1996.

Robertson, James C. *Introduction to Fire Prevention.* 5th ed. Upper Saddle River, N.J.: Brady/Prentice Hall Health, 2000.

Roush, William R., ed. *Principles of EMS Systems.* 2nd ed. Dallas, Tex.: American College of Emergency Physicians, 1994.

Sargent, Chase. *Confined Space Rescue.* Upper Saddle River, N.J.: Fire Engineering Books and Videos, 2000.

Worsing, Robert A., Jr., ed. *Basic Rescue and Emergency Care.* Park Ridge, Ill.: American Academy of Orthopaedic Surgeons, 1990.

2 Evaluating local risks and planning for the necessary resources

Brunacini, Alan V. *Fire Command.* Quincy, Mass.: National Fire Protection Association (NFPA), 1985.

Coleman, Ronny J., and John A. Granito, eds. *Managing Fire Services.* 2nd ed. Wash-

ington, D.C.: International City Management Association, 1988.

Commission on Fire Accreditation International. *Fire and Emergency Service Self-Assessment Manual.* Fairfax, Va.: International Association of Fire Chiefs, 2000.

Fire Risk Analysis: A Systems Approach. Emmitsburg, Md.: National Fire Academy, July 1984.

Foley, Stephen N., ed. *Fire Department Occupational Health and Safety Standards Handbook.* Quincy, Mass.: National Fire Protection Association (NFPA), 1998.

Gerard, John C., and A. Terry Jacobsen. "Reduced Staffing: At What Cost?" *Fire Service Today* (September 1981): 15–21.

Granito, John A. "Evaluation and Planning of Public Fire Protection." In *Fire Protection Handbook®: NFPA Codes, Standards and Recommended Practices.* 18th ed., 10-29 to 10-42. Quincy, Mass.: National Fire Protection Association (NFPA), 1997.

Granito, John A. "How to Rate Your Fire Department." *Firehouse* (May 1998): 86–93.

Justis, Robert T., Richard T. Judd, and David B. Stephens. *Strategic Management and Policy: Concepts and Cases.* Englewood Cliffs, N.J.: Prentice Hall, 1985.

Kipp, Jonathan D., and Murrey E. Loflin. *Emergency Incident Risk Management: A Safety and Health Perspective.* New York: John Wiley and Sons, 1996.

National Fire Protection Association (NFPA). NFPA 1500, Standard on Fire Department Occupational Safety and Health Program, 2002 ed.

Phoenix Fire Department. *Fire Department Analysis Project (FireDAP).* Phoenix, Ariz.: December 1991.

Teele, Bruce W., ed. *NFPA 1500 Handbook.* Quincy, Mass.: National Fire Protection Association (NFPA), 1993.

U.S. Fire Administration. *Risk Management Practices in the Fire Service.* Emmitsburg, Md.: December 1996.

Virginia Beach Fire Department. *Risk Management Plan.* Virginia Beach, Va.: 1999.

3 Leadership strategies for the political process

ahBerman, Evan B., Jonathan P. West, and Stephen J. Bonczek, eds. *The Ethics Edge.* Washington, D.C.: International City/County Management Association, 1998.

Clay, Franklin. "Managers and the Volunteer Fire Service: Sharing Common Ground." *Public Management* 80 (July 1998): 16–20.

DePree, Max. *Leading without Power: Finding Hope in Serving Community.* San Francisco: Jossey-Bass, 1997.

Hoetmer, Gerard J., ed. *Fire Services Today.* Washington, D.C.: International City/County Management Association, 1996.

Snook, Jack W., and Jeffrey D. Johnson. *Cooperative Service through Consolidations, Mergers and Contracts: Making the Pieces Fit.* York, Pa.: Emergency Services Consulting Group, 1997.

West, Jonathan, Evan Berman, and Anita Cava. "Ethics in the Municipal Workplace." In *The Municipal Year Book 1993.* Washington, D.C.: International City/County Management Association, 1993.

4 Organizing and deploying resources

Brunacini, Alan V. *Essentials of Fire Department Customer Service.* Stillwater, Okla.: Fire Protection Publications, Oklahoma State University, 1996.

Compton, Dennis. *When in Doubt, Lead! The Leader's Guide to Enhanced Employee Relations in the Fire Service.* Stillwater, Okla.: Fire Protection Publications, Oklahoma State University, 1999 (part 1), 2000 (part 2), 2001 (part 3).

Cote, Arthur E., ed. *Fire Protection Handbook®: NFPA Codes, Standards and Recommended Practices.* 18th ed. Quincy, Mass.: National Fire Protection Agency (NFPA), 1997.

Edwards, Steven T. *Fire Service Personnel Management.* Upper Saddle River, N.J.: Prentice Hall, 2000.

Matarese, Leonard A. "Forecasting the Outcome of Police/Fire Consolidation." *MIS Report* 23 (April 1991).

McManis Associates and John T. O'Hagan and Associates. *Dallas Fire Department Staffing Level Study.* Washington, D.C.: McManis and Associates, June 1984.

National Fire Protection Association (NFPA). NFPA 1500, Standard on Fire Department Occupational Safety and Health Program, 2002 ed.

———. NFPA 1901, Standard for Automotive Fire Apparatus, 1999 ed.

Steen, John E. "What about Consolidation?" *The International Fire Chief* 48 (November 1982): 17–19.

U.S. Department of Labor, Occupational Safety and Health Administration. Occupational Safety and Health Administration Regulations (Standards 29 CFR), Respiratory Protection. 1910.134, Procedures for IDLH Atmospheres (section g3), and Procedures of Interior Structural Firefighting (section g4).

Whitehead, Alfred K. *IAFF Fire Police Consolidation Manual.* Washington, D.C.: International Association of Fire Fighters, January 1986.

5 Human resource management

Bachtler, Joseph R., and Thomas F. Brennan, eds. Chapters 7–10 in *Fire Chief's Handbook.* 5th ed. Saddle Brook, N.J.: Fire Engineering Books and Videos, 1995.

Benoit, John, and Kenneth B. Perkins. "Managing Conflict in Combination Fire Departments." *IQ Service Report* 32 (July 2000).

Cascio, Wayne F. *Managing Human Resources.* 5th ed. Boston: Irwin McGraw-Hill, 1998.

Dessler, Gary. *Human Resource Management.* 9th ed. Englewood Cliffs, N.J.: Prentice Hall, 2002.

Fisher, Cynthia D., Lyle F. Shoenfeldt, and James B. Shaw. *Human Resource Management.* Boston: Houghton Mifflin, 1996.

Levering, Robert. *A Great Place to Work: What Makes Some Employers Good (And Most So Bad).* New York: Random House, 1988.

Personnel Management for the Fire Service, Course Guide. Emmitsburg, Md.: National Fire Academy, 1994.

Peterson, William. "Fire Department Administration and Management." In *Fire Protection Handbook®: NFPA Codes, Standards and Recommended Practices.* 17th ed. Ed. Arthur E. Cote and J. L. Linville, 9-42 to 9-54. Quincy, Mass.: National Fire Protection Association (NFPA), 1991.

6 Fiscal management

Ayers, Douglas W., and Leonard G. Marks. "Budgeting, Finance, and Cost Containment." In *Managing Fire Services.* 2nd ed. Ed. Ronny J. Coleman and John A. Granito. Washington, D.C.: International City Management Association, 1988.

Chartered Accountants of Canada / Public Sector Accounting and Auditing Board. *An Illustrative Guide to Municipal Accounting and Financial Reporting.* Toronto: Public

Sector Accounting and Auditing Board, 1997.

Eggars, William D., and John O'Leary. *Revolution at the Roots.* New York: The Free Press, 1994.

A Guide to Funding Alternatives for Fire and Emergency Medical Service Departments. Emmitsburg, Md.: U.S. Fire Administration, Federal Emergency Management Agency, 1993.

Hewitt, Terry-Dawn. *Fire Loss Litigation in Canada.* Scarborough, Ontario: Carswell, 1997.

Mintzberg, Henry. *The Rise and Fall of Strategic Planning.* New York: The Free Press. 1994.

7   Capital resource management

Evans, Eric. "When to Buy?" *American Public Works Association Reporter* (August 1998): 16–17.

Peters, William C. *Fire Apparatus Purchasing Handbook.* Saddle Brook, N.J.: Fire Engineering Books and Videos, 1994.

Peterson, Carl E. "When Should Fire Apparatus Be Replaced?" *The Times* (NFPA) (January 1994): 5.

Phoenix Fire Department. *Five-Year Plan 1997–2002.* Phoenix, Ariz.: Phoenix Fire Department, 1997.

Safety and Health Considerations for the Design of Fire and Emergency Medical Services Stations. Emmitsburg, Md.: U.S. Fire Administration, 1997.

8   Leading and managing

Blanchard, Ken, and Michael O'Connor. *Managing by Values.* San Francisco: Berrett-Koehler Publishers, 1997.

Compton, Dennis. *When in Doubt, Lead! The Leader's Guide to Enhanced Employee Relations in the Fire Service.* Stillwater, Okla.: Fire Protection Publications, Oklahoma State University, 1999 (part 1), 2000 (part 2), 2001 (part 3).

Heifetz, Ronald A. *Leadership without Easy Answers.* Cambridge, Mass.: Belknap Press of Harvard University Press, 1994.

Hewitt, William J. *Recreating the Fire Service.* Ottawa, Ontario: Kendall Publications, 1995.

Jaques, Elliott. *Requisite Organization: A Total System for Effective Managerial Organization and Managerial Leadership for the 21st Century.* Arlington, Va.: Cason Hall & Co., 1997.

Jones, Patricia, and Larry Kahaner. *Say It and Live It: The 50 Corporate Mission Statements That Hit the Mark.* New York: Currency-Doubleday, 1995.

Knauft, E. Burt, Renee A. Berger, and Sandra T. Gray. *Profiles of Excellence: Achieving Success in the Nonprofit Sector.* San Francisco: Jossey-Bass, 1991.

Levinson, Harry. "Organizational Character." *Consulting Psychology* 49 (fall 1997): 246–255.

Morgan, Gareth. *Images of Organization.* Thousand Oaks, Calif.: Sage, 1997.

Nanus, Burt. *Visionary Leadership: Creating a Compelling Sense of Direction for Your Organization.* San Francisco: Jossey-Bass, 1995.

Paulsgrove, Robin. "Delicate Balance." *NFPA Journal* 92 (May/June 1998): 50.

_____. "Evaluating Our Services." *NFPA Journal* 90 (May/June 1996): 49.

_____. "Recruiting and Retaining Fire Department FPEs." *NFPA Journal* 87 (January/February 1993): 58–63.

_____. "Take This Job and Love It." *Fire Chief* 36 (August 1992): 48–53.

_____. "That Vision Thing." *NFPA Journal* 90 (Feb 1996): 33.

_____. "Working Relationships." *NFPA Journal* 91 (January/February 1997): 37.

Romig, Dennis. *Breakthrough Teamwork: Outstanding Results Using Structured Teamwork.* Austin, Tex.: Performance Research Press, 1996.

_____. *Side by Side Leadership: Achieving Outstanding Results Together.* Atlanta, Ga.: Bard Press, 2001.

Tichy, Noel M. *The Leadership Engine.* New York: HarperBusiness, 1997.

Tosi, Henry L., and Stephen J. Carroll. *Management: Contingencies, Structure, and Process.* 2nd ed. New York: John Wiley and Sons, 1982.

10   Performance measurement and organizational improvement

Ammons, David N., ed. *Accountability for Performance: Measurement and Monitoring in Local Government*. Washington, D.C.: International City/County Management Association, 1995.

_____. *Municipal Benchmarks: Assessing Local Performance and Establishing Community Standards*. Thousand Oaks, Calif.: Sage, 2001.

Gay, William. *Benchmarking: A Method for Achieving Superior Performance in Fire and Emergency Medical Services*. Herndon, Va.: Public Management Group, 1993.

Handbook for Basic Process Improvement: Tools for Basic Process Improvement. Washington, D.C.: U.S. Department of the Navy, December 1992.

Hatry, Harry P., Louis H. Blair, Donald M. Fisk, John M. Greiner, John R. Hall Jr., and Philip S. Schaenman. *How Effective Are Your Community Services? Procedures for Measuring Their Quality*. 2nd ed. Washington, D.C.: The Urban Institute and International City/County Management Association, 1992.

Hatry, Harry P., James R. Fountain Jr., Lorraine Kremer, and Jonathan M. Sullivan, eds. *Service Efforts and Accomplishments: Its Time Has Come; An Overview*. Norwalk, Conn.: Governmental Accounting Standards Board, 1990.

National Highway Traffic Safety Administration. "A Leadership Guide to Quality Improvement for Emergency Medical Services (EMS) Systems." Washington, D.C.: U.S. Department of Transportation, July 1997.

Perry, Robert W. Jr., et al. *Service Efforts and Accomplishments: Its Time Has Come; Fire Department Programs*. Norwalk, Conn.: Governmental Accounting Standards Board, 1991.

Robson, George D. *Continuous Process Improvement: Simplifying Workflow Systems*. New York: The Free Press, 1991.

Rummler, Geary A., and Alan P. Brache. *Improving Performance: How to Manage the White Space on the Organization Chart*. San Francisco, Jossey-Bass, 1990.

12   Comprehensive prevention programs

Ahrens, Marty. *The U.S. Fire Problem Overview Report: Leading Causes and Other Patterns and Trends*. Quincy, Mass.: Fire Analysis and Research Division, National Fire Protection Association (NFPA), April 2000.

Fire Inspection Management Guidelines. Quincy, Mass.: National Fire Protection Association (NFPA) and the Fire Marshals Association of North America, in cooperation with the U.S. Fire Administration, 1982.

Fire Prevention 2000: Challenges and Solutions. Quincy, Mass.: Fire Marshals Association of North America and the National Fire Protection Association (NFPA), 1998.

Fleming, Joseph M. "A Code Official's View of Performance-Based Codes." Paper presented at the National Fire Protection Research Foundation symposium on fire suppression and detection research, Orlando, Florida, February 12–14, 1997.

Rossomando, Christina. *Reaching High Risk Groups: The Community-Based Fire Safety Program*. Alexandria, Va.: Rossomando and Associates, 1990.

Schaenman, Philip S. *International Concepts in Fire Protection: New Ideas from Europe*. Arlington, Va.: TriData Corporation, 1993.

_____. *International Concepts in Fire Protection: Practices from Japan, Hong Kong, Australia and New Zealand*. Arlington, Va.: TriData Corporation, 1985.

_____. *Proving Public Fire Education Works*. Arlington, Va.: TriData Corporation, 1990.

Shaw, Deborah, ed. *Conducting Fire Inspections: A Guidebook for Field Use*. 2nd ed. Quincy, Mass.: National Fire Protection Association (NFPA), 1989.

A View of Management in Fire Investigation Units. Vols. 1 and 2. Prepared for the Federal Emergency Management Agency and the U.S. Fire Administration by TriData Corporation. Washington, D.C. U.S. Government Printing Office, 1990, 1992.

13   Regulations, standards, and issues of liability

Brodoff, Maureen. "Legal Issues." In *Fire Protection Handbook®: NFPA Codes, Standards and Recommended Practices*. 18th ed. Ed. Arthur E. Cote. Quincy, Mass.: National Fire Protection Association (NFPA), 1997.

Cote, Arthur E., and Casey E. Grant. "Building and Fire Codes and Standards." In *Fire Protection Handbook®: NFPA Codes, Standards and Recommended Practices*. 18th ed. Ed. Arthur E. Cote. Quincy, Mass.: National Fire Protection Association (NFPA), 1997.

Foley, Stephen N., ed. *Fire Department Occupational Safety and Health Standards Handbook.* Quincy, Mass.: National Fire Protection Association (NFPA), 1998.

Guide to Developing an Emergency Service Infection Control Program. Washington, D.C.: U.S. Fire Administration, Federal Emergency Management Agency, 1992.

Guide to Managing an Emergency Service Infection Control Program. Emmitsburg, Md.: U.S. Fire Administration, Federal Emergency Management Agency, 2002.

Infection Control for Emergency Response Personnel: The Supervisor's Role. Emmitsburg, Md.: National Fire Academy, February 1992.

Kipp, Jonathan D., and Murrey E. Loflin. *Emergency Incident Risk Management: A Safety and Health Perspective.* New York: John Wiley and Sons, 1996.

National Fire Protection Association (NFPA). NFPA 472, Standard for Professional Competence of Responders to Hazardous Materials Incidents, 1997 ed.

_____. NFPA 473, Standard for Competencies for EMS Personnel Responding to Hazardous Materials Incidents, 1997 ed.

_____. NFPA 600, Standard on Industrial Fire Brigades, 1996 ed.

_____. NFPA 1001, Standard on Fire Fighter Professional Qualifications, 1997 ed.

_____. NFPA 1002, Standard for Fire Department Vehicle Driver/Operator Professional Qualifications, 1993 ed.

_____. NFPA 1003, Standard for Airport Fire Fighter Professional Qualifications, 1994 ed.

_____. NFPA 1021, Standard for Fire Officer Professional Qualifications, 1997 ed.

_____. NFPA 1041, Standard for Fire Service Instructor Professional Qualifications, 1996 ed.

_____. NFPA 1051, Standard for Wildland Fire Fighter Professional Qualifications, 1995 ed.

_____. NFPA 1403 Standard on Live Fire Training Evolutions, 1997 ed.

_____. NFPA 1404, Standard for a Fire Department Self-Contained Breathing Apparatus Program, 1996 ed.

_____. NFPA 1405, Guide for Land-Based Fire Fighters Who Respond to Marine Vessel Fires, 1996 ed.

_____. NFPA 1521, Standard for Fire Department Safety Officer, 1997 ed.

_____. NFPA 1561, Standard on Fire Department Incident Management System, 1995 ed.

_____. NFPA 1581, Standard on Fire Department Infection Control Program, 1995 ed.

_____. NFPA 1582, Standard on Medical Requirements for Fire Fighters, 1997 ed.

_____. NFPA 1971, Standard on Protective Ensemble for Structural Fire Fighting, 1997 ed.

_____. NFPA 1975, Standard on Station/Work Uniforms for Fire Fighters, 1994 ed.

_____. NFPA 1976, Standard on Protective Clothing for Proximity Fire Fighting, 1997 ed.

_____. NFPA 1977, Standard on Protective Clothing and Equipment for Wildland Fire Fighting, 1993 ed.

_____. NFPA 1981, Standard on Open-Circuit Self-Contained Breathing Apparatus for Fire Fighters, 1997 ed.

_____. NFPA 1982, Standard on Personal Alert Safety Systems (PASS) for Fire Fighters, 1998 ed.

_____. NFPA 1983, Standard on Fire Service Life Safety Rope and System Components, 1995 ed.

_____. NFPA 1991, Standard on Vapor-Protective Suits for Hazardous Chemical Emergencies, 1994 ed.

_____. NFPA 1992, Standard on Liquid Splash-Protective Suits for Hazardous Chemical Emergencies, 1994 ed.

_____. NFPA 1993, Standard on Support Function Protective Clothing for Hazardous Chemical Operations, 1994 ed.

_____. NFPA 1999, Standard on Protective Clothing for Emergency Medical Operations, 1997 ed.

National Institute for Occupational Safety and Health. *Pocket Guide to Chemical Hazards.* Publication DHHS No. 85-114. Washington, D.C.: Public Health Services, U.S. Department of Health and Human Services, September 1985.

Smeby, L. Charles, ed. *Hazardous Materials Response Handbook.* Quincy, Mass.: National Fire Protection Association (NFPA), 1997.

Stress Management Model Program for Maintaining Firefighter Well-Being. Emmitsburg, Md.: Federal Emergency Management Agency, U.S. Fire Administration, February 1991.

Teele, Bruce W., ed. *NFPA 1500 Handbook.* Quincy, Mass.: National Fire Protection Association (NFPA), 1993.

Washburn, Arthur E., Paul R. LeBlanc, and Rita F. Fahy, "1997 FireFighter Fatality Report." *NFPA Journal* (June/July 1998).

15   Communication systems and emergency response centers

Public Safety Wireless Advisory Committee. *Report of the Technology Subcommittee.* Federal Communications Commission, June 12, 1996.

16   Intergovernmental cooperation

Atkins, Patricia S. "Local Intergovernmental Agreements: Strategies for Cooperation." *MIS Report* 29 (July 1997).

Benoit, John, and Kenneth B. Perkins. *The Future of Volunteer Fire and Rescue Services: Taming the Dragons of Change.* Stillwater, Okla.: Fire Protection Publications, Oklahoma State University, 1996.

Blankenship, Ronnie. *A Study of: Implementation of Automatic Aid.* Emmitsburg, Md.: Executive Fire Officer Program, National Fire Academy, February 1995.

Campbell, Cary E. *Career/Paid-on-Call Fire Departments—Mutual Aid, Automatic Mutual Aid or Merger.* Emmitsburg, Md.: Executive Fire Officer Program, National Fire Academy, June 1996.

Cooper, Michael F. *Implementing an Automatic Aid Agreement between Fire Departments.* Emmitsburg, Md.: Executive Fire Officer Program, National Fire Academy, October 1998.

Furasek, Richard J. *Mutual Aid: Providing Better Fire and Rescue Protection for Citizens.* Emmitsburg, Md.: Executive Fire Officer Program, National Fire Academy, June 1998.

Kirin, Dennis E. *Automatic Aid: Is It a Feasible Service Alternative for Southwest Lorain County?* Emmitsburg, Md.: Executive Fire Officer Program, National Fire Academy, May 1997.

Kurtz, Thomas S. *Intergovernmental Cooperation Handbook.* Harrisburg, Pa.: International City Management Association Clearinghouse Report, April 1990.

Purchase, David J. *Automatic Aid: Moving Forward to Improve a Community's Response.* Emmitsburg, Md.: Executive Fire Officer Program, National Fire Academy, May 1996.

Stoffel, Robert. "Automatic Aid Dispatch in Under a Minute? Here's How. . . ." *APCO Bulletin* 65 (January 1999): 18–20.

List of contributors

Persons who have contributed to this book are listed below with the editors first and the authors following in alphabetical order. A brief review of experience and training is presented for each author. Because many of the contributors have published extensively, books, monographs, articles, and other publications are omitted.

Dennis Compton (Editor) is currently the fire chief in Mesa, Arizona. He previously served as assistant fire chief in the Phoenix (Arizona) Fire Department. During a career that spans more than thirty-one years, Chief Compton has been an active participant in the international fire service. Among other things, he is chair of the National Advisory Committee of the Congressional Fire Services Institute, immediate past chair of the Executive Board of the International Fire Service Training Association (IFSTA), and a member of the board of the National Fire Protection Association (NFPA). A charter member of the Arizona Fire Service Hall of Fame, he was selected as the American Fire Sprinkler Association's Fire Service Person of the Year 2000 and as the Year 2001 Distinguished Alumnus of the Year by the University of Phoenix. He is a well-known speaker and the author whose significant experience in management, consulting, and teaching covers a wide variety of disciplines and subjects in the public and private sectors.

John Granito (Editor) has worked in the fire service in many roles, ranging from fire officer to state supervisor of fire training, and from fire commissioner to national lecturer. For the past fifteen years he has been a consultant on municipal fire-rescue protection to several hundred communities and special facilities in the United States and abroad. A well-known author and coeditor of the second edition of *Managing Fire Services,* he is a member of the International Association of Fire Chiefs, both the New York and Florida Chiefs' Associations, and coordinator of the National Fire Protection Association's (NFPA's) Urban Fire Forum. He is professor emeritus and retired vice president of the State University of New York.

Maureen Brodoff (Chapter 13) is associate general counsel for the National Fire Protection Association (NFPA). An attorney since 1980, she has practiced law in both private practice and the public sector, including service as an assistant attorney general with the Office of the Attorney General in Massachusetts. She holds a bachelor's degree from Antioch College and a law degree from Northeastern University School of Law.

Timothy R. S. Campbell (Chapter 15) is a consultant with USIS, Inc., of Falls Church, Virginia. He serves as a subject matter expert and instructor with the U.S. Department of State, Bureau of Diplomatic Security's Antiterrorism Assistance Program, Weapons of Mass Destruction First Responder Training. In cooperation with the Pacific Northwest National Laboratory, he managed the curriculum development of the First Responder Operations training program offered to foreign capital emergency service teams at the HAMMER training facility in Richland, Washington. He has instructed at and assisted in course development for the National Fire Academy, the Emergency Management Institute, and the Pennsylvania State Fire Academy. He served for nineteen years as director of emergency services in Chester County, Pennsylvania. He has served on several boards and commissions, has written numerous trade publication articles, and has authored a chapter for a 2001 publication on defensive strategies against terrorism.

Steven C. Carter (Chapter 3) is currently the city manager of Champaign, Illinois. He previously served as city administrator in Moline, Illinois; assistant city manager in Sioux City, Iowa; project director for the International City Management Association, and intern and management assistant in Phoenix, Arizona. The author of numerous articles on council-manager government, environmental management, and productivity improvement, he has spoken at several conferences on these topics as well as on intergovernmental cooperation, workforce diversity, and ethics in local government. He has served on several professional committees at the state and national levels and is a past president of the Illinois City and County Management Association. He holds a bachelor's degree from Indiana State University and a master's degree from the University of Iowa.

William H. Clark (Chapter 6) has been with the Winnipeg Fire Service for the past twenty-nine years, working primarily in the core area of the city with one of the busiest firefighting units in North America. A rescue specialist, he was influential in developing the technical and water rescue programs and hazardous materials response for the city. Before being promoted to director of the Fire Academy, he worked as a fire prevention officer and as fire service instructor. In 1998 Mr. Clark seconded to the Financial and Business Initiatives Section of Winnipeg's Finance Department, where he was responsible for developing alternative service delivery policy and programs. In 2000 he returned to the new City of Winnipeg Fire Paramedic Service, an amalgamated fire and ambulance department, where he undertook the responsibilities for risk assessment, research, and planning. He has also assisted with the comprehensive risk assessment of two major Canadian cities. Mr. Clark has studied in the fields of administrative studies and political science and has a master's degree in public administration.

Jim Crawford (Chapter 12) is the fire marshal for the city of Portland, Oregon, and a member of the Standards Council for the National Fire Protection Association (NFPA). He began his twenty-six years of experience in the fire service as a volunteer and then became a paid firefighter. He has served as president of the International Fire Marshals Association, president of the Oregon Fire Education Association, administrative coordinator of the National Fire and Burn Education Association, and secretariat of the North American Coalition for Fire and Life Safety Education. He has also been a special consultant to the U.S. Fire Administration and an adjunct faculty member at the National Fire Academy, where he has worked on several design committees for course development. His articles on fire prevention planning and evaluation have been published through national trade journals, and he is frequently a speaker at prevention seminars around the nation. A recipient of the Fire Command Fellowship from NFPA, he holds an associate's degree in fire science and a bachelor of science degree in business management and communications.

David T. Endicott (Chapter 10) is owner of Endicott and Associates, a consulting firm to government and industry specializing in public safety and emergency services management, operational performance improvement, and performance measurement. With more than thirty years of experience in fire, emergency medical, and emergency management services, he has held progressively responsible operational, administrative, and executive positions (including planning chief, training chief, communications chief, field battalion chief, personnel officer, budget officer, and deputy coordinator of emergency services) with responsibility for project and program conception, design, development, implementation, and evaluation at the local, state, and federal levels. He developed the model for setting service delivery standards on the basis of customer needs and a process for assessing how changes in the land use plan affect service delivery capability. He also created the analytical methodology for determining and modeling the impact of workload capacity and response unit travel time on service delivery performance measures. Mr. Endicott is chairman of the National Fire Protection Association (NFPA) Technical Committee on Fire Fighter Professional Qualifications and a member of the NFPA Correlating Committee for Professional Qualifications that oversees the fire service professional qualifications standards system; he is also a member of the National Fire Service Incident Management System Consortium. He holds a master's degree in management.

Stephen N. Foley (Chapter 13) serves as a senior fire service specialist with National Fire Protection Association (NFPA) International, with responsibility integral to firefighter health and safety, and fire service organization and deployment. In addition he responds as a member of NFPA's Fire Investigation Unit, and serves as chair of the standards development and coordination subcommittee in the CBRNE arena for the Inter-Agency Board for Equipment Standardization and Interoperability. Prior to working for NFPA, he served in various capacities within the municipal fire service, spending the last twelve years of his career as fire chief in Longmeadow, Massachusetts. In addition to undergraduate and graduate degrees, he has completed the Executive Fire Officer Program in conjunction with the Kennedy School of Government at Harvard University. Mr. Foley has edited and authored numerous texts related to the field of public fire protection. He continues to instruct and lecture both in the United States and abroad.

Douglas P. Forsman (Chapters 9 and 16) is fire chief of the Union Colony Fire/Rescue Authority, which protects all of Greeley, Colorado, and the surrounding area. For most of the past decade, he served as director of Fire Service Programs at Oklahoma State University (OSU), where he was responsible for the university's extension activities related to fire service training, including the publishing of the International Fire Service Training Association (IFSTA) training materials. From 1980 to 1992, he served as fire chief for the city of Champaign, Illinois. He also served as the volunteer fire chief of Wabash Township, Indiana, and Norfolk, Massachusetts. His work experience includes professional positions at Purdue University and the National Fire Protection Association (NFPA). He is chair of the NFPA Fire Service Professional Qualifications project and a member of the NFPA Board of Directors; he is also a past member of the NFPA Standards Council and a past chair of the IFSTA Executive Board and the International Fire Service Accreditation Congress. Mr. Forsman holds degrees from OSU in fire protection technology, and in trade and industrial education.

P. Michael Freeman (Chapter 4) is fire chief of the Los Angeles County Fire Department, having been appointed to that position in 1989 after serving with the Dallas Fire Department for more than twenty-four years. The L.A. County Fire Department, one of the largest local fire departments in the country, provides fire protection and emergency medical services for fifty-seven cities and the unincorporated areas of the county, which make up 2,200 square miles and include a population of more than 3 million residents. Chief Freeman led the establishment of the department's Swiftwater Rescue, Urban Search and Rescue (USAR), Emergency Support Teams programs, and the department's air operations service. He is chairman of the California FIRESCOPE Board of Directors; a member of the Federal Emergency Management Agency's National USAR Advisory Committee; a recently appointed member of the Gilmore Commission; chairman of the International Association of Fire Chiefs Terrorism Task Force; and the mutual aid coordinator for a five-county area in Southern California. He is a graduate of Southern Methodist University.

Robert P. Gannon (Chapter 6) has been the chief financial officer for the city of Winnipeg since March 1997. Prior to that he was in the private sector: from 1990 to 1996 he was the vice president of finance and treasurer of James Richardson and Sons Ltd.; from 1979 to 1990 he worked with Inter-City Gas Corporation, starting as controller of the manufacturing division and working his way up to become president of Keeprite, Inc., the company's manufacturing subsidiary; and before that, he held financial and administrative positions in a number of companies, including K-Tel, Great West Life, and Arthur Anderson, where he earned his chartered accountant (C.A.) degree. He also holds a bachelor of arts degree and a master's degree in business administration; in addition, he was elected as a Fellow of Chartered Accounts and is a Fellow of the Life Management Institute. He has been on a number of corporate and industry boards, has held leadership positions with a number of charitable and nonprofit organizations, and has participated in various seminars and presentations.

Bob Hart (Chapter 8) is the city manager of Huntsville, Texas, where he has served since 2000. Previously, he served as city manager in the Texas cities of Georgetown, Pampa, Sweetwater, and Sundown. He has been active in the field of emergency management, having served as an instructor from 1990 to 1995 at the Emergency Management Institute in Emmitsburg, Maryland, as well as in the fields of budgeting, asset management, economic development, healthy communities, electric restructuring, and organizational development. He was a speaker on Awareness and Preparedness for Emergencies at the Local Level at the United Nations Environmental Programme. He served on the advisory committee for the Natural Hazards Research and Applications Information Center, University of Colorado, to develop the *Holistic Disaster Recovery Handbook*. He also serves as the International City/County Management Association's representative to the American Public Works Association Accreditation Council, where he is chair. The author of articles in numerous publications, he holds a bachelor of science degree from Baylor University and a master's degree in public administration from the University of North Texas, where he was selected as the outstanding alumnus of 2000.

William M. Kramer (Chapter 5) has been a career firelighter, rising through the ranks to assistant chief in Cincinnati, and serving as fire rescue chief for the Indianapolis International Airport and the Deerfield Township Fire Department, Warren County, Ohio. Simultaneously he has been a tenured professor and longtime director of fire science at the University of Cincinnati. He has authored several books and articles over the years, and he serves as technical advisor and educational commentator for the *Working Fire* video series. He holds bachelor's degrees in industrial management and business administration, a master's degree in industrial relations, and a doctorate in administrative management from the University of Cincinnati; he also holds an MBS from Xavier University.

Murrey E. Loflin (Chapter 2) is battalion chief with the Virginia Beach Fire Department in Virginia Beach, Virginia. He has a master of science degree in occupational health and safety and an associate in applied science degree from Marshall University in Huntington, West Virginia. He is past chairman of the National Fire Protection Association (NFPA) Fire Service Section and is current chairman of NFPA's Fire Service Medical and Health Technical Committee. An adjunct faculty member and a course developer for the National Fire Academy in Emmitsburg, Maryland, he has published numerous articles on firefighter safety and health and has coauthored a book on emergency incident risk management.

Wm. D. Morrison (Chapter 14) is currently in his twenty-third year as the senior systems analyst for the Dallas Fire Department, which he helped to establish as a leader in the use of technology and innovation by overseeing the development and implementation of fire computer-assisted dispatch, mobile data computers with global positioning satellite receivers, a fire hydrant maintenance system, a tactical information system, a fire incident reporting system, an emergency medical incident patient reporting system, and a fire security system. For seventeen years he has been a member of the National Fire Information Council (NFIC), and for six years he has served as chairman of the NFIC Systems Committee, which worked with the U.S. Fire Administration's National Fire Data Center to develop the new NFIRS Version 5 reporting standard. He is also a member of the National Fire Protection Association (NFPA) 901 Committee on Standard Classifications for Incident Reporting and Fire Protection Data. He holds a bachelor of science degree in economics from the University of Plano in Texas.

James O. Page (Chapter 1) began his career as a firefighter in 1957 and worked his way through the ranks of the fire department while completing undergraduate education and law school. He served as a chief officer in three fire departments before retiring in 1989. He is the founder of JEMS Communications, which publishes *JEMS (Journal of Emergency Medical Services)* and *Fire-Rescue Magazine*. Over the years, he has published five books, written more than 200 magazine articles and editorials, and given

more than 700 public speeches. In 1995, the International Association of Fire Chiefs made him the first recipient of its "James O. Page Award of Excellence," and in 2000, *Fire Chief Magazine* included him on its list of people who had the greatest influence on the American fire service in the twentieth century. Mr. Page has retired from publishing and is currently a practicing attorney and partner in a California law firm.

Robin Paulsgrove (Chapter 8) has been fire chief of the Arlington (Texas) Fire Department since 1997, where he focuses the organization's resources on community involvement—getting "out of the station, into the community." He began his fire service career in 1976 with the Austin Fire Department, rising through the ranks to become fire chief in 1994. A frequent author and public speaker, Paulsgrove was invited to author the "Fire Department" section in the 1997 *World Book Encyclopedia*. He has authored management chapters in two books and writes a regular "Leadership" column in a fire service periodical. In 1997, he was appointed to the Board of Directors of the National Fire Protection Association (NFPA), and in 1999, the Metropolitan Fire Chiefs, an exclusive group of fire chiefs from the largest cities in North America and throughout the world, elected him as their chairman. He holds a bachelor's degree from Western Illinois University.

Kevin M. Roche (Chapter 7) is the resource management administrator for the Phoenix (Arizona) Fire Department. He manages support service functions such as purchasing, fleet management, equipment management, and logistics. Other activities include developing firefighter safety instructional materials, speaking on fire service procurement and equipment issues, and working with fire service statistics. He has a bachelor's degree in fire protection and safety engineering technology from Oklahoma State University, and a master's degree in political science with a certificate in public administration from the University of Florida.

Russell E. Sanders (Chapter 2) serves as central regional manager of the National Fire Protection Association (NFPA), where he is responsible for promoting the adoption and use of NFPA codes, standards, education programs, and membership in nine U.S. states. He is also executive secretary of the NFPA/International Association of Fire Chiefs Metropolitan Fire Chiefs Section (Metro Section), in which capacity he coordinates activities and organizes meetings for the section members. And he is an NFPA representative to Europe, where he works with fire officials throughout the Continent to promote education programs and safety codes and standards. He recently coauthored a comprehensive text on structural firefighting, which was published by NFPA. In addition to the above duties, he serves as one of six vice presidents on the International Technical Committee for the Prevention and Extinction of Fire (CTIF). He graduated from the University of Louisville with a bachelor of arts degree, a master of education degree, and a master of science degree. In addition, he is a graduate of the National Fire Academy's Executive Fire Officer Program and of Harvard University's Senior Executive in State and Local Government Program.

James L. Schamadan, M.D. (Chapter 11) served as the medical advisor to the Phoenix Fire Department for almost twenty years. He established Arizona's first emergency physicians' group and was the founding president of the Arizona chapter of the American College of Emergency Physicians. In 1974 he took leave to fulfill a gubernatorial appointment as the first director of the Arizona Department of Health Services. Later he managed the health and hospital projects for a large multinational organization in Africa, Europe, and the Middle East. After returning to the United States, he served for more than a decade as president and chief executive officer of the Scottsdale Memorial Hospitals, where he created a strategic alliance with the Mayo Clinic. In 1994, he retired from the Scottsdale Hospitals as its president emeritus and became a trustee of its foundation. In September 1999, he was appointed by the governor as the acting director of the Arizona Department of Health Services. Dr. Schamadan was a military pilot during the Korean conflict and served as a medical officer in Vietnam. In 1991 he was a member of the American Voluntary Medical Team in Kuwait during Desert Storm. Following the events of September 11, 2001, Dr. Schamadan was selected by Arizona Gov. Jane Dee Hull to coordinate that state's Homeland Security efforts. A recognized authority on heat stress disease, he has published numerous scientific articles and coauthored two textbooks. He received his bachelor of science degree in engineering and his M.D. *cum laude* from Ohio State University. He is board certified in occupational and environmental medicine, a Fellow of the American College of Preventive Medicine, and a graduate of the Management Institute, University of California at Berkeley.

Gail Stephens (Chapter 6) is the first chief administrative officer (CAO) at the city of Winnipeg. Prior to her appointment at the city of Winnipeg, she was the vice president and chief financial officer of the Economic Innovation and Technology Council and also acted as the director of finance for the government of Manitoba's first special Operating Agency. Ms. Stephens played a leadership role in the provincial government by developing a framework, called "Manitoba Measures," for introducing performance measurement and business planning into all departments and programs. In 1997, she was appointed city auditor. Since her CAO appointment in January 1998, she has promoted a vision of innovative, affordable, and responsive public service, initiating corporate planning, departmental business planning, and a call for alternative service delivery opportunities, while making significant structural changes. Ms. Stephens graduated on the Dean's Honour List from the Faculty of Education, University of Manitoba, in 1973 and received the Manitoba Gold Medal for the highest level of excellence in the Certified General Accountants (CGA) Program in 1989. In 1998, she received the inaugural Public Sector Award for CGA Manitoba, recognizing her outstanding contribution to further the accounting profession in the public sector, and in 1999, she was named a Fellow of the CGA Association of Canada.

Lyle J. Sumek (Chapter 3) is president of Lyle Sumek Associates, Inc., a consulting organization that specializes in strategic goal setting for local governments, developing more effective governing bodies and governance processes; and assisting local governments and fire departments as they work with their communities. After receiving his bachelor's and master's degrees from San Diego State University, he worked in the office of the city manager in San Diego. He then received a doctorate in public administration from the University of Southern California (USC). He has taught at USC and Northern Illinois University, and he was associate professor and assistant dean for the Graduate School of Public Affairs at the University of Colorado at Boulder. Over the past twenty years, he has developed a national clientele of cities and counties. He has published articles on the changing environment facing local public managers, and he has developed materials and conducted numerous workshops for the National League of Cities, National Association of Counties, International City/County Management Association, and more than twenty-five state municipal leagues and county associations.

Illustration and table credits

Chapter 1   Figures 1–1, 1–4: Photos by Mike Wieder. Figure 1–2: Courtesy of the Saint Paul (Minnesota) Department of Fire and Safety Services. Figure 1–3: Picture of AED courtesy of Saramed, Inc.; photo by Bob Hart. Figure 1–5: Photos courtesy of KTLA television.

Chapter 3   Figures 3–1, 3–3, 3–4: Lyle Sumek Associates, Inc., 2000. Figure 3–2: Courtesy of the Phoenix (Arizona) Fire Department. Figure 3–5: Courtesy of the City of El Cerrito, California.

Chapter 4   Figure 4–1: Courtesy of the California Department of Forestry and Fire Protection. Figures 4–2, 4–7: Photos by Mike Wieder. Figure 4–5: Courtesy of the Los Angeles County Fire Department. Figure 4–8: (Left) Photo by John DeLeon; (right) Photo by Ken Morris. Figure 4–9: Photos by Andrea Booher/Federal Emergency Management Agency News Photo.

Chapter 5   Figure 5–3: William M. Kramer, "Training and Education," in *Fire Chief's Handbook,* ed. Joseph R. Bachtler and Thomas F. Brennan, 5th ed. (Saddle Brook, N.J.: Fire Engineering Books and Videos, 1995), 328. Copyright © 1995. Reprinted with permission of Fire Engineering Books and Videos, Tulsa, Oklahoma.

Chapter 6   Figure 6–3: Adapted with minor revisions from the Mesa (Arizona) Fire Department. Figure 6–5: Henry Mintzberg, *The Rise and Fall of Strategic Planning* (New York: The Free Press, 1994), 37. Reprinted with the permission of the Free Press, an imprint of Simon & Schuster Adult Publishing Group. Copyright © 1994 by Henry Mintzberg. Figures 6–8 and 6–11: Courtesy of the City of Winnipeg. Figure 6–9: Adapted from the management reference model service identification process developed by Chartwell, Inc., Toronto, Canada, in 1997. Figure 6–15: Adapted with minor revisions from T. D. Hewitt, *Fire Loss Litigation in Canada: A Practical Guide* (Scarsborough, Ontario: Carswell, 1993), chap. 5, pp. 27–28. Reprinted with permission of Carswell Publishing through the Canadian Copyright Licensing Agency (CANCOPY).

Chapter 7   Figures 7–1(a), (b), and 7–2 (left): Photos by Mike Wieder. Figure 7–1(c): Courtesy of American LaFrance (Ephrata, Pa.). Figure 7–1(d): Courtesy of SVI Trucks (Loveland, Colo.). Figures 7–1(e) and 7–2 (right): Courtesy of the Phoenix (Arizona) Fire Department.

Chapter 8   Figure 8–4: Adapted with permission from Dennis A. Romig, *Sponsoring Breakthrough Teams* (Austin, Tex.: Performance Resources, Inc., 1997), 8–9.

Chapter 9   Figure 9–1: Photo courtesy of the Phoenix (Arizona) Fire Department.

Chapter 10   Figures 10–1 and 10–14: Adapted from Harry P. Hatry et al., eds., *Service Efforts and Accomplishments Reporting: Its Time Has Come; An Overview* (Norwalk, Conn.: Governmental Accounting Standards Board [GASB], 1990), 10, 12–13; reprinted with permission of the GASB, 401 Merritt 7, P.O. Box 5116, Norwalk, CT 06856–5116. Complete copies of this publication are available from the GASB. Figure 10–2: Adapted from Harry Hatry, performance measurement definitions handout, ICMA Performance Measurement Consortium meeting, February 7, 1995. Figures 10–3 and 10–4: ICMA Center for Performance Measurement © 2001, pages 22 and 42–43. Figures 10–5 and 10–6: Geary A. Rummler and Alan P. Brache, *Improving Performance: How to Manage the White Space on the Organization Chart* (San Francisco: Jossey-Bass, 1990), 9 and 167; reprinted by permission of John Wiley & Sons, Inc. Figures 10–7 and 10–8: David T. Endicott, © 1990, 2001. Figure 10–9: *1990 Comprehensive Plan, Fire and Rescue Element* (Prince William County, Va., August 24, 1990), FR-32. Figure 10–10: William G. Gay, "Benchmarking: Achieving Superior Performance in Fire and Emergency Medical Services," *MIS Report* (ICMA) 25 (February 1993): 6. Figures 10–11 and 10–12: Dorothea St. John, *Breaking the Ice: First Interim*

Report of the Tricom Consortium (Prince William County, Va., February 1998), 9. Figure 10–15: *City of Portland Service Efforts and Accomplishments: 2000–01,* Report #280 (Portland, Ore.: Audit Services Division, City of Portland, 2001), 7–10. Figure 10–16: Adapted from Harry Hatry, Craig Gerhart, and Martha Marshall, "Eleven Ways to Make Performance Measurement More Useful to Public Managers," *Public Management* 76 (September 1994): S15–S17. Figures 10–17 through 10–22: Adapted from *Handbook for Basic Process Improvement: Tools for Basic Process Improvement* (Washington, D.C.: Total Quality Leadership Office, U.S. Department of the Navy, 1992). Figure 10–23: Adapted from the Department of Fire and Rescue, proposed budget (Prince William County, Va., February 2000).

Chapter 11   All photographs courtesy of the Phoenix (Arizona) Fire Department.

Chapter 12   Figure 12–1: Reprinted with permission from *The (Louisville) Courier-Journal,* May 24, 1993, page B3, © *The Courier-Journal.* Figure 12–2: Courtesy of the Oakland (California) Fire Department. Figures 12–3 and 12–4: Courtesy of Robert Cantwell, Phoenix fire marshal. Figure 12–5: Courtesy of Palm Beach Gardens (Florida)

Fire Department. Figure 12–6: Courtesy of the City of Portland (Oregon) Fire Prevention Division. Figures 12–7, 12–10, 12–12, and 12–13: Courtesy of Portland (Oregon) Fire and Rescue. Figure 12–8: Courtesy of Tualatin Valley (Oregon) Fire and Rescue. Figure 12–9: *Risk Watch*®, its logo, and icons are copyrighted by the National Fire Protection Association (NFPA). © 1998. NFPA, Quincy, MA 02269. All rights reserved. Figure 12–11: Courtesy of Portland (Oregon) Fire and Rescue and Plumbers Local 290.

Chapter 13   Figures 13–2, 13–3, and 13–4: Paul R. LeBlanc and Rita F. Fahy, Ph.D., *Report on Firefighter Fatalities—2001* (forthcoming July 2002), reprinted with permission from the National Fire Protection Association (NFPA), Quincy, MA 02269. All rights reserved.

Chapter 14   Figures 14–4 and 14–5: *1990 Survey of Metropolitan Members, All Incident Data* (National Fire Information Council, 1990). Figure 14–6: Courtesy of the Dallas (Texas) Fire Department. Table 14–3: National Fire Information Council System Committee, 1993.

Chapter 15   Figures 15–1 (top and bottom), 15–3, 15–4: Courtesy of Motorola.

Index

Municipal Management Series

**Managing Fire and
Rescue Services**

Text type
Times Roman, Helvetica

Composition
EPS Group Inc.
Easton, Maryland

Printing and binding
Edwards Brothers
Ann Arbor, Michigan

Design
Herbert Slobin

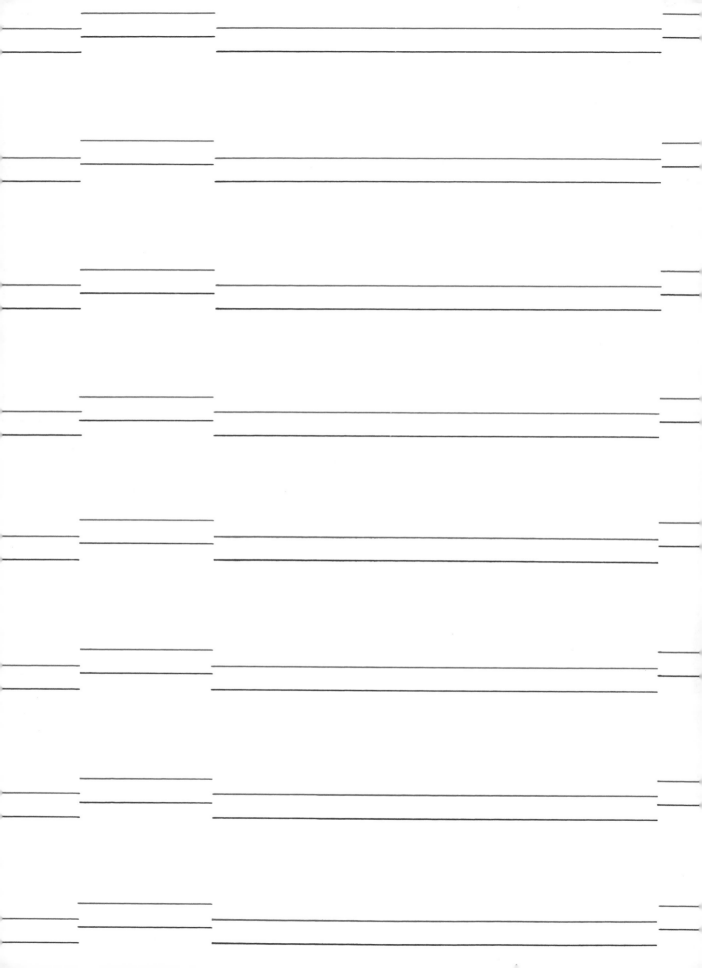